WHAT THE BIBLE TEACHES

Contributors

JOHN HEADING

John Heading was born and brought up in Norwich, though he now lives and is employed in Aberystwyth, Wales. He has written in book form many of the Bible study sessions that he has conducted in the assembly in Aberystwyth; these are commentaries on Chronicles, Daniel, Luke, Acts, First Corinthians, Second Corinthians, Hebrews, Revelation. He has written many magazine articles, and has produced a "Dictionary of New Testament Churches"; he has been co-editor of the magazine Precious Seed since 1962.

HAROLD PAISLEY

Harold S. Paisley was born into a Christian home in N. Ireland. Following his conversion, he became an earnest preacher of the Gospel. In the early sixties he emigrated to Canada, where the Lord has continued to bless his ministry in preaching, teaching, and in exposition of the Scriptures. As well as a book on Daniel, Mr. Paisley has written numerous articles for magazines.

WHAT THE BIBLE TEACHES

with
Authorised Version
of
The Bible

IN ELEVEN VOLUMES
COVERING THE NEW TESTAMENT

VOLUME 2

JOHN RITCHIE LTD
KILMARNOCK, SCOTLAND

ISBN-13: 978 1 904064 39 8
ISBN-10: 1 904064 39 6

WHAT THE BIBLE TEACHES

40 Beansburn, Kilmarnock, Scotland

www.ritchiechristianmedia.co.uk

Re-typeset and printed 2007
Reprinted 2021

Typeset at John Ritchie Ltd., 40 Beansburn, Kilmarnock.
Printed by Bell and Bain, Glasgow.

CONTENTS

MARK

ABBREVIATIONS

AV	Authorised Version of King James Version 1611
JND	New Translation by J.N. Darby 1939
LXX	Septuagint Version of Old Testament
Mft	New Translation by James Moffat 1922
NASB	New American Standard Bible 1960
NEB	New English Bible 1961
Nestle	Nestle (ed.) Novum Testamentum Graece
NIV	New International Version 1973
NT	New Testament
OT	Old Testament
Phps	New Testament in Modern English by J.B. Philips 1962
RSV	Revised Standard Version 1952
RV	Revised Version 1881
TR	Textus Receptus or Received Text
Wey	New Testament in Modern Speech by R.E. Weymouth 1929

PREFACE

They follow the noblest example who seek to open the Scriptures to others, for our Lord Himself did so for those two dejected disciples of Emmaus (Luke 24:32). Whether it is the evangelist "opening and alleging that Christ must needs have suffered, and risen, from the dead" (Acts 17:3) or the pastor-teacher "expounding ... in all the scriptures the things concerning himself" (Luke 24:27) or stimulating our hope "through patience and comfort of the scriptures" (Rom 15:4), he serves well in thus giving attendance to the reading of the Scriptures (1 Tim 4:13).

It is of course of equal moment to recognise in the exercise of able men, the continued faithfulness of the risen Head in giving gifts to the Church, in spite of her unfaithfulness. How good to recognise that "the perfecting of the saints ... the work of the ministry...the edifying of the body of Christ" need not be neglected. Every provision has been made to ensure the well-being of the people of God. And every opportunity should be taken by the minister of Christ and those to whom he ministers to ensure that the saints "grow up into him in all things, which is the head, even Christ" (Eph 4:15).

At various times in the post-apostolic period, certain teachers have come to prominence, sometimes because they succumbed to error, sometimes because in faithfulness they paid the ultimate price for the truth they had bought and would not sell. Some generations had Calvin and Luther, others Darby and Kelly, but in every generation God's voice is heard. It is important that we hear His voice today and recognise that He does speak through His servants. The contributors to this series of commentaries are all highly-respected expositors among the churches of God. They labour in the Word in the English-speaking world and have been of blessing to many throughout their years of service.

The doctrinal standpoint of the commentaries is based upon the acceptance of the verbal and plenary inspiration of the Scriptures so that their inerrant and infallible teachings are the only rule of conscience. The impeccability of Christ, His virgin birth, vicarious death and bodily resurrection are indeed precious truths worthy of the Christian's defence, and throughout the volumes of this series will be defended. Equally the Rapture will be presented as the Hope of the Church. Before the great Tribulation she will be raptured and God's prophetic programme will continue with Jacob's trouble, the public manifestation of Christ and the Millennium of blessing to a restored Israel and the innumerable Gentile multitude in a creation released from the bondage of corruption.

May the sound teaching of these commentaries be used by our God to the blessing of His people. May the searching of the Scriptures characterise all who read them.

The diligence of Mr. J.W. Ferguson and the late Professor J. Heading in proof-reading is gratefully acknowledged. Without such co-operation, the production of this commentary would not have been expedited so readily.

T. WILSON
K. STAPLEY

MATTHEW

J. Heading

MATTHEW

Introduction

1. Technical
2. Author's Apology
3. Religious and Political Background
4. Survey of Matthew's Gospel
5. Outline
6. Quotations from the Old Testament
7. Bibliography

1. Technical

Today, when an author's manuscript has been set up in type by the printer's compositor using the latest sophisticated electronic equipment, thousands of copies are then run off on an offset litho printing press. All these copies will be identical. Moreover if proof-reading has ensured that the compositor's work has been perfectly corrected, then every printed copy will likewise be correct; no subsequent errors or alterations can have crept into the printing process. But in the early days of the Christian church, the production of even one copy of a long book was a laborious and time-consuming process.

For a scribe had to produce a careful handwritten copy from a previously-made handwritten copy. The original manuscripts produced by the NT authors have either decayed with time, or have never been discovered, assuming that they were not destroyed. The same may be said about the first copies made from the originals. Thus what now remain are thousands of incomplete parts of the NT in Greek, together with a number of more or less complete copies made at different times throughout the early centuries. Investigations into this mass of evidence separate these manuscripts into families, and from the many variations experts have sought to produce what is most likely to have been the original text. Coupled with these Greek manuscripts, many very old translations exist (such as Latin, Syriac, Coptic, Armenian, Ethiopian and Arabic), from which may be deduced what was actually before the eyes of the translators as they translated from the Greek text. Thirdly, evidence can be gleaned from the writings of the so-called Fathers, since they quoted liberally from the Scriptures.

In their investigations to arrive at the original Greek text, different experts have adopted different lines of enquiry using different methods and differing basic assumptions, some of which appear to the author to lack the basic requirements of logic. Some of these investigators have been believers, but others have been academics with no faith in divine inspiration or in the preserving hand of God that has maintained His Word over the centuries. After all, throughout the millennia God has maintained life on the earth, with all its characteristics being passed down throughout the generations by means of the genetic code. It would be very strange if life in the Word were not similarly preserved by the same God who is over all, blessed for evermore.

Thus different editors have produced different Greek texts. These differ in the spelling of words, in the choice of individual Greek words used, in the order of words, whether some words should be present or not, whether short phrases, certain sentences, and even longer passages should or should not be in the text. The Greek text that was "standard" for many centuries was that printed in 1550 by Stephanus in Paris. In 1633, a Latin preface was printed to this text, in which the reader was informed that "the text which is now received by all" lay before him, and hence its name "The Received Text" (Textus Receptus – TR). Since then, more manuscripts have come to light, thereby suggesting many alterations to the TR. Editors have regarded these more recently discovered manuscripts as the "best", though what is "best" is usually a matter of taste and conviction, since not all Christians agree on the matter. Such opinions are not based on logic, and the editors themselves must be assessed by the Lord's words, "a corrupt tree bringeth forth evil fruit … neither can a corrupt tree bring forth good fruit" (Matt 7:16-20). Modern translations are usually based on these more recent amendations, though the AV was based on the TR.

Translations differ amongst themselves, not only because of the Greek text used, but also because of the translators' styles and theological convictions. Often in these modern translations, the Person of Christ, instead of being exalted and being reverenced as pre-eminent, is demoted and treated in a derogatory manner. Most Christians know nothing of manuscript and translation problems, and on linguistic and historical grounds they are in no position to judge between various translations (though these problems present a certain fascination to those interested to read about them). But believers have much more than such academic considerations to guide them: they have the Holy Spirit to guide into all truth. If a believer is confronted with a textual or translational variation, let him ask himself; which of the AV, RV, JND, or modern translations give the rightful pre-eminence to Christ? Which is more consistent with the rest of Holy Scripture? Which fits best into the context? The arguments of academics cannot surpass this approach, for at the best their arguments are based on many assumptions and a balance of probabilities judged by a rational mind, but faith transcends these arguments of the modern day. Faith should have the final say, though faith was not the ultimate arbiter in the work of most editors and translators. The simple believer, confronted with these editorial doubts on every hand, should be able to say with confidence, "I have more understanding than all my teachers' (Ps 119:99). Of course, if one little piece of leaven in the form of heresy appears in a modern translation, then since " a little leaven leaveneth the whole lump' (1 Cor 5:6), the whole translation should be treated with great caution, since the translators' minds are proved to be doctrinally polluted by this heresy, which usually denigrates the Person of Christ. These observations have guided the author in the preparation of his commentary on Matthew's Gospel.

2. Author's Apology

The author has sought to achieve a balance between devotional and practical material on the one hand, and technical material on the other, particularly when both appear in the same paragraph. The technical material is concerned with background information, together with doctrinal and linguistic explanations. Where Greek words are quoted, the dictionary forms are given rather than the inflected forms, namely the nominative singular of nouns, the nominative masculine singular of adjectives, and the first person singular active of the present tense of verbs, with a few exceptions where a departure from this rule appears advantageous. The Lord said, "with all thy heart, and with all thy soul, and with all thy mind" (Matt 22:37); this justifies a balanced mixture of devotional, practical and technical matter.

In dealing with variant readings in the Greek text, it is common practice to declare that "the best texts" give so-and-so, as distinct from the TR (the basis of the AV translation), though which manuscripts are "best" is often a matter of opinion, sometimes depending on the difference between flesh and spirit, between unbelief and faith in the contending parties. Where manuscripts differ, we shall adopt the wording, "some Greek texts give". It is tragic that much work on the Greek manuscripts, and on translations based on the work of the editors of the Greek text, has been done by unbelievers, no doubt expert linguists and theological scholars, but with their work deeply influenced by failure to perceive that the "words ... are spirit" (John 6:63), and that these are "the words ... which the Holy Spirit teacheth" (1 Cor 2:13). One appropriate test of the spiritual validity of a translation is the rendering of Ps 2:7 and Heb 1:5 . If the heretical rendering "You are my Son; today I have become your Father" appears, then the whole translation should be treated as suspect, not being suitable for detailed Bible study.

In preparing this exposition, the author has consulted the works of various expositors, though he has not been a slave to other people's ideas and opinions. It is important to distinguish between an expositor's dogmatic interpretation of a verse or passage and a suggested interpretation. When

Scripture provides its own interpretation, we must abide by it – this is dogmatic; when no interpretation is given, we must make suggestions consistent with the context and with the rest of Scripture. In this case, other authors may make other suggestions – herein lies the richness of Scripture – but under these circumstances no one has the right to be dogmatic that his suggestion is the only correct one. Some authors do not recognise this important point, and some of their readers may not appreciate the difference between

1. what is suggestive and presented as a suggestion,
2. what is suggestive but presented as dogmatic and unalterable, and
3. what is rightly dogmatic and cannot be altered.

This is particularly important when dealing with the parables, typology, prophecy presented in figurative language, the "spiritualisation" of historical passages, and even aspects of doctrine and practice. The author trusts that he has not gone beyond what is honest in this matter.

Some of the parables are difficult to deal with. To take a parable out of its context, and to present spiritual and practical lessons from it is relatively easy. To leave a parable in its context, and to explain it in its context, is much more difficult. In an overall exposition of a Gospel, the latter is more important than the former. The author has not therefore necessarily followed the opinions of others, but has sought to present the interpretations of parables according to the onflowing unfolding of truth according to Matthew's objective in presenting Christ as the King of the Jews.

Some parts of Scripture are not without their difficulties; many are well known and "standard". In dealing with Matthew's Gospel verse-by-verse, all such difficulties have had to be faced, so the author has not deliberately glossed over any of them; he has presented in some cases his own solutions, without, however, overlooking solutions proposed by others.

The most difficult decision that had to be taken was that of the Name to be used whenever the Lord Jesus Christ is referred to. Though this Gospel is the Gospel of the King, Matthew has referred only sparingly to this title. Other expositors have used the title "King" throughout their works, though this appears to be forcing an issue beyond what is written. We have used the title "King" in the overall subject headings, but only sparingly after that. The Name used in the Gospel narratives is, of course, "Jesus", but the Epistle-writers for Christian readers have used this Name only occasionally. In keeping with the post-resurrection confession, "It is the Lord" (John 21:7), we have decided to use the title, "the Lord", with occasional exceptions, when referring to Him in historical contexts. If this appears to some readers to be a personal preference, then their acquiescence will be appreciated, even if they think, preach, teach and write differently.

3. Religious and Political Background

The roots of Matthew's Gospel are found in the OT. When Aaron was the high priest and when David later was king, the choice of religious and regal leadership had been made by God (Heb 5:4; 1 Sam 16:12). However, there were forces at work then (as now) that were antagonistic to the concept of divine choice. Thus 1 Samuel opens with Eli as the high priest, indeed a descendant from Aaron, but stemming from Aaron's son Ithamar through whom the high priestly line was not chosen to descend. Thus Eli's name is not found in the list of high priests given in 1 Chron 6:3-15. In David's time, Zadok was the high priest, and he was in the chosen position as descending from Eleazar, another son of Aaron (Num 25:11-13). A similar situation arose with respect to royalty. After Solomon, there were two kings, Rehoboam (son of Solomon) over Judaea, and correctly a descendant of David in the regal line leading to Christ. The second king was Jeroboam (1 Kings 12:16-33), a rival king over the northern tribes. All the subsequent northern kings were given to idolatry, until the nation disappeared under the Assyrian captivity (2 Kings 17:1-41). In Jerusalem, faithfulness and unfaithfulness characterised the various kings who were rightly in David's line, until the Babylonian captivity, after which no king in David's line sat upon the throne in Jerusalem. Like Eli and Jeroboam, the high priests and kings in the NT were not chosen by God, but ultimately were Satan's choice.

During the Babylonian captivity, manifestations of the divine knowledge regarding the future were granted to the kings of Babylon, and Daniel interpreted dreams and the writing on the wall. In his old age Daniel too had visions (Dan 7:2-14), showing God's foreknowledge regarding the empires (mainly future relative to the time of the vision, but mostly past relative to our present standpoint) which should dominate that part of the world.

The metals in Dan 2:31-35, 38-45, and the beasts in 7:2-8 represent these kingdoms and their kings. Although the Jews returned to Jerusalem after the Babylonian captivity, they were never again their own masters with a king ruling over them. They were at the mercy of the succession of Gentile powers who had ultimate authority. The four empires were

1. The Babylonian empire under Nebuchadnezzar; this ended in Dan 5:30-31 when Daniel was an old man.

2. The Medo-Persian empire; under Cyrus the Jews returned to Jerusalem to rebuild the temple, and later the walls of the city.

3. The Grecian empire, whose first king was Alexander the Great (Dan 8:21).

4. The Roman empire, the dominant power when the Lord was here; though after several centuries it collapsed, it is to rise again in the future having

> the beast of Rev 13:1 as its head. This empire is described as "The beast that thou sawest was, and is not; and shall ascend out of the bottomless pit" (Rev 17:8, 11).

Their representative beasts are a lion, a bear, a leopard, and a nameless beast "dreadful and terrible, and strong exceedingly; and it had great iron teeth". This Roman kingdom, relatively young when the Lord was here and when Paul engaged in his missionary journeys, will be abolished with its king in the future by the Son of man coming in glory to establish His own kingdom (Dan 7:9-14, 22, 27; 2:44-45).

Many OT Scriptures refer to these kingdoms; the following list is not comprehensive, but it gives an indication of the wide application found in the OT. The Babylonian empire was announced prophetically to Hezekiah one hundred years before it dominated the world scene in the Middle East (2 Kings 20:12-19). Its attacks on Jerusalem are described in 2 Kings 24:8 onwards, while 25:1-21 describes the later destruction of the temple and city. See also 2 Chron 36:6-21; Jer 52. Subsequent events after the emergence of Babylon as a world power are found in 2 Kings 25:22-30; Ps 137; Jer 38:17-28; chs. 39-44; Lam chs. 1-5; Ezek chs. 1-48; Dan chs. 1-5; 7-8.

The early events relating to the Medo-Persian kingdom are described in Isa 44:28; 45:1-4 (prophetically); 2 Chron 36:22-23, Dan 6:9-12; Ezra, Nehemiah, Esther, Haggai, Zechariah, Malachi.

The Grecian empire rose and fell during the inter-testamental period; its history is found neither in the OT nor in the NT. Prophetically it is seen as the "third kingdom of brass, which shall bear rule over all the earth" (Dan 2:39) and as the "leopard ... the beast had also four heads; and dominion was given to it" (Dan 7:6). It is also seen as the "he goat" (Dan 8:5) that destroyed the ram, standing for the Medo-Persian empire. This goat is defined to be the king of Greece, its great horn being its first king, namely Alexander the Great (Dan 8:21). When he died, the vast empire was divided into four parts. Later Antiochus Epiphanes arose, and desecrated the temple in Jerusalem (Dan 8:9-12). During this period, the kings of the north (Assyria) and of the south (Egypt) were in constant warfare throughout the land of Judaea and Jerusalem, described prophetically in Dan 11:3-35 (what is now past history is also a prophetical view of future history after the church has been taken to be with the Lord).

The fourth empire was the Roman kingdom; in Dan 7:7-8 it is seen as extending right up to the time of the establishment of Messiah's glorious kingdom. No name is given to the fourth beast, since no real animal could adequately depict the cruel propensities of this kingdom. Its brutality and its conquests distinguish it from all previous empires. Although Rome is not mentioned by name in OT prophecy, this kingdom must be Rome (appearing so often in the NT), since it followed the Grecian kingdom which gradually collapsed over the century preceding the birth of the Lord Jesus as King of the Jews. And no further empire amongst men is foreseen in Dan 2:44; 7:8-9; Messiah's kingdom will follow. The God of heaven shall set up a kingdom, to be ruled over by the Stone (Dan 2:44, 45). The last beast shall be slain, to be replaced by God's King, the Son of man in glory (Dan 7:11-13). It is essentially this Roman kingdom that Satan offered to the Lord Jesus during the time of His temptation (Matt 4:8-10). It was Rome that crucified its criminals, that crucified the Lord Jesus under that unjust procurator Pilate, that put Paul to death under emperor Nero, that destroyed Jerusalem and its temple in 70 AD, that slaughtered millions of Jews, and that persecuted Christians causing many to be put to death. The Roman emperors ruled over all – North Africa, the Middle East, and southern Europe. Ultimately Rome polluted the church, and became papal Rome. Throughout the subsequent centuries, it is papal Rome that has dominated Christendom, though in the future the world scene will be dominated by political Rome as well as by religious Rome.

When the NT opened, Rome was the occupying power in Judaea, and men longed for divine intervention to rid them of this burden, just as God had delivered them from bondage in Egypt long ago. The hope of the kingdom, predicted by the prophets both morally and in glorious display with Messiah at its head, was longed for by the Jews. Men "looked for redemption in Jerusalem" (Luke 2:38); the Pharisees wanted to know "when the kingdom of God should come" (Luke 17:20); towards the end of His life, some "thought that the kingdom of God should immediately appear" (Luke 19:11); the two men on the Emmaus road thought that He "should have redeemed Israel" from the Roman yoke (Luke 24:21), while just before His ascension, the apostles still hoped that He would "at this time restore again the kingdom to Israel" (Acts 1:6). We know now what the disciples did not know when He was here: that the Roman yoke would remain, and that the liberty of Messiah's kingdom in glory would have to wait until the church has been completed and gathered into His presence.

This contrast between the Roman kingdom and Messiah's kingdom colours much of Matthew's Gospel, the rejected King pointing to the righteous and glorious kingdom to come in the future, not in the period when He was present in the days of His flesh. His kingdom was " not of this world" John (18:36) and the chief priests readily confessed, "We have no king but Caesar" (John 19:15).

The world-political scene was, then, entirely dominated by Roman jurisdiction. The Roman empire consisted of hundreds of satellite states, each of which was linked to Rome by negotiated arrangements. During the two-and-a-half centuries before Christ, these annexed states gradually grew in number, as the Roman tentacles spread out far and wide, with Rome as their centre. In order, these annexed states embraced Sicily, Sardinia, Corsica, Spain, North Africa, Macedonia, Achaia, Asia, Bithinia, Cyrene, Illyricum, Cilicia, Pontus, Syria, Gaul, the Rhine area, Egypt, the Danube states, Galatia, Cappadocia, Judaea and Britain. Many of these names appear in the book of the Acts. By the time the NT opened, the whole of the Mediterranean area and southern Europe was under the ultimate authority of the Roman emperor. These states were administered by Roman governors or proconsuls, whose duties included:

1. public order and military security (the Jews feared Roman intervention if their own administration could not control the people; see John 11:48, "the Romans shall come and take away both our place and nation");

2. taxation — taxes were collected for Rome by the "publicans" who constituted a hated minority amongst the Jewish population;

3. Roman justice, by means of Roman tribunals, the best-documented one in the NT being the trial of the Lord before Pilate.

The emperors ruled from Rome. The Caesars were a family that maintained the emperorship from Julius Caesar to Nero. Those named in the NT are: Caesar Augustus (Luke 2:1) whose decree ensured that the Lord's birth would take place in Bethlehem south of Jerusalem rather than in Nazareth up north in Galilee; Tiberias Caesar (Luke 3:1) who was in power during the Lord's ministry; Claudius Caesar (Acts 11:28; 17:7; 18:2) during Paul's early missionary journeys; Nero (Acts 25:11, 21, 25; 2 Tim 4:16-17) who was the cruellest of them all. Note : the word "Augustus" (*ho Sebastos,* Acts 25:21) is not the same as that in Luke 2:1 (*Augoustos*). Nero was the emperor implied by the word *"ho Sebastos",* translated "emperor" in the RV. *"Sebastos"* is the Greek equivalent of Augustus, and means "worthy to be reverenced", a designation used by many Roman Emperors.

John the Baptist's ministry opened in Luke 3:1-2, Pontius Pilate being "governor" of Judaea. Emperor Tiberias had appointed him to be the fifth procurator of Judaea; he had full control of the province, and was in charge of the Roman army of occupation stationed on the coast at Caesarea which contained a heathen Roman temple. There was also a garrison at Jerusalem in the fortress of Antonia north of the temple precincts. During the Jewish feasts, Pilate resided in Jerusalem, with additional troops to maintain order in the city. He appointed the Jewish high priests, and managed the temple funds. Many of his acts caused him to be thoroughly disliked by the Jews, although the Jewish leaders were glad of his unjust co-operation at the trial of the Lord. King Herod and Pilate had been mutual enemies until the Lord's trial, after which they were friends again (Luke 23:12). Because of his excesses Pilate was recalled to Rome, at which time Tiberias died; it is on record that Pilate ultimately committed suicide. Felix was procurator in Caesarea for eight years, mainly during Nero's emperorship (Acts 23:24), followed by Festus' two years (24:27; 25:1-27; 26:24-32).

In addition to Roman authority, the Jews were able to exercise their own authority. Firstly we shall discuss the pseudo-authority of the Jewish kings (*not* of the line of David), and later the Jewish council known as the Sanhedrin. Herod the Great was born in 73 BC, and reigned through the period 40-4 BC. His father Antipater was of Edomite descent, and Herod was a Jew by religion. Antipater was procurator of Judaea, and he appointed his son Herod to be military prefect of Galilee. The Romans then appointed him king of the Jews, and he retained the throne in Judaea for 33 years, having taken three years of warfare to secure it. He was disliked by the Jews. He engaged in building projects at home and abroad; in particular, he rebuilt the Antonia fortress north of the temple precincts, the temple in Jerusalem, and many heathen temples in other parts. He was well-known for his murderous pursuits, and just before his death that resulted from a serious illness, he was responsible for the Bethlehem massacre of young boys, from which the Lord Jesus was delivered by divine intervention (Matt 2:12-18). He was followed by his elder son Archelaus (Matt 2:22), who was removed from office by Rome because of his repressive policies, a Jewish deputation having been sent to Rome to inform on his activities. Another son of Herod the Great, called "Herod the tetrarch" in Luke 3:19, then ruled over the Galilaean and Peraean regions of his father's kingdom. This is the Herod that appears throughout the ministry of John the Baptist and that of the Lord Himself. He, too, was a great builder; Tiberias on the Sea of Galilee was built by him in 22 AD before the Lord's ministry commenced. He also was deposed from office by emperor Gaius in 36 AD after the Lord's death, and was succeeded by his son "Herod the king" (Acts 12:1), who ruled over an area approximately equal to that of his grandfather Herod the Great. His sudden death in Acts 12:23 brought his son Agrippa to the throne in due course, receiving the title of king from emperor Claudius; his territories were increased later by Nero. He appears in the NT in Acts 25:13 to Acts 26:32. He, rather than the Roman procurators, appointed the high priests, and during the war that resulted in the destruction of Jerusalem in 70 AD, he remained loyal to Rome; his kingdom was therefore further extended. None of these Herods had, of course, any divinely-given right to the throne; the Lord Jesus will ultimately take "the throne of his father David" (Luke 1:32). The authorities feared His title as "King of the Jews", and yet taunted Him with it.

Jewish religion can be described as a dual system – temple and synagogue; this dual system appears throughout the Gospels, and was always at variance with the doctrine of the Lord Jesus. Solomon's temple had been burnt to the ground by Nebuchadnezzar (2 Kings 25:9; 2 Chron 36:19; Isa 64:11 prophetically). At the end of the captivity, Cyrus had decreed that the temple should be rebuilt in Jerusalem (Isa 44:28; Ezra 1:2-3), and through many difficulties this was achieved in Ezra chs.3-6. It is known as Zerubbabel's temple, since he was the leader of the Jews who returned from the captivity. The Jews refused the help of the Samaritans in the rebuilding, who then erected a rival temple on mount Gerizim (John 4:20). Herod the Great built a substitute temple on mount Moriah, surpassing in magnificence the former two temples which had stood on the same site. Even after forty-six years the temple was not complete (John 2:20). The surrounding courts were arranged on successively lower levels, the mount of Olives on the east forming a vantage point from which the whole structure could be viewed looking west across the Kidron valley (Matt 24:1-3). As we have said, the high priests were chosen by Pilate in opposition to the true Aaronic high priesthood, where the choice was made by God. Annas had been deposed by Pilate, being replaced by Caiaphas, but the Jews regarded both as high priests (Luke 3:2) and both took part in the Lord's trial before the Jewish Sanhedrin (John 18:13, 24). The temple service was a rich elaboration of that which had been instituted by God in the OT; in particular, morning and evening sacrifices were offered daily on the altar throughout the Lord's ministry, and this continued right up to the evening of the temple's destruction by the Romans in 70 AD. Since then these sacrifices have ceased completely.

In the OT, the Levitical sacrifices were full of typical foreshadowings of the sacrificial death of the Lord Jesus; God perceived them as such as long as they were offered by men of faith. But they meant nothing to God when men of idolatry and unbelief offered them (Isa 1:10-15; Lam 2:7; Mal 1:8, 13-14). After the return from the captivity idolatry was not practised again, but a cold formalism of unbelief later replaced the zeal and faithfulness of those who had originally returned, and of those who stood for their faith during the persecutions stemming from the evils of Antiochus Epiphanes. But the sacrifice of the Lord Jesus brought about the complete end of the Jewish sacrificial system as far as God was concerned. After His death, the priests perpetuated it, and even Christians went back to it, but in 70 AD it came to a complete end. Ceremony today is therefore an anathema to God, since it is a rival to the pre-eminence of Christ.

The second component of the Jewish religious system was the synagogue. This originated after the return from the captivity, primarily to provide the opportunity for instructing the people in the knowledge of the law. Synagogues were built wherever Jews were found, though Philippi seems to have been an exception (Acts 16:13); when Jerusalem was destroyed in 70 AD, there may have been over 400 synagogues in the city. Each synagogue was governed by elders, who had the authority to punish members (John 9:22; 12:42) both by scourging and by excommunication. An "ark" contained the scrolls of the OT Scriptures for public reading. References to the synagogue and its service are found throughout the historical NT books. A typical service on the Sabbath day would embrace a prayer, the reading of the law and the prophets, an interpretation from the Hebrew into Aramaic, an exposition of the passages, and a concluding benediction. This formal arrangement was not followed in the services of the early church, where spiritual liberty was rightly exercised; yet later the church introduced formal arrangements into its own services, a practice that has remained to the present day in most ecclesiastical systems of Christendom, for men love to have it so. This shows how quickly departure from early church principles developed, largely copying temple and synagogue practice, whereas the Spirit of God had introduced a new thing. Once the principle of copying had been established, it was of course impossible to eradicate it.

Religion had its hold on Jewish administration, and on the various groupings and parties amongst men.

The Sanhedrin was the council exercising the highest Jewish authority, possessing religious, judicial and administrative powers. In NT times, its sphere of influence extended over Judaea, but not over Galilee where most of the Lord's ministry was accomplished. Its roots are said to extend back to the seventy elders who helped Moses (Num 11:16-24), and the rulers and elders in Ezra and Nehemiah are supposed to have formed a body that developed into the Sanhedrin. A responsible representative body amongst the Jews existed under Greek domination, but under the Romans it attained the status and authority seen so often throughout the NT historical books. Membership consisted of the high priest and men who had previously been high priests, Pharisees and Sadducees, and legal experts known as scribes or lawyers. Their religious convictions determined how they would react to matters under investigation (Acts 23:7-10). The president of the Sanhedrin was the high priest (Acts 5:17; 7:1; 9:1; 22:5; 23:2; 24:1). The council could exercise judgment in criminal matters according to Jewish law, though the Roman procurator had to confirm death sentences; in all cases, the Romans could interfere if necessary. There were formal procedures laid down for the conduct of the trial of a prisoner, with votes being taken for acquittal or condemnation of a prisoner.

The Pharisees were a group who adhered scrupulously to the law of Moses, and avoided politics, hating the Roman dominion over their country, and the rule of the pseudo-kings, the Herods. According to them the law of Moses contained 613 commandments, and all had to be formally observed. To them the law was not only the written law, but also oral tradition that interpreted the written law. They believed in resurrection (Acts 23:8), though not of course in the Christian doctrine of resurrection. In Matt 23:13-33 the Lord branded them as hypocrites owing to their inconsistency: their interpretation of the law only highlighted the ungodliness of their lives.

The Sadducees were more numerous than the Pharisees as members of the Sanhedrin, and they appear to have been derived from priestly families. They were mainly interested in secular power, and rejected the oral tradition favoured by the Pharisees. In their more materialistic outlook, they were more severe in their punishment of crime, and rejected the concept of resurrection or anything of a spiritual nature. They disappeared from history when Jerusalem was destroyed in 70 AD.

Scribes and Lawyers. The terms "scribe" (*grammateus*) and "lawyer" (*nomikos*) were synonymous. As experts in the study of the law of Moses, scribes were originally priests as was "Ezra the priest the scribe" (Neh 8:9). Some were members of the Sanhedrin. Their duties included preserving the law according to their oral tradition; they instructed pupils in the law, using the temple precincts for this purpose (Luke 2:46), and they administered the law as members of the Sanhedrin. They belonged to the Pharisaical party, though forming a distinct grouping.

The Herodians (Matt 22:16; Mark 3:6; 12:13) formed a party allied to the Pharisees when they could mount a joint attack on the Lord's teaching. They were supporters of the Herods, seeking to avoid any confrontation with Rome.

The Samaritans inhabited the territory between Judaea and Galilee. In the OT after Solomon's death, the kingdom north of Judaea was formed under king Jeroboam. He installed an idolatrous religious system, complete with temple, priests and feast days (1 Kings 12:26-33), so as to prevent the people returning to Jerusalem. Some 250 years later, the idolatry was so bad that God delivered the nation into the hands of the Assyrians (2 Kings 17:23). Later the land was repopulated by peoples from other nations (v.24), and they "possessed Samaria, and dwelt in the cities thereof", Samaria being the capital city of the northern kingdom. A priest was also repatriated, so as to teach them his own particular brand of idolatry (vv.27-41). These people became the Samaritans, possessing the Pentateuch and a temple on mount Gerizim. In the NT the Jews had no dealings with the Samaritans (John 4:9); often Jews would not pass through such enemy territory, but crossed to the east of the river Jordan so as to by-pass Samaria. In the parable, the priest and the Levite copied this convenient method of by-passing unpleasant things (Luke 10:31-33), but the good Samaritan did not by-pass the man wounded by thieves. Neither did the Lord in His ministry! In John 4:3-5 He passed through this territory, knowing that He would meet the woman and the men from the city Sychar. Though the Lord received the Samaritans, there was no reciprocation; as He passed through from the north with His face set steadfastly to go to Jerusalem they would not receive Him (Luke 9:51-53). Later He gave instructions that the gospel should spread out to Samaria (Acts 1:8); thus Philip preached Christ there, and there was great joy when people believed and were baptised (Acts 8:5, 12).

Into this confused political and religious scene the Lord entered.

4. Survey of Matthew's Gospel

The differences between the first three Gospels, by Matthew, Mark and Luke, and the Gospel by John are very marked. The amount of common material is very limited. The study of the similarities in, and differences between, the first three Gospels is known as the Synoptic Problem, but such an academic study usually reckons without the overall work of the Holy Spirit of inspiration. John concluded his Gospel with the statement that, if everything that the Lord Jesus did were recorded, then "the world itself could not contain the books that should be written" (John 21:25). Thus the actual amount that is recorded is very limited, yet sufficient for all subsequent readers. The selection and arrangement of material, together with the details given for each paragraph or subject, lay within the province of the Holy Spirit, who used the memory, experience and research of the authors, as well as their individual styles of writing, to produce the four

Gospels that provide details of the life and death of the Son of God when here on earth.

Most of the Lord's time was spent in Galilee (north of Judaea and Samaria), and the writers of the three Synoptic Gospels concentrated upon the Lord's ministry in that area. The OT law demanded that male Jews should go up to Jerusalem at the principal annual feasts (Exod 23:14-17), and that is what the Lord Jesus did. John, in his Gospel, concentrated upon the Lord's ministry during His visits to Jerusalem. Apart from John 1, only chs. 2:1-12; 4; 6; 21 deal with events outside the immediate vicinity of Jerusalem. In fact, the only miracle common to the four Gospels is that of the feeding of the 5,000, recorded in Matt 14:15-21; Mark 6:32-44; Luke 9:12-17; John 6:5-14. The various visits to Jerusalem in John's Gospel cannot all be pinpointed with certainty as to where they should be placed in the three Synoptic Gospels. Assumptions have to be made, particularly if a map is to be drawn showing the complete recorded itineraries of the Lord during His lifetime and in His resurrection. (It is easier to trace the missionary journeys of the apostle Paul on a map.) Different expositors and cartographers produce different schemes. However, the Holy Spirit does not ask believers to concern themselves with uncertainties, since faith is not disturbed thereby, and the building up of believers in their faith rests upon more sure and certain foundations.

The fact that there are four Gospels – and not three or five – has attracted attention since early times. No doubt imagination has crept in with the attempts to explain the number. Thus the one river in Eden parted "into four heads" (Gen 2:10-14), similar to the one Lord of glory from heaven watering the earth under four different aspects of His ministry. Moreover, four is the number of universality: there are four principal directions of the compass, and four seasons throughout the year. In Dan 2:32, 33, 37-40 we read of four great world empires under the figure of metals; in Dan 7:3-7 they are typified by beasts – the Babylonian, Medo-Persian, Grecian and Roman empires. In the parable of the sower (Matt 13:3-8, 18-23), the field, divided into four types of soil, is the world.

The four Gospels have often been likened to the four living creatures in the vision in Ezek 1:10, "As for the likeness of their faces, they four had the face of a man, and the face of a lion, on the right side: and they four had the face of an ox on the left side; they four also had the face of an eagle". The face of the lion speaks of the Gospel by Matthew, the Gospel of the King: "behold, thy King" (Zech 9:9; Matt 21:5; John 19:14). The face of the ox speaks of the Gospel by Mark, the Gospel of the Servant: "Behold my servant" (Isa 42:1; 52:13) The face of a man speaks of the Gospel by Luke, the Gospel of the Man Christ Jesus: "Behold the man" (Zech 6:12; John 19:5). The face of the eagle speaks of the Gospel by John, the Gospel of heaven, of the Son of God: "Behold your God" (Isa 40:9).

The structure of the Gospel by Matthew can be visualised in various ways:

Chapters 1-4 relate the unrecognised first advent of the King, together with

His early rejection. We find the mutual testimony both by John the Baptist and by the Lord Himself that the kingdom of heaven was at hand (3:2; 4:17). Repentance leads to the Sermon on the Mount in chs.5-7, laying the basis for conduct in the kingdom on the grounds of righteousness, rather than on the grounds of grace for believers associated with a risen and ascended Lord.

Chapters 5-12 consist of the Lord's teaching mingled with miracles (but not parables). The more specific object of the Gospel commences with ch.8. In chs.8-12, the testimony of the kingdom is proclaimed to "the lost sheep of the house of Israel" (10:6-7). The antagonism of the religious and political leaders in Israel grows, as the elders, priests and Pharisees become aware of a superior Authority in their midst. Their antagonism ends in blasphemy, when they accuse the Lord of casting out demons (*daimonion,* not "devils") "by Beelzebub the prince of the demons" (12:24). Such a generation of vipers is condemned by their own words (12:34, 37), and the Lord withdraws from the sinful scene into a ship apart.

In Matt 13:1 to 20:29, the New Order is introduced by the rejected Lord; here His ministry consists of teaching mingled mainly with parables (with very few miracles). The kingdom is seen in mystery form in ch.13, the truth being known only by revelation, and hidden from the wise and prudent (13:10-17). New concepts are introduced, such as Christ being the Son of the living God (16:16); the reception of truth by revelation from the Father (16:17); the introduction of the church as the building of Christ (16:18); the first direct announcement of His forthcoming death and resurrection (16:21); the glorified Christ as He will appear in His future kingdom no longer in mystery form, when He will be vindicated in open display (17:2). These new concepts are introduced only to His own disciples. Chapters 18-20 introduce principles of conduct suitable for those who confess the Son of God. The church as the Lord's holy property (16:18) is seen in ch.18 as the local church on earth, so this chapter deals rather fully with mutual relations between the Lord's people in local assembly fellowship. But the Lord is to occupy a position of glory by decreasing that He may increase. Matt 20:26-28, at the end of the section dealing with the New Order, shows the graduation of increase by the words " great", " chief", " Son of man". Yet this is to be attained by the Lord taking the decreasing position denoted by the words, "minister", "servant" (that is, bond servant), "give his life" .

Matt 20:30 returns to the Jewish position again; if the parenthesis of the New Order were removed, this verse would join on to the end of ch.12. Hence, up to the end of ch.25, the Lord is seen again in relation to the Jews; the King, in fact, comes into Jerusalem, "the city of the great King" (5:35). Since the King was rejected by the Jews then (as He is today), this section leads up to the day of restoration at His second advent, and to the gathering unto Himself of His elect (24:31), as well as to His triumphant throne of glory and judgment over the nations (25:31).

The last three chapters, chs. 26-28, show the final crescendo of hatred against the Lord by the Jewish religious authorities. He is falsely tried, condemned to death, and crucified by soldiers of the occupying power, the Romans. God's power is far greater than the puny efforts of men; the King is raised, no longer to be seen by His Jewish subjects, but by chosen witnesses who would commence to herald forth the truth of the gospel throughout the world.

The healing of the two blind men in Matt 20:30-34 is a pivot in the dealings of God with His people. It is at this point that Jewish relationships are taken up again, shown by the recorded cry of the blind men, who own the Lord as " Son of David" (v.30), a title that relates the Lord to the Jews as King in the regal line from David. Note that this title is taken up by these blind men at the end of the Lord's ministry on earth. It recalls a similar but distinct incident near the beginning of the Lord's ministry in Matt 9:27-31, where again we find two blind men who confess Him as "Son of David". These titles occur in those sections of Matthew's Gospel where the Lord is seen more particularly in His relation to the Jews; see also Matt 22:41-45.

This Gospel makes a difference between the Lord's dealings with the Gentiles and with the Jews, both then and in the future. But now, while grace reigns prior to His coming again for the church, there is no difference between Jew and Gentile; both are under sin (Rom 3:9); in the local church "there is neither Jew nor Greek ... ye are all one in Christ Jesus" (Gal 3:28); in the matter of salvation "there is no difference ... the same Lord over all is rich unto all that call upon him" (Rom 10:12). But later, prophecy that relates to the Jews in God's kingdom on earth is taken up again, and this order is followed in Matthew's Gospel where prophetical matters are dealt with in detail in chs.24-25

The miracle of healing accomplished by the Lord in these blind men speaks of this future day of restoration. The veil is taken away (2 Cor 3:16), enabling the elect of the nation to see Him (Rev 1:7). Blindness in part has happened to Israel until the fullness of the Gentiles is come in; but in the future, they shall see Him and be saved (Rom 11:25-26). In that great day when the desert shall blossom like a rose, "then the eyes of the blind shall be opened" (Isa 35:5); the Lord's Servant will "open the blind eyes" (Isa 42:7). Hence this miracle in Matt 20:30-34 is recorded as a picture of the nation when their faith recognises the Lord to be their King. The King entered Jerusalem in ch.21, and in spite of circumstances suggesting His public acclamation, He knew that it would lead almost immediately to His rejection and death.

Some expositors separate Matthew's Gospel into sections based on the five major teaching sessions recorded in the Gospel. These are:

1. Matt 5-7, the Sermon on the Mount, concluding with "when Jesus had ended these sayings" (7:28);

2. Matt 10:5-42, the Lord's instructions for the apostles when they were sent forth to evangelise, concluding with "when Jesus had made an end of commanding his twelve disciples" (11:1);

3. Matt 13:1-52, the parables of the kingdom presented in mystery form, namely known only to the initiated by revelation, and not in open display, concluding with "when Jesus had finished these parables" (13:53);

4. Matt 18, relationships between the Lord's people, concluding with "when Jesus had finished these sayings" (19:1);

5. Matt 24-25, two prophetical chapters dealing with events after the church has been taken, and when the King returns in glory, concluding with "when Jesus had finished all these sayings" (26:1).

The similarity between the five conclusions is very noticeable, showing that Matthew was using these discourses as building bricks for the structure of his Gospel.

The Gospel by Matthew, the book of the Acts, the Epistles to the Romans and to the Hebrews, and the book of the Revelation, are particularly rich in quotations from, and indirect allusions to, the text of the OT. Such quotations cannot be ignored in the careful study of any NT passage, since they often supply the spiritual key to unlock the treasures hidden in the passage, which a superficial reading may fail to notice. All such quotations are noted in our exposition, and in section 6 a list is supplied of all major quotations from and allusions to the OT in Matthew's Gospel.

5. Outline

Chapters 1 to 4

The King Comes to His People

I.	*The King's Regal and Legal Genealogy*	1:1-17
	1. From Abraham to David	1:1-6
	2. From David to the Babylonian Captivity	1:6-11
	3. From the Babylonian Captivity to Christ	1:12-17
II.	*The Birth of Jesus Christ*	1:18-25
	1. The Angelic Message to Joseph	1:18-21
	2. The King's Birth—Prophecy and Fulfilment	1:22-25
III.	*The King's Early Rejection*	2:1-23
	1. Worship by the Wise Men	2:1-12
	2. Temporary Sojourn in Egypt	2:13-23

IV.	*The Ministry of John the Baptist*	3: 1- 17
	1. Baptism of the Multitudes	3:1-12
	2. Baptism of the Lord Jesus	3:13-17
V.	*Commencement of the Lord's Ministry*	4: 1-25
	1. The Temptation in the Wilderness	4:1-11
	The First Temptation	4:1-4
	The Second Temptation	4:5-7
	The Third Temptation	4:8-11
	2. The Lord Commences His Public Ministry	4:12-25

Chapters 5 to 12

The King's Ministry—Teaching with Miracles

I.	*The Sermon on the Mount: Part 1*	5:1-48
	1. The Beatitudes	5:1-12
	2. Salt and Light—Effect on the World	5:13-16
	3. Superiority of the Lord's Teaching	5:17-48
	Not to Destroy the Law, but ...	5:17-20
	Not to Kill, but ...	5:21-26
	Not to Commit Adultery, but ...	5:27-32
	Not to Forswear, but ...	5:33-37
	An Eye for an Eye, but ...	5:38-42
	Love thy Neighbour, Hate thine Enemy, but ...	5:43-48
II.	*The Sermon on the Mount: Part II*	6:1-34
	1. Not Alms before Men	6:1-4
	2. Not Prayers before Men	6:5-15
	3. Not Fasting before Men	6:16-18
	4. Singleness of Purpose	6:19-24
	5. A Question of Priorities	6:25-34
III.	*The Sermon on the Mount: Part III*	7:1-29
	1. Hypocrisy and Judgment	7:1-5
	2. Features of Kingdom Conduct	7:6-14
	3. False Prophets	7:15-23
	4. Foundations—Rock or Sand	7:24-29
IV.	*Works of Authority*	8:1-34
	1. The Healing of the Leper	8:1-4
	2. The Healing of the Centurion's Servant	8:5-13
	3. Miracles and Discipleship	8:14-22

III.	*The Final Condemnation of the Pharisees*	23:1-39
	1. The Self-importance of the Pharisees	23:1-12
	2. The Seven Woes upon the Pharisees	23:13-33
	3. The Prophets and the House Desolate	23:34-39
IV.	*The Second Advent of the King in Glory*	24:1-51
	1. The Olivet Discourse—the Past and the Future	24:1-3
	2. Events during the Last Seven Years	24:4-28
	3. The Coming of the King as the Son of Man	24:29-41
	4. The Necessity of Watching	24:42-51
V.	*Parables Relating to the King's Return in Glory*	25:1-46
	1. The Parable of the Ten Virgins	25:1-13
	2. The Parable of the Eight Talents	25:14-30
	3. The Parable of the Sheep and the Goats	25:31-46

Chapters 26 to 28
The King's Crucifixion and Resurrection

I.	*The Night before the Lord's Death*	26:1-75
	1. Evil without and Worship within	26:1-16
	2. The Passover and the Breaking of Bread	26:17-35
	3. The Garden of Gethsemane	26:36-56
	4. The Trial before the Sanhedrin, and Peter's Denial	26:57-75
II.	*The Trial before Pilate, and the Crucifixion*	27:1-66
	1. The Suicide of Judas	27:1-10
	2. The Judgment before Pilate	27:11-31
	3. The Crucifixion of the Lord	27:32-50
	4. Events between the Lord's Death and His Resurrection	27:51-66
III.	*The Resurrection of Christ*	28:1-20
	1. The Resurrection Day	28:1-10
	2. Events after the Resurrection	28:11-20

6. Quotations from the Old Testament

We here give a list of the more important quotations from, and allusions to, the OT in Matthew's Gospel. We also show how the quotation is introduced, and by whom (in brackets).

Matthew	OT reference	Introduction of Quotation, and by whom
1:23	Isa 7:14	"that it might be fulfilled which was spoken of the Lord by the prophet, saying" (Matthew)
2:6	Mic 5:2	"thus it is written by the prophet" (priests and scribes)
2:15	Hos 11:1	" that it might be fulfilled which was spoken of the Lord by the prophet, saying" (Matthew)
2:18	Jer 31:15	"Then was fulfilled that which was spoken by Jeremy the prophet, saying" (Matthew)
2:23	Isa 11:1 (?)	"that it might be fulfilled which was spoken by the prophets" (Matthew)
3:3	Isa 40:3	" this is he that was spoken of by the prophet Esaias" (Matthew)
4:4	Deut 8:3	"It is written" (the Lord)
4:6	Ps 91:11-12	"for it is written" (the devil)
4:7	Deut 6:16	"It is written again" (the Lord)
4:10	Deut 6:13	"for it is written"' (the Lord)
4:15-16	Isa 9:1-2	"that it might be fulfilled which was spoken by Esaias the prophet, saying" (Matthew)
5:21	Exod 20:13	"it was said by (to) them of old time" (the Lord)
5:27	Exod 20:14	"it was said by (to) them of old time" (the Lord)
5:31	Deut 24:1	"It hath been said" (the Lord)
5:33	Exod 20:7	"it hath been said by (to) them of old time" (the Lord)
5:38	Exod 21:24	"it hath been said" (the Lord)
5:43	Lev 19:18	"it hath been said" (the Lord)
7:23	Ps 6:8	(the Lord)
8:17	Isa 53:4	"That it might be fulfilled which was spoken by Esaias the prophet, saying" (Matthew)
9:13	Hos 6:6	"what that meaneth" (the Lord)
10:35-36	Mic 7:6	(the Lord)
11:10	Mal 3:1	"of whom it is written" (the Lord)
11:14	Mal 4:5	(the Lord)
12:3	1 Sam 21:6	"Have ye not read?" (the Lord)
12:5	Num 28:9-10	"have ye not read in the law?" (the Lord)
12:7	Hos 6:6	"what this meaneth" (the Lord)
12:18-20	Isa 42:1-3	"that it might be fulfilled which was spoken by Esaias the prophet, saying" (Matthew)
12:40	Jon 1:17	"the sign of the prophet Jonas" (the Lord)
12:42	1 Kings 10:1	(the Lord)
13:14	Isa 6:9,10	"in them is fulfilled the prophecy of Esaias, which saith" (the Lord)
13:35	Ps 78:2	"that it might be fulfilled which was spoken by the prophet, saying" (Matthew)

Matthew	OT reference	Introduction of Quotation, and by whom
15:4	Exod 20:12	"For God commanded, saying" (the Lord)
15:4	Exod 21:7	"For God commanded, saying" (the Lord)
15:8, 9	Isa 29:13	"well did Esaias prophesy of you, saying" (the Lord)
17:11	Mal 3:1	(the Lord)
18:16	Deut 19:15	(the Lord)
19:4	Gen 1:27	"Have ye not read" (the Lord)
19:5	Gen 2:24	"he which made them … said" (the Lord)
19:7	Deut 24:1	"Why did Moses then command" (Pharisees)
19:18	Exod 20:12	(the Lord)
19:19	Lev 19:18	(the Lord)
21:5	Zech 9:9	"All this was done, that it might be fulfilled which was spoken by the prophet, saying" (Matthew)
21:9	Ps 118:26	(the multitudes)
21:13	Isa 56:7	"It is written" (the Lord)
21:13	Jer 7:11	"It is written" (the Lord)
21:16	Ps 8:2	"have ye never read?"(the Lord)
21:42	Ps 118:22, 23	"Did ye never read in the scriptures?" (the Lord)
22:24	Deut 25:5	"Moses said" (the Sadducees)
22:32	Exod 3:6	"have ye not read that which was spoken unto you by God, saying" (the Lord)
22:37	Deut 6:5	(the Lord)
22:39	Lev 19:18	(the Lord)
22:44	Ps 110:1	"How then doth David in spirit call him Lord, saying" (the Lord)
23:35	Gen 4:8	(the Lord)
23:35	2 Chron 24:21	(the Lord)
23:38	Ps 69:25	(the Lord)
23:39	Ps 118:26	(the Lord)
24:15	Dan 9:27; 11:31; 12:11	"spoken of by Daniel the prophet" (the Lord)
24:29	Isa 13:10 Joel 3:15 Ezek 32:7	(the Lord)
26:31	Zech 13:7	"for it is written" (the Lord)
26:64	Dan 7:13	(the Lord)
27:9, 10	Zech 11:13	"Then was fulfilled that which was spoken by Jeremy the prophet, saying" (Matthew)
27:35	Ps 22:18	"that it might be fulfilled which was spoken by the prophet" (Matthew)
27:46	Ps 22:1	(the Lord)

7. Bibliography

Books on Matthew's Gospel

Bellett, J.G. *The Evangelists: being Meditations upon the Four Gospels.* London: G. Morrish.

Brown, David. *The Four Gospels.* The Banner of Truth Trust, 1969.

Bullinger, E.W. (?) *The Companion Bible. Part V. The Gospels.* Oxford University Press.

Darby, J.N. *Synopsis of the Books of the Bible. Volume III. Matthew—John.* London: G. Morrish

Darby, J.N. *Notes on the Gospel of Matthew.* London: G. Morrish.

Dickson, David. *A Brief Exposition of the Evangel of Jesus Christ according to Matthew.* The Banner of Truth Trust, 1981.

Hendriksen, William. *The Gospel of Matthew.* The Banner of Truth Trust, 1973.

Henry, Matthew. *The Four Gospels.* London: Hodder and Stoughton, 1974.

Henry, Matthew. *Commentary on the Whole Bible.* Basingstoke: Marshall, Morgan and Scott, 1960.

Ironside, H.A. *Expository Notes on the Gospel of Matthew.* U.S.A.: Loizeaux.

Jamieson, Robert, Fausset, A.R. and Brown, David. *A Commentary. Critical and Explanatory, on the Old and New Testaments.* London: William Collins.

Kelly, William. *Lectures on the Gospel of Matthew.*

Miller, Andrew. *Meditations on the Beatitudes.* London: G. Morrish, 1878.

Morgan, G. Campbell. *An Exposition of the Four Gospel Narratives.* London: Oliphants, 1956.

Tasker, R.V.G. *The Gospel according to Matthew.* Tyndale New Testament Commentaries. Leicester: Inter-Varsity Press, 1961.

Ryle, John Charles. *Expository Thoughts on the Gospels. Volume 1. Matthew and Mark.* London: William Hunt, 1887.

Other Books Referred to, and Books Useful for Reference

Arnot, William. *The Parables of our Lord.* London: Nelson, 1874.

Douglas, J.D. *The New Bible Dictionary.* London: Inter-Varsity Press, 1962.

Edersheim, Alfred. *The Temple.* London: James Clarke, 1959.

Habershon, Ada R. *The Study of the Parables.* London: James Nisbet, 1904.

Heading, J. *From Now to Eternity, the Book of Revelation.* Canada: Everyday Publications, 1978.

Heading, J. *Understanding 1 & 2 Chronicles.* U.S.A.: Walterick Publishers 1980.

Heading, J. *The Book of Daniel.* Canada: Everyday Publications, 1982.

Heading, J. and Hocking, Cyril (Eds.) *Treasury of Bible Doctrine.* Precious Seed Publications, 1977.

Ironside, H. A. *Expository Notes on the Prophet Isaiah.* U. S. A.: Loizeaux, 1952.

Josephus. *The Jewish War.* Penguin Books, 1959.
Kelly, William. *An Exposition of the Book of Isaiah.* London: Weston, 1897.
Naismith, Archie and Naismith, W. Fraser. *God's People and God's Purpose.* Kilmarnock: John Ritchie, 1949.
Savage, John Ashton. *The Kingdom of God and of Heaven.* London: G. Morrish.
Souter, Alexander. *The Text and Canon of the New Testament.* London: Duckworth, 1913, 2nd edn. 1954.
The Treasury of Scripture Knowledge. London: Samuel Bagster.
Trench, Richard Chenevix. *Notes on the Parables of our Lord.* London: Kegan Paul, Trench, Trübner, 1898.
Trench, Richard Chenevix. *Notes on the Miracles of our Lord.*
Vine, W.E. *An Expository Dictionary of New Testament Words.* London: Oliphants, 1940.
Wilson, Walter Lewis. *Wilson's Dictionary of Bible Types.* London: Pickering & Inglis, 1957.

Text and Exposition

CHAPTERS 1-4
THE KING COMES TO HIS PEOPLE

I. The King's Regal and Legal Genealogy (1:1-17)

1. *From Abraham to David* 1:1-6

v.1 "The book of the generation of Jesus Christ, the son of David, the son of Abraham.
v.2 Abraham begat Isaac; and Isaac begat Jacob; and Jacob begat Judas and his brethren;
v.3 And Judas begat Phares and Zara of Thamar; and Phares begat Esrom; and Esrom begat Aram;
v.4 And Aram begat Aminadab; and Aminadab begat Naasson; and Naasson begat Salmon;
v.5 And Salmon begat Booz of Rachab; and Booz begat Obed of Ruth; and Obed begat Jesse;
v.6 And Jesse begat David the king; and David the king begat Solomon of her *that had been the wife* of Urias;"

The King would come to His own people according to the OT promises; they would even be waiting for Him, but when He would come, they would not recognise Him. The Roman authorities would ask, "Art thou the King of the Jews?" (27:11); the soldiers would mock Him as "King of the Jews" (27:29); on the cross, His accusation would be written, "This is Jesus the King of the Jews" (27:37). To the Jews, Pilate would say in mockery, "Behold your king" (John 19:14), to which the chief priests would answer, "We have no king but Caesar" (John 19:15). On one occasion, the people would try and make Him king by force, but the Lord would not accept honour from men (John 6:15), waiting for the time when God will say, "Yet have I set my king upon my holy hill of Zion" (Ps 2:6). Truly, "no man taketh this honour unto himself, but he that is called of God" (Heb 5:4).

The nation was blind to the implication of OT prophecy. They were waiting, of course, for the promised Messiah. They expected Him to come in power and glory with highly political overtones, believing that the promised One would deliver them from the Roman yoke under which they were suffering (Luke 2:38; 24:21). The fact that there would be three comings of their King was something quite unknown according to their interpretation of their own OT Scriptures.

"The King of glory shall come in" had been the exalted cry of the psalmist David of old (Ps 24:7), but the following three-fold coming of the King of the Jews was blurred in the understanding of the Jewish theologians.

1. "Thou, Bethlehem Ephratah ... out of thee shall he *come forth* unto me that is to be ruler in Israel" (Mic 5:2), was quoted by the priests and scribes in Jerusalem without realising that the event had already taken place (Matt 2:6).

2. The Lord riding in triumph into Jerusalem at the beginning of the last week partially fulfilled the prophecy, "Behold, thy King *cometh* unto thee, meek, and sitting upon an ass, and a colt the foal of an ass" (21:5; Zech 9:9). Indeed He came to His own city, the city of the great King, but men gave Him a cross for a throne.

3. Only at the end, at His second advent, will He be openly manifested as King. Men shall "see the Son of man sitting on the right hand of power, and *coming* in the clouds of heaven" (26:64). This is the time when He comes as "King of kings, and Lord of lords" (Rev 19:16), when "the Lord shall be king over all the earth" (Zech 14:9). This is the ultimate prospect of a world torn by sin, strife and warfare, but at the present time the Lord has no throne on earth, unless it be in the hearts of His people who recognise His power and authority.

Matthew 1 sets out the miraculous credentials of the One to be born the King of the Jews, Verses 1-17 trace the legal and regal genealogy of the King, verses whose details reveal the miraculous overruling power of God that preserved the genealogical tree from Abraham, through David, up to Christ, abundant grace being shown on many occasions. Verses 18-25 narrate the angelic announcement to Joseph of the miraculous conception that would result in the birth of "Emmanuel ... God with us" (v.23).

In this first chapter, the names Jesus, Christ and Emmanuel are used, but not the title "King of the Jews", yet this is implied. As "King" and "son of David" His genealogy is traced back to David; as "of the Jews" and "son of Abraham" it is traced back to Abraham. As "Son of man" it is traced back to Adam (Luke 3:38); as "Son of God" He is seen as the Word displayed in eternity (John 1:1-2), coming into the world and dwelling among men, without any human genealogy being necessary to attest His connection with eternity past.

1 By writing "The book of the generation of Jesus Christ" Matthew does not imply, of course, that the Lord had only a finite existence. By tracing the family tree back to Abraham only, Matthew is proving that the Lord's credentials were those of a Jew. Statements such as "Before Abraham was, I am" (John 8:58), and "having neither beginning of days" (Heb 7:3) show the Lord's pre-incarnate and pre-creatorial existence. Again, the word "book" (*biblos*) cannot mean in the context the whole Gospel by Matthew, but only this first genealogical paragraph (contrast this with Mark 12:26; Acts 7:42 where the singular word " book" denotes several books — of Moses and of the prophets).

Matthew divides the generations between Abraham and Christ into three parts. The complete OT genealogy is found in the opening chapters of 1 Chron. In particular, 1:1-27 traces the names from Adam to Abraham — omitted by Matthew but included in Luke 3:34-38 in the reverse direction. The three parts are:

1. **From Abraham to David** (vv.2-6), containing 14 names inclusively, with none omitted when compared with the OT list in 1 Chron 1:34; 2:1-15. This period was characterised by the fact that there was no true king in this line ruling over Israel. There were patriarchal leaders, Moses who was "king in Jeshurun" (Deut 33:5), Joshua, the judges and Samuel who was "a prophet of the Lord" (1 Sam 3:20). Saul was chosen by God to be king, because the people wanted to be like the nations around them, but he was not of the pre-Davidic line, being of the tribe of Benjamin.

2. **From David to Jechonias** (vv.6-11) at the beginning of the Babylonian captivity. Jechonias is the same as the OT Jechoiachin (or Jeconiah, Coniah); see 2 Chron 36:8,9; 1 Chron 3:16,17; Jer 22:24,28. There are 14 names in this list up to Jechonias, not counting David. The complete list is found in 1 Chron 3:1-16, from which Matthew omits several names, such as Ahaziah, Joash and Amaziah, between "Joram ... Ozias" (Matt 1:8). With the number "fourteen" in his mind, Matthew, under the inspiring control of the Holy Spirit, adjusted the number of names in this list showing that the word "begat" does not necessarily imply an adjacent family connection of father-son. This period was characterised by kings reigning over Jerusalem and Judah in the Davidic line. Many were good kings, but some were bad, such as Ahaz and Manasseh. They should all be distinguished from the inevitably bad kings of the northern kingdom, which separated from Judah and Jerusalem after Solomon's reign. The period ended with king Zedekiah reigning over Jerusalem, after which the monarchy ceased with the Babylonian captivity (2 Chron 36:11-21).

3. **From Jechonias to "Jesus, who is called Christ"** (vv.12-16). Here we have 14 names inclusively (not counting Mary), commencing with Jechonias and ending with Christ. The commencement of this list is found in 1 Chron 3:17-19, though difficulties in the text can be explained only by making assumptions. The rest of the list is not found in the OT, so Matthew must have used intertestamental sources from which to compile his list. This

period is characterised by the fact that there was no true king in Jerusalem after the Babylonian captivity. There were leaders, such as Zerubbabel (OT spelling), Ezra and Nehemiah, Zerubbabel being in the Davidic line and part-architect of the Jewish restoration after the return from the captivity (Ezra 2:2; Hag 1:1; Zech 4:6-9). Later the Herods ruled, but these were not in the Davidic line.

2 The word "beget" (*gennaō*) in the NT is used both in a physical and in a spiritual sense. In this list, the word usually implies a father-son relationship though here and there one or more intermediate links are omitted. Certainly the word is not used in v.16 where there was no physical relationship between Joseph and Christ.

Love, purpose and grace are evident in the choice of Abraham, for it appears that Satan was determined to break the line between Adam and Christ with as many evil devices as possible. The exact line had been predetermined by God, as He could look forward over the forthcoming vicissitudes throughout the centuries. Adam's sin of disobedience was the first attack, but God's purpose remained unchanged; He spoke of "her seed; it shall bruise thy head" (Gen 3:15). If Abel, a man of faith (Heb 11:4), were in the genealogical line leading to Christ, then he would be eliminated as soon as possible, Cain being the instrument of his murder (Gen 4:8). But the chosen line would pass through Eve's subsequent son Seth, and Eve seems to have realised this when she said "God … hath appointed me another seed" (Gen 4:25). Knowing that death was inevitable, Satan then ensured that "all flesh had corrupted" God's way on earth (Gen 6:12) trusting thereby to entrap the vital men in the line. But Noah "was a just man … and Noah walked with God" (Gen 6:9); he and his sons were saved through the flood. Satan knew that the line leading to Christ had to pass through Noah's sons, so he tempted Noah to drunkenness, hoping thereby to bring down a curse upon the particular son in the line; in the event Shem was blessed and Ham cursed (Gen 9:20-27).

Satan's masterpiece was to corrupt the whole earth with idolatry, and this engulfed even Abram and his forefathers. Joshua referred to this when he said "the gods which your fathers served on the other side of the flood … the gods which your fathers served" (Josh 24:14-15); such a state of affairs is described by Paul in Rom 1:18-23. Abraham became a man of faith (Heb 11:8-19), attested in the OT in Gen 15:6, "And he believed in the Lord; and he counted it to him for righteousness" upon the promise that he would have a son in his old age. Yet Sarah was barren (Gen 11:30). Her statement "the Lord hath restrained me from bearing" (Gen 16:2) may represent opinion rather than true knowledge. In fact, Satan may have interfered with the normal reproductive processes, since this formed part of the genealogical line leading to Christ. Abraham's having a son Ishmael by other means was not of faith (Gen 15:1-4; 15-16), interpreted by Paul as "bondage" (Gal 4:22-25). Only the miraculous power of God working through

Abraham's and Sarah's old age enabled them to have their son Isaac in the line leading to Christ (Gen 17:15-21; 21:1-5; Rom 4:18-22; Heb 11:11-12).

The seed of Abraham is a theme that pervades the NT:

1. The Pharisees were self-satisfied in claiming "We be Abraham's seed", "Abraham is our father" (John 8:33, 39), adding, "we have one Father, even God" (v.41). The Lord Jesus reversed their assumption, "Ye are of your father the devil" (v.44).

2. Paul was "of the stock of Israel ... an Hebrew of the Hebrews" (Phil 3:5) though he counted such an apparent privilege and gain as " loss for Christ".

3. Others had the same status, such as false apostles and ministers of Satan "Are they the seed of Abraham? so am I" (2 Cor 11:13-15, 22).

4. Believers today are children of Abraham in a spiritual sense – faith being the common thought: "they which are of faith, the same are the children of Abraham", fulfilling the promise "In thee shall all nations be blessed" (Gal 3:7-8; Gen 12:3). Elsewhere Paul wrote, "the faith of Abraham; who is the father of us all" (Rom 4:16).

As far as "Abraham begat Isaac" is concerned, God promised blessings "to thy seed" for ever (Gen 13:15; 17:8). The unwary reader may suppose that this referred only to the nation that should be born, but Paul interpreted it quite differently: "He saith not, And to seeds, as of many; but as of one, And to thy seed, which is Christ" (Gal 3:16). Christ was "of the seed of David according to the flesh" (Rom 1:3), but of the seed of Abraham according to purpose and promise. Moreover, "he took on him the seed of Abraham" (Heb 2:16),

1. so as to be able to enter into death to destroy him that had the power of death (v.14), and

2. to "be a merciful and faithful high priest" (v.17).

"Isaac begat Jacob": God knew the order in which the twin sons Esau and Jacob would be born, for He announced to Rebekah that "the elder shall serve the younger" (Gen 25:23). It is a dangerous thing to seek to achieve God's purpose in one's own way. First of all Jacob took advantage of Esau's physical weakness to gain the transfer of his birthright (Gen 25:29-34), and then, taking advantage of his father's blindness, he deceitfully obtained the blessing due to the firstborn (Gen 27:1-29). Thus God's will was achieved, though hardly done; this should be contrasted with the way in which the Lord achieved His Father's will, saying, "Thy will be done".

"Jacob begat Judas and his brethren": Leah was Jacob's first wife, bearing in order Reuben, Simeon, Levi and Judah (Gen 29:32-35). It is interesting to note that the priestly tribe and the kingly tribe originated from the same mother, the two sons being born consecutively. No doubt "and his brethren" is added because *all* the sons of Jacob led to the nation of Israel, whereas this was not true of the sons of Abraham and Isaac. We do not know when Jacob, in his turbulent life, realised that Judah was the destined son to lead to Messiah, but at the end of his life his faith looked to "the last days" (Gen 49:1) and said of Judah, "The sceptre shall not depart from Judah ... until Shiloh come; and unto him shall the gathering of the people be" (v.10).

3-4 "Judas begat Phares and Zara of Thamar". In view of Judah's sinful and troubled life, we do not know whether he realised that God's purpose for the Messianic line passed through one of his sons. At least his sons were born before he offered himself to be a prisoner in Egypt in place of Benjamin (Gen 44:33). Certainly in his younger days Pharez must have wondered how Judah was both his father and his grandfather. Lot was in a similar position with respect to his sons and grandsons Moab and Ben-ammi (Gen 19:35-38). For Judah had three sons Er, Onan and Shelah (Gen 38:1-11); the first two died at the hand of the Lord because of sin, and Er's wife Tamar would remain a widow until Shelah was grown up to become her husband. But Judah changed his mind regarding this proposal. As a result, Judah had twin sons by Tamar his widowed daughter-in-law who (unbeknown to him at the time) was posing as a harlot (Gen 38:13-30). At their birth it appeared that Zarah would be the firstborn, but in the event it was Pharez, his name meaning "breach". Thus Pharez came to be in the Messianic line; truly "where sin abounded, grace did much more abound" (Rom 5:20). Judah's sin could not be overlooked, but divine grace took up Pharez to prevent the Messianic line from collapsing through men's folly and Satan's endeavours.

The remaining names in vv.3-4 appear only infrequently in the account of the wilderness wanderings in the Pentateuch, but they were not lost in the divine purpose that was always at work preserving the line leading to Christ. Using the OT spelling, we note that Hezron appears in Num 26:21 in connection with the second numbering of the people. Amminadab occurs only in connection with his son Nahshon (e.g. Num 1:7; 2:3). Nahshon is recorded as head and prince of the tribe of Judah (Num 1:7, 16), as captain (2:3), as bringing an offering at the dedication of the altar (7:12, 17), and as being "over his host" on the first wilderness march (10:14).

5 "Salmon begat Booz of Rachab". A brief and clear genealogy of this period is given in Ruth 4:18-22. Nahshon, who as we have seen was active in the wilderness, had a son Salmon who therefore must have lived in Joshua's day. There is difficulty in determining how the generations between Salmon and David (Boaz, Obed and Jesse) can span the 450 years mentioned by Paul as lying between the entering into Canaan and Samuel the prophet (Acts 13:20). Expositors offer suggestions, to none of which we need be committed. It is clear that "Rachab" the wife of Salmon must be the Rahab of Jericho in the book of Joshua. This fact is not stated in the OT, but the NT often provides such supplementary information (e.g. Jude 14-15); we trust in the inspiring Holy Spirit of truth for the veracity of these statements.

The harlot Rahab acted "by faith" when she received the spies, not perishing with the unbelievers in Jericho (Heb 11:31); James describes her as being "justified by works" (James 2:25). Rahab is called a harlot in Josh 2:1; 6:17. Matthew knew that he was later going to quote the Lord's words, "the publicans and the harlots go into the kingdom of God before you" (Matt 21:31), spoken to the chief priests and elders. The Lord added that "the publicans and the harlots believed" John the Baptist (v.32). Consequently he included Rahab in the genealogy, to show divine grace displayed to harlots who repented, manifesting faith and good works.

"Booz begat Obed of Ruth". Now Ruth was a woman of Moab (Ruth 1:4), a nation that derived from the incestuous relationship between Lot and his elder daughter (Gen 19:37; Lev 18:6). Through Moses, God had made it clear that the daughters of the nations round about were not to be given in marriage to the men of Israel (Exod 34:16); this is interpreted in 1 Kings 11:1-2 as including Moab. Marriage therefore, then as now (1 Cor 7:39), was to be "in the Lord". Moreover, a Moabite was not to "enter into the congregation of the Lord; even to their tenth generation ... for ever" (Deut 23:3-4). What then can be said of Boaz marrying Ruth? Evidently through Naomi's influence, Ruth was converted, as proved by her testimony, "whither thou goest, I will go; and where thou lodgest, I will lodge: thy people shall be my people, and thy God my God" (Ruth 1:16). The commands of God against Moab were therefore suspended in respect of Ruth, as He had said, "showing mercy unto ... them that love me" (Exod 20:6), for she had become spiritually a suitable woman to be included in the Lord's legal and human genealogy (Luke 3:32).

6 "Jesse begat David the king" contains the only mention of "king" in Matthew's genealogy of Christ. Samuel would have chosen Jesse's son Eliab (1 Sam 16:6) thinking that he was "the Lord's anointed", but God made known His choice of David according to His purpose, "ruddy ... of a beautiful countenance, and goodly to look to", saying to Samuel, "Arise, anoint him: for this is he" (v.12). Satan was then active, working through Saul on many occasions to seek to kill David because he was of the Messianic line (1 Sam 21-24). But God's purpose could not be deflected, for "he refused the tabernacle of Joseph, and chose not the tribe of Ephraim: But chose the tribe of Judah, the mount Zion which he loved ... He chose David also his servant, and took him from the sheepfolds" (Ps 78:67-70). Note that David was anointed king first "in the midst of his brethren" (1 Sam 16: 13). Then when Saul had died "the men of Judah ... anointed David king over the house of Judah" (2 Sam 2:4); finally, several years later, "the elders of Israel

… anointed David king over Israel" (2 Sam 5:1-3). Thus it was in stages that David became king over all the tribes, after which he took the stronghold of Zion, the city of David, and established his throne there (vv.6- 10), also introducing the worship of God there by bringing up the ark (2 Sam 6:1-19). Prophetically, the throne of David looked forward to Messiah's kingdom: "I have exalted one chosen out of the people. I have found David my servant" (Ps 89:19-20); "the Son of the Highest: and the Lord God shall give unto him the throne of his father David" (Luke 1:32).

2. *From David to the Babylonian Captivity* 1:6-11

v.6 "And Jesse begat David the king; and David the king begat Solomon of her *that had been the wife* of Urias;
v.7 And Solomon begat Roboam; and Roboam begat Abia; and Abia begat Asa;
v.8 And Asa begat Josaphat; and Josaphat begat Joram; and Joram begat Ozias;
v.9 And Ozias begat Joatham; and Joatham begat Achaz; and Achaz begat Ezekias;
v.10 And Ezekias begat Manasses; and Manasses begat Amon; and Amon begat Josias;
v.11 And Josias begat Jechonias and his brethren, about the time they were carried away to Babylon:"

6 "David the king begat Solomon of her *that had been the wife* of Urias". Many Greek manuscripts omit the words " the king", and this is reflected in translations; thus the RV and JND omit the words, though JND inconsistently retains them in his French translation. There are no Greek words in the manuscripts that correspond to the English words in italics. All that occur in the Greek are two definite articles in the genitive case, the first feminine and the second masculine, *tēs tou*, which grammatically convey the same meaning as the English paraphrased words. Bathsheba is the woman implied—the fourth woman in the genealogy. The sins hidden in these words are the most odious that appear behind the scenes.

David's firstborn son in Hebron was Amnon (2 Sam 3:2); neither he nor others born in Hebron were destined to continue the Messianic line. Rather the second son by Bathsheba had been foreseen and chosen by God before the event (2 Sam 7:12-16; 1 Chron 28:4-6). Through him David's throne would be established for ever (2 Sam 7:16). Moreover, God said of this one to be born, "I will be his father, and he shall be my son" (v.14), a verse used in Heb 1:5 to refer to the Son of God. (This is an example of the NT changing the meaning of an OT quotation from its context.)

David's sin originated by his interest in a woman "very beautiful to look upon"; it led to adultery and the contrived murder in battle of her husband Uriah (2 Sam 11:2, 4, 15, 17). This is an example of the order "lust … sin … death" (James 1:15). Clearly David needed not only the commandments "Thou shalt not kill. Thou shalt not commit adultery" (Exod 20:13, 14; Matt 5:21, 27), but also the

Lord's deeper assessment, "whosoever looketh on a woman to lust after her ..." (Matt 5: 28). Grace does not mention this sin in 1 Chron, but 2 Sam presents the governmental repercussions. Later, David confessed, "I have sinned against the Lord", to which Nathan replied, "The Lord also hath put away thy sin; thou shalt not die" (2 Sam 12:13). However God's governmental dealings with David stated in vv.10-12 would be fufilled, so chapters 13-19 present all the troubles that David endured at the hands of his son Absalom who usurped the throne. Yet what comfort comes to believers today. David's great psalm of confession and repentance (Ps 51) leads to blessedness, "Blessed is he whose transgression is forgiven ... Blessed is the man unto whom the Lord imputeth not iniquity" (Ps 32:1-2), quoted by Paul for all believers as an example of faith "without works" in Rom 4:4-8.

The first son, conceived in sin and adultery, died (2 Sam 12:18), but the second was conceived in legitimate wedlock (2 Sam 11:27; 12:24). The name Solomon means " peaceful", contrasting with David who had been a man of war (1 Chron 28:3). The Lord loved Solomon, and sent Nathan to call "his name Jedidiah, because of the Lord" (2 Sam 12:25), this name meaning "Beloved of the Lord". Thus by means of these events the Messianic line continued through David and Solomon.

7 The lives of the kings from Solomon to the Babylonian captivity are fully treated in the author's book *Understanding 1 & 2 Chronicles: The House of God and its Service – Book 2.*

Solomon was "young and tender" (1 Chron 29:1) when he came to the throne, and he had been chosen by God to build the Lord's house (1 Chron 28:6). Satan was active in many ways, intending to break the Messianic line if at all possible. Thus as soon as David was old, "Adonijah ... exalted himself, saying, I will be king" (1 Kings 1:5), though his venture soon came to an end. At the beginning of his reign, Solomon failed spiritually, for he led the people to the arkless tabernacle at Gibeon, a structure that God had previously forsaken (2 Chron 1:1-6; Ps 78:60-61); the ark, symbol of God's presence, was then on mount Zion in a tent that David had erected. Later, Solomon married Pharaoh's daughter; obviously he had a bad conscience about this, since he said, "My wife shall not dwell in the house of David ... because the places are holy, whereunto the ark of the Lord hath come" (2 Chron 8:11). Moreover, Solomon appreciated religious relics in holy surroundings, for at the dedication of the temple he arranged for the forsaken tabernacle to be brought up to Jerusalem, as if this would enhance the status of the temple (1 Kings 8:4). Finally, when he was older, Solomon loved and married "many strange women" in defiance of God's will (1 Kings 11:1-8); these turned his heart to idolatry, and he built many false altars on the mount of Olives. God's judgment fell; the kingdom would be rent from Solomon's son, and be given to a man not in the Messianic line. Satan's triumph appeared to be complete, but God immediately added, "I will not rend away all the kingdom; but will give one tribe to thy son for David my servant's sake, and for Jerusalem's sake which I have chosen" (1 Kings 11:11-13). Of this one tribe, Judah, God later said "that David my servant may have a light alway before me in Jerusalem, the city which I have chosen me to put my name there" (1 Kings 11:36).

Rehoboam (we adopt the OT spelling throughout) soon established himself as a dictator (2 Chron 10:10-11); God used this event to "perform his word". Jeroboam gathered the northern tribes around him, establishing his idolatrous kingdom originally in Shechem (1 Kings 12:25-33). Unwittingly in conformity with God's purpose for the Messianic line, Rehoboam made his son Abijah chief dispersing all his other sons to prevent them from making mischief (2 Chron 11:22-23). Later "he forsook the law of the Lord", doing evil "because he prepared not his heart to seek the Lord" (2 Chron 12:1, 14).

Abijah recognised that God "gave the kingdom over Israel to David for ever" (2 Chron 13:5), and sought to retake the northern kingdom by warfare. He gained a great victory, but could not join together again what God had separated.

Asa did what was " good and right" at the beginning of his reign, taking away "the altars of the strange gods" and trusting entirely on God's help against a million men of the invading Ethiopian army (2 Chron 14:2, 3, 9-12). By way of contrast, towards the end of his reign Israel invaded Judah and Asa used the treasures of the Lord's house to induce Syria to help him (2 Chron 16: 1-3). A seer rebuked him for not relying on the Lord who was "strong in the behalf of them whose heart is perfect toward him" (2 Chron 16:9). In a rage Asa imprisoned the seer, and in his terminal disease "sought not to the Lord, but to the physicians" (vv.10, 12). Yet this king was in the Messianic line although he fell from faithfulness to unfaithfulness.

8 Jehoshaphat is described as walking "in the first ways of his father David" (2 Chron 17:3-4; 20:32) but his faithfulness was vacillating. He "joined affinity with Ahab", the idolatrous king of the northern tribes (2 Chron 18:1), and both went to war against Syria. He was rebuked by a seer, who said, " Shouldest thou help the ungodly, and love them that hate the Lord?" (2 Chron 19:2). Subsequently, when an invasion by Ammon, Moab, and mount Seir seemed imminent, Jehoshaphat engaged in prayer in the house of the Lord (2 Chron 20:5-13); a seer encouraged him, saying, "set yourselves, stand ye still, and see the salvation of the Lord" (v.17). So they worshipped the Lord, and singers in holy attire went out before the army (v.21). God arranged that the invading armies destroyed themselves, so Jehoshaphat returned to Jerusalem to the house of the Lord (vv.27-28). How fickle is the human heart! Jehoshaphat once again joined himself to the king of Israel "who did very wickedly". This time it was a mercantile commercial venture, but a seer said, "the Lord hath broken thy works" (vv.35-37). In spite of this vacillation Jehoshaphat was firmly entrenched in the Messianic line.

The kingdom passed to Jehoram the firstborn (2 Chron 21:3), a follower of the idolatry of the northern kingdom (v.13). To remove any possibility of the kingly line passing to his brothers, he slew them all with the sword (v.4). Later, the Philistines, Arabians and Ethiopians came up and killed all the king's sons except the youngest Jehoahaz (Ahaziah) (v.17). With no brothers, only one son left alive, and the king ready to die, the Messianic line was reduced to the slenderest thread, but God was in overall control.

The fact that the youngest son Ahaziah was all that remained is restated in 2 Chron 22:1. This name does not occur in Matt 1:8; he was slain during a visit to the northern kingdom, a destruction that "was of God" (vv.7-9), at which time the sons of Ahaziah's brothers were also killed. Satan then caused Athaliah, Ahaziah's mother, to destroy "all the seed royal of the house of Judah" (v.10). It would thus appear that the Messianic line had come to an abrupt termination. Once again God was in overall control; Ahaziah's sister Jehoshabeath, wife of the faithful priest Jehoiada, stole away Ahaziah's young son at the massacre, and hid him for six years in the house of God (vv.11-12). When he was seven, he was proclaimed king, "God save the king" (2 Chron 23:11; 24:1-2); so the slender thread was preserved.

Neither Joash nor his son Amaziah is mentioned in Matt 1:8. Because of the latter's idolatry, God was determined to destroy him (2 Chron 25:16), but the vital seed of the Messianic line was preserved. By comparing the 15 years in v.25 with the 16 years in 26:1, it can be seen that Uzziah was born either just before or just after God's threat of destruction.

Uzziah (as Ozias) appears at the end of Matt 1:8. As long as he sought the Lord he prospered (2 Chron 26:5). But he aspired after the priesthood, and "went into the temple of the Lord to burn incense upon the altar" (v.16), so he died a leper as cut off from the house of the Lord. No one in the Messianic line of the house of Judah could be a priest, since these stemmed only from the house of Aaron of the tribe of Levi. Only Christ would rule, *and* be a priest and that for ever after the order of Melchizedek (Ps 110:2, 4).

9 Ahaz was born before king Jotham came to the throne (2 Chron 27:1; 28:1). Ahaz, who must have watched him doing "that which was right in the sight of the Lord", determined to walk " in the ways of the kings of Israel" as soon as he came to the throne. Ahaz was one of the most wicked kings in Jerusalem, yet God allowed the Messianic line to pass through him. He ordered Urijah the priest to build a copy of a great heathen altar that he had seen in Damascus (2 Kings 16:10-16), and shut up the doors of the house of the Lord (2 Chron 28:24). Hezekiah was nine years old when Ahaz commenced his reign, so witnessed all that Ahaz had done, and was resolved to rectify things for the Lord as soon as he came to the throne.

Hezekiah restored the house of the Lord and cleansed it, keeping the Passover and re-establishing the collection of the tithes for the upkeep of the Levites. Later he trusted in the Lord for deliverance from Sennacherib of Assyria. However, *before* his son was born Hezekiah was "sick unto death", and Isaiah said, "thou shalt die, and not live" (2 Kings 20:1). He was healed and given another fifteen years of life (v.6), not only because of his prayer and plea, but also because of God's purpose that he should have a son to maintain the Messianic line.

10 To Hezekiah it had been prophesied that all his house would be carried away into Babylon, "nothing shall be left" (2 Kings 20:17). It was Manasseh who brought this about; he did evil above the heathen nations round about (21:10-16) in spite of having witnessed the faithful walk of his father. God determined to "forsake the remnant of mine inheritance" (v.14); what would become of the Messianic line in the process of judgment? Later Manasseh repented recognising that "the Lord he was God" (2 Chron 33:13), but this did not repeat the pronounced judgment of God against the nation.

Amon continued in the evil ways "more and more", and did not humble himself as Manasseh his father had done (2 Chron 33:23), although he had evidently witnessed it.

Josiah was only eight when he began to reign, but had not been seduced by his father Amon (2 Chron 34:1, 2). Desiring to walk "in the ways of David his father"
he cleansed the temple, read the book of the law, put the ark into its proper place within the vail (35:3), and reintroduced the Passover. A suitable man indeed to be found in the Lord's regal genealogy, though he was killed in a battle in which he should not have been engaged (vv.20-24).

11 "Josias begat Jechonias and his brethren, about the time they were carried away to Babylon" is full of meaning, because other kings are involved in the OT record. As we trace the names through, it would appear that the Messianic line had come to an irretrievable end.

Josiah's son Jehoahaz was taken captive by Pharaoh-nechoh after a reign of only three months; he remained in Egypt until he died (2 Kings 23:34). He was not destined to be in the line leading to Christ.

Jehoiakim, Jehoahaz' brother, was made king over Jerusalem by the king of Egypt (2 Chron 36:4). The judgment pronounced in the days of Manasseh now commenced to be fufilled (2 Kings 24:3). He was carried in chains into captivity at Babylon (2 Chron 36:6).

His son Jehoiachin (the NT Jechonias) reigned for three months, and he was taken away into Babylon (2 Chron 36:9, 10). He was also named Coniah, and of him the Lord said, "Write ye this man childless ... for no man of his seed shall prosper, sitting upon the throne of David, and ruling any more in Judah" (Jer 22:30). Thus it appears that the Messianic line could not pass through Jehoiachin.

Finally, the king of Babylon made Zedekiah king. 2 Kings 24:17 states that he was Jehoiakim's brother, and 1 Chron 3:15 shows that he was Josiah's third son which is confirmed in Jer 37:1. (Thus three of Josiah's sons were the final kings in Jerusalem, accounting for the words "and his brethren" in Matt 1:11). But the

Chaldeans "slew the sons of Zedekiah" (2 Kings 25:7) and deported him blind to Babylon, where he remained in prison until he died (Jer 52:11). Thus to all intents and purposes, at least as assessed by man without the revelation of God, the Messianic line had come to an end. Had Satan triumphed through the idolatrous sins of the latter kings over Jerusalem?

3. *From the Babylonian Captivity to Christ* 1:12-17

v.12 "And after they were brought to Babylon, Jechonias begat Salathiel; and Salathiel begat Zorobabel;
v.13 And Zorobabel begat Abiud; and Abiud begat Eliakim; and Eliakim begat Azor;
v.14 And Azor begat Sadoc; and Sadoc begat Achim; and Achim begat Eliud;
v.15 And Eliud begat Eleazar; and Eleazar begat Matthan; and Matthan begat Jacob;
v.16 And Jacob begat Joseph the husband of Mary, of whom was born Jesus, who is called Christ.
v.17 So all the generations from Abraham to David *are* fourteen generations; and from David until the carrying away into Babylon *are* fourteen generations; and from the carrying away into Babylon unto Christ *are* fourteen generations."

12 The Babylonian captivity lasted for seventy years. Originally Daniel had been taken to Babylon, together with "the king's seed" (Dan 1:1-3) namely Jehoiakim's sons who were not destined to be in the Messianic line. Yet Matthew states that the line was perpetuated in Babylon by Jehoiachin begetting Salathiel (1 Chron 3: 17). This is remarkable, since he had been declared "childless" in Jer 22:30. In fact, after 37 years in prison in Babylon, he was released, and he occupied a throne above that of other kings in Babylon, though he no longer had a throne in Jerusalem (2 Kings 25:27-30). It must have been after his release that he had his sons (1 Chron 3:17-18), though it is not clear to compilers of Bible dictionaries and concordances whether Salathiel was a son or grandson of Jehoiachin. This means that Jer 22:30 must be interpreted in a special way. God did not mean "childless" in the sense of never having off-spring; rather, no child would sit upon the throne of David in Jerusalem. Thus the Messianic line was preserved! In fact, a few verses later in Jeremiah, God said, "the days come ... that I will raise unto David a righteous Branch, and a King shall reign and prosper, and shall execute judgment and justice in the earth ... he shall be called The Lord our righteousness" (Jer 23:5-6). This is obviously a reference to Christ; being raised "unto David" means that He had regally to be descended from David by the regal genealogy.

Salathiel occurs in the OT only in a phrase such as "Zerubbabel the son of Shealtiel" (e.g. Ezra 3:2; Neh 12:1; Hag 1:1). By this means God was stressing that the Messianic line had been taken up again unbroken.

Zerubbabel was one of God's chosen leaders in Jerusalem when the Jews returned from their captivity in Babylon. He is called "governor of Judah" (Hag 2:21), but there is no evidence for the theory that the Jews made him king, an uprising that was subjugated by the Persians who had absolute control as the second beast of Dan 7:5. He was in the lead in building the altar and in laying the foundation of the temple (Ezra 3:2, 8, 10), as well as in the building of the temple after a considerable delay (Ezra 5:2).

13-15 The remaining names are outside the OT record. Yet the preserving hand of God was upon this Messianic line through times of considerable difficulty. Some of the prophetical parts of the book of Daniel refer to this period, and in particular the activity of the Syrian king Antiochus Epiphanes; this is described in detail in chs. 8, 11 of the author's book *The Book of Daniel.* Having been defeated in Egypt, Antiochus returned to Syria humiliated. He took revenge on Jerusalem where he killed thousands, causing the temple worship to cease (Dan 11:31), setting fire to the city, and insisting that the Jews worship only the Greek god Jupiter. He erected an altar for a heathen god, and faithful Jews were tortured if they did not observe it. Antiochus gained the apostate Jews (v.32), but the faithful remnant stood firm (their tribulations being described in 1 and 2 Maccabees in the OT Apocrypha). Heb 11:35 refers to these events, "Others were tortured, not accepting deliverance", an example of the Spirit of inspiration using profane Jewish sources. Thus in 2 Macc 6:19, the old man Eleazar was forced to eat "swine's flesh" for deliverance; "But he, choosing rather to die gloriously ... spit it forth, and came of his own accord to the torment" . He also refused to eat ordinary meat as a deception, " that in so doing he might be delivered from death" (v.22). In ch. 7, seven brothers died before their mother for a similar reason, refusing to eat for deliverance. With tongues and hands about to be cut off, their faith said, " these had I from heaven ... from him I hope to receive them again" (v.11). The seventh son was handled "worse than all the rest ... and put his whole trust in the Lord" (vv.39, 40). In other words, they expected to "obtain a better resurrection" (Heb 11:35). Those preserved in the Messianic line must have been present when these abominations were taking place.

16 Thus Joseph was safety reached, about 1900 years after Abraham, about 1000 years after David, and over 500 years after the end of the Babylonian captivity. The genealogy represents an extended divine miracle, showing God's purpose and triumph over Satan's attempts to block the coming of Messiah to His own people. The wording of v. 16 is very precise and careful. Unlike all the preceding names it is *not* said that "Joseph begat"; rather, Mary is introduced "of whom was born Jesus". The reader is thereby prepared for the account of the miracle in the following verses. Legally, but not physically, Joseph was the father of Jesus, and he is recognised as one of His parents in Luke 2:41, being called "thy father" by Mary (v.48). Again, Joseph was "the husband of Mary". The word *anēr* means an adult male, implying "husband" when the context demands it. It describes the *later* relationship of Joseph to Mary, and certainly *not* that appearing in v.18.

Note the names and titles given to the Lord in the opening two chapters: Jesus, Christ, Emmanuel, King of the Jews, Governor, Nazarene. In John 1, the names and titles are even more numerous: Word, God, Light, the only begotten of the Father, Jesus Christ, Lamb of God, Son of God, Rabbi, Messias, the Christ, Jesus, Jesus of Nazareth, Son of Joseph, the King of Israel.

17 The number 14, used to define the three groupings in the genealogy, has given rise to many explanations by the expositors, because Matthew's intention is not explained. We are not therefore committed to any particular suggestion. For example, the number acts as an artificial aid to memory. The number impresses David's name upon each group, for in Hebrew the numerical values of the letters in his name add up to 14. For those who perceive that numbers in the Scriptures have a very deep meaning, it has been observed that 14 = 2 x 7, witness coupled with completeness, and 14 = 10 + 4. the testing of responsible man.

Throughout the whole genealogy, it can be said, "what he had promised, he was able also to perform" (Rom 4:21).

II. The Birth of Jesus Christ (1:18-25)

1. *The Angelic Message to Joseph* 1:18-21

v.18 "Now the birth of Jesus Christ was on this wise: When as his mother Mary was espoused to Joseph, before they came together, she was found with child of the Holy Ghost.
v.19 Then Joseph her husband, being a just *man*, and not willing to make her a publick example, was minded to put her away privily.
v.20 But while he thought on these things, behold, the angel of the Lord appeared unto him in a dream, saying, Joseph, thou son of David, fear not to take unto thee Mary thy wife: for that which is conceived in her is of the Holy Ghost.
v.21 And she shall bring forth a son, and thou shalt call his name JESUS: for he shall save his people from their sins."

18 These verses present Joseph's side of the story prior to the birth of Christ, while Luke 1:26-56 present Mary's side. The introduction to the miracle is contained in the words "Mary *was espoused* to Joseph". This word *mnēsteuō* (RV "betrothed") is not the same as that used by Paul in 2 Cor 11:2. It appears in the NT only here and in Luke 1:27; 2:5, all three occasions relating to Mary. It implies to promise in marriage, a period prior to the actual marriage. The words "husband" (v.19) and "wife" (v.20) must be understood as referring to premarital conditions. They were not living together at the time; indeed, Mary spent three months living in the home of Elizabeth and Zecharias (Luke 1:40, 56), returning to "her own house" as distinct from that of Joseph. This is the meaning of the phrase "before they came together", the verb *sunerchomai* implying to assemble (Mark 14:53) or to cohabit. It answers to "Take unto thee" (vv.20, 24), namely to

Joseph's home. Some Greek authors use the word with a more intimate connotation, but it is best to understand our verse to mean that the couple were not living together.

During this period, she "was found with child of the Holy Ghost". Of course Mary knew what was happening; Gabriel had revealed to her God's purpose that her womb should be the vehicle for bringing into the world the Son of the Highest (Luke 1:28-33). Mary was a virgin, having no intention of breaking her virginity during the period of espousal, and confessed this to Gabriel by saying "seeing I know not a man" (Luke 1:34). The miracle would be accomplished by the Holy Ghost coming on Mary, so that the holy thing to be born would be called the Son of God (v.35). Evidently Mary kept this holy information to herself, and did not inform Joseph of Gabriel's message. While in her home, "she was found with child of the Holy Ghost", so both Matthew and Luke bring the Holy Spirit into the miraculous conception. She must have confided in Elizabeth, for Elizabeth called her "the mother of my Lord" (Luke 1:43).

19 Mary was faithful during the period of espousal and so was Joseph, being called "just", containing a lesson for younger believers today as surrounded by opposing forces and opinions in a world of darkness. Upon her return to Nazareth, Joseph must have wondered what Mary had been doing in her absence, and evidently suspected unfaithfulness. A public example might have led to stoning, particularly if the Jews had been as demanding as those in John 8:5. However, to do something secretly was the result of his consideration.

Now Matthew alone uses this word "put away" (*apoluō*) in connection with Joseph's relationship with Mary, and it implies the formal breaking of the espoused state, as distinct from the breaking of a married state. It is noteworthy that only Matthew includes the well known exception clause, "saving for the cause of fornication", and he does so twice (Matt 5:32; 19:9). We understand this to mean that divorce (the breaking of the marriage bond) is not in keeping with God's will, but if unfaithfulness (fornication) takes place during the period of espousal, then the wife can be put away.

20 The fact that Joseph thought like this suggests that he did not inform Mary of his intentions, nor did Mary inform him of Gabriel's revelation that would have explained the position. If God could reveal something to Mary, so could He to Joseph. So "an angel" (not "the" angel) appeared to him in a dream. God often used dreams as a means of communicating with men, whether heathen or saint. Some dreams need interpretation, as Pharaoh's dream (Gen 41:1), Nebuchadnezzar's dream (Dan 2:1), and Daniel's dream (Dan 7:1). Joseph's four dreams were direct, and had no need of interpretation (Matt 1:20; 2:13, 19, 22). The angel used the title "son of David", a title that would pass on to the Lord

Jesus; it recalled to Joseph his family tree leading back to David, and implied that the one to be born would be the Messiah as well as the Saviour. The miraculous conception achieved by the power of the Holy Spirit is announced by the verb "is conceived", the aorist passive participle of the verb *gennaō,* used throughout the preceding genealogy.

21 The son would be born in less than six months' time, for at least three months had passed already (Luke 1:56). The fact that His name would be "Jesus – Saviour" had previously been announced to Mary (Luke 1:31). This should be compared with the birth of John the Baptist, when both parents knew that his name would be John (Luke 1:13, 60-63). Very few cases are recorded in Scripture where a name was known long before the birth; see Josiah (1 Kings 13:2), Cyrus (Isa 44:28; 45:1). It should be pointed out that the use of capital letters for the name Jesus (Matt 1:21, 25; Luke 1:31 AV, RV, but not JND) is a device of the translators not found in the Greek manuscripts (as also Exod 3:14; Matt 27:37; Rev 17:5; 19:16).

No doubt Joseph, with many other Jews, was expecting Messiah to come to save His people, for the Jewish nation was suffering under the oppression of Rome. Many were looking "for redemption in Jerusalem" (Luke 2:38), namely redemption from the Roman yoke. This will be accomplished only at His second advent (Matt 24:30) when the power of the fourth beast of Dan 7 and the first beast of Rev 13 will be finally broken so that Messiah can reign triumphantly.

The first advent was quite different; by means of the sacrifice of Himself He came to "save his people from their sins". The collective future response of the people will be as in Isa 53:4-9, "with his stripes we are healed". In the angel's words is also contained the gospel for the individual, as announced by Peter and Paul in the Acts (2:21; 3:26; 10:43; 13:23, 38). What a difference this Saviour presents when contrasted with the saviours in the past whom God sent to deliver His people out of the hand of their enemies (Neh 9:27).

2. *The King's Birth—Prophecy and Fulfilment* 1:22-25

v.22 "Now all this was done, that it might be fulfilled which was spoken of the Lord by the prophet, saying,
v.23 Behold, a virgin shall be with child, and shall bring forth a son, and they shall call his name Emmanuel, which being interpreted is, God with us.
v.24 Then Joseph being raised from sleep did as the angel of the Lord had bidden him, and took unto him his wife:
v.25 And knew her not till she had brought forth her firstborn son: and he called his name JESUS."

22 Here is the first of many OT quotations occurring throughout Matthew's Gospel. Thereby the writer shows how the events in the life of the King were embedded in the OT. If all the OT quotations appearing in the four Gospels are extracted and rearranged, a very sizeable and complete life of Christ can be formulated. The fact that this can be done is another example of the miraculous in ch. 1. It was "the Spirit of Christ" in the prophets which testified beforehand of the birth and sufferings of Christ (1 Pet 1:11); "they were moved by the Holy Ghost" (2 Pet 1:21). Note that the AV "spoken *of* the Lord *by* the prophet" is better rendered "spoken *by* the Lord *through* the prophet".

23 In Isa 7:10-16, that evil king Ahaz would not ask for a sign when invited by God to do so. This contrasts with the Pharisees who asked for a sign when none would be given to them by the Lord (Matt 16:1-4). A sign had to be miraculous, otherwise it would not stand out from ordinary events on the earth or in the heavens. "Behold, a virgin shall conceive, and bear a son, and shall call his name Immanuel". This is exactly what the angel was describing to Joseph, and what was happening to his wife Mary. But if the miraculous can be toned down, then that is what some expositors wittingly or unwittingly seek to do. The Greek word for virgin (*parthenos*) definitely has this meaning, and the LXX for Isa 7:14 uses this word. But in the Hebrew OT things are different. The Hebrew word *bethula* (not used in Isa 7:14) is translated in the AV "maid" 7 times, "maiden" 5 times and "virgin" 38 times. The Hebrew word *almah* (*used* in Isa 7:14) is translated "damsel" once, "maid" twice, and "virgin" 4 times. The result of this is that some expositors and translators minimise the force of Isa 7:14 and use the words "young woman" or similar variant. This would then cease to be a sign and a miracle. Ironside, in *Expository Notes on the Prophet Isaiah,* writes, "It is only unbelief that would try to nullify the force of this passage by reading in place of "virgin" a "young woman" and attempting to make that young woman to be the wife of the prophet, and the son born to be his son through her. It is perfectly true that the word rendered virgin might also be rendered *maiden,* but every maiden is presumably a virgin – if not, something is radically wrong – so that the prophecy here clearly and definitely declared that an unmarried virgin should become a mother and the child should be named *God with us*" Kelly, in *An Exposition of the Book of Isaiah,* examines the matter in detail. He writes, "It is well known that the Jews have made desperate efforts to evade this luminous testimony to the incarnation of their own prophet … In the present instance the context requires the sense of virgin with the utmost precision; for in a young married woman's bearing a son there is no sign of wonder . . .".

The name given to the Son, "Emmanuel – God with us", is vital in the recognition of the full deity of Christ. Such an essential truth is denied and every relevant Scriptural quotation is twisted by heretics. It is important for all believers to know what quotations directly (and there are plenty of indirect ones too) support the holy doctrine of the equality of Father and Son in the Godhead. The following should be committed to memory: "My Father worketh hitherto, and I work … making himself equal with God" (John 5:17-18); "I and my Father are one … thou, being a man, makest thyself God" (John 10:30, 33). In other words, the Jews knew the true implication of the Lord's words. "Child – Emmanuel" (Matt 1:23; Isa 7:14) answers to "a child is born … The mighty God" (Isa 9:6); "the Word was God" (John 1:1); "My Lord and my God" (John 20:28); "Christ came, who is over all, God blessed for ever" (Rom 9:5); "That blessed hope … the great God and our Saviour Jesus Christ" (Titus 2:13); "Unto the Son he saith, Thy throne, O God, is for ever and ever" (Heb 1:8; Ps 45:6); " His Son Jesus Christ. This is the true God, and eternal life" (1 John 5:20). Anything else is false teaching, corresponding to "another Jesus... another spirit... another gospel" (2 Cor 11:4). Heretics are quick to point out that in the Greek of John 1:1 " the Word was with God, and the Word was God" *(ho logos ēn pros ton theon, kai theos ēn ho logos),* there is no definite article before the second occurrence of God, hence they translate it "the Word was a God". That this is a false conclusion can be seen from John 20:28, where "My Lord and my God" is, in Greek, *Ho kurios mou kai ho theos mou,* namely with the definite article before God. Similarly in Matt 1:23 " God with us" is in Greek *Meth ēmōn ho theos*, namely with the definite article before God.

It should be pointed out that, as Matthew's Gospel begins with God present with His people, so it also ends with the words "I am with you alway" (Matt 28:20).

24-25 No question or argument arises in Joseph's mind, as in Zecharias' case (Luke 1:18). The angel had given one command only, "fear not to take unto thee Mary thy wife", and Joseph obeyed, "and took unto him his wife". Namely, he took her to his home to live as husband and wife, but he " knew her not till she had brought forth her firstborn son" . This was not part of the angelic command, and shows Joseph's spiritual sensitivity to the miraculous work of God. It is dangerous to draw conclusions that are not in the text. Some expositors state that because Jesus was the "firstborn", therefore Mary had no further children, and that there were no marital relations between Joseph and Mary after this birth. This is to accommodate an ancient belief in the perpetual virginity of Mary, and requires that the four men who are called the Lord's brethren (Matt 12:47; 13:55; John 7:3, 5, 10) were either Joseph's sons by a former marriage or were near relatives. However, additions to Scripture should not be made merely to account for tradition.

The adjective "firstborn" is used of Mary's son in its normal physical sense. When an ordinary word is imported into Christian doctrine, its ordinary meaning is usually modified spiritually. In "firstborn" as applied to Christ in Col 1:15, there is *no* implication in any sense that the Lord came into existence in eternity past; rather He pre-existed before all creation which He Himself created.

III. The King's Early Rejection (2:1-23)

1. *Worship by the Wise Men* 2:1 -12

v.1 "Now when Jesus was born in Bethlehem of Judaea in the days of Herod the king, behold, there came wise men from the east to Jerusalem,
v.2 Saying, Where is he that is born King of the Jews? for we have seen his star in the east, and are come to worship him.
v.3 When Herod the king had heard *these things,* he was troubled, and all Jerusalem with him.
v.4 And when he had gathered all the chief priests and scribes of the people together, he demanded of them where Christ should be born.
v.5 And they said unto him, In Bethlehem of Judaea: for thus it is written by the prophet,
v.6 And thou Bethlehem, *in* the land of Juda, art not the least among the princes of Juda: for out of thee shall come a Governor, that shall rule my people Israel.
v.7 Then Herod, when he had privily called the wise men, enquired of them diligently what time the star appeared.
v.8 And he sent them to Bethlehem, and said, Go and search diligently for the young child; and when ye have found *him*, bring me word again, that I may come and worship him also.
v.9 When they had heard the king, they departed; and, lo, the star, which they saw in the east, went before them, till it came and stood over where the young child was.
v.10 When they saw the star, they rejoiced with exceeding great joy.
v.11 And when they were come into the house, they saw the young child with Mary his mother, and fell down, and worshipped him: and when they had opened their treasures, they presented unto him gifts; gold, and frankincense, and myrrh.
v.12 And being warned of God in a dream that they should not return to Herod, they departed into their own country another way."

1 These were "the times of the Gentiles" (Luke 21:24); there was no king of the Davidic line occupying the throne in Jerusalem. The four kingdoms represented by the four beasts in Dan 7:4-7 were rising successively and replacing each other. The Babylonian, Medo-Persian and Grecian kingdoms that once had dominated that part of the world had passed away, and the fourth beast – the Roman empire – exercised authority over the world. It is described as "dreadful and terrible, and strong exceedingly; and it had great iron teeth: it devoured and brake in pieces" (v.7). The Roman authorities appointed kings over various occupied countries. Originally, Herod the Great governed in Galilee, but he was made king of Judaea in BC 40. His strength and cruelty matched the description of Rome in Dan 7:7, though he did commence the building of the temple in Jerusalem that was still unfinished in the time of the Lord's ministry (John 2:20).

Herod was reigning at the time of the Lord's birth (Matt 2:1); he had four sons:

1. Archelaus (Matt 2:22) who reigned briefly during the Lord's early childhood;

2. Philip (Matt 14:3; Luke 3:1);

3. Herod the tetrarch who reigned during the Lord's ministry (Luke 3:19; Matt 14:1; Luke 13:31; 23:7);

4. Aristobulus, whose son Herod reigned after the Lord's ascension (Acts 12:1). In turn, his son was Agrippa II (Acts 25:13 to 26:32).

God gave no revelation concerning the birth of Christ to the Roman authorities, to these wicked Herods, or to the Jewish religious leaders and teachers in Jerusalem and Judaea; it was hidden "from the wise and prudent" (Matt 11:25).

The end of the Messianic line having been reached, Satan was active again. The King was attacked almost immediately after His birth, in keeping with Rev 12:1-5, where the woman (Israel) brought forth the man child (the Messiah) whom the "great red dragon" (Satan) sought to devour. Herod the Great was commissioned by Satan to carry out this plan. Its inevitable failure led to the next conflict, the temptation in the wilderness (Matt 4:1-11), with a similar result. Then Satan moved the evil hearts of men to crucify the Lord, and, when He died, victory seemed to be complete, but the power of God in resurrection showed that Satan's victory was only apparent. Since then, he has attacked the church as the body of Christ, using physical and doctrinal means, but the church remains intact, awaiting the rapture. In the future, Satan, knowing that his time is near, will incite men to "make war with the Lamb", seeking to abolish Him as He comes in power and glory – ending in their own destruction (Rev 17:14; 2 Thess 1:7-9). Satan's final attack will occur after the millennium. He will gather the nations against "the camp of the saints ... the beloved city" supposing the Lord to be there, only to meet their final end (Rev 20:7-10). At every stage, Satan has no power over Christ.

"**When** Jesus was born in Bethlehem" has been bound up with tradition, namely with the date December 25th. But starting from the known date of "the course of Abia" (Luke 1:5), it has been strongly argued (as in Appendix 179 to The Companion Bible; Part V. The Gospels) that, allowing 9 months for the birth of John the Baptist and another six months for the birth of Christ, the nativity took place at the end of September.

More important is how the events in Matt 2 are dovetailed with the events in Luke 2. For in Matt 2:23 the family came to Nazareth after its stay in Egypt, while in Luke 2:39 the record passes straight from Jerusalem to Nazareth. Truly the Lord was laid in a manger, " because there was no room for them in the inn" (Luke 2:7), all available space being occupied by an influx of people coming to Bethlehem for the enrolment. But we can rightly assume that they moved to a "house" (Matt 2:11) as soon as such accommodation became free. The days of Mary's "purification" according to the law were forty (Luke 2:22; Lev 12:2-4) after which they went to Jerusalem where the moving scenes with Simeon and Anna took place. They then returned to Bethlehem, and the events recorded in Matt 2 took place, ending with the family's return to Nazareth.

The number of the "wise men", or magi, is not stated; the fact that three types of treasures were presented does not imply that only three wise men were involved. The magicians, astrologers, sorcerers and Chaldeans (Dan 2:2) had their own methods for interpreting dreams and understanding the signs of the stars; they were helpless in retrieving Nebuchadnezzar's dream, a thing that only Daniel could do through divine revelation. These wise men were different. They were indeed Gentile astrologers, but converted by a supernatural event to seek the true King and worship Him; (cp. Rom 10:20, "I was found of them that sought me not"). Since the natural man does not receive the things of the Spirit of God (1 Cor 2:14), the truth of the birth of Christ was withheld from kings, priests Pharisees and men of learning. Only to Zacharias, Mary, Joseph, the shepherds, Simeon, Anna, and the wise men was anything revealed and made known.

Note that the wise men came "from the east to Jerusalem". They saw the "star in the east" – namely *when they were in the east* relative to Jerusalem, the star itself was in the west. To start with, the star did not lead directly and clearly to Bethlehem; it gave general guidance only, and they came to Jerusalem because this was the capital city of the Jews. Their journey commenced when the Lord was born, and may have lasted a considerable time before they reached Bethlehem; in fact, four months were needed for Ezra to travel from Babylon to Jerusalem (Ezra 7:9).

2 Their use of the title "King of the Jews" shows that the wise men were looking beyond the kings of the nations and the emperor of Rome. Had they known Dan 9:24-25, they would have looked away from the times of the Gentiles, knowing that "Messiah the Prince" had been promised. References to the Lord being "King, King of the Jews, King of Israel" are: Matthew – 9 times; Mark – 6 times; Luke – 5 times; John – 14 times. It is remarkable that John's Gospel – that of the Son of God – should contain more references to the King than Matthew's Gospel – that of the King of the Jews.

These men recognised that it was "his star" (*autou ton astera*), as distinct from the myriads of other stars. Speculation and theory do not help here. A comet bright enough to engage attention has been suggested; a planet or a conjunction of planets (it has been calculated that Jupiter, Saturn and Venus were in conjunction in BC 7); a supernova (a star that suddenly becomes brighter). But all these rotate with the sun, and would not fix a direction for the guidance of the wise men, particularly as the last few miles from Jerusalem to Bethlehem ended with the star exactly over the house where the young Child lay. One theory has used the method of bird migration, direction being fixed the sun and stars even though they are always rotating. We believe that "his star" was something miraculous for a miraculous occasion, near enough to the earth for the wise men to have taken a vertical bearing from the star to the house exactly underneath when it became stationary (Matt 2:9). So it may have been the "cloud of glory" that rested over the tabernacle, and that gave guidance to the children of Israel in their wilderness march from Egypt. Balaam had predicted, "there shall come a Star out of Jacob, and a Sceptre shall rise out of Israel" (Num 24:17), these being the Messiah Himself, having dominion over the nations. Similarly in Isa 60:3, "the Gentiles shall come to thy light, and kings to the brightness of thy rising". To us, the Lord is "the bright and morning star" (Rev 22:16).

"We ... are come to worship him" is of great spiritual significance. Such Gentile participation had been announced in the OT: "There shall be a root of Jesse, which shall stand for an ensign of the people; to it shall the Gentiles seek" (Isa 11:10), amplified by Paul in various quotations in Rom 15:9-12; "Ye kings ... ye judges ... Serve the Lord with fear ... Kiss the Son" (Ps 2:10-12). Right from the beginning of the gospel story God would establish this, so the Gentiles came up to Jerusalem to worship, as the queen of the south came up to king Solomon (Matt 12:42). On the other hand, this King was rejected by the Jews through Herod, meaning that the Lord learnt from an early age the tragedy of being rejected.

3-4 Those who are in a position of authority, and who hold to the principle of power politics, will do everything to maintain their position of authority. The beasts in Dan 7:4-7 maintained their power until they were overthrown. The beast of the future, who "shall ascend out of the bottomless pit" (Rev 17:8), will seek to maintain, and even to extend, his authority and kingdom at the battle of Armageddon. In this he will be supported by the anti-Christ who makes men worship an image of the beast (Rev 13:15). No wonder then that at the mention of the King of the Jews Herod was troubled. Such a cruel and wicked king would not stop at a multitude of murders to maintain his position as king, allowing no rival to emerge even as a newborn child. And how easily a leader can affect his subjects, for "*all* Jerusalem" was troubled with him. Similarly, how easily Solomon influenced "*all* the congregation" to leave the ark in Jerusalem to go to the arkless tabernacle in Gibeon (2 Chron 1:3), though evidently he could not easily bring them back again, for only he returned to the ark in Jerusalem (2 Chron 1:13; 1 Kings 3:15). Herod's attitude poisoned the minds of the people; although they expected the coming of Messiah, they now permanently rejected the King of the Jews. Later "*all* the city" was moved at the coming of the King, but shortly afterwards Peter accused "*all* ye that dwell at Jerusalem" of being responsible for the Lord's death (Matt 21:10; Acts 2:14). How careful should local church leaders be; in weakness they can so easily drag the flock downwards, "speaking perverse things, to draw away disciples after them" (Acts 20:30)

Notes

The Lord is not King of the church nor of His people today, in spite of many uses of this title for rhyming purposes in popular hymns. Rather he is Lord of the individual believer, and He is Head of the church implying a living relationship absent from the title King. In worship we recognise His character as King, "unto the King eternal, immortal, invisible, the only wise God" (1 Tim 1:17); "King of kings, and Lord of lords; Who only hath immortality" (1 Tim 6:15-16). "King of saints" (Rev l 5:3) should read "King of nations" (*hagiōn* being replaced by *ethnōn*).

Just as Nebuchadnezzar and Belshazzar had recourse to their astrologers (Dan 2:2; 4:7; 5:7), so Herod consulted his religious advisers – the chief priests and scribes. The latter were responsible for making handwritten copies of the OT Scriptures, so they would know every verse, and could call upon their knowledge with ease. But formal and academic knowledge is not spiritual knowledge. "The letter killeth, but the spirit giveth life" (2 Cor 3:6), and certainly in this case the letter of the OT caused Herod to kill. One can know the contents of the OT, without knowing its meaning according to the Spirit. Paul, as Saul the Pharisee, knew the OT thoroughly, but after his conversion he had to go into Arabia alone, so that his understanding should be completely reorientated to see Christ in all the OT Scriptures (Gal 1:17). Today, many may study the text, but do not believe it. "Ye do err, not knowing the scriptures", said the Lord (Matt 22:29), in spite of the vast knowledge of the Sadducees. Similarly, the people of Jerusalem "knew him not, nor yet the voices of the prophets which are read every sabbath day" (Acts 13:27). Reading does not imply faith, though it leads to it in those who are exercised. So in Herod's day, unbelief was quite sincere in its reading of Mic 5:2, but this did not enable them to perceive the King of the Jews in their midst. Later, others too quoted this OT verse (John 7:40-43), knowing that Jesus came from Galilee, but not knowing that he had been born in Bethlehem.

5-6 Without hesitation they answered "Bethlehem", without hesitation they knew that this would be the fulfilment of the words of the prophet Micah. They did not believe it, else they would have gone to worship. But Herod believed it sufficiently to take steps to preserve his throne: "the devils also believe" (James 2:19). It was not a question of "be ye doers of the word, and not hearers only" (James 1:22), but hearers, and then antidoers.

References to Bethlehem span the OT Scriptures. The name means "house of bread, or food"; its earlier name was Ephrath (Gen 35:19), the name Ephratah meaning "fertility, fruitbearing". It was near to Bethlehem that Rachel died in childbirth (Gen 35:16-20), so it held memories of death and tragedy. It was here that tragedy turned to happiness in the story unfolded in the book of Ruth. It was here that David was anointed king (1 Sam 16:4, 13). When the Philistines occupied Bethlehem, David's three mighty men broke through the Philistine army to draw water from the well at the gate (2 Sam 23:14-17). It was here that David first heard of the ark situated in Kirjath Jearim, and because of his exercise God promised, " Of the fruit of thy body will I set upon thy throne" (Ps 132:6, 11). And this was the place where the ultimate "fruit" of David's body would be born. God chose Micah to announce this in the days of Jotham, Ahaz and Hezekiah, kings of Judah (Mic 5:2). The reader should compare Mic 5:2 with the actual words and quotation used by the priests and scribes. They omitted "whose goings forth have been from of old, from everlasting", since this points to the divine character of the King just born, and this they would desire to avoid with its reminder of Isa 57:15, "the high and lofty One that inhabiteth eternity". The context of the verse in Micah should be noted. The nation would go into captivity in Babylon, with many nations gathered against it; yet the Lord would deliver His people, who would then "thresh" the nations (Mic 4:10-13). This would be accomplished by the birth of Messiah, ultimately to become ruler and governor, though in the meanwhile they would be "among the Gentiles" until their hand be lifted up upon their adversaries (Mic 5:8).

7-10 Herod relied on the testimony of the wise men for *the time* of the King's birth (namely, when the star first appeared, perhaps the same glory-sign seen by the shepherds in Luke 2:9), and on the OT Scriptures for *the place* of the King's birth. His scheme was full of deceit, and the wise men were completely deceived (as was Joshua by the men of Gibeon who worked "wilily" and told lies, Josh 9:3-27). Note that Herod used the word "young child" (*paidion*) as does the angel later in v.13, contrasting with the angel's description "babe" (*brephos*) to the shepherds in Luke 2:12.

Herod "enquired diligently", and requested the wise men to "search diligently". In the first, only one word *akriboō* occurs in the Greek, meaning to learn by exact enquiry. In the second, *two* words appear – an adverb and a verb – *akribōs exetazō*, accurately to seek out. Herod wanted the fullest possible information, to carry out strictly his odious deed (i.e. restricted to the one particular Child, if the relevant information were available), but falsified to the wise men as a desire to "worship" (*proskuneō*), namely, to do homage.

Worship is either false or true. In Mark 15:17-19, the Roman soldiers dressed the Lord as King in mockery, complete with a crown of thorns; they addressed Him as "King of the Jews" and spat on Him, and bowing their knees they "worshipped" Him. Concerning the formal religious paraphernalia of the Jews, the Lord said, "This people draweth nigh unto me with their mouth ... but their heart is far from me. But in vain they do worship me, teaching for doctrines the commandments of men" (Matt 15:8-9). Little do such men realise that in a coming day all in earth and under the earth will have to "confess that Jesus Christ is Lord, to the glory of God the Father" (Phil 2:10-11). But there is true worship "in spirit and in truth" (John 4:24). Thus the leper (Matt 8:2), those in the ship (14:33), the woman of Canaan (15:25), the women who held Him by the feet (28:9) all worshipped Him. In the coming day of His kingly power men "shall worship the Lord in the holy mount at Jerusalem" (Isa 27:13), and God says "all flesh (shall) come to worship before me" (66:23). See Zech 14:16-19.

As the wise men departed from Jerusalem, the guidance of the star became more precise, suggesting that they did not really need the information from Micah provided by the scribes. It "went *before* them", leading them to the town. Then " it ... stood *over*" the house, leading them to the very spot where the Child was. This shows that the star was stationary and very near the earth, like an apparent stationary orbit of a fixed satellite though much lower. The sight of the star leading them to their goal caused rejoicing and "exceeding great joy" quite unlike the fleshly rejoicing of the world (John 16:20); this reaction must have been similar to that of the shepherds when they glorified and praised God (Luke 2:20).

11 Upon entering the house, the men saw both the young Child and Mary His mother. How clear is Scripture when it describes the direction of worship: they "worshipped *him*" with *no* mention of Mary, so the Roman Catholic dogma is thereby nullified. In Matt 14:33, after the storm and Peter's walking on the sea, the disciples' worship was but *for a moment in time*; in Matt 27:54, after the earthquake and the Lord's death, a similar expression by the centurion was again just *for a moment in time.* But the worship of the wise men *looked forward through the ages.*

The three kinds of gifts spoke of Kingship, Deity and Manhood. The gold was a fitting tribute to the King, reminding us of excellence in tabernacle and temple. The frankincense was an emblem of divine fragrance in worship (Exod 30:7; Lev 2:1-2). The myrrh was a witness to His death, being used for embalming (John 19:39). The glitter of false religion can also use these things; Gold, odours, frankincense form part of the merchandise of Mystery, Babylon the Great, the Mother of Harlots, after the rapture of the church (Rev 18:12-13).

We read of gifts in many places in Scripture. In Neh 8:10, when the law was read by Ezra, men sent "portions" because of rejoicing; this is the Word Declared. In Esther 9:19, 22, when the Jews slew Haman's sons and their enemies, there was gladness and feasting, and " sending portions one to another"; this is the World Defeated. In Rev 11:10, when the two witnesses are killed, the earthdwellers shall rejoice, and "shall send gifts one to another"; this is the Witnesses' Death. As far as the wise men are concerned, this is the Worshippers' Devotion. See also 1 Kings 10:25 (presents to Solomon); 1 Chron 16:3 (from David to the people); 2 Chron 17:5 (Judah to king Jehoshaphat); 2 Chron 17:11 (enemies to Jehoshaphat); Isa 39:1 (king of Babylon to Hezekiah).

12 Just as God had preserved the Messianic line in the OT, so here He preserved the Child-Messiah against the evil designs of Herod. After the dream, the wise men might not have realised the danger that Herod had planned, but they were not disobedient to the voice of God. Perhaps only one man had the dream, and they all reacted to it, just as in Acts 16:9-10 Paul only had the vision "Come over into Macedonia, and help us", but the whole party then sought to go into Macedonia. Departing to their own country "another way" was not without its difficulties for the wise men. A glance at a map showing main roads at that time proves that the main road went from Bethlehem to Jerusalem, from Jerusalem to Jericho eastwards, and then over the Jordan northwards from the top of the Dead Sea. To reach the top of the Dead Sea "another way" would mean crossing inhospitable mountainous country east of Bethlehem. Obedience to God's voice does not always bring a bed of ease.

Other words of security in the NT spoken at night-time may be mentioned. In Acts 18:10 the Lord spoke to Paul "in the night by a vision", stating that there would be no danger to him in Corinth. In Acts 27:23-24 an angel spoke to Paul by night, promising security to Paul and all those on the ship during the storm.

2. *Temporary Sojourn in Egypt* 2:13-23

v.13 "And when they were departed, behold, the angel of the Lord appeareth to Joseph in a dream, saying, Arise, and take the young child and his mother, and flee into Egypt, and be thou there until I bring thee word: for Herod will seek the young child to destroy him.
v.14 When he arose, he took the young child and his mother by night, and departed into Egypt:
v.15 And was there until the death of Herod: that it might be fulfilled which was spoken of the Lord by the prophet, saying, Out of Egypt have I called my son.
v.16 Then Herod, when he saw that he was mocked of the wise men, was exceeding wroth, and sent forth, and slew all the children that were in Bethlehem, and in all the coasts thereof, from two years old and under, according to the time which he had diligently enquired of the wise men.
v.17 Then was fulfilled that which was spoken by Jeremy the prophet, saying,
v.18 In Rama was there a voice heard, lamentation, and weeping, and great mourning, Rachel weeping *for* her children, and would not be comforted, because they are not.
v.19 But when Herod was dead, behold, an angel of the Lord appeareth in a dream to Joseph in Egypt,
v.20 Saying, Arise, and take the young child and his mother, and go into the land of Israel: for they are dead which sought the young child's life.
v.21 And he arose, and took the young child and his mother, and came into the land of Israel.
v.22 But when he heard that Archelaus did reign in Judaea in the room of his father Herod, he was afraid to go thither: notwithstanding, being warned of God in a dream, he turned aside into the parts of Galilee:
v.23 And he came and dwelt in a city called Nazareth: that it might be fulfilled which was spoken by the prophets, He shall be called a Nazarene."

13-15 By comparing v.13 with v.16, it appears that the angel warned Joseph *before* Herod realised that the wise men would not return and that he waited for them in vain. The first dream contained instructions to cohabit with Mary (1:20) the second contained instructions to flee to Egypt; the third to return to the land of Israel (2:20), and the fourth to move up to Galilee (v.22). The first, second and fourth dreams contained information and instructions that fufilled the OT Scriptures. In Gen 12:10, Abram should not have gone into Egypt – he had his back to the altar. In Gen 45:28, Jacob was not wrong to go to Egypt, for unknown to Jacob this move was setting the scene for bondage to give place to redemption in Exodus, God's great plan to prefigure redemption through the blood of Christ. In Exod 16:3 and Num 11:5 the desires of the people looked back to Egypt; in the second case, apparent blessing turned into judgment (v.33). After the Babylonian captivity, men left in Judaea planned to escape the warfare saying, "we will go into the land of Egypt" (Jer 42:14). The Lord said, "Go ye not into Egypt" (v.19), but the disobedient people "came into the land of Egypt: for they obeyed not the voice of the Lord" (43:7), and judgment followed. How different the case of Joseph, with Mary and the young Child. Unlike the OT examples, Joseph was obedient to the command to go into Egypt, firstly to preserve the recently-born Messiah, and secondly to fulfil the OT Scripture.

The quotation from Hos 11:1, "When Israel was a child, then I loved him, and called my son out of Egypt", may appear strange at a first reading. The context deals with the Assyrian invasion of Israel the northern kingdom. Some of Israel would go into Egypt (Hos 8:13; 9:3, 6); others would not go into Egypt but the Assyrian would control their destiny (11:5). In the midst of this calamity, God recalled the first time when He brought up His people out of Egypt in the book of Exodus (Hos 2:15; 11:1). Israel was then a child, loved by God and called His son (Exod 4:22), though they turned to idolatry afterwards. Thus the similarity with the Lord's case is very restricted. Yet this demonstrates a principle behind some quotations from the OT occurring in the NT, a principle authorised by the Holy Spirit. A sentence can be taken out of its OT context, and made to refer to Christ. Needless to say, we have no liberty to do this with any other OT phrase or sentence. "My son" appears in Matthew's Gospel for the first time in our verse; a relationship within the Godhead is implied, to appear again in Matt 3:17. This first mention also occurs in Mark 1:1; Luke 1:32; John 1:18.

Just as the Lord was hidden in Egypt for a season, recall that Moses was hidden from the Egyptians for three months (Exod 2:2), Joash was hidden in the house of God for six years (2 Chron 22:12); the disciples were hidden in the upper room (Acts 1:13), while our life "is hid with Christ in God" (Col 3:3).

16-18 As he waited for the return of the wise men, the flesh in Herod rose to a peak described by the words "exceeding wroth". So as to attempt to kill the one Child whom he knew to be a divine rival, he extended the net in both space and time: *in space,* not only to Bethlehem, but to its neighbouring borders; *in time,* to children of not only a few months, but children aged up to two years. So his heartless cruelty knew no bounds. The word for "child" previously in the chapter has been *paidion,* a diminutive neuter, used also of a girl in Mark 5:39. But in our verse, the masculine word *pais* is used; the RV translates it as "male children". This word is also used of Jesus when He was twelve years old (Luke 2:43).

The quotation from Jer 31:15 is very interesting. Although Jeremiah largely deals with the captivity of Judah, yet in the opening part of ch.31 the subject of the captivity of the northern kingdom of Israel (Ephraim) is under consideration. It appears in v.15 (and Matt 2:18) that weeping at *both* captivities is being described, for Ramah was in the northern kingdom, and Bethlehem (near which Rachel died) was in the southern kingdom. But in v.16 weeping is restrained, and eyes no longer shed tears, because there is the promise of restoration through the new covenant made with *both* the house of Israel *and* the house of Judah (v.31). But Matthew quotes only the verse of weeping (v.15) and not the verses of rejoicing, because as far as the mothers in Bethlehem were concerned only tragedy had hit them. The later return of the Messiah from Egypt bypassed them, for He returned northwards to Nazareth.

19 Herod never lived to discover his mistake. Instead of reigning victoriously with no danger from his rival, he died of an unpleasant disease. God's rapid judgment fell on a man whose motive was to kill the King of the Jews, the Son of God. "He taketh the wise in their own craftiness" (Job 5:13), and "He that sitteth in the heavens shall laugh: the Lord shall have them in derision" (Ps 2:4) when the kings of the earth set themselves against the Lord and His anointed. Herod's motives were all known to God; the king was a religious man as seen in his building of the temple, but it was a religion without God, and he overlooked the fact that "all things are naked and opened unto the eyes of him with whom we have to do" (Heb 4:13). Similarly the Lord knew the motives of the Jewish leaders, when He said, "Why go ye about to kill me?" (John 7:19); always He knew the thoughts of men (Matt 9:4; 12:25; Luke 6:8; 9:47).

20-22 God's eye of jealousy watched over His Son in Egypt; the angel knew exactly where to go, when he visited Joseph in a dream. Judgment had fallen, and the danger had ceased. The angel said, "...*they* are dead which sought the young child's life", implying that the plot was not only Herod's but of many. God's judgment had fallen on them all, to ensure physical safety for the Lord Jesus until His ultimate sacrifice. Joseph knew, of course, who the Child was, and a tremendous responsibility rested upon his shoulders; we cannot blame him for fearing to go into Judaea when he learnt that Archelaus reigned there. After two years Archelaus was deposed by the Roman authorities, who then administered Judaea by procurators. The next Herod (Luke 3:1) ruled over Galilee.

A further warning from God in another dream caused Joseph to go into Galilee, where the Lord was safe in His childhood and in His early ministry, as He was in Judaea and Jerusalem when He returned there.

23 Nazareth was the city where Mary had received the message from Gabriel (Luke 1:26), the city they had left prior to the Lord's birth (Luke 2:4). At last they returned with the Child, so that He should be called a Nazarene. Usually, this word is *Nazōraios*, but four times it is *Nazarēnos*; both are used in the title "Jesus of Nazareth". Linguistically, the subject is a difficult one, and readers should consult a comprehensive dictionary, such as the *New Bible Dictionary* (Inter-Varsity Fellowship). On spiritual grounds, this name associates Christ with various OT passages speaking of Him as the "Branch", such as "a Branch shall grow out of his (Jesse's) roots" (Isa 11:1); this idea certainly fits in with the genealogy in Matt 1. The name Nazareth may derive from the Hebrew *nēser*, meaning "branch".

IV. The Ministry of John the Baptist (3:1-7)

1. *Baptism of the Multitudes* 3:1-12

v.1 "In those days came John the Baptist, preaching in the wilderness of Judaea,
v.2 And saying, Repent ye: for the kingdom of heaven is at hand.
v.3 For this is he that was spoken of by the prophet Esaias, saying, The voice of one crying in the wilderness, Prepare ye the way of the Lord, make his paths straight.
v.4 And the same John had his raiment of camel's hair, and a leathern girdle about his loins; and his meat was locusts and wild honey.
v.5 Then went out to him Jerusalem, and all Judaea, and all the region round about Jordan,
v.6 And were baptized of him in Jordan, confessing their sins.
v.7 But when he saw many of the Pharisees and Sadducees come to his baptism, he said unto them, O generation of vipers, who hath warned you to flee from the wrath to come?
v.8 Bring forth therefore fruits meet for repentance:
v.9 And think not to say within yourselves, We have Abraham to *our* father: for I say unto you, that God is able of these stones to raise up children unto Abraham.
v.10 And now also the axe is laid unto the root of the trees: therefore every tree which bringeth not forth good fruit is hewn down, and cast into the fire.
v.11 I indeed baptize you with water unto repentance: but he that cometh after me is mightier than I, whose shoes I am not worthy to bear: he shall baptize you with the Holy Ghost, and *with* fire:
v.12 Whose fan *is* in his hand, and he will throughly purge his floor, and gather his wheat into the garner; but he will burn up the chaff with unquenchable fire."

1 Matt 3; Mark 1:1-11; Luke 1:5-25, 40-80; 3:1-22; John 1:6-36; 3:23-36, and other shorter passages, relate to the birth, life and service of John the Baptist, while Matt 14:3-12; Mark 6:14-29; Luke 9:7-9 give details of his death and subsequent events.

Strictly John was a priest, as his father had been, but God called him to be a prophet and a preacher. He did not go to the crowds in the synagogues and temple courts in Jerusalem, but he expected exercised multitudes to come to him in the wilderness near the Jordan river.

2 John's message, "Repent ye: for the kingdom of heaven is at hand", should be compared with the Lord's initial ministry using the same words (Matt 4:17). This must be taken as a summary, for in Mark 1:15 the initial teaching of the Lord was, "The time is fufilled, and the kingdom of God is at hand: repent ye, and believe the gospel". Repentance is the first step to salvation – a turning around from the will of men to the will of God, from the affairs of the flesh and the world to the things of the Spirit of God and of His Word. "Repent", said Peter in Acts 2:38; "repentance toward God, and faith toward our Lord Jesus Christ", was Paul's message (Acts 20:21).

"The kingdom of *heaven*" should strictly be "the kingdom of the *heavens*"; Matthew writes *tōn ouranōn* not *tou ouranou*, a phrase restricted to Matthew's

Gospel, for elsewhere the phrase used is "the kingdom of God", *hē basileia tou theou*. Whereas "the kingdom of heaven" may be used in Matthew, yet in the parallel passage in Mark " the kingdom of God" is used; for example, Matt 13:11 and Mark 4:11. Again, in Matthew "the kingdom" by itself is used about eight times, and "the kingdom of God" occurs five times (6:33; 12:28; 19:24; 21:31, 43). Some authors assert that this feature is linguistic in character only, and that there is no difference between "the kingdom of heaven" and "the kingdom of God". But this does not explain why Matthew uses *both* expressions in one context (Matt 19:23, 24); clearly they meant something different to Matthew, as well as to the Spirit of inspiration.

There are several "heavens" in Scripture. In English, the words "sky" and "the skies" tend to convey a different meaning than " heaven " and " the heavens". The former refer to the physical creation, while the latter have a poetic sense, and a spiritual sense to the believer. But in other languages, as French, German and NT Greek, two sets of words do not exist, and the one word (and its plural form) *ciel, Himmel, ouranos* must refer both to the physical and the spiritual. Thus the first heaven refers to the local atmosphere surrounding the earth (Gen 7:11). The second heaven refers to the stellar heavens (Ps 8:1, 3). The third heaven refers to the eternal dwelling place of God (2 Cor 12:2; Heb 9:24).

Savage, in his book *The Kingdom of God and of Heaven,* sees one kingdom and its four aspects: (1) the kingdom of God, (2) the kingdom of heaven, (3) the kingdom of the Son, (4) the Father's kingdom. In (1), the kingdom is seen in its widest and fullest aspect, with the entire rule of God presented throughout all ages; it is the generic term including (2), (3), (4). For example, "Thine is the kingdom, O Lord, and thou art exalted as head above all" (1 Chron 29:11); "Thy kingdom is an everlasting kingdom" (Ps 145:13; Dan 4:3). In (2), the kingdom's ruling power originates in heaven and comes down from heaven; it is heavenly in character, contrasting with the rule of kings on earth. For example, "The God of heaven shall set up a kingdom"; "The heavens do rule" (Dan 2:44; 4:26); "The Lord hath prepared his throne in the heavens; and his kingdom ruleth over all" (Ps 103:19). It refers to OT and NT history, to the present rule from heaven in the lives of His people, and to the future millennial reign of the Lord Jesus.

3 John's mission was based on OT predictions (Isa 40:3-11), though this passage looks to millennial conditions, " the glory of the Lord shall be revealed ... Behold your God!" (vv.5, 9). But vv.3-4 describe the voice crying in the wilderness, the place where Rome dominated, and where the religious abomination "Mystery, Babylon" will rule (Rev 17:3-5). From a modern standpoint, John had to describe the making of a motorway – it had to be straight and level, with the far end visible from the beginning. In Luke 3:5 we find embankments and cuttings, with curves and all obstacles removed, the highway possessing a good surface. This picture shows the removal of different forms of sin, such as the depths of sin and Satan (Rev 2:24), the heights of pride, the deviative course such as Jacob's cunning, the rough surface implying the lack of love. Unless removed by repentance, all this would prevent a vision of "the salvation of God" (Luke 3:6).

4 John's clothing and food were characterised by lack of finance and worldly fashion, far from being clothed "in soft raiment ... in kings' houses (Matt 11:8). The Lord's needs in this respect were met by many women who ministered unto Him (Matt 27:55). In Paul's case, his hands ministered to his necessities (Acts 20:34), but when finance ran out he suffered "hunger and thirst ... cold and nakedness" (2 Cor 11:27). The sister adorned with "gold, or pearls, or costly array" (1 Tim 2:9; 1 Pet 3:3) is hardly like John the Baptist; remember that good works from the hidden man of the heart are of great price in the sight of God (1 Tim 2:10; 1 Pet 3:4).

This simple clothing with "a leathern girdle about his loins" reminds us of Elijah in 2 Kings 1:8. John's character was similar to that of Elijah, and he is compared with him in Matt 17:11-13; Luke 1:17; no wonder the Jews thought that John was Elias (John 1:21). Locusts were allowed as food (Lev 11:22), they were like a very large grasshopper, coloured red-brown or yellow. Truly, John came "neither eating nor drinking" (Matt 11:18).

5 Multitudes from Jerusalem, Judaea, and the region around Jordan flocked out to hear John. They were people, publicans, privates, priests and Pharisees. The first three groups found in Luke 3:10-14 were branded by John as selfish. All three aspects have money as their basis: some were over-indulgent in thinking of their own property; some used for their own advantage the taxes collected for the Romans; some were not satisfied with their income. The priests came out to ascertain exactly who John was (John 1:19), while evidently the Pharisees came to ensure that John did not undermine their own religious superiority and authority.

6 John baptised in the river Jordan, the place being selected "because there was much water there" (John 3:23). He had been sent by God to baptise—it was not of his own invention. (1:33). The actual symbolism behind John's baptism is not explained in the NT; of the eight different baptisms in the NT only the symbolism behind believers' baptism is developed in detail; it speaks of death and rising again (Rom 6:4-6). John's baptism of repentance was intended to lead to faith in the One who was to come (Acts 19:4). The "doctrine of baptisms" in the OT (Heb 6:2), relating to the ceremonial washings of the priests and the sacrifices, suggests that there was always the picture of forgiveness in baptism (except, of course, in the Lord's case). Ultimately, forgiveness could derive only from the cross, but the people did not know that at the time. John's preaching extended to the cross, when he said, "Behold the Lamb of God, which taketh away the sin of the world" (John 1:29). Baptism by itself cannot yield forgiveness; this only the Lord can give (Luke 5:20; 7:48).

7 In addressing the Pharisees and Sadducees, John was unequivocal: "O generation of vipers". The Lord used the same description of the Pharisees (Matt 12:34); He also called them "a wicked and adulterous generation" (16:4); He accused them with, "Ye are of your father the devil" (John 8:44); on Cyprus Paul declared, "thou child of the devil" (Acts 13:10). By using the word "vipers", John implied that there was likeness to the serpent in Gen 3:1. Actually he had not been warning *them* to flee from the wrath to come, for they had come to maintain their religious status. No doubt John's preaching was coupled with the testimony and warnings of the OT prophets. "The wrath" appears to refer to the judgment prior to the coming millennial kingdom, thus cleansing the world for the King's reign.

8 If repentance were real, it would be proved by its fruits; a new life had to contrast with the previous works of darkness. In Mark 1:15, "repent ye, and believe the gospel" stresses that faith rather than fruit follows repentance, the same order being found in Acts 20:21. Yet Paul could write of the "work of faith" (1Thess 1:3), and "faith which worketh by love" (Gal 5:6).

9 Fruit or faith does not bask in self-satisfaction. Here is religious conceit, since they derived from Abraham their father. Similar Pharisaical conceit in John 8:39 is interpreted by the Lord as equivalent to having the devil as father (v.44). Even the stones could be given more life than these Jews had (perhaps alluding to the stony hearts of the Gentiles later to be brought into salvation). After all, Adam had been made from the dust (Gen 2:7), and that which is earthy will give place to that which is heavenly (1 Cor 15:48). Admittedly, the Lord would not turn stones into bread for His own use (Matt 4:4), but the stones would cry out if the children were silent (Luke 19:40).

10 There would be an elimination of trees that could not produce good fruit. This had already happened to Israel, the axe being the Assyrian nation (Isa 10:15). Later, grace would bear long with the Jews; a delay in this judgment (as in Luke 13:7-9) would show grace waiting for like to produce like, until a good tree produced good fruit (Matt 7:18).

11 By saying, "he that cometh after me is mightier than I", John spoke well of Christ, taking a lowly position and desiring to become even lowlier, "He must increase, but I must decrease (John 3:30); later, the Lord spoke well of John (Matt 11:9-11). John contrasted himself completely with the Lord, as to His Person, His worthiness, and His capacity to baptise. John was not worthy even to stoop down before Him, because "He that cometh from above is above all" (twice repeated, John 3:31).

John's baptism with water gave place to baptism by the Lord's disciples (John 3:22; 4:12); this took place *before* the cross, and was the beginning of what later was believers' baptism in the Lord's Name *after* the cross (Acts 2:41). John looked beyond the physical act of baptism; he could see two further kinds of baptism: (1) "with (or *in*) the Holy Spirit", the Lord Himself repeating this promise after His resurrection (Luke 24:49), and also just prior to His ascension (Acts 1:5, 8); (2) "With (or *in*) fire". This does not refer to the cloven tongues like as of fire on the day of Pentecost (Acts 2:3), speaking of new fervency in testimony. Rather it refers to judgment, and the burning up of the chaff "with fire unquenchable" (Matt 3:11, 12; Luke 3:17). These two baptisms are separated by the whole of the church period, forming what is commonly called " the prophetic gap", a period of which the prophets were silent.

Note that baptism is *"in"* and not *"with"*. The Greek preposition *en* generally means *"in"* positionally; only a few times can it mean *"with"*, for example, *"with* the sword" (Luke 22:49). Compare "John did baptise in the wilderness" (Mark 1:4); the people "were all baptised of him *in* the river" (v.5) and hence "I indeed have baptised you *in* water", not with water (v.8) The translation *"with* water" arises from the common but false rite of sprinkling infants, the translation having been adopted to conform to an unscriptural practice.

12 The fan is a simple device for separating the wheat grains from the chaff after a harvest, referring to the rapture of the church, to the battle of Armageddon and the Lord's return in glory. The destinies of men will differ – the garner or the fire, heaven or hell. The Lord's object is to have the wheat for Himself; Satan wanted the chaff, engaging in his own sifting process to obtain it (Luke 22:31). Clearly John's ministry was often a warning ministry – "wrath, axe, burn, fire".

2. *Baptism of the Lord Jesus* 3:13-17

v.13 "Then cometh Jesus from Galilee to Jordan unto John, to be baptized of him.
v.14 But John forbad him, saying, I have need to be baptized of thee, and comest thou to me?
v.15 And Jesus answering said unto him, Suffer *it to be so* now: for thus it becometh us to fulfil all righteousness. Then he suffered him.
v.16 And Jesus, when he was baptized, went up straightway out of the water: and, lo, the heavens were opened unto him, and he saw the Spirit of God descending like a dove, and lighting upon him:
v.17 And lo a voice from heaven, saying, This is my beloved Son, in whom I am well pleased."

13 The Lord was "about thirty years of age" (Luke 3:23) when He left Galilee to come to John where he was baptising. Thirty was the age at which the Levites commenced their public tabernacle service in the wilderness (Num 4:3). This journey from Nazareth may have been anything up to 60 miles, and was the first of many to be made by the Lord between Galilee, Samaria and Jerusalem, aptly described by "in journeyings often" (2 Cor 11:26). According to the Baptist's own testimony, he did not know Jesus (John 1:33) until he saw the Spirit descending upon Him at His baptism. He had known Him as a relative, but after His baptism he knew Him identified as the Lamb of God and as the Son of God (vv.29, 34), and as the Baptiser in the Holy Spirit.

14 John knew of the Lord's moral excellency, so unlike himself and all those whom he was baptising unto repentance. This baptism was not for the Lord! And who could baptise John, save One far better than he? John was perplexed as he contrasted this Person with the people, publicans, privates, priests and Pharisees who came out from Jerusalem and Judaea.

15 By way of explanation, Jesus did not reveal His Person to John; that would come shortly afterwards. Rather He said, "for thus it becometh us to fulfil all righteousness". Note that He said "us" – both He and John were involved. This explanation clearly satisfied John, though expositors differ in their understanding of it. Some suggest that because He was to be made "sin for us" (2 Cor 5:21), He had to put Himself entirely in our place, to bear our sins in His own Person. But John's baptism was not connected with sin-bearing, neither did the Lord do anything vicarious prior to His sacrifice. The Lord's righteous life was the same *before* His baptism as it was *afterwards,* unlike the lives of the people who were supposed to be changed through repentance at their baptism. By being baptised, He would be accepted as a Teacher; had He not been baptised, they would have accused Him of claiming to be more righteous than they themselves. This would be demonstrated by His life and works, but the Lord would not give them even an unjustified cause for complaint. He wanted to be accepted as a Teacher, and this baptism of a righteous Man supported this objective.

16 Jesus did not linger in the water after His baptism; He left it immediately, "praying" as Luke adds (Luke 3:21), a feature that characterised Him during the great events in His life. It was then that the heavens were opened "unto him", and "he" saw the Spirit descending; the Baptist also saw this in John 1:32. This opening of heaven was an indication of God's infinite pleasure in the previously hidden life of His Son on earth. This opening showed divine communication and vision, cp: "the heavens were opened, and I saw visions of God" (Ezek 1:1) "ye shall see heaven open" (John 1:51); "Peter … saw heaven opened, and a certain vessel descending" (Acts 10:11); "a door was opened in heaven" (Rev 4:1); "I saw heaven opened, and behold a white horse" (Rev 19:11).

The Trinity was manifested – distinct Persons in absolute unity: the Son was baptised, the Father spoke, the Spirit descended. We must not think that the Lord did not possess the Spirit before this event! He could not have been in a lesser state than John, who was filled with the Spirit from his birth (Luke 1:15) rather the Son possessed the Spirit not by measure (John 3:34). The descent of the Spirit was a mark of identification – this happened to *none other but* the Son

(John 1:33). Moreover, it was a prelude to the Lord's service, "he hath anointed me to preach the gospel to the poor" (Luke 4:18; Isa 61:1). The outward appearance of this manifestation was "in a bodily shape like a dove" (Luke 3:22). This showed the Lord in the midst of wolves "as harmless as doves" (Matt 10:16); it showed Him as One who was harmless in His life, causing no adverse effects in men (Heb 7:26). The dove was the opposite of the raven feeding on the flotsam of the flood; the Lord's meat was to do the Father's will.

17 The voice from "heaven" shows its status, origin, authority and truth. In Matt 3:17; 17:5; Mark 9:7; Luke 9:35, the voice said, " *This* is my beloved Son " speaking *to John and the apostles* in the respective incidents, but in Mark 1: 11 Luke 3:22 the words *"Thou* art my beloved Son" were *to the Son*. At His baptism, this was the Father's commendation of His Son's life *prior* to His public ministry; on the mount of transfiguration, the reference was to His *subsequent* life of perfect ministry. We recall Isa 42:1, "mine elect, in whom my soul delighteth; I have put my spirit upon him". The Lord always possessed the Spirit in Himself, but here the Spirit comes upon Him. The difference is seen in connection with the oil of the meal offering, "upon it" and "mingled with oil" (Lev 2:1, 4, 5). Internal oil speaks of essential and absolute possession, external oil speaks of anointing for specific service.

The Father describes this blessed One as "my beloved Son" (*ho huios mou ho agapētos*). The description "beloved" stretches back to eternity (John 17:24).

The title "Son" refers to relationship, not to any heretically-suggested origin; the Name goes back beyond the creation (Luke 3:38). The first Adam was created by God, but the last Adam came forth from God as uncreated in His Person, though born into Manhood. Always suspect any Bible translation that renders Ps 2:7 and Heb 1:5 as "You are my Son; Today I have become your Father". Such false theology is heretical; moreover it cuts across Paul's inspired interpretation that "this day have I begotten thee" refers to the Lord's manifestation into public service after His baptism (Acts 13:22-37).

V. Commencement of the Lord's Ministry (4:1-25)

1. *The Temptation in the Wilderness* 4:1-11

a. *The First Temptation (vv.1-4)*

v.1 "Then was Jesus led up of the Spirit into the wilderness to be tempted of the devil.

v.2 And when he had fasted forty days and forty nights, he was afterward an hungered.

v.3 And when the tempter came to him, he said, If thou be the Son of God, command that these stones be made bread.

v.4 But he answered and said, It is written, Man shall not live by bread alone, but by every word that proceedeth out of the mouth of God."

1 Before the Lord's public service commenced, the following events had to take place:

1. The Lord had to attain 30 years of age to be outwardly acceptable to the Jews.

2. His baptism to show, not a need for repentance, but an on-going life of open righteousness.

3. The Father's commendation - *about* and *to* the Son.

4. His anointing to special service.

5. Proof had to be given to Satan of what heaven knew already – that the Lord *could not* and *would not* sin.

6. On account of sin and weakness all around, He had to experience what it meant to be "in all points tempted like as we are, yet without sin" (Heb 4:15).

We should trace briefly the subject of the Spirit in the life of the Lord Jesus up to and including His initial ministry. Mary was found "with child of the Holy Ghost" (Matt 1:18). There was revelation to Simeon "by the Holy Ghost" that he would see the Lord's Christ (Luke 2:26). "The child grew, and waxed strong in spirit" (2:40). There was the Spirit "descending like a dove, and lighting upon him" (Matt 3:16). Jesus was "led up of the Spirit into the wilderness"; in Mark 1:12 this reads " immediately the Spirit driveth him into the wilderness". After this, "Jesus returned in the power of the Spirit into Galilee" (Luke 4:14). In the synagogue at Nazareth, He said, "The Spirit of the Lord is upon me" (4:18).

The temptation was not the first encounter of One divine with Satan. In Job 1:6; 2:1 Satan presented himself "before the Lord"; in Zech 3:2 he was rebuked by the Lord. Satan lost both these encounters, since God was managing affairs on the earth. In Matt 4 an even greater lesson was presented to Satan; here the divine Man on earth was involved. In this paragraph, the evil one is called "the devil; the tempter; Satan" .

2 Fasting is an explicit manifestation that there is no trust in, nor contact with, even necessary things in the world. In Acts 13:2, the prophets and teachers in Antioch fasted as they "ministered to the Lord"; when there was contact with

Him and not with the world, they were used by the Spirit. In Matt 17:20-21, the Lord showed that unbelief could not be overcome except by prayer and fasting. Dispensing with even necessary things proves that one is in the world but not of it.

The Lord's fasting was for "forty days and forty nights"; forty is the number of probation. Those circumstances, that in Christ led to perfection, would lead a man of the flesh downwards to disaster. The children of Israel were in the wilderness for 40 years, and passages such as Num 21:4-9; 25:1-18 show that they had learnt no lesson. Moses was in the mount for 40 days (Exod 24:18); the people were tested, and fell into idolatry (32:1-35). Thus the Lord was tested by His circumstances, showing that He could not be found wanting; He was also prepared for many forms of contact with evil during His years of service, yet always remaining undefiled.

The temptation of the Second Man should be contrasted with the temptation of the first man Adam. Adam was in a place of advantage (a plentiful supply of food in the garden); the Lord Jesus was in a place of disadvantage (no food in the wilderness). The temptation of Adam and Eve (to know good and evil), and the temptations of the Lord were offers of apparent gain. Eve's response "God hath said" (Gen 3:3) proved ineffective; the Lord's "It is written" was completely effective. While angels ministered to the Lord Jesus, the cherubim and a flaming sword guarded the garden against human intrusions.

Of all the quotations that could have been made to counteract Satan's temptations, the Lord used only one small context in Deuteronomy, namely 8:3; 6:16; 6:13; 10:20. These were spoken by Moses at the end of the 40 years, just as they were spoken by the Lord at the end of the 40 days. At the end of 40 years Israel still needed teaching; at the end of the 40 days, the Lord triumphed with the Word against Satan. The three temptations relate to the misuse of Self-Sustenance, of Scripture, and of Service; they contain moral, religious and national implications.

Only at the appropriate times would the Lord

1. *Partake of bread.* He sat at meat in Matthew's house (Matt 9:10); He "came eating and drinking ... a friend of publicans and sinners" (Matt 11:19); He desired to eat the passover with His disciples before He suffered (Luke 22:15); after His resurrection He took fish "and did eat before them" (24:43).

2. *Come to the temple.* Having entered into Jerusalem in triumph, "Jesus went into the temple of God" (Matt 21:12); "the Lord ... shall suddenly come to his temple" (Mal 3:1).

3. *Inherit the kingdoms.* This would not take place by men trying to make Him king by force (John 6:15). Rather in a day yet to come, God will give Him the

heathen for His inheritance, and the uttermost parts of the earth for His possession (Ps 2:8); the kingdom (singular, not plural) of this world is to become the possession of the Lord (Rev 11:15) at the sounding of the seventh trumpet.

The lessons are that believers should await the time of God for the necessities of life, for service in the local assembly, and for ultimate exaltation of the humble.

There is an interesting connection between these three temptations and Isa 58. The people fasted for self (v.3), seeking their own pleasure (v.13). Rather, they should give bread to the hungry and satisfy the afflicted soul (v.10), delighting in the Lord (v.14). The results are given in v.14: God would feed them (answering to the first temptation); they would "ride upon the high places" (answering to the second temptation); theirs would be "the heritage of Jacob" (answering to the third temptation). Moreover they would be "like a watered garden" (v.11) answering to the angels ministering to the Lord Jesus when the temptations were over.

3 The Lord provided miraculously for others, but not for Himself alone. In mercy and grace He fed the 4,000 and the 5,000; He provided the tribute money, not just for Himself, but for Peter's sake (Matt 17:27). All of the Lord's actions were governed by the great principle, "Look not every man on his own things, but every man also on the things of others. Let this mind be in you, which was also in Christ Jesus" (Phil 2:4-5).

When Satan said, "If thou be the Son of God", the Greek word *ei* is used for "if" (as also in v.6), but in v.9 *ean* is used. Satan is not expressing a doubt, nor is he seeking to place a doubt in the Lord's mind; rather the meaning is, "since you were called Son after your baptism, let there be a miraculous demonstration of this fact" . The same may be said about Luke 23:37, 39: "If (*ei*) thou be the king of the Jews, save thyself", and, "If (*ei*) thou be Christ, save thyself and us". The other word for "if" (*ean*) - used far more often by the Gospel writers – does express a doubt or uncertainty, such as in the third temptation, "*if* thou wilt fall down and worship me".

The Lord would do no miracle on the wilderness stones because the suggestion came from Satan. Note that temptation of itself is not sin – yielding to it is. Moreover, temptation may be either Satan's voice (as in the Lord's experience), or the natural inclination and desire within the human heart (this was *not* so with the Lord). Temptation may be an evil seed sown by the voice of Satan, but such seed could not be received by the Lord, so it certainly could not germinate in His heart which was so perfect, divine and pure. In man's case, when lust has conceived, it brings forth sin and death (James 1:15).

Miracles could be performed on stones, whether literal or metaphorical. Water came out of the rock to provide drink for the children of Israel; David's one stone hit Goliath accurately because God was behind the projectile's path; God could have raised children to Abraham from the stones around (Matt 3:9), the stones would have cried out if the children had held their peace (Luke 19:40).

4 In reply, the Lord quoted the written word of God: "It is written" (*gegraptai*) namely the Greek passive perfect tense, implying a past act with its effects lasting to the present (this tense is often translated by a present tense in English, though this device cannot bring out the full meaning). The Lord therefore meant that this written word still had its same power, authority and value, else it would merely be of academic interest to quote it. The Lord's reply from Deut 8:3, "that he might make thee know that man doth not live by bread only, but by every word that proceedeth out of the mouth of the Lord doth man live", has an interesting context. The people needed 40 years for the lesson to be taught and learnt (v.2). The Lord allowed hunger among the people, so that they could learn priorities and that He keeps according to His will. When they would eat bread in the land after 40 years, either they would " bless the Lord" (v. 10) or they would forget the Lord by not keeping His commandments (v.11). But after 40 days, the Lord showed the path of a Man who fufilled all righteousness. For us, the lesson of priorities is important. The Lord taught that life is "more that meat (food)"; hence, "seek ye first the kingdom of God, and his righteousness; and all these things shall be added unto you" (Matt 6:25, 33). Martha was cumbered about much serving, but Mary had chosen "that good part" (Luke 10:40-42). "Seek those things which are above … Set your affection on things above, not on things on the earth" (Col 3:1-2).

b. *The Second Temptation (vv.5-7)*

v.5 "Then the devil taketh him up into the holy city, and setteth him on a pinnacle of the temple,

v.6 And saith unto him, If thou be the Son of God, cast thyself down: for it is written, He shall give his angels charge concerning thee: and in *their* hands they shall bear thee up, lest at any time thou dash thy foot against a stone.

v.7 Jesus said unto him, It is written again, Thou shalt not tempt the Lord thy God."

5 In this temptation, "the holy city" is called "Jerusalem" in Luke 4:9; elsewhere it is called "the city of the great King" (Matt 5:35), and "Sodom and Egypt, where also our Lord was crucified" (Rev 11:8). It is remarkable that the Lord allowed Himself to be taken into the city and set on the pinnacle; what a contrast with v.1 where He was led by the Spirit into the wilderness. Satan appears as a priest, similar to the second beast in Rev 13; in the third temptation he appears as a king deified, similar to the first beast in Rev 13. In Luke 2:27 the Lord was brought into the temple as a Babe; later He was in the temple at the age of twelve (2:46). In this temptation, He was brought to the top of the temple of such architectural fame, a fame soon to pass when not one stone would remain on another (Matt 24:2). In its precincts there were wilderness conditions, with nothing for God except, on occasions, a faithful remnant such as Zacharias, Simon and Anna.

The Greek word for "pinnacle" is *pterugion,* the diminutive neuter form of *pterux,* meaning "a wing". JND translates the word as "edge"; others use "parapet". There is speculation as to what this pinnacle was, but the use of the word " edge" eliminates the thought that it was anything special. The word used for "temple" (*hieron*) means the whole fabric and precincts of the structure on mount Moriah. This represents the outward visible part, with the courts where the people congregated. Whenever the Lord entered the temple, it was only into the *hieron* (Matt 21:14; 24:1). The second word for "temple" is *naos,* meaning the inner sanctuary where *only the priests could enter* (Matt 27:5, 51). Paul used this latter word metaphorically when he wrote of the believer's body being "the *temple* of the Holy Spirit" (1 Cor 6:19); it is used of the local assembly "ye are the *temple* of God" (3:16, 17), and of the universal church growing "unto an holy *temple* in the Lord " (Eph 2:21).

6 The temptation to cast Himself down from the uppermost part of the temple, thus to appear to come into His temple from on high with spectacular display (with complete disregard of the revealed prophetic programme found in the OT), was amplified by Satan by a false quotation from Ps 91. There, the Lord dwells in the secret place of the Most High (v.1); Jehovah is His refuge and fortress (v.2); He can have no fear on earth with Jehovah as His habitation (vv.5, 9). Consequently there is the promise of all deliverance (vv.3, 6, 10, 11-12), the last of which refers not to deliverance from falling physically from the pinnacle, but to deliverance from stumbling blocks caused by men and Satan. Because the Lord's love was directed to His Father, "therefore will I deliver him: I will set him on high" (v.14). In other words, only God raises Him – certainly not Satan or men: "he raised him from the dead, and set him at his own right hand in the heavenly places" (Eph 1:20). Hence the angelic ministration in Ps 91 is spiritual, and the Lord perceived its misapplication by Satan.

7 The Lord's response, "Thou shalt not tempt the Lord thy God", was taken from Deut 6:16, the context showing that the keeping of the commandments before God "shall be our righteousness" (v.25). The context also rebuked Satan, "Ye shall not go after other gods" – Satan himself being the god of this world (v.14). Thus the Lord instructed Satan (1) not to tempt God to fulfil Ps 91 when there was no necessity to do so, and (2) not to tempt Christ to put Ps 91 into practice. His quotation "the Lord thy God" referred to Himself, proving His deity, a fact that Satan knew though many religious men today appear to reject or doubt such a glorious truth.

c. *The Third Temptation (vv.8-11)*

v.8 "Again, the devil taketh him up into an exceeding high mountain, and sheweth him all the kingdoms of the world, and the glory of them;
v.9 And saith unto him, All these thing will I give thee, if thou wilt fall down and worship me.
v.10 Then saith Jesus unto him, Get thee hence, Satan: for it is written, Thou shalt worship the Lord thy God, and him only shalt thou serve.
v.11 Then the devil leaveth him, and, behold, angels came and ministered unto him."

8 How different is this scene from that in Matt 17:1. In the former, Satan took the Lord up the mountain to show Him the glory of the ordered kingdoms of the world. In the latter, the Lord took the three disciples up so that they might see His glory. The fact that the Lord was shown "all" the kingdoms of the world " in a moment of time" (*en stigmē chronou,* a prick or point of time, Luke 4:5) means that it was a special form of vision on the mountain top. There was no natural high mountain from whose summit all the existing kingdoms could be seen. Satan, a liar from the beginning, had no authority to bestow such promised earthly power and glory. In fact, he showed the Lord not the glorious Babylonian kingdom but the Roman corresponding to the fourth beast in Dan 7, something that the Lord knew already as well as its ultimate destruction. Nebuchadnezzar described the glory of his kingdom as " this great Babylon, that I have built for the house of the kingdom by the might of my power, and for the honour of my majesty" (Dan 4:30); later he spoke of "the glory of my kingdom" (v.36) corresponding to the gold of his dreams and of his image (2:32, 37- 38, 3:1). But in the Lord's time the " glory" of the nations was hardly something to be desired, for that kingdom is described as having "great iron teeth" devouring the "whole earth" and treading it down (Dan 7:7, 23). This was Rome, constituting the imperial authority over men; Greece (no longer a world empire) constituted the wisdom and unbelief of men. The character of such nations was the opposite of that of the nations which will bring their "glory and honour" to the holy Jerusalem during the millennial kingdom (Rev 21:24). Both now and in the past, power over nations attracts the basest of men and power-hungry dictators. In contrast to what Satan offered, Christ is King on Zion, awaiting the day of His possession of "the uttermost parts of the earth" granted by His Father God (Ps 2:8; 82:8), though originally all rulers were against Him (Ps 2:1-2). We should point out that in Dan 2 we have the kingdoms of earth as seen through Satan's eyes, while in Dan 7 they are seen through God's eyes.

9 Satan wanted personal worship. The worship of Satan and the glory of self were the objects of many worldly rulers – many OT kings were taken up with idolatry. Thus Nebuchadnezzar set up a huge image of gold, and all people were commanded to worship it (Dan 3:1-7).

10 In His reply, the Lord quoted Deut 6:13; only the Lord God should be worshipped and served. In that chapter, the people had to beware of forgetting the Lord; they were not to go after other gods (vv.12, 14). Rather, they had to love the Lord their God (v.5), a verse quoted by the Lord when resisting the Pharisees (Matt 22:37). This love was always the experience of the Lord, so He said, "Get thee hence, Satan". Such resistance to and rebuke of Satan may be found elsewhere; see Zech 3:2; Matt 16:23; 1 Pet 5:9. The word for "serve" in "him only shalt thou *serve*" is *latreuō*, and is used in many places in the NT for service Godward; Paul wrote, "whom I *serve* with (or in) my spirit in the gospel of his Son" (Rom 1:9).

11 So the devil left the Lord; Luke adds that he "ended all the temptation" (Luke 4:13). The temptation was complete as demonstrating to Satan his impotence before such an infinitely-superior, divine Being in Manhood. But the temptation was ended only for a season. By attacking the disciples afterwards, he was in effect attacking the Lord. Satan tempted Him through men, when they said, "save thyself" (Matt 27:40); when Peter said, "pity thyself" (Matt 16:22 marg); when His brethren said, "shew thyself" (John 7:4). Thus Satan used men where he himself had failed, and of course the failure continued.

The ministration of the angels was, no doubt, both spiritual and physical. Angels were active at these special points in the Lord's experience; for example, at Gethsemane, at His resurrection and His ascension, but not at the cross during the hours of darkness. The verb "ministered" (*diakoneō*) involves the service of works; it is usually employed for the service of the Lord's people in a local assembly.

2. *The Lord Commences His Public Ministry 4:12-25*

v.12 "Now when Jesus had heard that John was cast into prison, he departed into Galilee;
v.13 And leaving Nazareth, he came and dwelt in Capernaum, which is upon the sea coast, in the borders of Zabulon and Nephthalim:
v.14 That it might be fulfilled which was spoken by Esaias the prophet, saying,
v.15 The land of Zabulon, and the land of Nephthalim, *by* the way of the sea, beyond Jordan, Galilee of the Gentiles;
v.16 The people which sat in darkness saw great light; and to them which sat in the region and shadow of death light is sprung up.
v.17 From that time Jesus began to preach, and to say, Repent: for the kingdom of heaven is at hand.
v.18 And Jesus, walking by the sea of Galilee, saw two brethren, Simon called Peter, and Andrew his brother, casting a net into the sea: for they were fishers.
v.19 And he saith unto them, Follow me, and I will make you fishers of men.
v.20 And they straightway left *their* nets, and followed him.
v.21 And going on from thence, he saw other two brethren, James *the son* of Zebedee, and John his brother, in a ship with Zebedee their father, mending their nets; and he called them.

v.22 And they immediately left the ship and their father, and followed him.
v.23 And Jesus went about all Galilee, teaching in their synagogues, and preaching the gospel of the kingdom, and healing all manner of sickness and all manner of disease among the people.
v.24 And his fame went throughout Syria: and they brought unto him all sick people that were taken with divers diseases and torments, and those which were possessed with devils, and those which were lunatick, and those that had the palsy; and he healed them.
v.25 And there followed him great multitudes of people from Galilee, and *from* Decapolis, and *from* Jerusalem, and *from* Judaea, and *from* beyond Jordan."

12-13 Before John was cast into prison, many other events had taken place, for example, the miracle in Cana (John 2:1-11), and the Lord's visit to Jerusalem at the Passover (2:13-25); also the interview with Nicodemus (John 3:1-21), for John was still baptising and preaching in John 3:23-36; 4:1. John's outspoken denunciation of Herod's brother, "It is not lawful for thee to have her" (Matt 14: 3-4), caused Herod to imprison him, and he would have killed him, typical of dictators with bad consciences who seek to remove those more righteous than themselves. In prison, John was still interested in the works of Christ (Matt 11:2-6), until his untimely death at the request of Herod's brother's wife (Matt 14:6-11). Luke adds that John's condemnatory words also concerned "all the evils" that Herod himself had done (Luke 3:19-20). (Note: Luke's order of events cannot be chronological, for John's imprisonment is recorded before the Lord's baptism.) There also appears to be a deeper reason for John to disappear from the scene of public ministry. God would not have two focal points of interest—John and Christ; John's work was effectively concluded when the Lord became prominent, and to maintain this prominence, John had to disappear from the public eye: "Ye sent unto John, and he bare witness unto the truth. But I receive not testimony from man … He was a burning and a shining light" (John 5:33-35).

So the Lord "departed into Galilee". "From where?", we may ask. Perhaps from the Jerusalem area, since He spent most of His time in Galilee and Judaea. Although He had been brought up in Nazareth, this became a place of hostility, because of His outspoken testimony to the truth: "No prophet is accepted in his own country" (Luke 4:24). The Lord then dwelt in Capernaum about 20 miles northwest from Nazareth, towards the north of the sea of Galilee. It was in these environs that "most of his mighty works were done" (Matt 11:20-23), Capernaum being described as "exalted unto heaven", yet Sodom will be treated more tolerably in the day of judgment.

14-16 Matthew has added "in the borders of Zabulon and Nephthalim" so that the relevance of his quotation from Isa 9:1-2 should be more apparent. This NT quotation should be compared with the OT: "*when at the first he lightly afflicted* the land of Zebulun and the land of Naphtali, *and afterward did more grievously afflict her* by the way of the sea, beyond Jordan, in Galilee of the nations" (AV);

"In the former time he brought into contempt the land of Zebulun and the land of Naphtali, *but in the latter time hath he made it glorious,* by the way of the sea, beyond Jordan, Galilee of the nations" (RV); *"at the time he at first lightly, and afterwards heavily, visited* the land of Zebulun and the land of Naphtali, – the way of the sea, beyond the Jordan" (JND). The words in italics are omitted by Matthew, no doubt for good reason, to avoid the apparent conflict of meaning: "did more grievously afflict her" and "hath he made it glorious". (A glance at the English meanings of the Hebrew word *kabad* in a concordance will show the reader what is at stake.) In any case, both translations are valid. For the AV, the first light affliction occurred in 1 Kings 15:20 or perhaps 2 Kings 15:29, while the second, more grievous, affliction occurred in 2 Kings 17:6, representing the final dissolution of the northern kingdom. The RV "made it glorious" is entirely prophetical; this certainly did not take place historically in the OT, but refers to the presence of the glorious Lord in the days of His flesh, and to the future advent of the Lord coming in His glory.

Taken together, Isa chs. 8-9 describe the lowest and highest positions. The Assyrians had passed through the northern kingdom and Judaea. At that time, the Lord was "a stone of stumbling ... to both the houses of Israel" (8:14); there was "no light in them" (8:20) when the word of God was refused. This was moral and religious darkness, contrasting with other verses such as, "the Lord of hosts, which dwelleth in mount Zion" (8:18), "The people ... have seen a great light" (9:2). Ultimate redemption occurs in 9:6, "the government shall be upon his shoulder" referring to the millennial reign of Christ.

The "great light" is the Person of Christ Himself. This designation does not appear elsewhere in Matthew; rather John is the exponent of the Lord as the Light (John 1:9; 8:12; 9:5).

17 The Lord's initial teaching, "Repent: for the kingdom of heaven is at hand", was identical to that of John the Baptist (3:2). "At hand" is not an adverbial phrase, but forms part of the verb *engizō*, a common verb in the NT meaning to approach either in space or in time. The perfect tense *ēngiken* is used here, with the sense that the event had present effects. The presence amongst them of the Lord, issuing teaching of conduct compatible with His presence, shows that the kingdom of heaven could be appreciated by faith while He was on earth. This teaching is wholly consistent with the quotation from Isa 9:1-2, for the passage passes on to "the government" (v.6), a necessary ingredient of the kingdom of heaven. This "government" refers to the kingdom in its future millennial aspect.

18-20 The name "Jesus" in v. 18 is omitted in the RV and the Greek texts from which the translation is made. These three verses form a very abbreviated summary of the fuller passage in Luke 5:2-11. The Lord was "walking by the sea of Galilee" for a particular purpose – He knew the events that would happen there. The river Jordan flows through this sea, which is about 13 miles long from north to south. Its other names are the Lake of Gennesaret, the Sea of Tiberias and the Sea of Chinnereth. It was a place for fishing, though subject to severe winds blowing down the valleys of the surrounding hills.

We can discern various stages in the divine call to service.

1. *The call to discipleship* (John 1:35-42): Andrew and another heard John the Baptist's cry, "Behold the Lamb of God", and they with Peter followed the Lord. The events in John 2-4 (the miracle at Cana, Nicodemus, the woman at Sychar's well) must have taken place during this initial stage.

2. *The call to general service* (Matt 4:18-20; Luke 5:2-11): The first stage did not amount to total consecration to the Lord. Back at their original haunts, they returned to their past trade of fishing, so the Lord must have been walking alone. After Peter's confession of sin (Luke 5:8), the call to be "fishers of men" was issued. Compare this with Isa 6, where a confession of sin led to the prophet being sent (vv. 5,8).

3. *The call to apostleship* (Luke 6:13; Matt 10:1), namely, *the call to special service.* Out of *all* His disciples, the Lord chose *twelve* whom he called apostles, sent ones. In Paul's case these three stages may be found in Acts 9:4-9; 9:17-22 and 13:1-4 respectively.

The meaning of Peter's name must be particularly noted. His original name Simon means "hearing". The Lord gave him a new name in John 1:42, "Thou art Simon the son of Jona: thou shalt be called Cephas, which is by interpretation, A stone". *Cephas* is the Aramaic word for stone, while the Greek interpretation is *Petros,* meaning a detached piece of rock or boulder. In the NT, this word *Petros always* refers to the apostle, and *never* to a stone, for which the words *lithos* and *psēphos* are used. It should never be confused with the similar Greek word *petra* (feminine) meaning a mass of rock, occurring 16 times, literally in Matt 27:51, 60 (*rocks* being rent apart and the tomb hewn out in the *rock*) and metaphorically in Matt 7:24 (a house built on a *rock*) and 1 Cor 10:4 (*Christ*). We shall discuss this again in Matt 16:18.

Peter became the most prominent apostle – his was "the apostleship of the circumcision" (Gal 2:8), with God working effectively in him. Apart from the name "A stone" in John 1:42, the name Peter, *Petros,* appears the following numbers of times in the books of the NT: Matt (24), Mark (19), Luke (20) John (34), Acts (58), Gal (5), 1 Pet (1), 2 Pet (1), the total being 163. By contrast, John the Baptist's name occurs 92 times, John the apostle's 36 times, John Mark's 4 times, and John the chief priest's once. Again, the apostle Paul's name appears 162 times, and his former name Saul 17 times.

Peter's brother Andrew has a different history, his name occurring 13 times. Unlike Peter, Andrew is described as being one of John the Baptist's disciples (John 1:35). He therefore possessed the teaching that John had preached, including a knowledge of the prophecy of Isaiah which must have taken in Isa 53:7, "he is brought as a lamb to the slaughter", enabling Andrew to recognise the Lord as the "Lamb". Both he and Peter then followed the Lord, though not with complete priority. However, their ordinary occupation was transformed by the Lord into a spiritual occupation; from being "fishers" of fish they became "fishers of men". First they had to obey the call "Follow me". This is the only time in the NT that the verb *deute* is translated "follow" ("come ye after", RV). The other 12 occurrences are uniformly translated "come", such as "*Come* unto me" (Matt 11:28). Thus when we read that these two men "followed" Jesus, the more common verb *akoloutheō*is used; in the four gospels this word is used 76 times of following Christ, both literally and metaphorically as a disciple. It is used in the Lord's command "Follow me" on other occasions (e.g., Matt 8:22; 9:9; Mark 2:14; Luke 5:27). Thus the command to Peter and Andrew is singled out as something special, possibly because they are the two named disciples in John 1 who had the opportunity of this second call.

21-22 It is not certain whether James and John had been disciples of the Lord before this event, since their names do not occur. There is no direct evidence that they were among the "disciples" referred to in John 2:2 at the wedding in Canal Expositors suggest, however, that John is the unnamed disciple who, with Andrew, heard John the Baptist say, "Behold the Lamb of God" John 1:35-40), on account of the oblique way in which John refers to himself in the writing of his Gospel, such as "the disciple … whom he loved" (John 19:26), "he that saw it bare record" (v.35). If this is so, then John would have been at Cana; he would have included himself when he wrote "his disciples remembered" (2:17, 22). This event by the sea of Galilee would then have been John's second call, though we cannot deduce that this experience was also that of James.

James later was called to apostleship (Matt 10:2). Peter, James end John were the three privileged to witness the raising of Jairus' daughter (Mark 5:37), to be with the Lord on the mount of transfiguration (Matt 17:1), and to be with Him in the garden of Gethsemane (Matt 26:37). The mother of James and John wanted her two sons to share the places of privilege on the throne of the Lord's coming kingdom but she was rebuked, for privilege is granted "to them for whom it is prepared of my Father" (Matt 20:20-23). James was the first martyr amongst the apostles (Acts 12:1), while John lived to a ripe old age.

Before their call they were occupied with things (nets) and with men (Zebedee their father). Priorities had to be changed, if they would follow the Lord. Having put their hands to the plough (Luke 9:62) there could be no looking back; affections had to be on things above and not on things on earth (Col 3:1-2); treasures had to be in heaven, not on earth (Matt 6:19-20). If this was indeed

John's second call, it appears that his father had a hold upon him, reminding us of the call of Abram, who left Charran for the land only "when his father was dead" (Acts 7:4). Later, Peter, on behalf of them all, could boast, "We have forsaken all, and followed thee" (Matt 19:27), seemingly having forgotten the stages by which he had followed the Lord.

The verb "mending" in v.21 is *katartizō* employed 13 times in the NT, two noun derivatives occur, each once only: "we wish ... your perfection" (2 Cor 13:9), and "the perfecting of the saints" (Eph 4:12). The verb means "to adjust thoroughly", "to bring into its proper condition". The variety of renderings in the AV shows its wide-ranging applications. Thus the nets were "mended" praise was "perfected" (Matt 21:16); those overtaken with a fault should be "restored" (Gal 6:1); the Corinthians should be "perfectly joined together" (1 Cor 1:10); "a body hast thou prepared me" (Heb 10:5) – namely formed to perfection as a completely perfect vessel for the Son of God.

23-25 The word "synagogue" is a transliteration of the Greek *sunagōgē,* formed from *sun* ("together with") and *agō* ("to bring"). It usually referred to a building for Jewish congregations, unlike the word *ekklēsia* ("church") which *never* refers to a building in the NT. Originally, no doubt, they were used as houses of prayer far away from the temple in Jerusalem, but a large number were also built in Jerusalem. In the temple courts there was an altar but no pulpit, but in the synagogue there was a pulpit for preaching but no altar for sacrifice. A typical service consisted of a short exhortation, many prayers, readings from the law and prophets, a sermon and a blessing. There were "rulers", such as Jairus (Mark 5:22) and those who invited Paul to preach in Antioch (Acts 13.15), an "attendant" (Luke 4:20), and the rabbis, the recognised teachers in the synagogues. Thus the Lord taught in such buildings, until they judged His teaching too spiritual for their ears, when they cast Him out (Luke 4:28-29). Paul also preached in the synagogues, until his message of Christ and Him crucified and risen again was rejected by the Jews (Acts 13:44-52). His object was to take converts out of the *sun* ("together with") of the synagogue and into the ek ("out of") of the *ekklēsia,* a complete reversal!

The Lord preached "the gospel of the kingdom". The word *euangelion* means "good news", and the verb *euangelizō* means "to announce good tidings". Corresponding English words are *evangel* and *evangelise.* (Note the word angel" firmly rooted in these words – since this means "messenger".) There are many *aspects* of the gospel, but to Paul there was but *one* gospel (Gal 1.6-8). It is remarkable that in the gospels the noun appears only in Matt and Mark, the verb only in Luke (and Matt 11:5 exceptionally). Both words appear dozens of times in the Acts and in the epistles. No designation such as "of heaven" or "of God" is attached to "kingdom" here; it was divine rule beyond the cold rigidity of the law, based on mercy and sympathy.

The miracles of the Lord were characterised by three features that distinguished them from the works of men: (1) they were instantaneous, (2) they were complete, and (3) they were lasting. Men who claim to possess this ability of alternative medicine today should test their efforts by these three requirements before asserting that they are miracle-workers. This general statement about the Lord healing people is the *first* reference in this Gospel to His miraculous powers; later, of course, specific miracles are recorded. The first miracles in Mark (1:23-27), Luke (4:33-36), and John (2:1-11) are specific examples and not general statements. Such miracles demonstrate the Lord's authority over body and mind.

In vv.23-24, the various words denoting illness should be noted:

1. Sickness (*nosos*), found 12 times in the NT, is the regular word for illness and disease.

2. Disease (*malakia*), means "softness" or "weakness", and hence debility and disease. The word appears only three times in the NT, all in Matthew's Gospel; they all refer to general complaints and not specific ones.

3. Sick people (*kakōs echō*), "evilly to have", is applied to sickness 12 times in the Synoptic Gospels.

4. Divers (various) diseases. As *nosos* above.

5. Torments (*basanos*). Literally this was a material for testing metals. Only once used of illness, it occurs on two other occasions, referring to torment in hades (Luke 16:23, 28). The verb *basanizō* is also used of sickness (Matt 8:6), but mainly of divine judgments (Rev 14:10 etc.).

6. Possessed with devils (*daimonizomai*), occurs 13 times. Men could be possessed in body and mind by demons – evil spirits – under the control of Satan; demons were particularly active when the Lord was here. The word "devils" should *not* be used in this connection, because the word *diabolos* is used *only* of Satan, the accuser.

7. Lunatick (*selēniazomai*). Strictly, this means " to be moon-struck", and hence "epileptic" (RV); it occurs twice only (Matt 4:24; 17:15). It is derived from the word for moon (*selēnē*), occurring 9 times in the NT, only one of which is in Matt, "the moon shall not give her light" (24:29).

8. Palsy (*paralutikos*), "suffering from a paralytic stroke", occurs sometimes as a noun (10 times) and sometimes as a verb (5 times).

In all this activity, we find the initial introduction of the King to His people; towards

the end of His life, the working of miracles became less frequent. They were used to attract people to the message that He brought; they were never used for entertainment or mere outward display. To meet the needs of men is valid; to pander to their pleasures is not.
Thus the Lord's fame (*akoē*) spread abroad. The English word "fame" occurs 8 times in the Gospels (AV), translating four different Greek words.

1. *Akoē* means "a hearing", and hence a report.

2. *Phēmē* means "saying, rumour", from the common word "say": the people talked about Him, as in the case of Jairus' daughter, when the "fame" of the miracle went abroad (Matt 9:26; Luke 4:14).

3. *Echos*, meaning "sound, noise" occurs as the "fame of him" (Luke 4:37); "a sound from heaven" (Acts 2:2); "sounding brass" (1 Cor 13:1); "the sound of a trumpet" (Heb 12:19); "the sea and the waves roaring" (Luke 21:25).

4. *Logos* is only once translated "fame" (Luke 5:15); the RV gives "report".

And so "there followed him great multitudes" (v.25). Following alone does not constitute true discipleship, it must be subject to an acid test: Do the people like His teaching, and do they continue to follow Him? If not, then they are interested in merely material and physical relief, with the heart untouched. This is seen clearly in John 6:66; having seen His miracle in feeding the 5,000, and having listened to the conversation afterwards, "many of his disciples went back, and walked no more with him". Only the twelve apostles remained, since they (apart from Judas) knew that the Lord had "the words of eternal life" (v.68). How true that only a few were on the narrow pathway!

CHAPTERS 5-12
THE KING'S MINISTRY—TEACHING WITH MIRACLES

I. The Sermon on the Mount: Part 1(5:1-48)

1. *The Beatitudes* 5:1-1 2

v.1 "And seeing the multitudes, he went up into a mountain: and when he was set, his disciples came unto him:
v.2 And he opened his mouth, and taught them, saying,
v.3 Blessed *are* the poor in spirit: for theirs is the kingdom of heaven.
v.4 Blessed *are* they that mourn: for they shall be comforted.
v.5 Blessed *are* the meek: for they shall inherit the earth.
v.6 Blessed *are* they which do hunger and thirst after righteousness: for they shall be filled.

v.7 Blessed *are* the merciful: for they shall obtain mercy.
v.8 Blessed *are* the pure in heart: for they shall see God.
v.9 Blessed *are* the peacemakers: for they shall be called the children of God.
v.10 Blessed *are* they which are persecuted for righteousness' sake: for theirs is the kingdom of heaven.
v.11 Blessed are ye, when *men* shall revile you, and persecute *you*, and shall say all manner of evil against you falsely, for my sake.
v.12 Rejoice, and be exceeding glad: for great *is* your reward in heaven: for so persecuted they the prophets which were before you."

This first major discourse of the King outlines the moral and spiritual constitution of the kingdom, then, now and in the future millennial reign. At all times His people submit themselves to a heavenly rule far higher than rule by men on earth. Discernment is necessary when the details of the manifesto are examined. An overall blanket application leads to confusion; rather we must ask, which details apply to His people *then,* which to His people *now,* and which to His people *in the future?* Space is not available to answer these questions for every verse; readers must consider the principles involved, and provide answers for themselves.

It is obvious that Luke 6:20-49 forms what we may designate an abbreviated sermon on the mount. The occasions are clearly different – in Matt 5:1 "he went up into a mountain", but in Luke 6:17 "he ... stood in the plain". Truth is always worth repeating to different groups of people, since the needs are the same. The epistles 2 Pet and Jude have much in common, such truth being repeated by different writers.

There are two different sets of nouns, adjectives and verbs translated "bless, blessed, blessing, blessedness" in the NT with entirely different meanings. A concordance or dictionary should be consulted, but here we give the adjectival forms.

1. *Eulogētos* means praised by being well spoken of. It is applied to God: "Blessed be the Lord God of Israel" (Luke 1:68), both the noun and the verb are used in 1 Cor 10:16, "The cup of *blessing* which we *bless*".

2. *Makarios* denotes a pronouncement of happiness. This is the word used in the Beatitudes; it is applied even to God, "the glorious gospel of the *blessed* God" (1 Tim 1:11), and "the *blessed* and only Potentate" (6:15).

There are many ways in which the Beatitudes may be studied. Bearing in mind the fact that the constitution of the kingdom of heaven contrasts with the rule of kings and emperors on earth, we shall understand the Beatitudes to stand in sharp contrast to the objectives, ideals, policy and treatment of its subjects by the fourth beast of Dan 7 – the Roman empire under the Caesars. In Dan 7:7, this beast was seen prophetically by Daniel in his first vision. But in NT times, this beast dominated the Mediterranean area end Judaea and Galilee in particular. It dominated much of Europe and Africa in the early centuries of the church; presently the beast "is not" for a season (Rev 17:8), and it will yet dominate the world after the church has been raptured and prior to the millennial reign of the King (Rev 13:1-10). In this sense, the Beatitudes span a wide range of circumstances from the past into the future.

Moreover, not only are the character and circumstances of the disciples of the kingdom described, but the King Himself can be seen shining through His own teaching. Note too that the blessings of the Beatitudes are countered by the woes of ch. 23, just as the blessings in Luke 6:21-23 are countered by the woes of vv.24- 26.

1-2 The "multitudes" are those noted in Matt 4:25, distinct from the disciples who then permanently followed Him. So in v.1, the Lord separated His disciples from the multitudes to teach them privately on the mountain (see also Matt 13:36 where a house was used as a place for separated teaching). In other words, He was not going to give "that which is holy unto the dogs" (Matt 7:6). The reader should seek out the other mountain scenes in the Gospels.

The physical posture of being seated (*kathizō*) was habitual for teaching; two other cognate Greek words (*kathēmai, kathezomai*) are also used. A concordance must be used to note whether the act of sitting down or the state of being seated is being described. As far as *teaching* is concerned, we may note the examples: "he went into a ship, and *sat*" (Matt 13:1-3); "he *sat* upon the mount of Olives" (24: 3-4); "I *sat* daily with you teaching in the temple" (26:55). In Luke 4:16, 20, the Lord "stood up for to read" but afterwards sat down to teach.

3 In discussing "poor in spirit", we suggest that this is an inward character known to God, while "meek" (v.5) is an outward demonstration of discipleship known by men. Being "poor in spirit" stands in contrast to the arrogance of the empire-leaders of the times of the Gentiles. This is seen in the pride of Nebuchadnezzar, a "king of kings" and the "head of gold" (Dan 2:37, 38), the "tree ... whose height reached unto the heaven" (4:20), as he mused on the glories of his kingdom "for the honour of my majesty" (4:30). The third kingdom, "the he-goat", was "very great: and ... strong" (8:8), its great horn representing the first king Alexander the Great (8:21), his self-opinionated glory is the opposite of what is required by the Lord in His kingdom. Some of the Roman emperors lived in the pomp and pride of their achievements, and the "little horn" of the future "shall wear out the saints" (7:25). When the Lord was here, His disciples were living under the conceit of the Pharisees, of Herod, and of the Roman emperor holding sway over the land. The disciples could have no part in that kingdom, but their opposite character was entirely fit for the kingdom of heaven.

4 The mourning of the Lord's people commenced at the beginning of the times of the Gentiles: "By the rivers of Babylon, there ... we wept, when we remembered Zion" (Ps 137:1); "She weepeth sore in the night ... The ways of Zion do mourn" (Lam 1:2, 4). This is mourning for past sins and for present circumstances, but with the promise of comfort, "To appoint unto them that mourn in Zion, to give unto them beauty for ashes ..." (Isa 61:3). The Lord wept over Jerusalem (Luke 19:41), while Paul was the weeping apostle in his service: he wept while working (Acts 20:19), while warning (v. 31), while writing (2 Cor 2:4) and while walking (Phil 3:17-18). But he was comforted by God (2 Cor 1:4).

5 "The meek" stand in contrast to the outward manifestation of power and authority by the Gentile emperors. By his activity against the Jews' religion, temple and sacrifices, Antiochus Epiphanes (of the third kingdom) "magnified himself" (Dan 8:11), while Rome is described as "dreadful and terrible, and strong exceedingly; and it has great iron teeth..." (7:7). Though this describes the Roman emperor of the future (Rev 13:1-10), yet it also describes the uninhibited activity of Rome during the Lord's time on earth and afterwards (see 2 Tim 4:17, where Paul describes the abominable emperor Nero as "the lion"). But the Lord's disciples present an opposite way of life; so did the Lord when He said, "I am meek and lowly in heart" (Matt 11:29). They do not interfere with the politics of men, and do not strive for greatness. Work in the kingdom of heaven is quite different; in the future, His people will rule over the nations with Him (Rev 2:27), having their part in the governmental authority of the Holy Jerusalem (Rev 21:9-27). Even today, most men say "We have no king but Caesar" (John 19:15), but the Lord's people willingly submit to the fact that all power is given to Him. This is true meekness. Believers of the present age will not "inherit the earth" for theirs is a heavenly inheritance (Eph 1:11); they will reign over the earth, but the Jewish nation will inherit the earth during the millennial reign of Christ.

6 Hungering and thirsting "after righteousness" stands opposed to the power hungry emperors described in Dan 7, with their seeking after territorial aggrandisement. Nebuchadnezzar had thirsted after "people, the nations, and the languages" (Dan 3:7); the Medo-Persian empire had pushed "westward, and northward, and southward" (8:4). The Grecian empire under Alexander spread "toward the south, and toward the east, and toward the pleasant land" (8:9), reaching even to India. Later, Rome dominated most of southern and western Europe, together with northern Africa. Such conquests could not be achieved without much unrighteousness. The Pharisees were no better; the Lord's condemnation in Matt 23 shows that they knew nothing of practical righteousness. Thus those who seek true righteousness can have no fellowship with, and can offer no help to, those who seek leadership with the object of gaining possessions, lands, nations, even the world. Such disciples will be filled with the right quality of life that does not seek "treasures upon earth"

(Matt 6:19), nor bigger barns for much fruit, as did the farmer who sought "treasure for himself" (Luke 12:16-21).

7 Sometimes the Lord's people who seek to be "merciful" have to live under dictatorial régimes which are maintained by leaders dispensing anything but mercy. Thus Nebuchadnezzar had no mercy on Daniel's three friends when their faithful conduct seemed to undermine his authority (Dan 3:13-23). In his old age, Daniel was shown no mercy by the "presidents ... the governors, and the princes, the counsellors, and the captains" of the Medo-Persian empire (6:7). The murderous activity of Antiochus Epiphanes of the Grecian empire is well known (8:11-12). As for Rome, with teeth of iron and nails of brass, it devoured the whole earth (7:19, 23); as the little horn of the future it will make war with the saints (v.21). Those who show no mercy will receive no mercy, and the end of this beast is the lake of fire (Rev 19:20). In the Christian era, Nero was the chief exponent of cruelty to believers. But God is rich in mercy to them that fear Him. His people experience this spiritually, though not from men, but in their dealings with men they follow the example of Christ and not of the world. "Be ye therefore merciful, as your Father also is merciful" (Luke 6:36).

8 What a contrast "the pure in heart" make, when viewed in the light of the most evil of men. Their thoughts are described by Paul in Phil 4:8: "whatsoever things are true, honest, just, pure, lovely ... think on these things". But the evil hearts of men are naked and opened before the eyes of Him with whom they will have to do. As far as the emperor of the fourth beast-kingdom is concerned, the blackness of his heart "shall speak great words against the most High" (Dan 7:25); He will open "his mouth in blasphemy against God" (Rev 13:6). However, to the saints who endure, the promise to "see God" is given. Thus Daniel, who would not defile himself inwardly or outwardly (Dan 1:8), was privileged to see "the Ancient of days" and "one like the Son of man" (7:9, 13).

9 The noun "peacemaker" (*eirēnopoios*) occurs only once in the NT. It is derived from *eirene* (peace) and *poieō* (to make). Throughout the times of the Gentiles, national leaders have essentially been men of war, talking of peace but usually seeking conquests, causing empires to rise and empires to fall. The four great empires in Dan 7 derived their territory and authority by war. There is no peace to the wicked, but we must "follow after the things which make for peace" (Rom 14:19), and "Follow peace with all men" (Heb 12:14). The corresponding verb *eirēnopoieō* occurs once, in Col 1:20, referring to God, "having made peace through the blood of his cross". The "children of God" should be translated "sons of God" (*huioi Theou*). Of course, those who believe on His name are "children of God" (*tekna Theou*, John 1:12); but sonship comes by spiritual adoption (Gal 4:5-6). We therefore feel that the Lord implies that we experience sonship when we are peacemakers, the call of God by His Spirit enabling us to enter more into the blessed relationship in the family of God.

10-12 Verses dealing with persecution remind us of Paul's declaration for the Christian era, "all that will live godly in Christ Jesus shall suffer persecution" (2 Tim 3:12), and "if we suffer, we shall also reign with him" (2:12). Our v.10 deals with persecution "for righteousness' sake", namely because the outward life of the disciple is consistent with the Lord's description of life in the preceding Beatitudes; this is discipleship by conduct. But v.11 deals with persecution "for my sake", namely because of testimony for Christ. Such persecution was often foreseen by the Lord, and He would suffer first: "If they have persecuted me, they will also persecute you" (John 15:20). Thus in John 8:59 the Lord was *first* cast out, *then* the man who had been healed was cast out (9:34), to be found by the Lord in the outside place (9:35).

As far as men of faith living in the times of the Gentiles are concerned, Heb 11: 35-38 presents what evil men do to the people of God. Such persecutions had taken place during the intertestamental period, and now Satan was raising up men against Christ, as later he would against the church, and finally against the remnant during the great tribulation period (Rev 6:9-11; 11:3-13; 13:16-17). Such persecutions are by political and religious adventurers who seek to remove men who have a testimony for Christ.

A " reward in heaven" is promised though not necessarily an earthly deliverance. In the early Christian era there was no deliverance for Stephen or James (Acts 7:58-60; 12:2), and Paul was kept in prison in Rome under Nero until the time of his departure (2 Tim 4:6). All these could anticipate a rich reward in heaven; they would reign with Christ. Faith in the coming of the Lord brought comfort (1 Thess 4:14); there would be no more death, crying or pain in that day (Rev 21:4). The Lord stressed that those who suffer persecution are in good company, for the OT prophets had suffered likewise (Matt 23:31); these form a great cloud of witnesses whose lives should stimulate others passing through similar tragic circumstances.

2. *Salt and Light: Effect on the World* 5:13-16

v.13 "Ye are the salt of the earth: but if the salt have lost his saviour, wherewith shall it be salted? it is thenceforth good for nothing, but to be cast out, and to be trodden under foot of men.
v.14 Ye are the light of the world. A city that is set on an hill cannot be hid.
v.15 Neither do men light a candle, and put it under a bushel, but on a candlestick; and it giveth light unto all that are in the house.
v.16 Let your light so shine before men, that they may see your good works, and glorify your Father which is in heaven."

13 When the disciples of the kingdom were sent forth to testify that "The kingdom of heaven is at hand" (Matt 10:7), they were "as sheep in the midst of wolves" (v.16). In other words, these disciples were not to be cloistered as hermits or monks, but their characters and lives were to be in open display; they would be in the world but not of it. Hence their effect on the world is described by metaphors of salt and light. Not that they could change for the better the whole Jewish nation or the Roman empire or the whole world: yet any forthcoming good, whether moral or spiritual, would be worth while.

Salt is understood as the principle of preservation in spite of rottenness around. The Lord visualised a kind of rock containing salt, but age and damp can wash away the particles of actual salt, leaving nothing but the tasteless base mineral. Hence salt is a pervading substance, and we think of it as the outward manifestation of testimony by life and lip by the Holy Spirit in a disciple (Gal 5:25). "Ye are the salt of the earth" suggests a divine work in His disciples for testimony amongst men. He also said, "Salt is good ... Have salt *in* yourselves", suggesting a divine work in each disciple, bringing peace (Mark 9:50). "Let your speech be alway with grace, seasoned with salt", Paul wrote, suggesting divine inward power (Col 4:6). The danger is that the salt can lose its savour, namely the manifestation of divine power can be absent because the Spirit is grieved or quenched. For example, the Galatians had begun in the Spirit, and were now seeking completion by the flesh (Gal 3:3). Believers who return to the law can have but little testimony in a religious world dominated by law. Such salt (that is, the base mineral) is fit only to be cast out of such a life, for those who sow to the flesh shall of the flesh reap corruption (Gal 6:8).

14-15 "The light of the world" shows the disciples to be a radiating moral and spiritual influence in a world of darkness. The Lord employs two metaphors to illustrate this: (1) a city on a hill, and (2) a candle (properly "lamp"). The most striking example of such a city is the Holy Jerusalem, descending out of heaven to form the centre of government over the millennial earth; its glory and light are described in Rev 21:9-11, 23-24, and the nations on earth "shall walk in the light of it". No one on earth will fail to realise the reality of such superior authority placed permanently above them. But in the present men love darkness rather than light, so sometimes the influence of the believer's light is but minimal. In the Lord's case, "the light shineth in the darkness; and the darkness comprehended it not" (John 1:5).

As we have said, the word "candle" is properly " lamp" (*luchnos*), a portable oil lamp; to gain height in a room it would be placed on a "lampstand" (*luchnia*), not a "candlestick". It would be quite illogical to place such a lamp under a "bushel", namely a corn measure containing about two gallons or nine litres; its influence would be nil. In Luke 8:16, the additional metaphor "No man ... putteth it under a bed" is used. If hidden by the outward manifestation of the world and the flesh, the light becomes darkness, with no beneficial effects spreading outwards to men.

The Lord Himself said to the Pharisees, "I am the light of the world" John 8: 12); only those who followed Him would benefit. Again, He said, "I am come a light into the world" (John 12:46), adding that those who would profit from this light would be those that believe. Elsewhere He qualified this statement; "As long as I am in the world, I am the light of the world" (John 9:5), implying that He had the *open* character of light only during the days of His flesh. This is confirmed in John 12:35, "Yet a *little while* is the light with you. Walk *while* ye have the light". When the Lord left this scene, this direct light of the world was taken away. *Now* it is His disciples who are the light of the world; by their conduct and testimony, men see Christ in and through them. They are like the moon, radiating light from the true source, the sun. Hence it is not quite correct to sing the well-known hymn with the repeated line, "The Light of the world is Jesus". *He* is not here now, but *we* are in "the midst of a crooked and perverse nation", among whom we "shine as lights in the world" (Phil 2:15).

16 Clearly the "men" in this verse are not disciples and believers; the Lord does not say "their" Father, but "your" Father. This Father-relationship is not one of faith, but of providence and head-knowledge. The Lord states two objects of this moral and spiritual shining before them:

1. "That they may see your good works". These "works" are restricted, since later alms, prayers and fasting (Matt 6:1, 5, 16), which are to be done in secret, are excluded. Rather He implies those features of godly character and activity that distinguish His disciples from the ungodly of the world. Men notice such well-marked-out features, hence one's manner of life must be "honest among the Gentiles" (1 Pet 2:12).

2. That they may " glorify your Father which is in heaven " . Even the unsaved may glorify God if they are exercised by what they see and hear. Thus Paul wrote that unbelievers, present in an assembly meeting and beholding the spiritual order of those taking part with gifts endowed by the Spirit, would fall down and "worship God" (1 Cor 14:24, 25). Rahab exhibited this testimony when she said to the spies, "the Lord your God, he is God in heaven above, and in earth beneath" (Josh 2:9-11). Peter takes the matter further " that … they may … glorify God in the day of visitation" (1 Pet 2:12), i.e. in a day of divine intervention, whether for blessing or judgment (Luke 1:68; 19:44). The ultimate shall be when every tongue shall "confess that Jesus Christ is Lord, to the glory of God the Father" (Phil 2:11).

Note that the Lord said "*your* Father". Strictly this does not refer to the Christian position, for that could be a reality only after the Lord had been crucified and raised, and after the giving of the Spirit. This is clearly brought out in John's Gospel, where the language is always "*my* Father" and "*the* Father" until John

20:17, when the Lord said, "my Father, and *your* Father" – the first positive mention of "your" Father in that Gospel.

3. *Superiority of the Lord's Teaching* 5:17-48

a. *Not to Destroy the Law, but ... (vv.17-20)*

v.17 "Think not that I am come to destroy the law, or the prophets: I am not come to destroy, but to fulfil.
v.18 For verily I say unto you, Till heaven and earth pass, one jot or one tittle shall in no wise pass from the law, till all be fulfilled.
v.19 Whosoever therefore shall break one of these least commandments, and shall teach men so, he shall be called the least in the kingdom of heaven: but whosoever shall do and teach *them*, the same shall be called great in the kingdom of heaven.
v.20 For I say unto you, That except your righteousness shall exceed *the righteousness* of the scribes and Pharisees, ye shall in no case enter into the kingdom of heaven."

17 The disciples of the kingdom were to live in contrast, not only to the policies and activities of the Roman fourth-beast kingdom around them, but also to the religious policies and activities of the Pharisees. These Pharisees had the OT law, together with their interpretation and applications of it. The Lord's interpretation and applications were infinitely higher. His disciples had to know this, so, before He entered into details regarding the divine interpretation of the OT legal requirements, inner motivation as well as outward activity, He gave these preliminary verses by way of clarification. The Pharisees' cold, hard, rigid methods in codifying their detailed applications of the law led to "heavy burdens ... grievous to be borne" (Matt 23:4). They legislated against plucking ears of corn and rubbing them in the hand on the Sabbath day (Matt 12:1-2; Luke 6:1-2). They insisted upon the trivial "tithe of mint and anise and cummin" (Matt 23:23). They loved "holding the tradition of the elders" (Mark 7:3). The Lord summed it all up when He accused such hypocrites of "teaching for doctrines the commandments of men" (Matt 15:9). Thereby they "omitted the weightier matters of the law ... mercy, and faith" (Matt 23:23), whereas when the commandments were given God introduced mercy (Exod 20:6). Such self satisfaction led to the breaking of the law, and hence to dishonouring God (Rom 2:23). The disciples of the kingdom had to adopt higher standards than those of the hypocrites. Thus from v.21 onwards, whenever the Lord expounded higher principles from the law, the disciples were to understand that He was not destroying (*kataluō*, "to destroy utterly", "to overthrow completely" as the temple in Matt 24:2) the OT law and the prophets (as it would appear to them because the Pharisaical interpretation with which they had been brought up was being destroyed) but fulfilling them.

Particularly in matters relating to Himself (the law showing God's mind regarding holy living reflected in His life, the typology of the tabernacle and its sacrifices, the prophetical forthtellings of His birth, life, death, resurrection and coming again in glory), all this would be fulfilled.

18 The phrase "verily I say unto you" occurs frequently in the three Synoptic Gospels, whereas in John's Gospel it is "verily, verily, I say unto you". The difference is characteristic of the spiritual depths described in these Gospels, just as the words "miracle" and "mighty works" translate *dunamis* in the Synoptic Gospels and *sēmeion* in John's Gospel. The word "verily" translates *amēn*, meaning "truth"; the duplicated form "verily, verily" occurs 25 times in John's Gospel. The word "amen" appears at the end of prayers and doxologies (particularly in the epistles), and in the AV it terminates nearly every NT book, though the RV, in following different Greek texts, uses it very sparingly at the end of books.

The Lord makes it clear that the existence of the law cannot be tampered with by men; the law as written will remain in that form while heaven and earth exist. The "jot" (*iōta* in Greek; *yod* in Hebrew) means the smallest letter of the Hebrew alphabet; the "tittle" (*keraia*, a little horn) is a small stroke on certain Hebrew letters. The preservation of these small marks implies that the whole written law is safeguarded under God's hand, even if the mass of Pharisaical additions should be swept aside. In Luke 16:17, this truth is expressed thus: "it is easier for heaven and earth to pass, than one tittle of the law to fail". In Matt 24:35 the Lord goes further: "Heaven and earth shall pass away, but my words shall not pass away". We do not know the form in which God's Word will be preserved in heaven for all eternity; whether the sacred alphabets will be transported into heaven, or whether God has His own distinct means for recording truth in the heavenly books. In the latter case, the jots and tittles will cease to be needed, but the Word of God abides for ever. At least, all must be fufilled before the physical heaven and earth pass away (Heb 1:10-12; 2 Pet 3:10; Rev 20:11).

19-20 It appears to the author that in these verses the Lord is describing four classes of men. He is not describing the Christian position; that truth was yet to be revealed especially after His glorification: thus he spoke of "*your* righteousness", rather than the "righteousness of *God*" imputed to believers as expounded by Paul in Romans.

1. The "least in the kingdom of heaven" — sincere, honest, mistaken, perhaps having been deceived, not keeping some commandments that to them appear irrelevant, and teaching the same thing. In the Christian era, Apollos appears to have had this character until corrected by Aquila and Priscilla (Acts 18:24-26). One must distinguish this least position from the position of John the Baptist: "he that is least in the kingdom of heaven is greater than he" (Matt 11:11). There is no connection between the contexts, since

John was both a keeper and a teacher of the law. There is an application today, for there are those who teach that much of the NT is irrelevant for believers!

2. The "great in the kingdom of heaven" – the Lord's assessment of those who "do and teach". James was an exponent of this: "be ye doers of the word, and not hearers only" (James 1:22). A blessing is promised to those who "read, hear, keep" (Rev 1:3). Of course, self-greatness has no place in the Lord's commendation; of himself, Paul could write "though I be nothing" – his greatness lay in the service that the Lord carried out through him (2 Cor 12:11).

3. The Pharisees and scribes, "being ignorant of God's righteousness, and going about to establish their own righteousness" (Rom 10:3). Such had no place in the kingdom of heaven.

4. Those whose righteousness did not exceed that of the Pharisees – the moral outcast who had been given up by God, described by Paul in Rom 1:18-32.

b. *Not to Kill, but … (vv.21-26)*

v.21 "Ye have heard that it was said by them of old time, Thou shalt not kill; and whosoever shall kill shall be in danger of the judgment:
v.22 But I say unto you, That whosoever is angry with his brother without a cause shall be in danger of the judgment: and whosoever shall say to his brother, Raca, shall be in danger of the council: but whosoever shall say, Thou fool, shall be in danger of hell fire.
v.23 Therefore if thou bring thy gift to the altar, and there rememberest that thy brother hath ought against thee;
v.24 Leave there thy gift before the altar, and go thy way; first be reconciled to thy brother, and then come and offer thy gift.
v.25 Agree with thine adversary quickly, whiles thou art in the way with him; lest at any time the adversary deliver thee to the judge, and the judge deliver thee to the officer, and thou be cast into prison.
v.26 Verily I say unto thee, Thou shalt by no means come out thence, till thou hast paid the uttermost farthing."

21 "It was said *by them* of old time" has the alternative rendering *"to them"* (RV, JND), the Greek being merely the dative plural *tois archaiois.* "To them" is better, since God spoke in Exod 20:1 and Moses in Deut 5:1. "Thou shalt not kill" appears in Exod 20:13; offenders are liable to the judgment, since those who have sinned in the law shall be judged by the law (Rom 2:12), indeed they are "guilty before God" (or, subject to the judgment of God, 3:19).

22 But it is not only a question of the letter of the law, but of the spirit. The Lord analyses being "angry with his brother without a cause" referring, in the context, to one Jew against another – "his brother". Some Greek MSS omit "without a cause" (*eikē*, occurring six times in the NT, usually translated "in vain"), the RV relegates it to the margin, but JND retains it, translating it as "lightly". The concepts behind "angry, Raca, fool" represent downward stages in the loss of self-control in one's description of the character of another man. In effect, the man's character is being murdered! Raca (a transliteration of *raka*) is a term expressing complete contempt, ascribing intellectual emptiness of mind; it is similar to James 2:20 "O vain man", though there properly applied and a different Greek word is used. OT examples are Jud 9:4; 2 Sam 6:20. "Thou fool" continues the downward trend. This is the word *mōros*, describing a wicked, graceless, abandoned wretch, a worthless scoundrel in heart. The word is used 13 times in the NT, by Paul and by the Lord legitimately. In the Gospels, it occurs only elsewhere in Matt regarding the man who built his house on the sand (7:26), and the Pharisees (23:17, 19). OT examples are Abner (2 Sam 3:33) and Amnon (13:13), though we do not say that these ascriptions were "without a cause" .

The words " judgment, council, hell fire" signify three degrees of punishment recognised among the Jews, increasing in severity. The "council" was the Jewish sanhedrim which had authority to deal with crime. "Hell fire", translating *gehenna*, was strictly a valley south of Jerusalem where the bodies of criminals who had been stoned were afterwards burnt. Hence the name was also used for the place of eternal punishment, the lake of fire (Rev 20:15). The word should never be confused with the other Greek word *hadēs*, also translated "hell", the regions containing departed spirits of the lost awaiting judgment, and of the faithful prior to the Lord's ascension.

23 Such lack of control of the emotions has important consequences. The Lord visualises the Jewish setting where a man brings a sacrifice to the temple altar in keeping with the OT Levitical sacrificial system. The man bringing the gift is the man who was so badly treated in v.22; "thy brother" is the man who used the objectionable words. After all, this latter man may also be formally bringing a gift; God will refuse all things that He once commanded if they are offered with false motives mixed with animosity (Isa 1:12-18; Mal 1:6-14).

24 This advice is offered to the man who suffered the wrong and slander, not to the man who used the offending language, though he also needed such advice. An application can be made to the Lord's people in assembly fellowship. It is not unknown for bad feelings to exist between brethren, sisters and families; both parties apparently sit down together at the Lord's supper, but this is not true fellowship if the hearts of those involved are not in tune the one with the other. "Be of the same mind in the Lord" (Phil 4:2) demands reconciliation between saints. In our verse, reconciliation is effected by the offended party, not by the one giving offence. This is the constitution of the kingdom of heaven; men in the world think it should be the other way around. In a Christian sense, God has been offended by sin, yet He has made the way of reconciliation through the Lord Jesus. (Note: in Matt 5:24, a special verb for "reconcile" is used, the passive of *diallassō*, occurring only once in the NT; the usual word is *katallassō*. The former contains the thought of mutual reconciliation if necessary, while the latter verb does not, since God is never reconciled to men.)

25 The term "adversary" (*antidikos*) is used in a legal sense, this man still being the offending party. If no agreement is effected by the guiltless party, the opportunity of returning to the altar to offer the gift to God acceptably may be irretrievably lost, for the adversary may seek to justify himself, and count the guiltless as guilty. This is a device in the law courts: counsel for the defence may so question the witnesses as to throw guilt upon them, thus to confuse and deceive the jury. Well might Asaph observe that "the ungodly ... prosper in the world" (Ps 73:12). In our verse, the only stated failure of the man is that he failed to gain reconciliation, or did not think it necessary to seek it. He finds himself before the judge, perhaps with false witnesses testifying against him, and condemned. He is then delivered to the "officer" (*hupēretēs*, an "under-rower", so a minister or attendant under superior authority, in the synagogue, Luke 4:20, or in a law court, or spiritually as "ministers of Christ", 1 Cor 4:1). Thus the man is cast into prison, and the chance of offering the gift lost. In other words, the consequences of divided hearts between brethren can be disastrous!

26 This does not refer to "hell fire" from which there can be no escape. No doubt the prison sentence came to an end, though " the uttermost farthing" had to be accomplished. There were plenty of jots and tittles in the law, and plenty of farthings in a prison sentence. None could be overlooked! In a Christian sense, it is good when reconciliation between brethren is effected, and when fellowship can be resumed in worship and service.

c. *Not to Commit Adultery, but ... (vv. 27-32)*

v.27 "Ye have heard that it was said by them of old time, Thou shalt not commit adultery:

v.28 But I say unto you, That whosoever looketh on a woman to lust after her hath committed adultery with her already in his heart.

v.29 And if thy right eye offend thee, pluck it out, and cast *it* from thee: for it is profitable for thee that one of thy members should perish, and not *that* thy whole body should be cast into hell.

v.30 And if thy right hand offend thee, cut it off, and cast it from thee: for it is profitable for thee that one of thy members should perish, and not *that* thy whole body should be cast into hell.

v.31 It hath been said, Whosoever shall put away his wife, let him give her a writing of divorcement:

v.32 But I say unto you, That whosoever shall put away his wife, saving for the cause of fornication, causeth her to commit adultery: and whosoever shall marry her that is divorced committeth adultery."

27 In these verses, the Lord regulates the affections between opposite sexes. Sin has marred the beauty and the typical implications of the subject. Since sin came into the world, sexual sins have dominated. Verse 27, quoted from Exod 20:14 means what it says, " Thou shalt not commit adultery" . The Lord is not diminishing the requirements for the discipline of His disciples, rather He is strengthening them. It is good that the minds of young believers be taught in days of youth, while there is emotional stability, before any dangerous testing time of emotion and stress arises, when rational thought on the matter may not come easily. Marriage must be "in the Lord" (1 Cor 7:39): the partners must not only be saved, but must walk together in all aspects of doctrine, fellowship and service. How this contrasts with David in 2 Sam 11:2. He saw a beautiful woman, found out that she was married, and then fell into grievous sin, the consequences of which lasted to the end of his life. Truly, "whatsoever a man soweth, that shall he also reap" (Gal 6:7). Today, alas, corruption and mental temptation are found almost everywhere. The corruption of such a holy relationship is used for financial gain through advertisements, pleasure and entertainment; the natural man in the unsaved person falls for it without moral and rational consideration, but believers are raised to higher levels in their outlook and practice.

God's order is clear. In Gen 1:26-28 we find the natural purpose of sex given in the beginning; male and female are to be fruitful and multiply. In Gen 2:23-24, we find the purpose of sex in affection and typology. Both of these passages are used by the Lord in Matt 19:4-5, a chapter wholly given over to various aspects of the subject. In v.6 the marriage bond is indissoluble, "What therefore God hath joined together, let not man put asunder". Verses 7-8 refer to Moses' regulation of existing practice regarding divorce; he did not command. In v.9 the Lord states the vital principle regarding putting away, similar to Matt 5:32. In vv.10-12 there are some who will not marry for the sake of their service; this position is given them from the Lord. In vv.13-15 the children resulting from marriage are blessed. In vv.16-22 the law is quoted on adultery, and the necessity to honour father and mother. In vv.27-30, father, mother and children are not held dearer than devoted discipleship for His Name's sake.

28-30 The Lord also goes to the heart without minimising the outward act of adultery. Yet v.28 is largely treated as irrelevant in the world today, while adultery in v.27 is common and of appeal through entertainment. The heart begins it all: "out of the heart proceed evil thoughts, murders, adulteries, fornications" (Matt 15:19). But the believer will not yield his members "as instruments of unrighteousness unto sin"; rather he will yield himself "unto God" (Rom 6:13).

The " right eye" and the " right hand" are most dear and necessary possessions, but if the eye does not see by faith, and if the hand does not handle by faith the Word of life (1 John 1:1), then they may be ready to follow the downward pathway. These members may "offend thee" (*skandalizō*), that is they may prove to be a snare or stumblingblock. The Lord is speaking metaphorically when He states "pluck it out" and "cut it off", for He would not suggest mutilating a body which, in the case of a believer, is the temple of the Holy Spirit (1 Cor 6:19). Rather, if friends, pursuits, interests, talents or employment distract from Him and the true principles of discipleship, then they must be abandoned, so as to "glorify God in your body" (6:20). As far as being cast into "gehenna" is concerned, this refers to the unbeliever who hears the Lord's words "and doeth them not", being like a foolish man building his house on the sand. The ultimate winds of judgment cause all to collapse, and the great fall corresponds to the ultimate destiny of the unbeliever (Matt 7:26-27).

31-32 Verse 31 is a reference to Deut 24:1-4 and Jer 3:1. But in Matt 19:7-8 the Lord makes it clear that this practice was not "from the beginning", and that Moses regulated an existing practice. This was a by-product of the existence of sinful hearts, not an institution of God. Divorce was forbidden

1. if a man falsely accuses his wife of premarital unfaithfulness (Deut 22:13-19); "he may not put her away all his days";

2. if a man and an unbetrothed virgin are unfaithful before marriage, and if her father compels them to be married, then "he may not put her away all his days" (22:28-29).

But putting away was insisted upon when the returning exiles had married pagan wives (Ezra 9-10; Neh 13:23-30). By His statement in v.31, the Lord recognised that the Jews allowed various reasons for divorce. But in His response in v.32 He makes the disciples' path narrower than that of the law. This is amplified in Matt 19:4-9, when the Lord was answering a question from the Pharisees.

Adultery (verb *moichaō;* noun *moicheia*) refers to unlawful intercourse with another's spouse. Fornication (*porneia*) embraces all other acts of intercourse outside the marriage bond; some dictionaries state that it includes adultery, though it is difficult to accept this where both words occur in the same context The Lord implies that divorce leaves the wife (Matt 5:32) and the husband (19:9) potentially available for adultery. The exception clause "saving for the cause of fornication", has caused great difficulties to expositors, overcome by prejudice and seeking to justify their own particular moral and social outlook.

1. Some suggest that a ground for divorce is unfaithfulness in marriage, thereby equating fornication with adultery. Both ideas are used in Jer 3 and Ezek 23 in connection with Judah and Israel and their attachment to idols.

2. Some suggest that the reference is to marriage within the prohibited relationships listed in Lev 18:6-20.

3. In the light of the fact that this exception clause is not found in Luke 16:18, and that it is peculiar to Matt, an explanation must be found in Matthew's Gospel. Moreover, if 1 or 2 were correct, then the Lord would be merely repeating the OT, with no updating. Yet updating is just what He is doing as indicated by the word "but". The clue lies in Matt 1:19-20, where Joseph, a just man, suspected unfaithfulness in Mary "his espoused wife", namely unfaithfulness under premarital, yet espoused conditions. This appears to satisfy the Lord's teaching. However, if in doubt about the Lord's teaching then don't, for what is not of faith is sin.

In individual cases, mercy was seen to transcend general rules. In John 4:16-26, the woman who had had five husbands had Christ revealed to her. In John 8:11, the woman was not condemned: "go, and sin no more". In Luke 7:48-50 the sinner in the Pharisee's house was forgiven with the words "Thy faith hath saved thee; go in peace". But this does not justify a Christian couple going the downward pathway; they should think of the consequences of their action, and the difficult responsibility that they are placing upon the elders of their local assembly. Mercy can hardly overlook a downward pathway deliberately taken in opposition to known divine principles.

d. *Not to Forswear, but ... (vv.33-37)*

v.33 "Again, ye have heard that it hath been said by them of old time, Thou shalt not forswear thyself, but shalt perform unto the Lord shine oaths:
v.34 But I say unto you, Swear not at all; neither by heaven; for it is God's throne:
v.35 Nor by the earth; for it is his footstool: neither by Jerusalem; for it is the city of the great King.
v.36 Neither shalt thou swear by thy head, because thou canst not make one hair white or black.
v.37 But let your communication be, Yea, yea; Nay, nay: for whatsoever is more than these cometh of evil."

33 This is the third time that the Lord said, "ye have heard that it hath been said by them of old time", namely *tois archaiois*, "to the ancients". "Thou shalt not forswear thyself ..." is not a direct quotation, but an illusion to Lev 19:12, "ye shall not swear by my name falsely, neither shalt thou profane the name of thy God", an application of the commandment "Thou shalt not take the name of the Lord thy God in vain" (Exod 20:7). The false use of the name of God is equivalent to taking His name in vain. To swear is solemnly to appeal to God as a witness, either that the person making the oath is telling the truth, or that he will carry out what he promises to do. Clearly, the oath has meaning only if the person making it believes that God is, otherwise His name is being taken in vain; one feels that this is usually the case in law courts today. To "forswear" means to sware falsely, stating under oath that something is true when the person knows it to be false. The verb *epiorkeō* (derived from *epi,* against, and *orkos,* an oath) occurs in the NT only once, but the noun appears in 1 Tim 1:10, where Paul states that the law is made "for perjured persons", namely for those taking an oath falsely. Pilate put the Lord Jesus under an oath (Matt 26:63). Previously the Lord had been silent, but in keeping with Lev 5:1 He then answered Pilate, expressing of course the truth about His person and power.

34-36 "But", says the Lord, "swear not at all". The need to swear really indicates a reluctant truth-teller. The Lord is teaching that the disciples of the kingdom can do better than the law allowed. He, in effect, forbids it, as does James who uses almost the same words and examples (James 5:12). Many today try to make exceptions to the Lord's command, but the Lord gave no exceptions. The law of the land today insists on swearing for many legal purposes, although it is meaningless for unbelievers. But the law of the land also allows anyone to "affirm" under all circumstances, i.e. to declare without using the Bible or the name of God that the truth is being stated. Oaths could be taken by other methods apart from the name of God; the Lord excludes them all.

1. Not by heaven; being the place of God's throne, it use is almost equivalent to using the name of God.

2. Not by the earth; this is so low down as to have no higher authority than the person concerned.

3. Not by Jerusalem, the only divinely-chosen city on earth; since it is His city, the city of the great King, to swear by it would be almost equivalent to swearing by the great King.

4. Not by one's head – the seat of personal witness, having no higher authority than the person himself. The hairs remain white or black, just as positive facts and negative facts remain unaltered.

37 The better way is to adopt the principle "Yea, yea; Nay, nay", namely to state all facts as they are. Anything outside this principle cannot be correct. The Greek is *"nai nai, ou ou"*. Paul uses a similar expression in 2 Cor 1:17 though inserting twice the neuter definite article: *"to nai nai, kai to ou ou"*. In that context it means to use lightness in expressing a purpose, as if it does not matter whether or not it is carried out; just to change one's mind capriciously.

e. *An Eye for an Eye, but … (vv. 38-42)*

v.38 "Ye have heard that it hath been said, An eye for an eye, and a tooth for a tooth:
v.39 But I say unto you, That ye resist not evil: but whosoever shall smite thee on thy right cheek, turn to him the other also.
v.40 And if any man will sue thee at the law, and take away thy coat, let him have *thy* cloke also.

v.41 And whosoever shall compel thee to go a mile, go with him twain.
v.42 Give to him that asketh thee, and from him that would borrow of thee turn not thou away."

38 "An eye for an eye, and a tooth for a tooth" is taken from Exod 21:22-25. The Lord does not quote the circumstances (if a man hurt an expectant woman, and "if any mischief follow"), but merely quotes a general principle. Not only is an eye or a tooth involved, but also "hand, foot, burning, wound, stripe". Lev 24:17-20 adds "breach" and "blemish", while Deut 19:21 adds "life". In these verses there is *no* command to exact retribution, but only that the proper penalty and no more be exacted. The Jews thought that this was proper authority to take redress into their own hands, rather than through the magistrates. The Pharisees wanted retribution in financial terms.

39 But the principle of the kingdom is "resist not evil". There are to be no revengeful feelings or acts. How blessed to see the example of Christ who left "us an example", for "when he was reviled, (he) reviled not again; when he suffered, he threatened not" (1 Pet 2:21-23). The smiting on one cheek and the turning of the other implies that, after one indignity, there is submission should another follow. There is no implication that another indignity should be sought after. In John 18:22-23, the Lord was struck unjustly by an officer. His submissive answer corresponds to turning the other cheek.

40 The "coat" was the inner garment (*chitōn*), less valuable than the "cloke" the outer garment (*himation*). The thought of "evil" still persists, so this verse envisages an unjust act of suing; in other circumstances there may be a just act of suing, perhaps in payment of a debt. In Exod 22:26-27, the outer garment could not be taken and kept since this was the man's covering during sleep. So the Lord implies, "Give up the better and more useful of the two".

41 Being compelled to go a mile reflects on a Persian and Roman custom (two of the beast-kingdoms in Dan 7). Officialdom could demand people to act as slaves, providing personal attendance and carriages for authorities on an official journey. Go further than the distance intended; submit even beyond unreasonable demands.

42 Here the Lord visualises unreasonable asking, either for possession or for borrowing, perhaps by a beggar. There should be no unmerciful refusal to meet a real need. Thus in Acts 3:3 the lame man "asked an alms", and Peter went further using the power of Christ instead of silver and gold.

Overall, the lesson is: Don't insist on one's rights; go further than expected, following the example of Christ.

f. *Love thy Neighbour, Hate thine Enemy, but . . . (vv.43-48)*

v.43 "Ye have heard that it hath been said, Thou shalt love thy neighbour, and hate thine enemy.
v.44 But I say unto you, Love your enemies, bless them that curse you, do good to them that hate you, and pray for them which despitefully use you, and persecute you;
v.45 That ye may be the children of your Father which is in heaven: for he maketh his sun to rise on the evil and on the good, and sendeth rain on the just and on the unjust.
v.46 For if ye love them which love you, what reward have ye? do not even the publicans the same?
v.47 And if ye salute your brethren only, what do ye more *than others?* do not even the publicans so?
v.48 Be ye therefore perfect, even as your Father which is in heaven is perfect."

43 How careful is the Lord! He does not say, "It is written", regarding "Thou shalt love thy neighbour, and hate thine enemy". The former is quoted from Lev 19:18, "thou shalt love thy neighbour as thyself", stated by the Lord to be "the second" commandment (Matt 22:39). But, "hate thine enemy" is a Jewish addition, rather in conflict with the previous verse (Lev 19:17), "Thou shalt not hate thy brother". Many would hate the Jews, but it is God's prerogative to deal with them, and not the responsibility of the children of the kingdom to reciprocate in kind (Deut 30:7).

44 The text of this verse should be noted. The words "bless them that curse you, do good to them that hate you" and "despitefully use you, and" occur in the TR, but not in many other Greek texts. Hence they are omitted in the RV, and they are bracketed in JND. The Greek verb *agapaō*, used here for "love", is always to be distinguished from the other Greek word *phileō*. The former is either moral love, or Christian, divine and spiritual love revealed in the NT. The latter involves personal and tender affections. The former is recognised by its fruit. In our verse, the inner motivation must produce fruit even when dealing with enemies and those involved in persecution. No doubt the good Samaritan manifested this kind of love to the man fallen amongst thieves (Luke 10:25-37). In the gospel divine motives towards sinners are far deeper and higher: "for God so *loved* the world" (John 3:16); "God commendeth his *love* toward us" (Rom 5:8); "not that we loved God, but that he *loved* us" (1 John 4:10). Hence we ought to love one another (v.11).

45 To be "children of your Father" should read "sons" (*huioi*), and cannot refer to the Christian relationship revealed in the epistles. Rather it denotes an intelligent understanding of the providential care of God lavished upon all men. The providential goodness of God (the sun and the rain) is granted to all, and no difference is made between good and evil men (except in times of judgment that have been visited upon nations, particularly in the OT). Examples of such care are: "seedtime and harvest ... summer and winter ... shall not cease" (Gen 8:22); "Oh that men would praise the Lord for his goodness, and for his wonderful works to the children of men" (Ps 107:8); "he did good, and gave us rain from heaven, and fruitful seasons" (Acts 14:17); "he giveth to all life, and breath, and all things" (17:25).

46-47 See also Luke 6:31-35. If a disciple loves those who love him; if he greets his fellow-disciples only; if he does good only to those who do good to him; if he lends only to those who can reciprocate, then the conduct of that disciple is not much removed from the general standards of conduct found amongst many in the world. The "publicans" (*hoi telōnai*) were the despised tax-gatherers, collecting taxes for the Roman authorities, yet they exhibited this general standard of conduct when seen through unprejudiced eyes. The disciple needs great self-control to advance on this conduct, having the Lord as the true example. With opportunity, we must do good to "all men" (Gal 6:10).

48 The disciple will thereby be "perfect" (*teleios*); not perfect in the sense of being without spot or sin morally, but complete in every responsible part of his being. The Father sets a copy, and no part of this copy is omitted by the disciple. Luke mentions just one phase of this copy: "Be ye therefore merciful, as your Father also is merciful" (Luke 6:36). Note the RV and JND have "your heavenly Father" and not "your Father which is in heaven"; the TR has *"ho en tois ouranois"*, whereas other texts have *"ho ouranios"*. However, the TR has *ouranios* in Matt 6: 14, 26, 32; 15:13.

II. The Sermon on the Mount: Part II (6:1-34)

1. *Not Alms before Men* 6:1-4

v.1 "Take heed that ye do not your alms before men, to be seen of them: otherwise ye have no reward of your Father which is in heaven.
v.2 Therefore when thou doest *thine* alms, do not sound a trumpet before thee, as the hypocrites do in the synagogues and in the streets, that they may have glory of men. Verily I say unto you, They have their reward.
v.3 But when thou doest alms, let not thy left hand know what thy right hand doeth:
v.4 That thine alms may be in secret: and thy Father which seeth in secret himself shall reward thee openly."

This chapter deals with reward for responsible kingdom conduct; commendation from men is not to be sought, rather the "Well done" from the Lord. In vv.2-18 there is a reward from the Father when alms, prayer and fasting are done in secret. The "open" reward is not necessarily characteristic of this present scene on earth; more particularly, such reward is "treasures in heaven" (v.20). Conversely in vv.25-34, God knows the disciples' need of food and clothing, and He provides openly in this scene when we are occupied with the things of God (v.34). "My God shall supply all your need" (Phil 4:19).

1 This verse is really a general principle, illustrated by three examples in vv.2-18. Instead of the AV " alms" (*eleēmosunē*), the RV has " righteousness" (*dikaiosunē*); JND has "alms" in his text, but "righteousness" in his footnote which he admits is probably right. In the context, v.2 would have but little meaning if "alms" were correct in v.1. The disciple must question the motives behind all his righteous acts. Are they being done for God, or to be seen of men? Any public work should be severely examined by the worker himself. Paul's attitude "not as pleasing men, but God" (1 Thess 2:4) contrasts with that of the Pharisees "all their works they do for to be seen of men" (Matt 23:5).

2 The word "hypocrite" (*hupokritēs*) originally referred to an actor wearing a mask, so came to mean a false pretender claiming to be different from what he actually is. The sounding of a trumpet in the synagogues and streets might have had as its object the summoning of the poor, but hypocrisy would turn it into arrogant ostentation. (It is reported of one rabbi that he carried alms in a bag on his back, so that the poor might help themselves!) All takes place under divine scrutiny; in Mark 12:41 the Lord saw rich men casting much into the treasury. This was done to be seen, and the Lord saw also. But the widow cast in her two mites, not to be seen of men; yet the Lord saw this and commended her. Today, large gifts as philanthropy may make news headlines, but the Lord's people would wish their gifts to be known only by themselves and the Lord. For the hypocrites "have their reward" now on earth; the glory they receive from men is their reward. Their account is closed; nothing goes forward to heaven.

3-4 The left hand not knowing what the right hand is doing is an expressive idiom, denoting absolute secrecy. In an assembly sense, one believer does not know what another gives; if for some reason the treasurer knows, this is a matter of absolute confidentiality. Certainly the "goods works" done before men (Matt 5:16) are *not* these alms done in secret. In 2 Cor 8:1-5 Paul boasted of the Macedonian collection to the Corinthians, and in 9:1-5 of the Corinthian collection to the Macedonians, but this was not referring to individuals, and amounts were not disclosed. As far as the divine recompense or reward is concerned, the word "openly" is omitted in vv.4, 6, 18 by the RV and JND. If it takes place on earth, the world will know nothing about it; if it takes place in heaven this will enhance the glory of Christ. We may quote the following as examples of recompense: "...shall receive an hundredfold" (Matt 19:29); "It is more blessed to give..." (Acts 20:35); "God is able to make all grace abound toward you...all sufficiency in all things" (2 Cor 9:8); "his righteousness remaineth for ever" (v.9); "...enriched in every thing to all bountifulness" (v.11). The same principle applies to the believer's time devoted to the Lord's service: either to work "as unknown" (2 Cor 6:9), or to spend time on self, gain and advancement.

2. *Not Prayers before Men* 6:5-15

v.5 "And when thou prayest, thou shalt not be as the hypocrites *are:* for they love to pray standing in the synagogues and in the corners of the streets, that they may be seen of men. Verily I say unto you, They have their reward.
v.6 But thou, when thou prayest, enter into thy closet, and when thou hast shut thy door, pray to thy Father which is in secret; and thy Father which seeth in secret shall reward thee openly.
v.7 But when ye pray, use not vain repetitions, as the heathen *do:* for they think that they shall be heard for their much speaking.
v.8 Be not ye therefore like unto them: for your Father knoweth what things ye have need of, before ye ask him.
v.9 After this manner therefore pray ye: Our Father which art in heaven, Hallowed be thy name.
v.10 Thy kingdom come. Thy will be done in earth, as *it is* in heaven.
v.11 Give us this day our daily bread.
v.12 And forgive us our debts, as we forgive our debtors.
v.13 And lead us not into temptation, but deliver us from evil: For thine is the kingdom, and the power, and the glory, for ever. Amen.
v.14 For if ye forgive men their trespasses, your heavenly Father will also forgive you:
v.15 But if ye forgive not men their trespasses, neither will your Father forgive your trespasses."

5 In vv.5-8, note the alternating use of the singular and plural forms. "thou, you, thou, ye", a feature quite lost in modern translations which use "you" throughout, thereby losing accuracy and, to many, reverence when addressing Deity. (Some Greek manuscripts and the RV, but not JND, have the plural form "you" throughout v.5). There are dozens of examples in both the OT and the NT where "thou, thee, thy, thine" and "ye, you, your, yours" occur in the same verse or context; see Matt 23:37; 26:64 for example.

As in v.2 the synagogues and outside open spaces were used for arrogant ostentation when engaging in prayer; such hypocrites loved being on a pedestal to show their superiority to their fellows. God did not hear them, but men did: this was their reward – indeed what they wanted. It was a case of treating God as a matter of convenience, merely for self-glory. Of course, the Lord is not condemning prayer in public places when it is necessary. This is what Solomon did before the congregation in the courts of the Lord's house then being dedicated (1 Kings 8:12, 54-55; 2 Chron 6:12-13). This was also done in the days of Ezra and Nehemiah (Neh 9:1–3). Again, Paul prayed with a large company, kneeling down "on the shore" (Acts 21:5). But the public idolatrous worship ordered by Nebuchadnezzar before his image of gold was really supposed to be directed to himself as a deified heathen king (Dan 3:1–7): it was to enhance his personal glory.

6 There is a contrast for the disciples of the kingdom and their method of praying. The personal prayer of the individual believer is a private matter between himself and the Father. The Lord visualises the home, with a private room and a closed door, but the Father knows the secrets of the heart in such a secret place. Paul (as Saul) immediately after his conversion was in a house in Damascus, but the Lord knew what was happening: "behold, he prayeth" (Acts 9:8–11, 17). The Lord's example should be noted: He "departed into a solitary place, and there prayed" (Mark 1:35); in the garden of Gethsemane, the Lord "went a little further" to be alone (Matt 26:39). This principle does not contradict the position of Daniel in his old age; with the windows open towards Jerusalem, he prayed three times a day and was seen by the authorities (Dan 6:10). Again, Nehemiah was working in public, but prayed secretly to God (Neh 2:4). All faithful prayer receives a reward; prayer is answered, so often testified by men of faith in the Scriptures, and by the Lord's people throughout history.

7 Activity in prayer by the Lord's disciples must be distinct from that of "the heathen (*hoi ethnikoi,* Gentiles RV). In vv.5–6 it is *where;* here it is *how,* namely using "not vain repetitions". An OT example is found in 1 Kings 18:26–29; the prophets of Baal called upon his name "from morning even until noon…until…the evening sacrifice"; they thought that Baal would answer, "but there was neither voice, nor any to answer". By contrast, Elijah made one prayer of faith (vv.36-37) which was answered immediately when the fire fell. A NT example is found in Acts 19:34; for two hours the people of Ephesus repeated "Great is Diana of the Ephesians". By contrast, Paul prayed only three times that the thorn in the flesh should depart from him; here was no vain repetition, for the Lord answered by saying "My grace is sufficient for thee" (2 Cor 12:8-9). The Lord prayed three times in Gethsemane, "saying the same words" (Matt 26:44); an angel appeared strengthening Him (Luke 22:43).

8 Believers should not be like the Gentiles, whose motives are false. For the Father knows already, and can answer even *while* the prayer is being made; see Dan 9:20, 23, "*whiles* I was speaking, and praying"; "*At the beginning* of thy supplications". However, Christendom largely thrives on endless repeated prayers, uttered from printed books, leaving no room for personal exercise amongst both so-called clergy and laity. "Pray without ceasing", exhorted Paul (1 Thess 5:17), but this does not imply endless repetition.

9 The example prayer in vv. 9–13 has been greatly misunderstood, taken hold of by the ritualists and made into a vain repetition. The thoughts expressed at any time in prayer suit the dispensation in which the prayer is made; they suit the point to which the mind and purpose of God have been unfolded. In reading these verses, we must examine the thoughts expressed, and ask, Are they relevant to the period *before* the cross, or *after* it? Are they expressive of the situation under law in the OT, of the extended morality of the Sermon on the Mount, or of the period of grace after the cross and the Lord's ascension? The prayer was not given for men blindly to copy, but to take note of its structure, its simplicity, its length, its spirituality and its dispensational character.

Under different circumstances, the prayer appears again in Luke 11:2–4, though there various Greek texts differ greatly from the TR in that certain phrases are omitted (see RV). Moreover, in Luke the prayer was given in response to the disciples' question, "Lord, teach us to pray", not *what* to pray, but *actually to pray*.

In the prayer, we have thoughts Godward *first* – "thy"; *then* thoughts manward – "us". We have the divine Person, Purpose, Provision, Pardon and Protection. Their mode of expression was bound up with the then present situation. Today, similar thoughts would be moulded by the fact that the Lord's sacrifice has been accomplished, and that the Holy Spirit has been given.

In "Our Father", the heights of the knowledge of the Fatherhood of God as revealed in the Epistles had not yet been reached. The God of glory, providence, goodness and mercy – yes, but not the "Abba, Father" to whom the Spirit introduces us (Rom 8:15).

The phrase "which art in heaven" – strictly plural, "the heavens" (*Ho en tois ouranois*) – shows that the Father is above His own creation (1 Kings 8:27). Viewed from on earth, the description suggests a position of distance, outside the tabernacle and temple. Paul does not use the description, for we have been brought nigh, as seated in the heavenlies with Christ (Eph 2:6).

"Hallowed be thy name" (namely, "sanctified") implies that the Father is set apart from everything opposing His intrinsic character of perfection and goodness. He is apart from all the profanities of men. Thus this Name was not to be taken in vain (Exod 20:7); the Son referred to Him as "Holy Father" (John 17:11), while the heavenly praise is "Holy, holy, holy" (Rev 4:8). Today, only the Holy Spirit enables a believer to use this Name (Gal 4:6; Rom 8:15).

10 "Thy kingdom come" refers to a prayerful desire that the rule of God should be established in the form that is in keeping with the character of the dispensation in which the petition is made. In particular it referred to the Lord's teaching that the kingdom was "at hand", until Matt 13 when the kingdom was introduced in mystery because the King had been rejected by man's use of blasphemy. In Luke 17:20, the Pharisees wanted to know "when the kingdom of God should come", but the kingdom was not as yet going to come in open display. Today, the kingdom is moral (Rom 14:17), this sphere of His authority being disliked by men who want to exercise their own authority. The Lord's people have the hope of His coming before their hearts, but we do not pray for the coming of His glorious kingdom, since the times are in God's hands. This future kingdom will come through judgment and power (Rev 2:27). See Rev 11:15.

"Thy will be done in (*epi,* on) earth, as it is in heaven". In the third heaven, all moves in keeping with the divine will from the throne. In the physical heavens or skies, it is the same: "fire, and hail; snow, and vapour; stormy wind fulfilling his word" (Ps 148:8). When the Lord was here, His pathway was governed by His Father's will (Heb 10:7; John 5:30; Matt 26:39). For Christians today, the will of God is an important concept; we must say "If the Lord will, we shall live, and do this, or that" (James 4:15); it affects service, as Paul said, "I will return again unto you, if God will" (Acts 18:21). At a deeper level, "it is God which worketh in you both to will and to do of his good pleasure" (Phil 2:13; Heb 13:21; 1 Pet 4:2). But men will not be subject to His will, until all that offend are removed; then God's will will be done on earth.

11 "Give us this day our daily bread", or "give us to-day our needed bread" (JND). The previous expressions of Godward worship and desire now give place to a collective exercise of personal need. The needed bread for today had been known by God beforehand (v.8), and would be added if the disciples' priorities were correct (v.33). Recalling the manna in the wilderness, the psalmist said that He "had rained down manna upon them to eat" (Ps 78:24), even when the people murmured. "Thou…satisfieth the desire of every living thing" (Ps 145:16), the heathen included (Acts 14:17). However, such bread is useful only for a season, "Your fathers did eat manna…and are dead" (John 6:49); spiritually, if a man eat of the Bread of life, he shall not die (v.50). If ordinary bread is required daily, how much more is spiritual food (Acts 17:11). Paul teaches that all food should be received "with thanksgiving" (1 Tim 4:3-4).

12 To "forgive us our debts, as we forgive our debtors" the corresponding petition in Luke 11:4 is "forgive us our sins; for we also forgive every one that is indebted to us". The disciple is seen as owing something to God on account of sins, but nothing can be given that would merit forgiveness. "Forgive us" is a plea to God not to hold sin against a man when this would lead to eternal judgment. In the OT, David acknowledged his sin, and knew that "thou forgavest the iniquity of my sin"; sin was covered, and there was no imputation of sin (Ps 32:1-5). He pleaded for washing and cleansing, with sin blotted out (51:2, 7, 9). In the Gospels, *actual prayer* for forgiveness appears to be transitional, asked *before* the Lord died on the cross. Today we do not pray for forgiveness on the grounds that we also forgive others; this would amount to salvation by works. Now, we confess our sins, and He is faithful to forgive us our sins (1 John 1:9). The present order under grace reverses Matt 6:12, and this is completely overlooked by those who repeat this prayer indiscriminately; "forgiving one another, even as God for Christ's sake hath forgiven you" (Eph 4: 32; Col 3:13). Thus we forgive because we have been forgiven, not in order to be forgiven.

13 "Lead us not into temptation". The Greek word for "temptation" (*peirasmos*) has several shades of meaning. It may be a test or trial, sent or permitted by God; thus these trials proved the faith of Peter's readers (1 Pet 1:6-7). Abraham was tested when he had to offer up Isaac (Gen 22:1; Heb 11:17), and his faith did not fail. In such cases, it would not be proper to pray "lead us not into temptation", for it was God's will that such testing should take place. Likewise the church at Smyrna was going to be tried (God using the devil to effect it), but they had to remain faithful unto death (Rev 2:10). We suggest that the reference is to Matt 4:1, where the Lord was led by the Spirit to be tempted of the devil in the wilderness. He was victorious, but such temptation is outside the scope of the ordinary disciple to endure, so there is the prayer that it should never fall upon him.

In "Deliver us from evil", the definite article appears in the Greek, *apo tou ponērou,* "from the evil". This may refer

1. to the evil religion and wicked generation round about, or
2. to Satan as the evil or wicked one (1 John 2:13, 14; 3:12; 5:18). The Lord prayed this for His people in John 17:15.

Although the doxology "For thine is the kingdom, and the power, and the glory, for ever. *Amēn*" occurs in the TR and the AV translation made from it, it does not appear in the RV and JND and the Greek texts used for these translations. It appears to be a summary of 1 Chron 29:11, occurring in David's last great psalm of praise, "Thine, O Lord, is...the power, and the glory...thine is the kingdom"; this refers to His inheritance and intrinsic character. It stands in complete contrast to "a kingdom, power...and glory" given by God to Nebuchadnezzar, the king of the first beast-kingdom (Dan 2:37).

14-15 Both the reasons for forgiveness and the order in which forgiveness is granted were characteristic of the particular height that had been reached in the revelation of God's ways. Forgiveness or non-forgiveness was the portion of a man, depending upon forgiveness or non-forgiveness shown by him to others. That this was characteristic of the period *right up to* the cross is seen from Mark 11:24-26, where the Lord made the *same* statements during the *last* week. A similar statement is made in Luke 6:37. After the cross, our blessing is based on free grace and not on works: "forgiving one another, even as God for Christ's sake hath forgiven you" (Eph 4:32). We then are responsible to be "followers (imitators) of God" in this matter (5:1). When we forgive others, it means that we act towards our brother as if his sin against us had never been committed, though we rightly expect no repetition. But if there is repetition, forgiveness must be "until seventy times seven" (Matt 18:22); this is still applicable though the conclusion of the following parable could only be applicable to the period before the cross: "likewise shall my [not your] heavenly Father do also unto you, if ye from your hearts forgive not every one his brother their trespasses" (v.35).

3. *Not Fasting before Men* 6:16-18

v.16 "Moreover when ye fast, be not, as the hypocrites, of a sad countenance: for they disfigure their faces, that they may appear unto men to fast. Verily I say unto you, They have their reward.

v.17 But thou, when thou fastest, anoint thine head, and wash thy face;

v.18 That thou appear not unto men to fast, but unto thy Father which is in secret: and thy Father, which seeth in secret, shall reward thee openly."

16 Fasting was prominent in the OT, particularly on the Day of Atonement, the verb "to afflict the soul" referring to fasting (Lev 16:29, 31). After the return from the Babylonian exile, other annual fast-days were organised. In the NT, Pharisees fasted every Monday and Thursday (Luke 18:12). In Isa 58 there was both false and true fasting. The people complained that the Lord did not recognise their fasting (v.3), which they called "an acceptable day to the Lord" (v.5). Rather, true fasting is described in terms of good deeds (vv.6-7); then "shall thy light break forth as the morning", and such people will be "like a watered garden, and like a spring of water" (vv.8, 11). In the NT, the hypocrisy of the Pharisees knew no bounds. The outward signs of fasting were deliberately amplified and paraded before men; their reward was that of self-glory.

17-18 If fasting has as its object to get it over and done with as quickly as possible, so as to get back to the old life of overabundant food and drink, then this is no true fasting. True fasting is not observed outwardly. As one has commented, "Do openly whatever is commanded, that men may glorify God: do secretly all else, that men may not glorify thee". In the Christian era, fasting is not a matter of command, nor is it scripturally associated with a defined period such as Lent in the so-called church calendar. It is a matter of personal honest exercise should a believer feel it an advantage before God to fast for a particular reason in his life and service. Thus in Antioch they fasted while waiting for guidance in service (Acts 13:2); Paul and Barnabas "prayed with fasting" when the first elders were recognised at the end of their first missionary journey (14:23). Yet other aspects of fasting are perpetual and not merely spasmodic. The apostles had "forsaken all", and the Lord commended those who had left "houses, or brethren, or sisters, or father, or mother, or wife, or children, or lands" for His name's sake (Matt 19:27, 29).

4. *Singleness of Purpose* 6:19-24

v.19 "Lay not up for yourselves treasures upon earth, where moth and rust doth corrupt, and where thieves break through and steal:

v.20 But lay up for yourselves treasures in heaven, where neither moth nor rust doth corrupt, and where thieves do not break through nor steal:

v.21 For where your treasure is, there will your heart be also.
v.22 The light of the body is the eye: if therefore thine eye be single, thy whole body shall be full of light.
v.23 But if thine eye be evil, thy whole body shall be full of darkness. If therefore the light that is in thee be darkness, how great is that darkness!
v.24 No man can serve two masters: for either he will hate the one, and love the other; or else he will hold to the one, and despise the other. Ye cannot serve God and mammon."

19 No doubt these "treasures upon earth" partly refer to the "glory of men" (v.2) received by those who give alms, say prayers and appear to fast before their inferiors' gaze. Their reward is their treasure on earth, with no hope of this ever being transferred to heaven. The verb "lay up" (AV, RV, JND) really means "to treasure up", as in Luke 12:21, "he that *layeth up treasure* for himself". The Greek root appears in our English word "thesaurus", a storehouse of knowledge, especially of words. Literally, the meaning is, "Treasure not up for yourselves treasures" (*mē thēsaurizete humin thēsaurous*). Moth and rust are biological and chemical agents that produce damage and corrosion over the years; the precious metals may appear to be safe from corrosion, but thieves will be active if left for too long. Nothing is safe now, and nothing will be safe from the final conflagration that will end this world's existence (2 Pet 3:7, 10, 11), as far as the works of men are concerned. "Thy money perish with thee", said Peter to Simon of Samaria (Acts 8:20). Sudden judgment fell upon Ananias and Sapphira for laying up financial gain about which they lied to the Holy Spirit (Acts 5:1-10). The farmer who built bigger barns laid up treasure for himself, and judgment fell upon him that night, with the question, "whose shall those things be, which thou hast provided?" (Luke 12:20). In the OT, the vast riches of Solomon are described in 1 Kings 10:14-29. Alas, he took nothing away except a soul laden with idolatry, and much of this treasure was lost by his son Rehoboam, for the king of Egypt "took away the treasures of the house of the Lord, and the treasures of the king's house; he even took away all: and he took away all the shields of gold which Solomon had made" (1 Kings 14:26).

20-21 The converse also contains a duplication of the root "treasure": "treasure up for yourselves treasures". This would include the use of material possessions in the Lord's service, realising that we can carry nothing out of this world (1 Tim 6:7). In OT times, Moses esteemed "the reproach of Christ greater riches than the treasures in Egypt" (Heb 11:26), yet the people spoiled the Egyptians, taking "silver, and jewels of gold" (Exod 12:35), dedicating them later for the construction of the tabernacle (35:5), all the materials being given from "a willing heart" (vv.5, 21, 26) The tithes were compulsory, but were given to the Levites and priests so as to maintain the service of God; these were "consecrated unto the Lord" (2 Chron 31:6). Bringing "all the tithes into the storehouse" (Mal 3:10) corresponded to laying up treasures in heaven, for the windows of heaven were opened to pour out a blessing. Treasures gained by David in battle were dedicated to the Lord (1 Chron 18:11), while of his own personal possessions he had given to the house of the Lord (29:2–5). In the NT, Paul's gain was counted loss for Christ (Phil 3:7), while the gift from the Philippians was regarded by Paul as "fruit that may abound to your account" (4:17), being treasure in heaven since it was "an odour of a sweet smell...wellpleasing to God" (v.18). On a different plane, Paul sought no glory from men, but the Thessalonians would be his treasure in heaven – a "crown of rejoicing" at the Lord's coming (1 Thess 2:6, 19). Truly, the priorities of a disciple are shown up by the difference between Matt 6:19 and 20. "Set your affections on things above, not on things on the earth" (Col 3:2).

22-23 In v.22, "the light of the body" (*luchnos*) means a lamp, and "full of light" is an adjective (*phōteinos*), while "light" in v.23 (*phos*) is a noun. The Lord is using a picture to describe the moral state of a man – his body; the eye (lamp) describes the source of these inner contents of a man. A single eye or an evil eye yields a moral being either "full of light" or "full of darkness". The remarkable thing is that the Lord describes "light" as "darkness"; how can this be? What we have here is the strange physical property of light cancelling out light, to yield darkness. This is not a property of everyday experience, but the Lord knew all about it, though it was actually discovered by Newton. Press a lens against a flat piece of glass, and even in the most brilliant light there will be a small circle of darkness around the point of contact. These constitute "Newton's rings"; ordinary common sense would state that there must be light at such a spot. What is happening is that two waves of light are cancelling out each other, producing the rings of darkness. This is like two children pushing at a swing from opposite directions – the swing remains stationary.

Spiritually, the Lord is describing a disciple whose motives lead him to do either one thing, or two opposing things. If the eye is single, the motives of the heart are centred upon spiritual things; if the eye is evil, there are two motives, such as two masters, and a man is faithful to neither. The Lord had described two motives in alms, fasting and prayer – supposedly Godward and certainly selfward. In every such case, the effects cancel out, and nothing is left except great darkness. 1 Tim 6:17-19 describes a single-minded man, but vv.9-10 describe a double-minded man. Certainly "A double-minded man is unstable in all his ways" (James 1:8). After Peter's first call, he followed the Lord *and* engaged in fishing; this was the darkness of "a sinful man" (Luke 5:8). But Paul always had a single eye, unmarred by worldly ambitions and affections; "God forbid that I should glory (boast), save in the cross of our Lord Jesus Christ" (Gal 6:14).

24 The metaphor is changed to two masters, God and mammon; it is impossible to serve both or to love both. One will dominate, and darkness is produced by the attempt at serving both. "Mammon" (*mammōnas*) denotes riches, and was a common Aramaic word at that time. The Lord's motivation and service were unidirectional, "I have set the Lord always before me" (Ps 16:8); towards the end of Joshua's life, the people stated that they had the same single motive, "God forbid that we should forsake the Lord, to serve other gods" (Josh 24:16). For the believer today, there is danger that there may be rivalry in his affections; "love – hate" may mean "greater love – lesser love", as Luke 14:26. Many verses illustrate this danger of duality. In Isa 26:13, the people confessed that they had tried this dual mastership: "O Lord our God, *other* lords *beside* thee have had dominion over us", but they had changed to a single master, "but by thee *only* will we make mention of thy name". The church at Laodicea tried it, "I am rich…", wanting the best of both worlds, but the Lord rejected such an attitude (Rev 3:17). James summed it up; "friendship of the world is enmity with God" and "a friend of the world is the enemy of God" (James 4:4).

5. *A Question of Priorities* 6:25-34

v.25 "Therefore I say unto you, Take no thought for your life, what ye shall eat, or what ye shall drink; nor yet for your body, what ye shall put on. Is not the life more than meat, and the body than raiment?
v.26 Behold the fowls of the air: for they sow not, neither do they reap, nor gather into barns; yet your heavenly Father feedeth them. Are ye not much better than they?
v.27 Which of you by taking thought can add one cubit unto his stature?
v.28 And why take ye thought for raiment? Consider the lilies of the field, how they grow; they toil not, neither do they spin:
v.29 And yet I say unto you, That even Solomon in all his glory was not arrayed like one of these.
v.30 Wherefore, if God so clothe the grass of the field, which to day is, and to morrow is cast into the oven, *shall he* not much more *clothe* you, O ye of little faith?
v.31 Therefore take no thought, saying, What shall we eat? or, What shall we drink? or, Wherewithal shall we be clothed?
v.32 (For after all these things do the Gentiles seek:) for your heavenly Father knoweth that ye have need of all these things.
v.33 But seek ye first the kingdom of God, and his righteousness; and all these things shall be added unto you.
v.34 Take therefore no thought for the morrow: for the morrow shall take thought for the things of itself. Sufficient unto the day is the evil thereof."

25 In this section, we have the Introduction (v.25), the Illustration (vv.26–30), and the Implications (vv.31–34). The verb "to take thought" (*merimnaō*), appearing six times in these verses, is replaced by "to be anxious" in the RV; certainly we make preparation for the future according to God's will, but not anxious preparation as if His will were irrelevant.

The words "eat" and "drink" define the scope of the word "life" (*psuchē*); often translated "soul", it has a wide range of meaning. Here the functioning of the body is meant, as distinct from its form (referred to next under "raiment"). The importance of the life in this sense is relative, since eternal life transcends the needs of temporal life here below: "Labour not for the meat (food) which perisheth, but for that meat which endureth unto everlasting life" (John 6:27). He indeed provided food for the 5,000, but He also provided Himself as "the bread of life" (v.35). In John 4:8, 31-34 the disciples had gone away to buy food; the Lord's food was doing His Father's will. In Luke 10:38-42, whilst Martha was "troubled about many things", Mary sat and "heard his word". The same principle applies to the body. Now our bodies are "the temple of the Holy Spirit" (1 Cor 6:19), so a spiritual understanding of priorities would enable us to say, "having food and raiment let us be therewith content" (1 Tim 6:8). Paul would work with his own hands to meet his personal needs (Acts 20:34), yet there were occasions when he was "in hunger and thirst...in cold and nakedness" (2 Cor 11:27); he did not complain, for the work of apostleship came first. The fact that spiritual dress transcends physical dress is stressed in passages such as Eph 4:24; Col 3:12; 1 Tim 2:9-10; 1 Pet 3:3-4.

26-30 The Lord now provides some illustrations from nature. In the beginning, God created all living things, and arranged for their perpetuation. Constant provision was necessary for all included in Gen 1. "He giveth to the beast his food, and to the young ravens which cry" (Ps 147:9; 145:16; Job 38:41). For man things were different; because of the Fall, the ground was cursed, and man had to labour to acquire food (Gen 3:17-19). This daily toil for provision was the result of the governmental hand of God; it is still the same for believers today, though they can rise above the curse. We are therefore anxious about nothing, but prayer and thanksgiving rise unto God (Phil 4:6). We are better than the natural creation of birds and animals, since we are blood-bought, something that cannot be said of any other moving creature.

In v.27, "stature" (*hēlikia*) means a length of life, as well as physical height. We eat to live, but cannot go beyond our time which is in God's hands and of His ordering; He may intervene as in 2 Kings 20:5-6. We are utterly dependent upon Him; why act as if we were independent?

Similarly the need for "raiment" is the result of the Fall. The superior clothing and colouring of flowers existed both before and after the Fall, flowers having no means with which to toil and spin. Their submicroscopic perfection in design and structure implies that the hidden things show the glory of God as well as the infinite heavens. Yet men's work in beauty is poor when contrasted with God's, whether in buildings, metalwork or garments – all are rough and structureless when viewed at a microscopic level. But the beauty in God's creation – as the texture of a petal, a crystal, or a butterfly's wing – remains unimpaired through a microscope. What man glories in is an abomination to God, but He finds pleasure in His own creation (Rev 4:11). The glory of Solomon was wonderful – we cannot match it; yet the Lord was greater than Solomon (Matt 12:42), as He was greater than the magnificence of Herod's temple (v.6).

The fact that the Lord said "lilies *of the field*" and "grass *of the field*" suggests that the Lord had wild flowers in view, such as might be seen in a cornfield. Rich colourful flowers (***krinon***) possessed stems which, with other grasses, would be dried and used to fire ovens instead of wood. The lesson is now more pointed: if God clothes His own property in the field, which man burns up, how much more will He provide for His own people who possess eternal life? Only faith can turn this lesson into practice; acting otherwise, the disciples are but "of little faith", the motives behind their activity implying that God does not provide. Similarly they were "of little faith" when they cried as if He could not save them from the storm (Matt 8:26); Peter was "of little faith" when he started to sink into the waters (14:31); the apostles were "of little faith" when they doubted the Lord's ability to provide food (16:8). Indeed, the Lord had to say "Because of your unbelief" to some of the apostles (17:20).

31-34 The Lord concludes with implications and instructions for the disciples We are not to worry about these things as if we had two goals in life, each striving for mastery in our motives.

1. Because of God's providential provision in His creation – "Therefore".

2. This is characteristic of the carelessness of the last times (1 Cor 15:32; Matt 24:38).

3. Disciples must be distinct from the Gentile nations, and "unspotted from the world" (James 1:27).

4. The providential Father knows all the needs of His people.

Rather, "the kingdom of God, and his righteousness" must have first priority. Discipleship implies forsaking all that one has (Luke 14:33), not necessarily abandoning personal possessions, but regarding them as God's property and using them for Him and not for self. Thus in Acts 2:45; 4:32-37 the early church in Jerusalem sold all personal possessions, establishing a real fellowship between all believers. God provided by sending relief from Antioch (11:29), and stimulating exercise regarding the collection from the churches in Galatia, Macedonia and Corinth (Rom 15:25-27; 1 Cor 16:1-3; 2 Cor 8, 9). Discipleship may involve forsaking the opportunity of marriage, this being given to some men for special service (Matt 19:10-11). It may imply that one's employment must be forsaken if there is a call to service, or if its nature is inconsistent with that of the local church. It is to the separated "little flock" that the kingdom is given according to the Father's pleasure (Luke 12:32).

Preparation? Yes, but no anxious care for tomorrow; the disciple's outlook should be "one step enough for me". Thus we should examine our motives in all aspects of employment and earning; there should be no double motives, "not with eyeservice, as menpleasers; but in singleness of heart, fearing God" (Col 3:22). The trouble of tomorrow can be met when it comes, by a steadfast faith in God, and by being established in the truth; faith and anxiety are opposites that feed the dual motives that the Lord is seeking here to break.

III. The Sermon on the Mount: Part III (7:1-29)

1. *Hypocrisy and Judgment* 7:1-5

v.1 "Judge not, that ye be not judged.
v.2 For with what judgment ye judge, ye shall be judged: and with what measure ye mete, it shall be measured to you again.
v.3 And why beholdest thou the mote that is in thy brother's eye, but considerest not the beam that is in thine own eye?
v.4 Or how wilt thou say to thy brother, Let me pull out the mote out of thine eye; and, behold, a beam *is* in thine own eye?
v.5 Thou hypocrite, first cast out the beam out of thine own eye; and then shalt thou see clearly to cast out the mote out of thy brother's eye."

1 If believers seek to walk in the paths of practical righteousness that the Lord has been teaching in the Sermon on the Mount, those who are less righteous will seek to justify their position by judging harshly those who are more spiritual than they. Small issues may be raised to almost unbounded heights by this process. This is what the Pharisees sought to do with the Lord Jesus – except in His case there were no small issues or failures to attack, so they had to manufacture entirely false charges.

"Judge not" means that there should be no harsh and uncharitable judgment that would condemn a man. If our spiritual eyes are *not* closed, we *can discern* sin and failure in others, but our attitude must not be one of superior judgment. It has been suggested that the phrase "that ye be not judged" means that God will judge that man because of his own harsh judgment, but this seems to be rather a narrow interpretation; rather, those who deal hardly with others should expect to be similarly dealt with by God. "If any man defile (destroy) the temple of God, him shall God destroy" (1 Cor 3:17); "whatsoever a man soweth, that shall he also reap" (Gal 6:7); see Matt 18:33; James 2:13; 4:11-12.

2 Here the Lord shows that there will be reciprocation in kind. "Judgment" reflects upon the standard and harshness, while "measure" reflects upon the amount. Note that the AV "mete" should be translated "measure", to demonstrate the flavour of the Greek, for the root *kri* (judge) occurs *three* times in the first half of the verse, and the root *metr* (measure) occurs *three* times in the second half. This similarity of measure occurs at the end of the parable of the unmerciful servant: "his lord was wroth, and delivered him to the tormentors, till he should pay all that was due unto him" (Matt 18:34). Paul sums up the situation pertaining to those under law: "O man, whosoever thou art that judgest: for wherein thou judgest another, thou condemnest thyself; for thou that judgest doest the same things. But we are sure that the judgment of God is according to truth against them which commit such things" (Rom 2:1–2).

3-4 The Lord introduces a miniature, highly-exaggerated picture-story to stress the corresponding moral situation which, without exaggeration, can actually exist. (We do not call these verses a *parable,* since these do not commence in Matthew's Gospel until ch.13). The "mote" (*karphos,* from *karphō,* to dry up) denotes a very small piece of wool or dry stalk that the wind may blow into the unprotected eye; there is no exaggeration here. The "beam" (*dokos*) denotes a large piece of timber to support, for example, a roof; this is the exaggerated part of the picture. Verse 3 deals with the discernment of sin, while v.4 with the correction of sin. No doubt the Lord had particularly the Pharisees in mind – finding fault with others without paying any attention to their own state before God. Paul said that they sought to be "a light of them which are in darkness" (Rom 2:19), whereas they themselves were blind (John 9:40-41). They stole, yet taught that men should not steal; they made a boast of the law, yet dishonoured God by breaking it, thereby causing His Name to be blasphemed amongst the Gentiles (Rom 2:21-24).

5 Such men are hypocrites, pretending to be what they are not; claiming to be righteous, yet condemning as unrighteous others more righteous than themselves. It is a solemn thing for anyone, such as the elders in a local assembly, to have to discern failure and sin in another and then to have to deal in discipline with the offender. Some of the Pharisees learnt this lesson when the Lord said, "He that is without sin among you, let him first cast a stone at her", for they all went out one by one (John 8:7, 9). In a local assembly, overseers must be "sober, of good behaviour...not given to wine, no striker, not greedy of filthy lucre...not a brawler, not covetous" (1 Tim 3:2-3), a series of negative features of conduct indeed, but designed to ensure that there is no beam in the eye of an elder who must, with others, take decisions about discipline in an assembly.

It must be stressed that the Lord is not banning the process of discernment and decision-taking. Nathan said to David, "Thou art the man" (2 Sam 12:7), but he himself was qualified morally to be sent by God on such an errand. "O full of all subtilty and all mischief, thou child of the devil, thou enemy of all righteousness" said Paul to Elymas the sorcerer, knowing that he, the apostle, possessed the opposite character (Acts 13:10). Another example is in 1 Cor 5:3.

2. *Features of Kingdom Conduct* 7:6-14

v.6 "Give not that which is holy unto the dogs, neither cast ye your pearls before swine, lest they trample them under their feet, and turn again and rend you.
v.7 Ask, and it shall be given you; seek, and ye shall find; knock, and it shall be opened unto you:
v.8 For every one that asketh receiveth; and he that seeketh findeth; and to him that knocketh it shall be opened.
v.9 Or what man is there of you, whom if his son ask bread, will he give him a stone?
v.10 Or if he ask a fish, will he give him a serpent?
v.11 If ye then, being evil, know how to give good gifts unto your children, how much more shall your Father which is in heaven give good things to them that ask him?
v.12 Therefore all things whatsoever ye would that men should do to you, do ye even so to them: for this is the law and the prophets.
v.13 Enter ye in at the strait gate: for wide is the gate, and broad is the way, that leadeth to destruction, and many there be which go in thereat:
v.14 Because strait is the gate, and narrow is the way, which leadeth unto life, and few there be that find it."

6 Whereas much of the Lord's teaching was for the public ear, other truth was reserved only for the private ear of His own disciples; this is particularly so in matters relating to the church. There had to be discernment as to what was "holy" and who were the "dogs". The word "holy" (*hagios*, derived from *a*, without, and *gē*, earth) denotes the opposite of common. To be holy is to be separated to God and distinct from the things of men. The words saint, sanctify, sanctification, holiness, hallowed, all have the same root meaning. The word " dog", on the other hand, conveys an unpleasant meaning. The many references found in a concordance to the word "dog" show that this animal in the OT was a scavenger and engaged in the disposal of refuse (Exod 22:31; 1 Kings 14:11; 22:38). (The dog in Matt 15:26; Mark 7:27 seems to be a small pet dog, appearing in the NT *only* in the story of the Syrophenician woman.) The dog therefore represents what is defiled and unclean, such as the Gentiles (Matt 15:26); the antagonistic Jews (Phil 3:2); religious people who have sunk into sin (2 Pet 2:22); Christians today who exhibit hate and not love as they "bite and devour one another" (Gal 5:15); and all those outside the holy Jerusalem, for "without are dogs" (Rev 22:15). As we look around the world today, it is essential for the Lord's people to be spiritual enough to discern the difference between "dogs" and what is "holy", "that ye may put difference between holy and unholy, and between unclean and clean" (Lev 10:10). The "swine" in the OT were unclean (Lev 11:7); they could not be eaten nor offered in sacrifice unto God.

What is "holy" and the "pearls" represent truth held by the Lord's people that is particularly their property. The Lord would not have it otherwise. In the OT, only the priests had the privilege to enter into tabernacle and temple, on account of the holiness of the sanctuary. In Ps 137:3-4, the exiles beside the rivers of Babylon would not sing to the heathen the songs of Zion, for these songs were holy, so different from the "song of the drunkards" (69:12). The meanings of the parables of the kingdom were hidden from the Jews (Matt 13:11-15), but explained privately to the Lord's disciples alone (v.34-36). The vital truths regarding the Father and the Son were hidden "from the wise and prudent" (11:25-27). The prophetical discourse in Matt 24 was spoken only to the disciples (24:1). The holy discourse in the upper room was suitable for the Lord's apostles only after Judas had departed (John 13:30; 14-16). If the unsaved get hold of truth of this character, they will seek to damage it (2 Pet 3:16) as well as seeking to "rend" the believer in the sense of criticising the depths of his faith.

7-8 If we are enjoined to provide what is holy only to those who are holy, how much more will God provide needed blessings for those who are holy—His people. Hence in vv.7-8 we have our side in asking, and in vv.9-11 we have the Father's side in giving. To "seek, knock, ask" represent stages, showing an increase in eagerness and earnestness. To ask may involve an immediate reply; to knock, a short wait; to seek, perhaps a long wait. Note the following examples:

1. Peter cried, "Lord, save me" when he started to sink (Matt 14:30); there was an immediate response exactly as Peter asked.

2. The teachers in Antioch were engaged in prayer; shortly the Holy Spirit answered, showing that Paul and Barnabas were to depart for missionary work (Acts 13:1-3). Paul knocked by praying three times that the thorn in the flesh should depart. After this, his prayer was answered, but not as he had expected (2 Cor 12:8-9).

3. David said, "I waited patiently for the Lord; and he inclined unto me, and heard my cry" (Ps 40:1), suggesting a patient wait. Neh 1:4-6 is another example of this kind of prayer.

There are, of course, many conditions laid down in the NT for prayer to be answered, and it is instructive to prepare a list. A good thing asked (Matt 7:11); two or three agreeing (18:19); doubt not (21:21); believe that the things asked will be received (Mark 11:22-24); faith as a grain of mustard seed (Luke 17:6); to ask in His Name (as if He were asking), with the motive "that the Father may be glorified in the Son" (John 14:13-14); "if ye abide in me, and my words abide in you" (John 15:7); to bring forth lasting fruit (v.16); not to ask amiss (James 4:3); the one asking must be "a righteous man" (5:16); to keep His commandments, and to "do those things that are pleasing in his sight" (1 John 3:22); to ask "according to his will" (5:14). This is an impressive list, and must be taken in conjunction with the Lord's teaching in Matt 7:7-11.

9-10 In nature, all men, animals and birds are made so that they instinctively provide the right kind of food for their young (though many modern parents may have lost the instinct owing to traditional foods and processed foods tending to blind the instinct!). Natural kindness is shown in that proper foods and not "a stone…a serpent" are offered. To this list of bread and fish, Luke 11:12 adds "or if he shall ask an egg, will he offer him a scorpion?". The bread and fish refer forward to the feeding of the 5,000 (Matt 14:15-21). In that story, the Lord would provide exactly what was needed, as the manna had been provided in the wilderness. Note that the Lord did not turn stones into bread when He was in the wilderness (Matt 4:3-4), but He would provide bread and not stones for the multitude. A natural father treats his son with more love than to engage in a hollow act of mockery by providing a stone-like resemblance of a true loaf. Similarly, a fish and not a serpent shows that valuable food is provided by a normal father on earth. Again, the coiled body of a scorpion is white, like an egg. But natural human love never provides useless deceptive objects; it is the same with divine love that always provides a wholesome reality to meet any need.

11 The Lord now draws a similarity between an earthly father and the "Father which is in heaven". If a man, essentially evil, possesses instinct, logic, kindness and mercy, how much more will the Father demonstrate a suitable answer to prayer. In Rom 8:15 and Gal 4:6, it is the Father *who is worshipped;* here it is a Father *who gives.* As He knows the need before His people ask, so He provides what is good according to His estimate, both in daily life and in Christian service. As James 1:17 puts it, "Every good gift and every perfect gift is from above, and cometh down from the Father of lights".

12 This verse contains the "law of reflection": render to others only what you would like others to render to you. It is a rule by which to regulate our treatment of others. Speaking to Edom, the prophet Obadiah said, "as thou hast done, it shall be done unto thee: thy reward shall return upon thine own head" (Obad 15). Our treatment of others can be like a boomerang. Bring up children using rough and bad language, and this is the language they will use to their parents. Similarly the use of good, kind and polite language, with correct vocabulary and grammar, will become a two-way process. The same pertains in the moral sphere, in our interactions with men and society. There is a come-back of our deeds, whether good or bad. This is another way of expressing the second great commandment, "Thou shalt love thy neighbour as thyself" (Matt 22:39). It is an interesting fact that some Greek manuscripts of the letter in Acts 15:20 (but not in Acts 21:25) contain the extra sentence, "Do not do to others what you would not wish to be done to you". This has so little authority that it is not incorporated in the texts of the editors of the Greek manuscripts, yet it is to be found in the common Russian translation of the NT. This addition expresses in a negative way what the Lord said positively.

13-14 The "strait" gate and the "narrow" way are reversed to the "narrow" gate and the "straitened" way in the RV translation. The adjective applied to "gate" is *stenos*, appearing only three times in the NT, here and in Luke 13:24. This word means "narrow", and it describes the initial entrance to salvation and eternal life. It is narrow because God's method is unique, so distinct from the wide range of possibilities propagated by religious and heretical teachers. This "gate" is the beginning of the subsequent "way"; the gate is passed once, but the way is traversed throughout life. The gate is easily passed by and missed unless the seeking sinner is really exercised to find it. It is likened to "the eye of a needle" in Matt 19:24, the rich young ruler in the previous verses having sought the gate without finding it. The conditions of life to which he was attached prevented him from discerning the gate which the Lord placed before him. The Lord taught that entrance through the gate (or needle) was impossible by man's efforts, "but with God all things are possible". The relative "few" who find the gate are converts; they find the gate open by the grace of God. After that, the "way" is "narrow" (AV) or "straitened" (RV). This word is the perfect passive participle of the verb *thlibō* , occurring 10 times in the NT; the corresponding noun *thlipsis* (tribulation, affliction) occurs dozens of times. The verb means "to be pressed in", like a valley hemmed in by mountain sides to the right and left, with no room to move sideways. It is translated "throng" in Mark 3:9 reminding us of the way the multitudes surrounded the Lord. On this way, disciples find fellowship with their Lord, who passed along such a straitened way Himself; along His way "he stedfastly set his face to go to Jerusalem" with the cross at the end (Luke 9:51). It is God's grace and guidance that press His people into the confines of this way; "I being in the way, the Lord led me to the house of my master's brethren" (Gen 24:27).

The "wide gate" and the "broad way" stand by way of contrast. The word for "wide" (*platus*) suggests a unidimensional measure, while the word for "broad" (*euruchōros*) suggests a bidimensional measure – spacious in length and width. In other words, here is something easy for the multitudes to enter, and to swarm along in ease, but its end is "destruction" with no safety in numbers. The noun *apōleia* occurs 20 times in the NT, being translated by several words such as "waste", "perdition" and "damnation". It does not mean loss of existence, but ruin and loss of well-being. In Matthew's Gospel, those on this broad way are: the generation of vipers (3:7), "the children of the kingdom" (8:12), those not receiving the apostles' word (10:14), Capernaum and the other cities (11:21-24), the evil generation seeking a sign (12:39), the tares in the field (13:30), the bad fish (13:48), the nation who fell upon the stone (21:44), the hypocritical Pharisees (23:33), the goats (25:46).

Note: These words "strait" and "narrow" should not be confused with another word *sunechō* also translated "strait" or "straitened". This verb means "to hold together" as a constraint (Luke 12:50; Phil 1:23).

3. *False Prophets* 7:15-23

v.15 "Beware of false prophets, which come to you in sheep's clothing, but inwardly they are ravening wolves.
v.16 Ye shall know them by their fruits. Do men gather grapes of thorns, or figs of thistles?
v.17 Even so every good tree bringeth forth good fruit; but a corrupt tree bringeth forth evil fruit.
v.18 A good tree cannot bring forth evil fruit, neither *can* a corrupt tree bring forth good fruit.
v.19 Every tree that bringeth not forth good fruit is hewn down, and cast into the fire.
v.20 Wherefore by their fruits ye shall know them.
v.21 Not every one that saith unto me, Lord, Lord, shall enter into the kingdom of heaven; but he that doeth the will of my Father which is in heaven.
v.22 Many will say to me in that day, Lord, Lord, have we not prophesied in thy name? and in thy name have cast out devils? and in thy name done many wonderful works?
v.23 And then will I profess unto them, I never knew you: depart from me, ye that work iniquity."

15 Wherever there is light on earth, there will also be darkness, in a physical, moral and spiritual sense. Wherever the truth of the Word of God is taught, there will be the many who rise up with their false doctrines. In the Gospels, the Acts and the Epistles, there were men who rose up against the Lord, against the apostles and against Paul. To recognise this is either to adopt a could-not-care-less attitude, or constantly to follow the Lord's exhortation to "beware". In this case, He spoke of "false prophets" – supposedly speaking on behalf of God (as the men who prophesy in the Lord's Name in v.22), but there are many other kinds of false men, and we provide a list in the next paragraph. Some such men are obviously false—they are easy to recognise. But the subtle ones are more difficult to recognise, and we must know the truth in depth in order to perceive their errors. A toy coin (perhaps made of chocolate overlaid with gold paper) is obviously spurious, but a counterfeit pound note or coin is designed to resemble the real thing as accurately as possible; only an expert can distinguish it, yet it is completely false. Consequently the prophets in "sheep's clothing" appear to be near the truth, yet in reality they are completely false. In Matt 23:25-29, the Lord called the Pharisees "whited sepulchres" – outwardly appearing "righteous unto men", but within "full of hypocrisy and iniquity". We are not asked to unmask such men, rather we must "earnestly contend for the faith which was once delivered unto the saints" (Jude 3). The Lord sends His servants out "as sheep in the midst of wolves" (Matt 10:16), which by their subtle devouring activity seek to ruin the faith of Christians. Paul warned that the ministers of Satan are "transformed as the ministers of righteousness" with Satan "transformed into an angel of light" (2 Cor 11:14-15).

The Scriptures warn us of false Christs (Matt 24:23-24; 1 John 2:18), false apostles (2 Cor 11:13; Rev 2:2), false prophets (Deut 13:1-5; Isa 30:10; Ezek 13:16–

17; Matt 7:15; 24:11, 24; 2 Pet 2:1; 1 John 4:1), false evangelists (Acts 15:1; 2 Cor 11:4; Gal 1:7), false teachers (1 Tim 4:1-5; 2 Pet 2:1; Jude 4), false pastors (Ezek 34:1-10), false elders (Acts 20:29-30)—both externally as grievous wolves and internally as "of your own selves"—false brethren (Gal 2:4; 2 Cor 11:26). This is an horrific list, and the concerned reader should look up these references. Everything that God has ordained in the local assembly is liable to subtle attack, yet "greater is he that is in you, than he that is in the world" (1 John 4:4), and "the gates of hell shall not prevail against" the church of Christ (Matt 16:18). We recognise these men, not only by their doctrine, but by their "fruits".

16-20 The Lord often used agricultural, horticultural and arboricultural pictures to illustrate the truth being expounded. These related to common events and practices around Him, easily understood by the people listening, though sometimes designed so that they could not understand the spiritual implications (Matt 13:10–17). In the structure of vv.16–20 the truth "ye shall know them by their fruits" occurs at the beginning and the end with the illustration sandwiched in between. The principle behind the impossibility "grapes of thorns, or figs of thistles" goes back to the creation. Each tree created yielded "fruit, whose seed was in itself, after his kind" (Gen 1:12); this is the principle behind the transfer of life – like produces like. There may be variations in detail (used by men to produce better varieties), or there may be a manipulation of the genetic code by the experts, but this does not affect the principle stated by the Lord. Thorns and thistles were allowed by God because of the Fall (Gen 3:18), but these are also subject to the normal laws of nature.

This truth is expressed positively in v.17 and negatively in v.18. There are different Greek words for "good" in "good tree" and "good fruit". The first (*agathos*) refers to a fundamental nature that is beneficial in its outworking; the second (*kalos*) denotes what is pleasing, useful and profitable. Both words appear together in the same verse or context in several places: Luke 8:15; Rom 7:18. Similarly with "corrupt" and "bad"; here is a tree that is either old and cannot bear fruit, or a naturally-wild tree that produces fruit useless for man's consumption, perhaps even poisonous fruit. We think of Isa 5:2, where "wild grapes" were produced, useless to God. In a spiritual sense, Paul distinguishes between "the works of the flesh" and "the fruit of the Spirit" (Gal 5:19-23). The Lord implies that a false prophet is intrinsically rotten within; in spite of his mask, his outward actions will eventually match the nature of his doctrine. The Lord's disciples should therefore watch the outward manifestations of such a suspect, and act accordingly. In nature, bad trees are "hewn down, and cast into the fire" – a picture also used by John the Baptist in Matt 3:10. The Lord expands this statement in vv.21-23.

21-23 Verse 21 appears to apply to the time when the Lord was speaking, but v.22 suggests a future time of despair by the use of "in that day". These are the false prophets and miracle workers who bring forth evil fruit. In Luke 6:46 an abbreviated form of this statement occurs, still with the duplicated title "Lord, Lord". It appears again in Luke 13:25, the immediate context up to v.29 showing that the Lord was speaking about judgment prior to the millennial kingdom. At any time, the Lord recognises only those who call Him "Lord" by the Holy Spirit (1 Cor 12:3); any other use of this title by workers of iniquity is meaningless. Those on the narrow way love to call Him "Lord" in prayer, worship, service and obedience. But in a day of despair, men on the broad way faced with immediate judgment will adopt the same phrase. The Lord as the righteous Judge cannot be deceived; He will need no witnesses and no jury. For "the eyes of the Lord are in every place, beholding the evil and the good" (Prov 15:3); even the hearts of men are naked and opened to Him, whose eyes are as a flame of fire (Heb 4:13; Rev 1:14). During their life-time, such men have the opportunity to repent, and to change from the broad to the narrow way, though these men may not be allowed to play indefinitely with the longsuffering of God that leads men to repentance. Opportunity may be withdrawn, the door may be closed, and no amount of knocking will cause it to be opened again (Luke 13:25).

The issuing of false doctrine and the performing of false miracles are works of "iniquity" (*anomia*) or lawlessness. Some of these works are described in 1 Tim 4:1-3; 2 Pet 2:1-3. Anything out of the ordinary is too easily ascribed to God, whereas this cannot be so if those who perpetuate such things reject the fundamental doctrines of the Scriptures. It is solemn for the Lord to issue the disclaimer "I never knew you". This can never be so for Christians; He will confess us before His Father (Matt 10:32); He knows His own sheep (John 10:14, 27); "The Lord knoweth them that are his" (2 Tim 2:19).

The reader may care to consider the various duplicated names appearing in the OT and NT. "Jerusalem, Jerusalem" is related to sorrow (Matt 23:37); "Saul, Saul" is related to salvation (Acts 9:4); "Simon, Simon" is related to safety (Luke 22:31-32); "Martha, Martha" is related to service (Luke 10:41). To these we must add "Lord, Lord" in the verses under consideration, and "My God, my God" spoken by the Lord on the cross (Ps 22:1; Matt 27:46). Other examples occurring in the OT are "Abraham, Abraham" (Gen 22:11); "Moses, Moses" (Exod 3:4); "Samuel, Samuel" (1 Sam 3:10); "to Ariel, to Ariel" (Isa 29:1). All these demanded urgency in the speed of reply by those addressed.

4. *Foundations—Rock or Sand 7:24-29*

v.24 "Therefore whosoever heareth these sayings of mine, and doeth them, I will liken him unto a wise man, which built his house upon a rock:

v.25 And the rain descended, and the floods came, and the winds blew, and beat upon that house; and it fell not: for it was founded upon a rock.

v.26 And every one that heareth these sayings of mine, and doeth them not, shall be likened unto a foolish man, which built his house upon the sand:

v.27 And the rain descended, and the floods came, and the winds blew, and beat upon that house; and it fell: and great was the fall of it.
v.28 And it came to pass, when Jesus had ended these sayings, the people were astonished at his doctrine:
v.29 For he taught them as *one* having authority, and not as the scribes."

24-25 Throughout this Sermon on the Mount contrasts in abundance have been presented by the Lord; we now have the final contrast between the "wise man" and the "foolish man". Identical words describe the two groups of virgins in Matt 25:2. The word used for "wise" is not *sophos* but *phronimos*, meaning "prudent" or "practically wise"; the former is theoretical but the latter is practical. Hence this word suitably describes the activity of a man engaged on the building of a house on a solid foundation. This man both "heareth...and doeth" the Lord's sayings; James describes such a man as one who "looketh into the perfect law of liberty" (James 1:23-25), while the foolish man is described as one who examines himself in a mirror and then immediately forgets what he sees. Hearing and doing is an essential teaching in the NT, even if understanding is lacking; for example, in Rev 1:3 a blessing is promised to those who read, hear and keep the words of the prophecy.

There are many foundations in the Scriptures, giving perfect security to the buildings erected thereon, whether physical or spiritual. Exod 26:19, 21, 25 describe the 96 silver sockets to support the 48 boards of the tabernacle; these not only provided support but also separated the gold-coated boards from the desert soil, sand or rock. The foundation of Solomon's temple was laid in 1 Kings 6:37, while upon the return of the exiles to Jerusalem the foundation of their new temple was laid in Ezra 3:10. The Lord predicted that even the foundation stones of Herod's temple would be destroyed (Matt 24:2); this took place in AD 70. On a spiritual level, the foundations of the holy Jerusalem (the administrative centre over the earth during the millennial kingdom of Christ) are fully described in pictorial language in Rev 21:14, 19-21. On two occasions, Paul doubles the metaphor: "rooted and grounded in love" (Eph 3:17) and "rooted and built up in him, and stablished in the faith" (Col 2:7); the roots of a tree and the foundations of a building provide a double picture of strength. In love, in Christ and in faith form the substance of the foundation. For the local assembly, Christ is the one foundation that is laid (1 Cor 3:11), material that is so holy that only gold, silver and precious stones can properly be laid on Him to form a local assembly that grows through edification.

Some expositors suggest that the rock foundation in Matt 7:24 is Christ, but we feel that the Lord had not developed His teaching sufficiently at that point in His ministry to reach these heights. Rather we believe that it is His moral and spiritual teaching that constitutes the rock. With His teaching firmly in our minds and hearts there can be no danger of collapse, however awful the circumstances displayed against us. In language relating to the church and spiritual gifts, Paul wrote, "no more children, tossed to and fro, and carried about with every wind of doctrine, by the sleight of men, and cunning craftiness, whereby they lie in wait to deceive" (Eph 4:14).

26-27 The foundations of a house, bridge or a tall building cannot be seen. Despite this fact, no builder would seek to deceive deliberately, so as to cut the cost. Some central piers of huge bridges have had to be built under most awkward conditions; yet these foundations have remained for years as a testimony to the skill of the designers and builders long-since dead. The false prophets outwardly appeared to have good foundations, but when examined by the Lord these foundations were found to be nonexistent. The soft and shifting nature of sand causes it to be easily swept away by a flood, and the sawdust prophets likewise collapse when confronted by real trouble. When Paul wrote 1 Corinthians, many of the believers there were hardly built upon a rock. Their defective doctrine caused them to deny the resurrection; they were not built upon Christ raised and sins forgiven (1 Cor 15:16-17). As a result, everything else went wrong, both morally (ch.5) and as relating to their assembly service (chs.12-14). Only when the foundation of doctrine was corrected could Paul look forward to strength and stability; "be ye stedfast, unmoveable, always abounding in the work of the Lord, forasmuch as ye know that your labour is not in vain in the Lord" (15:58).

28–29 "When Jesus had ended these sayings", or some similar phrase, is typical of Matthew's style. The Sermon on the Mount concludes with this phrase. The teaching of ch.10 concludes with "when Jesus had made an end of commanding his twelve disciples" (11:1). The parables of the kingdom conclude with "when Jesus had finished these parables" (13:53). The Lord's teaching on the mutual relationships between brethren concludes with "when Jesus had finished these sayings" (19:1). The great prophetical discourse in chs. 24-25 concludes with "when Jesus had finished all these sayings" (26:1). Three times the word "sayings" occurs in this list, represented by the Greek word *logoi* ("words"). Some expositors sectionalise Matthew's Gospel around these five phrases, each section terminating with a discourse, after which another section begins, terminating in a similar manner.

The word translated "astonished" is *ekplēssō*, to be exceedingly struck in mind. In 5:1, the multitudes remained at the bottom of the mount, while the "disciples" ascended with Him. At the end, the "multitudes" were still there (8:1), but the word "people" should also be translated "multitudes" (*ochloi*), as the RV. During the Lord's discourse, some must have ascended the mount to be with the disciples. Well might they be astonished at His teaching; this was so new, so authoritative, so attractive, completely outclassing the scribes. These scribes, Pharisees and priests were the Lord's chief opponents during His life of teaching and miracles.

IV. Works of Authority

1. *The Healing of the Leper* 8:1-4

v.1 "When he was come down from the mountain, great multitudes followed him.
v.2 And, behold, there came a leper and worshipped him, saying, Lord, if thou wilt, thou canst make me clean.
v.3 And Jesus put forth *his* hand, and touched him, saying, I will; be thou clean. And immediately his leprosy was cleansed.
v.4 And Jesus saith unto him, See thou tell no man; but go thy way, shew thyself to the priest, and offer the gift that Moses commanded, for a testimony unto them."

In keeping with the OT predictions, the King is presented three times in Matthew's Gospel.

1. The first presentation was as a child: "out of thee shall come a Governor" (Mic 5:2; Matt 2:6).

2. The second presentation was as a light in Zebulon and Naphtali (Isa 9:1-2; Matt 4:15-16).

3. The third presentation was when the King entered Jerusalem in triumph (Zech 9:9; Matt 21:5).

There was a refusal of each presentation to Israel, and this rejection of the King is traced systematically through the Gospel. The King moulded His service and teaching according to the extent to which the rejection had developed.

Thus the wondrous *words* of chs.5-7 are followed by wondrous *works* in chs.8 onwards. He spoke with authority and He acted with authority. Chs.8-12 show the building up of opposition to the King and His ministry. (This record should be contrasted with that given in John's Gospel, where the build-up of opposition commences in 5:16-18, based on a miracle performed on the sabbath day and on the fact that the Fatherhood of God implied the Lord's deity.) Up to Matt 12, the kingdom was taught and manifested openly, but after that the kingdom was presented in mystery form. In fact, chs.8-12 reflect upon the outworking of the teaching given in chs.5-7; they anticipate the evil and the rejection of the people. The miracles that are recorded (with no parables) have moral and spiritual implications, both then, now, and in the future. The multitudes originally rejoiced and marvelled, but the Pharisees, scribes and priests gradually developed opposition, and swayed the multitudes against Him. This resultant opposition that led to His crucifixion has never been reversed; today we live in a world that is hostile to Christ, so we must not live as if we are of the world, but as those who are separated from it unto Him.

Thus we find that the power of Christ was rejected by the inhabitants beyond Galilee eastwards (8:34). The scribes accused the Lord of blasphemy (9:3). The Pharisees questioned the Lord about His eating with publicans and sinners (9:11). They accused the Lord of casting out demons through the prince of the demons (9:34). The treatment of the apostles by the cities corresponded to their treatment of Himself (10:25). The kingdom of heaven was violently attacked by religious men (11:12). Men accused Him of being "a man gluttonous, and a winebibber" (11:19). The accusation of blasphemy (12:24) caused the Lord to change His approach, thereby introducing parables in ch.13. Further truth is then developed relating to the kingdom, His Person, the Church, His death and resurrection, and prophetical matters in great detail. But this truth was essentially for His apostles only, and not for general consumption.

1 There had been no healing on this mount, just as there was healing only when the Lord came down from the mount of transfiguration (17:14). Usually mountain scenes were for the soul, and scenes below for the body, but there is a Contrast in 15:29-31 where multitudes were healed on a "mountain". Certainly the multitudes followed the Lord, since here was One different from the scribes (7:29). On the other hand, until the Spirit was given, too many followers would tend to hinder His work, and the Lord took precautions to prevent this in v.4.

2 Twelve cases of leprosy are mentioned in the NT: it was very common, and is thoroughly dealt with in the law in the OT. Authorities state that this disease in the Bible does not correspond to the disease with the same name in the present day. *Then* it was characterised by a rough scaly eruption on the skin, but *now* parts of the body may slowly be eaten away, such as the features, finger-joints and whole limbs – such a description is never found in the Bible.

Typically, leprosy speaks of sin, the manifestation of the flesh in a person. Miriam became leprous in Num 12:10 because she spoke against Moses; Gehazi became leprous because he subtly aspired after riches in the service of God (2 Kings 5:27); king Uzziah suddenly became leprous because he aspired after the priesthood, so was cut off from the house of the Lord (2 Chron 26:19-21). Lev 13 provides full details about the priestly discernment of leprosy, while ch.14 deals with its cleansing and the corresponding offerings that had to be offered. Specifically, leprosy denotes the working of sin; at its end it describes the state of being convicted of sin, and of being at the end of self. It introduces a fit subject for the grace of God. Palsy (Matt 8:6) denotes the incapability of doing good even though a man may know what is good (Rom 7:19), while fever (Matt 8:14) suggests the worries, turmoil and difficulties of life.

This leper "worshipped" the Lord. This verb *proskuneō* is common in Matthew, John and Revelation, but is almost absent from the Epistles. It appears in contexts where action is described rather than doctrine. Thus Deity is worshipped (Matt 28:9; John 4:21-24; 9:38; Rev 4:10); the dragon and the beast are worshipped (Rev 13:4); formal Jewish religion engaged in worship (John 12:20; Acts 8:27). But there were several occasions when men worshipped the Lord, not because they knew the truth of His Person, but on account of the respect in which they held Him because of His works. This leper was one such man, as was the ruler (Matt 9:18). Finally, there was worship in mockery (Mark 15:19)

The use of the title "Lord" (*kurios*) does not necessarily imply that the Holy Spirit is prompting its use (1 Cor 12:3). In the Gospels it was often a sign of respect for a superior as used here, by the centurion (8:6), by the blind men (9:28), and so on. It is translated "Sir" on occasions (John 4:11). But the leper realised that the Lord's power to cleanse was subject to His will. Moreover, the use of the word "clean" shows that the man had understanding, for removal of leprosy is always denoted by the verb "cleanse" (*katharizō*), except in Luke 17:15 where the ordinary verb to heal (*iaomai*) is employed. This is very significant, since this verb *katharizō* is used by John when he writes "the blood of Jesus Christ his Son *cleanseth* us from all sin" (1 John 1:7), to render the believer suitable for a new nature to dwell within.

3 The Lord's answer "I will" (*thelō*) shows that the leper's request was wellfounded in the divine will. This should mark the believer's prayer today: "if we ask any thing according to his will, he heareth us" (1 John 5:14; James 4:15). This was the prayer of the apostle Paul at the end of his second journey, namely "if God will" he would return to Ephesus (Acts 18:21), and this actually took place (19:1); see also Acts 21:14; 1 Cor 16:7. How the divine will responds to faith, when faith is founded in that will! The leper was cleansed with the Lord's word, a miracle marked by the description "immediately" (*eutheōs*). The Lord's miracles were always characterised by being immediate, complete and permanent. If an act today, claimed to be a miracle, does not satisfy these three criteria, then that act cannot be a scriptural miracle; usually it may be an act of the alternative medicine, perhaps at the moment without a scientific explanation. It would be presumption to call it a miracle; but sometimes presumption knows no bounds in order to deceive the people.

4 "See thou tell no man" the Lord instructed, apparently to safeguard His position. Fame drew curiosity, but miracles were not done to satisfy this. He would keep curious crowds away by such a command, since the Saviour was to be known not only through power but by the spiritual force of His words. In John 6:26 the people followed merely because they had been filled; the raising of Lazarus was the cause of many people being curious (John 12:18). Herod was desirous to see the Lord accomplish a miracle (Luke 23:8), but he was not satisfied and he went empty away. Mark 1:45 tells us that this leper "began to publish it much", contrary to the Lord's instructions, so the Lord remained in the desert places and would not come into the city. Disobedience can dispel the Lord's presence. Today, large numbers attracted by curiosity rather than by the reality of His presence can be no guide as to the spirituality of any work being done.

Finally, the man was still under the law; he had to act accordingly, showing himself to the priest for confirmation of the cleansing and for the offering decreed in Lev 14:4-32. We are not told whether this took place. Neither are we told whether the man "with a loud voice glorified God", as the one Samaritan leper did later (Luke 17:15-16).

2. *The Healing of the Centurion's Servant* 8:5-13

v.5 "And when Jesus was entered into Capernaum, there came unto him a centurion, beseeching him,
v.6 And saying, Lord, my servant lieth at home sick of the palsy, grievously tormented.
v.7 And Jesus saith unto him, I will come and heal him.
v.8 The centurion answered and said, Lord, I am not worthy that thou shouldest come under my roof: but speak the word only, and my servant shall be healed.
v.9 For I am a man under authority, having soldiers under me: and I say to this *man*, Go, and he goeth; and to another, Come, and he cometh; and to my servant, Do this, and he doeth *it*.
v.10 When Jesus heard *it*, he marvelled, and said to them that followed, Verily I say unto you, I have not found so great faith, no, not in Israel.
v.11 And I say unto you, That many shall come from the east and west, and shall sit down with Abraham, and Isaac, and Jacob, in the kingdom of heaven.
v.12 But the children of the kingdom shall be cast out into outer darkness: there shall be weeping and gnashing of teeth.
v.13 And Jesus said unto the centurion, Go thy way; and as thou hast believed, *so* be it done unto thee. And his servant was healed in the selfsame hour."

5 The Lord had been in Capernaum before (4:13), and now He returns to this city at the north end of the Sea of Galilee, a city "exalted unto heaven", where many of the Lord's "mighty works" would be done (11:23). The mention of a "centurion" recalls the fact that the fourth beast-kingdom (Dan 7:7) was dominant throughout the world. In order to sense the responsibility of a centurion, the following table explains matters clearly:

10 centuries = 1 cohort

10 cohorts = 1 legion

Each of the centuries contained 60-100 men, commanded by a centurion. The cohorts are called " bands" (Matt 27:27; Acts 10:1; 27:1). A legion could contain anything up to 6,000 men, though armies of that size remained outside Judaea until AD 66 (the year 2 Tim was written). Three different spellings are used for "centurion" in Greek:

1. *Hekatontarchos* (used in Matt, Luke and Acts);

2. *Hekatontarches* (used in Acts only);

3. *Kenturion* (used only in Mark).

In Luke 7:5, the Jews described this centurion as one who "loveth our nation, and he hath built us a synagogue", suggesting that he was a Jewish proselyte. Because he sincerely adhered to the Jews' religion, and evidently believed in the power of the Lord, he was ready to exercise faith when need arose. Later the centurion at Caesarea was devout, one that feared God, giving alms and engaging in prayer (Acts 10:2), a man ripe to receive the message of salvation.

6-7 The story is told more fully in Luke 7:1-10, where the centurion, feeling so unworthy, sent first the Jewish elders and then his friends to take his messages of faith to the Lord. In Matt 8:6-13, the story reads like a direct face-to-face conversation, but Luke implies that there were intermediaries, though the centurion may have been present when the Lord spoke the final words in v.13.

In v.6 a mere statement of fact is made: his servant was lying "at home sick of the palsy, grievously tormented". This is amplified in Luke 7:3, a request being made to the Lord that He would heal the servant. Mercy and grace were ready to meet Jew and Gentile alike when faith was operative, so the reply is given "I will come and heal him" (the word "will" being simply the future tense, unlike v.3 where we have seen that the "I will" denoted the divine purpose and intention).

8-9 This centurion was a man of authority in Roman circles, but he knew his true position before the Lord – he was not worthy for the Lord to enter into his house; it is not recorded that Peter took this attitude in v.14. Yet this man's faith was very deep; it was not a question of touch as in the case of the leper, but faith in the Lord's word acting over a distance. The Lord has power over a distance, something that can give confidence today when the Lord's physical presence and touch are absent. At His word, the creation came into being; by His word He upholds all things now (Heb 1:3); at His word the sea was calmed (Matt 8:26); at His word, Lazarus regained his life (John 11:43). Within the limitations of his knowledge, the centurion knew this, a fact that he illustrated with the brief word picture of his own authority. Because he had a position of authority, his soldiers and servant obeyed him immediately; the Lord had authority in wider spheres over nature, so His word was sufficient to cause nature to obey His commands. Now, He commands all men to repent, but alas, the heart of man is the one thing not subject to divine authority when faith is lacking.

10-12 This faith of a Gentile gave the Lord the opportunity to issue a prophetical statement, since even amongst the Jews such "great faith" could not be found. "Great faith" contrasts with "little faith" (Matt 6:30; 8:26; 14:31; 16:8); no wonder the apostles said to the Lord, "Increase our faith" (Luke 17:5).

The kingdom of heaven, of which the Lord speaks in v.11, is the sphere where the rule of heaven is recognised and appreciated, as distinct from the rule of men on earth, usually by governments, kings and heads of state which are atheistic, ecumenical or heathen. The precursor to this kingdom was found in the OT, when Abraham went out by faith to receive an inheritance (Heb 11:8-16). In the Gospels, this kingdom was at hand, since the Lord was present, declaring His manifesto for the conduct of His people. In the Acts, believers on earth formed part of the heavenly body the church, being subject not to the King but to their Lord and Head; to this heavenly body the Gentiles are introduced wherever faith is found (Eph 2:12-22). Paul was the apostle through whom this great truth was made known (Eph 3:1-9). In the future, the kingdom shall be manifested in glory, with the Lord reigning as "King of kings, and Lord of lords". Certainly "Abraham, and Isaac, and Jacob" will be there in that day. There will also be "a great multitude . . . of all nations, and kindreds, and people, and tongues" (Rev 7:9), who will have administrative thrones during the millennial reign (20:4). But "the children of the kingdom" are those possessing a natural inheritance, boasting that they are "Abraham's seed", yet accused by the Lord as being "of your father the devil" John 8:33, 44). In that coming day, only the elect out of the great tribulation shall be gathered "from the four winds, from one end of heaven to the other" (Matt 24:31); all will sit down with those who have gone before.

The Jews were always slow to understand that the Gentiles would be brought in, in spite of all the promises in the OT. The promise was made to Abram in Gen 12:3, and thoroughly made known by the prophets: "a root of Jesse . . . to it shall the Gentiles seek" (Isa 11:10); the Lord's servant would be "a light of the Gentiles" (42:6); "the Gentiles shall come to thy light" (60:3). Indeed the kingdom would be "given to a nation bringing forth the fruits thereof" (Matt 21:43), with the children of the kingdom broken and ground to powder. For the "outer darkness" is the destiny of unbelief, regardless of the privileges of natural birth (Rom 9:4-5). This is a destiny of darkness and remorse, as Jude puts it "the blackness of darkness for ever" (Jude 13).

13 The prophetic lesson came first; the miracle came second. Faith received its desire since this was in keeping with the will of God. This is a beautiful example of a miracle accomplished at a distance, and very suitable for the context, for the Gentiles were "afar off" (Eph 2:17).

3. *Miracles and Discipleship* 8:14-22

v.14 "And when Jesus was come into Peter's house, he saw his wife's mother laid, and sick of a fever.
v.15 And he touched her hand, and the fever left her: and she arose, and ministered unto them.
v.16 When the even was come, they brought unto him many that were possessed with devils: and he cast out the spirits with *his* word, and healed all that were sick:
v.17 That it might be fulfilled which was spoken by Esaias the prophet, saying, Himself took our infirmities, and bare *our* sicknesses.
v.18 Now when Jesus saw great multitudes about him, he gave commandment to depart unto the other side.
v.19 And a certain scribe came, and said unto him, Master, I will follow thee whithersoever thou goest.
v.20 And Jesus saith unto him, The foxes have holes, and the birds of the air *have* nests; but the Son of man hath not where to lay *his* head.
v.21 And another of his disciples said unto him, Lord, suffer me first to go and bury my father.
v.22 But Jesus said unto him, Follow me; and let the dead bury their dead."

14-15 Mark 1:29 informs us that they came out of the synagogue, and then entered into "the house of Simon and Andrew". Previously, they had come out of the house to the Lord (John 1:41), but now the Lord Himself enters the house. Most of the Lord's miracles and teaching were outside in the open, but occasionally a miracle (Matt 9:23-25) or teaching (13:36) was accomplished in privacy inside a house. Evidently Peter was married at that early stage in his life of service; certainly the other apostles also had wives, "as the brethren of the Lord, and Cephas" (1 Cor 9:5). There is liberty to be married "in the Lord" in His service, though Paul did not avail himself of such, believing that his service was best accomplished by remaining single. The general principle is "as God hath distributed to every man, as the Lord hath called every one, so let him walk" (1 Cor 7:17). So as a man of experience, Peter could write about wives and husbands (1 Pet 3:1-7), and even without personal experience Paul could rise to spiritual heights when writing on the subject (Eph 5:22-33).

When the miracle was accomplished, this mother of Peter's wife "ministered unto them" — strictly "unto him" (RV, JND); this was service directed uniquely to the Lord. So this woman took her place with others who regularly ministered unto the Lord (Matt 27:55; Luke 8:3), providing needful things for Him from their own substance. The word used for "minister" is *diakoneō*, what is accomplished by a "deacon" (*diakonos*). This is service in the widest sense – not only the service during assembly meetings, but beyond this practically in the home where the Lord's people may be in need, for "inasmuch as ye have done it unto one of the least of these my brethren, ye have done it unto me" (Matt 25:40). Do younger believers sometimes think that there is hardly anything for them to do in a local assembly? Then let them minister in this sense to others in need, instead of wasting valuable time in worldly pursuits, or in attending large ecumenical gatherings which are but precursors of mystery Babylon yet-to-be revealed. There may be older Christians housebound – here is true ministry to help them daily and weekly in their homes, with housework, shopping, cooking, electrical and plumbing repairs as well as necessary decorating. This is doing "good unto . . . the household of faith" (Gal 6:10).

16-17 This evening scene was hectic, for Mark 1:33 informs us that "all the city" was gathered at "the door" of Peter's house. The Lord was the centre of attraction, presenting such a contrast with Lot's house in Sodom, where men with evil intentions were pressing on the door of that house (Gen 19:4-11). Whereas "all that were sick" were healed at the door of Peter's house in Capernaum, yet the men at the door of Lot's house were smitten with blindness. But the contrast is really the reverse, for the land of Sodom shall be treated more tolerably than Capernaum in the day of judgment (Matt 11:23-24). Both the scenes in Gen 19 and Matt 8 took place in the evening, reflecting upon the moral state of the inhabitants. There were many evening scenes in the life of the Lord Jesus, and the reader is invited to search them out with a concordance.

When Matthew wrote his Gospel, he added a quotation from Isaiah, "Himself took our infirmities, and bare our sicknesses", taken from Isa 53:4 which reads, " Surely he hath borne our griefs, and carried our sorrows" . Often the NT writers quoted from the Greek LXX, but in this case Matthew certainly did not do so, for the LXX of Isa 53:4 reads literally "He bears our sins and is tormented for us".

Clearly the NT writers knew that Isa 53 referred to the Lord Jesus and His work on the cross (1 Pet 2:22-24), yet Matthew, when writing his Gospel, added this quotation from Isa 53, making it apply to His lifetime of miracles. Sometimes, prophetical statements have various fulfilments at different times and periods, and clearly this is one of them. Since the NT gives no indication that the Lord's body sustained illnesses taken from others as a result of His miracles, we interpret the quotation as referring to the Lord's grief and sympathy at the misery around Him. Such verses as "he was moved with compassion" (Matt 9:36; 14:14), "he groaned in the spirit . . . Jesus wept" John 11:33, 35) confirm this interpretation. Today, He is our High Priest who is " touched with the feeling of our infirmities" (Heb 4:15).

18-22 Here we have a "scribe" and "another of his disciples", in the corresponding passage in Luke 9:57-62 (placed after the transfiguration) there are three men. The scribe appears sincere, but the Lord tests his sincerity. The second man is not wholly sincere in his discipleship, but the Lord exhorts to greater sincerity. The scribe was evidently moved by the Lord's teaching and miracles, "I will follow thee" was easy to say at that stage of the Lord's life, but the man failed to realise the extent to which discipleship would have to go – even to Jerusalem and death, if "whithersoever thou goest" means anything. Later Peter showed such self-confidence, "I am ready to go with thee . . . to death" (Luke 22:33). This was beyond his capacity, for it is difficult to follow the Lord even in His life (as Matt 8:20 shows), and more difficult in His death, though Peter was ultimately crucified. The Lord provided habitats in nature for animals and birds but He did not provide such possessions for Himself (no doubt the women and the disciples who ministered to Him provided such things: a pillow on the boat (Mark 4:38) and a home for the night in Bethany during the last week). But would the scribe follow in this pathway? The rich young ruler would not (Matt 19:22), though Peter had forsaken all to follow the Lord (v.27). The early church in Jerusalem was like that (Acts 2:44-45; 4:34-37), but was later helped by the Gentile churches (11:27-30; Rom 15:25-27; 2 Cor 8-9). Not that every Christian has to sell all his possessions, otherwise there can never be the opportunity to help others. But there must be a willingness to leave all if God calls in that direction of service.

The second man is called "another" (*heteros*, meaning "another of a different kind"). The funeral and subsequent mourning would last several weeks

if the father had not yet died there would be a more considerable delay. The Lord will not have any delay in obedience to a divine call. Consider Abram: he went into the land only after his father Terah had died (Acts 7:4). The Lord will not have simple excuses; one must disentangle oneself from family ties if these prevent true discipleship. No doubt the Lord's reply, "let the dead bury their dead" is figurative: let those that are not disciples engage in that work. Under the law, touching the body of one dead brought uncleanness for seven days (Num 19:11), while a Nazarite was to "come at no dead body" (6:6).

4. *The Subduing of the Tempest* 8:23-27

v.23 "And when he was entered into a ship, his disciples followed him.
v.24 And, behold, there arose a great tempest in the sea, insomuch that the ship was covered with the waves: but he was asleep.
v.25 And his disciples came to *him*, and awoke him, saying, Lord, save us: we perish.
v.26 And he saith unto them, Why are ye fearful, O ye of little faith? Then he arose, and rebuked the winds and the sea; and there was a great calm.
v.27 But the men marvelled, saying, What manner of man is this, that even the winds and the sea obey him!"

The order of events is not necessarily identical in the three Synoptic Gospels. Their positions in these Gospels should be viewed relative to two key events:

1. the parable of the sower (Matt 13:1-23; Mark 4:1-20; Luke 8:4-15), and

2. the Transfiguration (Matt 17:1-13; Mark 9:1-13; Luke 9:28-36).

The story of the subduing of the tempest is found in Mark 4:36-41 and Luke 8:22-25, namely, *before* the parable of the sower in Matt, but *afterwards* in Mark and Luke. This fits in with the objective of the writers. In Matthew, the majority of the miracles are placed *before* the parable of the sower, but in Mark and Luke they are placed *before* the Transfiguration. Matthew's objective will become clear as we proceed.

The sea typically speaks of the unsubdued nations, and contrasts with the sea of glass in Rev 4:6 where all is subject to the throne. The wicked are like the troubled sea (Isa 57:20); "The waters . . . are peoples, and multitudes, and nations" (Rev 17:15); the Roman beast of the future will " rise up out of the sea" (13:1). The miracle is the first demonstration of the Lord's power over the physical forces of nature, indicating that He is Lord of all. Typically, it speaks of the future subduing of the nations by divine power.

23 Here is one of the occasions when the Lord sought to be separated from the multitudes; in Mark 4:36 He actually sent them away. There were occasions when He felt that "all nations compassed me about" (Ps 118:10). But the ship represents a little sanctuary, a place apart above the restless world.

24 The Lord was asleep. This shows that the phenomenon of sleep is not a result of sin, but was something introduced by God into the original creation. God Himself is above His creation, and neither slumbers nor sleeps (Ps 121:3-4). But for this blessed One manifest in flesh, "I will both lay me down in peace, and sleep: for thou, Lord, only makest me dwell in safety" (4:8). He "giveth his beloved sleep" and "wakeneth morning by morning" (Ps 127:2; Isa 50:4). So here was the Lord asleep during the storm, at peace among the nations surrounding Him in complete contrast to Jonah sleeping in the ship while running away from God who wanted to show grace to the nation of Assyria in its capital city Nineveh. Only on the cross would " all thy waves and thy billows" go over Him (Ps 42:7), the kings and rulers of the nations rising up against the Christ (2:1-2).

25 The disciples' cry "Lord, save" (many Greek texts omit "us") demonstrates a faith that trusts in a visible Man, but not in an invisible God. The Lord describes this as "little faith", "no faith" (Mark 4:40), and He asks "Where is your faith?" (Luke 8:25). Elsewhere we read "wherefore didst thou doubt?" (Matt 14:31); "Because of your unbelief" (17:20); "their unbelief" (Mark 16:14).

26 By rebuking the winds and sea, the Lord showed His power over the vast expanse, as distinct from His power over the restricted space of a human body, over the inanimate as distinct from the animate. After the storm in Ps 107:25-27 and the sailors' cry "unto the Lord in their trouble" (v.28), "He maketh the storm a calm, so that the waves thereof are still" (v.29). Again, "Thou rulest the raging of the sea: when the waves thereof arise, thou stillest them" (Ps 89:9). But Ps 46 presents the typical implication of this as pertaining to the nations: "though the waters thereof roar and be troubled" (v.3) is interpreted as "The heathen raged, the kingdoms were moved: he uttered his voice, the earth melted" (v.6), yielding a stream that would "make glad the city of God" (v.4). The winds speak of a Satan-like power over the nations, for Satan is " the prince of the power of the air" (Eph 2:2) even tempting believers "with every wind of doctrine" (4:14), tossing the children to and fro. But there will be eventually a millennial calm to replace the great tribulation described as " distress of nations . . . the sea and the waves roaring" (Luke 21:25); Isa 2:2-4 describes this calm as "nation shall not lift up sword against nation, neither shall they learn war any more"; see Mic 4:3.

27 By saying, "what manner of man is this?", the disciples began the development of a confession of the Lord's Person (a different development is found in John's Gospel). At that time the demons knew Him as "Jesus, thou Son of God" (v.29); the two blind men knew Him as "Thou Son of David" (9:27), and also in 12:23; 15:22; later the apostles called Him "the Son of God" because of His power over the storm (14:33), and finally, Peter confessed Him as "the Christ, the Son of the living God" by revelation from the Father (16:16).

What confidence this gives believers today; as David said, "O God . . . who art the confidence of all the ends of the earth, and of them that are afar off upon the sea . . . which stillest the noise of the seas, the noise of their waves, and the tumult of the people" (Ps 65:5-7).

5. *The Subduing of the Powers of Darkness* 8:28-34

v.28 "And when he was come to the other side into the country of the Gergesenes, there met him two possessed with devils, coming out of the tombs, exceeding fierce, so that no man might pass by that way.

v.29 And, behold, they cried out, saying, What have we to do with thee, Jesus, thou Son of God? art thou come hither to torment us before the time?

v.30 And there was a good way off from them an herd of many swine feeding.

v.31 So the devils besought him, saying, If thou cast us out, suffer us to go away into the herd of swine.

v.32 And he said unto them, Go. And when they were come out, they went into the herd of swine: and, behold, the whole herd of swine ran violently down a steep place into the sea, and perished in the waters.

v.33 And they that kept them fled, and went their ways into the city, and told every thing, and what was befallen to the possessed of the devils.

v.34 And, behold, the whole city came out to meet Jesus: and when they saw him, they besought *him* that he would depart out of their coasts."

28 The country of "the Gergesenes" is the same as that of "the Gadarenes" (Mark 5:1; Luke 8:26). A fuller account of this event is given in Mark 5:1-20, where only one man is mentioned. This country lay to the east of the Sea of Galilee, and Satan's special grip on men reached into that territory. By means of his demons he had the greatest entrance into human personality when the Son of God was present on earth. We must always distinguish demon possession from mental disorder which results from minute physical disorders of the brain. These two men blocked the pathway of anyone passing that way; in particular Satan was seeking to block the onward pathway of the Son of God. Later, through Peter, he sought to do the same thing (Matt 16:21-23) suggesting that He should not go to Jerusalem to be killed.

29 The confession of the demons contained the name "Jesus, thou Son of God", a confession greater than that implied in v.27. Silence was enjoined upon the demons (Mark 1:34), because they knew Him and believed (James 2:19). The fact of His Sonship would be hidden until the time was ripe for its manifestation; the source of such revelation was vital, the Lord would not accept testimony from men or demons. By saying "What have we to do with thee?", they showed a complete estrangement from divine things; a great void existed. They feared present judgment " before the time", their end being " everlasting fire, prepared for the devil and his angels" (Matt 25:41); other angels are "reserved in everlasting chains under darkness unto the judgment of the great day" (Jude 6).

30-32 The swine represented an unclean and appropriate abode for the demons; it appears that these demons needed some physical sanctuary. Deut 14:8 shows that swine were unclean; God's people were not to eat its flesh nor touch its dead carcase, and it could not be used for sacrifice. Isa 66:3 likens the offering of swine's blood to the blessing of an idol. The Lord Himself declared the incompatibility of holy pearls and swine (Matt 7:6). In the parable in Luke 15:15, 16 we find the great gulf between the swines' fields and the father's house. The result of the demons' request to be sent into the swine was that the behaviour of the swine was worse than that of the two men; they tormented and destroyed the swine. Note that Satan could not do this to Job; he suffered but was nevertheless protected. We may ask, "Why did the Lord allow these demons to enter into these harmless beasts?" It was visible proof that demons existed; a mere physical illness would be quite distinct. Also it showed the Jews that the keeping of swine was a snare as long as they were under the law. When he was at school, the author was taught that the swine behaved as they did only because of surprise at the new behaviour of the men – a miracle denied by an invented postulate to support unbelief!

33-34 Compare the testimony of these keepers that produced fear in the city with that of the Samaritan woman in John 4:28-30, 39-42 which resulted in the men's profession of "the Saviour of the world". The miraculous often caused fear: "they feared exceedingly" (Mark 4:41); "they were afraid" (5:15), a demonstration that they would not let the love of Christ cast out fear. Godly fear is in order, but here the Lord experienced His first open rejection, and had to depart. Yet the testimony remained, since the man had to go to his friends and tell them " how great things the Lord hath done" (Mark 5:19). Prophetically, the subject of demons and evil spirits is taken up again in Matt 12:43-45.

V. Further Miracles and Teaching (9:1-38)

1. *The Healing of the Man Sick of the Palsy* 9:1-8

v.1 "And he entered into a ship, and passed over, and came into his own city.
v.2 And, behold, they brought to him a man sick of the palsy, lying on a bed: and Jesus seeing their faith said unto the sick of the palsy; Son be of good cheer; thy sins be forgiven thee.
v.3 And, behold, certain of the scribes said within themselves, This *man* blasphemeth.
v.4 And Jesus knowing their thoughts said, Wherefore think ye evil in your hearts?
v.5 For whether is easier, to say, *Thy* sins be forgiven thee; or to say, Arise and walk?
v.6 But that ye may know that the Son of man hath power on earth to forgive sins, (then saith he to the sick of the palsy,) Arise, take up thy bed, and go unto thine house.
v.7 And he arose, and departed to his house.
v.8 But when the multitudes saw *it,* they marvelled, and glorified God, which had given such power unto men."

Prophetically speaking, this chapter reflects upon the continued traditional state of Israel and the necessity of a change that can come only through the work of Christ. At the same time, the moral and spiritual implications of the chapter also reflect on Christians today. The paralysed man denotes Israel in tradition and bondage, which only the Son of man can heal and forgive.

1-2 Further details are found in Mark 2:3-12. The rejected Lord passes over the Sea of Galilee to Capernaum, "his own city". "They brought to him a man" contrasts with Matt 8:2 where a man had come himself. This corresponds to sinners coming to the Lord; Peter was brought in John 1:41, but Cornelius came to Christ without being brought (Acts 10). On other occasions, the Lord found men directly, as in Matthew's case (Matt 9:9).

The man lay on a bed suffering from paralysis, speaking of a sinful state of bondage, being completely inactive for God. In Luke 5:18 those carrying him "sought means", implying that there is a variety of methods open for evangelists provided that they are spiritual means as described in 1 Cor 2:12-13. These men knew that they could not save the man; they could only bring him. But there was a barrier between this man and the Lord. The barrier (a roof) was below the man, and even this had to be broken up. The humbling of a sinner was essential as he descended still lower. The Lord recognised their faith, and unlike previous miracles went to the root of the matter first, "thy sins be forgiven thee", knowing the criticism that would arise immediately in the midst of the Pharisees (see Luke 5:21). Only twice in the Gospels did the Lord explicitly forgive sins,

1. in this passage where it was a question of faith, and

2. in Luke 7:48 where it was a question of repentance and love.

The verb forgive (*aphiēmi*) means "to send away", as typically sins were sent away in the form of the scapegoat on the day of atonement (Lev 16:21). Of course the cross was necessary, though men did not know that when the Lord said "thy sins be forgiven thee"; *now* we know that "we have redemption through his blood, the forgiveness of sins" (Eph 1:7).

3 The Pharisees could think only of the OT, where forgiveness is the work of God: "The Lord . . . forgiving iniquity and transgression and sin" (Exod 34:6-7); "thou forgavest the iniquity of my sin" (Ps 32:5). They desired no further light on the subject in the Man Christ Jesus, so objected by saying "This man blasphemeth" since "God alone" can forgive sins (Luke 5:21). The verb *blasphēmeō* has many translations in the AV: it is the act of those who speak contemptuously and evilly of divine things; when referring to men it is rendered "slanderously reported" (Rom 3:8), "being defamed" (1 Cor 4:13). To the Pharisees, here was a Man doing something that was uniquely the prerogative of God, for they failed to recognise the Person of Christ as God manifest in Manhood. This reasoning was a seed of religious opposition that would grow (Matt 9:34; 12:24).

4-5 The Lord had that divine capacity to know all thoughts, so He asked, "Wherefore think ye evil in your hearts?", to which the Pharisees knew the answer. In the OT we read, "The Lord knoweth the thoughts of man" (Ps 94:11; 139:23), and in the NT, "the word of God . . . is a discerner of the thoughts and intents of the heart" (Heb 4:12). In the early church, this was carried over into the gift of "discerning of spirits" (1 Cor 12:10), an example being found in Acts 13:10. The Lord continued the question, "whether is easier . . . ?", but provided no answer. Miracles are not presented in the NT as "difficult", but salvation is; for example, "It is easier for a camel to go through the eye of a needle, than for a rich man to enter into the kingdom of God" (Matt 19:24); "And if the righteous is difficulty saved" (1 Pet 4:18, JND). By saying, "Thy sins be forgiven thee", the Lord did an inward work that the Pharisees could not see outwardly; the miracle showed the Pharisees that He could work both outwardly and inwardly. Afterwards, of course, a change of heart and life would accompany forgiveness of sins (John 5:14; 8:11).

6 The divine Forgiver of sins called Himself "the Son of man", the name by which He usually designated Himself; it implies His absolute authority and control

both on earth and in heaven consequential upon His Manhood. In the OT it appears, for example, in Ps 8:4; Dan 7:13. In the four Gospels, the title first occurs in Matt 8:20; Mark 2:10; Luke 5:24; John 1:51 respectively.
The healed man had to do three things:

1. arise,
2. take up his couch (*klinē*, a bed, or a couch for reclining at meals or for carrying a sick person),
3. go into his house.

These actions would demonstrate the reality of the miracle; there was no delay, but immediate restoration (as in Acts 3:7-8).

7 The house would become a place for spiritual living, and for a display of the saving grace of God. Various occupations in a house are found in the Gospels in Matt 13:36; Mark 5:19; 7:17; Luke 10:38; 19:5; John 12:2. If service takes place in a house (as in Philem 2), and if service emanates from a house (Acts 10:23), there must be no skeletons in the cupboard. An example of such inconsistency is found in 2 Chron 8:11, where Solomon's Egyptian wife was out keeping with the sanctity of the house of the Lord in Jerusalem. In Luke 5:25 we read that the restored man obeyed the three commands of the Lord, "glorifying God" in so doing. He recognised the Source of his healing, but did not go as far as the blind man whose sight was restored in John 9:35-38, for he believed on the Son of God and worshipped Him.

8 The reaction of the people (as distinct from the Pharisees) was that of devout Jewish religionists; they failed to see the true source in Christ, perceiving only that God was working through "men". At least they "glorified God", as the man was doing: later the multitude "glorified the God of Israel" (Matt 15:31). At the same time, in Luke 5:26 they "were filled with fear" because the deed was so unusual; yet the Lord did not say "fear not" as He did so often to His disciples when they were fearful. Note, when Paul healed in Acts 14:11, men said that he and Barnabas were gods come down, but when Christ healed, men did not see Him as the Son of God come down from heaven.

2. *Transformation of Life* 9:9-17

v.9 "And as Jesus passed forth from thence, he saw a man, named Matthew, sitting at the receipt of custom: and he saith unto him, Follow me. And he arose, and followed him.
v.10 And it came to pass, as Jesus sat at meat in the house, behold, many publicans and sinners came and sat down with him and his disciples.
v.11 And when the Pharisees saw *it,* they said unto his disciples, Why eateth your Master with publicans and sinners?

v.12 But when Jesus heard *that,* he said unto them, They that be whole need not a physician, but they that are sick.
v.13 But go ye and learn what *that* meaneth, I will have mercy, and not sacrifice: for I am not come to call the righteous, but sinners to repentance.
v.14 Then came to him the disciples of John, saying, Why do we and the Pharisees fast oft, but thy disciples fast not?
v.15 And Jesus said unto them, Can the children of the bridechamber mourn, as long as the bridegroom is with them? but the days will come, when the bridegroom shall be taken from them, and then shall they fast.
v.16 No man putteth a piece of new cloth unto an old garment, for that which is put in to fill it up taketh from the garment, and the rent is made worse.
v.17 Neither do men put new wine into old bottles: else the bottles break, and the wine runneth out, and the bottles perish: but they put new wine into new bottles, and both are preserved."

9 Here, the man's name is called Matthew, meaning "gift of God", whereas in Luke 5:27 he is called Levi, usually interpreted as "joined". The Lord called His disciples one by one, not in one mass operation. He demonstrated that He could transform the most unlikely of men, calling them even when they were engaged in their unpleasant practices, for Matthew was "a publican" (Luke 5:27), or a tax-collector for Rome. These publicans often used their work to their own financial advantage. They were hated amongst the Jews and were counted as "sinners", the latter term being used do describe those engaged in the most disreputable occupations. Some were collectors of districts, with sub- contractors under them. Thus Zacchaeus (Luke 19:2) was an "arch-publican". John the Baptist had exhorted them not to go outside Roman law in their exploitation of the people for personal gain (3:13). The Lord's call "follow me" implies that the one who was so hated was now going to be used in the ministry of the gospel. Compare this with Aaron and Paul (as Saul) who were likewise transformed from the depths of sin to the heights of divine service (Exod 32:24; 1 Tim 1:15). In Matthew's case, there was a complete response: "he arose, and followed him". Luke 5:28 adds, "he left all". Sometimes new converts today have to leave certain kinds of employment which contain elements contrary to a true profession of faith – working as or under the modern form of "publican" is an example.

10 Hospitality immediately marked Matthew's changed life. Christians are exhorted to "use hospitality one to another without grudging" (1 Pet 4:9), and overseers in local assemblies must be "given to hospitality" (1 Tim 3:2). Mary, Martha and Lazarus used their home in Bethany to offer hospitality to the Lord; other examples are: Cornelius (Acts 10:24), Lydia (16:40), Aquila and Priscilla (18:2-3, 26; 1 Cor 16:19). In Matthew's case, the place is called "the house" (Matt 9:10), "*his* house" (Mark 2:15) and "*his own* house" (Luke 5:29). Matthew modestly describes the scene as "Jesus sat at meat", but Luke calls it a "great feast" (Luke 5:29). This was not just a social occasion, with undesirable publicans and sinners present at the meal. The Lord's time was better spent than that, and He explains later that He was present to engage in testimony and spiritual healing.

11 The presence of publicans and sinners in Matthew's house evoked criticism from the Pharisees who were always seeking occasion against the Lord. In Luke 5:30 their complaints were directed against the disciples, but here they complained about "your Master" (*didaskalos*, teacher). The overall accusation was equivalent to insinuating that the Lord was forming an unequal yoke (2 Cor 6:14), in the sense that the Pharisees were always occupied with maintaining separation from such folk according to their own definitions of ritualistic uncleanness.

12-13 Motives are all important; out of ignorant and hard hearts the Pharisees condemned the Lord by falsely assuming that they knew His motives. So the Lord explained in pictorial language and by an OT quotation why He was in such a company. It was *not* for the fellowship of feasting, but because He saw men as sick while He was a physician. The Lord regarded sin as Isa 1:5-6 puts it: "the whole head is sick, and the whole heart faint. From the sole of the foot even unto the head there is no soundness in it; but wounds, and bruises, and putrifying sores". Hence in that company His mission was "I am not come to call the righteous, but sinners to repentance". Of course, those who were righteous on their own accord formed an empty class of men. We read of the same class in Rom 2:7, "to them who by patient continuance in well doing seek for glory and honour and immortality, eternal life", but no man ever comes up to this standard, for "There is none righteous, no, not one" (Rom 3:10). Hence in the house of Matthew the Lord would call sinners to repentance, *never* being present to have a good time of feasting. Repentance is a practical turning of one's back on the past, facing forward instead unto the Lord. It is one of the ingredients of the gospel, though the full truth was available only after His death (Acts 20:21).

The Lord told the Pharisees to go and learn their own OT, "I will have mercy and not sacrifice" (Hos 6:6). Here, the word for "will" is not the future auxiliary, but *thelō*, expressing desire. A similar thought "to obey is better than sacrifice" appears in 1 Sam 15:22. In the two OT passages, the mercy and obedience are to be shown by men, such moral features transcending the formal offering of the Levitical sacrifices. But in the Lord's quotation, He appears to apply the showing of mercy to Himself; He was showing mercy by being present with sinners at the feast, a far more valuable occupation than being engaged in the temple services at the altar.

14-15 Verse 14 shows that there is sometimes far more behind a particular verse than contained in one Gospel only. Here, the question "Why do we and the Pharisees fast oft?" is asked by the disciples of John the Baptist, some of whom must have been present. In Luke 5:33 it appears that the Pharisees ask the question, but in Mark 2:18 the overall total is given: the disciples of John *and* the Pharisees ask the question. Such differences can be seen in the words placed by Pilate on the cross. The question contrasts the work of John with that of the

Lord. Both the disciples of John and the Pharisees fasted and prayed – John in the wilderness and the Pharisees in their religious circles. With John, repentance was there, so the exercises were true, while with the Pharisees it was formal and unacceptable. Christians too should pray without ceasing, but there is no bondage or formality about such exercise; unfortunately the lack of formality sometimes ensures that some may hardly engage in prayer at all.

The Lord answered the question by observing that the presence of the bridegroom should make everyone spiritually happy. But there is a hint of His death in this verse: "as long as the bridegroom is with them . . . when the bridegroom shall be taken from them". (There is another early hint of His death in John 2:19, "Destroy this temple".) When He was taken from them, then they would fast, and be "sorrowful" (John 16:20), though at that time "the world shall rejoice". Speaking along similar lines, John the Baptist said that "the friend of the bridegroom . . . rejoiceth greatly" (John 3:29), though in that statement he did not anticipate the Lord's death. Only in John 16:19-22 did the Lord imply His resurrection when the disciples' sorrow would be turned into joy.

But between His death and His subsequent resurrection, "then shall they fast". We assume that this is what they were doing in the upper room after His death waiting for something that their faith could not believe would actually happen.

16-17 In Luke 5:36-39, these two word-pictures are called "a parable". But Matthew avoids this word in the present context for a very good reason that is in keeping with the structure of his Gospel; not until ch.13 do we find parables in Matthew's Gospel.

The "new cloth" represents the new gospel message preached by the Lord; it cannot be used to patch up the failings of the outworking of the law, "an old garment" . Men may try to perpetuate the law, as in Acts 15, in Galatians, and in Hebrews. But the two materials are inconsistent the one with the other as can be seen by contrasting the old and the new covenants (Heb 8:1 to 10:18). The law would ensure that "Christ is dead in vain" (Gal 2:21), whereby no flesh can be justified. But the new material would ensure that the Spirit is received by the "hearing of faith" (3:2), that the Spirit now works in our hearts as sons (4:6) and that the Spirit leads us and brings forth His gracious fruit (5:18, 22).

The "new wine" speaks typically of joy in the Holy Spirit, possessed when things are new in Christ. He can come only on those blessed under the new covenant, not under the old. Otherwise the bottles would burst and perish. The Spirit would have fallen in judgment on the nation had He come before Pentecost: "whose fan is in his hand . . . he will burn up the chaff" (Matt 3:12); "that which beareth thorns and briers is rejected, and is nigh unto cursing" (Heb 6:8). But "new wine into new bottles" speaks of Pentecost, the Spirit taking up those who are a new creation in Christ: now, the believer's body is the temple of the Holy Spirit (1 Cor 6:19); "the Spirit of truth . . . dwelleth with you, and shall be in you" (John 14:17; 7:38-39). Luke 5:39 adds that men usually do not desire the new wine, saying "the old is better". In John 2:10 the new wine was better! The old nature of the Pharisees desired the old wine – their own religion of law and ceremony. Only converts desire the manifestation of the Spirit; they do not look back and claim that preconversion days were better (Num 11:4-6). This desire today can seek the best gifts of the Spirit (1 Cor 14:1) can seek the production of spiritual fruit (Gal 5:22), and can appreciate spiritual song (Eph 5:18-20). To return to the bondage of the law is to say "the old is better"; this describes any system of religion that is based on the OT with priests, altars, choirs, veils, incense, temples, vestments and so on.

3. *Two Miracles with the Number Twelve* 9:18-26

v.18 "While he spake these things unto them, behold, there came a certain ruler, and worshipped him, saying, My daughter is even now dead: but come and lay thy hand upon her, and she shall live.
v.19 And Jesus arose, and followed him, and *so did* his disciples.
v.20 And, behold, a woman, which was diseased with an issue of blood twelve years, came behind *him,* and touched the hem of his garment:
v.21 For she said within herself, If I may but touch his garment, I shall be whole.
v.22 But Jesus turned him about, and when he saw her, he said, Daughter, be of good comfort; thy faith hath made thee whole. And the woman was made whole from that hour.
v.23 And when Jesus came into the ruler's house, and saw the minstrels and the people making a noise,
v.24 He said unto them, Give place: for the maid is not dead, but sleepeth. And they laughed him to scorn.
v.25 But when the people were put forth, he went in, and took her by the hand, and the maid arose.
v.26 And the fame hereof went abroad into all that land."

A fuller account of these two miracles is contained in Mark 5:22-43 and Luke 8:41-56. In Luke 8:40, the people were "all waiting for him" to return, and "gladly received him". This is a prophetic picture of Israel; since both miracles contain the same number twelve, they refer to the same idea. Israel, as a nation in unbelief and spiritual death, awaits the Deliverer out of Zion, and faith will be formed when Messiah comes with healing.

18-19 Jairus is named in Mark and Luke; as a "ruler" (*archōn*) he was perhaps a priest presiding over the synagogue service, but formal religion was of no help either to salvation or to life. Yet his faith and humility were shown by his falling down at the Lord's feet and worshipping Him. The ruler knew by faith that the Lord could raise the dead! The number twelve in the story represents what God takes up for Himself out of the world, such as twelve tribes of Israel and the twelve apostles. Matthew's account is abbreviated, since at the beginning of the story in Mark and Luke the girl was "at the point of death" and "lay a dying" but here she was "even now dead".

There were, in fact, two messages: the first that she was dying, and the second that she was dead.

So the Lord "followed him", in contrast to v.9 where Matthew followed the Lord. Of course the Lord knew where Jairus' house was, but the story is told from the point of view of an observer watching the ordinary movements of men.

20 Whereas the girl as dead did not know of her state, here we find a woman who did know of her state. The fact that her distressing disease could not "be healed of any" (Luke 8:43) suggests spiritually that salvation is not of man: spiritual birth is not of the will of man, but of God (John 1:13); salvation is "not of works, lest any man should boast" (Eph 2:9); it is "not according to our works, but according to his own purpose and grace" (2 Tim 1:9). Today, many think that they have salvation through their works, but this results in ultimate disappointment, as in this woman's case who had "spent all her living upon physicians" (Luke 8:43), that is all her life had been devoted to seeking natural means for the healing of her perpetual haemorrhage. Natural means are available today, and there is nothing wrong in seeking such help.

21 It would appear that the woman wanted neither the people nor the Lord to know of her complaint. But there was faith, acting when the opportunity presented itself: "If I may but touch his garment, I shall be whole". The clothing possessed no intrinsic power in itself, but His raiment was such that it could shine with the light within on the mountain top (Matt 17:2). This recalls Isa 6:1, where "the train" (the hem of the divine garment) filled the temple. The touch can be likened to a lightning flash, when a pathway for the passage of electricity is first formed through the air, after which the electric power traverses it. Here, the touch was a pathway for the transfer of divine power. The contact was made by faith, providing a spiritual path for the free flow of salvation.

22 The verb "to be made whole" (*sōzō*) occurs three times in these verses; it is the usual verb "to save". The first time it was used by the women (in the *future* tense); the second time by the Lord (in the *perfect* tense); the third time by Matthew in his narrative (in the *aorist* tense). The perfect tense implies that the act was done, and its results continued afterwards—namely, there was no recurrence of the trouble, for a divine miracle is immediate, complete and lasting

In the Lord's statement, "be of good comfort; thy faith hath made thee whole", "good comfort" refers to the woman *mentally* since she was trembling in fear and awkwardness; "faith" refers to her *spiritually*, and "made whole" refers to her *physically* since the disease of twelve years standing had disappeared immediately. This recalls the God of peace preserving our "whole spirit and soul and body" until the coming of the Lord Jesus (1 Thess 5:23). After healing has come through faith, James 2:14 takes over. The answer to the question "Can faith save him?" is that faith is dead if there are no subsequent works. Certainly genuine faith accomplishes works, since a person cannot be the same after having received salvation as before it.

23-26 Here we find a special occasion, when only five were allowed to witness the Lord's work of power. Similarly, Peter was alone when Tabitha was raised (Acts 9:40); Elisha was alone when the miracle on the child was accomplished (2 Kings 4:33); Moses and Joshua alone ascended Sinai to receive the details of the law and the tabernacle (Exod 24:13); only Abraham and Isaac ascended Moriah for sacrifice (Gen 22:2); Peter, James and John alone were taken by the Lord into Jairus' house, up the mount of transfiguration (Matt 17:1), and into the garden of Gethsemane (26:37), so these three apostles saw His power, glory and sufferings.

In the house there were "minstrels" (*aulētēs,* a player on a pipe or flute); Mark 5:38 mentions "the tumult, and them that wept and wailed greatly", this being the Jewish method of showing grief; people were hired to make such an artificial tumult and wailing. There are two Greek words translated "sleep". Here in connection with the statement " the maid is not dead, but sleepeth", the word is *katheudō,* occurring 22 times in the NT, chiefly meaning physical sleep, but sometimes death (and also metaphorically in 1 Thess 5:10). The second word *koimaomai* occurs 18 times, and includes death (Matt 27:52; John 11:11; Acts 7:60; 1 Cor 15:6; 1 Thess 4:13, 14, 15). There may be a difficulty therefore, in that some expositors suggest that the girl was not dead, but only unconscious, because the Lord said "the maid is not dead" . Yet in the light of the miracle, we feel that the Lord implied "she is not irrevocably dead". Luke, being a physician, ascertained the facts, and in Luke 8:53 he wrote, "knowing that she was dead". Hence the tumult-makers "laughed him to scorn", a single word in Greek (*katagelaō*), meaning "derisive laughter". The word appears only three times in the NT (in this story in Matt, Mark and Luke), and several times in the OT (2 Chron 30:10, LXX).

"The people were put forth", since the miracle was not going to be done before the eyes of unbelief; (see Matt 21:12 and John 2:15 where the Lord drove men out of the temple courts). The Lord touched the girl's hand; here was passage of divine power direct from the infinite reservoir. In Luke 8:54, He addressed her directly, "Maid", as elsewhere He said "Young man" and "Lazarus" so that only those addressed should be raised from the dead. After the miracle, in Luke 8:56, the Lord charged the parents that "they should tell no man what was done"; there should be no direct testimony to those in unbelief on the outside. Of course, men would learn the news in due time, but not from the parents, who might have then been subjected to the same inquisition as were the parents in John 9: 18-23.

4. *The Blind, the Dumb and the Fainting* 9:27-38

v.27 "And when Jesus departed thence, two blind men followed him, crying, and saying, *Thou* Son of David, have mercy on us.
v.28 And when he was come into the house, the blind men came to him: and Jesus saith unto them, Believe ye that I am able to do this? They said unto him, Yea, Lord.
v.29 Then touched he their eyes, saying, According to your faith be it unto you.
v.30 And their eyes were opened; and Jesus straitly charged them, saying, See *that* no man know *it*.
v.31 But they, when they were departed, spread abroad his fame in all that country.
v.32 As they went out, behold, they brought to him a dumb man possessed with a devil.
v.33 And when the devil was cast out, the dumb spake: and the multitudes marvelled, saying, It was never so seen in Israel.
v.34 But the Pharisees said, He casteth out devils through the prince of the devils.
v.35 And Jesus went about all the cities and villages, teaching in their synagogues, and preaching the gospel of the kingdom, and healing every sickness and every disease among the people.
v.36 But when he saw the multitudes, he was moved with compassion on them, because they fainted, and were scattered abroad, as sheep having no shepherd.
v.37 Then saith he unto his disciples, The harvest truly *is* plenteous, but the labourers *are* few;
v.38 Pray ye therefore the Lord of the harvest, that he will send forth labourers into his harvest."

27 There are three miracles of a similar nature in the Synoptic Gospels, and they should not be confused one with another. The present event took place at or near Capernaum, and there were *two* blind men involved. The second event took place as the Lord was entering into Jericho; *one* blind man was involved (Luke 18:35-43). The third event took place as the Lord left Jericho; in Mark 10:46-52 *one* blind man was involved, named Bartimaeus, while in the corresponding account in Matt 20:30-34 *two* blind men were involved. The similarity is remarkable, but of course news spreads (Matt 9:31); what He had done once other blind men would learn about; faith would anticipate meeting Him, using the same words to gain His attention and sympathy. In our present verse, they said, "Thou Son of David, have mercy on us"; in Matt 20:31 they said "Have mercy on us, O Lord, thou Son of David"; in Mark 10:47 Bartimaeus said, "Jesus, thou Son of David, have mercy on me" (repeated in v.48), in Luke 18:37, 38, having heard that "Jesus of Nazareth" was passing by, the one blind man said "Jesus, thou Son of David, have mercy on me". In the last three references, the men had learnt that Jesus was passing by; they then provided the additional title "Son of David". This was the Lord essentially in His relationship as pertaining to Israel; it was a Messianic title. No doubt this title was common knowledge, but only men of faith could use it in any proper way. Alas, that His titles can often be thrown about without reverence!

28-31 These men knew what they wanted, and they had faith to obtain it. They compare favourably with the apostles at the foot of the mount of Transfiguration; their impotence caused the Lord to remark, "Because of your unbelief" (Matt 17:20). To such faith the Lord responded, He touched their eyes, as He did in many of His miracles of healing. By such contact, virtue or power went out from the Lord as an infinite divine reservoir of power accomplishing miracles according to His will. The details of this miracle must be contrasted with those of the healing of the blind man in John 9. At the start, it appears that the man did not have faith and he did not ask for healing, he merely followed instructions. In his testimony afterwards, he claimed that "this man" could do nothing if He were not of God (v.33), but he finally confessed "I believe" after the Lord had revealed Himself to him as the Son of God (vv.35-37). Spiritually this miracle speaks of evangelistic effort "to open their eyes" (Acts 26:18); prophetically, the miracle shows what will be done in the future to remove the blindness of the nation of Israel, "Then the eyes of the blind shall be opened" (Isa 35:5), "to open the blind eyes" (42:7). Note that the quotation "recovering of sight to the blind" made in the synagogue in Nazareth is not found in the Hebrew OT (Isa 61:1).

32-33 Whereas the previous miracle had been done in "the house" (v.28), this miracle on a dumb man was done outside in the public view. "Possessed with a devil" is one verb in Greek: *daimonizomai* – the word "demon" should always be used, not "devil". Demon possession was manifested in various ways – in this case, the man was dumb. Clearly this was not a physical defect, otherwise it would have been described differently (Mark 7:32). The removal of the demon enabled the man to speak, and the people claimed that nothing like that had been seen in Israel before. They may have been correct (at least in their experience), for only *after* this event are such miracles recorded (Matt 12:22; 15:30).

34 If the scribes had accused abominably the Lord of blasphemy (Matt 9:3), the Pharisees now engage in blasphemy themselves. This is repeated in Matt 12:24, causing the Lord to alter His whole approach to His ministry amongst men.

35 Yet the Lord waited long before He changed His tactics, just as the longsuffering of God had waited long in the days of Noah (1 Pet 3:20). For the reader should compare this verse with Matt 4:23, and note that they are almost identical. In other words, the methods of the Lord's ministry remained unchanged; He continued as He had started – *teaching with miracles,* until ch. 13 when the style of His ministry deliberately changes.

36 Yet even after the change in style of His ministry, the heart of love of the

Lord was still the same. The same description "moved with compassion" occurs in Matt 14:14, *after* the change of style in Matt 13 when parables were introduced, followed by the feeding of the 5,000. The same event appears in Mark 6:34, where the Lord was "moved with compassion", followed by the feeding of the 5,000. Yet the people being "as sheep having no shepherd" occurs *before* the change in style in Matt 9: 36, and *after* it in Mark 6:34. For the nation had no real leaders or pastors; the Herods, Pharisees and priests sought merely their own power, caring nothing for the multitudes under them politically and religiously. Later the Lord would present Himself as the Good Shepherd (John 10:14), the Great Shepherd (Heb 13:20), and the Chief Shepherd (1 Pet 5:4).

37-38 This compassion stretched to all "the lost sheep of the house of Israel" (Matt 10:6). Yet the Lord's ministry in His Manhood was deliberately restricted to serve only those who were in the immediate vicinity. He then changed the picture from a pastoral scene to a harvest scene. He used a similar picture in John 4:34-38; He was the One who had sown, while His disciples could reap the harvest. So the Lord called for prayer that labourers would be sent out to the fields. The same is said in Luke 10:2 under different circumstances. In the church, the Lord has many labourers, as Paul wrote, "we are labourers together" (1 Cor 3:9).

VI. The Apostolic Mission to Israel (10:1-42)

1. *The Apostles Empowered and Sent Forth* 10:1-6

v.1 "And when he had called unto *him* his twelve disciples, he gave them power *against* unclean spirits, to cast them out, and to heal all manner of sickness and all manner of disease.
v.2 Now the names of the twelve apostles are these; The first, Simon, who is called Peter, and Andrew his brother; James *the son* of Zebedee, and John his brother;
v.3 Philip, and Bartholomew; Thomas, and Matthew the publican; James *the son* of Alphaeus, and Lebbaeus, whose surname was Thaddaeus;
v.4 Simon the Canaanite, and Judas Iscariot, who also betrayed him.
v.5 These twelve Jesus sent forth, and commanded them, saying, Go not into the way of the Gentiles, and into *any* city of the Samaritans enter ye not:
v.6 But go rather to the lost sheep of the house of Israel."

1 The emergence of the twelve as a group, and the titles given to the group, deserve a detailed study. The title "apostles" or "twelve apostles" appears first in Matt 10:2; Mark 6:30 and Luke 6:13; it does not appear in John's Gospel. The name "apostle" (*apostolos*) is derived from the verb *apostellō*, to send forth. It was a technical name given to a very small band of men, including Paul from Acts 14:4 onwards. In a non-technical sense Barnabas was called an apostle (14:14) .

Apostleship was a spiritual gift (1 Cor 12:28; Eph 4:11), and there were false apostles (2 Cor 11:13; Rev 2:2). On occasions, this band of men were just called "the twelve" (John 6:67-71; 20:24). On other occasions (not in John) they were called the "twelve disciples" (Matt 10:1; 11:1; 20:17; Luke 9:1). The name "disciple" (*mathētēs*) is derived from the verb *manthanō*, to learn. In a nontechnical sense, the title was applied to many of the Lord's followers, but its use in the NT suddenly ceases in Acts 21:16 "an old disciple", leading some to suggest that this title should not be used of Christians today.

On occasions the Lord sent forth men who were not apostles; in Luke 10:1 He "appointed other seventy also, and sent them two and two before his face", these also were labourers sent into His harvest (v.2). The instructions given to these seventy (Luke 10:1-12) were similar to those given to the twelve apostles (Matt 10:5-15). To both groups the Lord gave the power to cast out unclean spirits and demons (Luke 10:17); whereas the apostles had power to "heal all manner of sickness and all manner of disease", yet this is not stated of the seventy. Not all disciples are gifted in every way (1 Cor 12:7-31).

Matt 10:1 is not the first time that this band of men had been called together; rather this had occurred previously in Luke 6:13-16 on quite a different occasion. There are, in fact, four stages by which a believer is called for a particular work; we illustrate this with reference to Peter and Paul.

Nature of call	Peter's case	Paul's case
1. A call to Christ	John 1:42	Acts 9:1-9
2. A call to general service	Luke 5:10	Acts 22:17-21
3. A call to special service	Luke 6:13-14	Acts 11:25-26
4. A call to particular service	Matt 10:1-5	Acts 13:1-4

2-3 The Lord called a large number of disciples, but only a small number of apostles, "many be called, but few chosen" (Matt 20:16). In this apostolic register, Peter is placed first, while Judas the betrayer is placed last. As a matter of interest, Peter occurs first in all the recorded lists of the apostles, including that in Acts 1:13. In any list it was easy for the writer to place Judas last, since his evil deed was long since past. But the Lord knew that he would be the traitor right from the beginning, "Have I not chosen you twelve, and one of you is a devil?" (John 6:70). In fact, none could be lost, except the son of perdition that the Scriptures might be fulfilled (17:12; Ps 109:7-8).

Space is not available to detail all the characteristics and activities of these apostles; interested readers can consult *God's People and God's Purpose,* by A. Naismith & W. F. Naismith. In this connection, we should mention "Simon the Canaanite" (*ho Kananitēs,* the Cananite, or *ho Kananaios,* the Cananaean, RV). In Luke 6:15 the name is "Simon called Zelotes" (*Zēlōtēs*, a zealot, full of zeal). "The Canaanite" title has no connection with the familiar Canaan of the OT.

5-6 The twelve were sent forth in six groups: "two and two" (Mark 6:7), as in the case of the seventy later (Luke 10:1). No doubt this was for companionship and fellowship, but spiritually because "the testimony of two men is true" John 8:17). Thus later Peter and John were together (Acts 3:1), as were Paul and Barnabas (13:2), Paul and Silas (15:40). John the Baptist was an exception, being a lonely single voice in the wilderness; the Lord too was an exception, His testimony and that of the Father being sufficient (John 8:16). The apostles' instructions were that they were not to go to the Gentiles or to the Samaritans. This was essentially the privilege of the Jews who, as a nation, had brought in Christ; it was to these "lost sheep" that He had been sent. At the beginning of the apostles' post-ascension testimony, this instruction was still kept. The gospel was "to the Jew first, and also to the Greek" (Rom 1:16); this was the historical order until Acts 13:46 when Paul said, "It was necessary that the word of God should first have been spoken to you . . . lo, we turn to the Gentiles". As Paul wrote elsewhere, the diminishing of the Jews was for the riches of the Gentiles (Rom 11:12), and it was in keeping with the Lord's command in Acts 1:8, "in Jerusalem, and in all Judaea, and in Samaria, and unto the uttermost part of the earth". Yet the Samaritans and Gentiles were not neglected before Acts 13:46, since the Lord brought salvation to the Samaritan woman and her city in John 4 and healing to the Gentile woman's daughter in Matt 15:21-29. And the Jews were not neglected after Acts 13:46, since Paul usually went into the synagogues on his missionary journeys (Acts 14:1; 17:1-2, and so on). Today, evangelists go where they are led by the Lord; it would be wrong to assert, as some do, that evangelists must now-a-days always go "first" to the Jews.

The NT always distinguishes the Samaritans from the Gentiles. They descended from those planted in the northern kingdom after the Assyrian captivity (2 Kings 17:24). Their own cult developed with the assistance of an imported priest (v.27); they had their own temple as a rival to that in Jerusalem, and possessed the Pentateuch though not the whole of the OT. But in these days of grace, the gospel goes out to all, and the " middle wall of partition" is broken down (Eph 2:14); the only division is between "the Jews . . . the Gentiles . . . the church of God" (1 Cor 10:32).

The organisation of the rest of the chapter should be noted:

vv.7-15 Details of that particular missionary journey amongst the cities of Israel, and under those special circumstances.

vv.16-23 The beginning of evangelistic activity in the Acts, leading on to the testimony of the remnant during the great tribulation (compare v.22 with 24:13).

vv.24-42 General principles of service for all times.

2. *The Mission of the Twelve* 10:7-15

v.7 "And as ye go, preach, saying, The kingdom of heaven is at hand.
v.8 Heal the sick, cleanse the lepers, raise the dead, cast out devils: freely ye have received, freely give.
v.9 Provide neither gold, nor silver, nor brass in your purses,
v.10 Nor scrip for *your* journey, neither two coats, neither shoes, not yet staves: for the workman is worthy of his meat.
v.11 And into whatsoever city or town ye shall enter, enquire who in it is worthy; and there abide till ye go thence.
v.12 And when ye come into an house, salute it.
v.13 And if the house be worthy, let your peace come upon it: but if it be not worthy, let your peace return to you.
v.14 And whosoever shall not receive you, nor hear your words, when ye depart out of that house or city, shake off the dust of your feet.
v.15 Verily I say unto you, It shall be more tolerable for the land of Sodom and Gomorrha in the day of judgment, than for that city."

7 The essential message was still the same, having been initiated by John the Baptist in Matt 3:2, and continued by the Lord in 4:17. The kingdom of heaven was "at hand" (*ēngiken*, has drawn near) because the opportunity was being offered to the Jews when the King was present amongst them, though this direct form of presentation would be removed in ch.13.

8 These special gifts were given both then and in the early church in the Acts during the transitional period leading to the time when spiritual gifts were operative for heart and soul rather than for the body. These gifts of healing, cleansing, raising and casting out had been "freely given". It is the same in the church, where God's servants are " ministers . . . even as *the Lord gave* to every man" (1 Cor 3:5). It was the same in the OT; the priests and Levites freely received their portion at the command of Hezekiah (2 Chron 31:4).

Of "freely give," one writer has quaintly put it, "the service we give is the rent that we pay for our room on earth". The service of the Lord's disciples must be free, otherwise there are some who will lose out, not being able to pay for such spiritual luxuries; "come ye, buy, and eat . . . without money and without price" (Isa 55:1). Paul would " make the gospel of Christ without charge" (1 Cor 9:18), even though this attitude would ensure that some of the Corinthians would reject his apostleship. The "flock of God" had to be fed "not by constraint, but willingly; not for filthy lucre, but of a ready mind" (1 Pet 5:2). Of course there must be provision made for the Lord's servants, for "the labourer is worthy of his hire" (Luke 10:7; Matt 10:10); evangelists should be able to "live of the gospel", if the work is not thereby hindered (1 Cor 9:12, 14). Such verses make no provision for a permanent religious employment with the assurance of a regular stipend which is the very opposite of faith in the Lord's service.

9-10 "Provide neither gold . . ." does not mean that nothing was to be taken on the journey. The word *ktaomai*, translated "get you" in the RV, means to procure for oneself, to acquire. The Lord is therefore talking about special *extra* provisions as distinct from those that are ready at hand. No time was to be spent on obtaining things that would be provided by others on the journey. Mark 6:8-9 implies that "nothing" should be taken except a staff, sandals and one coat. Certainly Peter and John had no silver and gold (Acts 3:6) because no-one in the early church had his own personal possessions. The word used for "purses" (*zōnē*) means a girdle or belt, and could be used for carrying money. The "scrip" (*pēra*) was a leather bag for the journey containing the traveller's possessions; it is translated "wallet" in the RV. The "two coats" (*chitō n*, an inner garment) implies that nothing extra was to be taken; the journey was to be commenced in haste with no special preparation; only one was to be taken (Mark 6:9). Similarly we understand by "shoes" that only one pair was to be taken, that being worn at the time (Mark 6:9). Strictly, the word for "staves" (*rhabdos*) is in the singular, but we understand this to be an extra one, since Mark 6:8 allows "a staff only".

We should ask the question, to what extent is this command applicable generally to all evangelical work, as distinct from this one specific occasion? Luke 22:35-36 recalls this event, when the apostles lacked nothing. Yet the Lord added, "But now, he that hath a purse, let him take it, and likewise his scrip (wallet)", implying that in the church period it would be quite legitimate for provision to be made for evangelistic missions. But there is a lesson: in all service, avoid the impression of prosperity over and above that of one's hearers.

During such an apostolic mission, "the workman is worthy of his meat" (*trophē* food, RV). In other words, the apostles had to look to divine provision in all things. The Lord opens the hearts of men to provide, but this does not mean that His servants must look to men and not to Him. Missionaries who go forth in faith need our prayers that they should not fall into trusting in organisations that furnish gifts regularly, even when they know the approximate date on which such gifts will be received. See 1 Cor 9:7-14 where Paul explains these principles in detail, though he would never avail himself of such provisions, working always with his own hands to supply his needs (Acts 20:34).

11-13 "Whatsoever city or town" (*polis* and *kōmē*) is translated in the RV as "city or village". The apostles had to seek out a worthy house and a worthy person. Here would be a household willing to receive the message; perhaps those who were disciples already would be living there. It is good to seek out the people of God in a strange place; thus Paul sought out Aquila and Priscilla in Corinth (Acts 18:2), and he found disciples in Tyre (21:4) and later at Sidon (27:3). This is fellowship that the Lord's people can show, offering hospitality to the Lord's servants passing through. We may quote: Paul joined himself to the disciples in Jerusalem (Acts 9:26-28); Peter came down to the saints at Lydda (v.32); Peter stayed in Caesarea, no doubt with Cornelius (10:48); Paul stayed in the home of Gaius in Corinth (Rom 16:23). A "worthy" house was a receptive house, suitable as a base for evangelistic endeavour. Additionally the peace of mind and heart that characterised the apostles was to promote a spiritual atmosphere in the house, for their attitude was gentle, patient and loving, as distinct from harsh, sharp and critical. Paul always greeted his readers with grace and peace – not the peace that the world formally offered, but the peace of Christ Himself (John 14:27). But if, upon further investigation, the house proved not to be worthy, then nothing was to be left in it since nothing had been received from it. The servants were to leave unruffled; they would depart in peace as they had arrived in peace, in keeping with 2 Tim 2:24, "the servant of the Lord must not strive; but be gentle unto all men, apt to teach, patient".

14 If the apostles and their words were rejected, then the house was to be given up; it had lost its opportunity, and all contact with the apostles was lost as they moved onwards. Typically, this speaks of the Jews as a nation in the OT. God had spoken to them by the prophets, and then by John the Baptist and finally by the Lord; but He will not always strive with men; see Prov 1:24-33 where there would be no answer from God. As a nation they had tasted the good word of God, but had fallen away, so the opportunity was lost (Heb 6:5-6). Today, a person or a household would not have had such an abundance of opportunities, so an evangelist cannot just give them up as if God had bypassed them. Alas that the apostles had to "shake off the dust of your feet", leaving the house entirely as it had been when they entered; how this contrasts with "How beautiful are the feet of them that preach the gospel of peace" (Rom 10:15). An example of this occurred in Antioch; the Jewish rejection of the word ensured that Paul and Barnabas "shook off the dust of their feet against them, and came unto Iconium" (Acts 13:51), though in the new era of Christianity they returned later (14:20-23).

15 Men today would regard such a house or city no doubt as moral and upright, when they compare such behaviour with that of Sodom and Gomorrha. But God's assessment in judgment is quite different. The sin of these OT cities was "very grievous" (Gen 18:20), though they had the testimony of "just Lot" in their midst, and though they had the opportunity of the natural creation that gave testimony to "his eternal power and Godhead" (Rom 1:20). But in Matt 10, the privileges of the Jews were greater, and seeing the Lord's "mighty works" was a further privilege. Thus all will be judged on account of sin, but there will also be taken into account the degree of response to revealed privilege. The deeper the privilege, the less tolerable it will be. This subject is developed further in Matt 11:20-24.

3. *Evangelistic Testimony through the Ages* 10:16-23

v.16 "Behold, I send you forth as sheep in the midst of wolves: be ye therefore wise as serpents, and harmless as doves.
v.17 But beware of men: for they will deliver you up to the councils, and they will scourge you in their synagogues;
v.18 And ye shall be brought before governors and kings for my sake, for a testimony against them and the Gentiles.
v.19 But when they deliver you up, take no thought how or what ye shall speak: for it shall be given you in that same hour what ye shall speak.
v.20 For it is not ye that speak, but the Spirit of your Father which speaketh in you.
v.21 And the brother shall deliver up the brother to death, and the father the child: and the children shall rise up against *their* parents, and cause them to be put to death.
v.22 And ye shall be hated of all *men* for my name's sake: but he that endureth to the end shall be saved.
v.23 But when they persecute you in this city, flee ye into another: for verily I say unto you, Ye shall not have gone over the cities of Israel, till the Son of man be come."

16 These verses take us right from the apostolic days when the Lord was here up to the remnant-testimony prior to the Lord's coming in glory. The Lord's servants would be as sheep amongst wolves – not sheep without a shepherd (Matt 9:36), but under the control of the Good Shepherd. Wolves would always be active, seeking to damage the true testimony, whether Pharisees (Matt 7:15) or those seeking entrance into the local assembly (Acts 20:29). They would be under the control of "the wolf", Satan himself (John 10:12), who would also appear as a "roaring lion . . . seeking whom he may devour" (1 Pet 5:8). Thus Paul had been a wolf before his conversion (Acts 9:1; 26:9-11). These sheep were to show wisdom and harmlessness – a hard combination. The word for "wise" (*phronimos*) is prudent and wise practically as distinct from doctrinal wisdom. This can, of course, be exercised in a bad sense as well, such as seen in the subtle activity of Satan. One therefore has to take great care in one's movements amongst the wolves, not only for one's own sake, but also not to preempt the opportunity of evangelistic work amongst these wolves. This can be seen in Phil 2:15, where the Lord's people must be "blameless and harmless . . . in the midst of a crooked and perverse nation", the examples of Christ, Paul, Timothy and Epaphroditus being cited to illustrate such behaviour.

17-18 "Beware of men" full of religious bigotry and opposition to the truth (2 Tim 4:15). Elsewhere, Paul wrote "Beware of dogs, beware of evil workers" (Phil 3:2), for there was opposition from both Gentiles end Jews. Such men would bring the Lord's servants before "the councils" (*sunedrion*, in its plural form). When in Jerusalem, this would refer to the Jewish Sanhedrin, consisting of a large number of priests, elders and scribes, having authority to try criminal cases. Thus Peter and John appeared before this council in Acts 4:5-22; 5:27-41, where they were threatened and beaten; Paul likewise appeared before this council in Acts 23:1-9. Such beatings took place in the OT (Matt 21:35); Paul records that he regularly suffered stripes, beatings and stoning (2 Cor 11:24-25); the church martyrs during the Reformation period suffered torture and death at the stake. So often this was done in the name of religion, "in their synagogues" as the Lord said. How often has religion been used as a cloke for the lust and cruelty that exist in the hearts of some men. But on several occasions the Lord warned that this would be so, at least during certain periods of testimony on earth: "If they have persecuted me, they will also persecute you" (John 15:20); "They shall put you out of the synagogues . . . whosoever killeth you will think that he doeth God service" (16:2). In Rev 11:7-8, the two witnesses will be overcome and killed in the great city, spiritually called Sodom and Egypt, where the Lord was crucified.

These sheep in the midst of wolves would be brought before the highest authorities in the land – "governors and kings" – for the Lord's sake. Thus James was killed by Herod, and Peter was imprisoned (Acts 12:1-4). Paul would bear the name of Christ before the Gentiles and kings (9:15), so he appeared before Sergius Paulus, Gallio, Felix, Festus and Agrippa, while at the end of his life he appeared before Nero, the cruel and abominable emperor in Rome. They were but following the footsteps of their Lord, against whom the kings and rulers had set themselves (Ps 2:1-2; Acts 4:27), a verse that has prophetical implications at the end times (Rev 17:14). The AV "for a testimony *against* them and the Gentiles" should read "to them" (RV), the Greek merely being the dative plural *autois*. God would use the evil designs of men to provide an opportunity for the truth to be presented to them, as in the case of Felix (Acts 24:25) and king Agrippa (26:12-23). Admittedly, it was "against" them as well, for Paul was "the savour of death unto death" (2 Cor 2:16).

19-20 When standing before such evil opponents of the truth, the disciples were not to take " thought how or what" they were to speak, namely, they were not to be anxious or careful, as in Matt 6:25. As the Father provides for the physical needs of His people when they seek first the kingdom of God, so He provides the words of testimony in times of special need. In a similar passage in Mark 13:9-11 (though spoken at a different time), " neither do ye premeditate" is added. Thus in Exod 4:12 the promise was made to Moses that God would be with his mouth to teach him what to say. In Jer 1:9 the Lord touched Jeremiah's mouth, saying "I have put my words in thy mouth". And such words will be by the Holy Spirit. Thus when Peter was before the council for the first time, his answer was given as "filled with the Holy Spirit" (Acts 4:8; 5:29). We recall that the inspiration of the Scriptures was achieved by holy men of God being moved by the Holy Spirit (2 Pet 1:21). Yet this does not imply that those who preach the gospel or minister the Word of God to the Lord's people need make no preparation beforehand. Luke wrote his

Gospel by inspiration, yet he did not just sit down and write at random trusting that he would be guided by the Spirit; rather, beforehand he had had the necessary benefit of diligent enquiry into the matters about which he was to write to Theophilus (Luke 1:1-4).

21 As well as persecution by the religious and political leaders, there may be persecution within families. Similar circumstances were predicted by the Lord in Luke 21:16. This does not appear to refer to the end times, since Luke 21:20, 24 suggest that AD 70 and the destruction of Jerusalem are in view. Certainly no such events are recorded in the Acts. On the mission field today, it may occur in lands where certain false religions hold sway. Turning to Christ and being baptised because of faith may lead to family persecution even unto death. In our country, lesser persecution may take place within the family circle when a young convert has parents who ridicule the truth of salvation through the blood of Christ. But take heart, many such parents have ultimately been saved!

22 This verse shows the ultimate of persecution and hatred, since "all" men are involved. Believers are not to be friends of the world, but they do not invite persecution during a period when no persecution is forthcoming. There has been speculation as to what "the end" may mean. Some suggest that it is personal referring to the end of the trial through which persecution takes a believer (1 Pet 1:4-7). Others suggest that it refers to the siege and destruction of Jerusalem by the Romans AD 70. Neither of these appeals to the author, since the next verse is prophetic—the time of the coming of the Son of man in glory. Hence we think that the end refers to the end period after the church has been taken, during the period known as the Great Tribulation. Certainly Matt 24:9, 13 refer to this period – being hated of all nations and "he that shall endure unto the end, the same shall be saved".

23 Under these circumstances, do not constantly strive with Christ-rejectors. The work of testimony is not abandoned, but is continued elsewhere. Thus Paul left Antioch, Iconium and Lystra (Acts 13:51; 14:6, 20), teaching "that we must through much tribulation enter into the kingdom of God" (v.22). When the Lord said, " Ye shall not have gone over the cities of Israel", He was thinking *far beyond* the mission on which He was sending His apostles. The period of the Great Tribulation will be limited to three and a half years, and difficulties will be such that the testimony of the faithful ones will not have spread over all the territory of the enemy, the population at large being deceived by the anti-Christ, the man of sin, sitting in the temple. We shall comment in greater detail on the coming of the Son of man in glory in Matt 24:30. This event will terminate the spread of true testimony against a background of persecution and rejection.

4. *General Principles of Service for all Times* 10:24-42

v.24 "The disciple is not above *his* master, nor the servant above his lord.
v.25 It is enough for the disciple that he be as his master, and the servant as his lord. If they have called the master of the house Beelzebub, how much more *shall they call* them of his household?
v.26 Fear them not therefore: for there is nothing covered, that shall not be revealed; and hid, that shall not be known.
v.27 What I tell you in darkness, *that* speak ye in light: and what ye hear in the ear, *that* preach ye upon the housetops.
v.28 And fear not them which kill the body, but are not able to kill the soul: but rather fear him which is able to destroy both soul and body in hell.
v.29 Are not two sparrows sold for a farthing? and one of them shall not fall on the ground without your Father.
v.30 But the very hairs of your head are all numbered.
v.31 Fear ye not therefore, ye are of more value than many sparrows.
v.32 Whosoever therefore shall confess me before men, him will I confess also before my Father which is in heaven.
v.33 But whosoever shall deny me before men, him will I also deny before my Father which is in heaven.
v.34 Think not that I am come to send peace on earth: I came not to send peace, but a sword.
v.35 For I am come to set a man at variance against his father, and the daughter against her mother, and the daughter in law against her mother in law.
v.36 And a man's foes *shall be* they of his own household.
v.37 He that loveth father or mother more than me is not worthy of me: and he that loveth son or daughter more than me is not worthy of me.
v.38 And he that taketh not his cross, and followeth after me, is not worthy of me.
v.39 He that findeth his life shall lose it: and he that loseth his life for my sake shall find it.
v.40 He that receiveth you receiveth me, and he that receiveth me receiveth him that sent me.
v.41 He that receiveth a prophet in the name of a prophet shall receive a prophet's reward; and he that receiveth a righteous man in the name of a righteous man shall receive a righteous man's reward.
v.42 And whosoever shall give to drink unto one of these little ones a cup of cold *water* only in the name of a disciple, verily I say unto you, he shall in no wise lose his reward."

24-25 Several times the Lord quoted what appears to be a proverb: "The disciple is not above his master". Here it is in connection with an abominable accusation; in Luke 6:40 it is in connection with moral and spiritual completeness; in John 13:16 it is in connection with humility in dealing with the needs of others, in John 15:20 it is in connection with hatred and persecution. Three social relationships are used in this picture: learner – teacher; servant – lord; the household and the master of the house (*oikodespotēs*), all of which can be spiritualised. If blasphemy was rendered against the Lord, so would it be against His followers. Beelzebub (*Beelzeboul*) was the name of an idol worshipped by the Philistines (2 Kings 1:2), and was used as a name for Satan by the Jews. No doubt in our verse the Lord is quoting what existed in the inward thoughts of the Pharisees; such a bud gave rise to the actual fruit in Matt 12:24 when the

Pharisees stated such an accusation openly. In John 8:48, they made their accusation face-to-face to the Lord Jesus: "thou . . . hast a devil (demon)". In both cases there was a similar reaction. After Matt 12, the Pharisees *remained in ignorance* because the parables were designed to hide the truth; in John 9:39 they *remained blind.* Hence the servants of the Lord could not expect to be treated better than the Lord; Paul wanted to learn "the fellowship of his sufferings" (Phil 3:10).

26-27 In spite of these accusations and persecutions, these self-satisfied religious bigots are not to be feared. These two verses are susceptible of two interpretations.

1. The efforts of men cannot hinder the progress of the gospel, even if temporarily they believe that they have an advantage. The word spoken by the Lord to His servants can be proclaimed openly, even when circumstances seem adverse. It is this attitude of boldness that saved Christianity from dying out long ago.

2. The hidden thoughts, counsels, sufferings of men will be openly manifested in the times of judgment, whether of the Lord's people (1 Cor 4:5), or of the Lord's enemies who hold thoughts of blasphemy and evil intentions against the Lord in their hearts.

28-31 If men are not to be feared, since they can kill only the body, yet we are to "fear him" – the one who can "destroy both soul and body in hell (gehenna, not hades)". Commentators have speculated upon the identity of this one whom we have to fear. Men can but "kill" the body, but this one can "destroy" the soul and body; this verb (*apollumi*) does not imply extinction, but ruin and loss, as in the case of the old bottles or skins (Matt 9:17) for example. Note also that the destiny is described as "gehenna", the lake of fire, not "hades", the past and present location of the dead who are unsaved. Some have argued that Satan is implied, but the ultimate condemnation to the lake of fire is found in absence from the book of life (Rev 20:12-15), and this implies that God the ultimate Judge is the One whom evangelists must fear. Not, of course, as relating to their own souls and bodies, but as contemplating Him who will judge those to whom they testify in the gospel if they continue to refuse to repent.

Again, one should not fear men because the protecting power of God is always around His servants, even if His will is the servants' suffering for His Name's sake, as in Paul's case (Acts 9:16). Two sparrows (two, no doubt, because the apostles were sent forth two-by-two) might be sold for food and killing, but even in the daily slaughter for food God knows all about it. The cost of such a purchase, "a farthing", was small, an *assarion* or a sixteenth of a Roman *denarius* (the daily wage of a labourer in Matt 20:2). The widow's mite was an eighth of an *assarion*. The size and value of a sparrow was therefore trifling, but God's estimate is the reverse of that of men. (Another such reversal is found in Luke 16:15.) Similarly with the hairs of the head – small in size, large in number, falling out and cut short with no regret – yet the care and protection of God are there, since everyone of them grows under the direction of His natural laws as He upholds everything. Similar thoughts are found in Luke 21:18 "there shall not an hair of your head perish", and Acts 27:34 "there shall not an hair fall from the head of any of you". How much more are the Lord's servants valuable and precious to Him. In unbelief and betrayal, the Lord was valued at thirty pieces of silver (Matt 27:3, 9), about two thousand times the "farthing" that the sparrows were sold for, but the value of the Son to the Father is infinite in its preciousness.

32-33 Although the confession in v.32 is a precious responsibility of all the Lord's people, yet the fact that the second person plural in v.31 changes to the third person singular in v.32 ("ye" to "him") suggests that the Lord is here referring to *the evangelised* rather than to *the evangelists,* to those who hear the message rather than to those who preach the message. The results in the testimony and lives of those who respond are found in several verses in this chapter. A Christian life is not something lived in a corner, as if such a life was not suitable to be seen by the world around; by life and lip, this new life is to be confessed "before men". We have again the principle of double-witness; a man's personal confession together with that by the Lord in heaven is sufficient to receive the Father's welcome in the coming day. "Behold I and the children which God hath given me" (Heb 2:13) will be His confession as He introduces us into the Father's presence. But the denial does not refer to a believer who in a moment of weakness fails to witness for his Lord before men. Rather it refers to those who do not receive the messengers or the messages, as in vv.14-15. The Lord's denial will occur in the future day of judgment. In this life, "the defiled and unbelieving" may try to give an impression that they know God, "but in works they deny him, being abominable, and disobedient" (Tit 1:15-16). In the future, they may say "Lord, Lord" (Matt 7:21), yet this will be a very one-sided confession; the principle of double-witness will still apply, with the Lord denying that He knows such men – "I never knew you . . . ye that work iniquity". In other words, their one-sided confession will be useless, and such men will have to depart from the Lord for evermore.

34-36 This distinction between faithful and unfaithful men also has its impact on the household. For in v.35 we find a household consisting of five people – two men and three women. The common cry of ecumenical religion, particularly at Christmas time, is "on earth peace, good will toward men" (Luke 2:14), but that peace is a millennial peace on earth in the future, for *now* there is no peace to the wicked – a common assertion by the three major prophets in the OT (Isa 48:22; Jer 6:14; Ezek 7:25). The common theme of religionists and politicians is always "Peace and safety" (1 Thess 5:3), but what will come is stated to be "sudden destruction". The Lord did not come to alter this situation, "Suppose ye that I am come to give peace on earth? I tell you, Nay; but rather division" (Luke 12:51). The only peace that He has available *now* is the "peace of God, which passeth all understanding" (Phil 4:7), something that He gives "not as the world" (John 14:27). This is a different Christ from the One that the world glibly talks about! It is the same within the family circle – not warfare, but division caused by those who have no faith in Christ, who are antagonistic to those who do exercise such faith (not, of course, the other way round). In such a household there can be no unity and no peace between its members; the Lord Himself has brought about this division by arranging that the gospel is brought into households. The unbelievers are the "foes" of the believing members – not in the sense of enmity, but a sense of difference brought about by distinct interests, occupations, affections, styles of life, friends and the service of God. See Mic 7:6.

37-39 Here are further characteristics of the true disciple of Christ. The Lord puts them in a negative sense – loving household members, not taking up his cross, finding his life. In v.37, we find love in both directions: upwards to parents, and downwards to children; (there seems to be a hint of this in Deut 33:9 when properly interpreted). The Lord comes *first* in the hearts of His people, so that He may have the preeminence in all things. Thus in the Ephesian assembly, they had left their "first love" (Rev 2:4); after His ascension He would test the direction and strength of Peter's love, by saying "lovest thou me more than these?" (John 21:15). As we sing in the hymn "Jesus calls us o'er the tumult":

"Still He calls, in cares and pleasures,
'Christian, love Me more than these!'

Give our hearts to Thy obedience,
Serve and love Thee best of all!"

In Luke 14:26, the word "hate" is used instead of "love more", but the implication is the same. Affections are relative, with "hate" meaning to "love less". See Rom 9:13 where a similar distinction is made between love and hate.

Verses 38-39 are repeated in Matt 16:24-25. In Matthew's Gospel, the Lord's cross has not yet been revealed in ch.10, but in 16:24 the truth is strengthened since the cross is revealed three verses previously. The disciples would know of the Roman method of execution, that criminals had to carry their own crosses to the place of crucifixion. So in the context of service, the disciple had to eliminate all impediments that would distract from sincere devotion and sanctification to the Lord. After His baptism, the Lord had left all His legitimate occupations of former years. In following Him, the disciples did not know that a cross really awaited Him at the end, but later Peter said that he was ready to go "to death" with his Lord (Luke 22:33) – and this meant a Roman cross when Peter said that, for the Romans had taken away the Jewish right to stone their own criminals to death.

In v.39, finding life and losing life are effectively past tenses, not present as in the AV. The "life" is not, of course, physical life, but life morally. The servant whose life is governed by the affairs, ease and joys of this world will find his life useless for the service of God. Believers, who have continued to live as in the world for years after their conversion and baptism, will find it difficult, if not impossible, to take up service when circumstances demand it later in life. Preparation for service commences when one is young, and natural advantages must be lost at this stage. A life lost in this sense will be productive, for the life will have been prepared for service whenever God chooses to make a call upon the time and ability of that man. Timothy was such an example: with a good report Timothy was available and ready for the time of the call to accompany Paul on his second missionary journey (Acts 16:1-3).

40-42 Here is the principle of reception. The man who receives the Lord's servants also receives the Lord Jesus and the Father who sent Him. The servants are described as "a prophet, a righteous man, one of these little ones". Reception is governed by receiving the prophet and his divinely-given message; receiving a righteous man and his moral standards learnt from the Lord; providing a cup of cold water – the simple basic necessities of life (as expected in v.9). Their future reward will be commensurate with their deeds. They will be rewarded as if they were prophets and righteous men (reward is dealt with more extensively in ch.25). Such men may not become prophets, but they should become endowed with some gift in the Lord's service; all men should exhibit moral righteousness in order to match their faith formed in the message brought to them. And all should demonstrate hospitality to the Lord's servants, at least when they have the means for so doing, whether it be a "great feast" (Luke 5:29), or a cup of cold water bought with the widow's mite. The Lord will reward according to that a man has!

VII. The Lord's Service Alone (11:1-30)

1. *The Lord's Testimony to and about John the Baptist* 11:1-19

v.1 "And it came to pass, when Jesus had made an end of commanding his twelve disciples, he departed thence to teach and to preach in their cities.
v.2 Now when John had heard in the prison the works of Christ, he sent two of his disciples,
v.3 And said unto him, Art thou he that should come, or do we look for another?
v.4 Jesus answered and said unto them, Go and shew John again those things which ye do hear and see:

v.5 The blind receive their sight, and the lame walk, the lepers are cleansed, and the deaf hear, the dead are raised up, and the poor have the gospel preached to them.
v.6 And blessed is *he,* whosoever shall not be offended in me.
v.7 And as they departed, Jesus began to say unto the multitudes concerning John, What went ye out into the wilderness to see? A reed shaken with the wind?
v.8 But what went ye out for to see? A man clothed in soft raiment? behold, they that wear soft *clothing* are in kings' houses.
v.9 But what went ye out for to see? A prophet? yea, I say unto you, and more than a prophet.
v.10 For this is *he,* of whom it is written, Behold, I send my messenger before thy face, which shall prepare thy way before thee.
v.11 Verily I say unto you, Among them that are born of women there hath not risen a greater than John the Baptist: notwithstanding he that is least in the kingdom of heaven is greater than he.
v.12 And from the days of John the Baptist until now the kingdom of heaven suffereth violence, and the violent take it by force.
v.13 For all the prophets and the law prophesied until John.
v.14 And if ye will receive *it,* this is Elias, which was for to come.
v.15 He that hath ears to hear, let him hear.
v.16 But whereunto shall I liken this generation? It is like unto children sitting in the markets, and calling unto their fellows,
v.17 And saying, We have piped unto you, and ye have not danced; we have mourned unto you, and ye have not lamented.
v.18 For John came neither eating nor drinking, and they say, He hath a devil.
v.19 The Son of man came eating and drinking, and they say, Behold a man gluttonous, and a winebibber, a friend of publicans and sinners. But wisdom is justified of her children."

1 This is the second time that the Lord finished a discourse, the previous occasion being in 7:28 and the next in 13:53. He commanded the twelve to go forth in 10:5; the rest of ch.10 is devoted to divinely-given instructions for their journeys and service. In 11:1, they commenced their mission, while the Lord "departed thence to teach and to preach in their cities". The return of the apostles is recorded in Mark 6:30 and Luke 9:10, though not in Matthew's Gospel. But we find the disciples with the Lord again in Matt 12:1, and we conclude that throughout ch.11 the Lord was alone in the continuation of His Galilean ministry.

2-3 John the Baptist had been bound and put in prison by Herod, because of his outspoken condemnation of the marital arrangements between Herodias and Herod's brother Philip (Matt 14:3-4). While in prison before his decease John kept in touch with the outside news regarding the fame of Jesus, and evidently was visited by some of his disciples; see Matt 25:36. He sent "two" of his disciples to the Lord, this being the number of adequate testimony. John wanted to know "Art thou he that should come, or do we look for another?". To note the nature of this question, consider the truths that John *did* know. He knew that in Jesus "all flesh shall see the salvation of God" (Luke 3:6), that He "shall baptise you with the Holy Ghost" (v.16); that He was "the Lamb of God, which taketh away the sin of the world" (John 1:29); that "this is the Son of God" (v.34), that "He that cometh from above is above all" (John 3:31), and that "grace and truth came by Jesus Christ" (1:17). Moreover, he knew that the Lord had been sent by God (John 3:34). John did not doubt a single one of these truths, his questions from prison did not indicate any lack of faith in any of these facts. Rather his questions were based on reports such as in Luke 7:16, "a great prophet is risen up". In other words, was this the One that had been promised in the OT? Was He the One of whom Moses spoke, "I will raise them up a Prophet from among their brethren"? (Deut 18:18). Was the Lamb, the Son, the Christ, also this Prophet? John wanted to extend his knowledge and faith, not (as some suggest) to bolster up a faith that was failing owing to his prison conditions.

4-6 The Lord's answer may appear to be oblique, but it was entirely satisfactory to meet John's enquiry. These two disciples were actually *there and then* hearing and seeing the Lord's works; see Luke 7:21, where miracles were performed *between* the disciples' questions and the Lord's answer. These miracles should have proved the truth to John about the One "that should come". For example John well knew the book of the prophet Isaiah; this prophetically informed him that he was the voice of one crying in the wilderness (Matt 3:3; Luke 3:4; John 1:23; Isa 40:3). Other portions would also be known to him, such as "a lamb to the slaughter" (53:7), and particularly "the eyes of the blind shall be opened, and the ears of the deaf shall be unstopped. Then shall the lame man leap as an hart, and the tongue of the dumb sing" (35:5-6) words spoken in amplification of the promise "God . . . will come and save you" (v.4). Thus the promised One was God working miracles. John would be "blessed" (*makarios,* happy) when he added this stock of spiritual knowledge to his faith. The proof to John was that miracles were being performed, and they corresponded to those listed in Isa 35:5-6. So indeed the Lord Jesus was the One that was to come; there could not be "another" (*heteros,* another of a different kind). The Lord added that faith must not be "offended" in Him. This word *skandalizō* means "to put a stumbling block in the way"; faith must not be stumbled in identifying the Man Christ Jesus with the promised One in the OT. The Lord's proof ended with the sweet observation, "the poor have the gospel preached to them". This goes beyond what is found in Isa 35:6, but contains more than a hint of Isa 61:1 "to preach good tidings unto the meek" (Luke 4:18). In other words, the Lord's physical miracles were mingled with His spiritual work.

7-9 Having satisfied these two disciples, the Lord then gave testimony concerning John to the multitudes, some of whom no doubt were still disciples of the imprisoned John, as can be deduced from the question "What went ye out into the wilderness to see?". Such men formed part of the multitude that had gone out to John to be baptised (Matt 3:5-6). So the Lord questioned their reasons for going out to John; in Luke 3:10 it was to ask "what shall we do then?", and in v.15 it was to assess whether John was the Christ. The Lord suggested three possibilities as to their motivation.

1. To see "a reed shaken with the wind" ? There were such reeds by the river Jordan where John baptised. Were these a picture of a weak and uncertain man, whose faith was blown about by every wind of new undigested doctrines and practices? Throughout the OT and NT there have always been winds of doctrine in religious circles (Eph 4:14; Heb 13:9; Jude 12).

2. To see "a man clothed in soft raiment"? A man like this would have the pomp, luxury and authority of the state, living at the expense of the king's subjects. Religion of that sort is condemned by the Lord, and its natural glory is similar to that of the future Babylon (Rev 17:4). Rather, John was roughly clothed, ill-housed and poorly fed (Matt 3:4), one who like Paul suffered hunger, was naked and had no "certain dwellingplace" (1 Cor 4:11; 2 Cor 11:27).

3. To see "a prophet"? Certainly, since "thou, child, shalt be called the prophet of the Highest" (Luke 1:76), he was a man who spoke from God by special revelation. The people knew of this, for "they counted him as a prophet" (Matt 14:5; 21:26).

Yet the Lord went beyond this; he was "more than a prophet"; compare this with what Paul wrote about Onesimus in Philem 16, "above a servant, a brother beloved".

10 John was the last of the OT prophets, with the special calling and privilege that he had been the only one to have seen the Lord face-to-face. Moreover, he was a "messenger" (*angelos,* usually meaning "angel"), in keeping with the last revealed prophecy in the OT, "Behold, I will send my messenger, and he shall prepare the way before me" (Mal 3:1); the subject of this verse then merges with the far prophetic future. Thus John had a special birth; he was a Nazarite (who remained unblemished throughout his life), and the spirit and power of Elijah were upon him. No other OT prophet had all these special characteristics at one and the same time.

11 Up to that time, no one " born of women" was greater than John (speaking of physical birth), this birth being an ordinary birth, but with the miracle of parenthood being conferred on both his mother and father. By these words, the Lord excludes Himself, since He was infinitely greater. The Lord was not "born of women" as such in this sense; rather He was " made of a woman", or literally "became of a woman" (Gal 4:4) without Joseph being involved. In spite of his greatness, John minimised himself by saying "I must decrease" (John 3:30), as indeed all believers must do, "Humble yourselves therefore under the mighty hand of God, that he may exalt you in due time" (1 Pet 5:6). Yet there is a difference in the dispensations: at that time, John was greatest in natural birth, calling, privilege and status. But to be in "the kingdom of heaven" (or "the kingdom of God" in Luke 7:28) is to be greater for this speaks of spiritual birth. Without this new birth, a man cannot see the kingdom of God (John 3:3). Today, members of the church are greater than the prophets; the bridegroom (the Lord) has the bride (the church), while the friend of the bridegroom (John) rejoices greatly (John 3:29). Now the "least" are sinners saved by grace after the sacrifice and resurrection of Christ, raising them to higher status according to the purpose of God.

12-13 The essential message of the law and the prophets, typically, morally and prophetically, was the coming glorious kingdom of the Messiah; prophecies of His birth and life blended with this prophetic future, thereby omitting the whole age of the church from Pentecost to the rapture. John's message was that the kingdom was at hand – the King was present. The kingdom would not be established in glory there and then (though a preview would be given in Matt 17:1-13), since it "suffereth violence, and the violent take it by force". We feel that the "violent" are the religious leaders who sought to dominate rather than bow to the unwanted authority and power of John the Baptist. They were not satisfied with the dominance of the Roman kingdom over the country, so would take advantage of anything better that was available. Men would claim that their works corresponded to entering into the kingdom of heaven (Matt 7:21-23), but morally and spiritually they were on the outside. They resembled the tares sown amongst the wheat by the enemy; both would exist side-by-side until the harvest (Matt 13:24-30). Note that this statement does *not* come in the parallel passage in Luke 7:28; rather it appears in Luke 16:16 in a different context. Here, "presseth" (AV) is translated as "entereth violently" (RV), and according to Vine, refers to men who "make an effort to enter the Kingdom in spite of violent opposition". But as far as the church is concerned, believers do *not* add themselves; it is God who adds (Acts 2:47; 5:13-14).

14-15 This reference to Elias (Elijah in the OT) could only be spiritually discerned, for the natural man cannot receive divine truth. " If ye will receive it" means the same thing as "He that hath ears to hear, let him hear"; spiritual ears and spiritual hearing are implied. In Rev 2-3, this statement "He that hath an ear" is made seven times; the singular "ear" suggesting that the spiritual hearing must be even more sharply focussed and discerning to understand the messages to the seven churches.

Elijah promised in the *last* message of the OT prophets (Mal 4:5), was associated with the *first* message in the NT from John the Baptist. Religious men in NT times were expecting Elijah, and were watching for an unusual man. Hence they thought that John was Elias (John 1:21), and later some thought that Christ was Elias (Matt 16:14). In Matt 11:14, the Lord's statement that John was the promised Elias must have fallen upon spiritually deaf ears. The three apostles Peter, James and John later exhibited no greater appreciation. After Elias had appeared in glory on the mount, they asked the Lord, "Why then say the scribes that Elias must first come?" (Matt 17:10); (note, they say "scribes" not the "Scriptures"!). The Lord gave two answers to this question:

1. that Elias "shall first come" referring to the prophetic *future;* some expositors think that one of the two witnesses in Rev 11:3-12 will be Elijah.

2. that "Elias is come already", referring to the past.

The Lord added that men "knew him not, but have done unto him whatsoever they listed", namely they killed him. Only then did the apostles realise that the Lord spoke of John the Baptist. Clearly John was not Elias personally in the flesh! The solution to this problem is found in the words of Gabriel to Zacharias in the temple: "he (John) shall go before him (the Lord) in the spirit and power of Elias, to turn the hearts of the fathers to the children" Luke 1:17), where Mal 4:6 is quoted. John, therefore, represented the "spirit and power" of Elijah. When Elijah was taken up to heaven, Elisha wanted "a double portion" of his spirit to be upon him (2 Kings 2:9). Afterwards, confession was made that "The spirit of Elijah doth rest on Elisha" (v.15), while his mantle represented the power (v.14). Perhaps only a single portion of the spirit fell upon Elisha, while the second portion fell upon John the Baptist much later, so that it would be "in the spirit and power" of Elias that John worked for God.

16-19 Both John's message and the Lord's message brought no response other than criticism from religious men at that time. We shall see in Matt 12 that this criticism worsened and reached a climax, at which point the Lord acted drastically. These religionists were the chief priests, scribes and lawyers who sought to destroy Him; they are to be distinguished from the common people who were attentive to hear Him (Luke 19:47-48). To illustrate the point, the Lord used a brief word-picture (the word "parable" is not used until ch.13) describing children playing games in the streets and cities. Here were games of weddings and funerals, but some of their friends refused to join in and provide the responses demanded in the games. By this word-picture, the Lord referred to the lack of response to two kinds of ministry, and to the personalities and conduct of the preachers. The Lord's ministry was one of joy in salvation, healing and comfort; John's ministry was one of judgment and stern rebuke. Verse 18 shows the religious leaders' actual thoughts of John, and indicates why there was no response, "He hath a devil (demon)". In other words, evil men discuss on their own level the supreme faithfulness of individual believers. These religious leaders recognised that John did not eat bread nor drink wine; this had been predicted by Gabriel in Luke 1:15, and was one of the OT's sternest degrees of abstinence. Hence John was self-denying, and refused social intercourse in any shape or form, since this would hinder his particular kind of testimony. Men likened John to the former state of those whom the Lord healed of demon possession. Moreover, these leaders would later accuse the Lord of this as well (Matt 12:24). By contrast, the Lord spoke likewise about them, that they were of their father the devil (John 8:44).

On the other hand, the Lord's life and ministry were quite different in a social context. As eating and drinking, He was *in* the world but not *of* it. Yet these religious leaders deliberately misunderstood and criticised Him – "a man gluttonous, and a winebibber, a friend of publicans and sinners". But the Lord acted on very definite spiritual principles when social occasions demanded His presence. It was a case of being disposed to go when invited to a feast (1 Cor 10:27); He always acted to help, never to partake in social wickedness. Thus the Lord would never have attended Belshazzar's feast (Dan 5:1); yet He went into Matthew's house (Matt 9:10), to a Pharisee's house (Luke 7:36, 11:37), to the home in Bethany (10:38), to Zacchaeus' house (19:5). The Pharisees exaggerated the charge of partaking even of ordinary food, when those in the house needed salvation, or if those in the house loved Him and provided for Him. "But wisdom is justified of her children", the Lord concluded. The motivation behind the life and service of God's servants, whether the divine Son or John the Baptist, was demonstrated to be right by the fruits of that service. For example, repentance and salvation were permanent and not rapidly passing away; fruit was thirty, sixty and a hundredfold (Matt 13:8); there was the Pharisees' fear that "all men will believe on him" (John 11:48).

2. *The Negative Response of the Cities* 11:20-24

v.20 "Then began he to upbraid the cities wherein most of his mighty works were done, because they repented not:

v.21 Woe unto thee, Chorazin! woe unto thee, Bethsaida! for if the mighty works, which were done in you, had been done in Tyre and Sidon, they would have repented long ago in sackcloth and ashes.

v.22 But I say unto you, It shall be more tolerable for Tyre and Sidon at the day of judgment, than for you.

v.23 And thou, Capernaum, which art exalted unto heaven, shalt be brought down to hell: for if the mighty works, which have been done in thee, had been done in Sodom, it would have remained until this day.

v.24 But I say unto you, That it shall be more tolerable for the land of Sodom in the day of judgment, than for thee."

20-24 The religious leaders were responsible for the spread of unbelief amongst the multitudes and throughout the cities. If in vv.16-19 the Lord criticised the Pharisaical leaders, here He criticised the cities that they had adversely affected. Capernaum lay on the north coast of the Sea of Galilee; Bethsaida lay also on the coast a few miles to the east, while Chorazin lay a few miles inland to the north of Capernaum. The Lord "began to upbraid" these cities. He had refrained from doing so previously, since His mighty works gave them time to repent. The verb "upbraid" (*oneidizō*) means "to reproach", in strong terms since predictions of judgment were issued by the Lord.

Chorazin and Bethsaida were cities that had had the greatest opportunities, and hence the greatest responsibilities. The Lord compared these with Tyre and Sidon, cities lying on the Mediterranean coast nearby. They are found, for example, in the OT, full of pride and business corruption (Ezek 26-28). The cities of Galilee had disregarded the Lord's great works, and this would bring greater judgment on them than on these cities of OT times which would have repented long ago had they had a similar opportunity. This the Lord knew, and it appears that future judgment will be based on *what they would have done had they had* the opportunity. Their repentance would have involved sitting "in sackcloth and ashes", a sign of deep humility and contrition, as in Job 16:15; Ahab in 1 Kings 21:27; David in Ps 30:11; and the king and people of Nineveh in Jonah 3:5-8. Later, local assemblies were formed in Tyre and Sidon (Acts 15:3; 21:2-7; 27:3), showing the good works of hospitality to Paul and his party as they passed through.

The same criticism was made of Capernaum; this city was "exalted unto heaven"

1. because of the Lord's presence and power, and

2. because of its pride and religious folly.

In Isa 14:12-15 a similar accusation was made against Babylon; it was likened to Lucifer who desired to ascend into heaven, to exalt his throne above the stars of God, and to be like the Most High; yet Lucifer would "be brought down to hell". Tyre, apparently a type of Satan, took the same attitude: that city said, "I am a God, I sit in the seat of God" (Ezek 28:2); its heart was lifted up because of its riches (v.5), yet this led to its being brought "down to the pit" (v.8). In all cases those who exalt themselves shall be abased.

So Capernaum was contrasted with Sodom (Gomorrha is included in Matt 10:15), because Capernaum had had an abundance of opportunities to repent through the Lord's teaching. What a contrast to Sodom! In Gen 13:10, Lot chose the well-watered plain, and "pitched his tent toward Sodom" (v.12). His testimony was "I pray you, brethren, do not so wickedly" (19:7), and he offered his daughters to their lust. Then he lingered in the city that was about to be judged (v.16). His spiritual testimony was non-existent, although " just Lot" was delivered from the overthrow (2 Pet 2:7). Sodom heard no spiritual testimony because Lot behaved as if he were almost one of them. Consequently, although Sodom suffered the vengeance of eternal fire as an example of the future judgment (Jude 7), yet there will be degrees of judgment in that day.

3. *The Lord's Response in Prayer and Appeal* 11:25-30

v.25 "At that time Jesus answered and said, I thank thee, O Father, Lord of heaven and earth, because thou hast hid these things from the wise and prudent, and hast revealed them unto babes.
v.26 Even so, Father: for so it seemed good in thy sight.
v.27 All things are delivered unto me of my Father: and no man knoweth the Son, but the Father; neither knoweth any man the Father, save the Son, and *he* to whomsoever the Son will reveal *him*.
v.28 Come unto me, all *ye* that labour and are heavy laden, and I will give you rest.
v.29 Take my yoke upon you, and learn of me; for I am meek and lowly in heart: and ye shall find rest unto your souls.
v.30 For my yoke is easy, and my burden is light."

25-26 Here we have one of the few occasions of divine and intimate communion that are recorded; John 17 is another. The Lord turned from the dark circumstances of earth to the eternal sunshine of His Father in heaven. In these verses, four titles are used: "O Father, Father, my Father, the Father". The title "my Father" occurs more than 50 times in the Gospels, many times the title "the Father" appears, while "Holy Father" and "righteous Father" are found in John 17:11,25. The proper use of divine titles shows spirituality, reverence and discernment. Sometimes today the unseemly repetition in prayer of the divine titles jars the hearts of those who are taught by Scripture. The Spirit enables us to say "Abba, Father" (Rom 8:15; Gal 4:6); vain repetition cannot be of the Spirit, and may result from habit or some subtle practice. The title "O Father" is a form of reverent address, "Father" of communion, "my Father" of relationship, and "the Father" of uniqueness recognised.

The additional title "Lord of heaven and earth" is the highest title in the universe, for God controls from heaven and on earth throughout His creation. In Luke 10:21, the additional words "Jesus rejoiced in spirit" occur; He rejoiced that the hiding and revealing of divine truth are according to the good pleasure of the Father. God does not force the truth on unwilling hearts, yet He reveals it to longing seeking hearts; this is a precursor of the introduction of parables in Matt 13. "These things" may relate to all the Lord's previous teaching, but in the context it appears to refer more particularly to the knowledge of the Son and the Father by men on earth (v.27). For "wise and prudent" minds are too full of earthly knowledge, and there is no room for heavenly knowledge. The words "wise" (*sophos,* the character of having a theoretical insight into the nature of things) and "prudent" (*sunetos,* manifesting a critical faculty in understanding) are used in a natural sense. Both words (and cognates) are used doubly in 1 Cor 1:19, "I will destroy the *wisdom* of the *wise,* and will bring to nothing the *understanding* of the *prudent*". Such minds cannot hear the still small voice; not many wise men after the flesh are called (v.26). Instead, God reveals these things to babes by His Spirit, to the weak things chosen to confound the mighty (2:10; 1:27). The Lord called them "babes" since here is self-weakness, knowing nothing but ready to learn (1 Pet 2:2).

27 In this verse, the Lord used the title "my Father" in connection with the fact that "all things" had been delivered unto Him. There are many verses which contain this title and also some of these "all things": John 8:28, 54; 10:17, 29; 20:21; Rev 2:27. Additionally in several verses this title is used in connection with what is done for, or given to, the Lord's people: Matt 16:17; 18:19; 20:23; John 6:32, 65; 14:21. Other things delivered to the Son are found in John 17: "the words" (v.8), His own (vv.9-12), glory (vv.22, 24). In our verse, the knowledge of the Son is confined to the Father – the One unknowable in the eternal nature of His Person, whom "no man can approach unto; whom no man hath seen, nor can see" (1 Tim 6:16). The fact that the Father also reveals the Son is made plain earlier (v.25), and also in Matt 16:17. As far as the knowledge of the Father is concerned, "the world hath not known thee" (John 17:25), only the Son ("As the Father knoweth me, even so know I the Father", John 10:15) and those to whom the Son will (*boulomai,* to exercise the will strongly) reveal Him. The Son's objective is to reveal the Father to His own people: "I have manifested thy name unto the men" (John 17:6). This shows that there is no natural knowledge of the Godhead amongst men; in fact, natural knowledge (through nature) leads sinful men into idolatry (Rom 1:21-23).

28 The cities previously considered thought that they could do as they liked; they cast off the "bands . . . cords" of divine restraint (Ps 2:3), failing to realise that this was bondage according to God's estimate. But if any individuals would become as "babes", here would be true liberty: "Except ye be converted, and become as little children" (Matt 18:3), "of such is the kingdom of heaven" (19:14). In this frame of mind we hear His voice, "Come unto me", being converted from bondage to liberty, from the OT law to the grace of the NT. The bondage of corruption changes to "the glorious liberty of the children of God" (Rom 8:21). The works and burden of law change to the rest of grace in the soul.

29-30 A yoke can be a yoke of bondage (keeping the law for salvation); see Acts 15:10; Gal 5:1. But a yoke (*zugos*) that is shared with One infinitely more powerful is a great blessing, for it cannot feel like a yoke at all. Christ had a yoke and a burden: the burnt offering with complete devotion to God's will was the yoke to God; the sin offering bearing sin was the burden from God, for He laid on Him "the iniquity of us all" (Isa 53:6). In Gethsemane's garden, "not as I will, but as thou wilt" was the yoke, but being "exceeding sorrowful, even unto death" was the burden (Matt 26:38-39). Now that His sacrifice is over, His yoke and burden that we share are easy and light. The yoke involves going where He goes and where He leads and calls; the burden, doing in service what He requires. What is easy and light is now the liberty of the believer, and there is freedom under grace to move according to the good will of God. This liberty arises from the presence of the Holy Spirit, for "where the Spirit of the Lord is, there is liberty" (2 Cor 3:17). This is not, of course, a pretext to do as we please but having the meekness and lowliness of Christ, we find it a joy to walk in His ways along pathways chosen by Himself. We should not seek to exchange yokes along this pathway, to exchange one that is easy for one that is really a burden: "Be ye not unequally yoked together with unbelievers" (2 Cor 6:14), an exhortation followed by five solemn examples.

These principles may be found in several passages in the Epistles.

1. "Stand fast therefore in the liberty wherewith Christ hath made us free, and be not entangled again with the yoke of bondage" (Gal 5:1); that is, do not return to the bondage of pre-conversion religion by building again the things destroyed (2:18). Liberty means the children of Sarah, but bondage the children of Hagar.

2. "Ye have been called unto liberty; only use not liberty for an occasion to the flesh, but by love serve one another" (Gal 5:13).

3. "As free, and not using your liberty for a cloke of maliciousness, but as the servants of God" (1 Pet 2:16). In other words, do not cover up any evil characteristic that is not compatible with the true service of a servant yoked with Christ in perfect liberty; in this respect, one cannot serve two masters, one giving liberty and the other bondage.

VIII. Crescendo of Pharisaical Opposition (12:1-50)

1. *The Pharisees and the Sabbath* 12:1-13

v.1 "At that time Jesus went on the sabbath day through the corn; and his disciples were an hungred, and began to pluck the ears of corn, and to eat.
v.2 But when the Pharisees saw *it,* they said unto him, Behold, thy disciples do that which is not lawful to do upon the sabbath day.
v.3 But he said unto them, Have ye not read what David did, when he was an hungred, and they that were with him;
v.4 How he entered into the house of God, and did eat the shewbread, which was not lawful for him to eat, neither for them which were with him, but only for the priests?
v.5 Or have ye not read in the law, how that on the sabbath days the priests in the temple profane the sabbath, and are blameless?
v.6 But I say unto you, That in this place is *one* greater than the temple.
v.7 But if ye had known what *this* meaneth, I will have mercy, and not sacrifice, ye would not have condemned the guiltless.
v.8 For the Son of man is Lord even of the sabbath day.
v.9 And when he was departed thence, he went into their synagogue:
v.10 And, behold, there was a man which had *his* hand withered. And they asked him, saying, Is it lawful to heal on the sabbath days? that they might accuse him.
v.11 And he said unto them, What man shall there be among you, that shall have one sheep, and if it fall into a pit on the sabbath day, will he not lay hold on it, and lift *it* out?
v.12 How much then is a man better than a sheep? Wherefore it is lawful to do well on the sabbath days.
v.13 Then saith he to the man, Stretch forth thine hand. And he stretched *it* forth; and it was restored whole, like as the other."

This chapter terminates the major section in which the Lord's teaching is mingled with miracles, those mighty works and signs that the cities of Galilee and the Pharisees so lightly disregarded. We subdivide the chapter into four paragraphs:

1. The Pharisees and the Sabbath (vv.1-13).

2. The Pharisees and their Council (vv.14-21).

3. The Pharisees and their Blasphemy (vv.22-37).

4. The Pharisees and their Demand of a Sign (vv.38-50).

No signs are promised, and the character of the Lord's ministry changes by the introduction of parables so as to hide the truth from unbelievers.

1 In John 5:16 the Jews caused trouble because the Lord had healed a lame man on the sabbath day. In the present paragraph the Pharisees caused further trouble, arising from this walk through a cornfield "on the sabbath day". The word sabbath means cessation. The Greek text reads *"tois sabbasin"*, the dative of the plural form *sabbata*. In other places the singular form *sabbaton* is used. The three Synoptic evangelists use both words throughout their Gospels but John uses only the singular form. In the corresponding passage in Luke 6:1 the adjective *deuteroprōtos* is added. The AV translates this as "the second sabbath after the first", but the RV gives only "on a sabbath". Modern translations resort to something like "on another sabbath". The variety of suggested words implies that translators are not certain what to make of the adjective. Segond's French translation reads "un jour de sabbat appelé second-premier", Luther's German has "an einem Sabbat"; JND has "on the second-first sabbath". Clearly a literal translation makes no sense, and expositors have invented suggestions to account for its appearance in the text: "A ghost-word which has crept into the text of many authorities by mistake", "an epithet of uncertain meaning, but probably appropriated to the sabbath following the first day of unleavened bread".

The disciples were hungry but simple food was available, so the Lord would work no miracle as He did in the cases of the feeding of the 5,000 and the 4,000 In a physical world where providentially God has prepared food all around in abundance, He expects self-help. Miracles were not accomplished needlessly neither were they intended to help the indolent. Luke adds that they "plucked the ears of corn . . . rubbing them in their hands". Separating the corn from the husks we would view pictorially as separating the doctrines of the OT and of the Lord from the doctrine of the Pharisees (Matt 16:6, 11-12). This exercise was certainly needed in this case, as it is often needed today.

2 This simple act raised the hostility of the Pharisees. Certainly such plucking of corn was legitimate in fields not of one's personal possession (Deut 23:24-25) even certain work associated with food preparation was allowed on the sabbath day, " no manner of work shall be done in them, save that which every man must eat" (Exod 12:16), referring to special sabbaths at the feast of unleavened bread. But the Pharisees added tradition in the form of husks, condemned by the Lord when He said, "Thus have ye made the commandment of God of none effect by your tradition" (Matt 15:6). The Pharisees' legal system stated that plucking was reaping, and that rubbing was threshing, so no wonder they complained if they watched very simple deeds as if they formed an extensive industry. These men loved the letter of the law (their law) but not its spirit; the mind but not the heart; legality but not mercy.

3-4 The Lord always had an answer to such false accusations, the Pharisees' own OT Scriptures themselves were a sufficient antidote to such charges. By quoting an event in David's life, the Lord expected its meaning to be understood by the Pharisees, since this somewhat ordinary historical event was full of spiritual meaning. The story is found in 1 Sam 21:1-6; David had come to the tabernacle at Nob, and being hungry he was given some of the showbread by the priest when, strictly, only the priests could partake of it. The story contained two lessons.

1. The house (Moses' tabernacle) was no longer really the house of God in David's time, since God had forsaken it previously when the ark had been taken captive by the Philistines (Ps 78:60). Only when God's presence dwelt in the tabernacle was this bread for the private use of the priests alone. Similarly, Herod's temple was not the real house of God in the Lord's time. The circumstances were parallel. Today, a religious building is quite distinct from a local assembly forming a spiritual temple consisting of God's people (1 Cor 3:16). So David was not really acting like a false priest, unlike Uzziah later (2 Chron 26:16-20).

2. The Lord said that it was lawful only for the priests to eat this showbread. But in the OT, the high priests in David's time (Ahimelech and Abiathar) were not genuine high priests, since they arose from Aaron's son Ithamar from whom Eli was descended; none of these appears in the high priests' genealogy (1 Chron 6:3-15). Similarly in the Lord's time: Annas and Caiaphas were not genuine high priests, having been appointed by men (the Roman authorities) and not by God. Today the same conclusion can be drawn in non-evangelical circles.

Thus David acted in the light of the fact that ceremony was at that time redundant, as the temple later became redundant when the Lord "cast off his altar" (Lam 2:7). The Lord too acted in the light of the redundancy of the sabbath.

1. when the needs of mercy were more important than legality, and

2. when the first day recognised in the Christian era would replace the seventh day of the Jewish era. As Lord of the sabbath, He could effect this.

5 To support His argument, the Lord then quoted another OT example in which it appeared that the sabbath was being profaned (*bebēloō,* to cross a threshold into a region that is unhallowed and polluted). However, appearances are deceptive if a judgment is made in ignorance of the Scriptures. The Lord was referring, for example, to the daily burnt offering that the priests also had to offer on the sabbath day (Num 28:9-10). This is singled out from the similar offerings that had to be made on the other days of the week (vv.2-8), so as to make it quite clear that the sabbath day was not excepted.

6 The Lord had thus quoted two events relating to the temple or house of God, events in which those disposed to argue might assert that the commandments were being broken; the Lord showed or insinuated that the law was *not* being broken, Yet He is greater than the temple, so what He allowed His disciples to do was quite legitimate. The word for "temple" used here twice is *"hieron"*, the external visible and public parts as distinct from the other word for temple, *"naos"*, meaning the inner sanctuary hidden from the eyes of ordinary men; this latter word is used in John 2:19 and always in the Epistles when it refers metaphorically to the church. Note that here the Lord is greater than the temple; elsewhere He is greater then Jonah (Matt 12:41), greater than Solomon (v.42), greater then Jacob (John 4:12) and greater than Abraham (8:53), these last two being in question form.

7-9 By saying "if ye had known what this meaneth", the Lord implied that a knowledge of the OT Scriptures would have saved the Pharisees from making such unfounded accusations. Once again He quoted Hos 6:6, the previous time being in Matt 9:13 in connection with the Pharisees' criticism that He ate "with publicans and sinners". The OT sacrifices offered from a cold heart were not acceptable; God wanted a warm heart that brought good to men. The former described the Pharisees and their approach to the law; the latter described the Lord.

In the light of the following miracle on the sabbath day, we may produce a list of all the reasons that the Lord gave for doing good on such a day.

1. **Need:** David partook of the showbread that he was not legally entitled to eat (Matt 12:4; Mark 2:26; Luke 6:1-5).

2. **Obedience:** the usual and the special sacrifices had to be offered on the sabbath (Matt 12:5).

3. **The heart transcends the mind:** "I will have mercy, and not sacrifice" (Matt 12:7).

4. **The Son of man is Lord:** there must be subjection to such divine authority even when spiritual and moral considerations demand that a command be interpreted in a way that runs counter to hard religious tradition (Matt 12:8; Mark 2:28; Luke 6:5).

5. **Preservation of life and compassion:** the sheep being drawn out of a pit, and a man being better than a sheep (Matt 12:11,12).

6. **The necessities of life:** an ox or an ass must be loosed and led out to water on the sabbath day (Luke 13:15).

7. **Salvation:** an ass or an ox fallen into a pit must be pulled out (Luke 14:1-6).

8. **Legal requirements:** a male child was circumcised on the sabbath day if this fell on the eighth day of life (John 7:22-23).

9. No further explanation was given in John 9:14. The time had come when no further concession could be made to the hardened hearts of the Pharisees their willing ignorance would remain, "your sin remaineth" (v.41).

In John 9, the Lord was already on the outside, since the Pharisees had cast Him out of the temple (8:59). But in Matt 12:9 rejection had not yet reached its height, so the Lord "went into their synagogue", still on the sabbath day, knowing that further accusations were about to follow.

10-13 Whether in the open field or in the synagogue, the Lord was subject to these Pharisaical accusations. Here they asked, "Is it lawful to heal on the sabbath days?" (the RV translates this in the singular, "the sabbath day"); in 15:2 the question was, "Why do thy disciples transgress the traditions of the elders?"; in 19:3 they tempted Him with the question, "Is it lawful for a man to put away his wife for every cause?"; in 22:17 the question was, "Is it lawful to give tribute unto Caesar, or not?". All these questions were concerned with *their* interpretation of the law, showing the legalistic rut along which their minds were always moving.

In Luke 6:6, the Lord was allowed to teach in the synagogue on the sabbath day, giving Him the opportunity to accomplish another sabbath day miracle. The man with the withered hand demonstrated a complete inability to serve, like the Pharisees both spiritually and morally. These leaders were not concerned with mercy, but with attempts at trapping the Lord by means of His answers to their accusing questions. How simply the Lord dealt with such men! He merely asked two questions by way of response, the first concerning a sheep in danger, and the second whether they considered a man better than a sheep. The Pharisees' question was like a boomerang; it was returned to them in the form of two questions which, had they answered, would have condemned themselves. The Lord Jesus drew the only conclusion, "it is lawful to do well on the sabbath days". A beaten and unconvinced opponent to the truth can be a dangerous man! So the Lord healed the man, knowing full well what the consequences would be. In John 5:18, the Jews "sought the more to kill him, because he not only had broken the sabbath, but said also that God was his Father, making himself equal with God". The same occurs here in Matt 12:13-14. The Lord knew the ultimate consequences of doing things that antagonised the Pharisees – it would lead to the cross. But for the sake of the truth, the Lord would never seek to be popular with the Pharisees; the conflict would lead ultimately to His death according to the will of God.

2. *The Pharisees and their Council* 12:14-21

v.14 "Then the Pharisees went out, and held a council against him, how they might destroy him.
v.15 But when Jesus knew *it,* he withdrew himself from thence: and great multitudes followed him, and he healed them all;
v.16 And charged them that they should not make him known:
v.17 That it might be fulfilled which was spoken by Esaias the prophet, saying,
v.18 Behold my servant, whom I have chosen; my beloved, in whom my soul is well pleased: I will put my spirit upon him, and he shall shew judgment to the Gentiles.
v.19 He shall not strive, nor cry; neither shall any man hear his voice in the streets.
v.20 A bruised reed shall he not break, and smoking flax shall he not quench, till he send forth judgment unto victory.
v.21 And in his name shall the Gentiles trust."

14 The Pharisees must have thought that their authority had been damaged before the people in the synagogue; so to preserve their own position, this Teacher and Miracle-worker had to be destroyed. Such plotting would increase until the Lord was crucified. The word for "council" (*sumboulion,* translated "took counsel" in the RV) means that they came together for consultation and mutual advice. After the raising of Lazarus, "Then gathered the chief priests and the Pharisees a council" (John 11:47), and "they took counsel together for to put him to death" (v.53). In John 11:47, the word for "council" (*sunedrion*) refers to the authoritative Sanhedrin in Jerusalem, but the second word "counsel" in 11:53 is the verbal form of the above noun *sumboulion,* describing the deliberations of the Sanhedrin. Although Ps 2:1-3 refers to the prophetic future when men and nations will fight against the Lamb (Rev 17:14), yet the heathen, people, kings and rulers taking "counsel together, against the Lord, and against his anointed", is interpreted by the apostles in Acts 4:25-28 as referring to "Herod, and Pontius Pilate, with the Gentiles, and the people of Israel". Additionally, it was what God's "counsel determined before to be done" (v.28), the word for "counsel" being *boulē*. Not that God's counsel justified the Pharisees' counsel for one moment!

15-16 Knowing the intentions of the Pharisees, the Lord would not allow these men to put them into effect, since His hour was not yet come. Hence He "withdrew himself". This verb (*anachōreō*) appears 14 times in the NT, usually translated " depart" . However, Vine states that the best rendering is "withdraw", and this implies departing with a motive to be at a distance. Of course, the Lord could not be alone, for "great multitudes" followed Him, and they had quite different intentions from those of the Pharisees. As in many other instances, the Lord "charged them that they should not make him known''. This request for secrecy characterised the earlier part of the Lord's ministry, and scholars speculate upon what they term the "Messianic secret". To the author it appears that the Lord often required that His Person, His capacity for miracles, and the place where He was residing and working, should not be spread abroad too much, so that evil men should have no opportunity to put Him to death before the time appointed in the divine calendar.

17 This request for no publicity was seen by Matthew as fulfilling Isa 42:1-3, though "unto victory" at the end of v.20 reads "unto truth" in the OT, and "he shall show judgment to the Gentiles" replaces Isa 42:4, "till he have set judgment in the earth: and the isles shall wait for his law".

18 This quotation shows

1. the divine assessment of the Son as Servant,

2. what He would not do,

3. what He will do.

Note the fourfold use of "my" in v.18: "*my* servant" and "*my* beloved" refer to the Son, while "*my* soul" and "*my* spirit" refer to God. The "servant" character of the Lord is made much of in the latter chapters of Isaiah, and is the characteristic feature of Mark's Gospel in keeping with Heb 10:7, "I come . . . to do thy will, O God"; He was given the title "thy holy Servant Jesus" by the apostles in Acts 4:27, RV. Moreover, God chooses only that which is valuable to Him, as "chosen of God, and precious" (1 Pet 2:4). "My beloved" recalls the testimony of the Father, "This is my beloved Son", at the baptism of His Son (Matt 3:17), and on the mount of transfiguration (17:5); the Son recognised this love in John 17:24 when He said, "thou lovedst me before the foundation of the world". "Well pleased" was also expressed at His baptism and at His transfiguration. The "spirit *upon* him" takes our minds to Isa 61:1 and Luke 4:18, "The Spirit of the Lord is *upon* me". Draw a distinction between the Spirit eternally *in* Him, and the Spirit *upon* Him for His particular ministry on earth; it is the same distinction as found in the typology of the meal offering, where wafers were *anointed* with oil (namely "upon") and the flour was *mingled* with oil (namely "within"); see Lev 2:4-6. Finally, "judgment to the Gentiles" implies that a distinction will be made between Gentiles who believe and those who do not believe. The message to the house of Israel will go forth to the Gentiles who will trust in His Name. The rejected King will have other subjects, over whom He will be Lord.

19 This verse, "He shall not strive, nor cry; neither shall any man hear his voice in the streets", appears to support the Lord's charge that He should not be made known. Under appropriate circumstances He "withdrew", so His voice was not heard. He would not force His teaching and claims upon unwilling men, nor would He seek publicity by popular preaching and by spectacular signs.

20-21 The reference to "a bruised reed . . . and smoking flax" has brought many suggestions from expositors. In Jamieson, Fausset and Brown's Commentary, we read "And whereas one rough touch will break a bruised reed, and quench the flickering, smoking flax, His it should be, with matchless tenderness, love, and skill, to lift up the meek, to strengthen the weak hands and confirm the feeble knees . . .". Another commentator has likened the reed to a man crushed under the burden and guilt of sin, while the flax is a man in whom the flame of grace is burning low, whose faith and love are barely alight, the Lord would bind up the bruised reed, and gently fan the smoking flax with no stern condemnation or bitter word. All this is true, but the present author interprets the reed and flax in the context, where things are quite different. The reed represents the Pharisees bruised by the winds of their own false doctrine (as in Matt 11:7); the Lord would not deal with them in judgment until His final victory. The smoking flax represents those already condemned, and after Matt 13 this condemnation remains unquenched until the future judgment day and His final victory. All this answers to the Lord withdrawing Himself, and the Pharisees could no longer hear the gracious words proceeding out of His mouth.

3. *The Pharisees and their Blasphemy* 12:22-37

v.22 "Then was brought unto him one possessed with a devil, blind, and dumb: and he healed him, insomuch that the blind and dumb both spake and saw.
v.23 And all the people were amazed, and said, Is not this the son of David?
v.24 But when the Pharisees heard *it*, they said, This *fellow* doth not cast out devils, but by Beelzebub the prince of the devils.
v.25 And Jesus knew their thoughts, and said unto them, Every kingdom divided against itself is brought to desolation; and every city or house divided against itself shall not stand:

v.26 And if Satan cast out Satan, he is divided against himself; how shall then his kingdom stand?
v.27 And if I by Beelzebub cast out devils, by whom do your children cast *them* out? therefore they shall be your judges.
v.28 But if I cast out devils by the Spirit of God, then the kingdom of God is come unto you.
v.29 Or else how can one enter into a strong man's house, and spoil his goods, except he first bind the strong man? and then he will spoil his house.
v.30 He that is not with me is against me; and he that gathereth not with me scattereth abroad.
v.31 Wherefore I say unto you, All manner of sin and blasphemy shall be forgiven unto men: but the blasphemy *against* the *Holy* Ghost shall not be forgiven unto men.
v.32 And whosoever speaketh a word against the Son of man, it shall be forgiven him: but whosoever speaketh against the Holy Ghost, it shall not be forgiven him, neither in this world, neither in the *world* to come.
v.33 Either make the tree good, and his fruit good; or else make the tree corrupt, and his fruit corrupt: for the tree is known by *his* fruit.
v.34 O generation of vipers, how can ye, being evil, speak good things? for out of the abundance of the heart the mouth speaketh.
v.35 A good man out of the good treasure of the heart bringeth forth good things: and an evil man out of the evil treasure bringeth forth evil things.
v.36 But I say unto you, That every idle word that men shall speak, they shall give account thereof in the day of judgment.
v.37 For by thy words thou shalt be justified, and by thy words thou shalt be condemned."

22 The Pharisees had by now caught up with the Lord again. The demon that possessed this man affected him physically – he was both blind and dumb. At the same time, he was a picture of the Jewish nation, for "seeing ye shall see, and shall not perceive . . . and their eyes have they closed; lest at any time they should see with their eyes" (Matt 13:14-15); "that they which see might be made blind" (John 9:39); with "eyes that they should not see" (Rom 11:8), manifesting that "blindness in part is happened to Israel" (v.25). For the man normal health was gained when the Lord had cast the demon out. We must not think that blindness, dumbness and deafness are usually caused by demons, far be the thought. Christians may suffer such physical infirmities particularly in old age, and because the Spirit of God dwells in their bodies no demon can simultaneously gain access. The healing of this man is a picture of conversion, bringing ability to see the Lord by faith and to confess His Name (Rom 10:9). The healing is also a picture of the healing of the nation in the future.

23-24 There were three kinds of reaction to this miracle.

1. The people (the majority) were amazed, saying, "Is not this the son of David?". They knew His genealogy, and perhaps His right to be the Messiah and King of the Jews.

2. Some of the Pharisees accused Him blasphemously.

3. The more devout of the Pharisees (although still in unbelief) desired a sign (v.38). This incident follows immediately after the miracle in Luke 11:14-16.

The accusation that demons were cast out "by Beelzebub the prince of the devils (demons)" was not only blasphemy, but it was also illogical as the Lord proceeded to show. Elsewhere, they said, "Thou hast a devil (demon)" (John 7:20; 8:48), though the Lord rapidly reversed this by saying, "Ye are of your father the devil" (8:44).

25-26 If the outward words of these men were not heard by the Lord, nevertheless He knew their inward thoughts; every heart is naked and opened before Him (Heb 4:13). In becoming Man, He did not empty Himself of the possession of this all-searching capacity. In v.25 the Lord gave two brief pictures to illustrate how illogical these Pharisees were in their attempt to discredit Him.

1. A kingdom with two opposing rulers cannot last. For example, the cases of Moses and Korah, of David and Absalom, of Solomon and Adonijah, had to be rectified, or there would have been a collapse in leadership. Both the beast and Babylon in Rev 13-19 ultimately had conflicting ideas, and both fell. In the OT, the kingdom was divided because there were two leaders, Rehoboam and Jeroboam, and the kingdoms remained as dry bones until Ezek 37: 1-17. They were divided in their policies, and there was war between their respective kings throughout the books of 1 and 2 Kings.

2. The same applies to " every city or house divided against itself", there cannot be two conflicting heads. In Jerusalem in AD 70, the division of the Jews into factions meant that there was no overall resistance and the city was ultimately taken by Titus. Domestically there can be disharmony through lack of mutual subjection, leading to the break-up of homes so frequent in the present day. In a local assembly as the house of God, divisions in the leadership exercised by the elders mean disaster; in Corinth, there was mixed adherence to Apollos, Peter and Paul and this lead to confusion (1 Cor 1:12).

Hence if Satan implants demons and Satan exorcises demons there is division. He does not put a demon in a man with one hand and cast it out with another. The Pharisees were not able to answer the question, "how shall then his kingdom stand?", so their blasphemous accusation fell to the ground.

27-28 The same accusation could be applied to "your children", namely "your sons" (*hüioi*) as in Luke 11:19. The twelve apostles and the additional seventy whom the Lord sent forth had the divinely-given power to cast out unclean spirits (Matt 10:1; Luke 9:1; 10:1,17). So if the Pharisees falsely accused the Lord, then they should also do so to these disciples, in keeping with the Lord's words, "If the world hate you . . . it hated me before it hated you" (John 15:18). With such superior power "they shall be your judges". Throughout the ages, simple saints with spiritual power in God's service have always shown up the barren activity of unsaved national religious leaders, and in the future, "the saints shall judge the world" (1 Cor 6:2).

There could be only one conclusion, that the Lord was casting out demons by the Spirit of God. It was not only in His Manhood (all that the Pharisees saw and recognised) that such work was done, but the three Persons of the Trinity were involved in the battle against the works of Satan. Thus the Spirit of Jehovah was upon Him to recover sight to the blind, with the attendant casting out of a demon if it were the cause (Luke 4:18), and it was through "the eternal Spirit" that He offered Himself without spot to God in the great work of destroying "him that had the power of death, that is, the devil" (Heb 2:14; 9:14). Truly the kingdom of God – the rule of God – was present, accounting for the manifestation of such power against the forces of evil. Today, it is the presence of the One that lets, or hinders, the development of the full flower of evil, the man of sin (2 Thess 2:7).

29 The conflict between the leaders, the Lord and Satan, is now described. The "strong man" is Satan, with his power, force and demons. The "house" stands for the attractive sphere of his powerful operations, since he is the god of this world and the prince of the power of the air. "His goods" refer to the souls of men, taken captive by him at his will. Babylon of the future will also have an interest in the "souls of men" (Rev 18:13). By contrast, in Luke 11:22 the Lord describes Himself as "a stronger than he". He was the One who would spoil principalities and powers, making a show of them openly (Col 2:15), through death annulling him that had the power of death (Heb 2:14). In the future, Satan will be bound and shut up in the bottomless pit, ultimately to be cast into the lake of fire (Rev 20:3, 10). This overcoming was achieved by the Lord's death on the cross in apparent "weakness and defeat", though the final manifestation of this victory is yet future. The Lord taught "now shall the prince of this world be cast out" (John 12:31) and "the prince of this world is judged" (16:11). To "spoil his house" means that during the present age of the gospel men can be rescued from Satan's bondage to become the property of God.

30 It is either Satan's kingdom or God's kingdom. Those motivated by Satan (his goods) are "against" the Lord, as particularly the Pharisees were in the context. In John 8:44, the Lord described them as "Ye are of your father the devil, and the lusts of your father will ye do". A man who scatters is like the hireling shepherd, but those who gather are like those who bring in the harvest (Matt 9:36-38). Apart from the Lord's harvest field, there can be no other place for true service. Everything else scatters, such as "false brethren unawares brought in" (Gal 2:4); "many deceivers" (2 John 7; 1 John 2:18); "men of corrupt minds" (1 Tim 6:5); "enemies of the cross of Christ" (Phil 3:18).

31-32 These two verses should be interpreted only in their context; the word "wherefore" makes this clear. The Lord indicated that there are two possibilities:

1. "All manner of sin and blasphemy . . . a word against the Son of man";

2. "blasphemy against the Holy Spirit . . . whosoever speaketh against the Holy Spirit".

The Lord spoke such solemn words because of the Pharisees' blasphemous accusation that the Lord cast out demons by Satan the prince of the demons (v.24), whereas in reality He had cast them out by the Spirit of God (v.28). Sin, blasphemy and speaking against the Son of man would occur when men, in ignorance, just did not know the truth of His Person, not knowing that He was the Son of God and hence divine. There was a sin-offering for a "sin through ignorance" (Lev 4:2) and such sin could be forgiven, not arbitrarily on the part of God, of course, but through the inevitable channels of confession, repentance and faith. Thus Saul had done many things contrary to the name of Jesus of Nazareth, compelling the saints to blaspheme (Acts 26:9-11), yet he was forgiven. But if men did know the truth of the Person of the Son of man, and yet rejected Him and likened the Spirit of God in Him to Satan, this amounted to blasphemy that could not be forgiven. Their sin had gone too far, and God's Spirit would not always strive with such men. The opportunity to repent would be taken away; these men would hear the truth in parables, and there would be no further hearing and seeing (Matt 13:14-15). In the context, the Pharisees were men in this category, and are completely condemned in Matt 23 for they could not escape the damnation of hell. As John wrote, "There is a sin unto death: I do not say that he shall pray for it" (1 John 5:16). An example in the future is the political beast in Rev 13:1-10, who will have " a mouth speaking great things and blasphemies", opening his mouth "in blasphemy against God, to blaspheme his name". The end of this emperor will be the lake of fire (19:20), with no possibility of repentance on the part of such an one who rises from the bottomless pit (17:8).

33 This verse refers to the inevitable state in which some men place themselves. In Matt 7:17-20 the Lord had distinguished between good and corrupt trees. The command "make" is remarkable, showing that men are responsible for the kind of tree into which they grow. When the gospel is preached to a man, he is what we may call "neutral" in the sense that he can go in either direction. Either he goes in the direction of eternal life through repentance and faith, or (like the Pharisees in the context) he rejects the truth through his own blasphemies. The mere rejection of truth means that the opportunity for repentance is still with him, but blasphemy against the Holy Spirit means that the opportunity has disappeared for ever. When a man is in such a state, we may not recognise it, but God does, assessing him by his fruit. In other words, unbelief can turn sour, and evangelists do well to warn their congregations that this danger could become a reality if the truth is rejected for too long a season.

34-35 These words "generation of vipers" were still being spoken to the Pharisees; John the Baptist used this description in Matt 3:7, and the Lord used it again in 23:33. They were as brute beasts ready to be destroyed, yet seeking to poison others through their teaching. The metaphor is changed, from a tree to the heart of man which reflects upon the very nature of his being. What the mouth speaks shows what exists in man's heart, it cannot be otherwise. A Christian will speak things worthy of his calling; an unbeliever will speak things consistent with his unbelief. "He that is of the earth is earthly, and speaketh of the earth" (John 3:31). The Lord expanded on this theme in Matt 15:11-20. A man who has "evil thoughts, murders, adulteries, fornications, thefts, false witness, blasphemies" (v.19) will speak of these things; another list is provided by Paul in Gal 5:19-21. These things have great entertainment value, since they meet a response in the hearts of those seeking entertainment. On the other hand, the heart of a believer is filled with quite different treasures. Paul supplied a list in Gal 5:22-23, calling them the "fruit of the Spirit". When he exhorts us to think on whatsoever is "true, honest, just, pure, lovely, of good report" in other believers (Phil 4:8), only a heart that has such treasures can respond. If, like the Pharisees, the heart contains hatred against the Lord, this will be manifested in speech that so often and easily takes the Lord's name in vain. If, like the apostle John, the heart contains love to the One who died on the cross, then this will be manifested in careful and reverent speech. One does not judge critically when one of necessity observes this difference in the speech of men around.

36-37 A man may speak millions of words in his lifetime, but there is a record kept. The word for "idle" is *argos*, derived from the negative particle *a* prefixed to *ergon* meaning work. Inactive and barren words do no useful work in those who hear; they can be mischievous words of unbelief and blasphemy (in the context) instead of words that are full of life and edification. For unbelievers, the record of life, conduct, words and deeds remains full; they may discard all thoughts of the day of judgment, stating that death is the end of it all. But the Lord said that an account will have to be given, evidently before the One seated on the great white throne. There will be no defence counsel, no jury to confuse, for the Judge will know all and will do right in judgment. Condemnation follows from words spoken in this present life, for they reveal the inner state of soul. And the same is true of believers; they will appear "justified", not of course before the great white throne, but before the judgment seat of Christ. "For with the heart man believeth unto righteousness; and with the mouth confession is made unto salvation" (Rom 10:10). To be justified means to be pronounced not guilty; this is the believer's portion now, since our confession shows that we are justified by grace (Rom 3:24), by faith (v.28), and by His blood (5:9).

4. *The Pharisees and their Demand for a Sign* 12:38-50

v.38 "Then certain of the scribes and of the Pharisees answered, saying, Master, we would see a sign from thee.
v.39 But he answered and said unto them, An evil and adulterous generation seeketh after a sign; and there shall no sign be given to it, but the sign of the prophet Jonas:
v.40 For as Jonas was three days and three nights in the whale's belly; so shall the Son of man be three days and three nights in the heart of the earth.
v.41 The men of Nineveh shall rise in judgment with this generation, and shall condemn it: because they repented at the preaching of Jonas; and, behold, a greater than Jonas *is* here.
v.42 The queen of the south shall rise up in the judgment with this generation, and shall condemn it: for she came from the uttermost parts of the earth to hear the wisdom of Solomon; and, behold, a greater than Solomon *is* here.
v.43 When the unclean spirit is gone out of a man, he walketh through dry places, seeking rest, and findeth none.
v.44 Then he saith, I will return into my house from whence I came out; and when he is come, he findeth *it* empty, swept, and garnished.
v.45 Then goeth he, and taketh with himself seven other spirits more wicked than himself, and they enter in and dwell there: and the last *state* of that man is worse than the first. Even so shall it be also unto this wicked generation.
v.46 While he yet talked to the people, behold, *his* mother and his brethren stood without, desiring to speak with him.
v.47 Then one said unto him, Behold, thy mother and thy brethren stand without, desiring to speak with thee.
v.48 But he answered and said unto him that told him, Who is my mother? and who are my brethren?
v.49 And he stretched forth his hand toward his disciples, and said, Behold my mother and my brethren!
v.50 For whosoever shall do the will of my Father which is in heaven, the same is my brother, and sister, and mother."

38 The scribes are now found with the Pharisees, and to judge from v.46 and 13:1 the scene took place in a house. Later in 16:1, Pharisees and Sadducees were joined together asking for a sign, an unusual combination since doctrinally they were enemies (Acts 23:6-9). Whereas Matthew places this event just *before* the parable of the sower, Luke places it well *after* the transfiguration (Luke 11:29).

Because of their unbelief, the Jewish religious leaders were not satisfied with the Lord's miracles; they wanted something even more spectacular. For example, they claimed that they would believe if the Lord had come down from the cross (Matt 27:42). The only signs given by the Lord were ones not particularly desired. They were, in fact, associated with His death and resurrection, such as "Destroy this temple, and in three days I will raise it up" (John 2:19), given in response to the Jews' request,

"What sign showest thou unto us?". This desire for signs demonstrated the people's unbelief, as if the unfamiliar and spectacular would provide a basis for faith. But the Lord would not form faith on that basis, and today any religious experience based on an unfamiliar happening and spectacular show is no sure basis for faith.

39-40 The Lord described the generation as "adulterous", namely they adhered to doctrines which were not divinely approved. The Lord would not help such men, except by quoting well-known OT events as signs. In fact, He would go further and confuse them by speaking in parables. The Lord thus quoted the OT story of Jonah, presenting it as a sign. The "great fish" that God had prepared in Jonah 1:17 is *kētos* in NT Greek, translated "whale". Strictly this word means a huge fish or sea-monster, evidently a special creation by God for a special purpose at a special time. Thus Jonah 2 was regarded as a type or sign of the Lord's death and resurrection (not that we can read types of Christ in all the activities of Jonah, for disobedience and complaint marked many of his actions). The Lord referred to the Son of man being "three days and three nights in the heart of the earth", reflecting both on the time and on the position that He would occupy in death. Some expositors interpret "the heart of the earth" as being the tomb where the Lord's body was laid; others interpret this as hades to which His soul was confined but not kept after the period was over (Acts 2:27). We do not care to adjudicate between these two interpretations. In Luke 11:30, the sign of Jonah is stated differently, "as Jonas was a sign unto the Ninevites, so shall also the Son of man be to this generation". He was a sign in the sense that his skin was coloured and pitted by the digestive juices within the fish. The Ninevites sew Jonah changed, a fact that led to their repentance. In the Lord's case, He had a glorious body in resurrection; this was unseen by sinners, whose repentance would be granted by the Spirit. His resurrection, preached but not seen, would be a sign to the Jews who "require a sign" (1 Cor 1:22-24).

41 The fact that "the men of Nineveh" will rise in judgment "with this generation" has important consequences, discussed in the following verse. Two preachers are contrasted—Jonah and One greater then Jonah (the Lord); two distinct results are contrasted—Nineveh's repentance and the Pharisees' refusal to repent.

42 The phrase "shall rise up in judgment" we must interpret as referring to the great white throne judgment, when John "saw the dead, small and great, stand before God" (Rev 20:12). How can this be? The queen of Sheba had faith, indicated by her words "Blessed be the Lord thy God . . . because the Lord loved Israel for ever" (1 Kings 10:9). This was a special Gentile faith, and the question is, When will such men and women as the queen of Sheba rise in judgment? Not being members of the church, they will not rise with the church at the rapture, nor will they rise at the "first resurrection" to enter into the kingdom established on earth nor into its sphere of administration from heaven (Rev 20:6). The Lord stated that their rising up will occur "with this generation", namely with the scribes and Pharisees in unbelief, who will be condemned by the men of Nineveh who repented and by the queen of the south who exercised faith. We feel that men such as these will then enter into life via the great white throne judgment, for Rev 20:11-15 does *not* state *nor* does it even imply that only unbelieving sinners will be there; certainly *no* member of the church will be there. Since the Lord was greater than Solomon, men should aspire to be greater in faith than the queen of Sheba; they should accept His teaching just as she had listened to the wisdom of Solomon. And if Nineveh repented upon seeing the sign of Jonah and hearing the words of a disobedient and complaining prophet, how much more should the Jews believe in the Person, works and teaching of Christ. At the great white throne, this city will show up the character of the Jewish unbelief at the Lord's teaching. While expressing this view, we recognise that expositors who explain Rev 20:11-15 in a different way will also explain these verses in Matt 12 in a correspondingly different way.

43-44 Verses 43-45 immediately follow v. 30 in the corresponding passage in Luke 11:23-26. This story, in which an unclean spirit leaves a man and later returns with seven others, has prophetical implications for the Jews. Some expositors have suggested that the man swept and garnished represents self reformation, but this hardly fits the context. Rather, the story shows how religious Jews were affected by Satan. The "unclean spirit" denotes the prevalent idolatry that characterised the nation at the close of the Jewish monarchy when Nebuchadnezzar king of Babylon destroyed Jerusalem and its temple (2 Chron 36:14). Upon their return to the land at the end of the allotted period of captivity, idolatry never again overtook the nation – they were "swept and garnished". Yet the nation remained in "dry places" after the period of faithful leaders like Ezra and Nehemiah; the unclean spirit ensured that the nation quickly became dead again after its restoration. Satan was not satisfied; if the idolatry of the nations around was kept out, then he would interfere with the actual Jewish religion through the Pharisees.

45 So the unclean spirit returned to attack the Jews, this attack with "seven other spirits more wicked than himself" making the nation worse than before, worse in the sense that they were now dealing so abominably with the Lord Jesus. Admittedly it was no longer idolatry as such, but the false legality of the Pharisees and their hypocrisy, highly esteemed amongst men but "abomination in the sight of God" (Luke 16:15). They were not antagonistic to the temple in Jerusalem, but to the true Temple in their midst, to the Lord Himself. The religious leaders would adhere to an OT ceremony completely abandoned by God upon the death and resurrection of His Son. In the OT they had killed many of the prophets, and now they were about to kill the true Prophet. The nation would thus be cast aside, enabling the Gentiles to enter into grace (Rom 11:17-22).

46-47 Clearly the Lord was inside a house, while His mother and brethren were outside. How different was His mother from His brethren. His mother had had a vision in Luke 1:28, so she knew the truth. But according to John 7:5 His brethren did not believe (at least prior to Acts 1 :14). Here we have representatives of two classes of people. No doubt they were seeking to persuade Him on a natural level to rest and to partake of some food, as in Mark 3:20-21.

This was like the disciples who once said, "Master, eat" (John 4:31), failing to understand that His food was to do God's will (v.34). An intermediary passed the message to Him, "thy mother and thy brethren stand without, desiring to speak with thee". "Desiring" carries with it one of two distinct attitudes of heart:

1. Knowing something about His Person without faith, as was the case of His brethren. Compare this with Herod, who had desired to see Jesus for a long time (Luke 23:8). So today, religious aspirations are not necessarily faithful and spiritual ones.

2. A true desire to find Him and to learn of Him, as the Greeks said, "we would see Jesus" (John 12:21), and as David said, "One thing have I desired . . . to behold the beauty of the Lord" (Ps 27:4).

48-50 The Lord's answer reflected upon the fact that the Pharisees had placed themselves outside any relationship with Himself, and that the new order would be founded upon new relationships far removed from natural ones.

In this answer, there is no mention of a "father" amongst His disciples, only "mother" and "brethren". In other words, He said nothing that would confuse others and distract from His Father in heaven. We do not attempt to spiritualise the two distinct words "mother, brethren", since the Lord only quoted the news that the intermediary had brought. He visualised here that relationship with Himself is based upon hearing and doing the Word of God. Such is "the will of my Father", namely receiving the seed and producing the fruit (Matt 13:8), or building a house on a rock (7:24), or hearing, believing and being baptised (Acts 18:8), or being a doer of the Word and not a hearer only (James 1:22). Yet there is a deeper sense in which He calls us "my brethren" (Matt 28:10; John 20:17; Heb 2:11-13); this corresponds to divine grace introducing us to the holy relationship "My Father, and *your* Father" .

CHAPTERS 13 TO 20:29
THE KING'S MINISTRY—TEACHING WITH PARABLES

THE NEW ORDER

I. The Parables of the Kingdom (13:1-58)

1. *The Parable of the Sower* 13:1-9, 18-23

v.1 The same day went Jesus out of the house, and sat by the sea side.
v.2 And great multitudes were gathered together unto him, so that he went into a ship, and sat; and the whole multitude stood on the shore.
v.3 And he spake many things unto them in parables, saying, Behold a sower went forth to sow;
v.4 And when he sowed, some *seeds* fell by the way side, and the fowls came and devoured them up:
v.5 Some fell upon stony places, where they had not much earth: and forthwith they sprung up, because they had no deepness of earth:
v.6 And when the sun was up, they were scorched; and because they had no root, they withered away.
v.7 And some fell among thorns; and the thorns sprung up, and choked them:
v.8 But other fell into good ground, and brought forth fruit, some an hundredfold, some sixtyfold, some thirtyfold.
v.9 Who hath ears to hear, let him hear.
v.18 Hear ye therefore the parable of the sower.
v.19 When any one heareth the word of the kingdom, and understandeth *it* not, then cometh the wicked *one,* and catcheth away that which was sown in his heart. This is he which received seed by the way side.
v.20 But he that received the seed into stony places, the same is he that heareth the word, and anon with joy receiveth it;
v.21 Yet hath he not root in himself, but dureth for a while: for when tribulation or persecution ariseth because of the word, by and by he is offended.
v.22 He also that received seed among the thorns is he that heareth the word; and the care of this world, and the deceitfulness of riches, choke the word, and he becometh unfruitful.
v.23 But he that received seed into the good ground is he that heareth the word, and understandeth *it;* which also beareth fruit, and bringeth forth, some an hundredfold, some sixty, some thirty."

1 After the blasphemy of the Pharisees in the previous chapter, the Lord's ministry now undergoes a considerable change. At least that is how Matthew under the control of the Spirit of God, chose to record events. The open ministry of the previous chapters mingled with many miracles now gives place to ministry of a different style. Parables are introduced in order to hide the truth from the wise and prudent. The first occasion on which the word "parable" occurs in Matthew's Gospel is in v.3. Throughout this major section, many new and holy things are introduced, that go beyond the Lord's ministry to the Jews. Ministry more particularly referring to the Jews commences again in 20:30, the major section commencing at that verse being concerned with the King's return.

2 To denote the change in the character of His ministry, the Lord left the house bypassing His mother and brethren, and sat by the edge of the Sea of Galilee. Multitudes were still present, though they would now find that much of His ministry was incomprehensible. He was now in a ship on the sea, typically amongst the nations who would later receive the Word of God and to whom further mysteries could be revealed. But the multitudes on the shore denote typically the Jews who were now distant and unbelieving.

3, 18 The word parable (*parabolē*, from *paraballō*, to throw or lay beside) denotes the placing of one thing beside another, the use of one set of circumstances to represent another set of circumstances. Sometimes this was to clarify or to simplify a spiritual or moral issue; other times it was to hide the spiritual truth from all except the initiated. According to Luke 8:11, the seed is "the word of God", but the "sower" is not defined in the Lord's explanation. It represents the Lord firstly, and secondly His servants after Him. In the second parable, the Lord defined the sower as "the Son of man", stating that "the field is the world" (Matt 13:37-38). He came into the world with the Word of God, teaching from the days when He was in the synagogue in Nazareth, up to the days in the temple courts in Jerusalem just before His cross. The seed was also sown by labourers chosen and sent forth into the field, such as John the Baptist, the twelve apostles and Paul (1 Cor 3:6; John 4:36-38), as well as the evangelists and teachers in the Acts, some of whom sowed while others reaped. As the seed, the Word of God has life and potential to produce more life, "born again . . . of incorruptible (seed), by the word of God" (1 Pet 1:23, James 1:18). The spreading of this seed is seen in passages such as Matt 10:5, and as in Acts 10:37 where it was "published throughout all Judaea"; see Paul's testimony in Rom 15:18-21. It is tragic that false teachers use the same method for distributing their false doctrine: in Matt 13:25 an enemy sowed tares among the wheat, while in Eph 4:14 the wind blows about the evil seed of weeds.

4, 19 No doubt the Lord could see in front of Him a field stretching down to the water's edge; there would be a patch around the field, trodden down by men and animals. There would be visible outcrops of rock, with other rocks overlaid with a thin layer of dry soil. There would also be cut-down clumps of bramble bushes and thorns with their roots remaining. The rest of the field would be good ground. The seed was scattered everywhere, with salvation available for all, namely "unto the uttermost part of the earth" (Acts 1:8).

Some seed "fell by the way side", or "along the way" (JND). The Greek is *"para tēn hodon"*, namely the path round the field. The word "side" in AV and RV sounds poetic and is traditional in this parable, but does not correspond to any word in the Greek, except the preposition *para;* "way side" appears again in Matt 20:30. This "way side" speaks of a hard heart that will not believe, the Word will not penetrate, not being mixed with faith. The birds rapidly devour what lies on the surface; namely, "the wicked one" (Matt 13:19), "Satan" (Mark 4:15) and "the devil" (Luke 8:12) ensures the removal of the seed. Thus "Satan hath desired to have thee" (Luke 22:31), and "the devil . . . (seeketh) whom he may devour" (1 Pet 5:8). The apostles were sometimes affected like this when the Lord was with them; thus in John 2:22 they failed to remember His words until He was risen, and in Luke 18:34 the plain and obvious truth about His death and resurrection "was hid from them", evidently by Satan, until the Spirit was given. The reader should note that the four types of ground reflect upon the work of Satan, self, sin and the Spirit.

5, 6, 20, 21 The word for "stony places" is *petrōdēs* rock lying beneath shallow soil; Luke 8:6, 13 uses the word *petra,* meaning rock. This speaks of a shallow heart, with no character, reality or earnestness. This is a surface religion, with a hard self-life underneath. Under these circumstances, there can be no question of being rooted and grounded in love (Eph 3:17), no possibility of being grounded and settled (Col 1:23), no possibility of taking root downward and bearing fruit upward (2 Kings 19:30). The Word will produce some effect, but not necessarily salvation. There may be joy outwardly for a season together with a kind of continuation. This can be brought about by crowd emotion, or when the gospel attracts the emotions rather than the conscience, or when outward miracles attract rather than a convicting message. The rock is a barrier to progress; such men may even "for a while believe" (Luke 8:13), yet this is not a saving faith, but a mental acknowledgement, proved invalid by the subsequent falling away under trials and tribulation. As examples, there were the disciples who went back and walked no more with Him (John 6:66), and Simon of Samaria who believed but ultimately perished (Acts 8:13, 20). Those to whom the Epistle to the Hebrews was written were not like that; in their weakness they were seeking ceremony, yet they believed, evidenced in things that accompanied salvation (Heb 6:9).

7, 22 Some of the scattered seed fell amongst thorns, that is amongst the roots of the thorns which were not necessarily visible above the ground if it had been outwardly cleared for sowing. Thorns speak of a worldly heart. Cares, riches and pleasures of the present materialistic life choked the full growth of the seed, and prevented fruit bearing. Only true faith overcomes the world and its tendencies and attractions (1 John 5:4), thereby enabling the believer not to love the things in the world (2:15). Cares and anxieties may speak of attempts to serve too much, with too little sitting at the Lord's feet (Luke 10:39). Many financial thorns appear in Luke's Gospel: riches brought disaster in the case of the rich farmer who had plentiful harvests but without God (12:16); mammon kept men from serving God alone (16:13); the rich man who fared sumptuously every day had good things in his lifetime, but nothing afterwards (16:19, 25); the rich ruler went away sorrowful (18:23). Financial problems in the early days of the church sprang from the same roots (Acts 5:1-2; 6:1; 8:18).

8, 9, 23 Good ground bringing forth much fruit was the object of God's creation; Isaac sowed and received "in the same year an hundredfold: and the Lord blessed him" (Gen 26:12). Spiritually, this suggests an honest and true heart. This ground was no mere natural ground, for the natural man does not receive the things of the Spirit of God (1 Cor 2:14). This heart had been prepared by grace; hardness was softened, shallowness was deepened, damaging roots were cleared away. Yet differing types of good soil had the capacity to produce differing yields. There is the capacity of the ground, as in the case of the differing talents (Matt 25:16-17), and the quality of faithfulness, in the parable of the pounds (Luke 19:16-18). The fruit of the Spirit is "in all goodness and righteousness and truth" (Eph 5:9; Gal 5:22), and this contrasts with the "unfruitful works of darkness" (Eph 5:11). As the seed, the Word will produce fruit "after his kind" (Gen 1:11). There was to be no confusion in God's natural creation, just as there should be no confusion in His spiritual creation. Men may engage in genetic manipulation which is a form of confusion, and pseudo-evangelists can attempt the same thing in spiritual work, but God desires only true fruit that arises on account of the grace of God: "by the grace of God I am what I am . . . not in vain; but I laboured more abundantly than they all" (1 Cor 15:10). No doubt Paul brought forth fruit an hundredfold, and lesser evangelists only thirtyfold, yet all such work is well done, and acceptable to the Lord who seeks such fruit.

In the three Gospels, note that the verb coming between hearing and bringing forth fruit is: "understand" in Matt 13:23; "receive" in Mark 4:20, and "keep" in Luke 8:15; compare these with the reading, hearing and keeping in Rev 1:3. By concluding the parable with the statement, "Who hath ears to hear, let him hear" the Lord implied that hearing must lead to responsible action. This should be taken in conjunction with the next paragraph; those who hear do not hear (v.13), while the ears of the apostles are blessed since they hear (v.16).

2. *Reasons for the Parabolic Method* 13:10-17

v.10 "And the disciples came, and said unto him, Why speakest thou unto them in parables?

v.11 He answered and said unto them, Because it is given unto you to know the mysteries of the kingdom of heaven, but to them it is not given.

v.12 For whosoever hath, to him shall be given, and he shall have more abundance: but whosoever hath not, from him shall be taken away even that he hath.

v.13 Therefore speak I to them in parables: because they seeing see not; and hearing they hear not, neither do they understand.

v.14 And in them is fulfilled the prophecy of Esaias, which saith, By hearing ye shall hear, and shall not understand; and seeing ye shall see, and shall not perceive:

v.15 For this people's heart is waxed gross, and *their* ears are dull of hearing, and their eyes they have closed; lest at any time they should see with *their* eyes, and hear with *their* ears, and should understand with *their* heart, and should be converted, and I should heal them.

v.16 But blessed *are* your eyes, for they see: and your ears, for they hear.

v.17 For verily I say unto you, That many prophets and righteous men have desired to see *those things* which ye see, and have not seen *them*; and to hear *those things* which ye hear, and have not heard *them*."

10 It is good to ask questions when one is in ignorance, particularly as we learn from v.23 that understanding is an integral part of the planted Word bringing forth fruit. Today, the implications of the parable of the sower are clear, in some measure at least, to every reader or hearer, whether he be younger or older. But to those early disciples this was not so; hence they adopted the strange attitude that, because *they* could not understand, therefore the Lord was speaking to the multitudes *only* and not to themselves. Note the word "them" in our verse contrasting with the word "you' ' in the Lord's answer in v.11. The change in the style of the Lord's ministry must have caused surprise to these disciples, and this gave rise to their question. This may be the experience of many believers today, upon reading, for example, the prophecy of Ezekiel for the first time. Yet the Lord offers understanding to those who have spiritual ears to hear, an idea that enters Rev 2-3 many times in connection with the figurative letters to the seven churches. In Mark 4:10, it was only when they were alone that they asked the Lord about the parable's meaning. In Luke 8 only one verse (v.10) explains why the Lord taught in parables, but seven verses (11-17) are devoted to this in Matt 13.

11-13 The Lord had been teaching the kingdom of heaven before, but from now on further specialised teaching on the subject would be reserved for the understanding of the disciples only. This further teaching is designated "the mysteries of the kingdom of heaven". According to Vine, the word "mystery" (*mustērion*) means "that which, being outside the range of unassisted natural apprehension, can be made known only by Divine revelation, and is made known in a manner and at a time appointed by God, and to those only who are illuminated by His Spirit". Thus it implies truth previously withheld but now revealed. For example, in the present dispensation there is the mystery of the church as one body consisting of Jews and Gentiles (Eph 3:1-11). A concordance can be used to search out all the mysteries recorded in the NT. The Lord implied that the mysteries of the kingdom of heaven were given in parabolic form to veil the truth from those outside the kingdom. Only the disciples would understand these mysteries hidden from the wise and revealed unto babes (Matt 11:25); the truth would be known only by the initiated. Many parables therefore were a veiled form of presentation of truth, so that "if any man be ignorant, let him be ignorant" (1 Cor 14:38). Not all parables, of course, had this purpose. Again Paul wrote, "Eye hath not seen . . . but God hath revealed them unto us by his Spirit" (1 Cor 2:9-10).

The parabolic method involved the principle of reversals. Matt 13:12 reads like a modern financial principle: those who have plenty of money can make more by expanding capital and increasing interest, while those who have but little money have to spend even that to make ends meet in times of rising prices. This may not appear to be fair, since those in the latter category may not have been responsible for bringing about their impecunious state. But spiritually this principle of reversals is very fair, because those who have and those who have not are responsible for their state of advantage or disadvantage respectively. Those who have the truth have it because they desire it; those who do not have the truth are in that state because they do not want it. (This does not refer to the heathen who have never heard the gospel, but to men like the Pharisees and the cities in Matt 11:20 who rejected the opportunity of participating in the truth.) As Amos 8:11-12 puts it, "Behold, the days come, saith the Lord God, that I will send a famine . . . of hearing the words of the Lord . . . they shall run to and fro to seek the word of the Lord, and shall not find it". The Lord enunciated this principle of reversals to the Pharisees in John 9:39 after the blind man's sight was restored, "I am come into this world, that they which see not might see; and that they which see might be made blind". See Matt 25:29.

The Lord was really perpetuating a condition that existed already in the pharisaical heart (Matt 13:13). They saw and heard the Lord's miracles and teaching, but they were spiritually blind and deaf. The use of parables and the fact that miracles were not going to be so prominent in the Lord's ministry after ch.13 had the end in view to maintain religious deafness and blindness in a spiritual sense. Later the Lord said to the argumentative Pharisees, "Why do ye not understand my speech? even because ye cannot *hear* my word" (John 8:43).

14-15 Further to prove the point, the Lord quoted from Isa 6:9-10. During the early stage of his first imprisonment in Rome, Paul also quoted these verses from Isaiah (Acts 28:25-27). The apostle provided the unbelieving Jews with a quotation from their own OT, "Well spake the Holy Spirit by Esaias the prophet unto our fathers". The quotation refers to lack of response; they would hear, but with their ears dull of hearing they would not understand – that is, they would not be able to discern Christ in the OT. Before Isa 6, king Uzziah had taken the decision to burn incense in the temple, something that only the priests were allowed to do. The heart of the king "was lifted up to his destruction: for he transgressed against the Lord his God" (2 Chron 26:16-21). The priest Azariah with eighty others went in after the king to preserve the sanctity of the ordinances and the house of God; the result was that the king was smitten with leprosy because he tampered with the holy things of God. A year after the king's death, Isaiah was permitted to see the Lord "sitting upon a throne, high and lifted up" (Isa 6:1). The glory was so great that only the hem of His garments occupied the temple, but the heavens above could not contain the fulness of the Godhead. The threefold nature of the Godhead is seen in the triple cry, "Holy, holy, holy, is the Lord of hosts". Isaiah himself would have been as unclean as king Uzziah but his iniquity was taken away by means of a "live coal" from off the altar. He then received the commission to go to a people just as unclean as Uzziah had been, and as he, Isaiah, had been. The difference would be that, whereas Isaiah had humbled himself in confession before the Lord, yet the nation would not repent. In Isa 6, the words of the quotation are the words of God Himself; there would be but little response to the message.

In using this quotation in Matt 13:14-15, the Lord was taking note of the previous blasphemous statement by the Pharisees (12:24). He slightly changed the last phrase of the quotation, saying "lest . . . they . . . should be converted, and I should heal them". In other words, the Lord is seen as the actual speaker of the quotation. This is confirmed by John 12:39-41 where Isaiah is stated to have said this "when he saw *his* glory, and spake of *him*"; in other words, the Lord Jesus is seen throughout Isa 6. Finally, in Acts 28:25, we note that the Holy Spirit was speaking in Isa 6. Hence, totally, the three Persons of the Godhead are seen in connection with this quotation, a remarkable feature that faith is not slow to grasp in these days particularly as the doctrine of the Trinity together with the Personality of the Holy Spirit is denied by many.

Paul used this quotation, not so much as applicable to individual Jews, but to the nation. "Lest they . . . should be converted, and I should heal them" means that there would be no further opportunity during the gospel-age for the Jews as a nation to turn again for spiritual healing. Admittedly this will be their happy portion in a day yet to come, but that is not the subject of Matt 13 and Acts 28; Rom 11 must be consulted for that aspect of truth. Paul implied that the Jews had thrown away their last opportunity collectively as a nation. This had already taken place in Antioch (Acts 13:46), and then it took place again in Rome. The Word was now wholly for the Gentiles, as well as for individual Jews brought into the kingdom; Paul's certainty was that "they will hear it". Quoting Isa 52:15, he had already written to the Romans, "To whom he was not spoken of, they shall see: and they that have not heard shall understand" (Rom 15:21).

16-17 By contrast, the apostles benefited by this. As far as the parable was concerned, their eyes were blind and their ears were deaf. As far as the meaning of the parable was concerned, their eyes could see and their ears could hear spiritually, only because its meaning was revealed privately to them. The word for "blessed" in this verse is *makarios* meaning happy, a word that occurs thirteen times in Matthew's Gospel, chiefly in the Beatitudes. (The other word for "blessed" comes from the verb *eulogeō* to speak well of, applied to the Lord in Matt 21:9; 23:39 as the coming King.)

These apostles had a great advantage over many prophets and righteous men who had either spoken prophetically of Christ. or who had sought for and seen those things by faith, as Abraham (Heb 11:13-19). The OT prophets had "inquired and searched diligently" concerning the sufferings of Christ and the glory that should follow (1 Pet 1:10-12), though, since they did not minister "unto themselves", a full vision and understanding was missing in their experience. As the Lord said, they "have not seen them . . . and have not heard them" obviously because the Lord was not present amongst them as a Man, manifest in the flesh. The apostles were special men, and carried the remembrance of the Lord's presence amongst them into their future years of ministry (2 Pet 1:16-18; 1 John 1:2). But all that the Pharisees carried into the post- resurrection era was unbelief that disregarded the Name of the Lord Jesus (Acts 4:18; 5:40).

3. *The Parable of the Tares* 13:24-30, 36-43

v.24 "Another parable put he forth unto them, saying, The kingdom of heaven is likened unto a man which sowed good seed in his field:
v.25 But while men slept, his enemy came and sowed tares among the wheat, and went his way.
v.26 But when the blade was sprung up, and brought forth fruit, then appeared the tares also.
v.27 So the servants of the householder came and said unto him, Sir, didst not thou sow good seed in thy field? from whence then hath it tares?
v.28 He said unto them, An enemy hath done this. The servants said unto him, Wilt thou then that we go and gather them up?
v.29 But he said, Nay; lest while ye gather up the tares, ye root up also the wheat with them.
v.30 Let both grow together until the harvest: and in the time of harvest I will say to the reapers, Gather ye together first the tares, and bind them in bundles to burn them: but gather the wheat into my barn.
v.36 Then Jesus sent the multitude away, and went into the house: and his disciples came unto him, saying, Declare unto us the parable of the tares of the field.
v.37 He answered and said unto them, He that soweth the good seed is the Son of man;
v.38 The field is the world; the good seed are the children of the kingdom; but the tares are the children of the wicked *one;*
v.39 The enemy that sowed them is the devil; the harvest is the end of the world; and the reapers are the angels.
v.40 As therefore the tares are gathered and burned in the fire; so shall it be in the end of this world.
v.41 The Son of man shall send forth his angels, and they shall gather out of his kingdom all things that offend, and them which do iniquity;
v.42 And shall cast them into a furnace of fire: there shall be wailing and gnashing of teeth.
v.43 Then shall the righteous shine forth as the sun in the kingdom of their Father. Who hath ears to hear, let him hear."

24, 36 All the verses from v.24 to v.33 form a connected discourse spoken to the multitudes. This second parable is described as "another" (*allos*), another of the same kind, since it related to the kingdom of heaven and was given to hide the truth; in this sense it was directly related to the first parable. In Mark 4:26-29 the parable coming between the parable of the sower and that of the mustard seed is quite different: we may almost call it the eighth parable of the kingdom, for it relates to good seed *only*, growing entirely under the hand of God, and even believers are unable to explain the mechanism whereby spiritual growth to the harvest takes place. Having just enunciated the fact that the understanding of parables would be outside the scope of mere human intelligence, the Lord sent the multitude away, and He went privately into a house to be alone with His disciples. Some enter a house spiritually (as David in 1 Chron 16:43), and others in a highly unspiritual state (John 7:53). Previously, the disciples had not asked for the meaning of the parable of the sower: they merely asked why the Lord spoke in parables (Matt 13:10); this time they ask for the meaning of the second parable. After the seventh parable, they confessed "Yea, Lord", they had understood everything; we cannot see that this was a perfectly correct answer!

Whereas in vv.31, 33, 44, 45, the word "like" (*homoios*) is just an adjective, yet in v.24 the word "is likened" is a verb (*homoioō*) in the past tense. The kingdom is not likened to the man by himself, but to the whole scene described in vv.24-30. The Lord's interpretation in vv.36-43 is given in great detail, showing how every part of the parable is susceptible to a spiritual meaning. No irrelevant padding occurs in the parable, inserted just for the sake of continuity and completeness; the reader may care to decide whether this attention to minute detail can be applied to every parable, particularly those which the Lord did not explicitly interpret.

We must understand what the word for "tares" (*zizanion*) really means. We quote Vine: this "is a kind of darnel, the commonest of the four species, being the bearded, growing in the grain fields, as tall as wheat and barley, and resembling wheat in appearance. It was credited among the Jews with being degenerate wheat. The Rabbis called it 'bastard'. The seeds are poisonous to man and herbivorous animals, producing sleepiness, nausea, convulsions and even death (they are harmless to poultry). The plants can be separated out, but the custom . . . is to leave the cleaning out till near the time of harvest".

25, 37-38 The kingdom of heaven is a sphere of profession that recognises the fact that divine rule originates from the heavens, contrasting with the rule of the beasts upon earth – particularly the Roman beast. "A man" is defined to be "the Son of man", a name designating the Lord in His position as having over-all authority over men on earth. "His field" is "the world", no longer seen as restricted to the house of Israel (Matt 10:5-6) since the King was rejected, but embracing the truth that "God so loved the world" (John 3:16). "Good seed" is defined to be "the children (*hoi huioi,* the sons) of the kingdom". In the previous parable, the seed was the Word of God; here disciples or believers are implied, those who by faith submit themselves to the rule from heaven, manifested in a manner consistent with the dispensation in which they live. This shows that a symbol in one parable need not have the same significance as the same symbol in another parable. "But while men slept" is not interpreted; this suggests that neither believers nor unbelievers will be in a state of watchfulness – the kind of circumstances when Satan can do his work. "His enemy" is "the devil", abiding his time secretly in the background, for had he been like a roaring lion his presence would have caused the disciples to take heed. The Lord stated that "the tares are the children (sons) of the wicked one (the evil one)". Unbelievers are seen as planted amongst believers; both are in the world together. Thus in Matt 15:13, the Lord spoke of plants that His Father had not planted; they would be rooted up, but in the meanwhile "Let them alone". Finally, with this insidious work complete, Satan "went his way". This is not interpreted, but it suggests that Satan quietly disappears from the scene, even his existence being denied by men who are the results of his planting and who are under his dominion.

26-30, 39-42 The parabolic conversation between the householder (*oikodespotēs*, master of a house) and the servants (*douloi,* bondmen) does not appear as a conversation in the interpretation, but we do not doubt that there will be such conversations in heaven (see 2 Chron 18:18-21). It would appear that this conversation took place before the fruit-bearing mentioned in v.26. It does not take long for the blade to appear and for the fruit to be brought forth. The fruit in the case of the good seed can speak of character and the spiritual graces (Gal 5:22-23), as well as of the 28 features of service given in 2 Cor 6:3-10 that "the ministry be not blamed". Likewise the fruit of the tares may be described as " the works of the flesh" (Gal 5:19), though these may be kept under so that the apparent fruit of the tares may resemble in some manner the fruit of the good seed, thereby causing deception and confusion. One of the Lord's last confrontations with the Pharisaical tares is found in Matt 23:13-33; they and their proselytes are described by the title "child of hell" (v.15), namely, "son of hell", and the oft-repeated name "hypocrites"; their end is "the damnation of hell" (v.33).

The "servants" are "the angels" in the interpretation; they question the risen Lord still in His capacity as Son of man. It may appear remarkable that the "angels" in v.27 have to ask the householder, "the Son of man", why tares have appeared in the field originally sown with good seed. They examined the earth and saw the results, but were not aware of the previous furtiveness of the enemy in secretly sowing the tares as a trespasser in the householder's field. The Lord offered no interpretation of this question, but since angels are not omniscient, omnipresent and omnipotent as is Deity, it would appear that not all angels are aware of what is taking place on earth at any particular moment. Again, in v.28 their question "Wilt thou then that we go and gather them up?" indicates that angels do not necessarily know the divine will on particular matters until that will is revealed, and that they cannot foresee the future, otherwise they would have known what would happen at "the end of the world". They are not allowed to gather the tares up before the harvest, lest mistakes be made in accidentally gathering up the wheat also. Deity can make no mistake in this or in any other connection, but angels not being omniscient and omnipotent could make mistakes unwittingly. The Son is "so much better than the angels" in this respect and in so many other ways as described in Heb 1:4-14. Hence the world will remain populated with good and bad, with faithfulness and unfaithfulness, with children of God and children of the devil, with light and darkness with spiritual and unspiritual, with the righteous and the unrighteous; until the harvest at "the end of the world" (v.39); they will "grow together until the harvest".

The "end of the world" (*sunteleia tou aiōnos*) is an expression occurring five times in Matthew's Gospel: 13:39,40,49; 24:3; 28:20. It also appears in Heb 9:26 where the word "world" is plural, and in 1 Cor 10:11 where "ends" is a different word altogether and "world" is in the plural. This must not be confused with the end of all things, as Peter described it in 2 Pet 3:7-13. In Matt 13, the word for "end" means the ultimate completion or consummation of a series of events; the word for "world" properly means "age", a period of time delineated by particular characteristics. When the disciples on the mount of Olives in Matt 24:3 asked about "the end of the world", the Lord's answer made no reference to the end of all things. Rather, His answer dealt with events just preceding His coming in glory, and with His actual descent in glory as King to establish His kingdom here on earth in open display. In other words, "the end of the world" terminates the long period when faithfulness and unfaithfulness exist side-by-side on the earth, from the days of Cain and Abel, through the OT centuries, through the lifetime of the Lord Jesus on earth, right through the period of the church on earth, and including the great tribulation when there will be a bright testimony for Christ amidst the great darkness around. Immediately after "the end of the world" will follow "the world to come", namely "the habitable world which is to come" (Heb 2:5), which does not mean the eternal state, but rather the millennial reign of Christ of 1000 years.

The "reapers" are "the angels" who gather the tares and cast them into "a furnace of fire". There will be several gatherings during the period of the end times. In 2 Thess 2:1, "our gathering together unto him" relates to the rapture of the church. In Matt 24:31, the gathering relates to His elect when the Lord comes in glory to establish His kingdom. In Matt 25:32, the gathering is that of the nations, when they are judged immediately after the battle of Armageddon. In John 12:32, the Lord lifted up would "draw all men" unto Him; this suggests a dragging process, when unbelieving men are forced to appear before Him and bow the knee. In Rev 14:14-20 there are two metaphors expressing reaping and gathering. The harvest of the earth is reaped by the Son of man sitting on a cloud; this refers to His elect at that time. The vine of the earth is gathered by an angel; this refers to the separation of the godless. apparently answering to the gathering of the tares, when angels "shall gather out of his kingdom all things that offend . . . and shall cast them into a furnace of fire". Today, men think that a utopia will come through human efforts, through love and the abandonment of war, and through accepted mutual international agreements. The Scriptures know nothing of this vain hope; the utopia will be the establishment of Christ's kingdom on earth, accomplished through judgment and the removal of all things that offend, when "the kingdom of the world is become the kingdom of our Lord, and of his Christ" (Rev 11:15, RV). At that time, God shall laugh, giving to His Anointed One the heathen for His inheritance, breaking them with a rod of iron, and dashing them in pieces like a potter's vessel (Ps 2:4, 8, 9).

43 By contrast, "the wheat into (his) barn" is interpreted as "the righteous ... in the kingdom of their Father". Those still on earth at the end of the great tribulation will enter into the kingdom as established on earth. But those who pass through death during that tribulation, and all members of the church of the Lord Jesus will reign with Him over the earth, the administrative centre being the "holy Jerusalem, descending out of heaven from God" and described in Rev 21:9-27. The saints will "shine forth as the sun", partaking of the glory that He gives (John 17:22), with bodies of glory (Phil 3:21), appearing in glory as did Moses and Elijah on the mount of transfiguration (Luke 9:30-31). The righteous will be "fair as the moon, clear as the sun" (Song 6:10). Strictly, Matt 13:43 looks beyond the millennial glory when the kingdom and the throne are those of Christ; "the kingdom of their Father" looks to the eternal state, when Christ "shall have delivered up the kingdom to God, even the Father" (1 Cor 15:24). This takes place at the end of Rev 20:9, introducing the new heaven and the new earth (21:1).

4. *The Remaining Parables of the Kingdom* 13:31-35, 44-50

v.31 "Another parable put he forth unto them, saying, The kingdom of heaven is like to a grain of mustard seed, which a man took, and sowed in his field:

v.32 Which indeed is the least of all seeds: but when it is grown, it is the greatest among herbs, and becometh a tree, so that the birds of the air come and lodge in the branches thereof.

v.33 Another parable spake he unto them; The kingdom of heaven is like unto leaven, which a woman took, and hid in three measures of meal, till the whole was leavened.

v.34 All these things spake Jesus unto the multitude in parables; and without a parable spake he not unto them:

v.35 That it might be fulfilled which was spoken by the prophet, saying, I will open my mouth in parables; I will utter things which have been kept secret from the foundation of the world.

v.44 Again, the kingdom of heaven is like unto treasure hid in a field; the which when a man hath found, he hideth, and for joy thereof goeth and selleth all that he hath, and buyeth that field.

v.45 Again, the kingdom of heaven is like unto a merchant man, seeking goodly pearls:

v.46 Who, when he had found one pearl of great price, went and sold all that he had, and bought it.

v.47 Again, the kingdom of heaven is like unto a net, that was cast into the sea, and gathered of every kind:
v.48 Which, when it was full, they drew to shore, and sat down, and gathered the good into vessels, but cast the bad away.
v.49 So shall it be at the end of the world: the angels shall come forth, and sever the wicked from among the just,
v.50 And shall cast them into the furnace of fire: there shall be wailing and gnashing of teeth."

31-32 In interpreting a parable containing the thought of large or excessive growth, we must always bear in mind the Lord's words about the narrow way, "few there be that find it" (Matt 7:14). Nothing else could be expected when the Lord was here, and during the church period true believers have always been in a minority. We must therefore not read into this parable and the one following any thought that suggests that the Christian testimony has expanded and exploded throughout the earth. The mustard seed is "less" (not "least") than other seeds, and its final growth is "greater" (not "greatest") of the herbs. In other words, there are other things doing the same in the world as this mustard seed and its tree. The minute mustard seed grew very quickly, yielding trees up to twelve feet high with branches suitable for birds to sit on. Such a system is based on doctrines quite different from the Lord's teaching and that of the apostles after Him. False religious teaching has always abounded, attracting men far more than the truth attracts them. As Wilson in his *Dictionary of Bible Types* has described it, "This figure represents the great religious group called 'the church'. It began with a very small group, but has spread all over the earth, and has become a monstrosity. Its members include atheists, idolaters and evildoers of every kind. Its branches reach out into every part of society, and in every nation. The birds in this church tree represent evil spirits ruling in church councils". This great system will head up into "Mystery, Babylon the great", described as sitting "upon many waters" which are "peoples, and multitudes, and nations, and tongues", and "with whom the kings of the earth have committed fornication, and the inhabitants of the earth have been made drunk with the wine of her fornication" (Rev 17:1, 2, 5, 15). "Come out of her, my people" (18:4) is the Spirit's exhortation to us today; Paul would write the same thing (2 Cor 6:14-18). The widespread cry today after ecumenicalism is really a desire after this tree where Satan's agents dwell. In the parable of the sower, birds represent Satan, and we see no reason for changing its meaning in this third parable. In Dan 4:11-12, a tree represented a huge political power, giving protection to the birds; the kingdom of heaven in its mystery form is likewise infiltrated with groups promulgating every form of departure in doctrine and practice.

33 Some expositors suggest that this is the one occasion in the Scriptures when leaven can be interpreted in a good sense, but only ecumenicalism endeavours to combine all brands of religion to lead to the salvation of the world. The Lord would not contradict Himself, for later He said to His disciples, "beware of the leaven of the Pharisees and of the Sadducees", this representing their doctrine (Matt 16:6, 12). Twice Paul wrote, "a little leaven leaveneth the whole lump", once describing evil practice in an assembly (1 Cor 5:6) and once describing evil doctrine (Gal 5:9). In the parable, the woman represents a leader of a religious system, such as Jezebel in Thyatira (Rev 2:20) and in an extended sense "Mystery, Babylon the great, the mother of harlots and abominations of the earth" (Rev 17:5). Early in the OT, Lot baked "unleavened bread" (Gen 19:3), and the passover lamb had to be eaten with "unleavened bread" (Exod 12:8). Leavened bread was the usual food in those lands, but on special occasions, moral typology had to take over. There was to be no leaven in the meal offering (Lev 2:11): this was seen in Gideon's example (Jud 6:19-21), and must also be implied in the restoration described in Ezek 45:24. Indeed, the meal offering in its various aspects had to be anointed or mingled with oil, speaking of the Holy Spirit (Lev 2:1, 2, 4, 5, 6). For Christ as the Bread of life is the food of His people. Unfortunately, throughout the ages His holy Person has been adulterated by the woman with leaven; these abominable insinuations have spread throughout Christendom, with only the few on the narrow way having escaped from these pollutions of doctrine. The system is ripe for judgment, though the parable does not reach to that event. Christ and His ways have been replaced by a continued development of spurious doctrine, of political attachment, of religious hierarchies resembling the OT priesthood, of formal services and of modern rationalism in many destructive forms.

34-35 Whereas the previous statement in vv.10-17 concerning the new use of parables had been made in response to questions from the disciples, yet here in vv.34-35 the insertion is due to Matthew as a historian-commentator. The multitudes heard parables only, and the interpretations were hidden from them. These multitudes were sent empty away in v.36, leaving only His disciples to hear an interpretation and the remaining three parables of the kingdom, only the seventh being given its interpretation in vv.49-50.

This secrecy was regarded by Matthew through the Spirit as fulfilling the words of the OT prophet (Ps 78:2) – compare this with Ps 49:4. Strictly, the author was Asaph, a temple singer chosen by David to sing the songs of the Lord (1 Chron 16:7; 25:2, 6, 9). Originally, he used psalms composed by David (16:7-37), though later Asaph developed spiritually so as to be able to compose psalms of his own (Ps 73-83). By writing "I will utter things which have been kept secret from the foundation of the world" (some Greek manuscripts omit "of the world") Matthew has departed from the OT Hebrew text and from the LXX. The AV has "I will utter dark sayings of old"; Ps 49:4 contains the same two words "parable" and "dark saying". JND's translation has, "I will utter riddles from of old". The Hebrew word *chidah* is translated "riddle" eight times in Jud 14:12-19 in connection with Samson's riddle, and "dark saying(s), speeches, sentences" in Num 12:8; Ps 49:4; 78:2; Prov 1:6; Dan 8:23. A "riddle" was a fact clothed in metaphor. To Asaph, the "dark sayings" or "riddles" were the history of the children of Israel in Egypt, in the wilderness and in the land, together with their failures and idolatry. The interpretation implied that the calamities that they suffered were really the judgments of God. In Ps 78:3-6, Asaph stated clearly that this interpretation had to be made known to every new generation. Matthew, on the other hand, gave only a restricted quotation. He did not use the LXX word *problēma* ("riddle"), but the one perfect participle *kekrummena* ("things hidden") standing for the AV "things which have been kept secret''. The opening up of these things would *not* be given to the multitudes, but to the disciples, as in Matt 13:36-43, whereas in Ps 78 the opening up of the implications of the past history of the nation would be given *to all* who should be born (v.6).

44 Many expositors see in this parable of the hid treasure and in the following parable of the pearl of great price a disciple seeking and finding true religion and even Christ Himself, by sacrificing all that he possesses to achieve this end. However, it is faith that finds Christ, not sacrifice; that comes later in the life of faith. We therefore see in the treasure and in the pearl what satisfies the heart of Christ – the two parables are from *His* point of view.

To the mind taken up with the letter and not the spirit, it may appear that the first four parables suggest that the kingdom is almost a failure: the unsatisfactory growth of the seed, the tares, the mustard seed and the leaven permeate everywhere. But divine pleasure is seen in treasure and in a pearl, eternally of value and unalterable. This could be revealed only in " the house" to the disciples; the psalmist only understood when he "went into the sanctuary of God" (Ps 73:17), when he desired in the house of the Lord "to behold the beauty of the Lord, and to inquire in his temple" (Ps 27:4). The field represents the world of men, and God knew those who were destined unto eternal life. But the evil one as the usurper took the field for himself, and the Lord came into enemy territory to seek and to save. The treasure remained hidden until the Lord had purchased the field and obtained the treasure for Himself. For example, Paul as the unconverted Saul was part of the treasure, but no one would have realised that until the Son of God found him on the Damascus road; he was hidden in the world until it pleased God to reveal His Son in him. Selling "all that he hath'' denotes the sacrificial work on Calvary's cross; there He gave Himself, a thought occurring six times, in Gal 1:4; 2:20; Eph 5:2, 25:1 Tim 2:6; Tit 2:14 (namely, twice in Gal, twice in Eph, and twice in the pastoral Epistles). Now that the treasure has been acquired, believers today "are not of the world" any longer (John 15:19). The sense in which the Lord bought the field should be noted. The righteousness of God by faith of Jesus Christ is "unto all" (namely, the world), but "upon all them that believe'' (namely, the treasure, Rom 3:22). Again, He died "for all'' (namely, the world), that "they which live . . ." (namely, the treasure, 2 Cor 5:14-15). The world was loved, but those who believe form the treasure (John 3: 16).

The nature of the treasure must be understood in the light of the prevalent dispensation. God's earthly people will be the treasure of the future: "my jewels" (Mal 3:17); among the Gentiles they will be like a bride adorned with jewels (Isa 61:10). Today, the church is the great eternal treasure of Christ, for believers are built on the one foundation which is Christ, and as edified they are gold, silver and precious stones, a spiritual character so precious to Him (1 Cor 3:11-12). Again, we are "living stones" built into a spiritual house, these stones being precious to Him, as He is precious to God (1 Pet 2:4-6).

45-46 The great city Babylon of the future will be decked with "precious stones, and pearls" (Rev 18:16), while the merchants of the world will become rich through trading in materials relating to her idolatry, including precious stones and pearls (vv.11-15). Other men purchase their merchandise, so they become rich through the abundance of their profiteering. But the merchant man in the parable does not become rich by selling to others, but he seeks and purchases for himself. Throughout the OT, God had been seeking amongst the nations, and had chosen Israel because of His love for them. But when the Lord was here, His seeking found the apostles with other faithful men and women, and He knew that these whom He loved would form the church after His departure. This was the "one pearl of great price", necessitating the giving of Himself (all that He had) so as to make it His own. Objects are valuable when they are scarce – here was one church and only one (not many church systems and denominations, as men view things), manifesting unity, glory and admiration, demonstrating the wealth of the Owner, for He gave His life and took it again, so He is eternally the richer as possessing the life that He gave, and also the church that He gained to be His bride throughout eternity. The aspirations of the psalmist should be those of the Lord's people today: "Let the beauty of the Lord our God be upon us" (Ps 90:17); "strength and beauty are in his sanctuary" (96:6); "Zion, the perfection of beauty" (50:2). By way of practical application, women in the church should not display "gold, or pearls, or costly array: but . . . good works" (1 Tim 2:9-10). Peter could write similarly, "not . . . wearing of gold, or of putting on of apparel; but let it be the hidden man of the heart . . . which is in the sight of God of great price" (1 Pet 3:3-4). God finds no delight in that materialistic kind of display, neither do fellow brethren and sisters in Christ.

47-50 The word for "net" (*sagēnē*) occurs only once in the NT; it refers to a long horizontal net, the ends of which are drawn in so as to enclose the trapped fish in a smaller and smaller volume. Hence its preferable name "drag-net". From the Lord's time here below up to the time of His return in glory (namely, at "the end of the world" – see our remarks on v.39), the kingdom proves to be very attractive to good and bad alike. False Christs, false apostles, false teachers, false prophets all attract men into a large sphere of profession; now this is Christendom, but in the future it will be the sphere of the harlot Babylon the great. At the end, the severing process will be the same as that for the wheat and tares. In this last parable of the seven, only the destiny of the bad fish is stated, unlike the second parable, where the destiny of the wheat is also explained.

5. *Understanding and Rejection* 13:51-58

v.51 "Jesus saith unto them, Have ye understood all these things? They say unto him, Yea, Lord.
v.52 Then said he unto them, Therefore every scribe *which* is instructed unto the kingdom of heaven is like unto a man *that is* an householder, which bringeth forth out of his treasure *things* new and old.
v.53 And it came to pass, *that* when Jesus had finished these parables, he departed thence.
v.54 And when he was come into his own country, he taught them in their synagogue, insomuch that they were astonished, and said, Whence hath this *man* this wisdom, and *these* mighty works?
v.55 Is not this the carpenter's son? is not his mother called Mary? and his brethren, James, and Joses, and Simon, and Judas?
v.56 And his sisters, are they not all with us? Whence then hath this *man* all these things?
v.57 And they were offended in him. But Jesus said unto them, A prophet is not without honour, save in his own country, and in his own house.
v.58 And he did not many mighty works there because of their unbelief."

51 Having explained only two of the seven parables, the Lord finally assessed the disciples' understanding. Being convinced that they did understand, they quickly answered, "Yea, Lord". This answer should be contrasted with that of the eunuch, "How can I, except some man should guide me?" (Acts 8:30-31). Both the disciples and the eunuch honestly assessed their own hearts, but it is easy to claim to understand, yet such men soon find it to be otherwise if they attempt to explain it to others or to put something into practice. Indeed vv.10, 36 show that the disciples did not understand a parable until it was explained. Moreover, Matt 16:6-12 shows that they still did not know what leaven meant as a symbol. In fact, men remain in ignorance of divine truth until they are taught by the Spirit of God (1 Cor 2:8-14).

52 Some regard this verse as an eighth parable in Matt 13, though it is not stated to be a parable as such. It was a word-picture, and its meaning was not intended to be hidden from the disciples. The work of the scribes was

1. to preserve the law particularly in times when the priesthood was corrupt;

2. to instruct pupils in the law;

3. as lawyers. to be occupied with the judicial aspects of the law.

Similarly, the Lord's disciples should act likewise in connection with the Lord's teaching. They should keep it pure in exposition; they should seek to pass it on to others, and they should ensure that its standards are maintained in their own lives and service as well as in the lives of others over whom they may be placed in spiritual matters. Of course, the Lord is the supreme "householder", for this is the same word as appears in the parable of the tares (13:27), and truly He exemplified the three aspects of the work of scribes just described. But He has many under-householders now on earth, and similar responsibilities fall upon them. Each one must keep the treasure safe; each one can show it to others provided it is not a case of casting pearls before swine (as did Hezekiah in 2 Kings 20:12-15), and each must judge what is true treasure, distinguishing this from the flotsam and jetsam of the world. We suggest that the "old" represents the OT, and the Lord's teaching up to Matt 12, while the "new" represents His teaching in Matt 13 and afterwards. We must not be like the man who says, "The *old* is better" (Luke 5:39), for the "new" takes us from the law up to the sacrificial work of Christ in His death and the introduction of the church which He would build (Matt 16:18, 21). The Lord was developing His teaching, soon to arrive at these higher truths.

53 So the Lord departed from the house of parables, to be rejected by all except the few exercising faith. No longer would the message be that the kingdom of heaven was at hand; rather He would be like a king travelling into a far country (Matt 21:33), preparing for His death, His church, and for the future kingdom in glory. Note that this is the third time in Matthew's Gospel that the Lord had "finished" a discourse; see Matt 7:28; 11:1; 19:1; 26:1.

54-56 In order to test the reaction to His new style of ministry with parables, the Lord came to "his own country", namely Nazareth. In spite of the events in the synagogue in Luke 4:28-29, He was still allowed to teach. In Luke 4:28 the reaction was "wrath", but here it is astonishment. By saying, "Whence hath this man this wisdom, and these mighty works", the people manifested unbelief by questioning the origin of divine power. This contrasts with that of the blind man whose eyesight was restored in John 9:33, " If this man were not of God, he could do nothing". But the people in the synagogue in Nazareth could not see anything other than a natural origin, this accounting for their astonishment. In Luke 4:22, men knew Him only as "Joseph's son"; here it is the "carpenter's son" and His mother, brethren and sisters were still living there. Why was He different from all others in the family circle? But ignorance knew not the revelation that Gabriel had brought to Mary many years before (Luke 1:31-33), and Mary had not been disposed to make this known (Luke 2:19, 51). In Matt 12:47-50 we have seen that the Lord would not allow natural relationships to be a substitute for spiritual ones; the same here: only unbelief would dwell on natural relationships, and Rome today adopts it as a principal tenet.

57 So these unbelievers were "offended in him" (*skandalizō*), namely they regarded Him as a stumbling stone. In this case, they were envious at what He could teach and what He could do. Later Peter would write, "a stone of stumbling, and a rock of offence, even to them which stumble at the word, being disobedient" (1 Pet 2:8), whereas for believers He is "a chief corner stone, elect, precious" (v.6).

The Lord knew that He was alone and rejected; this was characteristic of His own home city: "A prophet is not without honour, save in his own country, and in his own house". He had said this before in the synagogue of Nazareth, "No prophet is accepted in his own country" (Luke 4:24). We may observe that Paul was not accepted by the Jews, but he was accepted by the Gentiles. The same may occur in a local assembly that is determined to follow the ways of the world in service; an able spiritual brother may not be accepted by those who criticise his spiritual ministry, no doubt because this gives them a bad conscience. Yet he may be wholeheartedly received elsewhere by those who love the truth.

58 Hence the Lord "did not many mighty works there because of their unbelief". This contrasts with Matt 11:20, where the local cities of Galilee were those in which most of His mighty works were done. But lack of repentance and lack of faith brought about a lack of mighty works. In Mark 6:5, it is "he could there do no mighty work . . .", in the sense that it was contrary to the divine will to show power merely to satisfy the continued curiosity of unbelief. Unbelief was a hindrance to the reception of mercy and blessing. That is why all and sundry are not forgiven, for salvation and unbelief are incompatible.

II. Murder, Provision and Protection (14:1-36)

1. *Death of John the Baptist* 14:1-14

v.1 "At that time Herod the tetrarch heard of the fame of Jesus,
v.2 And said unto his servants, This is John the Baptist; he is risen from the dead; and therefore mighty works do shew forth themselves in him.
v.3 For Herod had laid hold on John, and bound him, and put *him* in prison for Herodias' sake, his brother Philip's wife.
v.4 For John said unto him, It is not lawful for thee to have her.
v.5 And when he would have put him to death, he feared the multitude, because they counted him as a prophet.
v.6 But when Herod's birthday was kept, the daughter of Herodias danced before them, and pleased Herod.
v.7 Whereupon he promised with an oath to give her whatsoever she would ask.
v.8 And she, being before instructed of her mother, said, Give me here John Baptist's head in a charger.

v.9 And the king was sorry: nevertheless for the oath's sake, and them which sat with him at meat, he commanded *it* to be given *her*.
v.10 And he sent, and beheaded John in the prison.
v.11 And his head was brought in a charger, and given to the damsel: and she brought *it* to her mother.
v.12 And his disciples came, and took up the body, and buried it, and went and told Jesus.
v.13 When Jesus heard of *it*, he departed thence by ship into a desert place apart: and when the people had heard *thereof*, they followed him on foot out of the cities.
v.14 And Jesus went forth, and saw a great multitude, and was moved with compassion toward them, and he healed their sick."

In this chapter, we see how the principles of the kingdom were worked out. The beheading of John (vv.1-12) demonstrates: the seed sown (parable 1) by John in Herod and Philip had been of none effect; the care of the world had choked the word and it became unfruitful. The wheat and tares (parable 2) can be likened to John and Herod. The leaven (parable 4) recalls the fact that things had become worse and worse in Herod's family, because of intermarriage and adultery. The feeding of the 5,000 (vv.15-21) recalls parable 1; in John 6:26-71 we find the word sown after the miracle that had been a sign to the people. Fruit had been brought forth in Peter as he made his great confession regarding "Christ, the Son of the living God", while the lack of fruit is seen in the fact that many went back and walked no more with Him (6:66,69). The walking on the water (Matt 14:22-34) shows the Lord seeking a treasure *in* the water (the disciples in the ship "in the midst of the sea" in v.24), and a pearl *on* the water (v.29).

1 Herod the king was in power when the Lord Jesus was born. One of his sons Archelaus (Matt 2:22) reigned for a short time during the Lord's childhood, after which another son "Herod the tetrarch" (Luke 3:1) reigned in Galilee during the Lord's ministry. He divorced his wife so as to marry Herodias, the wife of his half-brother Herod Philip. Although the fame (*akoē*, what is heard, a report) of the Lord took some time to reach Herod, yet this fame (the same Greek word) had already spread around Syria and Galilee (Matt 4:24; Mark 1:28). But once Herod had heard these things, "he was desirous to see him of a long season . . . and he hoped to have seen some miracle done by him" (Luke 23:8).

2 We are now given a few details of the superstitious religious ideas that existed in the mind of this political leader Herod. He had heard of the divine power and works from unfaithful witnesses; he was perplexed because there was no rational explanation for these works. Today, unbelief has had nearly 2,000 years in which to invent explanations of the Lord's miracles, so modern unbelievers cease to be perplexed. In Herod's day, the theory was not to deny miracles or to explain them by natural causes, but to assert that "This is John the Baptist; he is risen from the dead; and therefore mighty works do show forth themselves in him". In other words, he was doing miracles in this new form of existence, for resurrection was a popular doctrine except among the Sadducees. This was, of course, unsubstantiated imagination. Certainly in his lifetime, "John did no miracle" (John 10:41). In any case, John had denied being the Christ (John 1:20), for none can equal the Lord in the absolute uniqueness of Deity. Other men beside Herod had theories: some identified Christ with Elijah, since his coming had been promised by the last of the OT prophets (Mal 4:5), a popular supposition that had been quoted by the disciples (Matt 16:14). There could be no possibility of Elijah being on equality with the Lord, for he was a man of like passions with mankind generally (James 5:17). Another theory was that "one of the old prophets was risen again" (Luke 9:8), while Jeremiah was another speculative suggestion (Matt 16:14). In other words, superstition and rationalism can never fathom the Person of Christ.

3-6 Herod was a man who hated moral truth from the OT, and John was fearless in presenting this to him. The extent of Herod's sin goes beyond what is recorded in Scripture. Herodias' previous husband Philip was still alive, as was Herod's previous wife, who was the daughter of an Arabian king called Aretas. As a result of Herod's actions, there was war between Aretas and Herod. Moreover Herodias was niece both of her former husband Philip and of Herod, since she was daughter of their dead brother Aristobulus. Verses such as Lev 18:16 and 20:21 show quite clearly that Herod was acting contrary to the law of God, and hence John's denunciation, "It is not lawful for thee to have her". Here is an example of the fact that John displayed the "spirit and power of Elias" (Luke 1:17), this rebuking of Herod and Herodias being similar to what Elijah did to Ahab and Jezebel in the OT (1 Kings 18:18; 21:19, 23). In Mark 6:19, it was Herodias who would have killed John, and Herod would have agreed, but later realised that "he was a just man and an holy . . . and heard him gladly" (v.20). Instead, John was cast into prison. This had taken place some time earlier, almost at the beginning of the Lord's ministry (Matt 4:12; 11:2), evidently so that the power of John's ministry should not be seen in any sense to rival that of the Lord Jesus' ministry just commencing in Galilee and Jerusalem. Luke mentions the imprisonment in 3:20 of his Gospel. Herod's reaction was tempered by the reaction of the people, for they counted John "as a prophet" (Matt 14:5). We recall that Zacharias, filled with the Holy Spirit, had proclaimed, "thou, child, shalt be called the prophet of the Highest" (Luke 1:76), while the Lord Jesus had called him " more than a prophet" (Matt 11: 9).

Men of the flesh will celebrate birthdays according to the flesh. Herodias' daughter (Salome by name) brought entertainment by dancing "before them" (*en tō mesǭ* in the midst). This "pleased Herod" – the entertainment of the world always has this object, as well as its own highly-paid remuneration. Even in the Lord's service, there must never be any objective to please men, "if I yet pleased men, I should not be the servant of Christ" (Gal 1:10); "even so we speak; not as pleasing men, but God, which trieth our hearts" (1 Thess 2:4).

7-11 A promise with an oath can be a dangerous thing, particularly an open-ended promise "to give her whatsoever she would ask". Jephthah's vow was open-ended, "whatsoever cometh forth of the doors of my house to meet me" (Jud 11:30-31) was uttered without contemplating that it might be his only daughter. "Half the kingdom" was promised in Esth 5:3; 7:2; Mark 6:23. In Acts 23:12, some of the Jews bound themselves under an oath not to eat or drink until they had killed Paul, without contemplating whether such an act was possible. We are not told what ultimately happened to these men who uttered such an open-ended oath, since Paul was not killed, and arrived safely in Caesarea and then at Rome. Believers should never make rash promises, but contemplate intended decisions before the Lord, weighing up the consequences of their decisions beforehand.

This vile deed was really the result of a conspiracy between the two women Herodias and Salome (Mark 6:24), knowing that Herod would have to perform what they asked. They knew that he was capable of such a deed, for his nature was similar to the nature of their own hearts that could plan such a deed. It was a family united in immorality in every possible way. As the Lord said later, "out of the heart proceed evil thoughts, murders, adulteries" (Matt 15:19). Herod's sorrow was not godly sorrow, but merely because the deed would prove to be to his disadvantage. By this deed, Herod was copying men who had preceded him, as Stephen said just before his martyrdom, "Which of the prophets have not your fathers persecuted? and they have slain them which showed before of the coming of the Just One; of whom ye have been now the betrayers and murderers" (Acts 7:52). Men were resisting the Holy Spirit through John (v.51). The Lord predicted that men would kill and crucify some of the prophets sent to them (Matt 23:34); such prophets would be following in the footsteps of John the Baptist. And later the martyrs would be following the footsteps of the Lord Himself, "If they have persecuted me, they will also persecute you" (John 15:20). This would be done in the name of religion, for "whosoever killeth you will think that he doeth God service" (16:2).

12-14 They were sad disciples who buried the body of John. In place of "body" (*sōma*), some manuscripts have "corpse" (*ptōma*), as in Mark 6:29. He still awaits the resurrection. They were sad when Lazarus was placed in the tomb; he was raised, but later in death still awaits the resurrection. They were sad when they placed the Lord in the tomb, but in resurrection shortly afterwards He now lives in the power of an endless life: "ye shall weep and lament . . . but your sorrow shall be turned into joy" (John 16:20). But there was no joy for Herod, "be sure your sin will find you out" (Num 32:23). In AD 36, Herodias' father waged war against Herod's army, and he was heavily defeated. According to the Jewish historian Josephus, many Jews regarded this defeat as divine retribution for his murder of John the Baptist. He was sent into exile when "Herod the king" (Acts 12:1) took over an extended kingdom.

Of course the Lord knew exactly what was happening. The statement "his disciples . . . went and told Jesus. When Jesus heard of it" is written from the point of view of the disciples and Matthew. The Lord did nothing openly until they told Him the news; He desires to hear the exercises and trials of His people, although He knows about them beforehand. He would comfort the disciples by being alone with them in the boat and in the desert, prior to the arrival of the multitude who followed eastwards round the northern coast of the Sea of Galilee. According to John 6:2, they followed because they saw His miracles. And according to Mark 6:34, the Lord recognised that these people were "as sheep not having a shepherd", so He taught them many things. Moreover, He healed the sick, because He "was moved with compassion" towards them. This verb "to be moved with compassion" (*splanchnizomai*) is used twelve times in the NT, all in the Synoptic Gospels, and always referring to the Lord Jesus, except parabolically in Matt 18:27; Luke 15:20, where the interpretation is still of the divine.

2. *The Feeding of the Five Thousand* 14:15-21

v.15 "And when it was evening, his disciples came to him, saying, This is a desert place, and the time is now past; send the multitude away, that they may go into the villages, and buy themselves victuals.
v.16 But Jesus said unto them, They need not depart; give ye them to eat.
v.17 And they say unto him, We have here but five loaves, and two fishes.
v.18 He said, Bring them hither to me.
v.19 And he commanded the multitude to sit down on the grass, and took the five loaves, and the two fishes, and looking up to heaven, he blessed and brake, and gave the loaves to *his* disciples, and the disciples to the multitude.
v.20 And they did all eat, and were filled: and they took up of the fragments that remained twelve baskets full.
v.21 And they that had eaten were about five thousand men, beside women and children."

15 This is the only miracle that appears in all four Gospels (Mark 6:30-44, Luke 9:10-17; John 6:1-14). There are two such miracles, the second involving 4,000 men, recorded in Matt 15:32-39, Mark 8:1-9; the Lord recalled both miracles in Matt 16:9-10. For the 5,000, there were five loaves and two fishes while for the 4,000 there were seven loaves and a few fishes.

All that the apostles could see was a "desert place", but this could not be a desert when the Lord was there! It was not like the wilderness where the Lord had been tempted, when He would not make bread for Himself, neither was it like the wilderness where the woman "Mystery, Babylon the Great" was seated (Rev 17:3). Rather, it can be likened to the wilderness and the solitary place which will "blossom like a rose" (Isa 35:1). By intending to send the multitude away, and even instructing the Lord to do this by saying "send the multitude away", the apostles showed themselves to be entirely out of touch with the divine will. If not certain of His will, it is best to wait until this is manifested rather than express natural ideas and plans. To send the multitude away would be to send them away with nothing, contrasting with how the Lord had sent the apostles away full for service (Matt 10:1; Luke 22:35). By adopting a natural attitude in an apparent emergency, the apostles failed to appreciate Ps 132:15, "I will abundantly bless her provision: I will satisfy her poor with bread", and Luke 6:21, "Blessed are ye that hunger now: for ye shall be filled". Today, there is a danger of adopting materialistic ends to accomplish spiritual service, this shows a lack of faith in the power of God to do according to His will. Such apostolic lack of faith did not prevent the Lord working miracles, though this did not justify that lack of faith. And today, the ends do not justify the means when the Lord blesses service that is not carried out spiritually.

16-18 The Lord's simple command "give ye them to eat" shows that we must give what we have without question; it is bound to be small, but He does the rest, as with the "handful of meal in a barrel, and a little oil in a cruse" (1 Kings 17:12; 2 Kings 4:2). In John 6:5, the Lord asked Philip where bread could be purchased, "to prove him", but Philip gave no satisfactory answer. In Matt 14:16, "give ye them to eat " received no satisfactory response. To refer to five loaves and two fishes merely demonstrated the apostles' own inadequacy and lack of faith. There may be a parabolic implication here. The fish recall the miracle in Luke 5:1-11; by providing fish from the sea, the Lord showed evangelistically that the unsaved would be drawn from the nations, to become the people of God. The bread recalls 1 Cor 10:17, where the saints are seen as "one bread", namely the converted having been gathered into local assemblies.

19 In Luke 9:14, they had to sit down "by fifties in a company". Since there were "about five thousand men, beside women and children", there would have been many groups for whom the Lord provided comfort, fellowship and provision. The grass reminds us of the transient character of the natural creation (James 1:11; 1 Pet 1:24), contrasting with "that meat which endureth unto everlasting life" (John 6:27). Clearly a lot of personal organisation was necessary for the apostles to arrange this grouping, since more than 100 groups would be formed. With everything having been done decently and in order (1 Cor 14:40), the Lord now performed the miracle. Here is plenty of scope for the rational mind of unbelief to attempt to explain the Lord's act in non-miraculous terms. John 6:9 informs us that a lad provided the Lord with loaves and fish, so unbelievers suggest that his example encouraged other men to provide all the rest in their possession for general distribution. But the eye-witness John actually states that it was a miracle (John 6:14), and not a mere redistribution of food already possessed by the multitude.

The Lord looked "up to heaven", implying intimate communion with the Father before a great miracle; see John 11:41; 17:1. Here, the word "blessed" (*eulogeō*) means to speak well of the bread; it is also used in Matt 26:26 (for the bread),

Luke 9:16 (this same miracle), and Luke 24:30 (for the bread after His resurrection). In the NT, there is another word "give thanks" (*eucharisteō*); this is used in John 6:11 (this same miracle), Matt 15:36 (the feeding of the 4,000), Luke 22:19 (for the bread); Matt 26:27 (for the cup), and Acts 27:35 (on the ship). In the present miracle, obviously the Lord both blessed (with thoughts directed to the food) and gave thanks (with thoughts directed to God). It appears from the breaking and subsequent distribution that the miracle consisted of breaking off new pieces from the existing bread, and giving these new pieces to the disciples, rather than a vast amount of food suddenly appearing from nowhere. This is therefore similar to the one barrel of meal and the one cruse of oil not failing in Elijah's day (1 Kings 17:16 and the one pot enabling many vessels to be filled in Elisha's day (2 Kings 4:5-6). This is like the Word of God in the hands and hearts of believers: it is always full and never becomes empty.

The distribution process, "he . . . gave the loaves to his disciples, and the disciples to the multitude", is similar to the propagation of truth today. What Timothy had heard from Paul, he had to commit to faithful men who then would be able to teach others also (2 Tim 2:2).

20-21 None was excepted in the general distribution; no murmuring occurred as in the early church in Jerusalem (Acts 6:1). And there was plenty left over! Divine supplies are always over-abundant, as in nature, in divine providence and care, and in things spiritual (Exod 16:22-24; 36:7; 2 Cor 9:8-11; Eph 1:3, 23). Nothing was wasted, unlike what men do today who waste vast quantities of food because far more is grown than is needed. Gathering up the fragments is unlike the event in the parable where the son wasted his inheritance (Luke 15:13)

There are two different words for "basket" used in the Greek NT describing these miracles.

1. *Kophinos,* a word used six times only in the NT, all in the context of this miracle of the feeding of the 5,000. This was the smaller basket, one being carried by each of the twelve apostles for the left-overs.

2. *Spuris,* used four times in the second miracle of the feeding of the 4,000, and also in Acts 9:25 when Paul was let down from the walls of Damascus. This was the larger type of basket, capable of carrying a man. There were seven baskets, each one evidently corresponding to a loaf. Why such baskets were available is not clear.

Similarly, believers today should always have baskets full of what the Lord has originally provided, the treasures of His Word suitably broken up to suit every need.

In John 6:25-71 there is a long sequel to this miracle. The multitude had followed the Lord back to Capernaum, and He used the occasion to present

Himself as the Bread of life. The result was that many "went back, and walked no more with him" (v.66).

In the record, Matthew (that is the Spirit of God through Matthew) did not give exact numbers; the number was "about" 5,000 men. No census was taken by the apostles, since they had more important things to do. The same phenomenon may be observed in the numbering of the tribes of Israel in Num 1 and 26. In the feeding of the 4,000. this number is stated to be "about" (Mark 8:9). The same happened in the early church in Jerusalem; there were added "about three thousand souls" (Acts 2:41), and later the number was "about five thousand" (4:4). For the use of large numbers, see Rev 5:11. It is true that the Lord knows His sheep (John 10:14), that "The Lord knoweth them that are his" (2 Tim 2:19), and that sparrows and hairs are all numbered (Matt 10:29-30), but the Lord is satisfied with our use of round numbers when large numbers are concerned.

3. *Walking on the Water* 14:22-36

v.22 "And straightway Jesus constrained his disciples to get into a ship, and to go before him unto the other side, while he sent the multitudes away.
v.23 And when he had sent the multitudes away, he went up into a mountain apart to pray: and when the evening was come, he was there alone.
v.24 But the ship was now in the midst of the sea, tossed with waves: for the wind was contrary.
v.25 And in the fourth watch of the night Jesus went unto them, walking on the sea.
v.26 And when the disciples saw him walking on the sea, they were troubled, saying, It is a spirit; and they cried out for fear.
v.27 But straightway Jesus spake unto them, saying, Be of good cheer; it is I; be not afraid.
v.28 And Peter answered him and said, Lord, if it be thou, bid me come unto thee on the water.
v.29 And he said, Come. And when Peter was come down out of the ship, he walked on the water, to go to Jesus.
v.30 But when he saw the wind boisterous, he was afraid; and beginning to sink, he cried, saying, Lord, save me.
v.31 And immediately Jesus stretched forth *his* hand, and caught him, and said unto him, O thou of little faith, wherefore didst thou doubt?
v.32 And when they were come into the ship, the wind ceased.
v.33 Then they that were in the ship came and worshipped him, saying, Of a truth thou art the Son of God.
v.34 And when they were gone over, they came into the land of Gennesaret.
v.35 And when the men of that place had knowledge of him, they sent out into all that country round about, and brought unto him all that were diseased;
v.36 And besought him that they might only touch the hem of his garment: and as many as touched were made perfectly whole."

22-23 The multitudes had experienced a three-fold blessing:

1. their sick had been healed (v.14);
2. they had been taught (Mark 6:34);
3. they had been satisfied with food.

As a result, they claimed that the Lord was "that prophet that should come into the world'' (John 6:14). Above all, they attempted to make Him a king by force (v.15), an impossibility, since His enthronement would be by His Father God (Ps 2:6). The Lord departed from a multitude having such foreign designs, in order to be alone in a mountain apart to pray. Prior to this, "he sent the multitudes away". This contrasts with v.15; the disciples wanted the people to go away empty, but the Lord sent them away full. We learn from John 6:22 that the people remained in the vicinity, for only on the following day did they take shipping to cross the northern part of the Sea of Galilee to seek the Lord again on the opposite shore (v. 24). Well might the Lord say to them, "Ye seek me . . . because ye did eat of the loaves, and were filled" (v. 26).

24-26 The miracle is included in Matthew's Gospel to show the power of Christ, the weakness of faith, and the value of confessing the Son of God. And yet the whole story appears to be constructed so as to have a parabolic and prophetic ring about it. The sea represents the nations of the world, particularly the Roman empire holding sway over the Jews at that time. The boat and its contents represent God's earthly people in constant tribulation brought about by the Roman authorities. "Jesus went unto them" corresponds to His mission, coming to the lost sheep of the house of Israel. Peter stepping out of the boat demonstrates the faithful Jews who adhered to the Lord in His lifetime. The fact that he began to sink shows the kind of faithlessness amongst the Jews that brought about (in a practical way) the emergence of the church. The Lord caught him, and being together upon the sea represents the church, together with her Lord, and yet in tribulation during her earthly sojourn on earth amongst the nations. Coming to the boat speaks of the Lord coming to Israel at His second advent, the church coming with Him to share the administration of the coming kingdom in glory. Then will the nation confess their Lord, in keeping with such utterances as found in Isa 53. Then the power of the nations shall cease, suggested by the cessation of the wind. "Immediately the ship was at the land" (John 6:21) implies the fulfilment of God's purpose for Israel.

No doubt the most well-known storm-scene in the Scriptures is that in Jonah 1:4-17, this storm having been sent by God because of the presence of Jonah on the ship; a prophet was fleeing from God's presence. In the Lord's lifetime, the first storm-scene is in Matt 8:23-27, this occurring when a crossing of the Sea of Galilee was being made from west to east. Other sea-scenes are:

1. the miraculous draught of fishes (Luke 5:1-11; Matt 4:18-22);

2. the proclaiming of the parables of the kingdom (Matt 13:2);

3. the catching of the fish after the Lord's resurrection (John 21:1-8).

In Paul's experience, he recalled to the Corinthians, "thrice I suffered shipwreck, a night and a day I have been in the deep" (2 Cor 11:25), though when these events took place is not clear in the Acts. Finally there was the terrible storm in the Mediterranean during the voyage leading to Rome for Paul's imprisonment (Acts 27:14-44).

The Lord was omnipotent, having complete control over all the forces of nature as He upholds "all things by the word of his power" (Heb 1:3). The Lord walking on the sea demonstrated this power. Our faith now accepts the record, but for the apostles in the boat the recognition of what was happening was not quite so clear and simple. They had marvelled at His power over the storm in Matt 8:27, but were not prepared for this new manifestation of divine capability. Hence they "were troubled, saying, It is a spirit; and they cried out for fear". Fear often attaches unexplained happenings to a superstitious religion, whether they be genuine natural phenomena or actual divine interventions. The same happened in Luke 24:37 when they saw the Lord in resurrection for the first time; they "supposed that they had seen a spirit" .

27-32 The Lord would remove fear from His people's hearts, for He knows that fear is a natural emotion caused by the sudden emergence of the unknown, the unexpected and the unexplained. The announcement of His own identity stills all such fear: "I will fear no evil: for thou art with me" (Ps 23:3). "It is I" is *egō eimi* ("I am"). Similar expressions of identity are found in Mark 6:50; 14:62; Luke 22:70; 24:39 (with "myself" or "he" added); John 4:26 (literally, "I am, the One speaking to thee"); 6:20; 8:24, 28, 58; 13:19; 18:5, 6, 8, as well as various titles such as "I am the good shepherd". Peter's fear was removed and he was prepared to walk on the water if the Lord would call him. Fear of a different kind then manifested itself. The first fear was caused because they did not know it was the Lord; the second fear was caused, in the Lord's presence, by looking at the physical danger and not to the Lord who was controlling all things. However, that "little faith" reacted immediately in the face of great danger; a cry as "Lord, save me" was desperate, true and deep. This recalls Ps 107:23-31, where a storm is described, "Then they cry unto the Lord in their trouble, and he bringeth them out of their distresses. He maketh the storm a calm, so that the waves thereof are still".

33 The demons confessed "Jesus, thou Son of God" (Matt 8:29), but the true testimony of men was infinitely better. " Of a truth thou art the Son of God" is a testimony based on *power.* "Thou art that Christ, the Son of the living God" (John 6:69) is based on His *preaching.* "Thou art the Son of God; thou art the King of Israel" (1:49) showed Nathanael's *penetration.* "Thou art the Christ, the Son of God" (11:27) spoken by Martha, was based on His *promise.* Peter's confession "Thou art the Christ, the Son of the living God" (Matt 16:16) was on account of His *Person.* "Thou art my beloved Son" (Mark 1:11) was the Father's testimony concerning His *preeminence.*

34-36 The people received the Lord in Gennesaret, on the north-west side of the Sea, though they had rejected Him in the country of the Gergesenes on the east side of the Sea (Matt 8:34). Though the cities had been condemned (11:20-24), yet the men of Gennesaret still trusted the Lord as a miracle- worker. Their faith was rewarded. In Nazareth, He did not many mighty works because of the prevailing unbelief (13:58), yet here in Gennesaret all were healed. Even the touch of the hem of His garment was sufficient for healing power to flow from the eternal divine source, as it had done previously in the case of the woman in Matt 9:21. Not that His garments, no doubt provided by the faithful women who ministered unto Him of their substance (Luke 8:3), had any intrinsic power in themselves. Rather they offered no resistance to divine power flowing from Him, in just the same way as they became "white as the light" when He appeared in glory on the mount (Matt 17:2). Later, God allowed the same miraculous phenomena to occur through Paul. In Ephesus, He "wrought special miracles . . . from his body were brought unto the sick handkerchiefs or aprons, and the diseases departed from them" (Acts 19:11, 12). If there are those today who claim such powers, we would remind readers that divinely-accomplished miracles are instantaneous, complete and lasting. God does nothing less than this.

III. Dangers of Traditional Religion (15:1-39)

1. *The Heart of the Scribes and Pharisees* 15:1-20

v.1 "Then came to Jesus scribes and Pharisees, which were of Jerusalem, saying,
v.2 Why do thy disciples transgress the tradition of the elders? for they wash not their hands when they eat bread.
v.3 But he answered and said unto them, Why do ye also transgress the commandment of God by your tradition?
v.4 For God commanded, saying, Honour thy father and mother: and, He that curseth father or mother, let him die the death.
v.5 But ye say, Whosoever shall say to *his* father or *his* mother, *It is* a gift, by whatsoever thou mightest be profited by me;
v.6 And honour not his father or his mother, *he shall be free.* Thus have ye made the commandment of God of none effect by your tradition.
v.7 *Ye* hypocrites, well did Esaias prophesy of you, saying,
v 8 This people draweth nigh unto me with their mouth, and honoureth me with *their* lips; but their heart is far from me.
v.9 But in vain they do worship me, teaching *for* doctrines the commandments of men.
v.10 And he called the multitude, and said unto them, Hear, and understand:
v.11 Not that which goeth into the mouth defileth a man; but that which cometh out of the mouth, this defileth a man.
v.12 Then came his disciples, and said unto him, Knowest thou that the Pharisees were offended, after they heard this saying?
v.13 But he answered and said, Every plant, which my heavenly Father hath not planted, shall be rooted up.
v.14 Let them alone: they be blind leaders of the blind. And if the blind lead the blind, both shall fall into the ditch.

v.15 Then answered Peter and said unto him, Declare unto us this parable.
v.16 And Jesus said, Are ye also yet without understanding?
v.17 Do not ye yet understand, that whatsoever entereth in at the mouth goeth into the belly, and is cast out into the draught?
v.18 But those things which proceed out of the mouth come forth from the heart; and they defile the man.
v.19 For out of the heart proceed evil thoughts, murders, adulteries, fornications, thefts, false witness, blasphemies:
v.20 These are *the things* which defile a man: but to eat with unwashen hands defileth not a man."

1 Most of the Lord's ministry was accomplished in Galilee, commencing in Matt 4:12 and ending in 19:1, when His final journey to Jerusalem began (20:29; 21:1). Hence throughout the major part of Matthew's record, the King was outside "the city of the great King" (5:35). John's Gospel, however, displays quite a different picture, since the Lord is usually seen in Jerusalem throughout John's record. The reason is that, throughout His ministry, the Lord was presenting Himself as the One who fulfilled the OT, in particular relating to the major feasts: "Three times in the year all thy males shall appear before the Lord God" (Exod 23:14-17; 34:23). These were brief visits to Jerusalem, but John concentrated upon them in his record (John 2:13; 4:45; 5:1; 6:4; 7:2; 10:22; 11:55; 12:1). Thus the two records are complementary rather than supplementary, and this accounts for the almost totally different subjects found in these two Gospels. Because of this, the Pharisees in Jerusalem were well acquainted with the Lord's teaching learnt during the long conversations between the Lord and the Pharisees given in John's Gospel, that in John 5 being the last uninterrupted discourse. It appears that the scribes and Pharisees of Jerusalem now came north to Galilee, to check the nature of His teaching and its effects there, and to see how far it corresponded with His activities in Jerusalem.

2 The Pharisees loved the formal "tradition of the elders", and today also, adherents to any formal religious tradition delight in such a system since it detracts from the true spirituality of the Word of God. The word "tradition" (*paradosis*) means what is handed down. It has either a good meaning or a bad meaning – something to be loved or something to be hated.

1. It refers to the doctrine and practice given by God, and placed in permanent written form, so that it could be handed down without change. In 1 Cor 11:2, Paul used this word to denote his teaching regarding the assembly gatherings of the Lord's people; it is translated "ordinances" (AV) and "traditions" (RV). Paul exhorted the Thessalonians to "hold the traditions which ye have been taught" (2 Thess 2:15), relating in particular to the doctrine of the Lord's coming which had been falsely manipulated in a forged letter (vv. 1-2). Later, he wrote to the same church about brethren who walked

disorderly, and "not after the tradition which he received of us" (3:6). Thus we have three good examples of tradition – practice, doctrine, conduct.

2. It also refers to human ordinances, interpretations and additions handed down in rivalry to the authority of God. Usually, this kind of tradition has a very thin and damaged veneer of scriptural justification, though being completely off the mark, as the Lord showed in Matt 15:5-6. Before his conversion, Paul (as Saul) was "exceedingly zealous of the traditions of my fathers" (Gal 1:14), but this was "the Jews' religion" rather that the holy Scriptures of the OT. "Philosophy and vain deceit" which is "not after Christ" is called "the tradition of men" (Col 2:8), however much men may value this kind of approach to life. Peter wrote that redemption is "from your vain conversation (manner of life) received by tradition from your fathers" (1 Pet 1:18), these last six words being one compound word in Greek, *patroparadotos.*

The Pharisees interpreted the law with minute legalisms, and this was the body of doctrine handed down – such as washing hands when bread is eaten. This was not a matter of cleanliness, but of a formal religious rite. Fuller details are found in Mark 7:2-4, where various cooking utensils are also included. Matthew was writing for Jews who had been converted to Christ, so they did not need information about Jewish tradition, but Mark was writing for Gentile converts, and in several places he supplied information about Jewish practices so that his readers could understand. In Mark 7:3, the tradition was "except they wash their hands oft". the word for "oft" being *pukna*; other manuscripts have the word *pugmē*, meaning "with the fist", namely the fist of one hand diligently rubbing the hand of the other in the ceremonial washing process; the RV and JND both translate the word "diligently".

3 The Lord then showed that their tradition was opposed to the commandments of God in the OT; compare this with the Lord's treatment of the Pharisaical regulations about plucking, rubbing and eating corn on the sabbath day (Matt 12:1-8), and His condemnation of the Pharisaical details of regulating tithing, in contrast to the weightier matters of the law (Matt 23:23). Compare this with what men did in Jeremiah's time: the liberty granted by the law at the end of seven years was immediately turned into servitude again (Jer 34:13-17). Today much religious tradition and established practices are contrary to the liberty granted to believers by the Holy Spirit. Such practices are a copy of the old Jewish ritual dressed up to look and sound like Christianity, but contrary to the spiritual aspects of the house of God and its holy priesthood. The Lord issued three condemnations against the Pharisees:

1. they perverted the commandment of God (vv.4-6):

2. he quoted the condemnatory accusation of Isaiah (vv.7-9);

3. the nature of tradition is illogical; what is spiritual and not what is physical is required (v.11).

4-6 *Condemnation* 1. The Lord quoted the OT that showed the relationship that should exist between children and parents, though this was not a one-way process as Paul wrote in 2 Cor 12:14. The Lord quoted from the ten commandments (Exod 20:12): "Honour thy father and thy mother", the only positive commandment, all the others containing "no" or "not". It follows the commandment regarding the sabbath, this being the Pharisees' favourite accusation against the Lord. In Matt 19:19, "Honour thy father and thy mother" is adjoined to the over-all conclusion "Thou shalt love thy neighbour as thyself" The verb "honour" (*timaō*) means to value, with something being rendered to express that honour (1 Tim 5:3). The Lord's second quotation "He that curseth father or mother, let him die the death" is taken from Exod 21:17, (the AV and RV margin offer "revileth" instead of "curseth"). This is negative, and the Lord intended it to apply to the breaking of the positive commandment. Under God's care and provision, elderly parents merit such practical love by their children. But the tradition of the Pharisees had devised a means for avoiding their responsibilities in this direction, just as many do today who assume that the state has sole responsibility for elderly parents in need. The Pharisaical scheme was to forsake this duty to parents under the guise that the gift had to be made to God instead; the children then used the gift for themselves pretending that they were using it for God's service in their hands. The gift was stated to be "Corban" (Mark 7:11), a transliteration of the Hebrew and Greek words, meaning an offering. In the OT it is mostly used in Lev 1-7 and Num 7. The Lord viewed this as a stolen offering. Under the pretence of pleasing God, men forsook pleasing their parents by pleasing themselves instead. The commandment of God was thus nullified by the circular argument used by the Pharisees; see Rom 2:18-24, where men claim to hold to the law, yet in practice they do the opposite. To illustrate this with a human parable, it is like a school teacher and his duty to his class; under the guise of having some special work to do for his headmaster, he leaves the class for half an hour, spending the time drinking tea and smoking in the common-room entirely for his own satisfaction. In Acts 5:1-4, there was a gift to God being presented to the assembly, but part was kept back for the use of Ananias and Sapphira under a cloke of lies. And believers today may not be immune from this attitude: singing "Not a mite do I withhold" as if all has been presented to God or at least all used for Him and His service, yet with the house full of occupations and worldly pleasure that are far from God's satisfaction and service.

7-9 *Condemnation* 2. The title "hypocrites" (*hupokritēs*) occurs 20 times in the NT, mainly in Matthew's Gospel, and always spoken by the Lord Himself, showing His introspection of the inner motives of men. The word meant a play- actor, and hence morally one acting in pretence, a man whose words and deeds were in opposition to his inner motives. The Lord quoted Isa 29:13, which can be regarded as a perfect definition of hypocrisy. The pharisaical mouth and lips would engage in the synagogue services, appearing to be justified before men, but known to be otherwise by God; what is outwardly esteemed by men is regarded by God as an abomination (Luke 16:15), (this word being the same as that describing the image set up by the anti-Christ, Matt 24:15). Compare the words spoken to God by the Pharisee in the parable (Luke 18:11-12); there was no justification from God since the heart was far from Him. The context of Isa 29:13 is important: because of men's activities, God had poured out "the spirit of deep sleep", having closed their eyes, and having covered the prophets (v.10). Any vision was to them as a sealed book; in Isa 6:10 *the prophet* had to blind men, in Matt 13:15 *the people* blinded their own eyes, in John 12:40 *the Lord* had blinded their eyes. Thus if there is no reception of divine teaching, then there is a vacuum left to be filled with men's teaching, and then there can be no acceptable worship, for this flows from true hearts filled with true doctrine. The mouth and lips cannot make up for what is lacking in the heart. Thus the strong meat mentioned in Heb 5:14 leads to the sacrifice of praise in 13:15. The water that the Lord would give should lead to worship in spirit and in truth (John 4:14, 24). But time and again God would not accept offerings that He regarded as vain (Isa 1:11).

10-11 *Condemnation* 3. This was spoken to the multitude but no doubt heard also by the Pharisees. The Lord said, "Hear, and understand", but even the apostles failed to understand (vv.15-16), until the matter was explained to them; at least they had confidence to ask, though in Mark 9:32 they "were afraid to ask him". The Lord distinguished between two things: that which enters the mouth physically and that which leaves the mouth morally. The point is that food partaken without the observation of the Pharisees' ceremonial ritual of washing never harmed or poisoned a man (the Lord was not speaking of proper hygienic observations nor of such things as poisons). Under the law, some food was ceremonially unclean, but in Christ even this could not defile a man, since every creature is "good, and nothing to be refused" (1 Tim 4:3-5). Peter had to learn that lesson in Acts 10:11-16, "I have never eaten any thing that is common or unclean . . . What God hath cleansed, that call not thou common". By contrast, the Lord said, what emerges from the mouth reveals the state of the inner-self, and talk leads to practice, thereby defiling the man. But the Pharisees' tradition conveniently overlooked these weightier matters of the law.

12-14 Neither the Pharisees nor the multitude were allowed to hear the explanation of the parable, in keeping with the new principles introduced by the Lord previously in Matt 13:11. So this explanation took place in "the house from the people" (Mark 7:17). The Lord deliberately left them outside in ignorance.

By saying that "the Pharisees were offended", it appears that the disciples were gently rebuking the Lord, because they failed to understand the new principles under which He was directing His ministry. We must, of course, ensure that our lives and conduct do not offend unbelievers (Matt 17:27), but the truth even in parabolic form will offend or stumble if it is rejected.

The reference to the plant in v.13 shows that only what God has produced and planted can please Him (Gen 2:4-5); all others are like the tares (Matt 13:24-30) sown by the wicked one. Even though Paul claimed to have planted (1 Cor 3:6) yet it was as a minister of God that he did the work, recognising that the Corinthians were "God's husbandry" (v.9). Through Isaiah, God made mention of "the branch of my planting, the work of my hands" (Isa 60:21), in the future, His people will be called "trees of righteousness, the planting of the Lord" (61:3). Otherwise plants and trees, not being the planting of the Lord shall be rooted up; John the Baptist had used the metaphor of trees being hewn down and cast into the fire (Matt 3:10). The very last public pronouncement the Lord made before He was crucified was of a similar nature, "if they do these things in a green tree, what shall be done in the dry?" (Luke 23:31). But in Matt 15, the Lord was more particularly referring to the Pharisees; the plant's fruit was the pharisaical doctrines so contrary to the Lord's teaching.

The Lord's command to His apostles was "Let them alone", in the sense of trying to cleanse the world of such men and doctrines. Today, men are able, and will be able even more so, to eradicate the effects of various germs and viruses yet to eradicate the disease caused by *all* germs and viruses may well be impossible. But to eliminate all false doctrine from the world is an impossibility for such leaven expands and does not diminish. The crusades of the past were doomed to failure even before they commenced. God does not want His people to seek to cleanse the world, for only His Son will do this through judgment at His second advent. Thus the apostles had to live side by side with the Pharisees who were blind leaders of the blind, remaining separate from them and not imbibing their doctrines and practices. Thus during the last part of the wilderness journey up the east side of the Dead Sea, the children of Israel were not to "meddle" with the inhabitants of mount Seir (Deut 2:5), nor with the Moabites (v.9), nor with the Ammonites (v.19). We are not called upon to reform any heretical or formal religion. Believers possess gifts for preaching the gospel so that converts should come out of such religious environments. Blind leaders lead blind congregations, such leaders adhering dogmatically to error, for these blind leaders are those from whom the Lord took away the last shred of truth. Such men have placed themselves outside the kingdom of God, and their judgment lingereth for a while.

15-17 Peter was honest; he did not understand "this parable". By this he meant the parable in v.11 relating to the mouth and defilement, not that in v.13 relating to the plants. The Pharisees could not understand, but the apostles had the advantage of the Lord's teaching, so should have understood. Those who are spiritual should understand parables, once they have grasped the general principles of interpretation, fitting them into the Lord's moral and prophetical teaching. The implication of the Lord's answer is seen when the meaning of the word "draught" (*aphedrōn*) is appreciated. The AV, RV and JND all use this word. Even sizeable English dictionaries fail to define the word with the sense needed here; it is used in its obsolete sense by Shakespeare. The Greek word is derived from *apo* (separation) and *hedra* (seat), and hence means a privy, latrine, drain; see 2 Kings 10:27. Thus the human digestive processes accept chemical constitutives in food that are necessary for body-building and for energy provision, but other non-acceptable parts of food are rejected by the body. This takes place because the Creator arranged all things in order throughout the animal kingdom in the beginning. The Pharisaical legalism regarding ceremonial washing was irrelevant, and it tended to cast scorn on God's order and arrangement. A man was not defiled, because the body was designed to cope with impurities in food.

18-20 Rather, defilement is moral in its nature, arising from the heart which is desperately wicked (Jer 17:9). This wickedness comes out of a man, by word and deed, showing that he is defiled. Ceremonial religion can never cleanse such a state; guilt may be covered by the sin-offering, and the laver may sanctify in practice, but redemption through the blood of Christ is the only true and lasting answer to man's problems in his heart. The Lord provided a list of emanations that show defilement; other lists are found in Rom 1:18 to 3:20; 1 Cor 5:11; 6:9, 10; Gal 5:19-21; 2 Tim 3:2-9; 2 Pet 2:1-22. Several of these are dealt with by the Lord in a deeper measure in the Sermon on the Mount (Matt 5:21-37). Note that the use of the two words "adulteries, fornications" implies that they have different meanings, an important point in explaining Matt 5:32; 19:9, where we understand the former word to apply to sin within the marriage bond and the latter to sin outside the marriage bond including the period of espousal before marriage is formally contracted

Thus v.20 presents the conclusion of the issue. The Pharisees' attitude and doctrines were abolished by the Lord's logical reasoning. The disciples fully understood, but the Pharisees remained in ignorance, and even pharisaical converts later sought to introduce their doctrine into the church (Acts 15:1,

5), though the action of the Holy Spirit in that chapter saved Christianity from devolving into another Jewish sect.

2. *The Daughter of the Syrophenician Woman* 15:21-28

v.21 "Then Jesus went thence, and departed into the coasts of Tyre and Sidon.
v.22 And, behold, a woman of Canaan came out of the same coasts, and cried unto him, saying, Have mercy on me, O Lord, *thou* son of David; my daughter is grievously vexed with a devil.
v.23 But he answered her not a word. And his disciples came and besought him, saying, Send her away; for she crieth after us.
v.24 But he answered and said, I am not sent but unto the lost sheep of the house of Israel.
v.25 Then came she and worshipped him, saying, Lord, help me.
v.26 But he answered and said, It is not meet to take the children's bread, and to cast *it* to dogs.
v.27 And she said, Truth, Lord: yet the dogs eat of the crumbs which fall from their masters, table.
v.28 Then Jesus answered and said unto her, O woman, great *is* thy faith: be it unto thee even as thou wilt. And her daughter was made whole from that very hour."

21-22 Phenicia was a region to the west of Galilee. It was about 20 miles deep stretching northwards from Mount Carmel for over 120 miles along the Mediterranean coast; its principal cities were Tyre, Sidon and Ptolemais. References to the gospel reaching there and to the churches founded in these cities, may be found in Acts 11:19; 15:3; 21:2-7, 27:3. In NT times, Phenicia was part of the Roman province of Cilicia and Syria; it lay beyond the Lord's usual sphere of ministry, which was particularly concerned with "the lost sheep of the house of Israel" (Matt 10:6). This excursion into Gentile territory was therefore a precursor of what was to come after His death and resurrection when the Gentiles would receive the gospel in more abundant measure than the Jews. This is seen in John 10. In v.1 we have the *first* fold, consisting of Jewish believers and unbelievers mixed together. In v.7 we have the *second* fold, consisting only of Jewish disciples. In v. 16 we have the *third* fold, consisting of "other sheep", namely of the Gentiles. All would ultimately form one flock under one Shepherd.

Right from the start, this Syrophenician Gentile woman had faith, the Lord's fame must have spread into this territory, and she accepted Him and His power without question. The fact that her daughter was possessed with a demon shows that this affliction was not confined to Israel. But this woman was uncertain of the Lord's status. By calling Him "Lord, thou son of David", she was using a title that was preeminently a title that the Lord had in connection with the Jews. The blind men in Matt 20:30 used the same title, and this was legitimate in their case.

23-24 Hence the Lord answered nothing, until a proper relationship was formed by the woman's faith. Of course, this silence was not unkind: it was to draw out the woman in clearer confession. The disciples were always ready to ask that people be sent away if, to them, the people were merely of nuisance value; see Matt 14:15; 19:13. The Lord's response in v.24 appears to have been addressed to the disciples, not to the woman, although no doubt she heard the Lord's statement, and this added to her determination; like Jacob, she effectively said, "I will not let thee go" (Gen 32:26).

25-28 So the woman joined the leper (Matt 8:2), the ruler (9:18) with many others who worshipped Him. This word "worship" (*proskuneō*, derived from *pros*, towards, and *kuneō*, to kiss) occurs many times in the NT, particularly in Revelation. It means to make obeisance. The woman's cry "Lord, help me" contrasts with that of Peter, "Lord, save me" (Matt 14:30); the former was from a heart with growing faith, the latter from a heart that had momentarily turned backwards. The woman now used the proper title "Lord" suitable for Gentile lips. The Lord would then test her regarding His Jewish-Gentile relationships; the "children's bread" could not be cast to the "dogs". The "children" represented the Jews; the "bread" represented the blessings that the Lord provided; the "dogs" represented the Gentiles. The word used for "dog" is not the usual word *kuōn*, but *kunarion*, meaning a little dog, implying the lowly position that the woman was taking. The word "dog" is used in Phil 3:2 to refer to the Gentiles; to the Jews, this description carried the thought of moral and ceremonial uncleanness.

The woman's answer in v.27 shows not only the extent of her faith, but also the quickness of her reaction to a metaphorical situation, something that most believers lack. Evangelists are often well known for their ability to turn one statement into another so as to gain an advantage for the gospel. In this reply, we should point out that the Greek words for "Lord" and "master" are identical, namely *kurios*. In other words, she placed herself entirely under the authority of the Lord Jesus. His response was inevitable, the daughter was made whole immediately; another example of a miracle being accomplished at a distance. The Lord's will corresponded to the woman's will; this is the essence of a faith described as "great", a faith that was growing, unlike the description "little" (Matt 14:31) used of a faith that had suddenly diminished. A faith that "groweth exceedingly" is a matter for thanksgiving (2 Thess 1:3).

3. *The Feeding of the Four Thousand* 15:29-39

v.29 "And Jesus departed from thence, and came nigh unto the sea of Galilee; and went up into a mountain, and sat down there.

v.30 And great multitudes came unto him, having with them *those that were* lame, blind, dumb, maimed, and many others, and cast them down at Jesus' feet; and he healed them:

v.31 Insomuch that the multitude wondered, when they saw the dumb to speak, the maimed to be whole, the lame to walk, and the blind to see: and they glorified the God of Israel.
v.32 Then Jesus called his disciples *unto him*, and said, I have compassion on the multitude, because they continue with me now three days, and have nothing to eat: and I will not send them away fasting, lest they faint in the way.
v.33 And his disciples say unto him, Whence should we have so much bread in the wilderness, as to fill so great a multitude?
v.34 And Jesus saith unto them, How many loaves have ye? And they said, Seven, and a few little fishes.
v.35 And he commanded the multitude to sit down on the ground.
v.36 And he took the seven loaves and the fishes, and gave thanks, and brake *them*, and gave to his disciples, and the disciples to the multitude.
v.37 And they did all eat, and were filled: and they took up of the broken *meat* that was left seven baskets full.
v.38 And they that did eat were four thousand men, beside women and children.
v.39 And he sent away the multitude, and took ship, and came into the coasts of Magdala."

29-31 Back in Galilee, the Lord adopted His usual position, that of sitting down on a height so as to be able to teach the people. The multitudes were however more interested in His healing ministry, and Matthew compressed this vast activity into two verses. The previous verses had described just one miracle; the present verses describe many. Other examples of compressed description are found in Matt 4:23-25; 8:16; 9:32-38; 14:13-14, 34-36, forming part of "the books that should be written" (John 21:25). Mark's account of the same event concentrates on one such miracle only, that of healing a dumb man (Mark 7:31-37), ending with the people's confession, "He hath done all things well". In Matt 15:31, the result of the miracles was that "they glorified the God of Israel", a good thing to do, but it failed to recognise the deity of Christ present with them. In Luke 17:15, the one leper also glorified God, but appears to have gone further by falling at the Lord's feet and thanking Him. We can do the same when we see God working through one of His servants, as Paul wrote, "they glorified God in me" (Gal 1:24); this certainly did not imply the thought of deity, though the heathen may believe this on occasions (Acts 14:11-18; 28:6).

32-39 Here, the Lord gave the disciples no occasion to react adversely to the needs of the multitudes (as previously in Matt 14:15). By asking the question where bread could be purchased in the wilderness, the disciples had not learnt the lesson of the previous miracle when 5,000 were fed. For general comments on these miracles, the reader should see Matt 14:15-21. The events were similar; there could be no other way in which such miraculous provision could be distributed. The fact that there were two such miracles need not be surprising; there may have been more, but two are recorded, since two is the number of effective witness (John 8:17). And this effectiveness was necessary, since shortly afterwards the Lord would use these two miracles to illustrate an important principle regarding the leaven of the Pharisees and Sadducees (Matt 16:6-12).

IV. The New Revelation (16:1-28)

1. *Final Condemnation of the Pharisees' Doctrine* 16:1-12

v.1 "The Pharisees also with the Sadducees came, and tempting desired him that he would shew them a sign from heaven.
v.2 He answered and said unto them, When it is evening, ye say, *It will be* fair weather: for the sky is red.
v.3 And in the morning, *It will* be foul weather to day: for the sky is red and lowring. O ye hypocrites, ye can discern the face of the sky; but can ye not *discern* the signs of the times?
v.4 A wicked and adulterous generation seeketh after a sign; and there shall no sign be given unto it, but the sign of the prophet Jonas. And he left them, and departed.
v.5 And when his disciples were come to the other side, they had forgotten to take bread.
v.6 Then Jesus said unto them, Take heed and beware of the leaven of the Pharisees and of the Sadducees.
v 7 And they reasoned among themselves, saying, *It is* because we have taken no bread.
v.8 *Which* when Jesus perceived, he said unto them, O ye of little faith, why reason ye among yourselves, because ye have brought no bread?
v.9 Do ye not yet understand, neither remember the five loaves of the five thousand, and how many baskets ye took up?
v.10 Neither the seven loaves of the four thousand, and how many baskets ye took up?
v.11 How is it that ye do not understand that I spake *it* not to you concerning bread, that ye should beware of the leaven of the Pharisees and of the Sadducees?
v.12 Then understood they how that he bade *them* not beware of the leaven of bread, but of the doctrine of the Pharisees and of the Sadducees."

1 In vv.1-12, the Lord issued to His disciples His final condemnation of the doctrine of the Pharisees and the Sadducees; in 22:15-34 they were reduced to silence when they attempted to trick Him concerning His doctrine; in 23:1- 33 the Pharisees themselves were condemned to "the damnation of hell" (v.33). The Lord used the occasion in ch.16 to introduce many new aspects of truth, particularly, the truth of His Person (v.16), the truth of the church (v.18), the truth of His death and resurrection (v.21), and the truth of His coming in glory in His kingdom (v.28). The doctrines of men and the strange ideas about the Lord's Person (v.14) were quite baseless, while only the true revelation of the Father's purpose in Christ was of value.

A crescendo of questions and temptations had commenced in Matt 15:1. These men now wanted a spectacular phenomenon to appear in the heavens so as to prove something about the Lord's Person, although their request for such a sign had already been rejected (12:39). In 19:3 they would tempt Him about the subject of divorce, and in 22:17 about giving tribute to Caesar, attempting to trick the Lord into providing answers that they could construe as contrary to their law. Other questions also can be found in these subsequent chapters. By requesting a sign, they implied that they were not content with His miracles; however, they would not believe whatever happened! Even if a man rose from the dead, there would be no repentance nor faith (Luke 16:30-31); " they believed not on him" although He had done "many miracles before them" (John 12:37); the priests claimed that they would believe Him if He came down from the cross (Matt 27:42) – no doubt they would have been surprised and fearful, but faith is not built on emotions of that character.

2-3 The Lord drew a lesson from elementary observations in meteorology; the colour of the sky in the evening and morning give an indication as to the kind of weather to expect in the following hours. Both are effects of a common fundamental cause. Here are signs in God's creation that foretell the immediate future. Today, the weather, the tides, the times of sunrise and sunset, phases of the moon, eclipses of the sun and moon, the positions of stars and planets to a lesser or greater extent, are predicted mostly with great precision (apart from the weather) well into the future. Present conditions are a pointer to the future because of the inevitability of God's natural laws embedded in His creation. They are hypocrites (and more-so today with the growth of knowledge) who recognise these facts, and yet fail to "discern the signs of the times". These signs are the OT prophecies that relate to the Lord's lifetime and to His future coming in judgment to establish His kingdom. They were being worked out in His life, and they will be further worked out in that future day. The future was clearly foretold, both by the OT prophecies and by the Lord's present teaching. But these men were blind to these signs, and wanted something further of an astronomical nature.

4 The Lord used the same phraseology as in Matt 12:39; "adulterous" means that the Pharisees adhered to their own doctrine rather than to the Lord's. James used this description of believers who sought the "friendship of the world", rather than abiding in "the fellowship of his Son" (James 4:4; 1 Cor 1:9). The only sign that the Lord would provide such men was that of "the prophet Jonas". In Matt 12:38-42, He explained this sign, likening it to the Son of man lying in death for "three days and three nights", also expanding on the subject in relation to Nineveh and the queen of the south. But in our verse, no explanation was provided, in keeping with the Lord's new approach to parabolic and metaphorical utterances. Instead, "he left them, and departed". At that time, it was easy to leave, but later in Jerusalem departure would be more urgent when men sought to stone Him (John 8:59; 10:39). Note that the only "signs" provided by the Lord when men specifically asked for them were metaphorical and relating to His death; the other one occurs in John 2:19, "Destroy this temple, and in three days I will raise it up". Resurrection is implied there, though the disciples understood only when this event had taken place (v.22).

5-7 Another boat journey without incident brought them from Magdala (or Magadan) to "the other side", to the northern coast of the Sea of Galilee. Matthew stated that "they had forgotten to take bread", but in Mark 8:14 we find that they had not "more than one loaf" in the ship. In other words, they had what remained in their possession in Magdala, though there they had forgotten to buy any more. The Lord turned this to good advantage by warning them to "take heed and beware of the leaven of the Pharisees and of the Sadducees". The warnings introduced by "take heed" in the NT merit a special study by the reader (such as Matt 24:4; Acts 20:28; 1 Cor 3:10; Col 4:17). This leaven referred to ideas from Jewish sources ready to captivate the mind. The Pharisees were legalists; the Sadducees were materialists (denying the existence of spirits and resurrection, as in Luke 20:27; Acts 23:8); the Herodians were politicians (Matt 22:16; Mark 3:6). The "one loaf" may be typical of the fact that the disciples were not wholly immune from these things as yet. The reaction of the disciples showed their continued inability to interpret the Lord's words. "They reasoned among themselves" (a verb in the imperfect tense, showing a continued state of reasoning), perceiving materialistic circumstances only – they had "taken no bread". This verb *dialogizomai*, "to reason", usually refers to reasoning on a natural basis not on a spiritual basis, either by the disciples or by the religious leaders (Matt 21:25; Mark 9:33).

8-12 Reasoning based on the physical circumstances of the moment was called by the Lord, " little faith". After all, they had previously claimed to have understood the parable of the leaven, so they should have known its spiritual meaning (Matt 13:33, 51), as well as the typical implications of leaven in the OT; the letter but not the spirit was all that they could see (2 Cor 3:6). Rather, they should beware of all leaven from Jewish sources. Just as the Lord had provided abundantly when He had fed the 5,000 and the 4,000 with food of His special creating, so too He would provide all the doctrine that they needed to know: "the flesh profiteth nothing: the words that I speak unto you, they are spirit, and they are life . . . thou hast the words of eternal life" (John 6:63, 68). To stress this point, the sign of the miraculous feeding was given twice when 5,000 and 4,000 were fed as is recalled in our vv.9-10; the number of baskets of additional food is also recalled, in the form of two questions. All this the Lord had provided. Similarly, if He provides all necessary doctrine, then there is no need for any of His disciples to partake of extraneous doctrines emanating from the leaven of the Pharisees and Sadducees.

This doctrinal leaven was introduced and maintained by the various religious and political factions in rivalry the one with the other. Before his conversion, Paul had been taken up with this leaven as a Pharisee (Acts 26:5; Phil 3:5), but then he was completely converted to Christ and His word. These things of men expand because men delight in the things of men! Egypt was a place of leaven, and upon their departure from its bondage the children of Israel had to take no leavened bread or dough out with them (Exod 12:34, 39). The Greeks in Athens spent their time in acquiring new forms of leaven in the shape of "some new thing" (Acts 17:21), and they were quite content to believe that "Jesus, and the resurrection" came into this category. Some of the elders in Ephesus would propagate leaven in the form of "perverse things" to gain the attention of the disciples in the assembly there (Acts 20:30). Leaven was spreading amongst the Galatian believers; Paul wrote of those who "would pervert the gospel of Christ" (Gal 1:7) by bewitching them so that they "should not obey the truth" (3:1). Later, Paul called doctrinal leaven "every wind of doctrine" (Eph 4:14), and "profane and vain babblings: for they will increase unto more ungodliness" (2 Tim 2:16). Hence, as in Acts 15, we must take heed so as to stop the rot. If an assembly holds to the truth, then the influence of leaven will usually be presented from the outside, which is like a whirlpool of conflicting doctrines and practices. There is a strong movement of ecumenicalism abroad to compromise on the grounds of a desired unity, so unlike the unity that Paul describes in Eph 4:3-6. However, man's best level is equal to God's worst; millions seem to fall for it since it is an expanding leaven. But what are believers doing? Are they taking heed, or resting as if what happened in Paul's day can never adversely affect assemblies today? Weeds flourish in a garden when the gardener is not active. It is tragic if some believers shake hands with almost every doctrine and practice raised by man, because it appears to be more popular and acceptable than the doctrine and practice uniquely described in the NT. The safeguard is faith that accepts the Word of God without question, believing that the Lord provides the bread because He is the Bread of life. In our service, we must resolve to be like Peter who said, "such as I have give I thee" – and this came from God alone (Acts 3:6).

2. *Confession of the Truth of His Person* 16:13-20

v.13 "When Jesus came into the coasts of Caesarea Philippi, he asked his disciples, saying, Whom do men say that I the Son of man am?

v.14 And they said, Some *say that thou art* John the Baptist: some, Elias; and others, Jeremias, or one of the prophets.

v.15 He saith unto them, But whom say ye that I am?

v.16 And Simon Peter answered and said, Thou art the Christ, the Son of the living God.

v.17 And Jesus answered and said unto him, Blessed art thou, Simon Bar-jona: for flesh and blood hath not revealed *it* unto thee, but my Father which is in heaven.

v.18 And I say also unto thee, That thou art Peter, and upon this rock I will build my church; and the gates of hell shall not prevail against it.

v.19 And I will give unto thee the keys of the kingdom of heaven: and whatsoever thou shalt bind on earth shall be bound in heaven: and whatsoever thou shalt loose on earth shall be loosed in heaven.

v.20 Then charged he his disciples that they should tell no man that he was Jesus the Christ."

13 Caesarea Philippi was a city lying about 25 miles northwards from the Sea of Galilee. Apart from Sidon referred to in Matt 15:21, this city of Caesarea Philippi represents the most northerly point that the Lord reached in His journeys. The word for "coasts" is *merē*, meaning "parts", a very common word in the NT; it is distinct from the word *horia*, usually translated " coasts" and meaning "boundary" or "frontier" (Matt 15:22, 39; 19:1). Caesarea Philippi lay at the foot of Mount Hermon. The Roman emperor Augustus Caesar had given the town to Herod the Great, who built a temple there in his honour, though it was Philip who later gave it the name of Caesarea. To distinguish it from the city of Caesarea on the Mediterranean coast further to the south, Philip added the name "Philippi" after his own name.

It was here that the Lord tested what His disciples knew about the leaven that had spread around concerning His Person. The first question was not what the *disciples* knew or thought, but what men thought. In this question, He used His title " Son of man" – the usual title by which He referred to Himself. It is a title expressing His authority in Manhood, both when He was here in the days of His flesh, and when He returns at His second advent. It is not a title used of His relationship to the church; Stephen used it in Acts 7:56 and John in Rev 1:13, but that is all. Briefly, He is the Son of David to Israel, Son of God to the church and Son of man to the world.

14 As Man largely rejected by the religious and political leaders, He sought the disciples' views as to what men were saying about Him. Of course the Lord knew this already; He "needed not that any should testify of man: for he knew what was in man" (John 2:25). But it was useful for the apostles to contrast the leaven around with the revealed truth concerning His Person. The heart of man had already been laid bare in blasphemy (Matt 12:24), in the hypocrisy of mixing up legality and evil living (15:1-20), and in being the source of religious doctrinal leaven (16:1-12). Having dealt with all these things, the Lord was ready to announce some new things: the church, His death, His kingdom and glory. These new truths were made known to His own, but not to the world.

Previously, men had thought that John the Baptist was the Christ (Luke 3:15), though this had been refuted by John (John 1:20). Herod had suggested this theory to his servants (Matt 14:2). Peter rose above this confusion, for it was John's testimony through Andrew that had led him to Christ (John 1:37-42). Others thought that the Lord was Elias (i.e. Elijah). They confused Christ's miraculous power with the miracles that Elijah had been able to do in OT times. However, Elijah was once discouraged and had desired to die on account of the smallness of the testimony (1 Kings 19:4,10); he was a man of like passions as we (James 5:17). The Lord was not like this, and on the mount His glory eclipsed that of Elijah. The choice "Jeremias" does not appear in Mark 8:28 and Luke 9:19, and it is difficult to see why this theory was advocated. He did no miracle, but did denounce sin in Jerusalem before and after the capture of the city by the emperor of the first beast-kingdom, Nebuchadnezzar of Babylon; at the same time he painted a rosy picture of the future under the new covenant. The people may have associated this denunciation with the way in which the Lord denunciated the Pharisees. Lastly. "one of the prophets" was a vague suggestion. Of these Moses was greatest (Deut 34:10) and he had predicted that God would raise up a Prophet (18:18). On the mount of transfiguration he was displaced by the Son.

15-16 The second question asked by the Lord, "But whom say ye that I am?" was directed to the exercise and appreciation of His disciples. Note that it was addressed to them all, and not to Peter alone. Asking questions is a useful spiritual exercise, since answers are expected and they demonstrate the state of heart. Compare this with Matt 22:42, "What think ye of Christ?". 1 Corinthians is full of questions asked by Paul; in many cases no answer is provided. The Corinthians had to assess their own answers honestly, and by this means the apostle was ensuring that lessons were being learnt.

Peter rose to the occasion, not only as spokesman, but from vv.17-18 it appears that he alone had had this special revelation from the Father. "Thou art the Christ, the Son of the living God" is one of the choicest confessions in the NT. It contrasts with v.14 which represents the end of the leaven of men; here is the beginning of divine revelation. "Christ" declares the Lord to be the Messiah, the Anointed One, while Son expresses Deity and identification with the Father (John 5:18; 10:33). The use of the adjective "living" denotes the recognition of His eternal existence, one of the reasons why Peter later refused to contemplate the Lord's death (Matt 16:21-22). There are many testimonies to the Lord's Person found in the Gospels (see our comments on Matt 14:33). In Matthew's Gospel, we find the confession "Son of God" made by the demons (8:29); "Son of David" made by the blind men (9:27; 20:30), "the Son of God" made by the apostles (14:33); "the Son of God" made by the centurion (27:54). In John 1, there were many initial confessions of His Person: "the Lamb of God, the Son of God" by John the Baptist (vv.29, 34); "the Christ" by Andrew (v.41); "the Son of God . . . the King of Israel" by Nathanael (v.49). Further in John's Gospel, we find "Messias . . . Christ" by the woman of Samaria (4:25); "the Saviour of the world" by the men of the city (4:42); "that Christ, the Son of the living God" by Peter (6:69); "the Christ, the Son of God" by Martha (11:27). See also Acts 8:37 (a verse omitted in some Greek manuscripts), and Gal 2:20.

The title "Son" implies relationship with the Father. It is heresy to suggest that this title is only relative, referring to the incarnation and not to His eternal position in Deity. "Having . . . one son" (Mark 12:6) implies sonship before He came forth; the worlds were made by His Son (Heb 1:2); the Son was addressed in OT times before His incarnation (Heb 1:8), the Son had glory with the Father "before the world was" (John 17:5). The word "begotten" does not imply generation when used to describe the relationship Son-Father (Ps 2:7; John 1:14,18; 3:16); the old theologians of the fourth century employed the term "eternal generation" to avoid the concept of generation. Modern translations that give "You are my Son; today I have become your Father" (Ps 2:7; Heb 1:5) should be rejected as heresy, and not worthy of use in detailed Bible study. Ordinary human words with ordinary physical meanings are pressed into use to describe Deity and other spiritual concepts, but their literal physical meanings must not be imported into these spiritual realms. Thus "begotten" relates to a *state*, not to an *action*; it refers to external existence and relationship, and not to derivation as in human relationships in a created physical world governed by physical, chemical and biological laws.

17 The knowledge of divine truth is "revealed" (*apokaluptō*) meaning "to uncover". But spiritual truth is not revealed by natural processes. By "blood" is implied God's realm naturally (Acts 17:26), and by "flesh" man's realm naturally. Neither is competent to reveal divine truth, neither can achieve God's purpose or accomplish His work (John 1:13). Thus the Father is revealed by the Son (Matt 11:27); truth is revealed by the Father to babes (v.25), the Son is revealed by the Father (Matt 16:17); the gospel is revealed by the Lord Jesus (Gal 1:12); the Holy Spirit revealed a fact to Simeon (Luke 2:26); God reveals truth to us by His Spirit (1 Cor 2:10). This great fact must be grasped by evangelists and ministers of the Word alike. All they can do is to preach and to teach, their hearers may learn these things mentally (and this is good), but truth is learnt in the soul ultimately by revelation as a divine work.

Note that the Lord addressed Simon Peter as "Simon Bar-jona", that is, his natural name (John 1:42); correspondingly natural means, "flesh and blood", do not produce any spiritual result in a natural man prior to conversion.

18 This contrasts with "thou art Peter", the spiritual name that the Lord gave him at his first encounter with Him (John 1:42); correspondingly spiritual means, "my Father, I", are being used to convey deep spiritual truth to a spiritual man. Through failing to see this distinction, some writers have found great difficulty in this statement "thou art Peter". It has been made the basis of heresy, and it has even been suggested that the Greek words "*su ei petros*" (thou art Peter) should be abbreviated, altered and combined into "*su eipas*" (thou hast said), thereby removing the name of Peter altogether!

"Upon this rock I will build my church" has produced more heresy and conflicting claims than almost any other words of Scripture. These claims arise from the similarity of the Greek words for "Peter" (*Petros*, a piece of rock or stone) and "rock" (*petra*, a mass of rock). The former is small; the latter is large. To suggest that the building is on something small is not worthy of the One who builds on something large. To assert that early tradition held to the assumption that the church was to be built on Peter is false. A Roman Catholic scholar examined 85 writings of the early church Fathers, and found that 17 regarded Peter as the rock; 44 Peter's confession; 16 Christ; 8 all the apostles. We must note that the Lord claimed that "my church" was not to be built on "me" but on "this rock" – namely, not "on thee" nor "on me", but on a third concept. Physically, some buildings have artificial foundations laid in soil, today builders use concrete upon which the brickwork is to be placed. In this case, the foundation is part of the building. Where there is solid rock, the superstructure can be erected directly on that; under those circumstances the rock is not part of the building. Now Christ is part of the church, since He is Head of the body; hence we cannot interpret the "rock" as Christ. In the context, it can only be Peter's confession of his Person made in v.16. This is consistent with the use of the word "rock" in Matt 7:24, standing for divine words. This interpretation must not be confused with 1 Cor 3:10-11, where the foundation laid by Paul is Christ Jesus. The Lord's servants build on this foundation locally, enabled by God so to do, as were Bezaleel and Aholiab in the case of the tabernacle (Exod 31:1-6). In Eph 2:20, the church is not built on the "apostles and prophets", but on the foundation that they had laid, namely the teaching that had exalted the Lord Jesus as the "chief corner stone".

There are some expositors who insist that "my church" spoken of by the Lord does not refer to the church commenced in Acts 2. They assert that in the Gospel of the King, only Jewish concepts are to be found. But this is obviously not true, when we consider the wide-ranging scope of the Lord's ministry, which referred to

1. the Jews when he was present with them;
2. the period after His departure, the period of the church;
3. the time of the great tribulation after the rapture of the church; and
4. His kingdom in glory.

Rather, "my church" (*ekklēsia*, "a calling out of") refers to the whole company of the redeemed since Acts 2, commonly referred to as the mystical or universal church. It is to be distinguished from "the church" in Matt 18:17, where a local gathering of believers is implied in the context. Both meanings occur throughout the Acts and Paul's epistles, and the reader must always discern which aspect is being used. "My church" would be "a glorious church, not having spot or wrinkle, or any such thing" (Eph 5:27); Satan cannot tamper with such an absolute work of Christ. The troubles of the local churches in Paul's day, in Rev 2-3, throughout history, and in mustard seed growth of Christendom, cannot affect the spotless beauty of the mystical body of Christ. As the Lord said, "the gates of hell (hades) shall not prevail against it", the metaphor "gates" standing for power and authority. The power of death stands in contrast to "the living God" of Peter's confession. Certainly, Peter was excluded from the foundation; immediately afterwards he fell (vv.22-23), with Satan within savouring the things of men and not of God.

19 The distribution of the "keys" was not general, even among the apostles; the plural "ye" and "they" occur in vv.15, 20 but the keys were given to Peter alone (v. 19), as was the capacity to bind and loose (in contrast with 18:18, where "ye" is used). The keys imply a gate or door, and hence this stands in contrast to "the gates of hell" in v.18. Note that the entrance is not into the church, but into the kingdom of heaven. Only believers enter the church; no unbelievers can partake of the character "not having spot or wrinkle, or any such thing". But in keeping with Matt 13, in its mystery form the kingdom of heaven is a sphere of profession in which, by its very nature, both good and bad are found, to be separated at the end times. By means of Peter's preaching in Acts 2:14-36; 10:34- 43, the door was opened to Jew and Gentile. At first, only believers entered, and they also formed part of the church. But later, as true testimony waned, unbelievers were attracted to the more formal church structure organised by the Nicolaitans and the Jezebel (Rev 2:6, 15, 20). This does not form the church of Christ, whatever religious leaders may assert; it does form part of the kingdom of heaven during the present dispensation, awaiting cleansing through judgment to usher in the manifestation of the kingdom in glory.

Binding and loosing (*deō* and *luō*) as applied to Peter was a very solemn responsibility. Those brought in through his ministry were brought in permanently; those kept out through their attitude to his ministry were kept out permanently. None can claim to have the spiritual power to do this today, unless it be a claim of pure presumption. For Peter had to be in contact with the divine mind in heaven, to know exactly what the divine purpose was in these matters. It was no arbitrary choice on Peter's part, but a continuation of the Lord's work whereby certain of the Pharisees were kept in a state of blindness – they were bound. No evangelist today can know if an unbelieving soul is permanently blind; rather, the gospel is preached in season and out of season so that there should be every possibility of salvation entering unbelievers' hearts. Note that words "bound" and "loosed" are perfect participles in Greek (easily recognisable by the duplication of the first letter: de*demenon*, le*lumenon*); this implies permanence of state after the action.

20 Entry into the church would be by confessing that Jesus is the Christ, the Son of God. This important news regarding His Person was not to be publicised until the church was formed at Pentecost. There were, of course, others who knew this truth; Martha confessed, "thou art the Christ, the Son of God" (John 11:27). Later at His trial, the Lord was compelled by the provision of the law to answer the question, ". . . that thou tell us whether thou be the Christ, the Son of God" (Matt 26:63). He merely answered "Thou hast said" and immediately referred to His coming in power and glory as the Son of man. It appears that the high priest Caiaphas was one of those who had been bound never to be loosed. This prohibition upon telling men about His Person should be compared with

Matt 17:9, where there is a further prohibition about telling men about the vision of His glory on the mount.

3. *The Lord's Death, Resurrection, Glory and Kingdom* 16:21-28

v.21 "From that time forth began Jesus to shew unto his disciples, how that he must go unto Jerusalem, and suffer many things of the elders and chief priests and scribes, and be killed, and be raised again the third day.
v.22 Then Peter took him, and began to rebuke him, saying, Be it far from thee, Lord: this shall not be unto thee.
v.23 But he turned, and said unto Peter, Get thee behind me, Satan: thou art an offence unto me: for thou savourest not the things that be of God, but those that be of men.
v.24 Then said Jesus unto his disciples, If any *man* will come after me, let him deny himself, and take up his cross, and follow me.
v.25 For whosoever will save his life shall lose it: and whosoever will lose his life for my sake shall find it.
v.26 For what is a man profited, if he shall gain the whole world, and lose his own soul? or what shall a man give in exchange for his soul?
v.27 For the Son of man shall come in the glory of his Father with his angels; and then he shall reward every man according to his works.
v.28 Verily I say unto you, There be some standing here, which shall not taste of death, till they see the Son of man coming in his kingdom."

21 The word "began" (*archomai*) is very common in the Synoptic Gospels, though it is used only sparingly in describing the Lord's actions. Thus in Matthew's Gospel, He began to preach (4:17); He began to upbraid (11:20): He began to be sorrowful (26:37). The announcement of His sufferings, death and resurrection in Jerusalem was something new, to be revealed only after the truth of His Person had been made know. Previously He had announced His death using metaphorical language (Matt 12:40; John 2:19-22); the reference to a "cross" had not been associated with His own cross (10:38). At the same time, in the context the church to be built was closely linked to His death and resurrection. The full truth would come out later, when Paul wrote that both Jew and Gentile had been reconciled to God in one body by the cross (Eph 2:16), and that "he is the head of the body, the church: who is . . . the firstborn from the dead" (Col 1:18). The Lord disclosed the outward features of His sufferings; later the Spirit revealed the sacrificial nature of His cross.

Speaking some 100 miles north of Jerusalem, the Lord made it clear that He must go to Jerusalem in order to suffer, the word "must" indicating that the will of God would be done. Luke in particular traces this journey to Jerusalem: see Luke 9:31; 9:51 (where "he stedfastly set his face to go to Jerusalem"); 13:22; 17:11; 18:31; 19:11, 28, 37, 41. Not only did the Lord know the place, but He also knew the hour (John 13:1; 17:1). The religious leaders, "the elders and chief priests and scribes", would be responsible for His sufferings and death, when His body would be placed in the tomb, and when His soul would depart to hades, separated for a season until "the third day" when He would rise from paradise in the eternal state of resurrection to die no more. The fact that the Lord "began" to say this to His disciples means that He continually returned to the subject (see the next verse). In other words, the object of His ministry – His cross – was drawing nearer, and He prepared His disciples for this event.

22 Peter too "began" a certain course of action. Having enjoyed the period of being with the Lord in His ministry, he could not bear the thought of this coming to an abrupt end; hence his rebuke "Be it far from thee", or "God have mercy on thee" (RV marg), "[God] be favourable to thee" (JND). The Greek "*hileōs soi*" comes from a Hebrew expression, the first word meaning "propitious", "favourable", "merciful", the subject "God" being understood but not actually expressed. This reaction on Peter's behalf was the first of a long series of misunderstandings and manifestations of ignorance on the matter rectified only when the coming of the Holy Spirit had brought about a complete change in the apostles' understanding of the cross. "This shall not be" is a complete contrast to "thus it must be" (Matt 26:54). In Mark 9:9-10 they questioned one with another; in Mark 9:31-32 they understood not; in Matt 17:22-23 they were exceeding sorry; in Luke 9:44-45 it was hid from them (by Satan), and they perceived it not; in Luke 18:32-34 there was a continuous non-memory; in John 13:36-37 Peter thought that he could follow. No wonder after His resurrection the Lord could exclaim, "O fools, and slow of heart to believe" (Luke 24:25). Today there can be no excuse for similar ignorance amongst believers, since the Holy Spirit has been given to lead into all truth.

23 The Lord did not reply to "Simon" (his natural name), but to "Peter" (his spiritual name). In other words, he was fallible both before and after the revelation was given, although not, of course, when inspiration was operative. Peter's reaction and ignorance were due to Satan; the apostle did not always have divinely-motivated thoughts, in spite of the revelation he had in Matt 16:16. This difference is seen in 1 Cor 2:14, where spiritual discernment is needed to displace the thoughts of the natural man. Minding the things of the flesh and of the Spirit are contrasted in Rom 8:5-6. The minding of earthly things is in opposition to the thoughts of the heavenly citizens (Phil 3:19-20). We must mind those things above, and not things on the earth (Col 3:2).

Some suggest that Peter was instructed to get behind the Lord so that He could address Satan personally. This seems to be contrary to the following verse, where the Lord addressed His disciples, and Peter was not excepted. Rather, we feel the instruction is to Satan to get behind the Lord, so that Peter may remain out of temptation. After all, the Lord had said the same thing to Satan in the wilderness (Luke 4:8). The real offence came from Satan who used Peter as a vessel to pass on that offence. The verb "thou savourest" is merely the common word *phroneō*, meaning "to think" or "to mind"; the RV has "thou mindest".

24-26 The word "then" shows that the idea of "cross" is related to what the Lord had just said (in v.21) about His own death (though at that time the apostles no doubt thought of death by stoning rather than by the Roman method of crucifixion). In Matt 10:38 they probably did not associate the word "cross" with His own death. In other words, the apostles had to take up the will of God even if it meant their own suffering and death at the hands of men. Thus "the apostles . . . were appointed to death" (1 Cor 4:9); "in deaths oft" wrote Paul (2 Cor 11:23), adding that he took pleasure "in persecutions, in distresses for Christ's sake" (12:10). To "deny himself" means that the disciple has to abandon all thoughts that are contrary to the divine mind (as in Matt 16:22-23). His servants have to bring "into captivity every thought to the obedience of Christ" (2 Cor 10:5).

Saving and losing, losing and finding, are two vital principles that are opposite to what the world expects. "Life" does not necessarily mean one's physical life rather it means what the disciple has to live for in this world. A life of self interest is a life wasted for God; a life of spiritual interest is a life used for and by God. Any disciple can assess his own position by asking himself what he does with his spare time. These principles fit into the Lord's teaching in Matt 13:12: "whosoever hath (having lost his life and therefore having found it), to him shall be given . . . whosoever hath not (having saved his life and therefore having lost it), from him shall be taken away even that he hath". The Lord made similar statements elsewhere:

1. in Matt 10:39 where the subject of service was under consideration,

2. in Luke 17:33 of the future day when the Lord comes in glory and judgment. Men may scheme to preserve self, but God's final verdict will be death, while others who pass through the great tribulation will find that they have life abundantly in the glorious kingdom of the Son of man.

In v.26, the word for "soul" is the same word for "life" in v.25 (*psuchē*). To gain "the whole world" has been the object of many OT kings of the nations; such as Nebuchadnezzar; the first king of the leopard-kingdom Greece was Alexander the Great whose exploits enabled him to "bear rule over all the earth" (Dan 2:39; 7:6). Subsequent dictators right up to the twentieth century have had this object. In the end times, the beast will be given power over "all kindreds, and tongues, and nations" (Rev 13:7). All have lost, or will lose, all their possessions, so that the Son of God may possess "the uttermost parts of the earth" (Ps 2:8). Even if power on this scale cannot be achieved by the majority, yet man's ambition is essentially selfish, and all will ultimately fade away. The rich man in Luke 16:19 gained his life, but then lost it in hades. The rich farmer gained more and more as great profit, but lost his soul in one night having laid up treasure for himself (Luke 12:16-21). The rich young man in Matt 19:16-22 had "great possessions", but as far as we can assess he lost his own soul, going away sorrowful. Believers also cannot trifle with their lives, for "ye are not your own . . . ye are bought with a price" (1 Cor 6:19-20). Finally, having lost his own soul, what shall a man give in exchange for it? – namely, how can he regain it? In desperation he would seek to pay a ransom, but the world that he might possess is not enough. As Ps 49:6-8 puts it: wealth and riches cannot be given to God as a ransom to redeem a man, since the redemption of a soul is precious (namely, more than a man can give).

27 When the Son of man comes in glory, it will be too late for any man to seek to save his soul, to exchange worldly riches for his lost soul. Past works are the ground for reward in the millennial kingdom of Christ (Matt 25:19), but for those with a lost soul there will be "sudden destruction", and then there shall be no escape (1 Thess 5:3).

28 To press the point, the Lord changed the subject to "the Son of man coming in his kingdom". Not tasting of death is suggestive of those who pass through the great tribulation, who will see the Son of man descending in glory when "every eye shall see him" (Rev 1:7). The martyrs of that period will also be raised to share in the administration of that glorious kingdom (Rev 20:4). The transfiguration of Christ was a preview of that glorious descent, which Peter described as "the power and coming of our Lord Jesus Christ" (2 Pet 1:16).

V. Weakness of Faith, on the Mountain and below (17:1-27)

1. *The Transfiguration of Christ* 17:1-13

v.1 "And after six days Jesus taketh Peter, James, and John his brother, and bringeth them up into an high mountain apart,
v.2 And was transfigured before them: and his face did shine as the sun, and his raiment was white as the light.
v.3 And, behold, there appeared unto them Moses and Elias talking with him.
v.4 Then answered Peter, and said unto Jesus, Lord, it is good for us to be here: if thou wilt, let us make here three tabernacles; one for thee, and one for Moses, and one for Elias.
v.5 While he yet spake, behold, a bright cloud overshadowed them: and, behold, a voice out of the cloud, which said, This is my beloved Son, in whom I am well pleased; hear ye him.
v.6 And when the disciples heard *it*, they fell on their face, and were sore afraid.
v.7 And Jesus came and touched them, and said, Arise, and be not afraid.
v.8 And when they had lifted up their eyes, they saw no man, save Jesus only.
v.9 And as they came down from the mountain, Jesus charged them, saying, Tell the vision to no man, until the Son of man be risen again from the dead.
v.10 And his disciples asked him, saying, Why then say the scribes that Elias must first come?
v.11 And Jesus answered and said unto them, Elias truly shall first come and restore all things.

v.12 But I say unto you, That Elias is come already, and they knew him not, but have done unto him whatsoever they listed. Likewise shall also the Son of man suffer of them.
v.13 Then the disciples understood that he spake unto them of John the Baptist."

1 Tradition asserts that this "high mountain" was mount Tabor, a few miles to the east of Nazareth and 50 miles south of Caesarea Philippi, but this is very unlikely since there was a fort on its summit; another suggestion is mount Hermon near Caesarea Philippi. However, Scripture is silent on the matter, so mere speculation cannot be a spiritual exercise. Clearly the event made a profound impression on Peter since he recalled it (though not his failure) many years later (2 Pet 1:15-21). Then he insisted that the written word of prophecy is something "more sure" than a vision that fades.

Although the kingdom in open display would not appear until after the church era, far beyond the lifetimes of the apostles, yet this preview of divine glory would be given to "some" very shortly. Men at that time thought that "the kingdom of God should immediately appear" (Luke 19:11) to displace the Roman occupation, but in the meantime, the kingdom was not to come "with observation", but was to be "within, among you" (Luke 17:20-21). Nevertheless, this preview was intimated with the promise that the privileged ones would "not taste of death" prior to the heavenly vision. Compare the case of Simeon, who would not see death till "he had seen the Lord's Christ" (Luke 2:26). In the future, many will pass through death during the great tribulation period prior to the establishment of the kingdom by means of severe judgment, though others will not.

Matthew states "after six days", but Luke 9:28 states "about an eight days after", the word "about" showing that there is no conflict between these numbers. Six is the number of man, and the kingdom is established after the period of man's rule on earth; eight is the number of resurrection, which will be the portion of the martyrs of the great tribulation. Only three apostles were taken up the mount with the Lord, Peter, James and John. The others were not chosen to see the vision, no doubt because their faith was not up to the standard that was required (Matt 17:20). In a measure they are typical of those Jews in the great tribulation not entering into the kingdom. Note that the same three apostles were privileged to see the miracle of the raising of Jairus' daughter and to be with the Lord in the garden of Gethsemane (Luke 8:51; Matt 26:37).

2 On the mountain top the Lord prayed (Luke 9:29). The word "transfigured" (*metamorphoō*, "to change into another form") occurs also in Mark's account (Mark 9:2), though in Luke 9:29 "was altered" is used (*egeneto heteron*, "became different"). The word "transfigured" is used also of believers in Rom 12:2, "be ye transformed", and in 2 Cor 3:18, "transformed into the same images" (RV). The Lord was transfigured as never before to the apostles' gaze. Today, unbelief suggests that the sun's rays falling on the snow cast their dazzling effect upon the Lord. But faith knows that His intrinsic glory shone out on the mountain top (the nearest place on earth to heaven). We must distinguish this from the shining of Moses' face in Exod 34:29-35; it was not Moses' own glory, but that absorbed from the divine presence in the tabernacle. But in the Lord's case, His glory was burning through the very fabric of His Manhood body, and through His clothes. Moreover, "his face did shine as the sun", similar to "his countenance was as the sun shineth in his strength" (Rev 1:16). His raiment "white as the light" is called "white and glistering" in Luke 9:29. Paul also saw such a stupendous vision at his conversion, something that he never forgot; Luke described it as "a light from heaven" (Acts 9:3), while Paul recalled "from heaven a great light" (22:6), " the glory of that light" (v.11), " above the brightness of the sun" (26:13). After years of " no open vision" (1 Sam 3:1), the prayer "thou that dwellest between the cherubim, shine forth" (Ps 80:1, 3, 7, 19) had been answered.

3 On the mountain top, Moses, although no one knew of his grave (Deut 34:5-6), was typical of any man who had died. Later, Michael the archangel disputed with the devil about his body (not soul), see Jude 9, but this body remained safe until required, since this archangel was associated with resurrection to eternal life (Dan 12:2). Elijah (2 Kings 2:11) was typical of those who, being translated at the rapture of the church, will not die. Both of these men had been associated with fire and glory during their lifetimes, Moses in verses such as Exod 19:18; 34:29-35; 40:34-35; Lev 9:24, and Elijah in 1 Kings 18:38; 2 Kings 1:10, 12; 2:11. Now on the mount these two men also "appeared in glory" (Luke 9:31), a glory that was granted to them but not intrinsic as was the Lord's (John 17:22). They were thus made like the Lord (Phil 3:21), Moses being representative of the corruptible putting on incorruption, and Elijah of the mortal putting on immortality (1 Cor 15:53). On the mount, these two men were "talking with him", showing that the vision was not just for the eye but also for the ear. According to Luke 9:31, the subject of their conversation was "his decease which he should accomplish at Jerusalem". The Greek word for "decease" is *exodos*, meaning His way out from the world: "I leave the world, and go to the Father" (John 16:28). All the prophets testified of the sufferings of Christ (1 Pet 1:11), and both Moses before the tabernacle (Exod 27:1) and Elijah on mount Carmel (1 Kings 18:32) were men of the altar which spoke of His death. This exodus would take place "at Jerusalem", the place of God's choice (Deut 12:13-14), "for it cannot be that a prophet perish out of Jerusalem" (Luke 13:33).

4 Luke 9:32 records that the three apostles were "heavy with sleep", and that they saw His glory "when they were awake". We may ask: "Were they asleep because of the effects of the shining forth of glory causing their eyes to close, or were they actually tired?" The same three apostles slept in the garden of Gethsemane; there they were sleeping for sorrow, and the Lord said, "Watch and pray" (Matt 26:40-41). Finally, He said, "Sleep on now, and take your rest". In love and mercy He watched over them until the hour of betrayal arrived. This sleep is unlike that in Acts 12:6, where Peter slept peacefully prior to his expected execution.

While the Lord's glory still radiated forth, Peter was confused, and sought to retain the presence of Moses and Elijah on the same level as the Lord by suggesting the making of three tabernacles. Confusion in spiritual things can be disastrous, particularly if the phrase "if thou wilt" is added under the assumption that something false may be the will of the Lord. On one occasion Moses "spake unadvisedly with his lips" (Ps 106:33), and Elijah did the same (1 Kings 19:10, 14). Hence soberness is always necessary, so as to remain spiritually alert and intelligent, "Awake thou that sleepest . . . Christ shall give thee light" (Eph 5:14; Rom 13:11). The three tabernacles recall Lev 23:40, where the last of the feasts of Jehovah speaks of the prophetical ingathering of His people at His return in glory. This has the same implication as 2 Chron 7:9-10 at Solomon's dedication of the temple, namely, final rest in the land. Peter rightly associated the tabernacles with the kingdom age of the future, but in his remark there was no supreme and pre-eminent glory for Christ.

5 Upon so debasing a suggestion, "a bright cloud overshadowed them", a cloud shining like the Lord Himself, indicating a physical manifestation of the presence of God with the Son. In the Scriptures a cloud often relates to His coming in glory (Dan 7:13; Matt 24:30; 26:64; Rev 1:7; 14:14). Even the "cloud of witnesses" (Heb 12:1) may suggest the Lord's people coming with Him in His day of triumph and vindication, Moses and Elijah being but two amongst myriads. The Father's voice was heard from this cloud, like the voice from the cloud above the mercy seat (Num 7:89), and His presence in the cloud in the wilderness (Exod 13:21; 14:19). The Father said, "This is my beloved Son, in whom I am well pleased; hear ye him". Twice in each of the three Synoptic Gospels the Father's voice breaks forth from heaven and owns the Son. At His baptism the divine pleasure refers to the Lord's hidden life prior to His public ministry, here on the mount it refers to His public life of teaching and miracles. The Father's words "This is" were spoken about the Son to the apostles; similarly in Matt 3:17. In Luke 3:22, the words are "Thou art", spoken to the Son, while in Ps 2:7, the Son quotes the Father's words. "In whom I am well pleased" recalls God's words through the prophet, "in whom my soul delighteth" (Isa 42:1), also quoted in Matt 12:18. Such words of pleasure should cause all His people to hear Him, to give Him a unique place in their hearing as well as in their seeing. The promised prophet was the One to whom the people would hearken (Deut 18:15).

6-8 The existence of clouds on mountain tops is common; a climber can easily be immersed in mist within the cloud, but this phenomenon does not cause fear. In Luke 9:34 the apostles feared as they entered the cloud, and in Matt 17:6 the voice from the cloud caused the fear (see Exod 20:18-21). Fear is a natural emotion when circumstances without rational explanation present themselves. This the Lord knew and did not condemn, so many times He encouraged those who were fearful not to be afraid (Matt 14:27; Rev 1:17). When the apostles rose from their prostrate position, the vision was complete; there was no need for it to be prolonged. The continuous manifestation of glory must await the millennium and the eternal state. Hence there was no one else on the mount "save Jesus only". Peter's suggestion may have been partly responsible for the prompt termination of the vision.

9 Afterwards, only Peter's memory could recall this vision: "we . . . were eyewitnesses of his majesty" (2 Pet 1:16-18), adding that Scripture itself is a "more sure word of prophecy", since this was abiding, unlike the temporary manifestation of glory on the mountain top. Although Peter later recalled the vision for the sake of his readers, yet it had to be kept quiet until His resurrection. The vision really proved the truth of the Lord's resurrection prior to its taking place; yet He would not have proof by sight, rather by faith. In Mark 9:10, this statement caused the apostles to question "one with another what the rising from the dead should mean". At least, "they kept that saying with themselves" .

10-13 The question "Why then say the scribes that Elias must first come?" was prompted by the appearance of Elijah on the mount. This had been a preview of the Lord "coming in his kingdom", and hence Elijah also descended to take part in the kingdom. Yet according to the OT, Elijah had to come prior to this kingdom – the prophet had to be sent "before the coming of the great and dreadful day of the Lord" (Mal 4:5). The disciples could not see the connection between before His coming and at His coming. In the Lord's reply, the AV " Elias truly shall first come" is difficult to understand, but many Greek manuscripts omit the word "first", and this is followed by the RV. Hence we understand the Lord's answer in v.11 to refer, not to a prior return of Elijah, but to his actual return when the Lord comes in glory. By contrast, in v.12 the Lord referred to Elijah's previous return, typically in the person of John the Baptist, for John would go before the Lord " in the spirit and power of Elias" (Luke 1:17). That was past when the Lord spoke, though the scribes thought it was still future. The Lord used His answer to add something concerning Himself: what men had done to John (namely, putting him to death, as recorded in Matt 14:10), they would also do to the Son of man. We are not told whether the apostles understood this reference to His death, but at least they understood the Lord's reference to John the Baptist. Their interpretation of the OT prophetic Scriptures was now better than that of the scribes; this should be so today. Believers' understanding of the Scriptures should be far more advanced than that of merely academic theologians; believers are taught by God as having an unction from the Holy One, whereas the latter have just been taught in the schools of men; see Ps 119:99.

2. *Lunatic Cured, but not by Unbelief* 17:14-21

v.14 "And when they were come to the multitude, there came to him a *certain* man, kneeling down to him, and saying,
v.15 Lord, have mercy on my son: for he is lunatick, and sore vexed: for ofttimes he falleth into the fire, and oft into the water.
v.16 And I brought him to thy disciples, and they could not cure him.
v.17 Then Jesus answered and said, O faithless and perverse generation, how long shall I be with you? how long shall I suffer you? bring him hither to me.
v.18 And Jesus rebuked the devil; and he departed out of him: and the child was cured from that very hour.
v.19 Then came the disciples to Jesus apart, and said, Why could not we cast him out?
v.20 And Jesus said unto them, Because of your unbelief: for verily I say unto you, If ye have faith as a grain of mustard seed, ye shall say unto this mountain, Remove hence to yonder place; and it shall remove; and nothing shall be impossible unto you.
v.21 Howbeit this kind goeth not out but by prayer and fasting."

14 In v.4 we have seen the weakness of Peter on the mount; in vv. 16, 20 we find the weakness of the other nine apostles; in v.23 we have the weakness of all the apostles, while in v.25 we have the weakness of Peter again. A remarkable catalogue indeed, when compared with the abundance of revelations that they had received!

Coming down the mountain they found failure beneath, reminding us of the worse occasion when Moses, having received the details of the construction of the tabernacle, came down from mount Sinai and found a scene of faithlessness and idolatry (Exod 32:7-35). The man had been at fault, for he confessed that he had looked first to the disciples and not to the Lord (v.16). The disciples had been at fault, on account of their unbelief and lack of preparation (vv.20, 21). The man seems to have been the only one to have recognised his weakness, for he said, "Lord, I believe; help me thou mine unbelief" (Mark 9:24). Coming to the Lord, the man was "kneeling down to him", a good position showing self-weakness and utter dependence on the authority of the One approached. There are many examples of men and women kneeling or falling down before the Lord: in our verse there is absolute dependence when all else had failed; in Matt 2:11 the wise men fell down to worship; in Mark 1:40 the leper kneeled down in submission to the Lord's will; in Mark 5:22 Jairus fell down in faith; in Mark 5:33 the woman cleansed of the issue fell down in fear and trembling; in Mark 7:25 the Syrophenician woman fell down with the urgent desire of a Gentile; in Luke 5:8 Peter fell down in unworthiness; in John 11:32 Mary fell down in simplicity of faith. It is remarkable that the references in Matthew's Gospel corresponding to those in Mark do not contain these acts of kneeling or falling down before the Lord!

15 The word for "lunatick" (AV) or "epileptic" (RV) is *selēniazomai*, meaning "to be moon-struck,'; it appears only here and in Matt 4:24. Usually, this is a physical malady of the brain, but in this case it was demon possession (v.18), and Mark 9:17 shows that it was "a dumb spirit" . The time of the Lord's sojourn here seems to have been an occasion for great demon activity, exercising power over the body of the victim. A further manifestation of trouble was that the boy constantly fell into fire and water, symbolically speaking of judgment and death. In other words, demons lead one downwards and not heavenwards.

Here, the man used the title "Lord", though in Luke 9:38 the title "Master (Teacher)" was used. Evidently the man trusted the Lord as a worker of miracles; he was not thinking of himself, but only of his son, whom he called "mine only child" in Luke 9:38. The single word for "only child" (*monogenēs*) is the same as "only begotten" in John 3:16. This word means uniqueness in the affections of the father, and usually implies one child only. (But compare this with Gen 22:2, where Isaac is called "thine only son Isaac, whom thou lovest", though Abraham had other sons).

16 If this man was not a disciple as such, it is tragic that such a man condemned the apostles! It is tragic when a man of the world condemns a Christian through some lack of faith or consistency on his part! Originally, the apostles had been given power to cast out evil spirits (Matt 10:1), and Mark 6:13 records that this is what they did; afterwards, they returned and "told him all that they had done" (Luke 9:10). As a special gift, this continued into the church era: "In my name shall they cast out devils (demons)" (Mark 16:17), a gift that remained as long as it was God's will for His servants to have this capacity. It is a terrible tragedy when gift is inoperative on account of some weakness; here, the apostles "could not". Sometimes the work of Christ through His servants may be inhibited. For example, the disciples (including John) smugly thought that they were the only ones gifted to cast out demons (Luke 9:49). This was spiritual pride, which can quench the work of the Holy Spirit.

17 The Lord saw the root cause in the hearts of men. "O faithless and perverse generation" should be contrasted with "a wicked and adulterous generation" (Matt 16:4); the latter applied to the religious leaders, "faithless" to the apostles (17:20), and "perverse" to the multitude. The word "perverse" (*diastrephō*) means to distort or twist, and here, turned aside. What would they do when He was no longer with them? The answer would be given later; the Holy Spirit would be sent, and one of His ministries would be to strengthen the faith of those in whom He would dwell. The other question, "how long shall I suffer (bear with) you?", implies the Lord's longsuffering with the apostles in their weakness. Strictly, in both questions the words "how long" should be "until when"; the Lord had His cross before Him when He asked those questions.

18 The instantaneous character of the outworking of divine power is seen here; "from that very hour" is *apo tēs hōras ekeinēs*, "from that hour" (RV). Other cases may be noted, such as "healed in the selfsame hour" (Matt 8:13); "made whole from that very hour" (the same Greek words as just quoted, Matt 15:28); "immediately" (Mark 1:31, 42; 2:12). God's power in healing souls now has the same character as the power that healed bodies then. Exercise towards conversion may be a long experience, but conversion itself is a miracle that many can claim to have occurred "immediately".

19 Once again, the disciples approached the Lord "apart" (Matt 13:10, 36). They would seek no argument with the world in order to justify their weakness. Self is eliminated in His presence, and by taking heed to the contents of His answers.

20-21 The root cause of the apostles' impotence was "your unbelief". When the Lord was with them, their faith was not steadfast – it was flickering, as when Peter walked on the water (Matt 14:31), rather, faith should be "nothing wavering" (James 1:6). It should be like "a grain of mustard seed", when mountains would be removed and nothing would be impossible; see Matt 21:21; Luke 17:6. The least particle of genuine faith could work wonders if not inhibited by other factors. No doubt the "mountain" may refer to the removal of pride, since this always has an inhibiting effect on spiritual achievement. Possessing "all faith" (1 Cor 13:2) needs love if lasting results are to be achieved and if "mountains" are to be removed; yet faith that accomplishes exploits is a gift of God (1 Cor 12:9). Paul also wrote of "faith which worketh by love" (Gal 5:6). It must be pointed out that, in the church not all believers have this kind of faith which is a "gift". We all have that saving and living faith as those who are justified by faith (Rom 5:1), and this must be used in life and service, but the gift of faith that could work miracles was the privileged possession of only some in the early church. "Nothing shall be impossible unto you" did not mean that a reckless and wilful use of such gifts could be practised; miracles could only be done according to the will of God and in the Lord's Name.

Moreover, preparation was necessary in the form of "prayer and fasting". This was no last minute attempt to get the soul into a right state before God! We have discussed this when considering the Sermon on the Mount (Matt 6:5-18). Prayer is the continual contact of the heart with God; fasting is the continual lack of contact with the world. Even things normally regarded as necessary may have to be dispensed with if they hinder effective service (Matt 19:29). This, of course, has nothing to do with the so-called season of Lent, but Paul knew what fasting was (2 Cor 11:27), even remaining unmarried as an act equivalent to fasting (1 Cor 7:5-7). If any kind of fasting leads to a feeling of self-righteousness then it is false (Luke 18:11-12).

3. *Further Weaknesses of the Disciples 17:22-27*

v.22 "And while they abode in Galilee, Jesus said unto them, The Son of man shall be betrayed into the hands of men:
v.23 And they shall kill him, and the third day he shall be raised again. And they were exceeding sorry.
v.24 And when they were come to Capernaum, they that received tribute *money* came to Peter, and said, Doth not your master pay tribute?
v.25 He saith, Yes. And when he was come into the house, Jesus prevented him, saying, What thinkest thou, Simon? of whom do the kings of the earth take custom or tribute? of their own children, or of strangers?
v.26 Peter saith unto him, Of strangers. Jesus saith unto him, Then are the children free.
v.27 Notwithstanding, lest we should offend them, go thou to the sea, and cast an hook, and take up the fish that first cometh up; and when thou hast opened his mouth, thou shalt find a piece of money: that take, and give unto them for me and thee."

22-23 In these verses, we have the second direct reference in Matthew's Gospel to the Lord's forthcoming death and resurrection, the first being in Matt 16:21. The Lord was still dwelling in Galilee, awaiting the time when He would leave (19:1) to make His way to Jerusalem for the cross. The word for "betray" has appeared before in 10:4, "Judas Iscariot, who also betrayed him", and also at the end of the long discourse that followed the feeding of the 5,000 (John 6:70-71). The word for "betray" is *paradidōmi*, a very common verb in the NT usually translated "to deliver'', that is, the giving over of one person to another. It also means to betray, that is, to deliver treacherously as an act of betrayal. The context must determine when such evil motivations are involved. The corresponding passages in Mark 9:31 and Luke 9:44 have "delivered" in both cases. In other words, the translators were uncertain whether the sense of betrayal was included in the Lord's words. The RV of Matt 17:22 has " delivered" also.

In these direct references to His forthcoming decease in Jerusalem, the Lord never finished His remarks with His death: He also included His resurrection. In Acts 17:18, the Athenians thought the Paul's reference to the resurrection was the name of another deity! The apostles' reaction to the Lord's remarks continued to show uncertainty and weakness. Here they were "exceeding sorry": in Mark 9:32 they did not understand and were afraid to ask Him; in Luke 9:45 the saying was "hid from them, that they perceived it not: and they feared to ask him". Matthew recorded no reaction to the Lord's next reference to the subject (20:17-19), though in Luke 18:34 we find the continued state of non-memory on the part of the apostles. As far as believers are concerned, faith should accept what is not fully understood. As we grow in grace, there can be no excuse for lack of understanding, for the "eyes of your understanding" are enlightened (Eph 1:18).

24 Those who collected the tribute money were active even amongst those who were not permanently resident in Capernaum. All Jews over the age of twenty had to pay this annual sum, the *didrachmon* ("the half-shekel"), for the upkeep of Herod's temple in Jerusalem. It represented a human enlargement of the command in Exod 30:12-15; 38:25-26, the money being given when the people were numbered. Thereafter the house had to be kept going by tithes and gifts (Neh 10:39; 13:12). In the NT Herod's temple was no longer God's house, though the priests still expected income for its maintenance, and so it has been throughout history. Men in religious authority want money from their subjects. This can be seen in the activity of king Joash (2 Kings 12:4; 2 Chron 24:5). Hence in our verse these collectors approached Peter to ask him about "your master" or "teacher".

25-26 Peter quickly answered "Yes", and of course the Lord knew this answer even if He had not actually heard it. Another private house-scene was then enacted. If Peter was expecting to ask the Lord for His contribution, then the Lord "prevented him" (*phthanō*, "to anticipate"), namely, He spoke before Peter could. In fact, He asked a question, using a feature of the ordinary taxing system. The children of kings were not taxed, sharing in a royal privilege, for only people outside royal circles were taxed. An extended example of this principle is found in 2 Chron 8:7-9 regarding labourers who worked on Solomon's building projects. In this word-picture, "their own children (sons)" stand for "your master", and "the kings" for His Father. The Son of God was entirely free from the obligation to pay even a legitimate tax for the upkeep of God's house, and even more so under the circumstances in which Herod's temple was not God's house – He told the Jews it was "your house" (Matt 23:38). Peter gave the correct answer, "Of strangers" without realising the spiritual nature of the Lord's question. The Lord gave the spiritual conclusion, "Then are the children free" – there was no obligation for Him to pay the tax.

27 The Lord would not insist upon His divine rights if this would "offend them" (*skandalizō*, "to put a stumblingblock or snare in the way"). The Lord would not unnecessarily arouse the enmity of the Jews; He would not give them any material with which to accuse Him falsely. The sea and the fish are typical of earth and not of heaven, a natural origin (even though miraculous) would meet the demands of a natural situation, unlike the manna which came down from heaven (Ps 78:24). The "piece of money" was a "shekel" (*statēr*) being twice the value of the *didrachmon*. The Lord ensured that there was just enough to pay both for Himself and for Peter, so Peter paid the collectors, having learnt the lesson of freedom from religious bondage; see Acts 10:28. Since the Lord did not provide for the other apostles, some have suggested that all except Peter were under twenty years old; this accounts for John's long life afterwards.

VI. Mutual Relationships in the Kingdom and in the Church (18:1-35)

1. *Offences against the Greatest* 18:1-14

v.1 "At the same time came the disciples unto Jesus, saying, Who is the greatest in the kingdom of heaven?
v.2 And Jesus called a little child unto him, and set him in the midst of them,
v.3 And said, Verily I say unto you, Except ye be converted, and become as little children, ye shall not enter into the kingdom of heaven.
v.4 Whosoever therefore shall humble himself as this little child, the same is greatest in the kingdom of heaven.
v.5 And whoso shall receive one such little child in my name receiveth me.
v.6 But whoso shall offend one of these little ones which believe in me, it were better for him that a millstone were hanged about his neck, and *that* he were drowned in the depth of the sea.
v.7 Woe unto the world because of offences! for it must needs be that offences come; but woe to that man by whom the offence cometh!
v.8 Wherefore if thy hand or thy foot offend thee, cut them off, and cast *them* from thee: it is better for thee to enter into life halt or maimed, rather than having two hands or two feet to be cast into everlasting fire.
v.9 And if thine eye offend thee, pluck it out, and cast it from thee: it is better for thee to enter into life with one eye, rather than having two eyes to be cast into hell fire.
v.10 Take heed that ye despise not one of these little ones; for I say unto you, That in heaven their angels do always behold the face of my Father which is in heaven.
v.11 For the Son of man is come to save that which was lost.
v.12 How think ye? if a man have an hundred sheep, and one of them be gone astray, doth he not leave the ninety and nine, and goeth into the mountains, and seeketh that which is gone astray?
v.13 And if so be that he find it, verily I say unto you, he rejoiceth more of that *sheep*, than of the ninety and nine which went not astray.
v.14 Even so it is not the will of your Father which is in heaven, that one of these little ones should perish."

1 Because of the abundance of revelations that Paul had, there was the danger of exaltation above measure; hence he was given a thorn in the flesh to prevent this spirit of pride rising in him (2 Cor 12:7). Three of the apostles had also had such an abundance of revelations, having seen the Lord transfigured on the mountain top. The others had not had this vision. On account of this difference, the question arose as to who would be the greatest in the kingdom of heaven. From Matt 11:11 they would know that all in the kingdom were greater than John the Baptist. Later, the mother of James and John thought that her two sons should have the most exalted position in the kingdom in glory (Matt 20:21), while immediately after the institution of the breaking of bread there was strife among the apostles as to who should be the greatest (Luke 22:24). In both cases, the Lord's answer was similar. They seemed to have been thinking along the lines of the hierarchy in the priesthood where there was a high priest. Later,

John would have to cope with Diotrephes who wanted to have the preeminence (3 John 9) and he would write of the Lord's hatred of the deeds and doctrine of the Nicolaitans (Rev 2:6, 15). But the elements of the principle of clerisy existed in the apostles' hearts even when the Lord was with them.

2-5 The Lord knew that Isaiah prophesied of a "child" who would have the "government" upon his shoulder (9:6), and that in the coming kingdom of glory "a little child shall lead them" (11:6). Hence, to establish the principle of true greatness, the Lord set a little child in the midst of the apostles. His answer is quite general but He framed it around entry into and status in the kingdom of heaven, since the apostles had used this concept. The principle can also be applied to the local church, which is introduced in the next paragraph. The word for "converted" (*strephō*) is not the usual word for convert; on all other occasions the verb "turn" is used, including the RV of Matt 18:3. There had to be a turning of heart and attitude from that implied by the apostles – the seeking of status and the assumption that a man could be the greatest. One must turn from one attitude to another, to that possessed by little children, namely without pretension, not claiming or seeking to be anything other than what they really are. " Seekest thou great things for thyself? seek them not" (Jer 45:5). This governs entry into the kingdom of heaven. In the present state of the kingdom in mystery, there may be many adherents to the kingdom, such as those who propagate and practice ecumenicalism, but to adhere is not the same thing as to enter.

Based on this idea, the Lord drew a vital principle in v.4. He does not mean that the little child had humbled himself and that a convert must likewise humble himself; this the child could not do, for he was already humble naturally. Status must match status; the end result is in view, not the process by which it is attained. There must be no thought or desire for exaltation; only God may exalt and that in due time (1 Pet 5:6). Instead one should seek the lowest status—as one writer has expressed it, "This is true greatness, to serve unnoticed and to work unseen". Only then is a man "greatest"; strictly, the Greek has "the greater", as if the Lord does not take a man to the top, for He has the preeminence. A servant is great by being the servant of the saints (Matt 20:26-27), thereby reversing the attitude adopted by men in the world.

Then in v. 5, the Lord places responsibility on all disciples to recognise a fellow disciple who has taken this lowly position. To receive such a disciple in His Name is to receive Him. The desire to receive a man "with a gold ring, in goodly apparel" James 2:2), offering him a good place, is to be partial with evil thoughts. This is not reception in the Lord's Name, and the Lord is kept on the outside. In Corinth, there were some men who would not recognise the apostle because of his lowly life of service and sufferings; if he was unknown to these men and to the world, he was well known to God (2 Cor 6:9). If a man refuses to have the mind of Christ (who humbled Himself and was then highly exalted), that man can never be counted great by God (Phil 2:5, 8, 9).

6 Previously (vv.2, 3, 4, 5) the word for "little child" has been *paidion*. But now in vv.6, 10, 14 a different word is used, namely the plural of *mikros* meaning "little" The change has occurred because the Lord is no longer talking about little children with respect to age, but about His disciples who become similar to little children. Of course we must not offend little children, but that is not the point of the verse. Rather it is a question of offending a believer, perhaps an easy thing to do if that believer is humble and not aggressive. The word for "offend" is, as usual, *skandalizō*, "to cast a snare or stumbling block in the pathway". A similar passage occurs in Luke 17:1-2. One believer can either further the life of another, or he can hinder and damage it: thus Barnabas was stumbled by Peter (Gal 2:13). The "millstone" denotes a weight that is irresistible and permanent; it is something that drags down and keeps down out of harm's way. The Lord did not say that this would happen, but that this would be the best course. Grace prevents such an act of judgment falling, though this does not justify the believer's conduct. Rather, as believers, they lay aside every weight (Heb 12:1).

7-9 The difference in these verses must be noted. Verse 7 refers to an unbeliever in the world, vv.8-9 a particular disciple, and v.10 to the disciples generally. Men in the world may well attempt to stumble a spiritually-minded disciple that is humble as a little child. They attempted to do this to the Lord! Such offences *must* come; owing to human nature, it is inevitable that men act in unkind ways towards the Lord's people. The "woe" of judgment will fall upon such. We suggest that the rich man in Luke 16:19 was a man of this character, hindering Lazarus by providing nothing for his need. The "little ones" include Lazarus. It would be better (or profitable) to terminate the activity of these men, as in the case of the rich man, whose woe was to find himself in the fire of hades. Only mercy lengthens out the day of grace, allowing time for repentance.

By using "thy hand", "thy foot" and "thine eye" in vv.8-9, the Lord now addressed Himself to any particular disciple. Although the offence is against "thee", the context in v.10 shows "little ones" are still the dominant thought. A man is stumbled himself, if he stumbles another. The Lord issued similar exhortations in the Sermon on the Mount (5:29-30), though in a different context. Hands, feet and eyes are necessary members of the body physically. If the body is not kept under control, like the tongue, these members can defile the whole body (James 3:6). One hand can send forth sweet water, and the other bitter water (v.11). Cut off the member that offends by offending another believer. In other words, ensure that it is inoperative as an instrument of the flesh. How can this be done? In various circumstances Paul has supplied the answer: "It is good neither to eat flesh, nor to drink wine, nor any thing whereby thy brother stumbleth, or is offended, or is made weak" (Rom 14:21); "if meat make my brother to offend, I will eat no flesh while the world standeth, lest I make my brother to offend" (1 Cor 8:13); "Whether therefore ye eat, or drink, or whatsoever ye do, do all to the glory of God. Give none offence, neither to the Jews, nor to the Gentiles, nor to the church of God: Even as I please all men in all things, not seeking mine own profit, but the profit of many" (1 Cor 10:31-33).

The Lord's reference to "everlasting (eternal) fire" and "hell (Gehenna) fire" may appear difficult to interpret, since this could not be the fate of believers. Neither can a believer enter into resurrection life as lame, maimed. or with one eye, since the resurrection body will be without defect "fashioned like unto his glorious body" (Phil 3:21). Hence neither one possibility nor the other is literal. We suggest that the references are symbolic of the power of God or the power of Satan working in a disciple in his present life on earth, the former being so very far better than the latter. Paul shows the complete contrast between the fruit of the Spirit and the works of the flesh in Gal 5:19-24; the flesh has been crucified with its affections and lusts.

10 The final conclusion is that a believer must not "despise" another believer evidently more humble and spiritual than himself. The word "despise" (*kataphroneō*) means to think down upon someone; in Matt 6:24 it has the sense opposite to the verb "hold to" (*antechomai*) meaning to "to cleave to". For example, in Corinth many of the church despised the apostle Paul because of the special humble way in which he conducted his apostolic life and service, taking the position of being "the least of the apostles" (1 Cor 15:9). The meaning of "angel" (*angelos*) is "messenger" usually from heaven sent by God, but sometimes sent by men and even by Satan (2 Cor 12:7). Whereas we do not deny that children have their guardian angels (even in the Lord's case in Matt 2:13, 19), the primary application in the NT is to believers. In the context of our verse "their" refers to humble believers, and in Heb 1:14 angels are "ministering spirits, sent forth to minister for them who shall be heirs of salvation". Twice in the Acts the angel of the Lord opened prison doors, to the apostles (5:19), and to Peter (12:7-10). Even at that stage in the development of the church, some members had strange ideas, thinking that the sight of Peter was not really Peter but "his angel" (v.15). Angelic ministry is essentially one of protection; see Ps 34:7; 91:11; Dan 6:22; Matt 26:53. Their authority lies in being in God's presence, beholding the Father's face, and receiving commands directly from the divine Source to intervene in the affairs of men on earth (1 Kings 22:19-22).

11-14 The statement "For the Son of man is come to save that which was lost" is missing from some Greek manuscripts; it is therefore omitted in the RV, but not in JND The statement is, of course, perfectly true, and is found in Luke 19:10 referring to Zacchaeus having been sought and saved. A similar reference to a sheep having been lost and found occurs in the familiar parable in Luke 15:3-7. The reason why an occasional addition is found in some manuscripts is not hard to ascertain. A reader of a manuscript in which the phrase did not occur would insert a marginal note to prompt the memory that a similar narrative appeared elsewhere. Years later, if the manuscript was then copied by another scribe, this reference might be taken to be part of the text itself, and hence incorporated into it. We make references in the margins of our Bibles today, but our handwriting is so distinct from the printed text that it is impossible to confuse what is a mere note with what is actual text. But in those early days, both the text and the note were handwritten, and unwitting confusion could and indeed did occur in several places. To recognise this fact is not to deny inspiration; rather, we seek out what inspiration has actually provided in the first place, and linguistically this must be left to experts. Unfortunately some of the experts do not believe in inspiration, and this presents problems when manuscript evidence is weighed up by unbelievers. In some cases, the believer without linguistic knowledge can weigh up matters for himself, when he knows that there is a disputed word, phrase or even verse (even complete passages in two cases, namely Mark 16:9-20; John 7:53 to 8:11). We should ask, "Does the disputed word or phrase fit into the context?" It is the author's opinion that our v.11 does not fit into the context. In Luke 15:4 and 19:10 the word "lost" appears because the one sheep and Zacchaeus were lost. But in Matt 18:12-13, the sheep was *not* lost; it had only gone "astray", which is quite another matter. In that case, the word "lost" in v.11 seems out of place, suggesting that this verse was originally a marginal note that unfortunately later became incorporated in the text.

Verses 12-13 are not referring to lost sinners in the context; the Lord referred to "one of these little ones", namely a humble believer who had been stumbled either by a man in the world or by another believer who refused to humble himself.

In grace, the Lord concentrates upon one sheep that has gone astray. This one sheep is not lost in a multitude, but is an individual upon whom the love of Christ is placed. And however far the sheep may have gone, and however great the difficulties (mountains) to be encountered, the Lord seeks, and rejoices when the sheep is found, namely brought back to the spiritual state that was his before he was stumbled. But the Lord said, "*if*. . . he find it", implying the sad possibility that the sheep may have no desire to be found.

Thus the angel provides the protection; the Son of man provides the searching; the Father provides the will. The Father's will is that every believer should live a useful life, not that a believer should perish, namely become unsuitable for testimony and service. The same thought occurs in 1 Cor 8:11, "and through thy knowledge shall the weak brother perish, for whom Christ died". If a brother causes another to become unfruitful, then that brother has sinned against Christ (v.12). Is there any difference between that and sinning against the Holy Spirit (Acts 5:3)?

2. *Trespass in the Local Church* 18:15-20

v.15 "Moreover if thy brother shall trespass against thee, go and tell him his fault between thee and him alone: if he shall hear thee, thou hast gained thy brother.
v.16 But if he will not hear *thee, then* take with thee one or two more, that in the mouth of two or three witnesses every word may be established.
v.17 And if he shall neglect to hear them, tell *it* unto the church: but if he neglect to hear the church, let him be unto thee as an heathen man and a publican.
v.18 Verily I say unto you, Whatsoever ye shall bind on earth, shall be bound in heaven: and whatsoever ye shall loose on earth shall be loosed in heaven.
v.19 Again I say unto you, That if two of you shall agree on earth as touching any thing that they shall ask, it shall be done for them of my Father which is in heaven.
v.20 For where two or three are gathered together in my name, there am I in the midst of them."

15 The word "Moreover" shows that this subject follows on from that in the previous verses. The Lord still continued to deal with the stumbling activity of "thy brother" against "thee", namely the humble little one who is spiritually mature to resist the offence and not to go astray. Some Greek manuscripts omit the words "against thee", but they are retained in the RV and JND. They are certainly needed in v.21. The question is, what should this humble little one do under these circumstances? Leave things as they are, or invoke spiritual principles of discipline in a local church? Moses was the meekest man on earth, but God would not allow Miriam and Aaron to escape lightly when they complained about his authority (Num 12:1-13).

There are several forms of corrective discipline in the NT relating to the local assembly or church.

1. *Reproof and rebuke:* "Them that sin rebuke before all, that others also may fear" (1 Tim 5:20); "All scripture . . . is profitable . . . for reproof" (2 Tim 3:16). When this takes place, fellowship is maintained.

2. *Withdrawal:* "that ye withdraw yourselves from every brother that walketh disorderly, and not after the tradition which he received of us" (2 Thess 3:6), yet not counted "as an enemy" (v.15). There was to be no company with such a brother; the assembly leaves him, and he remains a lonely brother until there is repentance and rectification of conduct. Note that this is "in the name of our Lord Jesus Christ" (v.6).

3. *Excommunication:* as in the synagogue (John 12:42). For a list of sins leading to this, see 1 Cor 5:11; again Paul wrote, "in the name of our Lord Jesus Christ" (v.4). The man was delivered "unto Satan" (v.5), namely to his sphere on the outside of the local assembly. Thus Hymenaeus was "delivered unto Satan", having erred concerning the truth of resurrection (1 Tim 1:20; 2 Tim

2:17-18). Such a man is outside the immediate pastoral care of the assembly, but reached on the outside by prayer, leading to his repentance (2 Cor 2:6-8).

Thus three spheres result from these three aspects of discipline: fellowship, the lonely position, the world outside.

In our verse, the word for "trespass" is *hamartanō* properly meaning "to sin"; the RV and JND use the word "sin". The initiative for the restoration of a proper relationship is taken by the wronged, namely by the greater little one. This sin of course, does not cover every possible case of failure; a brother may sin morally or spiritually against the assembly rather than against an individual.

16-17 In v.15, there is a private entreaty that leads to restoration if the brother "shall hear thee". Alas, this may not always result, so the Lord prescribes a second stage in the process. A small circle of two or three witnesses, together with the humble brother, visit the one who has sinned. Their testimony must be true as based on the ninth commandment (Exod 20:16), where false witness is forbidden. The principle of double-witness was used by the Lord in John 8:13-18, "the testimony of two men is true". At the trial of the Lord, men deliberately disregarded this principle, otherwise they could have brought no charges against Him (Matt 26:59-61). The principle is stated in Num 35:30, "one witness shall not testify against any person". Paul invoked this principle in 2 Cor 13:1, to establish the error of the Corinthians and Paul's corrective intentions and warnings.

Thus these two or three witnesses listen to the conversation between the humble brother and the one who has sinned against him. Again there is the possibility of this brother neglecting "to hear them", in which case the humble brother has to "tell it unto the church", that is the local church. No doubt wisdom has to be exercised here, for some matters may not be suitable for the ears of the young or of new converts. Again, the man may "neglect to hear the church". Note that this neglect to hear is repeated three times, relating to the humble brother, the witnesses and the church. Church discipline must then be exercised. It is not stated whether this is withdrawal or excommunication; we suspect the former. Circumstances in any particular case will enable those who are spiritual to make a decision. One's treatment of the man must be the same as the treatment given to a "heathen man (Gentile) and a publican (tax collector)", namely the man needs the gospel to lead him to repentance. How different from Gal 3:28, where "there is neither Jew nor Greek, there is neither bond nor free".

18 The decision of the church is ratified in heaven if such a procedure is adopted. In Matt 16:19, this authority of binding and loosing was given to the apostle Peter in relation to the beginnings of the universal church, but here it is given to any local church. This requires that the local church be so in touch with the divine mind that it does exactly what the Lord Jesus would do; anything other than this is unspiritual presumption. This condition is laid down in 1 Cor 5:4 where the gathering had to be "with the power of our Lord Jesus Christ". Binding is a disciplinary measure whereby the offending man is treated practically as unsaved, until repentance and restoration bring about spiritual fruit again, when he can be loosed. In this matter, heaven and the local church do the same thing.

19 This verse explains how such a unity of thought and action can be achieved. The minimum for agreement must be at least two persons, no doubt referring to the two witnesses in v.16. Specifically, of course, the request in prayer refers to the binding and loosing of v.18, but as a principle, the verse goes far beyond church discipline. It is good to agree before prayer is made, as well as at the end when "Amen" is said. Thus in examples such as Acts 4:23-24; 12:5, 12, the Jerusalem church knew why it was praying, and the fact that answers were promptly received shows that these prayers were according to the mind of heaven. The secret behind successful prayer lies in the great principle enunciated by the Lord in John 14:13, "whatsoever ye shall ask in my name, that will I do, that the Father may be glorified in the Son".

20 Strictly this verse is intimately connected with the previous verses, yet it also forms an entity of truth in itself. Two or three are sufficient to form a local church. To gather in His name means that what is done and what is said are as good as if He were to do and to say what the church does and says. Anything else is carnal and not spiritual. He is present to direct solemn decisions, and since He is there, vv.18-19 must follow in order to maintain holiness in the gathering. The verb "gathered" (*sunagō*) is often used of assembly meetings: the breaking of bread (Acts 20:7), the prayer meeting (4:31), the meeting for teaching (11:26), the Bible reading or discussion meeting (15:30), the elders' meeting (15:6), the missionary meeting (14:27), the discipline meeting (1 Cor 5:4). It is important to note that Paul used the phrase "in the name of our Lord Jesus Christ" in two passages referring to discipline (1 Cor 5:4; 2 Thess 3:6). In fact, His Name should embrace everything that we do. For Paul wrote, "whatsoever ye do in word or deed, do all in the name of the Lord Jesus, giving thanks to God and the Father by him" (Col 3:17).

Certainly His Name is a gathering Name; even in the OT the people had to recognise that God would choose a place "to put his name there" (Deut 12:5), this being successively Shiloh, Zion and Moriah. It is a unifying Name; the devices and compromises of men do not unite spiritually. About twenty years ago, a placard "Courtesy is a curse" was raised when one high-ranking religious leader visited another of heretical persuasion. It is a ruling Name, for His people are subject to His authority. It is a displacing Name, for a believer cannot serve two masters, as the men of Judah tried to do in Isa 26:13. To act as if one can gather to any name amongst men, as did the Corinthians (1 Cor 1:12), is mere carnal religion.

The Lord "in the midst of them" *(en meso auton)* is very precious for the Lord's people. In Luke 2:46 it was in respect of instruction; in Matt 18:20 for association; in John 19:18 for salvation; in John 20:19 for resurrection; in Rev 5:6 for glorification.

3. *The Granting of Forgiveness* 18:21-35

v.21 "Then came Peter to him, and said, Lord, how oft shall my brother sin against me, and I forgive him? till seven times?
v.22 Jesus saith unto him, I say not unto thee, Until seven times: but, Until seventy times seven.
v.23 Therefore is the kingdom of heaven likened unto a certain king, which would take account of his servants.
v.24 And when he had begun to reckon, one was brought unto him, which owed him ten thousand talents.
v.25 But forasmuch as he had not to pay, his lord commanded him to be sold, and his wife, and children, and all that he had, and payment to be made.
v.26 The servant therefore fell down, and worshipped him, saying, Lord, have patience with me, and I will pay thee all.
v.27 Then the lord of that servant was moved with compassion, and loosed him, and forgave him the debt.
v.28 But the same servant went out, and found one of his fellow servants, which owed him an hundred pence: and he laid hands on him, and took *him* by the throat, saying, Pay me that thou owest.
v.29 And his fellow servant fell down at his feet, and besought him, saying, Have patience with me, and I will pay thee all.
v.30 And he would not: but went and cast him into prison, till he should pay the debt.
v.31 So when his fellow servants saw what was done, they were very sorry, and came and told unto their lord all that was done.
v.32 Then his lord, after that he had called him, said unto him, O thou wicked servant, I forgave thee all that debt, because thou desiredst me:
v.33 Shouldest not thou also have had compassion on thy fellow servant, even as I had pity on thee?
v.34 And his lord was wroth, and delivered him to the tormentors, till he should pay all that was due unto him.
v.35 So likewise shall my heavenly Father do also unto you, if ye from your hearts forgive not every one his brother their trespasses."

21 During the discourse in this chapter, the apostles had made no interruption, but a question arose at last in Peter's mind. The Lord had shown the responsibility of the offending brother, but what was to be the personal attitude of the offended brother, namely of the greater little one? Peter knew that he was responsible to forgive such an offending brother, but if this brother should later repeat the action, as if taking advantage of the forgiveness, then how many times should he be forgiven? In the OT, God "forgave their iniquity . . . many a time turned he his anger away" (Ps 78:38). So Peter opted for the number seven, perhaps remembering the "sevenfold" vengeance that would be taken against a man who murdered Cain (Gen 4:15); see Prov 24:16.

22-24 In Gen 4:24, Lamech boasted that he would be avenged "seventy and sevenfold", going far beyond the number associated with Cain. But the Lord spoke not of vengeance but of forgiveness with which He associated the number "seventy times seven", namely 490 times. No doubt this stands for a lifetime of forgiveness, for "threescore years and ten" are visualised for an ordinary life in Ps 90:10. Such repeated forgiveness would "confirm your love toward him" (2 Cor 2:8; see also v.10).

There is far more to forgiveness than meets the undiscerning eye. In the parable the Lord (*kurios*) forgave the servant (*doulos*) who therefore should have forgiven his fellow servant (*sundoulos*); its meaning was that God had forgiven His servant Peter who in turn must forgive others. To many parables can be appended the exhortation, "Go, and do thou likewise" (Luke 10:37).

The magnitude of debt of "ten thousand talents" may be evaluated bearing in mind the fact that when the tabernacle was made there were 29 talents of gold and 100 talents of silver (Exod 38:24-25). A talent was approximately equal to 30 kg or 66lb. If these ten thousand talents were of gold, their value in sterling would be of the order of forty thousand million pounds! Such is the divine estimate of the debt brought about by sin – "Her sins, which are many, are forgiven" (Luke 7:47). This vast sum should be contrasted with the tribute of thirty talents of gold that the king of Assyria laid upon Hezekiah (2 Kings 18:14), and with Solomon's income of 666 talents of gold annually (2 Chron 9:13). The other debt in Matt 18:28, "an hundred pence" (*dēnarion*), was trivial in comparison, amounting to only a few pounds.

25-27 Of course the servant could not pay; self-redemption is impossible, even with the humility and effort mentioned in v.26. We have been "bought with a price" (1 Cor 6:20), and the debt from which we have been absolved in this parable shows clearly the cost of our redemption. For we have been redeemed not "with corruptible things, as silver and gold . . . But with the precious blood of Christ, as of a lamb without blemish and without spot" (1 Pet 1:18-19); "In whom we have redemption through his blood, the forgiveness of sins, according to the riches of his grace" (Eph 1:7). These verses show the "compassion" of God towards us, and the fact that the blood of Christ is not something merely doctrinal but that it is infinitely more precious than gold in the abundance of millions. In Ephesians Paul continued, "forgiving one another, even as God for Christ's sake hath forgiven you" (4:32). Again, he wrote "forgiving one another" in Col 3:13. Those who are forgiven most also love the most, and so this love and grace are passed on to others.

28-30 At least in an ideal spiritual community this is so. This greater little one who was once so humble before the Lord and before his fellow-saints, can become trapped if he does not abide close to the One who loved him, and gave Himself for him (Gal 2:20). If a brother does not forgive in return, then Satan can "get an advantage of us: for we are not ignorant of his devices" (2 Cor 2:11). Thus to forewarn of this danger, the Lord in His parable limited forgiveness further than the seven times of Peter's question, and painted the worst possible picture. Instead of forgiving 490 times, the first occasion of stumbling caused by the offending brother is met with terrible retaliation, in opposition to the procedure laid down in vv.15-17. To "cast him into prison" (v.30) is the opposite of discussing "his fault between thee and him", acting like Diotrephes and casting him "out of the church" (3 John 10). Even the local church itself was not instructed to adopt this extreme measure of discipline (Matt 18:17). Thus the brother took the law into his own hands, when he had no authority to do so.

31-35 The "fellow servants" observed this deed; telling "their lord all that was done" corresponds to the local church placing the matter in prayer before God. It is the responsibility of a local church to note such an unforgiving spirit towards another brother, knowing that discipline should have passed to the two or three witnesses or to the church as a whole, at which stage complete repentance might have been gained.

Thus the greater little one has become a "wicked servant", and must be bound and "delivered to the tormentors, till he should pay all that was due unto him". This is equivalent to Gal 6:8, "he that soweth to his flesh shall of the flesh reap corruption". This does not refer to punishment after death, but to discipline exercised here below placing a brother outside the fellowship of the local church until complete repentance takes place. We must interpret v.35 on these grounds; eternal retribution cannot be in question where a saved sinner is concerned. But the Father will not allow such practical unholiness to exist in a church, which is responsible to recognise when it does and to put matters right in a scriptural way. To allow matters to continue without discipline would allow a little leaven gradually to leaven the whole lump (1 Cor 5:6), when the flesh would pervade the whole church introducing Laodiceanism at its worst (Rev 3:17-19).

VII. Giving up All (19:1-30)

1. *Marriage or not, but not Divorce* 19:1-12

v.1 "And it came to pass, *that* when Jesus had finished these sayings, he departed from Galilee, and came into the coasts of Judaea beyond Jordan;
v.2 And great multitudes followed him; and he healed them there.
v.3 The Pharisees also came unto him, tempting him, and saying unto him, Is it lawful for a man to put away his wife for every cause?
v.4 And he answered and said unto them, Have ye not read, that he which made *them* at the beginning, made them male and female,
v.5 And said, For this cause shall a man leave father and mother, and shall cleave to his wife: and they twain shall be one flesh?

v.6 Wherefore they are no more twain, but one flesh. What therefore God hath joined together, let not man put asunder.
v.7 They say unto him, Why did Moses then command to give a writing of divorcement, and to put her away?
v.8 He saith unto them, Moses because of the hardness of your hearts suffered you to put away your wives: but from the beginning it was not so.
v.9 And I say unto you, Whosoever shall put away his wife, except *it be* for fornication, and shall marry another, committeth adultery: and whoso marrieth her which is put away doth commit adultery.
v.10 His disciples say unto him, If the case of the man be so with *his* wife, it is not good to marry.
v.11 But he said unto them, All *men* cannot receive this saying, save *they* to whom it is given.
v.12 For there are some eunuchs, which were so born from *their* mother's womb: and there are some eunuchs, which were made eunuchs of men: and there be eunuchs, which have made themselves eunuchs for the kingdom of heaven's sake. He that is able to receive *it*, let him receive *it*."

1-2 This appears to have been the Lord's final departure from Galilee, initiating the journey that took Him to Jerusalem and the place of sacrifice. But he would return again. As He left Jerusalem for the mount of Olives on the night in which He was betrayed, He informed His disciples, "after I am risen again, I will go before you into Galilee" (Matt 26:32). The angel at the tomb announced that "he goeth before you into Galilee; there shall ye see him" (28:7), and there they went "into a mountain where Jesus had appointed them" (v.16). Also John 21 took place "at the sea of Tiberias", namely, the Sea of Galilee.

This journey commenced when the Lord "had finished these sayings"; this is the fourth time that Matthew has made a similar statement, the last time is in 26:1. He came to "the coasts of Judaea beyond Jordan", namely to the district of Peraea on the east side of the river, this river being the boundary between Judaea and Peraea. Great multitudes were still following Him, and although the record is concerned only with His teaching and parables at this stage, miracles were still being performed, for "he healed them there". Multitudes were still following Him as He crossed the river again, passing through Jericho (Matt 20:29) on His way up to Jerusalem.

3 The Pharisees were the Lord's chief opponents; in Matt 12:3 they questioned Him about an aspect of the law; in 12:38 and 16:1 they wanted the Lord to show a special sign from heaven; in 15:1,2 they questioned Him about another aspect of the law. In 19:3 they tempted Him about a further aspect of the law. The word for tempt is *peirazō*, namely, seeking to ensnare the Lord in His answers; the same happened again in 22:35, while in 22:15 their intention was to "entangle him in his talk". The more caustic or clever amongst unbelievers try to do this today, seeking to tempt or to entangle believers in their knowledge of the Scriptures.

Their question, "Is it lawful for a man to put away his wife for every cause?" caused division among the Jews, for it was not clear to them when divorce was lawful. Not that they wanted help from the Lord on the matter; rather, they hoped that His answer would in some way be contrary to their interpretation of the OT law. The verb "to put away" (*apoluō*) is translated "divorced" at 5:32 in several versions. Today, civil laws allow divorce with considerable ease, and it would appear from the utterances of non-evangelical religionists that they have never searched the Scriptures to ascertain the mind of God on the matter. The so-called marriage vows are cast aside as if they had never been made, though in a so-called church wedding these vows were supposedly made in the presence of God. Indeed, the present paragraph is sometimes used to justify the practice, whereas it really condemns it.

4-6 We have already commented on the Lord's teaching on this subject in the Sermon on the Mount (5:31-32), where the excepting clause "for the cause of fornication" occurs. The Lord's definitive teaching without the excepting clause is found in Luke 16:18; adultery is committed when either one or the other of a divorced pair marries again. Hence the readers of Luke's Gospel had to learn the divine mind on the subject, without the apparent advantage of knowing of the excepting clause. They would infer that divorce was not allowed, else it led to further sin.

In His answer, the Lord quoted what God had done in the beginning. He had created them "male and female" (Gen 1:27). Men may speculate why the two- sex system exists in animal and plant life, and their speculations must be governed by their adherence to the theory of evolution. But believers know more than all ungodly men (Ps 119:99), since the two-sex system was created by God in the beginning. Moreover, there were spiritual reasons why this should be so, since the union thus formed would be a typical picture of a deeper and eternal love between the Lord and His bride the church (Eph 5:25-32). Even before the first son or daughter was conceived, before Adam and Eve were actually father and mother, these names were used in Gen 2:24, "Therefore shall a man leave his father and his mother, and shall cleave unto his wife: and they shall be one flesh". The Lord quoted this verse as a question, and Paul also quoted it in Eph 5:31, calling it "a great mystery". The Lord's quotation shows that this was a statement made by God, not by Moses as a comment on the previous verse where Adam said "flesh of my flesh". The seed that would result from their union is referred to in Gen 3:15 looking forward to Christ. Events then passed quickly, and it appears that Adam first "knew" his wife in Gen 4:1 after sin had entered and they had been cast out of the garden. Not that childbearing is a result of sin being in the world, since before sin had entered into His creation God had commanded the couple to "be fruitful, and multiply" (Gen 1:28).

By answering thus, the Lord did not take sides with any of the theological schools of His day, in the same way as He did not take sides with political opinion (Matt 22:17-21). The answer was contained in the OT; the Lord would quote this, make a deduction, and let the Pharisees draw conclusions as to the answer to their own question.

The "one flesh" implied, of course, the consummation of the marriage relationship, else the partners would still be two bodies separately. The word "cleave" is *proskollaō* (or *kollaō* according to the editors of the Greek text), the same as the word " join" (*proskollaō*) in Eph 5:31. The most intimate union is implied. The Lord stated that this joining together is an act of God – a biological act indeed enrooted in creation and all subsequent beings, yet enlarged by love in human beings and far removed from the automatic compulsion observed in the acts of birds and animals. The verb "hath joined together" (*suzeugnumi*) is literally to yoke together, and metaphorically denotes the marriage union. This work of God was not to be undone; only death could dissolve the bond when a further marriage would not constitute adultery (Rom 7:1-3; Deut 25:5; Matt 22:24-26; 1 Cor 7:39). There are those who suggest that when a marriage breaks up, God has no longer joined the partners together, in which case they can be divorced through legal channels. But this is mere presumption to justify a desired practice. The Lord did not say that God unjoins what He has joined together.

7 The Lord's reply might have silenced the Pharisees, had they not been able to quote a verse that guided their own thoughts and principles on the subject of divorce. They used Deut 24:1, abbreviating it to Moses' command "to give a writing of divorcement, and to put her away". The particular circumstances in mind in Deut 24:1-4 were if a married man had "found some uncleanness in her", or "some unseemly thing" (RV, JND). (The Hebrew word *ervah* is translated " uncleanness " only once, but on 51 occasions it is translated "nakedness".) The word is used many times in Lev 18:6-20, 20:10-21, and clearly any form of premarital or postmarital false attachment is being described, not only with those in the immediate family but also with a "neighbour". The commandment "Thou shalt not commit adultery" (Exod 20:14, Deut 5:18) was broken. Hence, why did "Moses" command this in the light of the Lord's quotations from Gen 1:27; 2:24?

8-9 We too may have had difficulties in answering the Pharisees' question, but the Lord, of course, knew exactly why every command under the law had been given. By saying "from the beginning it was not so", He implied that His principles were based on what had preceded the details of the law. The commandments were based on the unalterable standards of God, and the one relating to adultery would not be altered as a standard. Failure because of the hardness of man's heart was no excuse, and such sin could never be justified. But the breaking of this commandment had so many after-effects, that the law regulated these after-effects as an act of mercy, otherwise uncontrollable family difficulties would have arisen. Hence Moses "suffered you to put away your wives".

As in the Sermon on the Mount, the Lord's standards went beyond those required by the law. In v.9 He based His declaration of standards, not on something that arose through the breaking of the law, but on absolute principles laid down by God in the beginning: "Whosoever shall put away his wife, except it be for fornication, and shall marry another, committeth adultery and whoso marrieth her which is put away doth commit adultery". Here, in remarrying, the husband who has been divorced commits adultery, and the new husband of the divorced wife commits adultery; the same appears in Luke 16:18. But in Mark 10:12 the divorced wife commits adultery when she remarries; see also Rom 7:3.

In other words, in the remarriage, adultery is committed because one of the partners had been previously married, and both of the new partners are guilty of adultery.

"And I say unto you" can be translated "But I say unto you" (JND). Apart from the emphatic "I" (*egō*), the structure of the argument is similar to that in the Sermon on the Mount (Matt 5:22, 28, 32, 39, 44), where a statement of the law has been made, followed by a higher assessment by the Lord. So in our v.9 He was presenting a contrasting practice to that which Moses allowed in the law. In this higher assessment, the Lord went back to the beginning, where no divorce was allowed, else adultery is committed upon remarriage. Thus the excepting word "fornication" must be interpreted in the context as not conflicting with this assessment. Some would interpret fornication as unfaithfulness after marriage, but this would be adultery, and the two words cannot be interchangeable. The only meaning left is that unfaithfulness occurs before the formal contract of marriage takes place, namely during the period of espousal, when the word "wife" is still used. In our day, we would use the word "engagement" for the period prior to marriage. To "put away" under these circumstances would be to break off the intention to marry, and does not constitute divorce. The Lord did not substitute a replacement condition for divorce; rather He was removing any condition for divorce whatsoever. We have seen in Matt 1:19 that Joseph intended to go through with this procedure as regards his espoused wife Mary, until instructed by the Holy Spirit as to the genuine cause for her being with child. The Lord was not therefore laying down an entirely new procedure; rather He was condoning an existing procedure that was not contrary to "the beginning" of creation.

We recognise that, in practice, any particular situation may be much more complicated, with many side-issues involved. These situations are becoming much more common in these days. There was to be no fellowship with a brother who was a fornicator (1 Cor 5:11), where the word is not used in any restricted context. "Fornicators . . . nor adulterers" shall not "inherit the kingdom of God" wrote Paul to the Corinthians (6:9). Yet he recognised that some of the Corinthians had been characterised by these sins (v.11); but when he was writing they had been washed, sanctified and justified (v.11). In other words, if these things were sins of the past, and not continuing into the present, then faith and fellowship were possible. In a sense, they were the product of their sinful environment, but the local church is quite a different environment, with a set of new spiritual principles for the conduct of life. During the Lord's ministry, He exercised considerable compassion on those who had fallen into these immoral ways. Thus publicans and harlots would enter the kingdom because they believed (Matt 21:31-32). The woman "which was a sinner" brought the alabaster box of ointment, and was forgiven because she loved much (Luke 7:37, 47). The woman who had had five husbands, the sixth not being her husband, made a great confession of faith, and became an evangelist in her city (John 4:18, 29). The woman taken in adultery was not accused by the Lord; rather, he said "go, and sin no more" (John 8:3,11). But elders who may have to deal with such cases, whether concerning those who seek fellowship in a local assembly and who had sinned before their conversion, or those who have sinned as believers and already in fellowship, cannot expect to find these particular cases dealt with in detail in the Scriptures. They must carefully and spiritually weigh the matter up before the Lord, endeavouring to assess the consequences of their decisions not only on those who cause the problem, but also on the local assembly: "Take heed . . . to all the flock" (Acts 20:28).

10 In v.8, the Lord addressed the Pharisees who had asked the question in the first place, but now we come to another house scene. "In the house" the disciples asked a similar question (Mark 10:10). The AV rendering, "If the case of the man be so with his wife, it is not good to marry", is a bit awkward to understand. Both the RV and JND give a similar construction, and it is a literal rendering of the Greek text. It means something like: "If such is the condition of a man with regard to his wife", or "If the marriage bond is so strictly binding", then it would be better for no marriage to take place – evidently to anticipate trouble and to avoid it.

11-12 The Lord replied by first observing that His answer applied only to some men, namely to those " to whom it is given" . Of the three possible cases, the first was given naturally, the second by the man himself or by other men and the third by divine exercise and calling. The word "eunuch" (*eunouchos*) has two meanings; the first refers to a court officer in high authority (Acts 8:27-39) occurring several times in the OT (seven times in Dan 1). The second meaning applies both physically and metaphorically. In v.12 the Lord outlined three possibilities.

1. Men who are born with a physical defect, rendering it impossible for them to beget children. The original cause of this defect (as with so many other defects to which a minority of newborn babes is susceptible) is not known. The speculation of the disciples that a man or his parents had sinned is without foundation (John 9:2), though it is well known that certain methods of contraception have led to physical deformities of a very grave nature.

2. Men who have been rendered eunuchs, unable to beget children, by methods such as castration – even attempted personally by men in times past. This may be done on farm animals ultimately for economic reasons, but to be done on men seems to be an abuse on the structure that God originally created. Sometimes it may be necessary on health grounds, and other times the result of an accident. The Lord may also have been applying this concept to a man (not a disciple) abstaining voluntarily from marriage for some reason or ideal.

3. A disciple who, for the kingdom of heaven's sake, does not marry. Here is no formal command enjoined upon a certain brand of clergy, evidently so that those in the higher ranks of a hierarchy can lord it over the lower ranks. It is for those servants of God who believe that their work can more effectively be carried out by remaining unmarried.

Certainly in the NT we do not find this situation very often. Paul had the liberty to have a Christian sister as a wife (1 Cor 9:5), as the other apostles. But he would not avail himself of this liberty, believing that his service as an apostle to the Gentiles would be more effective otherwise. His assessment of his position – and he was not putting this forward as a pattern for everyone – was "He that is unmarried careth for the things that belong to the Lord, how he may please the Lord" (1 Cor 7:32). Only some can receive this ideal, when spiritual aspirations before the Lord override physical necessities. A blanket statement "forbidding to marry" (1 Tim 4:3) is an example of departing from the faith, "giving heed to seducing spirits, and doctrines of devils (demons)".

2. *The Rich Young Ruler, and Lessons therefrom* 19:13-30

v.13 "Then were there brought unto him little children, that he should put *his* hands on them, and pray: and the disciples rebuked them.
v.14 But Jesus said, Suffer little children, and forbid them not, to come unto me: for of such is the kingdom of heaven.
v.15 And he laid *his* hands on them, and departed thence.
v.16 And, behold, one came, and said unto him, Good Master, what good thing shall I do, that I may have eternal life?
v.17 And he said unto him, Why callest thou me good? *there is* none good but one, *that is*, God: but if thou wilt enter into life, keep the commandments.
v.18 He saith unto him, Which? Jesus said, Thou shalt do no murder, Thou shalt not commit adultery, Thou shalt not steal, Thou shalt not bear false witness,
v.19 Honour thy father and *thy* mother: and, Thou shalt love thy neighbour as thyself.
v.20 The young man saith unto him, All these things have I kept from my youth up: what lack I yet?
v.21 Jesus said unto him, If thou wilt be perfect, go *and* sell that thou hast, and give to the poor, and thou shalt have treasure in heaven: and come *and* follow me.
v.22 But when the young man heard that saying, he went away sorrowful: for he had great possessions.

v.23 Then said Jesus unto his disciples, Verily I say unto you, That a rich man shall hardly enter into the kingdom of heaven.
v.24 And again I say unto you, It is easier for a camel to go through the eye of a needle, than for a rich man to enter into the kingdom of God.
v.25 When his disciples heard *it*, they were exceedingly amazed, saying, Who then can be saved?
v.26 But Jesus beheld *them*, and said unto them, With men this is impossible; but with God all things are possible.
v.27 Then answered Peter and said unto him, Behold, we have forsaken all, and followed thee; what shall we have therefore?
v.28 And Jesus said unto them, Verily I say unto you, That ye which have followed me, in the regeneration when the Son of man shall sit in the throne of his glory, ye also shall sit upon twelve thrones, judging the twelve tribes of Israel.
v.29 And every one that hath forsaken houses, or brethren, or sisters, or father, or mother, or wife, or children, or lands, for my name's sake, shall receive an hundredfold, and shall inherit everlasting life.
v.30 But many *that are* first shall be last; and the last *shall be* first."

13-15 Men of all sorts came continually to the Lord: in this chapter we have the Pharisees (v.3), the parents with the children (v.13), and the rich young ruler (v.16). In Mark 10:13-16 and Luke 18:15-17, the children were brought so that the Lord should touch them, but in our verse so that He should put his hands on them and pray. Perhaps the parents did not know why they wanted the Lord to do this, nor what results to expect; perhaps the children were ill. In some places, the laying or putting on of hands was for healing (Mark 6:5; 7:32, Luke 4:40 13:13. Acts 28:8); elsewhere it was for commendation to a particular sphere or field of service (Acts 6:6; 13:3). Those with the gift of prophesy revealed the gift that Timothy possessed, and he was commended by the elders by the laying on of their hands (1 Tim 4:14). The apostles Peter, John and Paul had the discernment to lay hands on those who were to receive the Holy Spirit (Acts 8:17; 19:6), though this was not necessary in Acts 10:44. It is sheer Nicolaitanistic presumption to assume that this has been necessary since, or that any others save a few of the apostles had, or have, this ability.

The Lord never turned away honest seekers, even if they proved to be a nuisance to the disciples. If *they* rebuked the parents, then the Lord gently rebuked *them*, saving "Suffer little children, and forbid them not". The verb "suffer" is the very common word *aphiēmi*, meaning "to send away" (but not in the present verse!); in Matthew's Gospel it is translated "suffer" in 3:15; 23:13, but otherwise it means "forgive", "leave", "let", "forsake", "omit". In our verse it means "permit". The Lord allowed children to come to Him because "of such is the kingdom of heaven" – i.e. the disciples of the kingdom should have a child- like character (Matt 18:3-4). In Matt 21:15-16, the temple children were singing the praises of the Son of David, God had perfected praise from these babes and sucklings, whereas the hearts of the chief priests and scribes were hard and barren. The wise and prudent had empty ignorant hearts, but divine truth was revealed to babes (Matt 11:25). No wonder the Lord wanted such children around Him, a moral and spiritual lesson for the disciples whom He would also have around Him, and whom He would bless. Yet He departed, for His journey would end in Jerusalem when His hour was come.

16 There are different kinds of rulers or officials in the Gospels: there were rulers in the synagogue, such as Jairus (Matt 9:18): rulers in the Jewish Sanhedrin, such as Nicodemus (John 3:1); political "princes'' or rulers amongst the Gentiles (Matt 20:25) According to Luke 18:18 this man was a "ruler" (*archōn*), and he was also "young" (Matt 19:22). Mark 10:17 says he came running, evidently to catch up with the Lord who had already left, and kneeled down to Jesus; the most elevated and rich amongst men can sometimes make haste to adopt a position of humility, though in this case to no avail.

The ruler said, "Good Master", the word for Master being, as usual, Teacher (*didaskalos*). Some Greek manuscripts omit the adjective "good" before "Master", and this is followed by the RV and JND. However, it is retained in the corresponding verses in Mark 10:17 and Luke 18:18. Evidently this ruler believed in good works as a means to eternal life; having been brought up under the law and regulating his life by it, he could not know anything better. He seems to have known Lev 18:5 quoted in Gal 3:12, "The man that doeth them shall live in them", but not Hab 2:4 quoted in Gal 3:11, "The just shall live by faith". Coming to the Teacher to improve his knowledge was a good thing, but the question he asked has a false ring about it. He knew the Lord was "good", and believed that his own works should be "good" to match the Lord Himself. But there is too much of self in the question: "I" is used twice. His attitude contrasts with that of the publican who said, "God be merciful to me a sinner'' (Luke 18:13), and with the despair of the Philippian jailor (Acts 16:29-30).

17-19 The Lord's reply, "Why callest thou me good? there is none good but one, that is, God" is repeated as such in Mark 10:18. But in Matthew, where the Greek text omits "good" in the previous verse, a difference must be made in v.17 so as to make sense. This revised Greek text is then translated "Why askest thou me concerning that which is good?'' (RV, JND). As if to say, "You know that already''. But the statement in Mark 10:18 has a deeper implication, for "good" applied to the one God only, and yet it also applied to the Lord, being a guarded reference to His divine Person. The ruler could have deduced from this that He and the Father were one. But the ruler was lacking in revelation; he was granted no special knowledge as was Peter (Matt 16:16) and the blind man (John 9:37). Outwardly the Lord would not fully accept the title "good", since it was not addressed to Him on the grounds of faith; even today, the Lord's titles must be derived from a heartfelt faith, otherwise their use is only formal and traditional.

The Lord then expounded a vital principle of the law "if thou wilt enter into life, keep the commandments", a statement often overlooked by evangelists today. Paul elaborated on this in Rom 2:6-10: "Who will render to every man according to his deeds: to them who by patient continuance in well-doing seek for glory and honour and immortality, eternal life . . . glory, honour, and peace, to every man that worketh good''. However, sin prevented this, for no one came or comes up to this standard. "by the deeds of the law there shall no flesh be justified in his sight'' (Rom 3:20). The standard is so high, that one is guilty of all even if one offends in one point only (James 2:10). The "commandment, which was ordained to life" led to death on account of sin (Rom 7:10).

The young ruler was puzzled, since he knew that outwardly he kept the commandments according to the letter. The Lord quoted the six commandments that are manward in their application (to be contrasted with Matt 22:37-39, where the commandments both Godward and manward are summarised from Deut 6:5 and Lev 19:18). It is interesting that the Lord altered the order of the commandments in Exod 20:12-17. The fifth commandment "Honour thy father and thy mother" was placed after the ninth, and the tenth "Thou shalt not covet . . ." was omitted, to be replaced by the summary "Thou shalt love thy neighbour as thyself". These two were placed last, since it was here that the young man failed, and he did not know it.

20 Without realising his limitations, the young man was satisfied that he kept the law. He had no idea about the balances of the sanctuary, even as people today have no concept of the gravity and all-pervasiveness of sin (adultery according to scriptural standards is so common, and people enter upon remarriage without giving the matter one thought). The man's motives had to be examined; his "great possessions" caused him to disregard v.19 entirely. We would judge that he provided nothing for his father and mother, and as for selling and giving to the poor, there was no love for his neighbour in his heart. In Mark 10:21 the Lord "loved him", and he should do likewise; he had a moral obligation to love others, but here he failed. A believer should manifest a "work of faith, and labour of love" (1 Thess 1:3), while "love is the fulfilling of the law" (Rom 13:10). Such love is very practical, going beyond even bestowing all one's goods to feed the poor (1 Cor 13:3).

21 To be "perfect'', the man must sell his possessions and give to the poor. The word "perfect" (*teleios*) means "to reach an end''. Serving mammon meant that he could not "serve God" (Matt 6:24); this was a barrier to faith, and consequently he could not reach the desired end, he could not attain to eternal life. Regarding riches, had he never read what David as an old man said: "Both riches and honour come of thee . . . for all things come of thee" (1 Chron 29:12,14)? Hence David returned them to the Lord for the building of the temple. As Hannah said, "The Lord . . . maketh rich" (1 Sam 2:7), while Moses warned, " it is he that giveth thee power to get wealth", lest the people should think that they had acquired everything through their own power (Deut 8:17-18). What is received from God should be used for Him and His service. But mechanical obedience is far from being sufficient; we have already quoted 1 Cor 13:3 as showing that true love goes beyond what is merely mechanical. Instead, the example of the Lord should be before the hearts of His people. Because He gave Himself, in so doing He loved those for whom He died: He was rich, yet for our sakes He became poor (2 Cor 8:9). The removal of distracting goods on earth has its antithesis in the accumulation of treasure in heaven, when one can follow Him without distraction (Matt 8:18-22).

22-26 And so the rich young ruler departed sorrowfully from the Lord. His riches stumbled him, and he was unable to pluck out his eye and cut off his hand (Matt 18:8-9). There is no record that this man whom the Lord loved had another opportunity to repent and to do works meet for repentance. His end may have been similar to that of the rich man in Luke 16:22-23 who had lived for himself.

The Lord then proceeded to draw some lessons from this sad event: "a rich man shall hardly enter into the kingdom of heaven". The word "hardly" is *duskolōs,* meaning "with difficulty" (JND). Peter wrote something similar, using the word *molis*. "if the righteous scarcely (*molis*, with difficulty) be saved, where shall the ungodly and the sinners appear?" (1 Pet 4:18). For the Lord knew the human heart, that it is difficult to turn it away from an attachment to the things of the world. To illustrate this forcibly, the Lord gave the little proverb about a camel passing through the eye of a needle – physically something impossible, as was the beam in a human eye (Matt 7:4). The interpretation that the eye was a small gate in a city wall is without foundation, an invention by those who want to eliminate the need for the power of God. Another similar "exaggerated" word-picture is to "swallow a camel" (Matt 23:24). The Lord thus unmasked the unbelief of the apostles (19:26), for salvation is not an ordinary event but a miraculous work transcending human explanation. All things are possible with God but not with men, as Gabriel said to Mary (Luke 1:37); see also Jer 32:17; Phil 4:13. The same power that raised Christ from the dead is available today (Eph 1:19-20).

27-30 Peter knew that he was far better than this ruler, so naturally wanted to know what he would have as a consequence (though he seems to have clung to his house and to his wife, Matt 8:14; 1 Cor 9:5). In fact, Peter placed too much stress on "we" (cp. Luke 9:10; Dan 4:30) unlike Paul in Acts 14:27. The "I" is crucified with Christ, so that He can live and work in a believer (Gal 2:20).

Nevertheless, the apostles were a very special chosen band of men, with Judas no doubt replaced by Matthias, who had also followed the Lord, to make up the number twelve (Acts 1:21-26). As a result, they will have a special position in the millennial administration, "in the regeneration". This word *palingenesia* means "new birth" (re-genesis), not used here in the sense of spiritual regeneration (Tit 3:5) nor as referring to the new heavens and the new earth of the eternal ages to come (Rev 21:1). Rather the word refers to the coming period when the world will return to the state that it had before sin entered, when the Jews and Gentiles will own the Lord, seated on "the throne of his glory", as King of kings: this is the period to which the prophets looked forward in their restoration prophecies. All believers will sit with Him on His throne (Rev 3:21), having power over the nations (2:26), but the apostles will be concerned with restored Israel.

Compare this with Rev 21:12, 14 where we find twelve gates inscribed with the names of the twelve tribes and twelve foundations bearing the names of the twelve apostles in the millennial city of heavenly administration over the earth. The same promise was made by the Lord in Luke 22:30 regarding Israel, but for the church, "the saints shall judge the world" (1 Cor 6:2).

Finally, in Matt 19:29, the Lord provided a list of things to be "forsaken", not necessarily physically (though this does happen) but spiritually as having the heavenly realities before the heart. According to Mark 10:29-30, this is also for the sake of the gospel, and there are also rewards "now in this time". No doubt the apostles who were first (1 Cor 12:28) will be first in kingdom status; while the repentant thief on the cross represents the last who shall be last (with no reward for works). The carnal Corinthians are among the first who will be last (1 Cor 3:1, 15), while Simeon who was a last to see Christ will be a first (Luke 2:26). In other words, do faithfulness and devotion increase or decrease?

VIII. Those who Want More (20:1-29)

1. *Dissatisfaction with one Penny* 20:1-16

v.1 "For the kingdom of heaven is like unto a man *that is* an householder, which went out early in the morning to hire labourers into his vineyard.
v.2 And when he had agreed with the labourers for a penny a day, he sent them into his vineyard.
v.3 And he went out about the third hour, and saw others standing idle in the market-place,
v.4 And said unto them; Go ye also into the vineyard, and whatsoever is right I will give you. And they went their way.
v.5 Again he went out about the sixth and ninth hour, and did likewise.
v.6 And about the eleventh hour he went out, and found others standing idle, and saith unto them, Why stand ye here all the day idle?
v.7 They say unto him, Because no man hath hired us. He saith unto them, Go ye also into the vineyard; and whatsoever is right, *that* shall ye receive.
v.8 So when even was come, the lord of the vineyard saith unto his steward, Call the labourers, and give them *their* hire, beginning from the last unto the first.
v.9 And when they came that *were hired* about the eleventh hour, they received every man a penny.
v.10 But when the first came, they supposed that they should have received more; and they likewise received every man a penny.
v.11 And when they had received *it*, they murmured against the goodman of the house,
v.12 Saying, These last have wrought *but* one hour, and thou hast made them equal unto us, which have borne the burden and heat of the day.
v.13 But he answered one of them, and said, Friend, I do thee no wrong: didst not thou agree with me for a penny?
v.14 Take *that* thine *is*, and go thy way: I will give unto this last, even as unto thee.
v.15 Is it not lawful for me to do what I will with mine own? Is thine eye evil, because I am good?
v.16 So the last shall be first, and the first last: for many be called, but few chosen."

This parable is judged to be difficult to interpret in detail, as distinct from gleaning from it only general principles. It commences with the word "For", implying that it follows on from the previous verse. In Matt 19:16-30 "eternal life" and heaven were certainly in view (vv.16, 17, 21, 29, where the word "everlasting" is the same as "eternal", namely *aiōnios* and not *aidios*, that is without end rather than without interruption). But the present parable deals with rewards for service rather than inheriting eternal life – rewards not only in heaven but "now in this time" (Mark 10:30), equivalent to what had been given up for the gospel's sake. The Lord added another dimension to Peter's question, "what shall we have therefore?" (Matt 19:27). It is not possible to interpret the scene in the parable as the judgment seat of Christ, on account of the complaint made against the householder in vv.11-15, which could not possibly pertain. Those who interpret this parable as referring to eternal life conveniently omit those parts that do not fit in, suggesting that they are only supplementary to the parable as a whole, but we do not view parables from this restricted point of view. The parable can be compared with that of the pounds where each had the same (Luke 19:12-27), and can be contrasted with the parable of the talents where each had something different (Matt 25:14-30).

The present parable deals with long service and bad motives (the first being last) receiving the same reward as short service and good motives (the last being first). Long service and good motives would no doubt gain a greater reward (the first being first), and we place the apostles into that category.

1 The "householder" (*oikodespotēs*) is the "goodman of the house" (v.11) and "master of the house" (10:25). The vineyard represents the sphere of service amongst both Jew and Gentile, both when the Lord was present and during the time of His absence. For the vineyard is "the house of Israel, and the men of Judah" (Isa 5:7), but later the Gentiles were involved (Matt 21:41, 43), and believers form the branches of the vine (John 15:5).

2 Here, then, is a sphere of service, and the Lord seeks labourers, calling them in His own chosen time. Some were chosen early, such as the apostles, most of whom lived long lives in the Lord's service. They planted and watered, and "every man shall receive his own reward according to his own labour" (1 Cor 3:8). The agreement for one penny shows that there was a spirit of bargaining from the beginning – this should *not* be so in the Lord's service. The Roman *dēnarion* was a small but sufficient wage for a day. Although many rewards for faithfulness are stated in Rev 2, 3, yet it is better for us today to be like Abraham, namely "not knowing" (Heb 11:8) what to expect for our labours except in general terms. The labourers were then "sent" to the place of their work. Since the Lord came to do the will of the Father who had sent Him (John 5:30; 9:4), how much more His servants (20:21)! Thus Paul was sent to preach (1 Cor 1:17), and quite generally, "how shall they preach, except they be sent?" (Rom 10:15).

3-7 There were "twelve hours" in a day (John 11:9); the period between sunrise and sunset was divided into twelve hourly intervals, so the precise subdivisions depended upon the season of the year. Without the means of defining the hours exactly, the word "about" is often used, so in this parable the word "about" is used of the third, sixth, ninth and eleventh hours. The third, sixth and ninth hours were also used to describe rougher subdivisions, while the eleventh hour described a last-minute event. Greater exactitude was not necessary for the Lord nor for the Spirit of inspiration.

On each occasion, the householder, realising that more labourers were required, found men standing "idle" (*argos*). This word is compounded from *a* (a negative particle) and *ergon* (work), carrying the thought of being inactive or barren. These men were not idle in the sense of laziness; rather they were unemployed and waiting for employment – "Because no man hath hired us". We are not told why they had not been hired previously that day – they may have been working elsewhere for a short period, or seeking employment elsewhere in which case the householder would not have found them. At least they must have been equipped for the work to which they were sent. The same is true of Christians today; younger believers do not have a specific service, rather they are preparing themselves for the Lord's service, and awaiting the call from the Lord. Thus Matthias had to wait for over three years before his call in Acts 1:26, and Paul had to wait for nearly ten years before he received the call to apostolic service in Acts 13:2-4 (during that period he was not called an apostle, neither had his name been changed from Saul to Paul). Although saved during Paul's first missionary journey, Timothy had to wait until the beginning of the second journey before he was called (Acts 16:1-3). Of course, in some cases the labourer may be occupied with idle pleasure, not being consecrated to the Lord; repentance must take place before he can be sent forth, but then there would have been only a little preparation of heart, life and mind for divine service.

These others were not told that they would receive "a penny", only what was "right" (*dikaios*, just), repeated twice in vv.4, 7. In v.7, some Greek texts omit the last clauses "and whatsoever is right, that shall ye receive". The RV omits them, and JND places them in brackets being unsure whether they are genuine.

8 We do not believe that the "even" represents death, nor that the appearing of the labourers before the "lord of the vineyard" represents the judgment seat of Christ, on account of the murmuring that took place amongst the recipients. In any case, these men were available for further work on the following day, and the parable does not include the advent of the King, as in Matt 25:19; Luke 19:15. The word for "hire" (*misthos*) means "reward" (Matt 10:41; 1 Cor 3:8, 14; etc), "wages" John 4:36; 2 Pet 2:15), and "hire", also used in Luke 10:7 "the labourer is worthy of his hire" (in this present life of service). In the parable instructions are given to start with "the last" and to end with "the first". This does not mean that this is always so; the object of the parable was to teach Peter a lesson on account of his self-confidence and self-satisfaction in Matt 19:27, "what shall we have therefore?".

9-15 The difficulties of the parable mainly centre around these verses. Trench in his *Notes on the Parables* observes that "It is a parable which stands only second to that of the Unjust Steward in the number and wide divergence from one another of the explanations that have been proposed for it; and only second to that, if indeed second, in the difficulties which it presents". The reader will find a wide range of these explanations in his book. To the dispensationalist who is not too much concerned about the context of a parable nor with its details, the suggestion that the Jews represent the first and the Gentiles the last will greatly appeal (Acts 20:21; Rom 1:16). But we believe that the context demands a much more practical explanation. The hire or rewards do not represent heavenly rewards in heaven, but heavenly rewards on earth after a period of service to which believers are called by the Lord. During the burden and heat of the day, motives and incentives may become mixed, and service may become mechanical rather than conducted in the state of spiritual freshness with which it commenced. If this is so, then these motives will be laid bare at the end of such a period of service.

Those who were hired at the eleventh hour received "a penny", and may well have been surprised, for it appears that they had not known this beforehand; no doubt they were thankful, knowing that they were unprofitable servants. They had done what they could in the time allocated, and men cannot do more. Those who had commenced work at the first hour watched what was happening, and the financial considerations of the flesh immediately became evident; they expected to receive more – perhaps twelve times more. It is the attitude of those not satisfied with their wages (Luke 3:14), but applied to spiritual work. It is, in fact, a Gehazi-like attitude (2 Kings 5:20-24). They desired to tear up a contract, and substitute something else. But the employer had the last word. He was "good" doing what was "lawful", namely he abode by the contract which was just when it had been drawn up.

Paul's reward in this life was quite distinct from the "crown of righteousness" that he would receive in the day to come (2 Tim 4:8). He asked, "What is my reward then?", and he provided the answer, "that, when I preach the gospel, I may make the gospel of Christ without charge, that I abuse not my power in the gospel" (1 Cor 9:18). His reward was to be made the servant of all. No natural man in the flesh would take such an attitude; Paul's exercise to make the gospel free when he preached came from the Holy Spirit, and at the end of a spell of service he was glad that it was so, and he was prepared to do more for the Lord with the same kind of reward. Men joined this grand service at different times, such as Timothy, Silas, Apollos, Aquila and Priscilla, together with the list in Acts 20:4, men who derived from Paul's first, second and third journeys. Some served longer, and others more briefly, yet none complained about their rewards. The details of their heavenly rewards on earth are not stated; that is irrelevant. What we do know is that these early servants of the Lord were spiritual men and women, with no seed-thought of complaint arising in their hearts. We can add Peter to the list who had commenced his service long before Paul, and John who served longer than they all, and whose reward was the patience of Jesus Christ (Rev 1:9) with the privilege of writing the Book of Revelation following the signifying of it to him by the angel (v. 1).

There is a danger than a man may have an "evil eye" (*ophthalmos ponēros*). In Prov 23:1-7, this occurs in the context of riches, and the setting of the eyes on that which flies quickly away. Similarly in Prov 28:22, "He that hasteth to be rich hath an evil eye". In Matt 6:19-23 the "evil eye" is that which looks on treasures laid up for self on earth, rather than on treasures laid up in heaven. In the list of evil things that come from the heart and defile a man, "an evil eye" is one such thing (Mark 7:22); in the light of these other references, we interpret this to refer to the greed of gain. And so in the parable, the desire for a greater reward than justified suggests an "evil eye". The Lord asked that as a question in the parable; He did not actually state that such a servant had an evil eye, though outwardly it appeared to be so. A Christian can appear to be carnal and to "walk as men" (1 Cor 3:1-3) in appearance, though this is a disgrace to the testimony.

16 The Lord concluded with the same statement as preceded the parable (Matt 19:30), "the last shall be first, and the first last". Only those who take the false attitude towards reward will be last. The last clause, "many be called, but few chosen" is omitted in some Greek texts; the RV omits it, but JND includes it. Many being called refers to the service of all believers, but the few being chosen refers, in the context, to those who have no ulterior motives and aspirations in their hearts. These thoughts also appear in Matt 22:14.

Although this parable does not refer to the judgment seat of Christ, readers may care to have a few details about this important subject. There are four main references:

1. Assessment of motives for service (1 Cor 4:5), when "every man" will have praise of God.

2. Assessment of service (1 Cor 3:13), when "every man's work shall be made manifest" and when fire "shall try every man's work of what sort it is".

3. Assessment of motives of conduct (Rom 14:10-12), when "every one of us shall give account of himself to God".

4. Assessment of conduct (2 Cor 5:9-10), when "we must all appear before the judgment seat of Christ; that every one may receive the things done in his body".

It is important to note that every believer is concerned.

2. *Greatness of the Humble Believer* 20:17-29

v.17 "And Jesus going up to Jerusalem took the twelve disciples apart in the way, and said unto them,
v.18 Behold, we go up to Jerusalem; and the Son of man shall be betrayed unto the chief priests and unto the scribes, and they shall condemn him to death,
v.19 And shall deliver him to the Gentiles to mock, and to scourge, and to crucify *him:* and the third day he shall rise again.
v.20 Then came to him the mother of Zebedee's children with her sons worshipping *him,* and desiring a certain thing of him.
v.21 And he said unto her, What wilt thou? She saith unto him, Grant that these my two sons may sit, the one on thy right hand, and the other on the left, in thy kingdom.
v.22 But Jesus answered and said, Ye know not what ye ask. Are ye able to drink of the cup that I shall drink of, and to be baptized with the baptism that I am baptized with? They say unto him, We are able.
v.23 And he saith unto them, Ye shall drink indeed of my cup, and be baptized with the baptism that I am baptized with: but to sit on my right hand, and on my left, is not mine to give, but *it shall be given to them* for whom it is prepared of my Father.
v.24 And when the ten heard *it,* they were moved with indignation against the two brethren.
v.25 But Jesus called them *unto him,* and said, Ye know that the princes of the Gentiles exercise dominion over them, and they that are great exercise authority upon them.
v.26 But it shall not be so among you: but whosoever will be great among you, let him be your minister;
v.27 And whosoever will be chief among you, let him be your servant:
v.28 Even as the Son of man came not to be ministered unto, but to minister, and to give his life a ransom for many.
v.29 And as they departed from Jericho, a great multitude followed him."

After the previous paragraphs that show how Peter and other servants hoped to receive a lot for having forsaken all, and for having engaged in such extensive service, the example of the Lord is given (vv.17-19), the One whose service took Him into death. Then James and John, using their mother for their purpose, desired the highest position with the Lord without being the minister of all. In other words, lessons were never learnt; the first still wanted to be first although they had false motives. The Lord was going to show them "the way of God more perfectly" (Acts 18:26).

17-19 This is the final announcement that the journey to Jerusalem was now taking place; it is also recorded in Mark 10:32-34 and Luke 18:31-34, being the conclusion of a series of announcements commencing in Matt 16:21. Although there were evidently multitudes with the Lord, the twelve disciples were taken apart privately to hear this communication. The history of the forthcoming days was unfolded: "to Jerusalem", reached in 21:10; "betrayed unto the chief priests and scribes", taking place in 26:47-50; "they shall condemn him to death", and this condemnation took place in 26:66 and 27:1 (note the Romans had at that time taken away the Jewish right to put men to death); "shall deliver him to the Gentiles" was done in 27:2; "to mock" took place when the soldiers dressed Him up to resemble a king even with a crown of thorns (27:31); "to scourge" took place in 27:26; "to crucify him" is recorded in 27:35; "the third day he shall rise again" is found in the announcement of the angel (28:6). Truly the Lord knew all things that were about to come upon Him.

Matthew made no comment upon the apostles' reaction to this prediction Perhaps having been there, he was too embarrassed to record their reaction, but Luke, who was not there, had no such inhibitions. Although they had heard this prediction before, and although the time was near, "they understood none of these things: and this saying was hid from them, neither knew they the things which were spoken" (Luke 18:34). We attribute to Satan this lack of understanding and memory on the part of the apostles.

20-21 If the Lord was thinking of His sufferings leading to glory (1 Pet 1:11), then James and John were thinking of glory without suffering. They were thinking of being the first who would be first, but without becoming last in order to achieve it. It is not stated whether James and John enlisted their mother's help to achieve their goal, or whether it was her own idea for the advancement of her two sons. At least, a woman came, firstly worshipping and then asking. The fact of the Lord's status, glory and authority in His coming kingdom must have been well known to this woman; either she had heard this teaching from the lips of the Lord Himself, or she had received it from her sons. She was determined that her two sons should have the preeminence over the rest of the apostles. It is true that overcomers will sit with the Lord in His throne (Rev 3:21), but there is no promise of special preeminence since that would distract from the preeminence of the Lord. Later, after the institution of the breaking of bread, there was "a strife among them, which of them should be accounted the greatest" (Luke 22:24). They had never learnt the lesson of what true greatness is.

Thus Peter had failed in the presence of glory on the mountain top (Matt 17:4), while the other two on that mountain failed later in our verse at the thought of kingdom glory. In both cases, there was a distraction from the preeminence of the Lord.

22-23 By using "Ye", the Lord made it clear that He knew that the two disciples were really behind this request. They knew not the nature of their desire, for the truth is: "If we suffer, we shall also reign with him" (2 Tim 2:12). So the Lord tested them about their preparedness and willingness to suffer, even as He would suffer. He asked them about His "cup" and His "baptism". Admittedly, the fulness of His cup and the depth of His baptism were to be unique; they could not participate to that extent. His sufferings were twofold, at the hands of men, and at the hands of God to effect our redemption. His question was therefore restricted to suffering at the hands of men. The Lord spoke of His cup in deeper measure when He prayed to His Father in the garden of Gethsemane (Matt 26:39); it was a cup that could not pass from Him because this was the Father's will. Relating to baptism, we sometimes sing "Baptised in death's dark waters" as referring to the Lord. The symbol of immersion was fitting to describe the depths into which the Lord went under the waters of suffering. It should be pointed out that the reference in Rom 6:4, "we are buried with him by baptism into death", does not refer to the suffering of believers at the hands of men, rather this baptism is the practical testimony of a believer that he reckons his old nature as crucified with Christ so that His resurrection life should be manifested instead.

By saying, "We are able", these two disciples exhibited a self-confidence that went beyond their faith and experience. All the apostles suffered in Acts 4:3, while James was martyred in Acts 12:1-2 by Herod. Peter considered that he could die with the Lord (Matt 26:35; John 13:37-38), but afterwards he forsook the Lord (Matt 26:56) and then denied Him (vv.69-75). However, later Peter wrote much about suffering in his first epistle, and referred to his own crucifixion in 2 Pet 1:14 as the Lord had shown him. Yet glory was promised after suffering In the last part of our v.23, the words in italics (AV) "*it shall be given to them*" do not appear in the Greek text. They have been inserted by the translators to make sense. Unfortunately they have also altered the actual sense! The AV reads as if it *will not be* within the Lord's capacity to exalt some of His people in glory. But commentators and JND (but not the RV) render the last half of v.23 as: "to sit on my right hand, and on my left, is not mine to give, but to them for whom it is prepared of my Father". In other words, the Lord will give these privileged positions to those of His people for whom it is prepared by His Father. The idea of just two such positions originated in the minds of James and John, and the Lord used this wording in His answer. For all will be able to sit with Him, though the twelve apostles will have special thrones in this position of nearness (Rev 3:21; Matt 19:28). The Lord as the Lamb will be in the midst (Rev 5:6), and the description of movement and activity in heaven excludes the idea of permanent left and right positions for two special believers! It is noteworthy, however, that John was nearest to the Lord at the last supper in the upper room (John 13:23-28).

24 The fact that "the ten" heard these words means that they had been directed solely to James and John. For Judas to enter into the condemnation was mere hypocrisy, since his heart was not right in spiritual matters – he was a thief with a heart prepared for Satan to enter (John 13:2). They were indignant because

1. by their request James and John had demonstrated that they thought that they were so superior to the others in standard and work as to warrant the highest reward;
2. they had nor learnt the lessons of the previous chapter;
3. they had given the Lord an occasion to issue a rebuke.

"They were moved with indignation" is one word in Greek, the verb *aganakteō* (derived from *agan* meaning "much", and *achomai* meaning "to grieve"). Literally the Greek text states "And having-heard, the ten were indignant about the two brothers". The word occurs as a verb seven times in the NT, where it is also translated as "sore displeased" or "much displeased". This reaction was that of the disciples in Matt 20:24; 26:8; Mark 10:41; 14:4; of the religious leaders in Matt 21:15; Luke 13:14 (in the temple and synagogue respectively), and of the Lord Himself in Mark 10:14 when the disciples rebuked the parents who brought their children to Him. In all six occasions when men were indignant, the flesh was operative at various levels. (Several different Greek nouns are also translated "indignation" on a minority of occasions, but these words should properly be rendered differently.)

25-28 Once again the Lord explained the principle of true greatness, yet still the apostles did not learn the lesson, for He had to repeat it in similar words in Luke 22:24-30 just after the institution of the breaking of bread. He quoted the example of the power-hungry amongst the Gentiles, and we remember that the fourth beast-kingdom of Dan 7:7 was operating at that time, the Roman empire with its emperor and lesser officials throughout its provinces. Men love power, and seek the top positions to wield it over the masses; having gained the positions and power, they strive in various ways to retain it, effectively doing Satan's work for him in the political and military fields. "The princes of the Gentiles" (*hoi archontes tōn ethnōn*) are the rulers of the nations. The two verbs "exercise dominion over" and "exercise authority upon" are *katakurieuō* (occurring in Mark 10:42; Acts 19:16; 1 Pet 5:3, the last reference negatively in a local assembly) and *katexousiazō* (also appearing in Mark 10:42). In these two verbs the reader will notice the two roots *kurios* (lord) and *exousia* (power, authority), respectively giving flavour to the officials' ambitions.

After stating that a believer must "not" engage in such worldly ambitions, the Lord showed that spiritual ambitions are attained only by means that reverse those of the world. There is a threefold process towards preeminence, the status rises upwards, but the steps lead downwards. As far as status is concerned, we have "great, chief, Son of man", the first two being applicable to disciples, while the last is the unique name and status of the Lord. The steps are: "let him be your minister . . . let him be your servant . . . to minister, and to give his life a ransom for many", the latter again being the sole prerogative of the Lord.

The word for "great" (*megas*) means "great in size and intensity" as in the English words megalith and megaphone, and "great in rank" of persons. The same word is used in v.25 to describe the "great" Gentile politicians. The word for "chief" (*prōtos*) means "first", such as "the chief man" of Melita (Acts 28:7) and "the chief women" of Thessalonica (17:4). The word for "minister" (*diakonos*) is the usual word in the NT for servant or deacon. In a local assembly, the word refers to all believers who serve the Lord in any way. The "servant" (*doulos*) is a bondservant having the lowest possible position; it is used of Paul (Phil 1:1) and of Christ Himself (Phil 2:7). In other words, one goes downwards to reach the top, as Peter wrote (having learnt the lesson), "Humble yourselves therefore under the mighty hand of God, that he may exalt you in due time" (1 Pet 5:6); see Matt 23:11-12; James 4:10.

The greatest lesson of all is seen in the way in which the Lord conducted His life of service that ended in a sacrificial death. Whereas the Gentile rulers expect their subjects to serve them, yet the Lord's attitude was exactly the opposite. Although He was Son of God and Son of man, He did not come to display His status so that men would have to minister to Him. The word for "ministered" here is the passive of *diakoneō*, namely the work of a *diakonos*. There were, however, several women who "ministered unto him of their substance", no doubt referring to food and clothing (Luke 8:3; Matt 27:55). Instead, the Lord would "minister", that is, engage in deacon work; in Luke 22:27, He said, "I am among you as he that serveth", the same word *diakoneō* being used in all the verses. The extent of the Lord's ministry was "to give his life a ransom for many". A ransom (*lutron*) is a payment made in order to set another free (the word is derived from *luo*, "to loose"). This is what the Lord accomplished when He gave His life on the cross. This ransom was "for many", reminding us of Matt 26:28 where His blood was "shed for many". Yet other verses use the words "all, every, whole", such as Rom 5:18; Heb 2:9; 1 John 2:2; 1 Tim 2:6. Of course there is no confusion of doctrine here. The work of Christ is available for all, but not all will believe; the "many" are those who believe. Paul distinguished this in Rom 3:22 when he wrote, "unto all and upon all them that believe". The first "all" is all-embracive amongst men; the second "all" is all-embracive amongst believers, standing for the "many" in the other verses.

The fact that the Lord "gave himself" is prominent in Paul's epistles. The expression occurs twice in Galatians, twice in Ephesians, and twice in the Pastoral Epistles. He "gave himself for our sins" (Gal 1:4); He "gave himself for me" (Gal 2:20); He has "given himself for us" (Eph 5:2); Christ loved the church and " gave himself for it" (v.25); He " gave himself a ransom for all" (1 Tim 2:6); He "gave himself for us" (Tit 2:14). Most of these have the thought of separation in the context, and many also have the thought of love.

Thus by means of this humbling of Himself whereby He became obedient to death, "even the death of the cross", He has now been highly exalted, "and given . . . a name which is above every name" (Phil 2:1-11). The lesson for the apostles could not have been concluded on a deeper or higher note. The higher note does not appear in Matt 20:28, but is found in verses such as Matt 24:30; 26:64 referring to the coming day of His triumph, glory and vindication.

29 The departure of the Lord with his disciples and the multitude terminates the section that commenced with the parables of the kingdom in Matt 13. Jericho is left behind as He ascends to Jerusalem. In the parable, the man went down from Jerusalem to Jericho, and fell amongst thieves (Luke 10:30); the Lord followed the reverse journey, and men took Him shortly after His arrival in the city.

CHAPTERS 20:30 to 25
THE KING'S ADVENT: PAST AND FUTURE

I. The Arrival in Jerusalem (20:30 to 22:14)

1. *Healing of the Blind Men* 20:30-34

v.30 "And, behold, two blind men, sitting by the way side, when they heard that Jesus passed by, cried out, saying, Have mercy on us, O Lord, *thou* son of David.
v.31 And the multitude rebuked them, because they should hold their peace: but they cried the more, saying, Have mercy on us, O Lord, *thou* son of David.
v.32 And Jesus stood still, and called them, and said, What will ye that I shall do unto you?
v.33 They say unto him, Lord, that our eyes may be opened.
v.34 So Jesus had compassion *on them*, and touched their eyes: and immediately their eyes received sight, and they followed him."

30-34 The narrative now joins on to the end of Matt 12; the intervening chapters have been concerned with the kingdom in mystery form, with the King unknown by the Jews. They correspond to the church age, with the nation put on one side until its future restoration. Now He was going to present Himself to His people in anticipation of the greater presentation and advent described in chs.24-25. At the second advent, the fulfilment of prophecy will be taken up again after the church age, when the King and kingdom in glory will be manifested in the world.

There are three stories of blind men being healed under similar circumstances:

1. In Matt 9:27-31 towards the beginning of the Lord's ministry;
2. In Luke 18:35-43 when the Lord was entering into Jericho, perhaps the same incident as in Mark 10:46-52, the man's name being Bartimaeus;
3. In Matt 20:29-34, where two blind men were healed as the Lord left Jericho.

In all cases, they addressed the Lord as " Son of David", namely the coming King in David's line. It need not be surprising that they all said the same thing; they were copying the successful call for help in Matt 9:27, and news spread that such faith met with success.

The miracle is a picture of the nation restored when faith takes Him up as King. For "blindness in part is happened to Israel, until the fulness of the

Gentiles be come in" (Rom 11:25), in keeping with the OT prophecies, "Then the eyes of the blind shall be opened" (Isa 35:5), and "to open the blind eyes" (42:7), predicting that physical healing will be replaced by spiritual healing. With their eyes opened, "they shall look upon me whom they have pierced" (Zech 12:10).

2. *The Lord's Entry into Jerusalem* 21:1-11

v.1 "And when they drew nigh unto Jerusalem, and were come to Bethphage, unto the mount of Olives, then sent Jesus two disciples,
v.2 Saying unto them, Go into the village over against you, and straightway ye shall find an ass tied, and a colt with her: loose *them*, and bring *them* unto me.
v.3 And if any *man* say ought unto you, ye shall say, The Lord hath need of them; and straightway he will send them.
v.4 All this was done, that it might be fulfilled which was spoken by the prophet, saying,
v.5 Tell ye the daughter of Sion, Behold, thy King cometh unto thee, meek, and sitting upon an ass, and a colt the foal of an ass.
v.6 And the disciples went, and did as Jesus commanded them,
v.7 And brought the ass, and the colt, and put on them their clothes, and they set *him* thereon.
v.8 And a very great multitude spread their garments in the way; others cut down branches from the trees, and strewed *them* in the way.
v.9 And the multitudes that went before, and that followed, cried, saying, Hosanna to the Son of David: Blessed *is* he that cometh in the name of the Lord; Hosanna in the highest.
v.10 And when he was come into Jerusalem, all the city was moved, saying, Who is this?
v.11 And the multitude said, This is Jesus the prophet of Nazareth of Galilee".

In Matt 21:1-17, the Lord's entry into Jerusalem and the second cleansing of the temple involve four OT quotations:

1. Verses 1-7: **The King;** v.5 is quoted from Zech 9:9. See also Isa 62:11, the great chapter in Isaiah dealing with the ultimate restoration of, and blessing upon Jerusalem.

2. Verses 8-11: **The Multitude;** v.9 is quoted from Ps 118:26. This Psalm is a holy conversation between the Lord and His people, rehearsing His sufferings and His triumph in resurrection.

3. Verses 12-13: **The Merchants;** v.13 is quoted from Isa 56:7, showing God's ideal for His house in the ingathering of Israel. The "den of thieves" (or "den of robbers") is found in Jer 7:11.

4. Verses 14-17: **The Children;** v.16 is quoted from Ps 8:2, showing the divine origin of all that gives Him pleasure, whether in creation or in praise.

The rest of the paragraphs in the chapter contain a similarity of thought.

> In vv.18-22, we find no fruit in Jerusalem, only in Bethany (v.17), a word meaning "house of dates or figs", contrasting with the barren fig tree in the way. We have here the Lord's authority in *cursing*.
>
> In vv.23-32, we find no fruit from the disobedient, only from the repentant. We have here the Lord's authority in *cleansing*, enabling the publicans and harlots to enter the kingdom.
>
> In vv.33-46, we find that there is no fruit from the Jews (the husbandmen, the "you" in v.43), only from a "nation bringing forth the fruits thereof". We have here the Lord's authority in *choosing*.
>
> In 22:1-14 we have a continuation of this theme, showing the Lord's authority in *clothing*.

A different point of view may be adopted. The parable in vv.28-32 is one of repentance; some Jews are not allowed in, while the others are brought in. The parable in vv.33-46 is one of foreknowledge; the Lord knew the treatment that the Jews would mete out to Him, and the fact that the Gentiles would bring forth fruit. This rejection enabled the Gentiles to be brought in. Finally, in 22:1-14 we find that it is grace that has brought in the Gentiles.

1 The Lord had previously said, "it cannot be that a prophet perish out of Jerusalem" (Luke 13:33), and hence at the beginning of the last week "they drew nigh unto Jerusalem". The disciples should have known what would transpire at this place of destiny, since just previously He had told them that they were now going up to Jerusalem where He would be crucified (Matt 20:17-19). Looking back on the event, the Spirit of prophecy would call this place "the great city . . . Sodom and Egypt, where also our Lord was crucified" (Rev 11:8).

The verse shows that the Lord came "to Bethphage", a village whose name means "a place of young figs". "Bethany" also means a "house of dates or figs "; these two villages on the slopes of Olivet contrast sharply with the barren fig tree on the way into Jerusalem (Matt 21:19). That these two villages are distinct is shown by Luke 19:29, where both are mentioned

How fitting that the King should enter His city via the mount of Olives. This mount was not only rooted in the spiritual history of the past, but also in the prophetical history of the future. For example, it had been both a place of weeping by the rejected king David (2 Sam 15:30), and a place of idolatry when the heart of Solomon went astray (1 Kings 11:7). Furthermore, it was the place of the Lord's ascension and promised return in like manner (Acts 1:11), and will be the place of His return to Jerusalem in glory (Ezek 43:4; Zech 14:4). The Lord knew all this as He humbly presented Himself as King for the last time, riding into the city from Olivet. Meanwhile, He still awaits this crowning day, although even now He is set as King upon the holy hill of Zion (Ps 2:6).

2-3 In sending the two disciples into the village, the Lord was adopting once again the two-by-two principle (Mark 6:7; Luke 10:1). He exhibited divine foreknowledge of immediate future events by saying, "ye shall find"; elsewhere, He had said, "thou shalt find" (Matt 17:27), and "there shall meet you a man" (Mark 14:13). The Lord lived the present in the light of known future events; see John 13:1. If this were possible for ordinary man, he might well seek to avoid the foreseen unpleasant things of life, but the Lord, knowing all things that were to come upon Him, went forth (John 18:4).

The ass and the colt were clearly two distinct animals, because of the word "them" in v.3. Mark recorded the colt only (11:2-7), as did Luke (19:30-35). John mentioned one animal, "a young ass", namely a colt (12:14). Clearly the Lord sat upon the colt, not upon the ass, and some interpret Matt 21:5 to mean, "sitting upon an ass, and that a colt the foal of a beast of burden". It should be pointed out the last word "ass" (*hupozugion*) of v.5 is not the same word as that used first in v.5 (*onos*). The first word is rightly the name of an animal, but the last word denotes its work, namely a beast of burden. Its responsibility as the mother ass was to follow its colt who carried the King. Such were ridden by kings and judges in times of peace, while horses were used in warfare (Rev 19:11).

The Lord instructed His disciples to confess Him as "the Lord". They were not to use the title Son of man which had reference to the glory of His kingdom power (Matt 25:31; 26:64), nor the title Son of David referring to His authoritative position amongst the Jews (Matt 22:42). Believers should always use the title most suitable to the occasion, learning the implications of the titles appropriate to His relationship with them. Thus the title "Lord" shows His relationship to a disciple living closely in subjection to the divine will. Compare the title "Master" (Teacher) in Matt 26:18.

4-5 We have here the first OT quotation, and Matthew was making it clear that these events were a fulfilment of prophecy. Indeed, in this Gospel more than ten events are said to fulfil some aspect of OT prophecy; see for example 13:35 from Ps 78:2, 27:35 from Ps 22:18. The OT can be taken to be a comprehensive prophetic map of the Lord's life when on earth.

The quotation is a dual one, consisting of two OT references, namely, " Say ye to the daughter of Zion, Behold, thy salvation cometh; behold, his reward is with him, and his work before him" (Isa 62:11), and "Rejoice greatly, O daughter of Zion . . . behold, thy King cometh unto thee: he is just, and having salvation; lowly, and riding upon an ass, and upon a colt the foal of an ass" (Zech 9:9). The splicing together of these two distinct verses occurs where "thy salvation cometh" is changed to "thy King cometh". Other examples of this splicing process are:

1. Rom 9:33 taken from Isa 28:16 and 8:14 and back again to 28:16; Peter separated these two OT quotations in 1 Pet 2:6, 8;
2. Luke 4:18, 19 taken from Isa 61:1-2 and 42:7.

The title "daughter" means "inhabitant". In His last public utterance prior to His crucifixion, the Lord called the great company of people and the women "daughters of Jerusalem" (Luke 23:28). Zion implies Jerusalem in the incomparable ways of God, but that this should be so demonstrates the amazing grace of God. Originally, Zion was a single hill in which God desired to dwell for ever (2 Sam 5:7; Ps 68:16), for there the ark rested during David's reign. But at the dedication of the temple, the ark was taken "out of the city of David, which is Zion" (1 Kings 8:1) to mount Moriah. At the same time Solomon confessed that Zion was still the rest of God for ever (Ps 132:13-14). This is not inconsistent, since from that time onwards God in grace named the whole of the city as Zion, thereby encompassing Moriah, the temple and the ark.

"Tell ye" appears (as "Say ye") in the greatest chapter of ultimate restoration (Isa 62), but "thy salvation cometh" is not quoted. Unknown to the people, He was coming to *accomplish* salvation on the cross; only in the future will He *bring* salvation to the restored nation (Isa 59:20). The rest of the quotation is taken from Zech 9:9. In Rev 19:11 we find the King of kings and Lord of lords coming, riding on a horse for battle to establish His kingdom. Following this, He comes on an ass as King of peace as pictured in Matt 21. In that day there shall no longer be a horse or battle in Jerusalem (Zech 9:10); He will then exercise His Melchisedec priesthood, being "King of righteousness, and . . . King of peace" (Heb 7:2).

The phrase "just, and having salvation" (Zech 9:9) is omitted in Matt 21, no doubt because this will be known only in the future. Had the Lord demonstrated in Matt 21 that He was just, then swift judgment would have fallen upon the rebellious nation. But He comes "the second time without sin unto salvation" (Heb 9:28), and then the complete quotation will be fulfilled. John 12:16 informs us that the disciples understood and remembered these things only when the Lord was glorified. In other words, the Holy Spirit was needed to show the disciples the connection between the Lord's activity and the OT prophetic Scriptures.

6-8 Garments were placed under the King as He sat upon the colt. Circumstances were different, but earlier Israel had cried, "Jehu is king", as they took every man his garment and put them under their newly-anointed king (2 Kings 9:13). We have here an eastern method of showing honour. Moreover the trees are named as palm trees in John 12:13, their fanlike leaves being much used in processions. Such trees had often been used in OT typology and figurative language. Ps 92:12 tells us that "the righteous shall flourish like the palm tree", illustrating the "just" character of Christ that had been omitted from Zech 9:9.

Moreover, in the temple all the walls were carved with palm trees (1 Kings 6:29), typical of the unknown One who would flourish in His own house. The people, in their enthusiasm and ignorance, acclaimed Him in His proper character.

9 We have here the second OT quotation. The multitudes who acclaimed their King were, without doubt, distinct from those who later cried "crucify him". These multitudes would comprise the passover pilgrims from Galilee, His immediate followers and disciples, those who knew of the raising of Lazarus (John 12:17), and the children of the temple courts. Psalms 113-118 were often quoted at the passover and the feast of tabernacles in the autumn. Ps 118 is used here because of the rejoicing, and certainly fitted the occasion. Unwittingly the people took up a psalm speaking both of His death and His resurrection, and of His people's response. In fact, the psalm consists of a holy mutual meditation by the Lord and His people, viewed from the resurrection side of death. The five subdivisions of the psalm are:

1. Vv.1-21: The Lord's rehearsal of His sufferings on the cross at the hands of men, and His resurrection in vv. 17-21.

2. Vv.22-24: His people acclaim the Stone's Headship, the Lord's doing, and the Lord's day.

3. V.25: The Lord's reply shows His desire for prosperity to follow His sufferings and resurrection.

4. Vv.26-27: His people expect His return, engaging in the sacrifice of praise and testimony in blessing from the house of the Lord.

5. Vv.28-29: The Lord's final reply, praise to His God for these results of His death, and a general leading of His people in thanks to the Lord.

The word "Hosanna" (taken from the Hebrew) means "save now"; it was quoted by the multitude from vv.25-26, using words both of the Lord and of His people in the psalm. No doubt the multitude's cry was traditional, but God would ensure that this was the genuine result of His death and triumph. For this psalm (vv.22-23) is quoted again in Matt 21:42, where the exalted Stone is seen choosing a nation to bring forth appropriate fruit in praise and service.

The Lord appeared to be unmoved by such outward rejoicing, although Luke 19:40 shows that He accepted the praise, otherwise the stones would have cried out. (We judge that the stones on the mount of Olives were still influenced by the fact that the glory of God had departed to that mount when He left the temple of Solomon for the last time in Ezek 11:23). The immediate effect on the

Lord was, however, that He wept over Jerusalem, as He contemplated its destruction. He knew that His throne in Jerusalem would be His cross; only when He was raised and received up would He receive true praise.

10-11 Here we find the reaction of the people. The city of Jerusalem did nor know Him, and the multitude could rise no higher than the description "Jesus the prophet" from Galilee; see also v.46. How much was lacking in their understanding of His Person! In Matt 16:14 the people's suggestion that He was a prophet was elevated by Peter to "the Son of the living God". In John 4:19 the woman's perception that He was a prophet was extended to know Him as the Christ (v.29). The healed blind man thought that He was a prophet (John 9:17) but the Lord later permitted him to know Him as the Son of God (vv.35-38). In other words, the outward manifestation of confession and praise can be developed in the heart by a revelation of Himself, since the Lord would have a true, yet feeble, faith grow more fully into the knowledge of His Person.

3. *The Merchants and the Temple Children* 21:12-17

v.12 "And Jesus went into the temple of God, and cast out all them that sold and bought in the temple, and overthrew the tables of the moneychangers, and the seats of them that sold doves,
v.13 And said unto them, It is written, My house shall be called the house of prayer; but ye have made it a den of thieves.
v.14 And the blind and the lame came to him in the temple; and he healed them.
v.15 And when the chief priests and scribes saw the wonderful things that he did, and the children crying in the temple, and saying, Hosanna to the Son of David; they were sore displeased,
v.16 And said unto him, Hearest thou what these say? And Jesus saith unto them, Yea; have ye never read, Out of the mouth of babes and sucklings thou hast perfected praise?
v.17 And he left them, and went out of the city into Bethany; and he lodged there."

12 As we trace the Lord entering the temple (*hieron*, not *naos* the "inner sanctuary") we must realise that there was no divine warrant for the existence of this temple; Herod had conceived it for outward show and beauty, an architectural masterpiece. When the Lord left this temple for the last time, He appropriately called it "your house" (Matt 23:38), in just the same way as what had once been a feast of the Lord was now termed a "feast of the Jews" (John 5:1). Generally speaking, this temple was not the house of God. In the OT the tabernacle had been the house of God, built by divine command, but it ceased to be His sanctuary after He had forsaken it in Samuel's day (Ps 78:60). The presence of David, a man of faith, transformed it temporarily into the house again (Mark 2:26), but this was an isolated occasion. Similarly, when God departed from Solomon's temple for the last time (Ezek 11:23) it was no longer His house, although it was still called by its traditional name during the years up to its destruction (2 Chron 36:19). Thus the Lord's presence temporarily transformed Herod's temple into "the temple of God", as previously it had been called "my Father's house" (John 2:16). It had been only the special presence of God that had transformed the burning bush into a sanctified place (Exod 3:2). Today, a building or an organisation may be called a "church" by tradition, but the vital question is, does the Lord's presence reside there in the congregation?

Essentially, the Lord entered the temple with the object of teaching the people (Matt 21:23; Luke 19:47), but its cleansing was necessary first; compare Josiah's cleansing in 2 Chron 34. The Lord's act was the same as He had accomplished in John 2:14-16 some three years before, but the heart of man would not receive correction, and had perpetuated the things that the Lord had judged.

No doubt the sale of items in Jerusalem for use in the temple had been instituted in the OT (Deut 14:25), thereby saving transport between a distant home end Jerusalem, but in Matt 21:12 the method employed by these men desecrated the house for the greed of financial gain, something not unknown even in the church in Jerusalem later (Acts 5:1-4). The sons of Eli had acted similarly in 1 Sam 2:12-17, placing the taste of a carnal appetite above the holy requirements of God. In Corinth, many had reduced the Lord's supper to the act of taking their own supper; "one is hungry, and another is drunken" (1 Cor 11:21). Judgment fell in every case where holy institutions were turned into an occasion for the flesh.

The moneychangers were concerned with the annual payments of half a shekel to the temple funds. Originally there had been one payment only (Exod 30:12-14). In Matt 17:24-27, the Lord provided payment both for Himself and for Peter to avoid offending the people. But God does not take payment from the Son, since the children are "free". In Matt 21, payment could be made only in Jewish coins, so moneychangers were necessary to effect this for pilgrims who had arrived from afar (Acts 2:9-11), but these changers were working for carnal profit, "supposing that gain is godliness" (1 Tim 6:5).

13 We have here the third OT quotation. In John 2:16, the house had been made a "house of merchandise"; there, the OT is not quoted, except the disciples' own recollection from Ps 69:9, "The zeal of thine house hath eaten me up". But here, on this the second such occasion, the Lord probed deeper, likening it to "a den of thieves". See Jer 7:11, where "den of robbers" appears. However, in John 2:25, "he knew what was in man"; suitable conduct in the house was impossible apart from being born again. These verses also show that moral holiness is just as necessary today for those who seek to serve in God's spiritual house, "How thou oughtest to behave thyself in the house of God, which is the church of the living God" (1 Tim 3:15). There can be no defilement of the temple of God, "for the temple of God is holy, which temple ye are" (1 Cor 3:17).

And now Isa 56:7 is quoted: "for mine house shall be called an house of prayer for all people". The context refers to those who please God (v.4). These have a place in His house, having been given an everlasting name (v.5), having joined themselves in true fellowship to the Lord by loving His Name (v.6). This results in acceptable prayer, worship and fellowship (vv.7-8). This is God's ideal, obviously in contrast to the state of affairs in Jerusalem when the Lord was there in the days of His flesh.

14-15 The blind and the lame that were healed were among those who formed the true temple, after that particular brand of ceremonial Judaism had passed away. The blind and lame sacrifices of Mal 1:8 could not be accepted, but the Lord anticipated a "pure offering" from the Gentiles (v.11), their offering up would be acceptable, "being sanctified by the Holy Spirit" (Rom 15:16).

In the temple courts, the activity of the children was in sharp contrast to the displeasure of the priests. The religious leaders possessed nothing, but the lowly and innocent had scriptural praise. It should be the same today. The cold formality of large religious precincts should be contrasted with the spiritual warmth found amongst the Lord's people gathered in His Name and in a much less imposing building that is not designated " a church". If official Christendom is displeased when it sees the Lord's servants far more able spiritually in evangelistic work and in the exposition of the Scriptures, let it note that such believers recognise that the gift and calling of God derive from the risen Christ and not from men and the training of their schools.

16-17 Here we have the fourth OT quotation. To the ignorant priests the Lord quoted from the Messianic Psalm 8. The "babes and sucklings" had not tasted the wisdom of the world, so could not be deflected from the true subject-matter of praise. These were the "weak things of the world" chosen by God "to confound the things which are mighty" (1 Cor 1:27). Thus no flesh should glory in His presence; thereby would be brought to nought the "things that are" (v.28), namely "the enemy and the avenger" (Ps 8:2). The mouth of the children referred to in this verse is like the mouth of David, the sweet psalmist of Israel, "The Spirit of the Lord spake by me, and his word was in my tongue" (2 Sam 23:2). The Lord Himself had previously intimated that this would be so observing that these things, hid from the wise and prudent, had been revealed "unto babes" (Matt 11:25).

The Lord knew that He was passing on to His decease, but this Psalm gives details of His ultimate vindication. Verse 6 indicates that He will have dominion over all, and that all will be placed under His feet. Heb 2:5-8 shows that this will be accomplished openly in "the world (age) to come", but meanwhile He is crowned with glory and honour. See Heb 1:13; 1 Cor 15:25-27.

Hence in v. 17 the Lord left a nation religiously barren, although still containing a remnant of praise, and departed to a place of love, namely Bethany. Moreover, this was a "place of dates or figs", a place of fruitfulness, contrasting sharply with the barren fig tree in the way found in the next paragraph.

4. *Fruitlessness and Repentance* 21:18-32

v.18 "Now in the morning as he returned into the city, he hungered.
v.19 And when he saw a fig tree in the way, he came to it, and found nothing thereon, but leaves only, and said unto it, Let no fruit grow on thee henceforward for ever. And presently the fig tree withered away.
v.20 And when the disciples saw *it*, they marvelled, saying, How soon is the fig tree withered away!
v.21 Jesus answered and said unto them, Verily I say unto you, If ye have faith, and doubt not, ye shall not only do this *which is done* to the fig tree, but also if ye shall say unto this mountain, Be thou removed, and be thou cast into the sea; it shall be done.
v.22 And all things, whatsoever ye shall ask in prayer, believing, ye shall receive.
v.23 And when he was come into the temple, the chief priests and the elders of the people came unto him as he was teaching, and said, By what authority doest thou these things? and who gave thee this authority?
v.24 And Jesus answered and said unto them, I also will ask you one thing, which if ye tell me, I in like wise will tell you by what authority I do these things.
v.25 The baptism of John, whence was it? from heaven, or of men? And they reasoned with themselves, saying, If we shall say, From heaven; he will say unto us, Why did ye not then believe him?
v.26 But if we shall say, Of men; we fear the people; for all hold John as a prophet.
v.27 And they answered Jesus, and said, We cannot tell. And he said unto them, Neither tell I you by what authority I do these things.
v.28 But what think ye? A *certain* man had two sons; and he came to the first, and said, Son, go work to day in my vineyard.
v.29 He answered and said, I will not: but afterward he repented, and went.
v.30 And he came to the second, and said likewise. And he answered and said, I *go*, sir: and went not.
v.31 Whether of them twain did the will of *his* father? They say unto him, The first. Jesus saith unto them, Verily I say unto you, That the publicans and the harlots go into the kingdom of God before you.
v.32 For John came unto you in the way of righteousness, and ye believed him not: but the publicans and the harlots believed him: and ye, when ye had seen *it*, repented not afterward, that ye might believe him."

The King having entered His own city to be crucified, He now used various opportunities to show the true state both of the Jewish nation as a whole, and of the Gentiles who would be brought in under grace. We have already pointed out the similarity of thought in the remaining paragraphs:

In vv. 18-22: the Lord's authority in *cursing;* there was no fruit in Jerusalem, only in Bethany.

In vv.23-32: the Lord's authority in *cleansing;* there was no fruit from the disobedient, only from the repentant.

In vv.33-46: the Lord's authority in *choosing;* there was no fruit from the Jews, only from the "nation" (v.43).

In 22:1-14: the Lord's authority in *clothing.*

18-22 The summer season for figs occurred well after the passover; as Mark 11:13 informs us, there were leaves but "the time of figs was not yet". Figs are a peculiarity amongst the wide variety of created things. Cultivated fig flowers are fertilised for fruit-bearing only by pollen from the wild fig tree, the pollen being carried from the flower of the wild fig to that of the cultivated fig by the small fig wasp. Lack of knowledge of the cycle brought failure, for example, when only the cultivated fig was introduced into America. Moreover, the flowers are so to speak inside out, being inside the pear-like green shapes on the tree. There can be two crops of figs. Those in spring were called "the hasty fruit before the summer" (Isa 28:4), or "the firstripe fig before the summer" (RV). This former crop precedes the leaves, which in turn precede the summer crop.

These details reflect upon the many facets of interpretation found in the incident where the Lord found no fruit but only leaves. The Lord longed for early fruit from His people but, apart from the remnant previously noted, there was none. There may have been leaves produced over the years since then, and more certainly will be produced in the future days; these leaves will herald the future restoration when "summer is nigh" (Matt 24:32).

The fig, vine and olive are distinct. In one sense, the vine refers to the *past* (Ps 80:8; Isa 5:1-7); the fig to the *present*, namely the leaves representing the state of the Jews without fruit, and the olive to the *future*, when the branches will be grafted in again (Rom 11:19). From another point of view, the following differences may be noted.

All three are found in Hab 3:17, and in Jud 9:8-13, where the olive, fig and vine refer to fatness, sweetness and wine to cheer respectively.

Again, the *fig* may speak of God's *national interests* on earth, since the fig was cursed in Mark 11:21, something that could never come upon God's spiritual interests. The Jewish national preeminence (Deut 28:13), according to which they would be "the head, and not the tail", would come under the curse (vv. 15-19), so that the nations would be the head and the Jews the tail (v.44). In the Lord's time there were leaves only, leaves of outward show (Gen 3:7), but in AD 70 even these withered, and Israel ceased from being a nation before the Lord even though a remnant had looked for "redemption in Israel" (Luke 2:38; 24:21; Acts 1:6). Yet the promise of restoration in His times and seasons will be fulfilled when summer has come (Acts 1:7).

On the other hand, the vine speaks of God's *spiritual interests* on earth. In Isa the Lord looked for spiritual fruit from His people the husbandmen, His vineyard being the sphere of service of the priests, prophets, Levites and shepherds (Matt 21:33). This service would pass to others who would bring forth fruit, this being now fulfilled by the branches abiding in the vine, which is Christ Himself (John 15:1-5).

Finally, the *olive* represents the *testimony* of God maintained on earth by the Spirit of God (of whom the oil speaks). The public testimony was first in the hands of the Jews, and then in the hands of the Gentiles in local assemblies. Rom 11:11-26 traces the history of the transfer of this testimony, showing clearly the position occupied by believers today. For the future, see Rev 11:3-4.

Hence the leaves in Matt 21:19 speak of a show of Jewish religious activity throughout the period of the Lord's ministry, and the withered-away state corresponds to the present age wherever the Jews conduct their religion without Christ. Since there was nothing for the Lord, He pronounced the words of judgment, "Let no fruit grow on thee henceforward for ever", that is, while in their conceited state of unbelief and national pride. The words "for ever" (*eis ton aiōna*) cannot exclude the blessing of future restoration, but this is not visualised in the story of the fig tree. Only a remnant shall be saved, while the rest of the nation will be judged as in deep apostasy. (We may compare this with Coniah, king Jehoiachin, who before his restoration was pronounced to be childless, with no hope of prosperity, and with no further son sitting on the throne of David, Jer 22:30. But mercy was promised immediately, that a righteous Branch would be raised to David, 23:5-6. So, after all, Jehoiachin had a son in the genealogy of the King, Matt 1:12, after his restoration, 2 Kings 25:27-30; 1 Chron 3:17.) In other words, we see now with a vision wider than that pictured in the incident of the fig tree; after the destruction of Jerusalem in AD 70, we see the great mercy of God that ultimately "all Israel shall be saved", namely the remnant passing through the great tribulation.

The Lord used the occasion for a lesson on the power of prayer (Matt 21:21-22). There is a particular condition given, under which prayer will be answered: "faith, doubt not, believing". The mountain may well be a physical mountain, if this were necessary in the will of God. (Geologically, mountains have exploded into fragments under volcanic activity, being deposited in the sea afterwards, but such circumstances were not the result of prayer). Mountains are removed in the judgment section of the Book of Revelation (Rev 6:14; 16:20), not as a result of prayer but demonstrating the intervention of God in judgment. The mount of Olives will split and move in that coming day when the Lord's feet shall stand on that mount (Zech 14:4). But the mountain may also be metaphorical, a mountain of pride, of difficulty, of unbelief. For if it refers to the heart, then this will be moved out of the way, "A new heart also will I give you, and a new spirit will I put within you: and I will take away the stony heart out of your flesh, and I will give you an heart of flesh" (Ezek 36:26). See also Luke 17:6; 1 Cor 13:2.

23-27 In the temple courts, the teaching of the King was now called into question since He taught "as one having authority, and not as the scribes" (Matt 7:29). The people recognised this difference, since they were attentive to hear Him as He taught daily in the temple (Luke 19:47-48). It was this fact that caused the leaders to withhold their hands from Him until His hour was come, for they feared the people. But the Lord had no man-given authority to teach, neither had He teaching or licence from the Rabbis; rather, "as my Father hath taught me, I speak these things (John 8:28). The Jews considered the Lord as "having never learned" (7:15), but it was with envy that the priests watched His authority. As it was then, so it is today. Unspiritual religious leaders trained in the schools of men tend to question any spiritual authority and ability in others who have been trained only in the school of God. Ordination by rite and by man is a denial of the liberty of the Spirit amongst His people, and Nicolaitanism, hated by the Lord, seems to answer to this practice (Rev 2:6, 15).

Chapters 21-22 represent the Lord's final conflict with formal religion, which He then condemned in ch.23. It is quite clear in chs. 21-22 that the Lord openly had the victory. The leaders sensed this; the Lord used their own arguments to reduce them to silence, but their developing antagonism led to His crucifixion.

Service originating from heaven, whether of John the Baptist or of the Lord Himself, is the basis of all true achievement, but this is thoroughly disliked by men who refuse to recognise this divine origin. Believers today should always have a sanctified sense of the origin of their service. It is true that "a man can receive nothing, except it be given him from heaven" (John 3:27); the Baptist said this of the Lord, but it also referred to himself. Similarly as ascended on high the Lord gave gifts unto men (Eph 4:8). Hence our testimony, as was that of the apostle Paul, should be, "I was not disobedient unto the heavenly vision" (Acts 26:19) As the apostle said to the Ephesian elders, "so that I might finish my course with joy, and the ministry, which I have received of the Lord Jesus, to testify the gospel of the grace of God" (Acts 20:24). Later he wrote, "I thank Christ Jesus our Lord, who hath enabled me, for that he counted me faithful, putting me into the ministry" (1 Tim 1:12). See also Gal 1:1, and 2 Tim 1:12 which we believe should be rendered, "I . . . am persuaded that he is able to keep that which he has committed unto me against that day".

28-32 We now have the first of three parables, followed by three questions asked by the religious leaders. Their common subject refers to those who thought that they were in the kingdom, whereas in reality they (the self-righteous Jews) were but the tares. Others morally outside to start with were brought in by grace. In vv.28-32, they would not obey unto repentance; in vv.33-46, they would not serve unto fruitfulness; in 22:1-14, they would not have their affections set upon the Lord's things. In vv.28-32, we have the Jews not in, and the Jews (a remnant) coming in. Conversely in vv.33-36, the Jews are not in, but the Gentiles are brought in.

Those not in. A certain man's second son said, "I go, sir: and went not". This had been the original intention of the nation, "we will do" (Exod 19:8). But they went not, for in practice they broke the law by boasting in it (Rom 2:23). Later, the Lord said of the scribes and Pharisees, "they say, and do not" (Matt 23:3). This is religious humbug and hypocrisy. Many may appear to acknowledge the "way of righteousness" (Matt 21:32), but although they know this way, yet they turn from it to become entangled with the pollutions of the world (2 Pet 2:21-22). Such are not walking in the way of the Lord, making His paths straight (Matt 3:3), neither are they on the way of holiness that the unclean shall not pass over (Isa 35:8).

Those coming in. By contrast, the first son repented and went into the vineyard. This is typical of those who ultimately recognise their sin and need, and exercise faith. For example, in Luke 3:12 publicans came to John saying, "what shall we do?", and without doubt they followed the instructions issued by John (Matt 3:6). Similarly the Lord received publicans and sinners (Luke 15:1-2), leading to repentance and faith as in the parable of the prodigal son. Hence in Matt 21:31-32, the Lord showed publicans and harlots entering the kingdom of God by faith, something that the Pharisees never desired to do. The Lord did not say the "kingdom of heaven", rather the "kingdom of God", the all-embracive sphere of His rule, being "righteousness, and peace, and joy in the Holy Spirit" (Rom 14:17).

Finally, we note that the Lord expected repentance in v.29, followed by faith in v.32. As Paul said in Acts 20:21 to the Ephesian elders, "repentance toward God, and faith toward our Lord Jesus Christ". This is the divine order available today in the gospel, namely repentance towards the One offended, and faith in the One who saves.

5. *The Vineyard and the Stone* 21:33-46

v.33 "Hear another parable: There was a certain householder, which planted a vineyard, and hedged it round about, and digged a winepress in it, and built a tower, and let it out to husbandmen, and went into a far country:

v.34 And when the time of the fruit drew near, he sent his servants to the husbandmen, that they might receive the fruits of it.

v.35 And the husbandmen took his servants, and beat one, and killed another, and stoned another.

v.36 Again, he sent other servants more than the first: and they did unto them likewise.

v.37 But last of all he sent unto them his son, saying, They will reverence my son.

v.38 But when the husbandmen saw the son, they said among themselves, This is the heir; come, let us kill him, and let us seize on his inheritance.

v.39 And they caught him, and cast *him* out of the vineyard, and slew *him*.

v.40 When the lord therefore of the vineyard cometh, what will he do unto those husbandmen?

v.41 They say unto him, He will miserably destroy those wicked men, and will let out *his* vineyard unto other husbandmen, which shall render him the fruits in their seasons.

v.42 Jesus saith unto them, Did ye never read in the scriptures, The stone which the builders rejected, the same is become the head of the corner: this is the Lord's doing, and it is marvellous in our eyes?

v.43 Therefore say I unto you, The kingdom of God shall be taken from you, and given to a nation bringing forth the fruits thereof.
v.44 And whosoever shall fall on this stone shall be broken: but on whomsoever it shall fall, it will grind him to powder.
v.45 And when the chief priests and Pharisees had heard his parables, they perceived that he spake of them.
v.46 But when they sought to lay hands on him, they feared the multitude, because they took him for a prophet."

The second parable of the trio shows the Lord seeking His Father's fruit, and knowing where this would ultimately be found. The parable provides a wide panorama of the purposes of God relating both to the Jews and to the church, as well as to Christ, the exalted Stone. The parable is a summary of the whole Bible!

It is important to notice the difference between the results effected by this parable and by the original parables in Matt 13. Although the prophetical implications of exaltation and grace were quite lost on the Pharisees, nevertheless they understood their own position in the parable, since "they perceived that he spake of them" (v.45). On the other hand, the parables of the kingdom in ch. 13 were designed to hide the truth from all, except those to whom a divine explanation was given (13:10-17); the Lord explained some of the parables only to His disciples (vv.18, 36).

33-36 In these verses the Lord described parabolically events that took place prior to His first advent. The vineyard evidently is distinct from the servants who worked in it. It represents the sphere of service in which men are responsible for fruitbearing relative to sacrifice, worship and sanctuary service. Indeed the nation had left Egypt for tabernacle service, to "hold a feast unto me in the wilderness" (Exod 5:1). The Lord had done everything possible to ensure the fruitfulness of this vine (Ps 80:8-11; Isa 5:1-2).

In the parable, the Lord did not take note of the decay of the vine, although this is prominent in the OT. Its hedges were broken down, and it was burned with fire (Ps 80:12, 16); it brought forth "wild grapes" (Isa 5:4); it became a "degenerate plant of a strange vine unto me" (Jer 2:21); it had become fuel for the fire (Ezek 15:6).

The householder went into a far country. This corresponds to the time when the Lord's glory departed from Israel, when there was no open vision (1 Sam 3:1; 4:22), and to the time when heaven was regarded as the divine dwelling place (1 Kings 8:30, 34, 36, 39, 43, 45, 49). To this nation, God then sent prophets priests and kings. He thus spoke "unto the fathers by the prophets" (Heb 1:1). For example, Isaiah was one who was ready to be sent (Isa 6:8). God sent to them "all my servants the prophets, daily rising up early and sending them" (Jer 7:25); He longed for their obedience.

But the parable continues to show that the prophets were subjected to beating, killing and stoning (Matt 21:35-36). The voice of the prophets seeking the fruits of obedience was not heeded; and the divine record in the NT takes note of this They suffered cruel mockings and scourgings, bonds and imprisonment; "they were stoned, they were sawn asunder, were tempted, were slain with the sword" (Heb 11:36-37). The Lord concluded His final condemnation of the religious leaders by stating that they were "the children of them which killed the prophets" (Matt 23:30-35). Stephen said the same thing, "Which of the prophets have not your fathers persecuted? and they have slain them which showed before of the coming of the Just One" (Acts 7:52). The sad thing is that all this was done in the name of religion, by those who took the name of God upon their lips, but knew not God. Such men thought that they did God service, "because they have not known the Father, nor me" (John 16:2,3). Even today, the testimony of those who trust wholly in the Word of God is discarded by those who make a show of rites of ceremonial religion.

37-39 We now come to the events that took place during the Lord's sojourn on earth. God still looked for fruit amongst the tribe that was left. Hence the "one son, his wellbeloved" (Mark 12:6) was sent, in order to seek worshippers of the Father. The fruit was His own property, rightly expected from His own vineyard. After all, the Son was appointed heir of all things (Heb 1:2), so He had the divine right to receive of His own. But the idea of possessions vested in Deity causes the spirit of jealousy to blossom forth in unregenerate men, in spite of the tenth commandment (Exod 20:17). If the Heir was cast out, then His possessions so near at hand could be seized. In this parable, the act of seizing means to turn spiritual matters to their own carnal advantage, and to seek domination and authority over the thoughts and lives of men, things that believers can also be prone to do in the present time (1 Cor 3:3; 11:21). Moreover, the priests and Pharisees would go to the ultimate end to achieve their objective, without realising that they were bringing down judgment upon themselves and the nation. Hence they cast out the Son from the vineyard and slew Him; even Pilate realised their motives, knowing "that for envy they had delivered him" (Matt 27:18). In the OT Joseph had suffered because of similar motives; his brethren had "cast him into some pit" (Gen 37:20). But he later became a fruitful bough by a well, the one who was separate from his brethren obtaining a crown of glory (Gen 49:22,26). How typical this was of the Lord who suffered without the camp, that He might bring forth "much fruit" (John 12:24), and "see of the travail of his soul" (Isa 53:11).

40-43 We now pass on to events that took place after the Lord's resurrection. A suitable question by the Lord, "what will he do unto those husbandmen?", provoked the Pharisees to condemn themselves out of their own mouths; such wicked men would be miserably destroyed. Men see sin in others, but not in themselves; see Luke 18:11, and compare David, who, concerning a parable relating to his own sin, had said, "the man that hath done this thing shall surely die" (2 Sam 12:5). The Pharisees were constrained to speak the truth, as Caiaphas also had to do (John 11:51). But at least it appears that the Pharisees at that point in the parable did not realise that the Lord was speaking against them. They realised this when the Lord said "you" in v.43. To what does "destroy" refer? It refers to the ultimate judgment of those concerned, but in the parable the time of the judgment is just after His ascension. Hence it may refer to the destruction of Jerusalem in AD 70 by the Romans, when all the cherished religious traditions of the Jews were swept away.

In v.42 the Lord quoted from the resurrection Psalm 118. It was much quoted by the people during Passover week, but its true spiritual implications could not have been understood by those who automatically repeated it. We have already analysed this Psalm when dealing with a quotation from it in v.9. The Lord quoted it to show the true position attained by the rejected King. There was a Part that the builders had rejected as unwanted, but the divine Architect had reserved the most prominent position for this Part, and would ensure that Christ became "the head of the corner" in resurrection glory. This resurrection should appear to us as something "marvellous in our eyes", something that demanded the greatness of His power to accomplish (Eph 1:19-20).

The fruits of his travail would be brought forth in another nation, as the Lord said in v.43. The book of the Acts relates how the opportunity for salvation spread forth from the Jews to the Gentiles, being rejected by the former, and accepted by the latter (Acts 13:46; 28:28). The other nation is the church which yields to Him the fruit of the Spirit, reminding us that it is always God who gives the increase (1 Cor 3:6). This fruit is also in worship and praise, Rom 15:9-11 showing the Gentiles engaged in this holy activity.

44 The conflict between man and the Stone eventuated in the Stone's exaltation in v.42, but in the judgment of man in v.44. None who enters into conflict with God can ultimately survive; God will always be victorious (Acts 9:39). Man first falls on the Stone in anger and envy, but the Stone then falls upon him in devouring judgment. In a different context, the nations first fell upon the Anointed of God (Ps 2:1-2), but later the Stone will break them into pieces (Dan 2:45). Moreover, as men are divided into Jews, Gentiles and the church of God (1 Cor 10:32), so the Stone is seen in relation to each of these classes. These distinctions are also found in 1 Pet 2:5-10, and in the OT passages quoted.

The Jews: "whosoever shall fall on this stone shall be broken". This refers to the break-up of the Jewish nation as a result of their crucifixion of their Messiah. They stumbled over this Stone by unbelief, disobedience and hatred, quoted in 1 Pet 2:8 from Isa 8:14, "a stone of stumbling, and a rock of offence". See Rom 9:32-33.

The Gentiles or nations: "on whomsoever it shall fall, it will grind him to powder'' This is of very wide application, as the word "whomsoever" implies. There is a correspondence with the dream in Dan 2:34 and its interpretation in v.45, as already pointed out. The Stone cut out without hands smote the image upon his feet of iron and clay, and broke them in pieces; the Stone then became a great mountain, filling the whole earth. But in 1 Pet 2:7, the apostle quoted Ps 118:22 in a different manner; the Stone disallowed and made head of the corner is seen in relation to the disobedient generally, namely those who obey not the gospel of the Lord Jesus Christ.

The church: "The stone which the builders rejected, the same is become the head of the corner". This headship refers to the new class of believers who afterwards brought forth the fruit of the vineyard. We contemplate the saints of the present day living in contact with their risen Head. 1 Pet 2:6 (quoted from Isa 28:16) contains the same idea of preciousness to those who believe, "Behold, I lay in Sion a chief corner stone, elect, precious: and he that believeth on him shall not be confounded". In Isa 28 the Stone is seen as a "sure foundation", whereas in Ps 118 He is the top-most Stone. The Lord has both positions at once, a Foundation and a Head to His people.

45-46 And so the Pharisees realised that the Lord was using the parable to condemn them. This is unlike John 10:6 where, after the parable of the sheepfold, the sheep, the porter and the shepherd, "they understood not what things they were which he spake unto them". However, they were quick on the uptake regarding other things! When the Lord referred to His Father, they knew that this implied the deity of the Son (John 10:33).

So in this parable, the Lord has introduced a pause: in His lifetime and at His second advent He will be King, but now His people see Him as their Lord and Head.

Even in those days, the Pharisees still dared not take Him, since they "feared the multitude" who believed the Lord to be "a prophet". However, after a few days, when His hour was come, this fear would be overcome. Before that, they would seek to discredit Him in front of the multitudes (Matt 22:15-46), but instead His answers would discredit them. Enmity against the Lord in this life can often be like a boomerang!

6. *The Parable of the Wedding Feast* 22:1-14

v.1 "And Jesus answered and spake unto them again by parables, and said,
v.2 The kingdom of heaven is like unto a certain king, which made a marriage for his son,
v.3 And sent forth his servants to call them that were bidden to the wedding: and they would not come.
v.4 Again, he sent forth other servants, saying, Tell them which are bidden, Behold, I have prepared my dinner: my oxen and *my* fatlings *are* killed, and all things *are* ready: come unto the marriage.

v.5 But they made light of *it*, and went their ways, one to his farm, another to his merchandise:
v.6 And the remnant took his servants, and entreated *them* spitefully, and slew *them*.
v.7 But when the king heard *thereof*, he was wroth: and he sent forth his armies, and destroyed those murderers, and burned up their city.
v.8 Then saith he to his servants, The wedding is ready, but they which were bidden were not worthy.
v.9 Go ye therefore into the highways, and as many as ye shall find, bid to the marriage.
v.10 So those servants went out into the highways, and gathered together all as many as they found, both bad and good: and the wedding was furnished with guests.
v.11 And when the king came in to see the guests, he saw there a man which had not on a wedding garment:
v.12 And he saith unto him, Friend, how camest thou in hither not having a wedding garment? And he was speechless.
v.13 Then said the king to the servants, Bind him hand and foot, and take him away, and cast *him* into outer darkness; there shall be weeping and gnashing of teeth.
v.14 For many are called, but few *are* chosen."

This passage forms the last of the three parables that we are considering. The self-righteous religious Jews thought that they were in the kingdom, whereas they really were but tares; others who had been morally on the outside were brought in through grace. This third parable contrasts with a similar one in Luke 14:16-24, where it was spoken in a house at supper to those who wanted a reward for well-doing; the Lord's lesson for them was "lest they also bid thee again" (v.12). The two parables are similar, but spoken on different occasions for different purposes.

In vv.1-7, we have the wedding feast empty, but in vv.8-14, the wedding feast filled.

1 Although the chief priests and Pharisees "sought to lay hands on him" (21:46), the Lord did not seek to escape or depart as in John 8:59; 10:39. In the present incident, by the word "again" He continued His parabolic teaching, knowing that these events furthered the near approach of His hour.

2 The king who made a marriage for his son represents the Father drawing souls unto Himself (John 6:44), so as to have communion with the joy of His Son. The bride is *not* mentioned; this is not the subject of the parable. Confusion of thought and of interpretation may arise if extraneous concepts are introduced into a parable together with their explanations. Moreover, in Matt 13 the Lord explained two of the parables, but when Scripture is silent as to its meaning we can but make suggestions, allowing other expositors to see other truth in the same parable. Such suggestions are valid only when:

1. they fit into the context of the parable, and

2. they concur with the overall truth of both OT and NT.

Additionally, in this case, the parable was spoken to the Jews in relation to kingdom truth as relating to themselves, so we must not expect to find complete parallels to what we now know as the more distinct church aspects of truth, even though we interpret the parable as referring to Gentiles being brought in to replace the Jewish nation in unbelief.

3 The servants sent by the king to call the guests were really "bondservants" (*doulos*), as the apostle Paul often called himself in the Epistles. These servants were essentially the apostles sent forth to call the Jewish nation during the Lord's lifetime; they were to go neither to Gentile nor to Samaritan, but to the "lost sheep of the house of Israel" (Matt 10:5-6). At the same time, on account of the previous parable (21:34-36), we must not rule out the possibility that the OT prophets may also be implied. The word for "marriage" (*gamos*) means either the wedding itself, or the subsequent wedding feast; the RV uses "marriage feast" as fitting the context.

In spite of the invitation (the verb "bidden" is the perfect passive participle of *kaleō*, "to call", implying a previous invitation that remained valid up to the time of the feast), the consistent testimony of the Gospels is that "they would not come". The same word *kaleō* is used for the actual summons to the feast. The Jews had no pleasure in the thought of the Son being their Messiah. Hence the world knew Him not, and His own people received Him not (John 1:10-11). When the implications of the divine teaching became too spiritual for them, they went back and walked no more with Him (John 6:66); although the Lord would have gathered them unto Him, yet they "would not" (Matt 23:37).

4 A second attempt was then made to gain the heart of the nation. "All things are ready" implies that the basis of communion had been accomplished; the oxen and fatlings point to the Lord's sacrificial death as the basis of grace, so the period immediately *after* His cross is visualised here. Hence the "other servants" sent forth speak of the further testimony to the Jews in the book of the Acts; for example, Philip, Stephen, Paul and Timothy appear as newly chosen servants of God. Originally, they still testified to the Jews, and the witness as a whole still circulated amongst the Jews, "preaching the word to none but unto the Jews only" (Acts 11:19). Even Paul's manner was to preach to the Jews first (17:2); in the beginning the divine order was "to the Jew first, and also to the Greek" (Rom 1:16; 2:9, 10).

In our verse, note that the word "bidden" is again the perfect passive participle as in v.3. The verb "have prepared" (*hetoimazō*) is in the aorist tense in some Greek manuscripts, namely, "I prepared", but in others, followed by the AV, RV,

JND it is in the perfect tense, "I have prepared". In other words, the preparation took place in v. 3, and this preparation remained until the second calling in v.4.

5 Making "light of it" (*ameleō*) means "not to care about it" or "to be negligent of it". This verb appears five times in the NT, such as "neglect not the gift that is in thee" (1 Tim 4:14); "How shall we escape, if we neglect so great salvation" (Heb 2:3), and "I will not be negligent to put you always in remembrance of these things" (2 Pet 1:12). In the parable, the Jews went "*their* ways", which contrasts with the similar parable in Luke 14, where the converse is stressed: "*my* house" and "*my* supper" (vv.23, 24). The motivation of man therefore contrasts sharply with the divine plan. The ways of men consisted of farming and merchandise; the cares of worldly enterprise came first; affections were set on things pertaining to self and not on the Lord's service. He had already set the proper perspective in Matt 6:31-34 where they were not to seek food or raiment at the expense of seeking first the kingdom of God and His righteousness. See Matt 6:19-21; Luke 10:40-42; 12:13-21.

6 The "remnant" (*hoi loipoi*, "the rest") were men who lived apart from business and mundane matters, but their attitude in dealing spitefully with the Lord's servants and killing them shows that they were religious men whose hard tradition caused them to eliminate the spiritual. That the servant would not be above his Lord was the warning He gave His own disciples in Matt 10:24. In the midst of wolves, they would be hated of all men, delivered up and scourged (vv.16-17) even to death. The Lord suffered at their hands *first of all* (as in the previous parable), and then the book of the Acts shows clearly that this persecution even unto death was perpetuated. Paul's witness of this treatment was that he was "buffeted ... reviled ... persecuted ... defamed ... made as the filth of the world" (1 Cor 4:11-13).

7 Hence the king in the parable destroyed those murderers and their city. This refers to the destruction of Jerusalem in AD 70 by the Romans, so often foretold in the NT. Their house would be desolated at that time, with not one stone left on another (Matt 24:2). Jerusalem would be compassed with armies, its desolation nigh (Luke 21:20). The Lord's last public utterance before His cross referred to this destruction of the city (Luke 23:28-31). The Chaldeans were the destroying invader in Hab 1:5, 6, and Paul quoted this in Acts 13:41, "Behold, ye despisers, and wonder, and perish", referring to what was to come upon the nation. The Romans in the parable under consideration are visualised as being "his armies", being used of God for His purpose in judgment; cf. Isa 10:5, 15 where the Assyrian army was "the rod of mine anger".

8 We now come to the second part of the parable in which the wedding feast was filled with guests. The feast being ready and those bidden being not worthy refers to the testimony after the Lord's death. These were men of the Jewish nation, "contradicting and blaspheming", from whom Paul turned away, since they had judged themselves "unworthy of everlasting life" (Acts 13:45-46). There was nothing good in themselves, and they were unwilling to avail themselves of the grace that justifies freely. Their eyes were closed, lest they should be converted (Acts 28:26-27).

9 Hence others would be bidden to the marriage feast from the highways. The two references to the Acts made in the previous verse both lead to the same result: "lo, we turn to the Gentiles" (Acts 13:46), and "the salvation of God is sent unto the Gentiles ... they will hear it" (Acts 28:28). In other words, we find here the whole purpose of God to maintain a testimony for Himself on earth, in spite of the rejection of Christ by the nation that He first called unto Himself. These new invitees correspond to the other nation in the previous parable (Matt 21:43).

The word "highways" consists of two nouns in Greek, namely, the accusative plural *tas diexodous tōn hodōn*, translated"the partings of the highways" (RV). Crossroads are implied, where more people could be contacted than on a road without junctions. Paul stopped to evangelise Thessalonica (Acts 17:1) since there the main east-west route crossed the main north-south route. In an extended sense, the crossroads in the parable refer to "all nations" (Matt 28: 19; Luke 24:47), and to "the uttermost part of the earth" (Acts 1:8). We should notice that at these crossroads the servants were to "bid" (***kaleō***) men to come – this is the proper work of the evangelist. On the other hand, in Luke 14:23, the one servant had to "compel" men to come in – this is the work of the Holy Spirit.

10 Both "bad and good" were gathered in. We see that Christendom responds to the invitation for its own ends. The wheat is found, but also the tares (Matt 13:24-26); both good and bad fish are caught together (13:47-49). All came in for the gain of communion, whether with spiritual motives, with carnal religious motives, or for material and financial advancement. Simon of Samaria came in for gain in his power of sorcery (Acts 8:9-24); false brethren came in to spy out the liberty of the saints (Gal 2:4); Diotrephes loved the pre-eminence, casting many out of the church (3 John 9-10).

But the reality of all who come in is tested. The "wedding garment" is the distinguishing feature of those who are His own. Such "have put on Christ" (Gal 3:27); they "have put on the new man" (Col 3:10; Eph 4:24). The "form of doctrine" (Rom 6:17) is like a mould, fashioning the believer under its influence unto Christ likeness. In the parable, the grace of wearing such a garment in the presence of the king was provided as an identity check, because of the wide-spread nature of the invitation. Believers today do not supply their own garment; even in the beginning God supplied garments evidently through death – the first sacrifice (Gen 3:21). In Luke 15:22, "the best robe" was provided by the father for the prodigal son who had returned, while in Zech 3:4, the promise was made, "I will clothe thee with change of raiment".

11 In the parable there now comes a second sifting. The *first* sifting had been when those called had refused to come, namely the Jewish nation kept on the outside, while a mixture of the Gentiles came in. The *second* sifting concerns those who did come in, but not in the fitness of Christ. The wedding garment speaks of being made fit for the Lord's presence. Believers possess imputed righteousness, this being the result of divine grace. Others may seek to establish their own righteousness (Rom 10:3), but this is not valid before God. In our v.11, the Lord came in "to see" the guests (*theaomai*, "to behold", RV), that is, to scrutinise them attentively and earnestly. At the present time, a man without a garment still has the opportunity to take the wedding garment unto salvation, since the Lord, whose eyes are a flame of fire, lingers in grace. But in the future, this opportunity will be lost, and judgment will follow.

12 The king called the man "Friend" (*hetairos*), a word occurring four times in the NT, all in Matthew's Gospel. For example, in Matt 26:50, the word is spoken to Judas, and means "companion, associate" but with no sense of endearment nor of attachment to the motives and deeds of the one addressed. The man became "speechless" before this scrutiny, reminding us of Rom 3:19, "every mouth may be stopped". Here is fear unrelieved in judgment, unlike the hand of grace that lifts up His own people when fear strikes for other reasons (Rev 1:17).

13 The word for "servants" (*diakonos*) is quite distinct from the previous one (*doulos*) in this parable. This word means "deacons, ministers", and does not refer to the evangelists suggested by the previous word in the passage. In fact, the NT is usually silent as to who accomplishes this fearful act of casting into outer darkness. In Rev 19:20; 20:15, the verb is in the passive voice; the one who casts in is not indicated. Admittedly, the saints shall judge the world (1 Cor 6:2), but in a millennial scene, and not touching on the judgment leading to outer darkness. Jude describes these men without a wedding garment as "wandering stars, to whom is reserved the blackness of darkness for ever" (v.13).

This is the principle of gathering out of the kingdom all things that offend (Matt 13:41); the angels there are described as casting them into a furnace of fire. "Outer darkness" is solemn to contemplate, since this is "everlasting destruction from the presence of the Lord" (2 Thess 1:9), and a "mist of darkness" reserved forever (2 Pet 2:17; Jude 13).

14 "Many are called, but few are chosen" also occurs in Matt 20:16, though there some editors of the Greek text omit it on manuscript evidence. But the phrase is completely genuine in the present parable. The many who are called are those who are bidden in vv.3, 9, Jews and Gentiles alike hearing the gospel message. Although there is only one man in the parable without a garment, he represents the many who will pass that way – called but not chosen. The few chosen ones are the "good", by grace having taken to themselves the wedding garment. The many are on the broad way, but the few are on the narrow way leading to life (Matt 7:13-14).

Various elements in these *three* parables have anticipated the *three* questions now to be put to the Lord by various religious factions. In the first parable, obedience was rendered (21:29), corresponding to rendering to God what is His due (22:21). In the second parable, there was no fruit, but resurrection (21:42), corresponding to the fact that there will be no children in resurrection (22:30-32). In the third parable, there was affection towards the king in those with a wedding garment, corresponding to "love" in the Lord's answer to the third question (22:37-40).

II. The Silencing of the Religious Leaders (22:15-46)

1. *The Herodians and the Tribute Money* 22:15-22

v.15 "Then went the Pharisees, and took counsel how they might entangle him in *his* talk.
v.16 And they sent out unto him their disciples with the Herodians, saying, Master, we know that thou art true, and teachest the way of God in truth, neither carest thou for any *man*: for thou regardest not the person of men.
v.17 Tell us therefore, What thinkest thou? Is it lawful to give tribute unto Caesar, or not?
v.18 But Jesus perceived their wickedness, and said, Why tempt ye me, *ye* hypocrites?
v.19 Shew me the tribute money. And they brought unto him a penny.
v.20 And he saith unto them, Whose *is* this image and superscription?
v.21 They say unto him, Caesar's. Then saith he unto them, Render therefore unto Caesar the things which are Caesar's; and unto God the things that are God's.
v.22 When they had heard *these words*, they marvelled, and left him, and went their way."

The first two of these three "trick" questions, and the concluding question posed by the Lord, appear in the three Synoptic Gospels Matthew, Mark and Luke. The background is more clearly presented in Luke 20:19-20. The intention of the priests to take the Lord was reaching a climax; His hour was drawing near. Their hatred had just been intensified, because they knew that the parable of the vineyard spelt out the end of their religious system (Matt 21:45; Luke 20:19). The fact that these leaders "feared the multitude" is extraordinary; they had a bad conscience before those who were attentive to hear the Lord's teaching.

15 Clearly there was still a big gap between the leaders and the people. In Luke 20:19, the priests sent forth "spies" – secret agents – to appear as just men. These agents were the Pharisees, Herodians and Sadducees. They conveniently forgot that the Lord had discerned the thoughts of men before, in which case, they could not possibly remain secret. Joshua had been deceived by the Gibeonites (Josh 9:15), but the Lord could never be deceived. Other men who deceived can be found in Acts 5:1-2; 20:30; Gal 2:4, and Tobiah in Neh 2:19; 13:4-5. If, in the Lord's answers, these priests had found one word out of place (an impossibility, of course), this would have been all that they needed to bring Him before Pilate. So in each case the Lord replied in such a way they could use nothing to their own advantage. This was like Festus later who had nothing against Paul to present to Caesar (Acts 25:26). But in the Lord's case, to achieve their end these religious leaders had to fabricate lies out of the Lord's answers, as in Luke 23:2 relating to the first question about the tribute money.

16-17 The Herodians were a party mainly political in nature, upholding the position of the Herods as the reigning power. The Pharisees formed the main religious party, having a strong hold over the Jewish interpretation of the law. Here both parties were bound together with a common interest, to try to trick the King of the Jews and the Son of God. A common bond between political and religious power can be a danger, as in Ps 2:1-2. It is this that reconciles the two passages Acts 9:23-24 and 2 Cor 11:32-33, where Paul had to escape by means of a basket from a common plot by the religious Jews and the political aspirations of the king of Damascus. Again, the two beasts in Rev 13 are political and religious leaders (the emperor of the revived Roman empire and the anti-Christ), moving in harmony with each other until their mutual destruction (Rev 19:20). Today, political control over a state church leads to unbelief, formality and barrenness.

These men approached the Lord with flattery, making statements that they did not really believe: "Master, we know that thou art true, and teachest the way of God in truth". The orator for the Jews in Acts 24:2-4 did the same thing. Everything that the Pharisees said was true, although emerging from hearts of unbelief. "Thou regardest not the person of men" is subtle, intended to place the Lord in an inconsistent position by attempting to get Him to minimise the authority and status of Caesar in Rome. They tried to place their required answer into His mouth even before posing the question. Privately, they objected to paying a tax to the Romans – in effect they hated the fourth beast of Dan 7:7. But they conveniently used the situation against the Lord; should their money be given to Caesar? (Consider things given or shown to the nations in the OT: by Asa, 1 Kings 15:18; by Jehoash, 2 Kings 12:18; by Ahaz, 2 Kings 16:8; by Hezekiah, 2 Kings 18:15; 20:13). If the Lord had answered, No, He would have been denying the authority of Caesar; to have answered, Yes, would have been in conflict with Jewish opinion. In either case, they would have taken action!

18-21 However, the Lord knew their motives, and would not become Involved in political matters. He commenced His answer by saying, "Why tempt ye me, ye hypocrites?", recalling the Lord's statement to Satan, "Thou shalt not tempt the Lord thy God" (Luke 4:12). When the people chided with Moses at Massah, this was equivalent to tempting the Lord, a fact recorded many times in the OT to indicate its solemn nature (Exod 17:1-2; Deut 6:16; Ps 78:18, 41; 95:8; 1 Cor 10:9). The tribute money was "a penny", that is, the Roman denarius. This amount was a daily wage (Matt 20:1-16); two of these coins were given to the inn-keeper by the good Samaritan (Luke 10:35). The coin had marked upon it both the name of the Roman emperor, and an image of his head. This was the fourth beast (both leader and empire) at that time (Dan 7:7), heading up ultimately in the future beast described in Rev 13:1-10. The image on the coin will be developed into a larger image in that future day (Rev 13:14-15), with life being given to it so that it will be worshipped; this shows the ultimate development of world politics.

Although the Lord asked, "Whose is this image and superscription?", He did not state that the coin, or its value in tax, belonged to Caesar. It is the responsibility of man to recognise what is due and to whom; certainly tribute must be paid (Rom 13:6). The leaders are God's ministers, whether or not they act responsibly (Rom 13:6). Thus Nebuchadnezzar was God's "servant" in spite of what he did (Jer 25:9; 27:6; 43:10). (Tribute was paid by the Lord in Matt 17:24-27, though this was a temple tax, and though He as the Son was "free".)

The Lord's answer implies that taxes are rightly paid to the authorities, provided that there is a proper balance of priorities (1 Pet 2:13-17), with each individual assessing what is due to God. Certainly David did this when he said at the end of his life, "all things come of thee, and of thine own have we given thee" (1 Chron 29:14). It was therefore up to the priests and scribes, the Pharisees and Herodians, to decide upon the legality of the tribute money; the Lord stated a principle, and they had to apply it.

22 His words could not be further pulled into pieces even by their false methods of thinking; rather, they had to apply the answer to their own lives. Hence "they went their way" in our verse, and they "held their peace" (Luke 20:26). In other words, they retired silenced and humiliated before the people; when they had regained their composure, they turned the Lord's answer into a lie before Pilate, "We found this fellow perverting the nation, and forbidding to give tribute to Caesar, saying that he himself is Christ a King" (Luke 23:2). Such men will be forever silenced at the judgment of the great white throne, but will then retire to the lake of fire.

2. *The Sadducees and the Resurrection* 22:23-33

v.23 "The same day came to him the Sadducees, which say that there is no resurrection, and asked him,
v.24 Saying, Master, Moses said, If a man die, having no children, his brother shall marry his wife, and raise up seed unto his brother.
v.25 Now there were with us seven brethren: and the first, when he had married a wife, deceased, and, having no issue, left his wife unto his brother:
v.26 Likewise the second also, and the third, unto the seventh.
v.27 And last of all the woman died also.
v.28 Therefore in the resurrection whose wife shall she be of the seven? for they all had her.
v.29 Jesus answered and said unto them, Ye do err, not knowing the scriptures, nor the power of God.
v.30 For in the resurrection they neither marry, nor are given in marriage, but are as the angels of God in heaven.
v.31 But as touching the resurrection of the dead, have ye not read that which was spoken unto you by God, saying,
v.32 I am the God of Abraham, and the God of Isaac, and the God of Jacob? God is not the God of the dead, but of the living.
v.33 And when the multitude heard *this*, they were astonished at his doctrine."

23 Men who were disunited in doctrine were now united in their efforts against the Lord. How universal this is! In the past, men offering ideologies from various nations were united against the Lord (Ps 2:1-3); Pilate and Herod were united against Him (Luke 23:12). In the future, men will have "one mind" against the Lord (Rev 17:13). In Paul's later days, differences in doctrine brought about different attitudes towards the apostle on the part of the Pharisees and the Sadducees (Acts 23:6-10), but against the Lord these parties provided in order a series of subtle tricksters. The Sadducees denied the resurrection, angels and spirits; their world was a materialistic one only, but "the Pharisees confess both" (Acts 23:8).

24-28 These Sadducees quoted the law of Moses to the Lord, attempting to show themselves righteously interested in the OT. But they wove an almost impossible situation around their quotation. The object of the law that they quoted was that the first husband's name should be preserved in Israel (Deut 25:5-6). If he died with no children as a result of his marriage, then his brother should become the first wife's new husband, rather than a stranger outside the family. The first son to be born would continue the name of the first husband. Thus Ruth's first husband Mahlon died, with no children. Hence she married Boaz "to raise up the name of the dead" (Ruth 4:10), although the first husband had been a man of Moab; this led to Obed being the firstborn. The Sadducees then made postulates for a trick question. The number "seven" of the brothers was *their* choice of a number, *not God's* choice. We cannot see therefore that the number has any special significance, though when the number seven is used by God it denotes completeness; perhaps the Sadducees had borrowed this concept from the OT. They systematically made these seven men, one by one, husbands of this one wife by quite a legal process! The situation was quite unlike what we find in John 4:18, where the woman of Samaria had had five husbands, and she knew that she was guilty.

Their question in v.28 implied something quite illogical to minds that rejected the doctrine of resurrection, for they thought that the woman would have seven husbands at the same time. This may have been a puzzle to them in their efforts to discredit the resurrection, and they may never have been satisfied by their opponents' answers. By using the words "*the* resurrection" in their question, they implied some kind of general resurrection, about which the Scriptures know nothing. In fact, there are different groups in resurrection: for example, Christ the firstfruits (1 Cor 15:23), followed by every man in his own order, namely the resurrection of believers at the rapture of the church (1 Thess 4:16); then the "first resurrection" at the Lord's coming in glory (Rev 20:4-5). Both are resurrections "*out from among* the dead", leaving the rest behind.

29 The Lord issued a three-fold condemnation:

1. "Ye do err",

2. they did not know the OT Scriptures,

3. they did not know the power of God (Eph 1:19-20).

The Greek verb for "err" is *planaō*, from which the English word "planet" is derived. It is quite a common word in the NT, with a variety of translations. In the active voice it means "to lead astray", "to deceive". In the passive voice it means "to be led astray", "to err" (as here). Others take it to be in the middle voice (namely, reflexive), "ye deceive yourselves". The Lord never excused the holding of false doctrine. The Corinthians adopted the principle: "what you cannot understand or explain rationally, deny", so they denied the future resurrection of the believer. Hence Paul used the whole of 1 Cor 15 to explain the position, linking the believer's resurrection with that of Christ – if the former was not possible, neither was the latter with all its terrible consequences. Later, doctrinal difficulties became established doctrinal error, "who concerning the truth have erred, saying that the resurrection is past already; and overthrow the faith of some" (2 Tim 2:18). It appears that such men were excommunicated as being unfit to have fellowship in a local assembly (1 Tim 1:20).

30 This verse corresponds to "ye do err"; vv.31, 32a correspond to "not knowing the scriptures"; v. 32b to "not knowing … the power of God".

The insinuations of the Sadducees were all wrong. There is no marriage ceremony in heaven, except in a spiritual sense between the Lamb and the church as His bride (Rev 19:7). By these remarks, the Lord did *not* fully answer the Sadducees' question about relationships formed on earth being transferred to heaven. Rather, the Lord stressed the fact that there is still life *after* death and *before* the resurrection – to add confusion to the Sadducees' minds rather than to enlighten them. In fact, those who have died in faith are "as the angels of God in heaven", or "equal unto the angels" (Luke 20:36). This does not imply that believers will be identical to the angels, but will have certain characteristics in common, namely living for ever, and having freedom from the necessities of earth such as food and marriage.

31-32 The Lord proved that there is life beyond physical death by one simple quotation from the OT. Note the differences in the three Synoptic Gospels: in our verse in Matthew's Gospel, it is "*God* spake unto *you*, saying, I am the God of Abraham"; in Mark 12:26 it is "*God* spake unto *Moses*, saying, I am the God of Abraham"; in Luke 20:37 it is "*Moses* called the Lord the God of Abraham". In Exod 3:6, the words are those of God. So Luke 20:37 must mean that Moses *recorded* this title of Deity when he wrote Exodus, but he did not call God directly by this title. The changing of the words "unto Moses" to "unto you" is quite a common feature in the NT. God's words to others in the OT are interpreted in the NT as words to NT believers; see Rom 4:23-24; Heb 10:15-16; 1 Pet 1:12.

The growth of this divine title, "Abraham", "Abraham, Isaac", "Abraham, Isaac, Jacob" is found in Gen 26:24; 28:13. The Lord's meaning is that, when God used this title, the men were *still* alive as to the spirit, though physically dead and awaiting the resurrection. This deduction hinges on the present tense "I am" (*egō eimi*) and not the past tense "I was"; in Mark 12:26 the present tense is implied, since *egō* "I" alone is used. Regarding life in this intermediate state, see Luke 16:22; Rom 14:8; 2 Cor 5:8; Rev 6:9. Thus "God is … the God … of the living" applies to all OT and NT believers who have passed from the scene of their labours and testimony.

33 This answer silenced the Sadducees (v.34), and the multitudes who were present heard it and were astonished at the doctrinal capability of the Lord. No doubt they were glad that one carefully-selected OT quotation could demolish the rationality of leaders who were humiliated with embarrassment before the common people. The Lord showed no mercy to men of that calibre.

3. *The Pharisees and the Great Commandment* 22:34-40

v.34 "But when the Pharisees had heard that he had put the Sadducees to silence, they were gathered together.

v.35 Then one of them, *which was* a lawyer, asked *him a question*, tempting him, and saying,
v.36 Master, which *is* the great commandment in the law?
v.37 Jesus said unto him, Thou shalt love the Lord thy God with all thy heart, and with all thy soul, and with all thy mind.
v.38 This is the first and great commandment.
v.39 And the second *is* like unto it, Thou shalt love thy neighbour as thyself.
v.40 On these two commandments hang all the law and the prophets."

34-35 As a result of the silencing of the Sadducees, the Pharisees entered into the conflict again, presenting moderate scribes (Mark 12:28; Luke 20:39), one of whom was a "lawyer" as spokesman. Scribes and lawyers were the same class of men; they formulated and preserved their rules of religion. No mention is made of this third question in Luke 20:39, only the conclusion, "Master, thou hast well said"; compare this with Mark 7:37, "He hath done all things well". On the other hand, Mark 12:28-34 contains a longer account of this event.

36 In asking "Master (Teacher), which is the great commandment in the law?", the lawyer evidently wanted one single answer, but in the Lord's reply He provided two, as in Matt 22:21, where both the Godward and manward sides appear. The Lord provided balanced answers to unbalanced questions, since the law itself was divided into two parts – Godward and manward aspects (Exod 20:2-11 and 12-17).

37-39 Both these aspects of the answer have appeared before, a lawyer having quoted them from the OT as a result of his own question, "what shall I do to inherit eternal life?"; the parable of the Good Samaritan was then given to define the word "neighbour" (Luke 10:25-28).

"Thou shalt love the Lord thy God with all thy heart, and with all thy soul, and with all thy mind" is quoted from Deut 6:5, where the words "heart, soul, might" occur. In Mark 12:30 all four words appear, "heart, soul, mind, strength", while in Luke 10:27 the order (spoken by the lawyer) is "heart, soul, strength, mind". The word "all" occurs before all these words, showing that God requires every part of a human personality to be directed pre-eminently towards Himself. The "heart" relates to the motivation and obedience of love; the "soul" to the spiritual character of love; the "strength" to the effort behind love (to distinguish it from a careless, easy-going attitude); the "mind" to the intellectual side (an aspect not to be discarded even by a believer). Each of these concepts is present in 1 Cor 13:5-7: "rejoiceth in the truth" is the heart; "believeth all things" is the soul; "endureth all things" is the strength; "thinketh no evil" is the mind. In just the same way as faith is shown by works, so too love Godward is shown by love manward; hence James also quoted "Thou shalt love thy neighbour as thyself", calling this "the royal law" (James 2:8). This quotation from Lev 19:18 was also used by the Lord both in Matt 19:19 when addressing the rich young ruler, and also in the Sermon on the Mount (Matt 5:43). The word "neighbour" appears several times in Lev 19:13-18; there general relationships between the children of Israel are in question (proper wages, no bribes), and in Matt 5:44, the Lord extended the scope to include one's enemies. In the parable of the Good Samaritan the neighbour is the man who showed such great mercy, and in James 2:5 "the poor of this world" rich in faith and chosen by God. Thus love is not restricted in the class of men to which it reaches. John described this love as not being in word or in tongue, but "in deed and in truth" (1 John 3:18), while Paul wrote, "As we have therefore opportunity, let us do good unto all men, especially unto them who are of the household of faith" (Gal 6:10).

40 The Lord's conclusion was that all the law and the prophets were based on these two commandments, and this can be traced in verses such as Exod 20:6; Deut 30:16, 20; Josh 22:5; Ps 145:20; Amos 5:15.

Mark 12:32-34 presents a quite different conclusion. The scribe was deeply touched by the Lord's response, saying, "thou hast said the truth". Such love towards God and towards one's neighbour "is more than all whole burnt offerings and sacrifices". The scribe partially echoed David in Ps 51:16-17, where the psalmist recognised that God no longer desired animal sacrifice or burnt offering, only the sacrifices of a broken spirit. The same sentiments are expressed in Ps 40:6-8 and Heb 10:5-9, where Messiah, delighting to do His will, is substituted for the four types of offerings. In Lam 2:7 the Lord had cast off His altar – a different kind of sacrifice was desired. In NT times, love and sacrifice are seen perfectly in Christ, for He "hath loved us, and hath given himself for us an offering and a sacrifice to God for a sweet-smelling savour" (Eph 5:2). Not that the scribe had reached that level of appreciation, yet he had answered "discreetly" (*nounechōs*, lit. having understanding), enabling the Lord to comment, "Thou art not far from the kingdom of God". Yet a barrier remained, for he failed to perceive that the One whom he was addressing was Christ.

4. *The Question to End all Questions* 22:41-46

v.41 "While the Pharisees were gathered together, Jesus asked them,
v.42 Saying, What think ye of Christ? whose son is he? They say unto him, *The son* of David.
v.43 He saith unto them, How then doth David in spirit call him Lord, saying,
v.44 The LORD said unto my Lord, Sit thou on my right hand, till I make thine enemies thy footstool?
v.45 If David then call him Lord, how is he his son?
v.46 And no man was able to answer him a word, neither durst any *man* from that day forth ask him any more *questions*."

41 The Pharisees still remained gathered together, in spite of the failure of their last spokesman. Perhaps they were plotting a further question, but they were forestalled by the Lord asking them a question that they could not even attempt to answer.

42 The first part of the Lord's question, "What think ye of Christ? whose son is he?", was intended to drive the Pharisees into their own hole of unbelief: "Whoso diggeth a pit shall fall therein" (Prov 26:27), "he shall fall himself into his own pit" (Prov 28:10). The Pharisees knew the Messianic promises in the OT, and knew that the Messiah would be "the son of David", but they remained in ignorance as to how such a promise could ever be put into effect.

43-45 Based upon the Pharisees' confession, the Lord then asked a subsequent question that stumbled them completely. Amongst men, the order of precedence was father-son; no father would look up to his son and address him as "My Lord". How, then, could Christ be David's Son, whom David called "my Lord" (Ps 110:1). By not being able to answer this question, the Pharisees showed their ignorance of their own Scriptures. Yet this divine One whom David called "my Lord" was his Son, in keeping with many Messianic prophecies, such as "The Lord hath sworn in truth to David ... Of the fruit of thy body will I set upon thy throne" (Ps 132:11); "a rod out of the stem of Jesse" (Isa 11:1); "I will raise unto David a righteous Branch" (Jer 23:5).

In Matt 22:43, it is "David in spirit" (*en pneumati*) – interpreted as "in the Spirit" in the RV; in Mark 12:36, it is "by the Holy Ghost", but in Luke 20:42, it is "in the book of Psalms", implying inspiration (2 Sam 23:2). The Lord quoted this Messianic Psalm 110 as He looked forward to His ascension when He will occupy the Father's throne, until He comes forth to subdue His enemies at the battle of Armageddon, when He will sit upon His own throne of glory.

David was in good company when he acknowledged his Son as "my Lord", for others said the same thing: Elizabeth just before His birth (Luke 1:43); Mary at the tomb (John 20:13); Thomas in the upper room (v. 28), and Paul (Phil 3:8). In all cases, the lesser owns His Person as the greatest.

The "right hand" was a position of status, nearness, identity, authority and exaltation; it occurs five times in the Epistle to the Hebrews (1:3, 13; 8:1; 10:12; 12:2), obviously referring to Ps 110. How, then, can this Lord be David's Son? The religious leaders knew nothing of this truth. For this Son was God manifest in the flesh, the Manhood of Christ according to the flesh deriving legally through the royal line (Rom 1:3), and physically through Mary. The question was an insoluble riddle apart from the incarnation.

46 No man could answer this question; the Lord had silenced these leaders completely, since no further questions were forthcoming. But the Lord did not let the matter end there; His final condemnation of the Pharisees is found in the next chapter. In other words, the Lord would not leave this scene without having issued this condemnation in very plain language.

III. The Final Condemnation of the Pharisees (23:1-39)

1. *The Self-importance of the Pharisees* 23:1-12

v.1 "Then spake Jesus to the multitude, and to his disciples,
v.2 Saying, The scribes and the Pharisees sit in Moses' seat:
v.3 All therefore whatsoever they bid you observe, *that* observe and do: but do not ye after their works: for they say, and do not.
v.4 For they bind heavy burdens and grievous to be borne, and lay *them* on men's shoulders, but they *themselves* will not move them with one of their fingers.
v.5 But all their works they do for to be seen of men: they make broad their phylacteries, and enlarge the borders of their garments,
v.6 And love the uppermost rooms at feasts, and the chief seats in the synagogues,
v.7 And greetings in the markets, and to be called of men, Rabbi, Rabbi.
v.8 But be not ye called Rabbi: for one is your Master, *even* Christ: and all ye are brethren.
v.9 And call no *man* your father upon the earth: for one is your Father, which is in heaven.
v.10 Neither be ye called masters: for one is your Master, *even* Christ.
v.11 But he that is greatest among you shall be your servant.
v.12 And whosoever shall exalt himself shall be abased: and he that shall humble himself shall be exalted."

This long chapter of denunciation appears only briefly in Mark 12:38-40; Luke 11:39-52; 20:45- 47. The very similar passage in Luke 11 was obviously spoken on another occasion — in a Pharisee's house who had marvelled that the Lord had not ceremonially washed before a meal. Hence in Matt 23 the Lord used the occasion to present a survey and a summary of previous denunciations, as a warning to formal religionists throughout the ages. For there were two kinds of religious men importantly strutting about the stage when the Lord was here: the priests who engaged in the formality of the ceremonial law, and the Pharisees who engaged in the formality of the moral law. In vv.1-12 we have the self-exaltation of the religious man; in vv.13-33 the hypocrisy of the religious man, and in vv.34-39 the judgment of the religious man. From v.13 to v.29 we have eight "woes", seven being the number of completion, and the extra one representing what is filled up, as in v.32. However, we should point out that v.14 (though it properly appears in Mark 12:40; Luke 20:47) does not appear in many Greek manuscripts, and is therefore omitted in the RV and JND; we have discussed how this phenomenon could come about under Matt 18:11.

1 The following paragraph was spoken about the Pharisees to the multitude and to the disciples, but no doubt in the hearing of the Pharisees. For from v.13 onwards, the Lord spoke directly to the Pharisees, no doubt in the hearing of the multitude and His disciples. The disciples would take this as a lesson — the Lord's assessment of religious failure in others when the scribes and Pharisees had placed themselves beyond the scope of correction.

2 These men sat "in Moses' seat", namely they taught the law of Moses and claimed to have the same authority as that great leader of the past had in his day. The difference was that Moses' authority came from God, but the Pharisees' authority derived from self. They claimed to be "Moses' disciples" (John 9:28), yet the Lord said that Moses in whom they trusted, accused the Pharisees, for if they really believed in the law of Moses then they would also believe in Himself (John 5:45-47). How different was Ezra, who was "a ready scribe in the law of Moses, which the Lord God of Israel had given" (Ezra 7:6).

3 The Greek manuscripts, and the RV and JND, make a change in the beginning of this verse. The first word "observe" is omitted, while "observe and do" is changed to "do and observe (keep)". Men in high places who do not believe that the Scriptures are the Word of God, may nevertheless speak correct things, but it is by their fruit that they are known. If they quote the Word of God, then we follow, not because of their word, but because it is the Word of God; not that their quotations of the Word justify their unbelief! For God's intention is that teachers should be consistent – they should be examples, their works being based on the Scriptures. Hearers of the Word must be doers of the Word also (James 1:22), otherwise their religion is vain (v.26). Jewish teachers boasted in the law, yet by breaking the law they dishonoured God (Rom 2:23). How different was the Lord's case; His works confirmed His teaching (John 10:38). Hence the Pharisees' works were not to be followed, even though they were leaders. For ourselves, as for Timothy, we must be "an example... in word, in conversation, in charity, in spirit, in faith, in purity" (1 Tim 4:12).

4 The Pharisees forced heavy burdens upon men, but they themselves refused to carry any, living an easy kind of life spelt out in the following verses. Here were traditions and rigidity, bound up in great bundles of heavy duties. They did not help others to carry out these duties, and did not lift a finger to help the Lord carry His cross. Simon of Cyrene was compelled to carry it when the Lord, because of the effect of the scourging, was unable physically to carry it. By contrast, disciples have to carry their crosses, and the Lord assures that this burden is light (Matt 11:30). The attitude of the Pharisees is still prevalent today; the majority of men find no interest in the denominationalistic structure of Christendom, because ritual is imposed on adherents, and strangers to such practice find it a burden.

5 Instead, the Pharisees' works were concocted for open display, "to be seen of men". In Matt 6, they gave alms, made prayers openly, and engaged in fasting, all before men, so as to receive glory – this was their reward, and certainly there would be no heavenly reward afterwards. Such an open display of religious carnality was the opposite of the principle under which the apostle Paul moved in his service, "as unknown, and yet well known" (2 Cor 6:9). The Lord's consistent attitude was, "I receive not honour from men" (John 5:41); He neither desired it nor sought it.

A phylactery (*phulaktērion*) was a piece of parchment attached to the forehead or left arm by a strap; on the parchment were written quotations from the law, so that these might be prominent before mind and heart. The proper motive of the wearer was that this phylactery should be for a testimony and not for self-glory

Speaking of the annual Passover feast, the Lord said to Moses, "It shall be for a sign unto thee upon thine hand, and for a memorial between thine eyes, that the Lord's law may be in thy mouth" (Exod 13:9). or "it shall be for a token upon thine hand, and for frontiers between thine eyes" (v.16). Moses said the same thing in Deut 6:8-9, adding, "thou shalt write them upon the posts of thy house, and on thy gates". Again, this appears in Deut 11:18, with the comment "Therefore shall ye lay up these my words in your heart and in your soul". But the Pharisees increased this ritual by their own additions, thereby removing the purpose and the motivation of the practice; it was an attitude of self-show and self-glory.

Similarly with "the borders of their garments". In Num 15:38-39, they had been commanded to make "fringes in the borders of their garments" and upon these to put "a ribband of blue"; men would look at these fringes, and "remember all the commandments of the Lord, and do them" – they were not to seek after their own heart or eyes. In order to boast in the law, the Pharisees were enlarging these borders, but as the Lord said, "they say, and do not" (Matt 23:3). The ritual, especially in its outward show, had been transcended by the Lord in Matt 5:16, "that they may see your good words, and glorify your Father which is in heaven". Moral light from heaven, not ritualistic heavenly blue, was to be seen and displayed.

6 The "uppermost rooms" were the chief reclining places at a table used for a feast, the Greek noun being *prōtoklisia*, with a variety of renderings in the AV and RV. Here was the outward Pharisaical pride in associating with the highest men at such feasts. When the Lord saw this practice in Luke 14:7, He gave instructions that men should take the lowest position, moving up in order of status only if invited to do so, for "whosoever exalteth himself shall be abased; and he that humbleth himself shall be exalted" (v.11). See 1 Pet 5:5-6 and the Lord's example in John 13:4-17. Today, some believers may forsake a small local assembly for the ostentation of a large one; the idea of "chief seats in the synagogues" (*prōtokathedria*) is also not unknown in a local assembly. James warns about such a practice (James 2:1-4), particularly where riches and superior clothing secure such recognition.

7-10 The religious self-exaltation of the Pharisees caused them to enjoy not only what men saw them to be but also how men addressed them. Evidently the ordinary people reserved a special form of greeting for the Pharisees in the public places of Jerusalem; they loved to have it so in order to preserve their status and reputation. The duplicated title "Rabbi" was a reverent form of address, also denoting an authorised teacher. But teachers amongst the Lord's people do not need titles granted by men as a sign of theological authority to teach; authority and ability to teach in spiritual things come from the Lord through the Holy Spirit, and not through the schools of men. Such titles, both then and now, distract from the pre-eminence of Christ over all those who are brethren in the family of God. The TR has *kathēgētēs* once in v.8 and twice in v.10, translated "Master" in the AV. But the editors of the Greek text amend v.8 to read *didaskalos* – "teacher" (RV), though JND uses "instructor" in all three places. The word *kathēgētēs*, occurring nowhere else in the NT, also means teacher, in the sense of a guide. Of course, believers in a local assembly must recognise those who are chosen by God to guide the flock, those "who have spoken unto you the word of God" (Heb 13:7), namely the overseers or elders who are "apt to teach" (1 Tim 3:2), and we know that such men are equipped by God for their work. But while the Lord was given the title "Rabbi" many times, these men in an assembly are never dignified by such an appellation.

In v.9, the Lord did not mean that men must not recognise their human fathers according to the flesh; parents are to be honoured (Eph 6:2). Rather, He meant: don't give them a position and status that distracts from the Fatherhood of God (Matt 10:37). The general principle therefore is, glory in One divine having these positions, but there should be no glorying in man as teacher, father or leader.

11-12 Verse 11 echoes Matt 20:27, where in the context the Lord is included as also ministering in a lowly position. But here, the word "greatest" should properly be "greater" (RV marg), implying that Christ, the greatest One, does not appear in the verse, only in the previous three verses. We are all brethren and we are all servants (*diakonos*); this excludes self-exaltation. God reverses what man would esteem. The exalted one shall be abased, the proud, mighty and rich are brought low (Luke 1:51-53). But the humble one shall be exalted, "He raiseth up the poor out of the dust, and lifteth up the beggar ... to make them inherit the throne of glory" (1 Sam 2:8). The former were the Pharisees, the latter the apostles. It is tragic if believers walk as men and emulate the Pharisees. This was the fault of the Corinthians in 1 Cor 14; all was done for outward show in their meetings, and therefore could not lead to edification.

2. *The Seven Woes upon the Pharisees* 23:13-33

v.13 "But woe unto you, scribes and Pharisees, hypocrites! for ye shut up the kingdom of heaven against men: for ye neither go in *yourselves*, neither suffer ye them that are entering to go in.

v.14 Woe unto you, scribes and Pharisees, hypocrites! for ye devour widows' houses, and for a pretence make long prayer: therefore ye shall receive the greater damnation.

v.15 Woe unto you, scribes and Pharisees, hypocrites! for ye compass sea and land to make one proselyte, and when he is made, ye make him twofold more the child of hell than yourselves.
v.16 Woe unto you, *ye* blind guides, which say, Whosoever shall swear by the temple, it is nothing; but whosoever shall swear by the gold of the temple, he is a debtor!
v.17 *Ye* fools and blind: for whether is greater, the gold, or the temple that sanctifieth the gold?
v.18 And, Whosoever shall swear by the altar, it is nothing; but whosoever sweareth by the gift that is upon it, he is guilty.
v.19 *Ye* fools and blind: for whether *is* greater, the gift, or the altar that sanctifieth the gift?
v.20 Whoso therefore shall swear by the altar, sweareth by it, and by all things thereon.
v.21 And whoso shall swear by the temple, sweareth by it, and by him that dwelleth therein.
v.22 And he that shall swear by heaven, sweareth by the throne of God, and by him that sitteth thereon.
v.23 Woe unto you, scribes and Pharisees, hypocrites! for ye pay tithe of mint and anise and cummin, and have omitted the weightier *matters* of the law, judgment, mercy, and faith: these ought ye to have done, and not to leave the other undone.
v.24 *Ye* blind guides, which strain at a gnat, and swallow a camel.
v.25 Woe unto you, scribes and Pharisees, hypocrites! for ye make clean the outside of the cup and of the platter, but within they are full of extortion and excess.
v.26 *Thou* blind Pharisee, cleanse first that *which is* within the cup and platter, that the outside of them may be clean also.
v.27 Woe unto you, scribes and Pharisees, hypocrites! for ye are like unto whited sepulchres, which indeed appear beautiful outward, but are within full of dead *men's* bones, and of all uncleanness.
v.28 Even so ye also outwardly appear righteous unto men, but within ye are full of hypocrisy and iniquity.
v.29 Woe unto you, scribes and Pharisees, hypocrites! because ye build the tombs of the prophets, and garnish the sepulchres of the righteous,
v.30 And say, If we had been in the days of our fathers, we would not have been partakers with them in the blood of the prophets.
v.31 Wherefore ye be witnesses unto yourselves, that ye are the children of them which killed the prophets.
v.32 Fill ye up then the measure of your fathers.
v.33 *Ye* serpents, *ye* generation of vipers, how can ye escape the damnation of hell?"

13 *The first woe*. The word *ouai* is an interjection, always translated in the NT as "woe" except in Rev 18:10,16,19 where it is rendered "Alas, alas, that great city". Hence it is normally used as a sign of denunciation, but in these last three occurrences as a sign of grief. The word appears almost exclusively in Matthew, Luke and Revelation; it is used for the three "woes" in Rev 8:13 as another name for the last three trumpet judgments.

The word "hypocrites" (*hupokritēs*) originally meant a stage-actor, so here it implies a religious actor where the externals and internals do not correspond. The word was used only by the Lord, and is recorded only by Matthew and Luke with a single occurrence in Mark 7:6. In Matt 23, the word occurs with all eight woes, except the fourth in v.16. If v.14 is omitted as previously explained, then the word occurs six times in the chapter, the number of man.

In Luke 20:20, these men attempted to "feign themselves justmen", this being the mark of a hypocrite. They sought to prevent men who were exercised towards the kingdom from entering in, in just the same way as today men of non-evangelical persuasion spurn the evangelical doctrine of salvation through the sacrifice of Christ. The Lord said a similar thing in Luke 11:52, where the lawyers had taken away "the key of knowledge" so as to hinder men who were entering in. Entering in must be by wholesome doctrine. At that time, the key was that interpretation of the OT that perceived Christ in all the Scriptures (Luke 24:27, 44-46); by insisting on their own interpretation, the Pharisees effectively blocked any true understanding of the inspired OT Scriptures. Later, "the Pharisees which believed" sought to do the same thing in the churches in Jerusalem and Antioch (Acts 15:1-5). No doubt this is an example of offending one of the little ones, but if they keep the truth from those who are exercised, then the Lord also keeps the truth from men of Pharisaical intent, by ensuring that they remain blind and ignorant – "that they which see might be made blind" (John 9:39).

14 As we have pointed out, this verse is missing in some Greek manuscripts, so it is also omitted from the RV and JND. However, it rightly appears in both Mark 12:40 and Luke 20:47 – both occasions being the same as that in Matt 23, so the words were actually spoken by the Lord. In Mark and Luke, the word "beware" is used rather than "woe".

The Pharisees gained the ear of devout widows by means of their pretended sanctity, and took of their substance to further their own ends. The fact that God was "against those that oppress ... the widow" (Mal 3:5) was conveniently overlooked. The word for "damnation" (*krima*) is properly "condemnation", and the Lord implied that there will be degrees of condemnation passed on unbelievers. This particular Pharisaical venture into widows' homes reminds us of Paul's warning later, that there will be men ready to "creep into houses, and lead captive silly women laden with sins" (2 Tim 3:6). Again, we have commented upon the making of long prayers in Matt 6:5,7; the Pharisee who stood and prayed "with himself" was neither heard not justified, rather he was abased because he exalted himself (Luke 18:10-14).

15 *The second woe*. All religious sects and political parties seek converts to their own persuasion. To "compass sea and land" does not necessarily mean that they went overseas seeking converts, but that when overseas visitors were in Jerusalem (for the feast days, for example), they were attacked by Pharisaical propaganda, no doubt warning them about the Lord's teaching. Of course, Christians also engage in this activity, and rightly so, for the Lord sent the apostles to "the uttermost part of the earth (Acts 1:8), saying "Go ye into all the world" (Mark 16:15). In the same way, Peter's teaching compassed sea and land on the day of Pentecost, for men from many nations were present (Acts 2:8-11). A "proselyte" (*prosēlutos*) was a convert from the Gentiles to the Jewish religion, mentioned in Acts 2:10 at the festival of Pentecost; they worshipped in the synagogues (Acts 13:42,43; 17:4); some were faithful such as the centurion in Capernaum, who built the Jews a synagogue (Luke 7:5), and Cornelius (Acts 10:2). But in our verse, the Lord was speaking of proselytes who had been gained for the Pharisees' particular brand of religion. The heathen became worse than their teachers, for they were not delivered from their own heathen vices and ignorance (unlike converts to Christianity, who are delivered from their pre-conversion conduct). In fact, they became "the child of hell", bringing forth nothing but the produce of death – "their throat is an open sepulchre" (Ps 5:9, Matt 23:27; Rom 3:13). Elsewhere, the Lord accused the Pharisees of being "of your father the devil" (John 8:44). It appears that it was easy to gain converts, for the minds of unconverted men can easily be swayed downwards, as is evident today in the rapid growth of false cults. Thus it was easy to cry out "Absalom reigneth in Hebron", and those who followed "increased continually" (2 Sam 15:10-12). It was only necessary for Adonijah to call out "I will be king", and some of David's leaders turned their allegiance to him (1 Kings 1:5-10). It was all so easy, since some men traded in the natural weaknesses and propensities of their fellows. But to gain a convert to Christ is far from easy, needing all the power of the Holy Spirit.

16-22 *The third woe*. The Lord's comments on the general method of swearing and on the Pharisaical method must be understood in the light of Matt 5:33-37 where He said to His disciples, "Swear not at all", not by heaven, earth, Jerusalem or one's own head, and also in the light of James 5:12, "swear not, neither by heaven, neither by the earth, neither by any other oath".

The Pharisees had a defined order of priorities by which they took oaths. They claimed that the gold was greater than the temple, and that the gift was greater than the altar (vv.16, 18). By His answers, the Lord was not condoning the existence of Herod's temple, nor the ritualistic practices that took place there. He was merely putting logic into the minds of the illogical Pharisees, and would no doubt think back to what was true of Solomon's temple in the OT which had been built by divine command. From this point of view, the temple was greater and so was the altar, each of which "sanctifies" the lesser. That is, the greater sets apart the lesser from common use. But the Pharisees had reversed this, proclaiming "he is a debtor" and "he is guilty" when a man swore by these lesser things. These expressions are identical in Greek, being the verb *opheilō*, and mean that the man was under an obligation to abide by the terms of his oath.

The Lord's conclusions are given in vv.20-22; v.22 stands in contrast to vv.20-21, since God did not dwell in such a temple made with hands (Acts 7:48-49); only the priests worked there; God dwells in heaven seated upon His throne of absolute authority. In v.20, the addition of "all things thereon" takes the thought from the greater to include the lesser, but v.21 takes the thought from the lesser to include the greater. Not that God dwelt in that temple, but the Lord was talking about ideal circumstances, no doubt looking back to Solomon's temple where God's presence was manifested in glory. But v.22 indicates an order of greatness that cannot be exceeded (Heb 6:13-14). It appears that if men swore by heaven, they overlooked the fact that God was greater, and this might have led to men taking the name of God in vain. Note that the Lord did not attempt to correct the Pharisees, by saying "Swear not at all" as He said to His disciples. In this series of woes, only vv.23, 26 contain a hint of correction. He knew that the Pharisees intended to carry on with their practices in spite of His denunciations.

23-24 *The fourth woe.* In the matter of tithing, the scribes and Pharisees were hypocrites because they regarded small ritualistic observances as being far greater than their great moral obligations before God and men. The proper principle is found in verses such as: "I will have mercy, and not sacrifice" (Matt 12:7; Hos 6:6); "To obey is better than sacrifice" (1 Sam 15:22); "to love him…to love his neighbour… is more than all whole burnt offerings and sacrifices" (Mark 12:33). Tithing was prominent under the OT law, in verses such as: "all the tithe of the land…is the Lord's: it is holy unto the Lord" (Lev 27:30), though in the seventh year nothing should be sown and nothing reaped (Lev 25:1-7) thereby excluding agricultural produce from the tithes that year. These tithes unto the Lord were to be given to the Levites and priests to maintain them in their service (Num 18:24), the tenth of the tenth being the portion of the priests (Neh 10:38). Additionally, there was a second tithe that the people themselves had to eat in the place that the Lord would choose (Deut 12:17, 18; 14:22-26), though in every third year this tithe had to be devoted to others (vv.28-29; 26:12). The OT Apocrypha shows how these tithes were regarded in later years: "But I alone went often to Jerusalem at the feasts . . . having the firstfruits and tenths of increase . . . The first tenth part of all increase I gave to the sons of Aaron . . . another tenth part I sold away . . . and spent it every year at Jerusalem: And the third I gave unto them for whom it was meet" (Tob 1:6-8).

But the ritualistic mind of the Pharisees legislated that this principle of tithing be applied even to the smallest garden herbs, when at the same time the heart was not affected with "weightier matters". These herbs were sweet-smelling mint (*hēduosmon*), anise (*anēthon*) – otherwise "dill" used for pickling – and cummin (*kuminon*) used to flavour dishes. For a more detailed description of these plants, see the *I. V. F. New Bible Dictionary*. On the other hand, the Lord commended small matters when they arose from a sincere and devoted heart, as in the case of the woman who could only offer "two mites" (Mark 12:41-44). Today, giving to the Lord does not have a legal basis but is spiritual, from the heart, as the whole of 2 Cor 8-9 amply demonstrates.

To illustrate this point, the Lord used an exaggerated word picture similar to the beam and the mote (Matt 7:3-5). "Strain at" (*diülizō*) should be rendered "strain out", as an act of filtering with a strainer. The "gnat" (*kōnō ps*) was a midge that bred in fermenting wine. Not that there was anything wrong in such filtering activity in normal practice. But the word-picture demonstrated that the Pharisees focussed their religious attention on matters so minute and trivial while allowing larger things, "a camel", to pass by unnoticed and seemingly irrelevant. In other words, "the first and great commandment. And the second" (Matt 22:38-39) had no place in the Pharisaical philosophy. Believers today should assess their own priorities, in the face of surrounding religious blindness and self-righteousness.

25-26 *The fifth woe.* Cleansing commences from the inside, and extends to the outside; compare this with 2 Chron 29:16-17, where Hezekiah in cleansing the house of the Lord, started with "the inner part" and ended with the "porch". The inside and the outside of the cup likewise had to be cleansed. For the Pharisees' religion was one of outward demonstration of self-righteousness, while the iniquitous interior of the heart became worse and worse – "full of extortion and excess". Such a religion of sight really demonstrates blindness, and so their sin remained (John 9:39-41). In fact, this kind of blindness glibly passes over things that are most offensive to God; yet He knows the interior state of the heart; He knows what is in man (John 2:25), for all things are "naked and opened" unto His eyes (Heb 4:13). So in v.26 the Lord placed the responsibility squarely upon the Pharisees. Not that a man can ultimately cleanse his own heart, but he can remove those elements that hinder a response to salvation.

27-28 *The sixth woe.* In Luke 11:44, the Lord likened the Pharisees to "graves which appear not" – that is, men failed to perceive that death marked the lives and character of such men. They were dead in trespasses and sins, yet men thought that they were upright and righteous. But in our v. 27, the Lord changed the metaphor. The tombs were certainly now apparent, since they were "whited sepulchres", as Paul described the high priest, "thou whited wall" (Acts 23:3). In the case of tombs, these were white-washed annually, so that men would notice that they were there, and thus avoid touching them; otherwise they would be defiled. In the case of the Pharisees, they were permanently in contact with their own deadness, but men saw only what was outward, having no idea that abominable corruption was resident within. These men were defiled by reason of their evil thoughts and blasphemies against the Son of man (Matt 15:18-20). "Hypocrisy and iniquity" dwelt in their hearts, unlike believers, whose bodies are the temple of the Holy Spirit (1 Cor 6:19), in whose hearts the Lord dwells (Eph 3:17), and in whom even the Father will make His abode (John 14:23).

29-33 *The seventh woe.* On the other hand, there were special ornamental tombs erected outside Jerusalem to commemorate the outstanding OT prophets and righteous men. By this means, the Pharisees would seem to be taking a stand for the prophetical message in the OT, and to be opposed to those who had taken the lives of such prophets long ago. They would not have committed such crimes had they been alive in those days. "They were stoned, they were sawn asunder, were tempted, were slain with the sword" (Heb 11:37) by men who were opposed to their lives and message. Stephen said the same thing, "Which of the prophets have not your fathers persecuted? and they have slain them which shewed before of the coming of the Just One; of whom ye have been now the betrayers and murderers" (Acts 7:52). This faithful man concluded his testimony by saying, "as your fathers did, so do ye" (v.51).

They were "children" (*huios*, sons) of those who committed these crimes in OT days. In a physical sense, they claimed to be related to Abraham, saying, "Abraham is our father" (John 8:39), so they lay in the line of Jewish descent. In a moral sense, in their hearts they knew that they would be prepared to do the same thing, for during this last week the leaders were preparing plots whereby they might take the Lord to kill Him. Yet the ordinary people did not know what was being hatched behind their backs. They would not have thought that their leaders could be capable of such a crime!

The Lord's conclusion was, "Fill ye up then the measure of your fathers". In other words, "the iniquity of the Amorites is not yet full" (Gen 15:16), that is to say, to the iniquity of the past, there had to be added still more before God would intervene in swift judgment. The murders committed by men in the OT had yet to be completed in the NT by the murder of the Son of God. Similarly in Rev 6:9-11, God would not intervene to avenge the blood of the martyrs shed during the coming great tribulation after the rapture of the church until their numbers had been completed: "for a little season, until...their brethren, that should be killed as they were, should be fulfilled". As long as time lasts, the efforts of the present are usually devoted to filling up activities of the past. Thus Paul knew when his end had come (2 Tim 4:6-7), but before that end he knew that he had to "fill up that which is behind of the afflictions of Christ in my flesh for his body's sake, which is the church" (Col 1:24), namely he had then not yet completed the sufferings that he had to pass through according to the will of God (Acts 9:16), but they had to be filled up to the brim.

The Lord finally called these Pharisees "Ye serpents, ye generation of vipers". John the Baptist had used this title (Matt 3:7), urging them to repent. The Lord had also used this title before (Matt 12:34), making it clear that nothing good could come out of their hearts. But here in v.33, the question implied that their portion would be "the damnation of hell", namely to be condemned to gehenna, the lake of fire. Heaven would not welcome one man walking a life of such blatant hypocrisy; the serpents would go the way of the serpent – "that old serpent, which is the Devil, and Satan...was cast into the lake of fire" (Rev 20:2, 10).

3. *The Prophets and the House Desolate* 23:34-39

v.34 "Wherefore, behold, I send unto you prophets, and wise men, and scribes: and *some* of them ye shall kill and crucify; and *some* of them shall ye scourge in your synagogues, and persecute *them* from city to city:
v.35 That upon you may come all the righteous blood shed upon the earth, from the blood of righteous Abel unto the blood of Zacharias son of Barachias, whom ye slew between the temple and the altar.
v.36 Verily I say unto you, All these things shall come upon this generation.
v.37 O Jerusalem, Jerusalem, *thou* that killest the prophets, and stonest them which are sent unto thee, how often would I have gathered thy children together, even as a hen gathereth her chickens under *her* wings, and ye would not!
v.38 Behold, your house is left unto you desolate.
v.39 For I say unto you, Ye shall not see me henceforth, till ye shall say, Blessed *is* he that cometh in the name of the Lord."

34 The filling up in v.32 came as a result of these servants being sent forth by the Lord. Thus in the OT, Moses (Exod 3:10,13,14,15), Isaiah (Isa 6:8), Jeremiah (Jer 1:7) and Ezekiel (Ezek 2:3) were sent. In the NT, the apostles were sent (Matt 10:5), as were Paul and Barnabas (Acts 13:4). The general principle is, "how shall they preach, except they be sent" (Rom 10:15). True service can be achieved only when the servant is sent by the Lord, otherwise service is mere presumption. Thus the Lord sent "prophets, and wise men, and scribes". The "prophets" were NT prophets (1 Cor 12:10, 28; Eph 4:11), men able to forthtell the mind of God before the NT Scriptures were complete in written form. The "wise men" (*sophos*) were nothing to do with the "wise men" in Matt 2:1 (*magos*). Normally in the NT this word is uncomplimentary, as in Matt 11:25, where divine truth was hidden from "the wise". But Paul was "a wise masterbuilder" (1 Cor 3:10); the corresponding noun "wisdom" (*sophia*) is promised by the Lord (Luke 21:15) as a gift of the Spirit (Acts 6:3; 1 Cor 12:8). The "scribes" were men able to maintain the truth and to teach it, though this word is not used in the Acts and the Epistles to refer to believers. Such men were far removed from the Jewish scribes so often seen in conflict with the Lord In the Gospels. In hatred, the Jewish leaders killed some of these, such as Stephen and James. The word "crucify" is remarkable, since this was the Roman and not the Jewish method of putting men to death; it suggests collaboration between Jews and Romans, as took place when the Lord was crucified. Paul was scourged by the Romans (Acts 22:24-26), while often he had to go from city to city suffering persecution, particularly on his first missionary journey (Acts 13:50; 14:5-6, 19).

35-36 The sum total of all murders recorded in the OT is now considered. The first "righteous blood" shed was that of Abel (Gen 4:8), a man who is called "righteous" in Heb 11:4. The last murder was that of Zacharias, the son of the faithful high priest Jehoiada (2 Chron 24:21-22); this high priest had saved the boy king Joash in the temple, yet when grown this king murdered God's servant Zecharias. This murder is recorded last because the order of books in the Hebrew OT is different from the order traditionally adopted today. Genesis was the first book, and Chronicles was the *last*. The Lord's mind thus spanned the whole history recorded in the OT. This activity of the scribes and Pharisees, together with the priests, reached a climax in the NT, with the crucifixion of the Lord Jesus. There was no safety in the temple or in its courts: Joab was killed clutching the horns of the altar (1 Kings 2:28), Uzziah became a leper inside the holy place (2 Chron 26:19), while Zacharias was stoned in the temple courts (2 Chron 24:21). It is not possible to be certain why "son of Barachias" appears in Matt 23:35, because quite a different man, Zechariah the prophet, was the son of Berechiah (Zech 1:1). If this is a copyist's error or insertion, it took place before the writing of existing manuscripts available today, for according to these the words are not open to textual doubt. The corresponding verse in Luke does not contain them (Luke 11:51). A similar difficulty exists in Mark 2:26, where Abiathar is stated to be high priest, whereas during the event there described his father Ahimelech was the high priest (1 Sam 21:1). When difficulties of this kind arise in a few places, faith remains unmoved by the theories of rationalists who use them to discredit the Scriptures; when a scriptural explanation does not exist, faith still remains undeflected — there are more important things to be concerned with than inventing explanations for the appearance of names in verses in which we would not expect them to appear!

"All these things shall come upon this generation" refers to the divine judgment for the shedding of righteous blood. This divine visitation did not necessarily happen in the time of the Acts; no doubt AD 70 is included in the view, on account of the Lord's words in Matt 24:2 relating to the destruction of the temple. But "this generation" stretches to the prophetic future, when the nation will suffer for its crimes against God's servants.

37 The repeated name "Jerusalem, Jerusalem" reminds us of other occasions when repeated names were used; we have supplied a list in our comments on Matt 7:21-22 where the duplicated title "Lord, Lord" appears. This lament over Jerusalem also occurs in Luke 13:34-35. In spite of the complete similarity, it is not the same occasion as that described here. In Luke 13 the lament was only preparatory, in anticipation of what He would say directly to the city in this later passage. The Lord lamented at the very thought of the outcome of the city's unfaithfulness; this outcome in judgment would be unrelieved, since the people would not have Him and His invitations. The idea of protection under the divine wings is found several times in the OT; see Exod 19:4; Deut 32:11; Ruth 2:12; Ps 17:8; 36:7; 63:7. As self-sufficient and trusting In their own ways, they "would not" – similar to Isa 30:15-16, "In returning and rest shall ye be saved; in quietness and in confidence shall be your strength: and ye would not. But ye said, No". Note that the singular "*thou* that killest...sent unto *thee*...*thy* children" is changed to the plural "*ye* would not...*your* house...I say unto *you*, *Ye* shall not see me henceforth, till *ye* shall say". The city as a whole becomes a city of responsible persons! In Jer 7:13, God said that He was "rising up early and speaking", but the people "heard not...answered not", so the desolations that came upon the tabernacle in Shiloh would come upon Solomon's temple. This rising up early and negative response on the part of the people occurs eleven times in Jeremiah: 7:13,25; 11:7; 25:3,4; 26:5; 29:19; 32:33; 35:14,15; 44:4.

38 So the house would be "desolate" (*eremos*), an adjective usually translated "desert"; it would become an uninhabited waste. This was the Lord's estimation of the character of the temple without His presence; He disassociated Himself from this house. Just prior to the destruction of Solomon's temple, God told the people to look at Shiloh's tabernacle which He had forsaken; He would do the same thing to the temple (Jer 7:12,14; 26:6; Ezek 11:23; Lam 2:8; 2 Chron 36:19). The final destruction of Herod's temple took place under the Romans in AD 70, referred to by the Lord in Matt 24:2. The OT often referred to such desolation: "the heathen are come into thine inheritance; thy holy temple have they defiled" (Ps 79:1); "Zion is a wilderness... Our holy and our beautiful house, where our fathers praised thee, is burned up with fire" (Isa 64:10-11). This desolation will remain until the end times, when the Lord will take its desolate character away when He enters in glory (Ezek 43:4). According to Mal 3:1, God's messenger will prepare the way (then comes the "gap" of the church age), and then the Lord "shall suddenly come to his temple".

Note that the Lord called this house "your house" – not His possession, but the Jews'. Similarly in John 5:1; 6:4; 7:2, we read of feasts "of the Jews" rather than "of the Lord". See Ezek 44:8, where the Lord's things were turned into their things. See also Ezek 16:6-14, where "my comeliness" is described; in the following verses, Jerusalem counted it as all her own, misusing it for the purposes of idolatry. Even in NT times, Paul wrote that the activity of the Corinthians was such that the Lord's supper was "not...the Lord's supper" (1 Cor 11:20); they had made it their own.

39 The Lord is now no longer going to teach in public; Matt 24-25 and John 13-16 were for the disciples' ears only. The people will see Him in public display no longer until they shall say, "Blessed be he that cometh in the name of the Lord" (Ps 118:26). They had said this in Matt 21:9 when He entered Jerusalem in triumph, but never will do so again until His future public manifestation in glory as the Son of man and King of kings. Only then will His weeping over Jerusalem give place to joy, "so shall thy God rejoice over thee" (Isa 62:5); "Weeping may endure for a night, but joy cometh in the morning" (Ps 30:5).

IV. The Second Advent of the King in Glory (24:1-51)

1. *The Olivet Discourse — the Past and the Future* 24:1-3

v.1 "And Jesus went out, and departed from the temple: and his disciples came to *him* for to shew him the buildings of the temple.
v.2 And Jesus said unto them, See ye not all these things? Verily I say unto you, There shall not be left here one stone upon another, that shall not be thrown down.
v.3 And as he sat upon the mount of Olives, the disciples came unto him privately, saying, Tell us, when shall these things be? and what *shall be* the sign of thy coming, and of the end of the world?"

The teaching of Matthew 24 appears in three separate parts in Luke's Gospel; we believe that the Lord repeated similar things in different places. Luke 12:42-48 (the last part of Matt 24) deals with the responsibility of servants; Luke 17:22-37 (the central part of Matt 24) provides details of the events at the Lord's return in glory and Luke 21:5-36 (the beginning of Matt 24) describes events prior to His coming. There are, of course, many differences in the details given in these two Gospels.

Since "the abomination of desolation" (v.15) is quoted from Dan 9:27, ch.9 of Daniel provides the necessary background of Matt 24. In Dan 9, Daniel's repentance and supplication on behalf of his nation led to a vision of the future granted through Gabriel (vv.20-23). This vision was concerned with "*thy* people" and "*thy* holy city" (v.24), namely the Jews and Jerusalem. The church is not seen in Daniel's visions and prophecy. Certainly all Scripture is for the church, but not all is about the church. The church is not a subject of prophecy (Eph 3:5), although certainly Christ, His sacrifice and His exaltation are. In fact, Matt 24 refers solely to the Lord's future coming in glory; only v.2 refers to the destruction of Jerusalem in AD 70. As is quite usual in prophecy, events near in time merge with events far distant in time, the gap in between not being indicated. Note that Matt 24:42 to 25:30 forms a parenthesis dealing with watching; this still refers to the future, but it contains important principles of application that bear upon the present testimony.

We must consider the "seventy weeks" in Dan 9:24. A fuller account will be found in the author's *The Book of Daniel*. A week represents a period of seven parts; here, they must be years so that the period reaches up to the cutting off of Messiah. The prophecy therefore deals with 70 x 7 = 490 years. Now a prophetic year consists of 360 days. This can be seen from the fact that the periods "a time, and times and half a time", "forty-two months" and "1,260 days" are identical (Dan 7:25; 12:7; Rev 11:2,3; 12:6; 13:5). This period of seventy weeks or 490 years commenced with "the commandment to restore and to build Jerusalem" (Dan 9:25), namely the decree in Neh 2:5-8. From that date there were 69 weeks (483 years each of 360 days) leading up to the last week of Messiah when He was crucified. Note that in Dan 9:26 "but not for himself" reads in the margin "and shall have nothing", that is, of the Jews and of the holy city. The gap that we know as the church age intervenes before the seventieth week of seven years commences after the rapture of the church. The fact that there would be a gap between the sixty- ninth and seventieth week was not obvious to Daniel, but it is certainly obvious to us in the light of NT revelation, since we look back to weeks 1-69 and forward to week 70.

The seventieth week represents seven years of unfulfilled prophecy, and the Lord described these years in Matt 24. In this chapter, the word "end" appears several times; it represents two different Greek words with different meanings.

1. in "the *end* of the world" (v.3), the word is *sunteleia*, in which several things coincide so as to reach their climax during the same period. Verses 4-28 represent this "end". This word also appears in Matt 13:39,40,49; 28:20. Daniel's vision in Dan 9:24-27 also deals with this end period.

2. The second word is *telos*, a common word in the NT, and means in Matt 24 the final completion of the end period just described — the final crash. It appears in the phrases "but the *end* is not yet" (v.6); "he that shall endure unto the *end*" (v.13): "then shall the *end* come" (v.14). Dan 7:13-14, when the Son of man comes with the clouds, deals with this event.

After the church has been taken to meet the Lord in the air (1 Thess 4:14-17), the great multitude converted during these last seven years will be opposed by "the prince that shall come" (Dan 9:26); he is the beast from the sea of Rev 13:1, the head of the revived fourth beast-kingdom in Dan 7, representing Rome. They will also be opposed by the lamb-like beast of Rev 13:11; he is the anti-Christ and the man of sin (2 Thess 2:3), claiming to be God in the temple of that time. There will be a covenant between the revived Roman empire and the apostate Jews (Isa 28:15-18) for the protection of the latter against the northern power, northern in relation to Jerusalem. The political and religious scene during the period of this covenant is described in Matt 24:4-14. Half way through the seven-year prophetical period, the covenant will be broken (Dan 9:27); there will be an idol "the abomination of desolation" in the temple and the "great tribulation" will commence, to last for the remaining three and a half years. Matt 24:15-28 describes this period. The conclusion is that Christ will then come in glory to sweep away all evil and opposition (Matt 24:29-41), with many being taken for judgment, and with the beast and the anti-Christ being cast into the lake of fire (Rev 19:20). The passage Matt 24:42 to 25:30 represents a parenthesis, showing various aspects of watching during that period. The prophetic narrative concludes with 25:31-46, returning to the Lord's second advent, when the nations remaining after the battle of Armageddon will be judged before the throne of His glory.

1 The Lord now departed from the temple (*hieron*) for the last time. Up to this moment, "the times of this ignorance God winked at" (Acts 17:30) or "God overlooked" (RV), but now, after the cross, judgment was near at hand. The temple and its system were now disowned; they were ripe for judgment: the rent veil demonstrated that the system was a sham, since there was no ark behind the veil in the holy of holies. The last departures recorded in the other Gospels should be noted. In Mark 13:1, He left the temple after having seen the false attitude taken by the rich in their giving. In Luke 21:37, He left for Bethany after His final session of teaching. In John 10:23, 39 He escaped from Solomon's porch, because the Pharisees rejected His deity and sought to stone Him for His assertions. This abandonment of the temple finds certain similarities in the OT. Thus God "forsook the tabernacle of Shiloh" (Ps 78:60), and later His glory returned to fill Solomon's temple at its dedication (1 Kings 8:10-11). The glory departed from Solomon's temple just before its destruction (Ezek 11:23), to return later in the prophetic future (43:4) from the mount of Olives.

By showing the Lord "the buildings of the temple", the apostles adopted a grossly materialistic outlook. There had been no divine command for its design nor for its construction; thus far, it had taken forty-six years to build so as to be of great architectural fame. In John 2:13-21, the Lord regarded it as valueless when contrasted with the temple of His body. In the present day, religious temples made with hands give Him no pleasure. The remarkable thing is that the cross was so near, yet the disciples were so materialistic in their thinking. This was manifested again in the upper room after the supper, when there was strife among them as to who should be the greatest (Luke 22:24). They failed to distinguish between what was heavenly and eternal on the one hand, and what was merely temporal on the other (2 Cor 4:18).

2 By answering "There shall not be left here one stone upon another, that shall not be thrown down", the Lord predicted the destruction of the temple by the Romans in AD 70. It was to be a repetition of what Nebuchadnezzar had done to Solomon's temple (2 Chron 36:19). The wall and palaces of Jerusalem had also been broken down, and this was included in the Lord's prophecy (Luke 19:44). Such destruction showed the divine estimate of material things that are not consecrated to Himself. By contrast, the material gifts in Phil 4:18 were "an odour of a sweet smell, a sacrifice acceptable, wellpleasing to God". The casting down of the temple in AD 70 represented the ultimate "fall", "casting away", and "breaking off" of Israel (Rom 11:12,15,17). The nation has remained "Lo-ammi" ("Not my people", Hos 1:9) ever since. In the church God's new order is for Jews and Gentiles alike; there is no temple made with hands in the present where God dwells, no temple service and ritual, no recognition of man in the flesh, no meats, drinks and observance of days. Over the centuries how hard has it been for man to learn this lesson – indeed, many have never learnt it, seeking to perpetuate the Jewish system of ritual under a veneer of Christianity.

3 The Lord's simple answer stirred up the minds of the apostles. It had always been their privilege to ask questions (particularly interspersing the Lord's discourses in John's Gospel). In Matt 22:46, unbelieving men could ask nothing further, until He appeared before the high priest and Pilate. The Lord always answered an honest enquiry, as in Matt 13:10,18, 36, 37, although others were sent empty away. Effectively, the apostles asked three questions.

1. "When shall these things be?" This referred to an event near in time, namely AD 70, though the disciples did not know that, and the Lord did not answer that part of the overall question. The fact that the church would spread to many parts, including Jerusalem and Rome, during the period between His death and AD 70 was something that could not be revealed, else the hope of the church in its early days would have been no hope at all.

2. "What shall be the sign of thy coming?" – namely of His second advent as King. His coming to receive believers unto Himself, as promised in John 14:2-3, had not yet been revealed. But they had already heard His teaching concerning the advent of the Son of man in Luke 17:20-37, so they were certainly asking a question of relevance: what events would precede His coming? See also Matt 16:28. In their minds, question 1 led to question 2, since the destruction of a temple had prophetic significance, as explained in our comments on v.1. The city being smitten (Ezek 33:21) led to visions of restoration (chs.40-48). The sanctuary being destroyed (Dan 9:26) again led to prophecies of restoration (12:2-3).

3. "What shall be the end of the world?" (*sunteleias tou aiōnos*, the completion of the age). They were not asking about the end of all things, but the end of the age to which prophecy referred, namely the age leading up to His kingdom in glory.

It was fitting that this prophetical discourse should take place on the mount of Olives on the east of Jerusalem. The summit overlooked mount Moriah on which the temple was built in Jerusalem; no doubt the temple, gleaming in the sunlight, looked such a solid structure, that it gave the impression that it was unmoveable and lasting. In that future day, the Lord's feet shall touch the mount of Olives, which will then split into two parts (Zech 14:4); He ascended from the mount of Olives (Luke 24:50; Acts 1:12), and there He shall return again in like manner, to restore again the kingdom to Israel (v.6). It will be from the mount of Olives that the Lord's glory returns to the restored temple (Ezek 43:4), since thither the glory had departed in Ezek 11:23.

2. *Events during the Last Seven Years* 24:4-28

v.4 "And Jesus answered and said unto them, Take heed that no man deceive you.
v.5 For many shall come in my name, saying, I am Christ; and shall deceive many.
v.6 And ye shall hear of wars and rumours of wars: see that ye be not troubled: for all *these things* must come to pass, but the end is not yet.
v.7 For nation shall rise against nation, and kingdom against kingdom: and there shall be famines, and pestilences, and earthquakes, in divers places.
v.8 All these *are* the beginning of sorrows.
v.9 Then shall they deliver you up to be afflicted, and shall kill you: and ye shall be hated of all nations for my name's sake.
v.10 And then shall many be offended, and shall betray one another, and shall hate one another.
v.11 And many false prophets shall rise, and shall deceive many.
v.12 And because iniquity shall abound, the love of many shall wax cold.
v.13 But he that shall endure unto the end, the same shall be saved.
v.14 And this gospel of the kingdom shall be preached in all the world for a witness unto all nations; and then shall the end come.
v.15 When ye therefore shall see the abomination of desolation, spoken of by Daniel the prophet, stand in the holy place, (whoso readeth, let him understand:)
v.16 Then let them which be in Judaea flee into the mountains:
v.17 Let him which is on the housetop not come down to take any thing out of his house:
v.18 Neither let him which is in the field return back to take his clothes.
v.19 And woe unto them that are with child, and to them that give suck in those days!
v.20 But pray ye that your flight be not in the winter, neither on the sabbath day:
v.21 For then shall be great tribulation, such as was not since the beginning of the world to this time, no, nor ever shall be.
v.22 And except those days should be shortened, there should no flesh be saved: but for the elect's sake those days shall be shortened.
v.23 Then if any man shall say unto you, Lo, here *is* Christ, or there; believe *it* not.
v.24 For there shall arise false Christs, and false prophets, and shall shew great signs and wonders; insomuch that, if *it were* possible, they shall deceive the very elect.
v.25 Behold, I have told you before.
v.26 Wherefore if they shall say unto you, Behold, he is in the desert; go not forth: behold, *he is* in the secret chambers; believe *it* not.
v.27 For as the lightning cometh out of the east, and shineth even unto the west; so shall also the coming of the Son of man be.
v.28 For wheresoever the carcase is, there will the eagles be gathered together."

4 In the Lord's answer (vv.4-14), we find the character of religious deception and persecution generally, and specifically at the end times, when there will be a heading up of all these things. The masses are referred to in vv.5-8, and individuals in vv.9-14. The bud in vv.5-8 brings forth fruit – the worst in vv.9-12, and the best in vv.13-14. The "beginning of sorrows" (v.8) will be religious (v.5), political and military (vv.6-7a), and natural (v.7b). The immediate results will be religious and international hatred (v.9), personal hatred (v.10), and the reign of false religion and iniquity (vv.11-12). Yet on behalf of the people of God at that time there will be endurance, salvation and testimony (vv.13-14). Hence men of all ages must "Take heed that no man deceive you". Deception is the enemy of all true doctrine. It can be self-inflicted (1 Cor 3:18; 1 John 1:8); it can be brought about by others (Rom 16:18; Eph 4:14; 2 Thess 2:3), and by Satan (Rev 20:3,8,10). We can "take heed" by knowing the truth in detail; otherwise there are chinks in the armour leaving us susceptible to deception.

5 The rise of false Christs and false prophets (vv.11, 24) is something that has dominated attempts to mar the true testimony throughout the ages. When the Lord Jesus was here on earth, no one is recorded as having arisen claiming to be Christ: Herod claimed that John the Baptist was Christ, but John strenuously denied this whenever such insinuations were made. There have been many antiChrists during the Christian era. John wrote, "even now are there many antichrists; whereby we know that it is the last time. They went out from us, but they were not of us" (1 John 2:18-19). A man was an anti- Christ if he denied "the Father and the Son" (v.22). The spirit of antiChrist does not confess "that Jesus Christ is come in the flesh" (4:3), and John added, "even now already is it in the world". He wrote the same thing in 2 John 7, concluding, "This is a deceiver and an antichrist". He also spoke of "false prophets" who had gone out into the world (1 John 4:1). Peter warned of the same class of men, "there were false prophets also among the people, even as there shall be false teachers among you, who privily shall bring in damnable heresies, even denying the Lord that bought them, and bring upon themselves swift destruction. And many shall follow their pernicious ways; by reason of whom the way of truth shall be evil spoken of" (2 Pet 2:1-2). The Lord referred to OT false prophets in Luke 6:26. All this characterises the assembly age now, with various cults claiming Christs, prophets and teachers, denying the truths that are basic to the faith of all believers. But after the church has been taken, there will arise the anti-Christ and the false prophet (the same person). This mystery of iniquity is already working (2 Thess 2:7), but when the Spirit of God is taken and restraint removed, "then shall that Wicked be revealed" (v.8). He will deceive those that perish. Satan will work "with all power and signs and lying wonders" through him, and God will cause men to believe "a lie" (strictly, "the lie", vv.9-11). This anti-Christ is the second beast, described in Rev 13:11-17, afterwards called "the false prophet (16:13; 19:20). The full activity of this enemy of God will take place during the last three and a half years, and many will be willing to follow his deceptions (Matt 24:11, 24). However, the end of the two beasts – the emperor and the anti-Christ – is described in Rev 19:19-20; they will be cast into the lake of fire without judgment, for they will be caught in the midst of their abominable activity by the coming of the King of kings.

6-8 The Lord proceeded to describe other afflictions that are called "the beginning of sorrows", meaning that worse things were to come, for "the end is not yet".

Wars and trouble between nations have been the curse of mankind ever since Cain slew his brother in Gen 4:8, which was the first war in miniature. In the OT, warfare characterised the four beast-kingdoms described in Dan 7, by that means the lust for territorial aggrandisement was satisfied, enabling the king of the third empire (Dan 8:21) to engulf all the world even to India (vv.4-8). On other occasions God used warfare as an act of judgment on nations opposed to His people. Wars still mark the present day, though not on a global scale. But the expressed desire of men and their leaders is for peace, though some desire warfare so as to achieve their ends. As the psalmist said, "I am for peace: but when I speak, they are for war" (Ps 120:7). Elsewhere, David wrote, "continually are they gathered together for war" (Ps 140:2). However, the world situation will be worse during the last seven years represented by the seventieth week. Men will say, "Peace and safety; then sudden destruction cometh upon them... and they shall not escape" (1 Thess 5:3).

Earthquakes were often seen as God's voice to men. Thus when the first covenant was given an earthquake gripped men's hearts with fear: "the whole mount quaked greatly" (Exod 19:18; Heb 12:18- 21). The death of the Lord Jesus that marked the basis of the new covenant was accompanied by an earthquake (Matt 27:51, 54). "A great earthquake" occurred to manifest the resurrection of the Lord and the empty tomb (Matt 28:2). At the future introduction of the new covenant earth and heaven will be shaken, so as to remove incompatible things, leaving the kingdom that cannot be moved (Heb 12:26-29). An earthquake will occur in that day when the Lord's feet touch the mount of Olives (Zech 14:4-5). So when the Lord mentioned earthquakes, He referred to the destroying and judging power of God prior to the establishment of His kingdom under the blessings of the new covenant made with the houses of Israel and of Judah (Rev 6:12).

The breaking of the seals in Rev 6 and their consequences appear to answer to these calamities mentioned by the Lord. Seal 1 shows a conquering religious leader with a crown, answering to the anti-Christ (Rev 6:2; Matt 24:5). Seal 2 shows a leader taking peace from the earth, answering to the wars and rumours of wars (Rev 6:4; Matt 24:6-7). Seal 3 and seal 4 deal with the price of food and with death due to hunger, answering to famines (Rev 6:6,8; Matt 24:7). Seal 5 shows the souls of those that are slain, answering to "they...shall kill you" (Rev 6:9; Matt 24:9). Seal 6 shows a great earthquake, answering to the earthquakes mentioned by the Lord (Rev 6:12; Matt 24:7). Prior to seal 7, we read of the sealing of the 144,000, and of those who have come out of great tribulation, answering to those who respond to the preaching of the gospel of the kingdom throughout the world (Rev 7:4,14; Matt 24:14).

9-10 These personal afflictions of the people of God at that time remind us of the Lord's similar words in Matt 10:21-22. For we have remarked that Matt 10 represents the history of testimony from the time when the Lord was here, through the period of the Book of Acts, right up to the end times "till the Son of man be come" (Matt 10:23). Even in families love will not be respected, while betrayal and hatred will be reciprocated amongst unbelievers.

11-12 We have commented already upon "false prophets". They will deceive men of the world; certainly the anti-Christ will deceive "them that dwell on the earth by the means of those miracles which he had power to do" (Rev 13:14). But we feel that the "many" who are deceived will also include believers in that era, for that is just what the unconverted Saul sought to do when he compelled Christians in weakness to blaspheme (Acts 26:11). The same may be said about the encompassing power of iniquity: "the love of many shall wax cold" does not appear to answer to unbelievers, since they would have no love to start with. In the present day, worldliness causes love for Christ to diminish, but in that day the pressures brought about by continual iniquity will weaken the love of those who are weak. The Lord knows all about such weakness – He had witnessed it in His apostles when He was here below. So the days will be shortened, else none would be saved (Matt 24:22).

13-14 In the phrase "he that shall endure unto the end", the word for "end" is *telos*, namely the absolute end of the tribulation period when the Lord intervenes to put an end to the rule of man on earth. We suggest that the word "saved" here refers, not to salvation of the soul, but to remaining alive until the Lord's return, thus to enter into the blessings of the earthly kingdom to be established at His advent.

Verse 14 deals with the testimony for God that will exist on earth during this future period. The word "gospel" is *euangelion*, meaning "good news", the corresponding verb being *euangelizō*, meaning "to proclaim the good news", or "to evangelise". The noun "gospel" occurs only four times in Matthew, namely, 4:23; 9:35; 24:14; 26:13, while the verb occurs only in 11:5. The Lord commenced by preaching "the gospel of the kingdom" (Matt 4:23; 9:35), after which the expression does not occur for a considerable period, then appears again here in a prophetic setting.

The particular message contained in "the gospel" depends upon the era in which the preaching is being carried out. In Paul's day, there was only one gospel (Gal 1:6-9); there was no other of the same kind (*allos*, "another" of the same kind in v.7), but many false ones, gospels of a different kind (*heteros*, "another" of a different kind in v.6). This message of the grace of God was fully revealed after the death and resurrection of Christ, being made known by the Holy Spirit. It led to the formation of the church purchased by the blood of His own Son (Acts 20:28); its goal was to glorify Christ in the church throughout eternal ages. The message Christ preached related to a kingdom which stood in sharp contrast to the kingdoms established by the emperors in Dan 2:37-40, 7:2-7. The four world-kingdoms thrived on warfare, cruelty and evil, whereas the kingdom of heaven, first preached in Matt 3:3; 4:17, thrived on the presence of the Lord, with moral and spiritual living characterising its citizens. The object of this gospel was to glorify Christ in His kingdom here on earth, the blessing of this gospel being based on the blood of the new covenant. However, this particular message ceased in the first half of Matthew's Gospel because of the attitude of the Jewish leaders, as we have explained in our exposition of Matt 12. After that, the kingdom was in mystery-form, namely hidden from the wise and prudent but revealed unto babes, with no prospect of it being manifested in glory there and then. This became a future expectation, so its preaching reappeared only in a prophetical passage. The substance of the message of this future good news will still be the efficacy of the blood of Christ, as seen in verses such as Rev 7:14; 12:11, and emphasised by the continual use of the title "the Lamb". It will also embrace the judgment of God necessary to cleanse the earth, such as the contents of "the everlasting gospel" (Rev 14:6-7). This gospel will direct the hearts of men to the scenes of peace and righteousness that will characterise the kingdom in that coming day of open display. The message will circulate around the world, in just the same way as evangelists now take the message of the value of the blood of Christ to the uttermost parts of the earth. Particular effects of this testimony in Jerusalem are described in Rev 11:3-12, where two witnesses are killed, but rise again to ascend into heaven.

15-28 We now have a description of specific events that will take place during the last three and a half years before the Lord's second advent in glory. The Lord quoted "the abomination of desolation" from the book of Daniel the prophet. The appearance of this idol in the temple (v.15) is followed by a flight to safety (vv.16-20), the unique character of this tribulation (vv.21-22) and the irrelevance of the claims of false Christs, since there will be no doubt whatsoever that it is He when He comes in the clouds with power and great glory (vv.23-28).

15 "The abomination of desolation" (*to bdelugma tēs erēmōseōs*) appears in Dan 11:31; 12:11, and in the plural in 9:27; it means "the abomination that maketh desolate", referring to the effects that it has upon men. This future evil in the temple was historically pre-enacted by the activity of Antiochus Epiphanes who desecrated the temple to the consternation of the Jews. Then, the daily sacrifice was taken away (Dan 8:11), and the sanctuary was polluted (11:31). The "abomination" was an idol placed in the temple; this word is used of the idols that Solomon erected on the mount of Olives (1 Kings 11:7), while in the days of Jeremiah, God complained that the people had "set their abominations in the house which is called by my name, to pollute it" (Jer 7:30). Not only will the anti-Christ as the man of sin sit in the temple claiming to be God (2 Thess 2:4), but he also will make an image of the beast (the final emperor in Rome) that can talk, insisting that all men should worship this image of the beast (Rev 13:14-15). Having said this, the Lord insisted that men "understand", no doubt taken from

Dan 12:10, "the wise shall understand"; this should be taken in conjunction with Rev 1:3, where blessing is promised to those who "read, hear and keep" the words of the prophecy.

16-20 If the unfaithful worship the anti-Christ and the image of the beast, then pressure of a most cruel kind will be placed upon the faithful in Jerusalem at that time. No wonder the faithful are exhorted to "flee into the mountains". This will be a flight into safety; under other circumstances, unbelievers will also seek refuge from the Judgments of God pouring down at the opening of the sixth seal, "the kings of the earth, and the great men...hid themselves in the dens and in the rocks of the mountains; And said to the mountains and rocks, Fall on us, and hide us from the face of him that sitteth on the throne, and from the wrath of the Lamb" (Rev 6:15-17); see also Hos 10:8; Luke 23:30. This warning in Luke 23:30-31 is very solemn, since it represents the Lord's last words to the people of Jerusalem before He was crucified, concluding with "If they do these things in a green tree (namely, crucifying Himself), what shall be done in the dry?" (namely, the calamities ultimately to befall the nation that crucified Him).

Safety for the faithful in Jerusalem and Judaea will be by fleeing from the evil around. That is what Lot did under pressure (Gen 19:15, 23); "the way of life would be for those who left the city (Jer 21:8- 9). In John the Baptist's testimony, there was the exhortation to flee from the wrath to come (Matt 3:7). In Luke 21:20-24, the corresponding passage contains further details regarding Jerusalem being "encompassed with armies" and "trodden down of the Gentiles", suggesting the destruction of the city and temple by the Romans in AD 70. Josephus, the Jewlsh historian, was an eye-witness of these dreadful events, which are fully documented in several chapters of his book *The Jewish War*. But the events of the prophetic future will be worse than those of AD 70, the description of which Josephus has left us. The flight is to be immediate, without stopping or returning for necessary things. In Rev 12:14, the "woman" flew into the wilderness from the power of Satan, and even the "earth" (some men amongst the nations) offered help in the time of her greatest distress. Verse 19 shows distress in the most intimate of family occasions; previously the parents of the Lord Jesus had to flee with the young Child from the evil designs of Herod the king (Matt 2:13). Winter weather would impede flight, or at least make it uncomfortable, and so would the Sabbath day; pious Jews would have scruples about travelling more than a Sabbath day's journey on that day. In v.20, the Lord provided no indication as to the outcome of prayer regarding such circumstances.

21-22 The unique character of this tribulation is shown by the words, "such as was not since the beginning of the world to this time, no, nor ever shall be". Ghastly calamities have occurred before, but the events of these last three and a half years will be worse than anything that has previously occurred. Dan 12:1 states, "there shall be a time of trouble, such as never was since there was a nation even to that same time". Yet in vv.1-2, this time leads to deliverance and resurrection. For God is in absolute and final control; the wicked cannot triumph for ever. The persecution of the godly who love "not their lives unto the death" (Rev 12:11) will last only for the predicted time. Those days will be "shortened", namely restricted to the three and a half years. Had it been longer, the elect (*eklektos*) would not survive in the flesh; all would die or be martyred. But the Lord will ensure that many will pass safely through that period (like Noah through the period of the flood), so as to form the nucleus of those entering the millennium, the final form of the kingdom on earth.

23-25 Not only will there be persecution, but there will be deception by false Christs and false prophets. Knowing that the godly expect the return of Christ, these evil men will claim "here is Christ, or there". This cannot possibly refer to Christians during the present period of grace, since they know that He will not come so as to be hidden in secret places; rather "we shall see him as he is" (1 John 3:2). However, believers can be led away by false apostles (2 Cor 11:13; Rev 2:2), by false teachers (Eph 4:14; 2 Pet 2:1-3) and by false evangelists (Gal 1:6-9). On the other hand, false Christs can be used to deceive only those who expect Him on earth – such as the Jews who expect Messiah to re-establish their nation; for this reason, and indeed because of the whole context, we interpret the "elect" in vv.22, 24 as referring to the Jewish elect (Isa 45:4) and not to the Christian elect (Rom 8:33; Col 3:12).

The deception will be by "great signs and wonders", so that the eyes and the mind can, if possible, be captivated. Pharaoh's magicians were capable of doing this, when God acted in power to bring His people out of Egypt. Simon of Samaria was hailed as being "the great power of God" because he bewitched the people of Samaria with his deeds and claims (Acts 8:9-10). Satan will work through the future man of sin, "with all power and signs and lying wonders" (2 Thess 2:9), and this anti-Christ will do "great wonders...and...miracles(Rev 13:13-15). Men's hearts are always ready to admire activity of this sort. Even today, men make claims to be able to do signs and wonders without scriptural authority, and this is even more disturbing when they are Christians who make these claims usually for the advantage of open display. All this is a mimic of the work of Christ when He was here, for He was "approved of God among you by miracles and wonders and signs, which God did by him in the midst of you" (Acts 2:22). Even in this future day, there can be no excuse for the godly remnant falling before such deception, for the Lord has given adequate warning: "I have told you before". There were other matters that the Lord told the disciples "before". He told them about the betrayal "before it come" (John 13:19), and about His return to the Father (John 14:28-29). Similarly, Paul told the Thessalonians "before" that they would suffer tribulation (1 Thess 3:4). It is good to have prior intimation of events from the Scriptures, so that God's people can be prepared for them beforehand.

26-27 In matters relating to prophecy, there are always men ready to come forth with false teaching. In Corinth, there were men who denied the resurrection of the saints (1 Cor 15:12); later this became a fully-developed doctrine, needing the excommunication of such teachers from the church (2 Tim 2:18). There were men who denied that there will be any divine intervention in the last days (2 Pet 3:4), while in Thessalonica some men were claiming that the persecution through which they were passing was actually the day of the Lord (2 Thess 2:1-3), using a forged letter as from Paul to establish their doctrine. During the great tribulation period, there will be those who will claim to know that the Lord has returned secretly. One suggested place will be the rooms of the assemblies of the false teachers – "the secret chambers" as in Ezek 8:8-12 where God showed Ezekiel what was taking place. This will mimic the fact that the Lord did take His own disciples into a house (Matt 13:36) and into "a large upper room" (Luke 22:12). Others may claim that Christ will be found "in the desert", but this will be a lie. This will mimic John the Baptist who testified in the desert places, and men went out to him thinking that he might be the Christ (Matt 3:1; 11:7). Men also went out to the Lord "into a desert place apart" (Matt 14:13). Today, of course the Lord is found with His people in wilderness conditions, and in the sanctuary of His house apart from men.

Such lying assumptions will be impossible because His coming will be seen by all. The lightning coming from the cast and shining right over to the west (v.27) is not indicative of suddenness, in the context, but rather of universal manifestation. This will be no almost private coming as at His birth in the stable in Bethlehem, nor will there be any need for Him to be pointed out by a voice crying in the wilderness. Few saw Him at His birth and at His resurrection. But in that future day, "every eye shall see him...and all kindreds of the earth shall wail because of him" (Rev 1:7); no deception will be possible. The "east" is a typical direction of His coming; there "the Sun of righteousness" shall arise (Mal 4:2); "the glory of the God of Israel came from the way of the east" (Ezek 43:1-4). Whereas the idea of speed is not involved here, yet for Christians today they know that the Lord's coming for them will be "in a moment, in the twinkling of an eye" (1 Cor 15:52).

The word for "coming" in v. 27 is *parousia*. This word occurs four times in Matthew's Gospel, in 24:3,27,37,39. It is derived from "with" and "being", and can mean either an arrival or the following presence – the context must decide which is implied. The word is translated "presence" in 2 Cor 10:10, and Phil 2:12 in contrast to "absence" (*apousia*). Three times the Lord's servants are seen as coming: Stephanas (1 Cor 16:17), Titus (2 Cor 7:6,7) and Paul (Phil 1:26). Once the coming refers to the man of sin (2 Thess 2:9). The other 17 times when the word is used apply to the Lord Jesus; the context must decide whether this coming is for the church or for the establishment of His kingdom. For example, 1 Thess 4:15 refers to the former, while the four references in Matt 24 apply to the latter. To note this vital prophetic distinction is to avoid much confusion in one's understanding of the Scriptures.

28 This verse occurs in quite a different position in Luke 17:37, which corresponds to its being placed just before Matt 24:42. In our v.28, the word "carcase" (*ptōma*) means "a corpse", "a dead body", and represents the mass of mankind who will not enter the kingdom when the Lord comes. In this word- picture, the Lord was describing a separation process, when all that offends will be removed. The useless flesh of the dead bodies of those judged at the battle of Armageddon (Rev 19:17,21) will be devoured (even physically) so as to cleanse the earth. There will be a great physical disposal, with hades receiving the souls of men until the judgment of the great white throne. This disposal will be a world-wide phenomenon, in just the same way as the "lightning" represents a world-wide manifestation of the Lord's power and glory.

3. *The Coming of the King as the Son of Man* 24:29-41

v.29 "Immediately after the tribulation of those days shall the sun be darkened, and the moon shall not give her light, and the stars shall fall from heaven, and the powers of the heavens shall be shaken:
v.30 And then shall appear the sign of the Son of man in heaven: and then shall all the tribes of the earth mourn, and they shall see the Son of man coming in the clouds of heaven with power and great glory.
v.31 And he shall send his angels with a great sound of a trumpet, and they shall gather together his elect from the four winds, from one end of heaven to the other.
v.32 Now learn a parable of the fig tree; When his branch is yet tender, and putteth forth leaves, ye know that summer *is* nigh:
v.33 So likewise ye, when ye shall see all these things, know that it is near, *even* at the doors.
v.34 Verily I say unto you, This generation shall not pass, till all these things be fulfilled.
v.35 Heaven and earth shall pass away, but my words shall not pass away.
v.36 But of that day and hour knoweth no *man*, no, not the angels of heaven, but my Father only.
v.37 But as the days of Noe *were*, so shall also the coming of the Son of man be.
v.38 For as in the days that were before the flood they were eating and drinking, marrying and giving in marriage, until the day that Noe entered into the ark,
v.39 And knew not until the flood came, and took them all away; so shall also the coming of the Son of man be.
v.40 Then shall two be in the field; the one shall be taken, and the other left.
v.41 Two *women shall be* grinding at the mill; the one shall be taken, and the other left."

29 We now come to that thrilling event to which so much of the OT and NT looks forward – the coming of the Son of man in the clouds of heaven. The word "immediately" implies that He comes exactly at the end of the three and a half years of the great tribulation. Astronomical events occur first; these can be understood in two ways.

1. *Physically*. The heavenly bodies will be darkened in various ways so that nothing can prevent men from having a sight of the Son of man in His glory. (Compare this with the position of John the Baptist. He had to be removed from the scene of his ministry so that nothing might detract from the ministry of Christ who followed him. "He was a burning and a shining light" (John 5:35), yet he had to decrease so that Christ might increase (John 3:30), since He was the light of the world.) In Acts 2:20 Peter quoted Joel 2:31, "the sun shall be turned into darkness, and the moon into blood", the latter no doubt being a coloration effect caused by volcanic activity on earth (Acts 2:19). All these physical phenomena will be due to the fact that God is in control of the forces of nature; see Rev 6:12 (the sixth seal) and Rev 8:12 (the fourth trumpet). At that time, the heavens will be shaken prior to the introduction of the new covenant made with the two houses of Israel (Heb 12:26-27), in just the same way as mount Sinai was shaken when the first covenant was given (Exod 19:18). By this means, the things that cannot be shaken will remain.

2. *Metaphorically*. Some expositors suggest interpretations for these heavenlv bodies, in the same way as they do for the symbols in the Book of Revelation. The sun being darkened corresponds to the darkening of a great ruling power at the end of the tribulation period. The moon giving no light corresponds to derived authority being in a state of final moral death. The failing of the stars corresponds to subordinate authority being in a state of open apostasy. The shaking of the heavens corresponds to the overthrow of all governmental order.

The heavens themselves need to be cleansed so as to prepare a passage through which the descending Son of man may pass.

30 When this has been accomplished, "the sign of the Son of man" shall appear in heaven; this will be a precursor of the Lord's return in glory. This is what the Pharisees wanted, but no sign was then granted (Matt 12:39; 16:1). Physically in that coming day, the sign shown in the heavenly bodies will be unambiguous even to the hardest unbeliever. In Gen 1:17, God set them to give light, to rule over the day and night, to be for "signs, seasons, days, years". Their movements are so common today, obeying regular natural laws that enable their positions to be calculated well in advance, that they are taken for granted. Such regularity in God's natural creation breeds contempt, and is no supporter of faith. People therefore ask, "Where is the promise of his coming?", because all things continue (apparently) as from the beginning of creation (2 Pet 3:4).

Consequently something extraordinarily startling will be necessary as a sign, perhaps relating to the heavenly bodies' brightness, orbits, positions, periods. If 30 stars were suddenly to appear in a straight line, men would remark, "This is the finger of God" (Exod 8:19), since no rational explanation would be possible. See Isa 13:9-10. Again, the sundial in Hezekiah's day indicated ten degrees backwards (Isa 38:8). In a battle with the Amorites, the sun stood still for a day; there was no day like it before or afterwards (Josh 10:13). There is ample evidence that God had moved, and hence will yet move, in unexpected ways in His own creation.

The central statement in this passage is "they shall see the Son of man coming in the clouds of heaven with power and great glory". References to this event are so numerous in both OT and NT that we must ask the reader to look them up for himself. In the OT, we may quote: Ps 2:6-9; 110:1-3; Isa 59:20; Ezek 43:1-4; Dan 7:13; Zech 14:1-4; Mal 3:1; 4:2. In the NT, we may quote: Matt 16:27-28; 17:2; 21:9; 23:39; 24:30-31; 25:31; 26:64; Mark 9:1,3; 11:9-10; 13:26-27; 14:62; Luke 9:29; 13:35; 17:24; 19:15, 38; 21:27; 1 Thess 5:2-3; 2 Thess 1:7-8; 2:8; 2 Pet 1:16; Jude 14-15. A full account has been given by the author in the chapter "The Lord's Coming in Glory" in *Treasury of Bible Doctrine* (edited by J. Heading and C. E. Hocking). In the book of Revelation, we may quote the passages: Rev 1:7; 11:15-18; 14:14-20; 19:11-21, full details of which will be found in the author's book *From Now to Eternity: The Book of Revelation*.

The clouds will be physical clouds as in Acts 1:9-11, where the Lord's return will be "in like manner" as He ascended into heaven (v.11). On the other hand, Heb 12:1 speaks of "so great a cloud of witnesses", in which case men of faith returning with the Lord as the armies of heaven may also constitute this cloud. This will be an open manifestation of the Son of man made known to all men; the armies of men at that time will turn their weapons upon the Lamb as they make warfare against Him (Rev 17:14); of course the Lamb "shall overcome them". This will be the first time that the world sees the Lord Jesus since they saw Him dead upon the cross. Indeed "all the tribes of the world (shall) mourn". In Rev 1:7, we read that "all kindreds of the earth shall wail because of him". Zech 12:9-14 describes this time when all nations that come against Jerusalem shall be destroyed. The mourning will be by "the inhabitants of Jerusalem", by "every family", "the family of the house of David", "their wives", "the family of the house of Nathan", "the family of the house of Levi", "the family of Shimei" (the LXX gives "Simeon"), and "all the families that remain… and their wives". They shall mourn for the One whom they had pierced, though the Lord told the women who "bewailed and lamented him" on the road to the cross, "weep not for me, but weep for yourselves, and for your children…" (Luke 23:27-29). This future weeping by the godly remnant will be but a prelude to their entrance into the kingdom, for "weeping may endure for a night, but joy cometh in the morning" (Ps 30:5).

31 When the law was given, "the voice of the trumpet sounded long, and waxed louder and louder" (Exod 19:19); it was a call to preparation and action. Similarly in Rev 1:10; 4:1, the Lord's voice to John was "as of a trumpet", calling him to attention and to action. There are trumps for the church: the voice of the Lord to the seven churches therefore constituted seven trumps (Rev 2-3), which can be interpreted as a prophetic history of the church throughout the dispensation. The "last trump" will be heard when the Lord comes for the church; the dead shall be raised incorruptible and the living shall be changed (1 Cor 15:52) when the Lord descends from heaven (1 Thess 4:16). There will also be seven trumps after the rapture, given in detail in Rev 8:2 to 11:15, the last of which corresponds to the climax when the kingdoms of the world become the kingdom of Christ. There are therefore two last trumps, each terminating a well-defined sequence, each sounding at different times and for different purposes. It is to the second of these that the Lord refers here. "The elect" represent in particular the remnant of God's earthly people who have survived the great tribulation. From the whole world, they will be gathered for the first time since the captivities of Assyria and Babylon, in keeping with Isa 27:13, "in that day...the great trumpet shall be blown, and they shall come which were ready to perish in the land of Assyria, and the outcasts in the land of Egypt, and shall worship the Lord in the holy mount at Jerusalem". Compare this with 2 Chron 30:10-11, where some from Israel would not come to Jerusalem, although many did accept the invitation. In the future the angels of the Son of man first gather up the tares for judgment (Matt 13:30, 40-42), this gathering corresponding to Matt 24:39- 41. The angels also shall gather in the wheat, namely the elect, into the kingdom of Christ; see Isa 11:12, where we read of the gathering of "the dispersed of Judah from the four corners of the earth".

32-33 At this point Luke 21:28 adds, "Look up, and lift up your heads; for your redemption draweth nigh", namely, the ultimate redemption from the Roman yoke, which they had sought when the Lord was here (Luke 2:38; 24:21; Acts 1:6).

The word for "tender, soft" (*hapalos*) appears only in v.32 and in Mark 13:28, A tender branch and the appearance of leaves are a precursor of summer. Such natural signs show the certainty of an event not very far in the future. Similarly in Matt 16:2-3, the colour of the sky suggests the kind of weather shortly to be experienced. Hence, when signs of the times are given, the Lord's people should be able to discern the nearness of subsequent events. We have described the implications of the fig tree in considering Matt 21:19-20. When the Lord was here, there was nothing from the Jewish nation that satisfied Him; the fig tree was cursed. But in the future, a restored branch will put forth leaves, a herald of fruit soon to come in the summer. The leaves speak of the experiences of the Jewish remnant during the great tribulation. When they see and pass through all these events, they must recognise that their Messiah is about to come forth.

Luke 21:31 states that they must recognise "that the kingdom of God is nigh at hand". The AV of Matt 24:33, "it is near, even at the doors", is retained by JND in his translation, but the RV reads "he is nigh, even at the doors". The Greek verb *estin* can mean either "it is" or "he is"; the translator must therefore insert his own interpretation; "it" would refer to the coming of the Son of man, while "he" would refer to the Son of man Himself. Certainly in Luke 21:31, the Lord's coming to establish His kingdom is the stated meaning, but Luke did not use the words "at the doors". However, we feel that Matthew had the Messiah more in mind, and we prefer the words "he is near". This is because John saw a door opened in heaven in Rev 4:1, and heaven was again opened in Rev 19:11 when the King of kings and Lord of lords comes forth, implying a door in John's vision. See Ps 24:7-10.

34-35 The Lord now stressed the certainty of the prophetic word. The word "generation" (*genea*) means a family, or members of a genealogy as in Matt 1:17, and extends to a race of people. In a prophetic sense, this last meaning is implied here: the nation of Israel will not disappear before the prophetic word has been fulfilled. It is the explanation as to why the Jews have existed over the centuries, and have never died out in spite of massive persecution against them. The nation of unbelief will pass away when the Lord comes, but those who are faithful at that time will be saved to enter the kingdom, as Paul wrote, "And so all Israel shall be saved" (Rom 11:26).

The prophetic word is more sure than God's natural creation (v.35). As Peter wrote, "We have also a more sure word of prophecy", more sure than events that could be seen and heard (2 Pet 1:19). In this statement, the Lord merely indicated that the natural creation shall pass away; His teaching did not include events at the end of the millennial reign, when this will take place (Rev 20:11; 21:1), with the kingdom having been delivered up to God, even the Father (1 Cor 15:24). What was created originally will perish (Heb 1:10-11), in contrast to the Lord: "thou remainest". Peter also wrote of this event, in connection with the day of judgment and perdition of ungodly men (2 Pet 3:7-13).

The continued existence of the natural creation as a proof of God's will in other directions is used in the OT. If the sun, moon and stars as ordinances depart from before God, "then the seed of Israel also shall cease from being a nation before me for ever" (Jer 31:35-36). After all, the seed had been likened to the stars in Gen 15:5, so we need not be surprised that the existence of one should go hand-in-hand with the prophetic existence of the other. In Jer 33:25-26, God said, "if I have not appointed the ordinances of heaven and earth; then will I cast away the seed of Jacob, and David my servant".

36 In this verse, the Lord spoke of the lack of knowledge of the timing of final prophetical events. He used the present tense "knoweth", meaning at the time when He was speaking, and as we now know, this was to continue throughout the church age. Whereas believers know that the coming of the Lord draws nigh, yet we do not know the exact time, neither can it be calculated, as some have mistakenly sought to do. If the date were known, then evil men would take advantage of it, and His own people would be slothful. The Lord said, "It is not for you to know the times or the seasons, which the Father hath put in his own power" (Acts 1:7); evidently the apostles were looking for the restoration of the kingdom to Israel, by the Messiah appearing in glory to sweep away the fourth beast-kingdom.

Matthew does not contain the remarkable addition found in Mark 13:32, ''neither the Son'', for which various suggestions have been put forward. But in the future, men of understanding will be able to deduce the year of the return of the Lord in glory, since the prophetic Scriptures are quite clear that when the great tribulation commences it will last for only three and a half years. Angels are prominent in the Book of Revelation, and when the last seven years start to unfold, they will be able to deduce when the end will come, though perhaps the exact "day and hour" may still be unknown. Throughout all the previous ages, the plan has been known within the counsels of the Godhead, but that great day of the vindication of Christ on earth remains hidden from men and angels, on earth and in heaven.

37-41 In the last seven years, the godly on earth will know when the end is coming, and through their reading of Scripture they will know the circumstances of the end. But the multitudes of unbelievers will have no idea that the end is near, in spite of suffering under the judgments that God will let loose upon mankind generally. In the last days, they shall mock, "Where is the promise of his coming?" (2 Pet 3:4), evidently at the testimony of the godly that the wrath of God is near at hand. This had been so in Noah's day, for the flood came unexpectedly upon the ungodly. Noah had "prepared an ark to the saving of his house; by the which he condemned the world" (Heb 11:7). He himself had been warned by God but others did not heed his testimony. Noah was "a preacher of righteousness" (2 Pet 2:5), and the Spirit of Christ preached through him to the ungodly whose spirits are now in prison in hades (1 Pet 3:18-20). The longsuffering of God waited while the ark was being built. The corresponding prophetical passage in Luke's Gospel adds the unexpected judgment of God against Sodom in the days of Lot (Luke 17:28-29).

In Noah's day, men were "eating and drinking, marrying and giving in marriage" as the ark was being built; in Lot's day, "they did eat, they drank, they bought, they sold, they planted, they builded" (Luke 17:28). These were not just the common features of life, but activities associated with gross sin and idolatry. When Aaron made the golden calf, "the people sat down to eat and to drink, and rose up to play (Exod 32:6), implying gross sexual immorality copied from the heathen around. The Lord's reference to marriage goes back to Gen 6:2, where "the sons of God saw the daughters of men that they were fair; and they took them wives of all which they chose". Though interpretations of this verse vary amongst expositors, yet strange results emerged in that there were "giants in the earth in those days" (Gen 6:4).

Thus the flood came when they were not anticipating it, and so shall the future judgment be at the coming of the Son of man; "in such an hour as ye think not the Son of man cometh" (Matt 24:44), "In a day when he looketh not for him, and in an hour that he is not aware of" (v.50), "watch therefore, for ye know neither the day nor the hour wherein the Son of man cometh" (25:13). As Paul wrote, "then sudden destruction cometh upon them, as travail upon a woman with child; and they shall not escape" (1 Thess 5:3).

The taking of "them all away" corresponds to the fate of the tares in Matt 13:30 and of the goats in Matt 25:41-46. It corresponds similarly with the taking of the one worker in the field, and the one woman grinding at the mill, while Luke 17:34 adds the one person of two in a bed. Unity will be broken, with people being taken for judgment from all works and walks of life; day and night will make no difference in this great sifting process. There will be identical outward occupations, but differing states of the inner heart, in keeping with the Lord's words, "Let both grow together until the harvest" (Matt 13:30). The two women "grinding at the mill" depicts a simple practice of that day; the lower millstone is fixed, and the upper moveable one is pushed back and forth by two people sitting opposite one another. In the Lord's word-picture, those that are "left" remain to enter the kingdom. The word translated "other" in the AV strictly, is just the word for "one", one person. But in Luke 17:35-36, the word *heteros* is used, another of a different kind. Moreover, in Luke 17:37, the reference to the body, and the eagles occurs as a picture of this sifting process.

4. *The Necessity of Watching* 24:42-51

v.42 "Watch therefore: for ye know not what hour your Lord doth come.
v.43 But know this, that if the goodman of the house had known in what watch the thief would come, he would have watched, and would not have suffered his house to be broken up.
v.44 Therefore be ye also ready: for in such an hour as ye think not the Son of man cometh.
v.45 Who then is a faithful and wise servant, whom his lord hath made ruler over his household, to give them meat in due season?
v.46 Blessed *is* that servant. whom his lord when he cometh shall find so doing.
v.47 Verily I say unto you, That he shall make him ruler over all his goods.
v.48 But and if that evil servant shall say in his heart, My lord delayeth his coming;
v.49 And shall begin to smite *his* fellowservants, and to eat and drink with the drunken;
v.50 The lord of that servant shall come in a day when he looketh not for *him*, and in an hour that he not aware of.
v.51 And shall cut him asunder, and appoint *him* his portion with the hypocrites: there shall be weeping and gnashing of teeth."

42 We now have a series of parables connected with watching and working, in the light of the fact that the *hour* of the Lord's return is not known. The context still demands that the reference must be to the faithful and godly remnant waiting through tribulation for the introduction of the kingdom in open display. But the principles involved in these parables are also applicable to the Lord's people today, as they too watch for the Lord from heaven. The overall lesson that must be appropriated is that the whole life must be lived in the light of the Lord's return. Moreover, in these parables we find reference to the ungodly, namely, "the goodman of the house" (v.43), "that evil servant" (v.48), the five foolish virgins (25:3), and the man with the one talent (25:26).

43-44 The word "goodman of the house" (*oikodespotēs*) occurs only in the synoptic Gospels, and is variously, translated "master of the house" (three times), "goodman of the house" (five times), and "householder" (four times); the corresponding verb occurs once in 1 Tim 5:14 as "guide the house". The implication of the words in v.43 is that the householder did not watch, and his house was broken up by the thief. The verb "broken up" (*diarussō*) strictly means to dig through, occurring in the NT only here and in Matt 6:19, 20; Luke 12:39. When houses were made with clay walls, it was easy to dig through the clay to gain an entrance rather than break down a door. In a vision, Ezekiel was confronted with a hole in the wall and a door, and he also had to dig (Ezek 8:7,8). Some expositors suggest that this householder represents the apostles. But we believe that he stands for the future Jewish religious leaders, whose work will be broken up in judgment, for the Lord will come unexpectedly, as a thief, both for the church at the rapture (Rev 3:3), and when He comes in glory, and judgment (1 Thess 5:2; Rev 16:15), as well as at the final dissolution of all things (2 Pet 3:10). But the godly at that time will be ready (as described in the following parables), they, will know of the end of the seven year period, though they will not know the actual "hour" of the coming of the Son of man.

45-47 The second man is the "faithful and wise servant" (*doulos*, a bondman), having responsibility to feed others in the household. In spite of many problems, this responsibility must be worked out until his lord comes, when he will be set over all his property. Those who have been faithful in that which is least will have occasion to be faithful in that which is much (Luke 16:10). For faithfulness during the difficulties of the last seven years there will be kingdom blessings of responsibility, they will reign with Christ (Rev 20:4) instead of being reigned over by the future beast.

Today, God expects His people to be faithful in their service: in the NT, the men who are called faithful are Paul (1 Tim 1:12), Timothy (1 Cor 4:17), Tychicus (Eph 6:21; Col 4:7), Epaphras (Col 1:7), Onesimus (Col 4:9) and Silvanus (1 Pet 5:12). We trust Him because He is faithful (1 Cor 1:9); He trusts us when we are faithful.

The service visualised here is that of giving "meat in due season". Today, this is the work of teachers and of elders who are apt to teach. Overseers must "feed the church of God" (Acts 20:28); the elders must "feed the flock of God which is among you" (1 Pet 5:2), for the edification of the assembly, conforming the Lord's people to the mind of Christ. The Lord expects this service to take place until He come, in the same way, as He expects the breaking of bread or the Lord's supper to take place until He come. For members of the church, there will be many rewards for faithful service.

48-51 The third man is "that evil servant", who deliberately renounces all superior authority. He represents men who set themselves up in high religious circles by tradition of men, but not by any divine calling. They are elected by men, and pay lip-service to the authority of' Christ by saying "My lord". By stating, "My lord delayeth his coming", the man shows that organised religion and its servants never make much of the promised coming of Christ: prophecy is a closed book to such men. Smiting his fellowservants (v.49) denotes persecution of those who hold the truth, while he has fellowship with the unsaved by eating and drinking with the drunken. Such eating and drinking is not part of the kingdom of God (Rom 14:17), but answers to what the Lord had said in Matt 24:38. However, a denial of the truth of His coming does not remove its glorious fact. The day and hour will arrive unexpectedly at the moment of unsanctified feasting (as took place in Dan 5). That man's portion will be with the wicked (as in Matt 13); religious unrighteousness shall not triumph, for the One who sits in the heavens shall laugh at man's puny efforts to work contrary to His will (Ps 2:4).

V. Parables Relating to the King's Return in Glory (25:1-46)

1. *The Parable of the Ten Virgins* 25:1-13

v.1 "Then shall the kingdom of heaven be likened unto ten virgins, which took their lamps, and went forth to meet the bridegroom.
v.2 And five of them were wise, and five *were* foolish.
v.3 They that *were* foolish took their lamps, and took no oil with them:
v.4 But the wise took oil in their vessels with their lamps.
v.5 While the bridegroom tarried, they all slumbered and slept.
v.6 And at midnight there was a cry made, Behold, the bridegroom cometh; go ye out to meet him.
v.7 Then all those virgins arose, and trimmed their lamps.
v.8 And the foolish said unto the wise, Give us of your oil; for our lamps are gone out.
v.9 But the wise answered, saying, *Not so*; lest there be not enough for us and you: but go ye rather to them that sell, and buy for yourselves.
v.10 And while they went to buy, the bridegroom came; and they that were ready went in with him to the marriage: and the door was shut.
v.11 Afterward came also the other virgins, saying, Lord, Lord, open to us.
v.12 But he answered and said, Verily I say unto you, I know you not.
v.13 Watch therefore, for ye know neither the day nor the hour wherein the Son of man cometh."

This parable is another of the "separation parables" that occur so frequently in Matthew's Gospel. Interpretations differ considerably, depending upon how the five wise virgins and the five foolish virgins are explained; even looked at from the point of view of the prophetic programme presented in our book there can be more than one interpretation, all full of practical exhortations for the Lord's people as they approach the coming of the Lord. We believe that the five wise and the five foolish represent classes of persons rather than individuals, the former being saved and the latter being unsaved.

1-2 For practical purposes, we shall consider the five wise virgins as representing the church, while the five foolish virgins represent the Jewish nation that is not saved. Other expositors may see these classes as both existing on earth during the last seven years, in which case the wise cannot represent the church, but rather the faithful Jewish remnant. We need not be surprised that the church can be seen in such a parable, for this has occurred before, for example in Matt 21:43, where "a nation bringing forth the fruits thereof" replaces "those wicked men".

The "lamps" are the spheres of testimony of these two groups, existing side-by-side since Acts 2, as Paul indicated in 1 Cor 10:32. Both groups went forth with differing aspirations. For the church, its hope was the coming of the Lord to the air, though this hope was largely lost during the long ages of church history since apostolic days. For the Jews, their hope was the coming of the promised Messiah, though their hearts were closed by unbelief to the fact that this Messiah was Jesus of Nazareth now exalted on the throne above. The state of the wise and the foolish has already been described in Matt 7:24-27, where acceptance or rejection of the words of the Lord forms the difference.

3-4 The kind of profession indicated by the lamps depends upon the contents of these lamps; either there is oil for light, or there is a lack of oil for darkness. These two verses show that all ten lamps possessed oil once, but there were also "vessels" (*angeion*, a small vessel, being a diminutive form of *angos*) intended to yield a continual supply of oil. In the OT the Jewish nation was a partaker of the Holy Spirit (Heb 6:4), not of course in the sense of Acts 2, but in the sense that the Spirit had been in the prophets (2 Pet 1:21) speaking to the nation. However, as Stephen said, "ye do always resist the Holy Spirit: as your fathers did, so do ye" (Acts 7:51). By contrast, the wise virgins had an abundant supply of oil; the Spirit of God is without measure, as believers throughout the church period have been baptised in the Spirit, and filled with the Spirit for Christian living, courage and service. The Spirit, alas, may be quenched (1 Thess 5:19) and grieved (Eph 4:30), but the abundant supply is never cut off, even when the testimony is weak.

5-6 The day of God's grace continued, and men in both spheres of religious profession "slumbered and slept". The first verb is *nustazō*, in the aorist tense, denoting the act of nodding off to sleep. The second verb is *katheudō*, in the imperfect tense: they were sleeping for a period. Outwardly there appeared to be no difference between the two classes of virgins. As Paul asked, "Are ye not carnal, and walk as men?" (1 Cor 3:3). This is not the state of those who are watching for the coming of the Lord. "Therefore let us not sleep, as do others; but let us watch" (1 Thess 5:6), but if there is failure, we need the exhortation "it is high time to awake out of sleep" (Rom 13:11). But the others are of the night and darkness, and "sleep in the night" (1 Thess 5:5,7). In the OT, David certainly did not sleep when there was important work before him (Ps 132:4), and the One who keeps Israel never slumbers (Ps 121:3).

The slumber and sleep visualised in the parable obviously are connected with the appreciation of the truth of the Lord's return. Over the centuries, the professing church has had no true concept of the rapture and the resurrection of believers, while Jews have had no true concept of the coming of their Messiah in glory for the NT Scriptures were quite unknown to them. This ecclesiastical ignorance can be seen in quotations from the old Book of Common Prayer. The collect for the First Sunday in Advent reads, "that in the last day, when He shall come again in His glorious Majesty to judge both the quick and the dead, we may rise to the life immortal". Again, the collect for the Third Sunday in Advent reads, "that at Thy second coming to judge the world we may be found an acceptable people in Thy sight". Such confusion of doctrine shows that those who wrote, perpetuated and said these prayers were asleep as far as the true doctrine of the rapture is concerned!

In the blackest hour of ecclesiastical and Jewish ignorance, the cry is made, "Behold, the bridegroom cometh; go ye out to meet him". Here is an awakening of some in the Christian profession, brought about by the Holy Spirit in these last days. True prophetical knowledge, so long hidden to the eyes of men, has been regained, and the hope of the church has been taught and proclaimed again as in Paul's day. The Spirit has been a teacher to us, and then He is a light shining out from us in testimony. Regarding the subject of prophecy, the Lord said in Rev 22:16, "I Jesus have sent mine angel to testify unto you these things in the churches", and this message has emerged from centuries of darkness, in the same way as the book of the law was found in Josiah's day (2 Chron 34:14-18).

7-9 Religious men and groups of all persuasions have to assess their position in the light of the revived teaching concerning the rapture and the return of the Lord in glory. What testimony will they render with their lamps? The wise virgins had oil for their lamps – their testimony, emanated in the power of the Holy Spirit. Of course, not all Christians are embraced by the five wise virgins, and not all Jewish unbelievers are embraced by the five foolish virgins. Many Christians, alas, still have no true understanding of prophecy, and some may have no interest in it either, but all will rise to meet the Lord in the air at the rapture. But the parable focuses attention on only certain Christians, namely, those whose hearts have been opened to receive the truth. The foolish represent only a group of the unbelieving Jews – those who hear the testimony that the coming of the Lord draws nigh. Through hearing the gospel message, they realise that they have no oil – that they are unsaved and do not possess the Holy Spirit. They recognise that their lamps "are going out"; their own testimony of the OT promises of a coming Messiah had grown dim, and was about to fade away through the excesses of unbelief.

The request "Give us of your oil" represents ignorance; there can be no transfer of oil from one to the other, no transfer of the Holy Spirit from one person to another. (The flowing out in John 7:38-39 does not represent a transfer, but testimony.) By saying "not enough", there is implied that each believer is filled with the Spirit dwelling in his body as a temple; God does not contemplate a half-filled believer, so sharing is impossible. Rather, the oil comes through acquisition from "them that sell"; it is the Father that gives the Comforter (John 14:16) and also the Son (15:26; 16:7; Acts 2:33). The idea behind buying has nothing to do with Simon's attempt to buy the Spirit from Peter and John with money (Acts 8:18); rather, it goes back to the OT concept of buying "without money and without price" (Isa 55:1).

10 Clearly this group of five foolish virgins was exercised about the matter, for the whole truth of the gospel lies behind this exercise. But God's Spirit does not always strive with men, and they were too late to acquire the blessings of God through the gospel message presented by the wise virgins. The Bridegroom came, and the five who were ready went in with Him to the marriage. In other words, at the rapture of the church believers enter in but unbelievers (here, unbelieving but exercised Jews) remain on the outside. The fact that "the door was shut" suggests that the opportunity to enter into blessing had been taken away; faith will be formed amongst the Jews during the last seven years, but not amongst this grouping. When the Lord shuts the door, no man can open it (Rev 3:7). Some expositors raise the question as to who the bride will be, and they provide different answers, because the bride is not mentioned in the parable. Jerusalem (Isa 62:1, 5) seems to be a satisfactory suggestion.

11-12 Later, this unbelieving group found themselves in a position where they were able to plead with the Lord. Their cry, "Lord, Lord", expresses urgency. They will claim to have engaged in religious activity in His name (Matt 7:21-23), but He will reply, "I know you not", or "I never knew you" (v.23). The reason is that, because of unbelief, they are those who "work iniquity", not having done the divine will. They had to depart, evidently into eternal judgment. This conversation will take place when the Lord comes in glory, when such Jews will hope to enter the millennial kingdom, but like the goats in Matt 25:41 they will be eternally on the outside.

13 The parable concludes with the implied lesson: "Watch therefore". As we have commented before, no one knows the day or the hour of His return, so it is dangerous to sleep as if His return is of no relevance. Some Greek texts (followed by the RV and JND) omit the last words "wherein the Son of man cometh". The interpretation that we have given suggests that this omission is valid, for the Lord does not take the character as "Son of man" in relation to the church, so if the rapture is implied in v.10 then this particular title is inappropriate.

2. *The Parable of the Eight Talents* 25:14-30

v.14 "For *the kingdom of heaven is* as a man travelling into a far country, *who* called his own servants, and delivered unto them his goods.
v.15 And unto one he gave five talents, to another two, and to another one; to every man according to his several ability; and straightway took his journey.
v.16 Then he that had received the five talents went and traded with the same, and made *them* other five talents.
v.17 And likewise he that *had received* two, he also gained other two.
v.18 But he that had received one went and digged in the earth, and hid his lord's money.
v.19 After a long time the lord of those servants cometh, and reckoneth with them.
v.20 And so he that had received five talents came and brought other five talents, saying, Lord, thou deliveredst unto me five talents: behold, I have gained beside them five talents more.
v.21 His lord said unto him, Well done, *thou* good and faithful servant: thou hast been faithful over a few things, I will make thee ruler over many things: enter thou into the joy of thy lord.
v.22 He also that had received two talents came and said, Lord, thou deliveredst unto me two talents: behold, I have gained two other talents beside them.
v.23 His lord said unto him, Well done, good and faithful servant; thou hast been faithful over a few things, I will make thee ruler over many things: enter thou into the joy of thy lord.
v.24 Then he which had received the one talent came and said, Lord, I knew thee that thou art an hard man, reaping where thou hast not sown, and gathering where thou hast not strawed:
v.25 And I was afraid, and went and hid thy talent in the earth: lo, *there* thou hast *that is* thine.
v.26 His lord answered and said unto him. *Thou* wicked and slothful servant, thou knewest that I reap where I sowed not, and gather where I have not strawed:
v.27 Thou oughtest therefore to have put my money to the exchangers, and *then* at my coming I should have received mine own with usury.
v.28 Take therefore the talent from him, and give *it* unto him which hath ten talents.
v.29 For unto every one that hath shall be given, and he shall have abundance: but from him that hath not shall be taken away even that which he hath.
v.30 And cast ye the unprofitable servant into outer darkness: there shall be weeping and gnashing of teeth.

The parable of the talents shows the differing capacities of men who receive something from the Lord; the parable of the pounds in Luke 19:12-27 implies common responsibility. Some expositors have thought that the two parables are identical, but the respective contexts demonstrate that they were spoken on different occasions. In Luke 19:11, the parable was spoken because some thought "that the kingdom of God should immediately appear"; it was given as the Lord left Jericho on His way to Jerusalem. But the parable of the talents was given a few days later on the mount of Olives. The former was spoken publicly to the people accompanying Him, but the latter to the disciples privately. Moreover, expositors differ in their interpretation of the parable, some even denying that the "outer darkness" in v.30 represents eternal punishment. The fact that the parable spans the time from the ascension of Christ (v.14) to His return (v.19) means that we can interpret the intervening period as that of the church age and not restrict it to the last seven years prior to His return in glory.

14 The words "the kingdom of heaven" do not correspond to any words in the Greek text; "For it is as if a man" is the rendering in the RV and JND, though "the kingdom of heaven" is implied as in v.1. "Travelling into a far country" is one word in Greek, being the verb *apodēmeō*, meaning to leave the country. The RV translates it as "going into another country", and JND as "going away out of a country". In v.15 this same verb is rendered "took his journey". The AV always inserts the word "far" when this verb appears (Matt 21:33; Mark 12:1; Luke 15:13; 20:9) though strictly the sense of "far" is not implied. But in Luke 15:13 and 19:13, the additional words "a far country" are used in the narrative, and are properly rendered in the English translation.

Once again, the "servants" are bondmen (*doulos*), and they receive the man's goods, suggesting that the talents are not all money in the parable, but these talents represent the worth of the goods; the man who received one talent definitely received "money" (v.18).

15 The distribution was uneven, showing that the man knew the capacity and faithfulness of these servants beforehand it was "to every man according to his several (or respective) ability". Expositors make so many suggestions as to what these talents represent, that their suggestions appear almost like guess-work, although since the Lord did not explain the parable we are at liberty to make sensible spiritual suggestions. Certainly, the servants did not possess the talents previously. We cannot therefore agree with J. C. Ryle in his book *Expository Thoughts on the Gospels: Vol. 1 Matthew,* where he writes: "Anything whereby we may glorify God is a talent. Our gifts, our influence, our money, our knowledge, our health, our strength, our time, our senses, our reason, our intellect, our memory, our affections". Of course these features must be used in the service of God for His glory, but they hardly represent extra talents received on account of the Lord's departure to heaven. We believe that these talents were far more positive, in keeping with the Lord's words after His resurrection, "Receive ye the

Holy Spirit" (John 20:22), translated into spiritual gifts when the Lord had ascended into heaven. The man with the one talent was a servant and responsible to God, yet not saved; he had the Spirit in the sense of John 16:8-11, where the Spirit is given to "reprove the world of sin, and of righteousness, and of judgment". One way in which the Spirit is manifested is through the spiritual gifts that are given to the Lord's people. In Rom 12:3 it is God who has "dealt to every man the measure of faith", and a list of gifts is then given. In 1 Cor 12:11 it is the Holy Spirit who has divided "to every man severally as he will", a list of gifts appearing in vv.8-11. In Eph 4:7 Paul wrote, "unto every one of us is given grace according to the measure of the gift of Christ", and a list follows. In 1 Pet 4:10, the apostle wrote, "As every man hath received the gift". Note the stress on "everyman" and the great fact that the three Persons of the Godhead are involved in the distribution. The original giving of gifts continues to the present, the particular gifts given depending on God's will, and not necessarily embracing all the original gifts that concerned the beginning of the church testimony.

16-17 The faithfulness of the first two men enabled them to duplicate the number of talents. Ability in divine service increases through the exercise of that ability; gift was not to be neglected (1 Tim 4:14), but it had to be stirred up into greater usefulness (2 Tim 1:6). Gifts were given for edification, not only of self, but particularly of other members of local churches. By this means the talents increased, a doubling in the parable, but a hundredfold in the case of the good seed (Matt 13:8). The labours of the apostle Paul enabled many churches to be formed, each consisting of many believers with developing gifts from the Holy Spirit. In the case of Rome, he desired to impart to them some spiritual gift for their establishment in the faith (Rom 1:11).

18 But the one talent was buried in the earth by the man who would not appreciate its value. The Spirit strives with men, but "ye would not" (Matt 23:37). This man was not a heathen, but one who knew of the existence of the talent. No doubt he was of the type that engages in religious pursuits, but without power since he was not saved. Contact with the earth is a convenient method for avoiding the convicting power of the Holy Spirit; the doctrine of the Holy Spirit would be known, but not the power leading to salvation. Treasures on earth were more to the taste of this man than treasure in heaven. Consequently, no work of grace could be accomplished in that man, and if no work was begun, then no work could continue; if no good work had begun, then this could not be finished before the day of Christ (Phil 1:6).

19 The Lord gave no indication as to the duration of the "long time". Heb 10:36-37 is very apt here; "after ye have done the will of God, ye might receive the promise. For yet a little while, and he that shall come will come, and will not tarry". Of course, the servants that were alive at the beginning of the church will not be here at the rapture; they "sleep in Jesus" until that day (1 Thess 4:14), and they shall rise first, to be followed by those who "are alive and remain unto the coming of the Lord" (v.15). The reckoning or assessment will take place at the "judgment seat of Christ" (Rom 14:10); we have discussed this in connection with Matt 20:16.

20-23 All three men commenced their statements by using the title "*Kurie*" – Lord. Today, other popular titles are in common use in some circles, but their constant repetition has no justification in Scripture. In that day, everyone will be constrained to use the title "Lord" (Phil 2:11). The first two men used identical words (apart from the numbers five and two), and the Lord used identical words in His responses to them. Without boasting, they used the word "I", unlike Luke 19:16,18, where "thy pound" was used. To say "I" is not boasting, but is a humble recognition of fact, as Paul wrote, "I laboured more abundantly than they all: yet not I, but the grace of God which was with me" (1 Cor 15:10); see also Gal 2:20. Before the Lord, they could point to the increase in the talents. Gift is developed in self, and used in service, as in Paul's case where he "increased the more in strength, and confounded the Jews ... proving that this is very Christ" (Acts 9:22). Gift was produced in Apollos (a man already possessing eloquence, and mighty in the scriptures), who then helped those in Achaia who had believed through grace (Acts 18:27). These gifts are "for the edifying of the body of Christ" (Eph 4:12), as members take up their own gifts through the stimulus of others who are more mature. The Lord recognises such men as "good and faithful" servants; faithfulness is the basis of the divine assessment. "It is required ... that a man be found faithful", wrote Paul (1 Cor 4:2); God counted Paul faithful (1 Tim 1:12), and at the end Paul declared that he had "kept the faith" (2 Tim 4:7). The divine assessment will be based on what a man has, and not on what he has not (2 Cor 8:12), since the original distribution was according to the Lord's will. No one should be jealous or even disappointed that he does not possess what another man may possess: "as God has distributed to every man, as the Lord hath called every one, so let him walk" (1 Cor 7:17).

A twofold reward is promised for faithfulness. We should point out that the commendation "Well done" (*eu*) should merely be "Well", whereas in Luke 19:17 "Well" (*euge*) should be "Well done" (RV). When full faithfulness has been worked out in life and service, millennial authority "over many things" is granted to both men. Faithfulness here leads to authority there, as Paul wrote, "we shall also reign with him" (2 Tim 2:12); a kingdom is appointed to us (Luke 22:29), and we shall have power over the nations (Rev 2:26; 5:10). The second reward is to enter "into the joy of thy lord". In ascension, the Lord entered into "pleasures for evermore" (Acts 2:28; Ps 16:11); this joy had been set before Him as He endured the cross and its shame (Heb 12:2). Faithfulness now often brings tribulation in this scene, but the contrasting reward will be eternal.

24-30 The explanation given by the third man does not take place at the judgment seat of Christ, the unsaved will not be there. Depending on circumstances, it takes place when the unsaved are gathered so as not to enter the millennial kingdom, or at the judgment of the great white throne that takes place at the end of the thousand years. The answer appears to be concocted for the occasion. The Lord certainly is not "hard", since it is His grace that provides the gift and His grace that enables it to be worked out; it is His grace that leads men to repentance and salvation by the Holy Spirit. And the examples of the first two men show that the Lord reaped and gathered where He had sown and scattered, for as the good Sower He provided the seed, together with the gifts and opportunities whereby His work was done. The Holy Spirit was given to convince men; lack of fruit was the fault of men – it was no reflection on the power of the Lord as this man insinuated. We doubt whether the man was "afraid" during his lifetime; attachment to the world was more desirable than the inward work of the Spirit, so the Spirit returned to Him that gave Him. As Paul wrote, "For of him, and through him, and to him, are all things" (Rom 11:36).

In the Lord's answer, the words "wicked and slothful" stand in contrast to the words "good and faithful". The Lord merely quoted the man's words, namely what he claimed to know. His doctrine was wrong, but on that basis he would be judged, "For by thy words thou shalt be justified, and by thy words thou shalt be condemned" (Matt 12:37). Verse 27 causes difficulty to the expositors. We feel that by hiding the talent the man was preventing the Holy Spirit from leading others to a knowledge of Christ and salvation. He passed his worldliness on to others, for such an attitude is very contagious. If the man did not want salvation himself, then he should not hinder the work of the Spirit in others. The Lord would then have received something at His coming. The Pharisees were like that: they would not enter themselves, neither would they allow others to enter in (Matt 23:13). The power of God can never be wasted; it will be needed during the millennial administration by those who are granted the authority to rule. It is withdrawn from the one-talent man, and given to the ten-talent man.

Verse 29 repeats what the Lord has said in Matt 13:12 – the growth of truth in those that possess it, and the taking away of truth from those who do not desire it. The same applies to the work of the Holy Spirit in men's hearts. These are words of encouragement to the Lord's people, and words of warning to the unconverted, but we seldom hear them presented to the unsaved! In that future judgment, such a man will be assessed as "unprofitable". In our present life, we should assess ourselves as "unprofitable servants" (Luke 17:10) with a deep sense of humility. Yet Mark could be "profitable" after a change in his previous attitude (2 Tim 4:11; Acts 13:13; 15:38), and Onesimus was now "profitable", having previously been unprofitable before he was converted (Philem 11). But if one remains unprofitable unto the end, there remains but the "outer darkness", "the blackness of darkness for ever" (Jude 13), with a remorse that can never be erased.

3. *The Parable of the Sheep and the Goats* 25:31-46

v.31 "When the Son of man shall come in his glory, and all the holy angels with him, then shall he sit upon the throne of his glory:
v.32 And before him shall be gathered all nations: and he shall separate them one from another, as a shepherd divideth *his* sheep from the goats:
v.33 And he shall set the sheep on his right hand, but the goats on the left.
v.34 Then shall the King say unto them on his right hand, Come, ye blessed of my Father, inherit the kingdom prepared for you from the foundation of the world:
v.35 For I was an hungred. and ye gave me meat: I was thirsty, and ye gave me drink: I was a stranger, and ye took me in:
v.36 Naked, and ye clothed me: I was sick, and ye visited me: I was in prison, and ye came unto me.
v.37 Then shall the righteous answer him, saying, Lord, when saw we thee an hungred, and fed *thee*? or thirsty, and gave *thee* drink?
v.38 When saw we thee a stranger, and took *thee* in? or naked, and clothed *thee*?
v.39 Or when saw we thee sick, or in prison, and came unto thee?
v.40 And the King shall answer and say unto them, Verily I say unto you, Inasmuch as ye have done *it* unto one of the least of these my brethren, ye have done *it* unto me.
v.41 Then shall he say also unto them on the left hand, Depart from me, ye cursed, into everlasting fire, prepared for the devil and his angels:
v.42 For I was an hungred, and ye gave me no meat: I was thirsty, and ye gave me no drink:
v.43 I was a stranger, and ye took me not in: naked, and ye clothed me not: sick, and in prison, and ye visited me not.
v.44 Then shall they also answer him, saying, Lord, when saw we thee an hungred, or athirst, or a stranger, or naked, or sick, or in prison, and did not minister unto thee?
v.45 Then shall he answer them, saying, Verily I say unto you, Inasmuch as ye did *it* not to one of the least of these, ye did *it* not to me.
v.46 And these shall go away into everlasting punishment: but the righteous into life eternal."

The Previous three parables of watching, waiting and working have formed a parenthesis; the concluding parable, in its subject matter, is linked to Matt 24:41. In particular, the title "Son of man appears once more, appropriate to the coming of the Lord in glory to Israel and to the world. This parable is one of judgment. There are many aspects of judgment found in the Scriptures, and they must not be confounded the one with the other. In just the same way as redemption plans had been made before the foundation of the world, since the Lamb had then been foreordained (1 Pet 1:19-20; Acts 2:23), so too had there been divine preparation for judgment. For example, there was the "everlasting fire, prepared for the devil and his angels" (Matt 25:41); the angels that had sinned had been delivered "into chains of darkness, to be reserved unto judgment" (2 Pet 2:4). Before the fall, God could say that Adam would die if he ate of the fruit of the forbidden tree (Gen 2:17); as a result of the fall "death passed upon all men, for that all have sinned" (Rom 5:12). Nevertheless, during the OT period there were always men of whom it could be written, "These all died in faith" (Heb 11:13), though of the rest, men were judged at the flood, at the Red Sea, at the making of the golden calf, at the rebellion caused by Korah, and so on; these await "the resurrection of damnation" (John 5:29).

In the NT, the prominent judgment of the present day concerns God's governmental judgment in local churches, for "judgment must begin at the house of God" (1 Pet 4:17). Examples are: Ananias and Sapphira (Acts 5:1-11); the Corinthians who desecrated the Lord's Supper by becoming drunken with the symbolic wine (I Cor 11:30-32); the chastening of sons for correction unto holiness and righteousness (Heb 12:6-11). After the rapture of the church, there will take place "the judgment seat of Christ" (Rom 14:10), when the motives and deeds of the Lord's people will be assessed for rewards. There will then follow God's governmental judgments on earth during the last seven years – His direct intervention amongst men on account of growing apostasy and sin; this is detailed in many chapters between Rev 6 and Rev 19. Conditions will be so bad, that Isa 1:9 will apply, "Except the Lord of hosts had left unto us a very small remnant, we should have been as Sodom".

The conclusion of these seven years will see what is called the warrior judgment of Christ, when He comes forth to destroy firstly the apostate religious system known as "Mystery, Babylon the great" (Rev 17; 18; 19:1-4) and secondly the armies of men gathered at the battle of Armageddon (Rev 16:14-16; 19:11-21), thus cleansing the world of power-hungry leaders so opposed to the introduction of His millennial kingdom. Then follows the judgment of "the quick" (*zontes*, the living), referred to by Peter in Acts 10:42, and the substance of the parable in Matt 24:31-46. This further stage in the divine administration is to cleanse the earth of all that defiles, so making it a suitable place for the reign of Christ. The church will reign with Christ over the earth, with administrative service granted by grace. During the millennium all men will be under the divine authority, though not all will be converted; this is shown at the end of the 1,000 years when there will be vast numbers amongst the nations ready to gather against the saints (Rev 20:8-9). The last judgment on earth then takes place – "fire came down from God out of heaven, and devoured them" – before the earth finally disappears. The "great white throne" judgment follows (Rev 20:11-15), corresponding to the "resurrection of damnation" (John 5:29). Here, all the unsaved shall appear; the trial will be so unlike all trials by men on earth where judge, jury and counsel for the defence have not witnessed the crime. But God will have seen all deeds of unbelief for which men are then to be tried, and the Judge of all the earth will do right.

31 The coming of the Son of man in glory, is that great event to which so much of the Scriptures points. A preview was granted in Matt 16:27, when the three apostles saw the Lord transfigured on the mountain top (17:2). The Lord spoke of the throne of His glory in Matt 19:28, adding that the apostles would sit upon twelve thrones, "judging the twelve tribes of Israel". In Matt 24:30 He had spoken of "the Son of man coming in the clouds of heaven with power and great glory", while in Matt 26:64 He said to the high priest that they should see the Son of man sitting on the right hand of power and coming in the clouds of heaven. At present He is seated on His Father's throne, but in that coming millennial day, He will sit on His own throne together with the overcomers in the church age (Rev 3:21).

32-33 All nations shall be gathered before Him, that is, those that remain after the judgment of God against the armies of the nations at the battle of Armageddon. The Lord described this dividing process in a different way in Matt 24:38-41: some are taken for judgment and the others left, and these others are distinct from the "elect" in v.31 who are also gathered together. There are, then, three groups of people: the elect, those taken for judgment, and those who remain. (In the parable of the wheat and tares there were only two groups.) These three groups are also found in our present parable. "My brethren" (Matt 25:40) correspond to "his elect"; "the sheep" correspond to those who are left at the sifting process; "the goats" to those who are taken away, as at the flood.

40, 45 "The least of these", "one of the least of these" are owned by the Lord as "my brethren"; they are those Jews who pass through the great tribulation refusing to have the mark, name or number of the beast (Rev 13:16-17). The beast is the final emperor with his headquarters in Rome; the anti-Christ in Jerusalem will seek to keep the beast's authority fully recognised in Jerusalem by insisting that the Jews worship the image of the beast in the temple, and causing that they cannot buy or sell without adopting the mark, name or number of the beast. These faithful ones form "the remnant" of the woman's seed, "which keep the commandments of God, and have the testimony of Jesus" (Rev 12:17). No doubt when Matt 12:46-50 is projected into the future, the Lord's words refer to these faithful Jews, "Behold... my brethren! For whosoever shall do the will of my Father...is my brother". Some of these brethren will die during the great tribulation, and will therefore share in the first resurrection at the Lord's return in glory (Rev 20:4). But those who remain are gathered out as the "elect" to enter into the kingdom (Matt 24:31).

34-40 The sheep likewise are those who have not received the mark of the beast, but who evidently at that time have not received the testimony of Jesus unto salvation. They are, to use a non-scriptural word, neutral. The Lord recognises what they did (vv.35-36) though it was done in ignorance, for in vv.37-39 they confess that they had no idea that they were serving the Lord by attempting to take care of His brethren, the Jewish remnant. Satan will be abroad in the earth at the time of their ministering, having been finally cast down to its surface (Rev 12:9). The faithful Jews will seek to escape (v.14 ; Matt 24:16) to where they will be "nourished" for the three and a half years composing the great tribulation (v.14). This nourishment will be accomplished by "the earth" that helps the woman (v.16), and we interpret "the earth" as denoting the sheep who have compassion on the Jews in their extremity of distress. In grace, the Lord interprets this as "ye have done it unto me". (The converse of this is also true, the persecution that Saul waged against the church was described by the Lord as, "why persecutest thou me?" in Acts 9:4, but this revelation led to Saul's conversion.)

Previously, the Lord had said, "He that receiveth you receiveth me" (Matt 10:40), so the ignorance of the sheep is turned to a glorious reality of knowing the Lord for the first time. We believe that they were saved there and then upon the sight of the Lord in glory (as was Saul), so He calls them "blessed of my Father", and in the parable they are called "righteous" (Matt 25:34, 37). They therefore enter the kingdom "prepared...from the foundation of the world". This expression involving "from" is also found in Rev 13:8; 17:8. In all cases it has reference to those who have a particular blessing on the earth, connected with God's natural creation. This stands in sharp contrast with such expressions as "before the world was" and "before the foundation of the world" (John 17:5, 24). Here are features of divine glory and love that are eternal and heavenly. And this word "before" equally applies to Christians, for "he hath chosen us in him before the foundation of the world" (Eph 1:4), so we are attached to heaven and eternity rather than to earthly blessings.

So these sheep enter into the kingdom, under the rule and authority of the King of kings and Lord of lords. They form the nations on earth at the beginning of the millennial reign of Christ, though subsequent generations will not necessarily be saved. At that time, "all nations shall come and worship before thee" (Rev 15:4); "the nations of them which are saved shall walk in the light of" the heavenly Jerusalem in its administration over the earth (Rev 21:24); "they shall bring the glory and honour of the nations into it" (v.26). But Zech 14:16-19 shows what will happen if there is indifference to the requirement that the nations come up to Jerusalem to worship the King annually.

41-46 On the other hand, the goats are those who receive the mark of the beast. They form the tares, and their names are not written in the book of life of the slain Lamb (Rev 13:8; 17:8). Some will be active in opposing the Lamb in open warfare (Ps 2:1-3; Rev 17:14), to be removed at the warrior judgment of Christ; the rest shall be gathered before the Lord the Judge when He sits on the throne of His glory. During the period of the great tribulation, the Lord will be watching their every motive and activity. There will be no good shown to their fellow human beings, and consequently the Lord will see them do nothing for Himself. With the mark of the beast upon them they could easily buy and sell, but nothing was used to meet the hunger and thirst of the Lord's brethren. Before this judgment throne, they address the Judge as "Lord" (as in Matt 7:22; 25:24). Realising at last their folly, they ask the same questions that the sheep had asked, adding "and did not minister unto thee?". The meaning is, of course, that since the Lord had not been there in person, they could not possibly have ministered unto Him! They conveniently forgot the brethren of the Lord.

Consequently, these are the "cursed", and have to depart "into everlasting fire, prepared for the devil and his angels" (Matt 25:41), called "everlasting punishment" in v.46. Scripture does not inform us whether this takes place there and then, or whether they enter hades prior to appearing again before a divine tribunal at the great white throne. The word "everlasting" means what it says; see 2 Thess 1:9; Jude 7, 13; Rev 14:9-11.

OT references to the judgment of the nations may be found in Dan 7:13-14; Joel 3:11-17, where "the valley of Jehoshaphat" near Jerusalem is mentioned as the venue of the judgment.

CHAPTERS 26-28
THE KING'S CRUCIFIXION AND RESURRECTION

1. The Night before the Lord's Death (26:1-75)

1. *Evil without and Worship within* 26:1-16

v.1 "And it came to pass, when Jesus had finished all these sayings, he said unto his disciples,
v.2 Ye know that after two days is *the feast of* the passover, and the Son of man is betrayed to be crucified.
v.3 Then assembled together the chief priests, and the scribes, and the elders of the people, unto the palace of the high priest, who was called Caiaphas,
v.4 And consulted that they might take Jesus by subtilty, and kill *him*.
v.5 But they said, Not on the feast *day*, lest there be an uproar among the people.
v.6 Now when Jesus was in Bethany, in the house of Simon the leper,
v.7 There came unto him a woman having an alabaster box of very precious ointment, and poured it on his head, as he sat *at meat*.
v.8 But when his disciples saw *it*, they had indignation, saying, To what purpose *is* this waste?
v.9 For this ointment might have been sold for much, and given to the poor.
v.10 When Jesus understood *it*, he said unto them, Why trouble ye the woman? for she hath wrought a good work upon me.
v.11 For ye have the poor always with you; but me ye have not always.
v.12 For in that she hath poured this ointment on my body, she did *it* for my burial.
v.13 Verily I say unto you, Wheresoever this gospel shall be preached in the whole world, *there* shall also this, that this woman hath done, be told for a memorial of her.
v.14 Then one of the twelve, called Judas Iscariot, went unto the chief priests,
v.15 And said *unto them*, What will ye give me, and I will deliver him unto you? And they covenanted with him for thirty pieces of silver.
v.16 And from that time he sought opportunity to betray him."

The last stage of the King's work on earth is reached in these chapters, for to use an expression prominent in John's Gospel, His "hour" had come (John 17:1), and the prophetic Scriptures concerning His death had now to be fulfilled. Matt 26 takes the narrative up to the end of the first part of the trial of the Lord. The history of the betrayal is given in vv.1-5, 14-16, 21-25, 47-56; 27:3-10. We have the supper in Bethany and the anointing of the Lord (vv.6-13), the last passover and the first breaking of bread (vv.17-30), Peter's denial of the Lord (vv.31-35, 69-75), the garden of Gethsemane (vv.36-46), and the Lord's trial before the high priest and the Jewish Sanhedrin (vv.57-68).

1 The words "when Jesus had finished all these sayings" occur here for the fifth time in Matthew's Gospel, terminating the five major discourses therein recorded. These are:

1. preaching on the mount (7:28),

2. preparation of the disciples for being sent forth (11:1),

3. parables of the kingdom (13:53),

4. personal relationships (19:1),

5. prophetical discourse (26:1),

It is necessary to start a work and to finish it, as in the creation (Gen 2:1). The Lord said in prayer, "I have finished the work which thou gavest me to do" (John 17:4; 4:34; 5:36), while when He died on the cross His final words were, "It is finished" (John 19:30). Paul could look back on his life's work, and comment, "I have finished my course" (2 Tim 4:7). Similarly for believers, a work taken up in the Lord's will must be completed with zeal and diligence.

No further teaching by the Lord takes place in Matthew's Gospel, though we know that there was the upper-room and subsequent ministry of John 13-16 that can be inserted in Matt 26:30.

2 The words "Ye know" are remarkable; compare "Jesus knew" in John 13:1. Certainly they knew that the Passover was near at hand; they were thoroughly acquainted with that annual ceremony for John has recorded their previous visits to Jerusalem for the Passover and other feasts during the Lord's ministry. But they did not know very well the fact of His impending death. The previous occasions on which He had explained this openly to them are in Matt 17:23; 20:17-19 (see Luke 18:31-34), but they always exhibited ignorance as to the meaning of such predictions (Luke 18:34). Today, religious ritual can take away the possibility of having a true spiritual knowledge of the sacrifice of Christ; ignorance of fundamentals is a serious matter. Apart from direct statements, there were also other clear hints that the Lord would return to heaven, such as John 2:19; 3:14 ("lifted up"); 8:28; 12:32; Luke 9:31 ("his decease"), yet the disciples were hardly prepared for the event.

Whereas the AV has "betrayed" in this verse, the RV and JND have "delivered" The reason for the difference is that the word *paradidomi* means both "to deliver" and "to betray" (as an act of treachery); the context must decide. In our verse, the context is not sufficiently clear. Certainly the forthcoming betrayal had been prominent in the Lord's thoughts (John 6:70-71; Matt 17:22), and in various ways it could be found in the OT, such as Ps 41:9; 69:25; 109:8; Zech 11:12-13. It caused the Lord to be "troubled in spirit" (John 13:21), though the disciples did not appreciate the enormity of the crime to be committed, each thinking that he might do it, as indicated by their asking, "Is it I?" (Matt 26:22).

3 Evil men had plotted before to put the Lord Jesus to death (John 11:47-53), yet they had been impotent to achieve anything. But now these evil leaders were doing their part at the exact time approved by God. This worst act of men had its place in the predetermined timetable of God; they had been restrained in their deeds until the arrival of the correct time, in the same way as now the Spirit of God withholds the manifestation of the man of sin until his time (2 Thess 2:6). Of course the prophetical forthtelling of the deeds of sinful men (usually the leaders) does not compel men to act in their sinful way. Rather, men are restrained in their deeds (circumstances are against them), until the restraint is removed; then their motivations and plans can be brought to fruition. It is like the opening of a barred gate to the enemy.

This was a meeting of the Jewish Sanhedrin (*sunedrion*), consisting of 71 members, namely the high priest, members of his family, elders and scribes, with Pharisees and Sadducees mixed together in spite of differences in doctrine. This body had great religious and legal authority, though the Romans had taken from it the authority to carry out capital punishment. The high priest was Caiaphas, son-in-law of the previous high priest Annas; both are named in Luke 3:2. The Roman authorities chose the high priests – quite unlike what happened in the OT, where the high priesthood ran through the Aaronic line involving Eleazar and Phinehas (1 Chron 6:3-15). The Romans had deposed Annas in 15 AD, replacing him by Caiaphas, though the Jews still recognised both as high priests, recalling the OT situation where Abiathar and Zadok were high priests together at the beginning of Solomon's reign, while Ahimelech and Zadok had been high priests earlier (2 Sam 8:17). Caiaphas had issued the famous prophecy that it was expedient that one man should die for the people, though he had meant something quite different from what his words convey to believers (John 11:50-52). He was a man who preferred Rome and Caesar rather than Christ.

4-5 The consultation took place in the "palace", properly the court (*aulē*) surrounding the dwelling. Peter sat "without" or "beneath" in this court (Matt 26:69; Mark 14:66). This word is used in the OT for the courts surrounding the tabernacle and temple (see Rev 11:2), This consultation took place in secret, for fear of the people (Luke 22:2), yet they had commanded the people to reveal where the Lord was so that they could take Him. It seems that there was a confusion of policy here – secretly or openly.

Hundreds of thousands of people would have come up to Jerusalem for the feast day; this was a duty originating from the first Passover in Exod 23:14; 34:23. In John 12:12 John used the description "much people that were come to the feast", and they were very interested in the Lord Jesus coming into Jerusalem.

Such large multitudes could have caused great trouble had they sided with Him against the leaders, who sought to avoid such an uproar by not taking the Lord on the feast day to kill Him. Their attitude amounted to: Don't let the people know what is being planned behind their backs; they were oblivious to the fact that God, the God whom they professed to serve, knew their intentions. "Not on the feast day" should read "Not during the feast" (RV, JND), namely not refraining just on the one day, but throughout the feast of unleavened bread. Because of the large crowds, the Roman governor Pilate (from Caesarea) was there to ensure that order was kept, thus fulfilling Ps 2:1-2 "the heathen ... the people ... the kings of the earth ... and the rulers", interpreted in Acts 4:25-26 as "the heathen ... the people ... the kings of the earth ... the rulers ... Herod ... Pontius Pilate ... the Gentiles ... the people of Israel"

6 This event in the house of Simon the leper in Bethany is not the same as that which took place in the house of Simon the Pharisee in Luke 7:36-50. Simon was a common name, and the conversation was completely different on the two occasions. Since an alabaster box of ointment had been broken in Luke 7:37-38, this would have encouraged repetition later under appropriate circumstances.

Neither do we believe that this is the same event as recorded in John 12:1-9: the conversations were similar but the deeds were different. The supper in John 12 took place just before the Lord rode into Jerusalem in triumph, but that in Matt 26 took place just before the Passover. In fact, there was often a duplication of similar events (and sometimes triplication). The cleansing of the temple is recorded in John 2 and Matt 21; the healing of the blind men is found in Luke 18:35 and Matt 20:30; there are two storm scenes (Matt 8:24 and 14:24); twice the Lord fed the multitudes (Matt 14:15-21; 15:32-39); some of the Beatitudes were spoken twice (Matt 5:3-13; Luke 6:20-23). So we need not be surprised that there were two suppers, with similar and yet with differing happenings at each.

7 In Luke 7:37, the woman "which was a sinner" produced a box of ointment, and her sins which were many were forgiven. In John 12:3, it was Mary who produced the ointment of spikenard, the sister of Martha and Lazarus, an event recalled in John 11:2. But in Matt 26:7, the identity of the woman was not announced. Whether a repentant sinner, a mature saint, or one largely unknown, we can all enter upon such acts of worship and adoration. The "alabaster box" (*alabastron*) was made of a marble-like stone found near Alabastron in Egypt; usually it was shaped like a flask with a long sealed neck. This neck was broken to gain access to the perfume or ointment – "very precious ointment" and worth "more than three hundred pence" (Mark 14:5). This ointment had been previously prepared, and as stored it was kept from contact with the world; it was only suitable for the Lord, like the holy anointing oil and the perfume "pure and holy" for use in the tabernacle (Exod 30:31-38). In Luke 4:18, the anointing of the Lord was in connection with His work of preaching the gospel to the poor. Ps 45:6-7, and Heb 1:8-9 speak of the Lord as having been "anointed with the oil of gladness above thy fellows": since the context speaks of the throne for ever and ever, we interpret the "fellows" as the OT kings in Jerusalem who were anointed as was David (1 Sam 16:1, 12-13). Certainly in Heb 1, the Lord has the pre-eminence in His Sonship (v.5). in His sovereignty (vv.8-9), and in substance (v.11).

Note the reverent and suitable posture adopted by the Lord under various circumstances: in v.7 He "sat" at the meal for fellowship (the Greek word is *anakeimai*, to recline at table, and is so translated in the RV). In v.20, He sat (reclined) down for the Passover and for the introduction of the breaking of bread. In v.55, He recalled that He "sat" daily teaching in the temple courts; here, the verb is the imperfect tense of *kathezomai*. In v.39, He fell in prayer, while in 27:11, He stood for testimony. Our own posture in service is not without its importance.

8-9 Differences are clearly seen between this event and that recorded in John 12:2-8. In Matt 26:7, the Lord's head was anointed; in John 12:3, His feet were anointed. In Matt 26:8, the disciples complained, but in John 12:4 it was Judas Iscariot. In Matt 26:9, the disciples assessed the value as "much", whereas the financial man Judas provided a suitable figure, "three hundred pence" (John 12:5). The disciples could not appreciate that this was a work of faith; nothing that is devoted to the Lord can then be wasted. The time Christians devote to worship and service today is not wasted, though it may not fit into the financial experts' estimation of what is good for the economy in a materialistic sense. The disciples would recall that the Lord had allowed nothing to be wasted after the miracles of the feeding of the 5,000 and the 4,000, and also His words to the rich young ruler, "sell that thou hast, and give to the poor" (Matt 19:21). The attitude of the woman can be described as "spiritual", that of the disciples as "carnal", and that of Judas as "natural", using adjectives found in 1 Cor 2:14; 3:1. The disciples manifested their usual weakness: here they seemed to have no understanding of worship; in Gethsemane where they slept they had no understanding of prayer in the sanctuary (Matt 26:40); later Peter had no true concept of testimony when he denied the Lord (vv.69-75). Worship Godward in Spirit and in truth cannot be replaced by good works, however valuable the latter may be; selling all one's goods to feed the poor is of no value if love is absent (1 Cor 13:3).

10 Here we have the divine assessment of such unjust criticism. No doubt the disciples voiced their criticism without letting the Lord hear, but He understood in the sense of "knowing their thoughts" (Matt 9:4), and of perceiving "in his spirit" (Mark 2:8). His sympathy was for the one who served faithfully, "Why trouble ye the woman?". He described the action as "a good work", not a good work that seeks salvation, but a good work resulting from faith that has already appropriated salvation. It would have been a bad work (like the wood, hay and stubble in 1 Cor 3:12) had the ointment been sold! Such works of faith are always desired by God; Paul wrote of "faith which worketh by love" (Gal 5:6) and "your work of faith" (1 Thess 1:3). In the case of this woman, her good work was done directly to His body; there was no intermediary between the woman and One divine as in the OT Levitical service, where service to the Lord was often done to Aaron the high priest, and through Aaron.

11 The Lord stressed that there must be a balance between opportunities; the first and great commandment comes before the second (Matt 22:37-39). Service Godward is despised by any who say, "Let us be practical". In the face of financial difficulties amongst the widows, was it profitable for the apostles to give themselves continually to prayer and to the ministry of the Word (Acts 6:4)? Was it profitable to minister to the Lord and to fast in Antioch, when there was still much to be done in that church (Acts 13:2)? Of course it was profitable, when such deeds are weighed in the balances of the sanctuary.

The poor would always be present, and could be helped at any time, but the Lord was shortly leaving them, and such opportunities to minister to His body would no longer be present. The existence of the poor is a feature of a fallen world that cannot be eradicated until the coming of His kingdom in equity. Social welfare cannot produce equality; if by some means equality was achieved by the efforts of men and leaders, this equality would be so unstable that differences would immediately appear again. The Christian position is to "remember the poor" (Gal 2:10), and to "do good unto all men, especially unto them who are of the household of faith" (Gal 6:10).

12-13 No doubt this woman was not one of those who prepared spices and ointments to bring to the sepulchre (Luke 23:56; 24:1) after His death; she made her contribution before He died. Certainly the Lord interpreted her act as: "she did it for my burial". The fragrance on His head and body would subsist until His sufferings on the cross were over; the woman seemed to know that His death was near, and by faith she acted accordingly. No doubt the precious ointment did not remain only on the Lord's head, but as we read elsewhere, "the precious ointment ... ran down ... to the skirts of his garments" (Ps 133:2).

The doctrine behind the message of "this gospel" is deeper now than it had been in previous references, since His cross was near at hand, and the faith of this woman realised it, whatever may have been the ignorance of the apostles. There was no reference to His death in Matt 4:17, 23 when in early days He preached the gospel of the kingdom, since this would have been an unknown subject to His listeners. But now we find the truth that His death and burial were very closely associated with the gospel, as Paul wrote when he declared the gospel to the Corinthians, "Christ died for our sins ... he was buried, and ... he rose again" (1 Cor 15:3-4). All the counsels of God in His Son with reference to believers and the church derive from His death, burial and resurrection. Previously the message had been to the lost sheep of the house of Israel, and not to the Gentiles (Matt 10:5-6); this restriction was now to be removed, and "the whole world" was now envisaged as the sphere for the preaching of the message. "Teach all nations" (Matt 28:19) was the new command; in Mark 16:15 we read, "Go ye into all the world, and preach the gospel to every creature", namely "in Jerusalem, and in all Judaea, and in Samaria, and unto the uttermost part of the earth" (Acts 1:8). All this is in keeping with John 3:16, "God so loved the world". The message would also reflect what "this woman hath done", namely that she acted on the faith that she had in His death. In other words, preaching the gospel does not only present doctrine and historical fact, but it also concerns faith that accepts and worships. Too often, only one of ten cleansed returns to glorify God in worship (Luke 17:18). The Father seeks worshippers, but sometimes new converts refuse to be found for this purpose.

14-16 If there was worship within, then there was evil and treachery without. Judas is described as "one of the twelve", a unique designation to single out a unique man. In v.47 he is again described as "one of the twelve", while in John 6:70 the Lord called him "one of you", v.71 ending with "being one of the twelve". This man "went unto the chief priests". Note the four occasions on which Judas "went". Here he "went" to the chief priests; in John 13:30 he "went" immediately out: and "it was night". In Matt 27:5 he "went and hanged himself". In Acts 1:25 he went "to his own place" as the son of perdition. Some have suggested that he will rise again to be manifested as the son of perdition, the anti-Christ and the beast out of the earth (Rev 13:11), while emperor Nero will ascend out of the pit to become the beast out of the sea, the last emperor of Rome (Rev 13; 17:8). This is, of course, mere speculation, but the reader may come across the idea in some books.

The order of events is as follows: the chief priests and the Pharisees had commanded men to give information as to where the Lord was so that they could take Him (John 11:57); Satan then entered into Judas "being of the number of the twelve" (Luke 22:3-6), who then contacted the leaders with the promise to betray Him "in the absence of the multitude". In the upper room, Satan showed Judas that the time had come to do this deed (John 13:2), yet then the Lord openly stated that He knew that one of them would betray Him. Being uncertain of their own hearts, they all asked, "Lord, is it I" (Matt 26:22), after which Judas went out (John 13:30), knowing that the Lord would go into the garden of Gethsemane without the multitudes being present – that most holy sanctuary of prayer was to Judas' mind a suitable place to arrange for the Lord to be taken.

The piece of silver was the *argurion*, used of money in general. There is a similarity to Exod 21:32 where thirty shekels of silver had to be paid in compensation to a master for the loss of a servant, and to Gen 37:28 where Joseph was sold to the Ishmeelites for twenty pieces of silver. The prophetical reference is to Zech 11:12-13, quoted in Matt 27:9. Expositors of the prophecy of Zechariah suggest that these two verses are the most difficult to explain, firstly in the context of the prophecy, and then in the application to the Lord Jesus and Judas. We need not be surprised that the immediate context and the prophetical application are different, since this feature often manifests itself in the use that NT writers make of the OT. A further difficulty arises in Matt 27:9 where "Jeremy the prophet" is mentioned and not Zechariah. The lesson, however, to believers is clear. If the priests and Judas valued the Lord on a rather low level financially, how do we value the Lord spiritually? He is the chiefest among ten thousand, with His head, hands and feet as gold (Song 5:10-16).

2. *The Passover and the Breaking of Bread 26:17-35*

v.17 "Now the first *day* of the *feast* of unleavened bread the disciples came to Jesus, saying unto him, Where wilt thou that we prepare for thee to eat the passover?
v.18 And he said, Go into the city to such a man, and say unto him, The Master saith, My time is at hand, I will keep the passover at thy house with my disciples.
v.19 And the disciples did as Jesus had appointed them; and they made ready the passover.
v.20 Now when the even was come, he sat down with the twelve.
v.21 And as they did eat, he said, Verily I say unto you, that one of you shall betray me.
v.22 And they were exceeding sorrowful, and began every one of them to say unto him, Lord, is it I?
v.23 And he answered and said, He that dippeth *his* hand with me in the dish, the same shall betray me.
v.24 The Son of man goeth as it is written of him: but woe unto that man by whom the Son of man is betrayed! it had been good for that man if he had not been born.
v.25 Then Judas, which betrayed him, answered and said, Master, is it I? He said unto him, Thou hast said.
v.26 And as they were eating, Jesus took bread, and blessed *it*, and brake *it*, and gave *it* to the disciples, and said, Take, eat; this is my body.
v.27 And he took the cup, and gave thanks, and gave *it* to them, saying, Drink ye all of it;
v.28 For this is my blood of the new testament, which is shed for many for the remission of sins.
v.29 But I say unto you, I will not drink henceforth of this fruit of the vine, until that day when I drink it new with you in my Father's kingdom.
v.30 And when they had sung an hymn, they went out into the mount of Olives.
v.31 Then saith Jesus unto them, All ye shall be offended because of me this night: for it is written, I will smite the shepherd, and the sheep of the flock shall be scattered abroad.
v.32 But after I am risen again, I will go before you into Galilee.
v.33 Peter answered and said unto him, Though all *men* shall be offended because of thee, *yet* will I never be offended.

v.34 Jesus said unto him, Verily I say unto thee, That this night, before the cock crow, thou shalt deny me thrice.
v.35 Peter said unto him, Though I should die with thee, yet will I not deny thee. Likewise also said all the disciples."

17-19 Luke 22:7-13 provides fuller details of this preparation for keeping the Passover. The day was "the day of unleavened bread, when the passover must be killed" according to Luke, and "the first day of the feast of unleavened bread" according to Matthew. Strictly, the Passover took place on the fourteenth day of the first month, and the feast of unleavened bread commenced on the fifteenth and lasted for seven days (Lev 23:5-6). So by NT times, the Jews commenced the feast of unleavened bread on the day of the Passover; certainly no leavened bread was to be eaten on that day (Exod 12:8,18). There was such a close connection between these first two of the seven annual feasts that Paul could write, "For even Christ our passover is sacrificed for us: Therefore let us keep the feast, not with old leaven … but with the unleavened bread of sincerity and truth" (1 Cor 5:7-8).

The disciples' question, "Where wilt thou that we prepare for thee to eat the passover?" was in response to the Lord's command, "Go and prepare us the passover, that we may eat" (Luke 22:8). The Lord's command brought about a sense of helplessness on the part of the disciples. This also occurred when the 5,000 were fed; the Lord said, "Give ye them to eat", but the disciples expressed their impotence to do anything about it (Luke 9:13). In point of fact, there were so many visitors to Jerusalem at the feast, that normally there would be no available room for latecomers. At the birth of the Lord Jesus, there had been "no room for them in the inn" (Luke 2:7), but there was in Jerusalem still a vacant "large upper room furnished" (Luke 22:12), and the Lord would ensure that this was available. The room chosen was "large" because the Lord knew that the disciples would continue to use it after His death and resurrection; this was the room where He manifested Himself to them again (John 20:19), and this was "*the* upper room" (not "*an* upper room", the definite article is present in the Greek) where many abode during the period between the ascension and the giving of the Spirit (Acts 1:13).

Peter and John were selected by the Lord to locate the room (Luke 22:8). As usual, two and not one were chosen for this work, in the same way as they were together in Acts 3:1; they are called "pillars" in Gal 2:9. The Lord used a simple, but distinctive, circumstance as a sign of guidance. Here was one man out of thousands flocking the streets at Passover time. The man was doing a woman's work, carrying a pitcher of water (Luke 22:10), no doubt returning home with the pitcher full of water perhaps later to be used by the Lord when He washed the disciples' feet (John 13:4-12). They addressed the man by referring to the Lord as "the Master" – namely Teacher (*didaskalos*) – as if the man would recognise Him by this title. Some expositors suggest that the Lord had made prior arrangements with the man, but we prefer to believe that the Lord's miraculous omniscience is implied. They also had to say, "My time (*kairos*) is at hand". In Luke 9:51, "when the time was come" should strictly read "when the days were being fulfilled", whereas in John's Gospel the Lord referred often to His "hour" (*hōra*, John 17:1)

So the two disciples "made ready the passover". The usual practice was that the lamb had to be slain in the temple courts, with no bones broken; unleavened bread also had to be obtained, no doubt plentiful in Jerusalem at that season. Today, preparations for the gatherings of the Lord's people are far less elaborate, but someone has to make them, such as obtaining the bread and the wine, and laying the table for the breaking of bread before anyone else arrives. This is a simple and regular service, and no doubt few give any thought as to who does it or when it is done. But the Lord knows, and what is done unto His brethren is also done unto Him.

20 This simple verse "...when the even was come, he sat down with the twelve" should be read in conjunction with Luke 22:14, "...when the hour was come, he sat down, and the twelve apostles with him". This was the legal hour in the beginning of the fourteenth day of the month Nisan. It was not quite the "hour" of John 17:1, though it fused with it, that being the time of God's great purpose in the sacrifice of His Son. "He sat down with the twelve" contrasts with "he sat down, and the twelve apostles with him". The points of view adopted in these two descriptions of the same event are different. Luke was describing the end of the old era, the last Passover, when men went to meet with God under the cover of the ceremony of the old covenant; see Exod 20:21; 19:17; 33:7. Hence in Luke's description the Lord sat down first, and then the apostles associated themselves with Him. But Matthew was describing the beginning of the new. He did not describe the Passover meal; rather, the theme is that of the Lord coming to meet with His people where they are; see Matt 18:20; John 20:19-26; Acts 2:1; John 14:23. Hence in Matthew's account, the apostles were there, and in grace the Lord closely associated Himself with them. The difference in the two points of view is seen in the words "with the twelve" and "with him". The former describes the position of local assemblies today.

21-25 Readers of Matthew's Gospel have been prepared from 10:4 to know that Judas would ultimately betray the Lord. The apostles had known since John 6:70 that one of their number was "a devil", though we do not read that they tried to ascertain who was the one. Yet the Lord knew all the time that Judas would do this, and even at this late hour He spoke of the betrayal as still future. Perhaps Judas did not know that he would do this deed until Satan entered into him. Yet Judas could not escape from the responsibility of having been the betrayer, even though it was through the determinate counsel and foreknowledge of God that the Lord was delivered (Acts 2:23). The men of Israel, Herod, Pilate, the Gentiles and the soldiers could not escape from the responsibility of having taken part in the crucifixion of the Son of God (Acts 4:27-28). Even though the betrayal had been the subject of OT prophecy, the responsibility of Judas remained. Thus in John 13:18-30, a Psalm is quoted, "He that eateth bread with me hath lifted up his heel against me" (Ps 41:9). Judas could never escape from the consequences of his deed, so the Lord stated, "woe unto that man by whom the Son of man is betrayed". Elsewhere, He said, "none of them is lost, but the son of perdition" (John 17:12), and hence "it had been good for that man if he had not been born".

The Lord's announcement that one of those partaking of the Passover with Him would be His betrayer caused them to be "exceeding sorrowful". It seems strange that all of them could not trust their own hearts. In Luke 22:23, they merely asked among themselves; in Matt 26:22, they all said "Lord, is it I", while in John 13:25 John asked personally, "who is it?", acting as spokesman for the others. Note that the eleven said, "Lord, Is it I", using the vocative *kurie*. But Judas did not dare to use this title implying such divine authority; rather, he said "Master" (Matt 26:25) and "Master, master" (Mark 14:45), namely, Rabbi. At this point, we should explain that there are six titles (as distinct from names) used in the NT when addressing the Lord:

1. *didaskalos*, Teacher, occurring a large number of times;

2. *despotēs*, Despot, with absolute ownership and authority, used by Simeon in Luke 2:29;

3. *epistatēs*, Commander, used only in Luke's Gospel such as 5:5, "Master, we have toiled all night";

4. *kathēgētēs*, Guide or Leader, only in Matt 23:8, 10;

5. *rabbei*, Rabbi, a courteous form of address;

6. *kurios*, Lord (or "Sir" when used by unbelievers), being in the LXX the word used for Jehovah.

Judas was identified:

1. in a general way, "He that dippeth his hand with me", "One of you which eateth with me" (Mark 14:18), and "the hand of him that betrayeth me is with me on the table" (Luke 22:21);

2. in the fact that the Lord gave a sop to Judas (John 13:26);

3. by the Lord's answer directly to Judas, "Thou hast said".

Even then the eleven did not know that Judas had been thus identified, thinking that the Lord had asked Judas to buy something, or to give something to the poor, since Judas acted as treasurer with the bag (John 13:29). Only John noted that Judas "went immediately out" (v.30), and we believe that this occurred before the Lord's Supper or the breaking of bread was instituted following the Passover meal.

26-29 These verses describe what is called the "breaking of bread" in Acts 2:42; 20:7, and "the Lord's supper" in 1 Cor 11:20. This is also found in Mark 14:22-24; Luke 22:19-20; 1 Cor 11:23-26. The reader should collate all these passages for a complete appreciation of the subject. It was instituted by the Lord in the Gospels; it was practised by the disciples in the Acts; its doctrine was given by Paul in 1 Cor 11. As far as its name is concerned, the "breaking of bread" (Acts 2:42; a verb in Acts 20:7) answers to *what* we do. The "Lord's supper" answers to *when* in a moral sense, for it was not a morning breakfast meal, but a night-time act, answering to the moral conditions around, from which believers are separated until the day dawn: "it was night" (John 13:30); "the night is far spent" (Rom 13:12). The word "Lord's" (***kuriakos***) does not have a genitive possessive meaning, it is an adjective meaning "dominical, pertaining to the Lord". The same word appears in "the Lord's day" (Rev 1:10), and the word occurs only twice in the NT. As in the institution, all believers in a local assembly take, break and partake, for it manifests communion as a common act. The cup is "the communion of the blood of Christ" and the bread is "the communion of the body of Christ" (1 Cor 10:16), though not all expositors understand these verses in 1 Cor 10 as referring to the breaking of bread.

The Lord said in Luke 22:19 that the partaking of the emblems is "in remembrance of me", a phrase that does not appear in the accounts by Matthew and Mark. It is found in 1 Cor 11:24, suggesting that Luke obtained this phrase from Paul who had received it directly "of the Lord" (v.23). The simplicity of the act is completely lacking in ritual for many men who love to perpetuate a modernised form of the OT ceremony. Thus they have invented transubstantiation (meaning, according to them but not according to the Scriptures, that the bread literally becomes the body of Christ whatever the eye may perceive). Such men seek to multiply the body of Christ upon a thousand altars so as to dupe the multitudes who are under the thumb of the priests, failing to see that the Lord's statement "this is my body" is akin to other metaphorical descriptions such as "that Rock was Christ" (1 Cor 10:4), and "I am the door" (John 10:9). Others invented consubstantiation, asserting that the bread and wine are still bread and wine, but that the body of Christ is present in the symbols at the same time. Calvin stated that the partaking of the symbols was an act of reception by faith of the sacrificial virtue of the work of Christ. The idea of a memorial was too low a point of view for the Reformers, yet that is just what the Scriptures imply. There is no question of reception of His actual body, else it would be a dead Christ with which we have to do. It is not a question of what we receive, but of what we give to God from the memorial of worship in our hearts as we contemplate the Lord's Person in His death in the past, and His glorious person in heaven above both now and eternally.

We should notice the two words "bread" and "bless" in Matt 26:26 and in other passages. The Greek word *artos* means bread as a material, and a loaf when baked in a particular shape; such a loaf was flat and it was broken and not cut with a knife. In the NT the word is usually translated "bread" (over 60 times) but it is translated "loaf" in all accounts of the feeding of the 4,000 and the 5,000 where numerical amounts are concerned. However, in the accounts of the breaking of bread, the word "bread" is always used, but the RV margin gives the alternative "loaf", which may appear to be preferable in some places in the light of 1 Cor 10:17 where "we being many are one bread, and one body", suggestive of unity being demonstrated by one loaf.

The word "blessed" is *eulogeō*, meaning to speak well of the bread. The word is used in Matt 14:19 and Luke 9:16 (regarding the bread in the feeding of the 5,000), and in Luke 24:30 (for the bread after His resurrection). There is a second word "give thanks" (*eucharisteō*) used in John 6:11 (the feeding of the 5,000), Matt 15:36 (the feeding of the 4,000), Luke 22:19 (for the bread), Matt 26:27 (for the cup), and Acts 27:35 (for the food on the ship). Hence, in the feeding of the 5,000, the Lord both blessed (His thoughts directed to the bread) and He gave thanks (His thoughts directed to God). Both words are also used in relation to the institution of the breaking of bread.

The reference to the "blood of the new testament" is important, for it stands in contrast to the blood of the Passover lamb relating to the old covenant. In Jer 31:31, the promised new covenant was to be made with Judah and Israel; it was therefore a promise for the future, when unconditionally God's law would be written in their hearts, and when all would know God. However, no information was provided in Jer 31 as to how this new covenant was to be inaugurated. Heb 9:15 to 10:18 shows that it is by blood (death), this being the basis for the putting into effect of a will, for "a testament is of force after men are dead" (Heb 9:17). Only in the upper room did the Lord reveal that His blood enables the provisions of the new covenant to be put into effect – this being future for Israel, but present for us, since His blood "is shed for many for the remission of sins".

In v.29, the Lord used the expression "this fruit of the vine" rather than "wine"; to the author the difference is not without its significance, for the former is what God produces through natural causes, the pure juice of the grape, while the latter is what man makes of the juice after treatment and fermentation. By saying "I will not drink henceforth ... until that day when I drink it new with you in my Father's kingdom", the Lord was only partially referring to His resurrection. Certainly the opportunity for fellowship with

His own over a meal was now past; the Lord's freedom was shortly to be taken away. In resurrection, He "did eat before them" (Luke 24:43), while Peter recalled that the apostles "did eat and drink with him after he rose from the dead" (Acts 10:41). But the Lord's words appear to go beyond this, containing a sense of unrevealed mystery. For the "Father's kingdom" is still future (Matt 13:43), and there is also the future "marriage supper of the Lamb" (Rev 19:9) for the church in resurrection.

30 The short walk over the brook Cedron (John 18:1) to the slopes of the mount of Olives was the last movement of the Lord in freedom; His return to Jerusalem was as a captive of the religious leaders. David had fled that way in 2 Sam 15:23, 30, though he later returned to see both the ark and God's habitation (v.25). God's glory had departed that way (Ezek 11:23), its return being yet future in the days of millennial restoration (Ezek 43:4).

The Lord was seeking a sanctuary in the garden of Gethsemane before being taken captive. His ultimate destination was the Father in glory, but first He would meet with the Father in the garden in the depths of anticipative suffering of soul. His ultimate destination was without geographical location, behind the cloud that would hide Him from the disciples' gaze. But the garden was well known both to them and to Judas, for this was "as he was wont" (Luke 22:39), and "Jesus ofttimes resorted thither with his disciples" (John 18:2).

In singing "an hymn", they would have used part of the Jewish Hallel consisting of Psalms 113-118, being appropriate Passover Psalms. "When they had sung an hymn" is one word in Greek (also in Mark 14:26), being the aorist participle of *humneō*. Psalms 113-114 would be sung at the beginning of the Passover feast: Jehovah was "high above all nations" (113:4), enabling Him to bring Israel "out of Egypt" (114:1). Ps 115 demonstrates a passion for the glory of God: "not unto us, but unto thy name give glory" (v.1), while Ps 116:8, 9 rehearses the deliverance from death to walk in the land of the living. Ps 117 is a brief expression of universal praise, while Ps 118 is a prophetical conversation between the Lord and His people, His death and resurrection being the subject (v.22). As they sung some of these Psalms, only the Lord knew how they applied to Himself – that He was about to fulfil their prophetical forthtellings.

31-35 The Lord had already shown that He knew that Judas (the worst) would fall by betraying Him: He now shows that the eleven would forsake Him, and that Peter (one of the best) would deny Him. The verb "shall be offended" is the usual word *skandalizō*, namely that the disciples would act as if He were a snare or stumblingblock causing them to fall. Certainly He was "a stone of stumbling, and a rock of offence" (1 Pet 2:8) to unbelievers; to the Jews Christ crucified was a stumblingblock (1 Cor 1:23), and those who fell upon that Stone would be broken (Matt 21:44). But here (v.32) full restoration was in view after the Lord's resurrection. He told them the worst about themselves, coupling it with the promise of His resurrection so as to make it easy for them to return. He would "refine them as silver is refined, and will try them as gold is tried" (Zech 13:9), a thought which follows the Lord's quotation from Zech 13:7. There, it is the sword that smites "my shepherd"; in Matt 26:31 the Lord speaks of the action of God, "I will smite"; in Isa 53:4 it is as "smitten of God", while in John 10:18 the Lord stated that "No man taketh it (my life) from me, but I lay it down of myself". All sides of the Lord's sacrifice are therefore embraced.

The sheep of the good Shepherd were about to be "scattered abroad", temporarily scattered by the wolf (John 10:12); the Lord's work would be to gather together in one those who were scattered abroad (John 11:52). For He promised to rise again, and to go before them into Galilee where they would see Him: "A little while, and ye shall not see me: and again, a little while, and ye shall see me" (John 16:16). Galilee was the sphere where most of the Lord's successful ministry had been accomplished, and this promise by the Lord was recalled later by the angel in Matt 28:7 and Luke 24:6.

Peter was still argumentative as the darkness was closing around and the hour of the Lord's sacrifice drew near. He had argued against the Lord's death in Matt 16:22, and had questioned the future of the apostle John's life (John 21:21). Today, men argue against the Scriptures and the Lord's words, adopting a similar or a worse attitude of unbelief. This shows an unreadiness to receive the divine testimony against the human heart. Peter was quite sincere in what he said: he would never stumble over the Lord Jesus! But sincerity is no sure guide to spirituality; sincere pride in self-effort is of no avail: "Pride goes before destruction, and a haughty spirit before a fall" (Prov 16:18). In the same context in Luke's Gospel, the Lord interpreted the situation as Satan's desire to sift Peter so as to gain the chaff for himself (Luke 22:31-32), but the Lord would gain the wheat after Peter's conversion. The Lord's reply to Peter's self-confidence indicated His divine knowledge of all future events, "this night, before the cock crow, thou shalt deny me thrice", implying a short time limit within which the denials would take place. Peter, and all the other disciples, were confident that they would never deny the Lord, rather accepting death if that were necessary. Previously, the Lord had taught, "whosoever shall deny me before men, him will I also deny" (Matt 10:33), while Paul wrote, "if we deny him, he also will deny us" (2 Tim 2:12). However awful this denial was, Peter recovered, with the result that "with great power gave the apostles witness of the resurrection of the Lord Jesus" (Acts 4:33). But it appears to have affected at least something of his teaching in his future service; thus in 1 Pet 5:1, he writes of being only a witness of the sufferings of Christ, but a partaker of the glory to be revealed; he could not write of being a partaker of the sufferings, for there had been an element of safety in his denial and forsaking of the Lord. Certainly Peter was peacefully facing death in Acts 12:1-6.

3. *The Garden of Gethsemane* 26:36-56

v.36 "Then cometh Jesus with them unto a place called Gethsemane, and saith unto the disciples, Sit ye here, while I go and pray yonder.
v.37 And he took with him Peter and the two sons of Zebedee, and began to be sorrowful and very heavy.
v.38 Then saith he unto them, My soul is exceeding sorrowful, even unto death: tarry ye here, and watch with me.
v.39 And he went a little further, and fell on his face, and prayed, saying, O my Father, if it be possible, let this cup pass from me: nevertheless not as I will, but as thou *wilt*.
v.40 And he cometh unto the disciples, and findeth them asleep, and saith unto Peter, What, could ye not watch with me one hour?
v.41 Watch and pray, that ye enter not into temptation: the spirit indeed *is* willing, but the flesh is *weak*.
v.42 He went away again the second time, and prayed, saying, O my Father, if this cup may not pass away from me, except I drink it, thy will be done.
v.43 And he came and found them asleep again: for their eyes were heavy.
v.44 And he left them, and went away again, and prayed the third time, saying the same words.
v.45 Then cometh he to his disciples, and saith unto them, Sleep on now, and take *your* rest: behold, the hour is at hand, and the Son of man is betrayed into the hands of sinners.
v.46 Rise, let us be going: behold, he is at hand that doth betray me.
v.47 And while he yet spake, lo, Judas, one of the twelve, came, and with him a great multitude with swords and staves, from the chief priests and elders of the people.
v.48 Now he that betrayed him gave them a sign, saying, Whomsoever I shall kiss, that same is he: hold him fast.
v.49 And forthwith he came to Jesus, and said, Hail, master; and kissed him.
v.50 And Jesus said unto him, Friend, wherefore art thou come? Then came they, and laid hands on Jesus, and took him.
v.51 And, behold, one of them which were with Jesus stretched out *his* hand, and drew his sword, and struck a servant of the high priest's, and smote off his ear.
v.52 Then said Jesus unto him, Put up again thy sword into his place: for all they that take the sword shall perish with the sword.
v.53 Thinkest thou that I cannot now pray to my Father, and he shall presently give me more than twelve legions of angels?
v.54 But how then shall the scriptures be fulfilled, that thus it must be?
v.55 In that same hour said Jesus to the multitudes, Are ye come out as against a thief with swords and staves for to take me? I sat daily with you teaching in the temple, and ye laid no hold on me.
v.56 But all this was done, that the scriptures of the prophets might be fulfilled. Then all the disciples forsook him, and fled."

36 "Gethsemane" means oil-press; the name occurs only here and in Mark 14:32. Luke refers only to "the place" (Luke 22:40), while John uses only the description "a garden" (John 18:1). It was not only the place of the Lord's agony, but also of the betrayal and His arrest by the Jewish authorities. The garden lay to the east of the brook Kidron, on the western lower slopes of the Mount of Olives. There were three classes of men, with the Lord separated "a little further":

1. the mass of men on the outside, mostly unbelievers, but some being His disciples;

2. the eight apostles whom the Lord left near the entrance;

3. the three special apostles taken into the garden by the Lord who remained separated from them in His agony of prayer.

We can liken these positions to the precincts outside the temple, the temple courts, the holy place, and the holiest of all. Broadly speaking, they may correspond to those who are natural, carnal and spiritual. The positions may correspond to Christ being popular, present and prominent, but He Himself must be pre-eminent.

37 Peter, James and John were given special prominence: they were taken into the garden to be specially with the Lord. Various suggestions (presented in the form of unanswered questions) can be given as to why these three were chosen. Were Peter and John given this special treatment since they would write part of the NT, and was James included because he would be the first martyr? On the other hand, were they the weakest of the eleven, needing special encouragement? For these were the only ones whom the Lord had to rebuke (Mark 8:33; Luke 9:55). Or did the Lord seek those who most of all could have provided comfort; or was the Lord building one more special occasion for the memory of these three, as He had done before at the raising of Jairus' daughter (Luke 8:51) and on the mount of transfiguration (Matt 17:1)?

As the "man of sorrows", the Lord began to be "sorrowful and very heavy". Words of this nature gain their meanings by the common experiences of mankind. Yet when the inner state of the Lord's soul is being described, there are no other words available except those in the natural languages of men. Words are poor things with which to express the inner sensitivities of One divine, particularly when these words are completely coloured by our own experiences. However, there was no other way to describe what was almost indescribable, and the Spirit of inspiration did the best with the verbal material available. "To be sorrowful" is the passive infinitive of *lupeō*, implying grief or sorrow. The noun and the verb are used more times in 2 Corinthians than anywhere else in the NT. The verb (and the adjective *perilupos*, "exceeding sorrowful") are used of the Lord only in this particular context; the verb and the noun are used also of the disciples, "they were exceeding sorrowful" (Matt 26:22), "sleeping for sorrow" (Luke 22:45). In the Lord's case, here was the deepest grief ever experienced on earth, yet revealed in a measure to the apostles. Paul wrote later, "As sorrowful, yet alway rejoicing" (2 Cor 6:10), yet in the Lord's case in the garden there is no written record of joy, though Heb 12:2 shows that there was the joy set before Him when He endured the cross. Again, the word for "very heavy" is *adēmoneō*, much distressed and depressed, almost overwhelmed with sorrow. The word is used only of the Lord in the garden, and of Epaphroditus (Phil 2:26). Of course, great care must be exercised as to how far human emotions implied in the word can be applied to the Lord's experience. No doubt we cannot tell, but humbly accept that the Spirit of inspiration chose the word to describe the state of the Lord's soul.

38 As already stated, "exceeding sorrowful" is one word in Greek, a strengthened form of adjective. It occurs five times in the NT: twice of the Lord in the Gethsemane narrative, twice of the rich young ruler (Luke 18:23, 24), and once of Herod because of his oath (Mark 6:26), thereby describing three completely different states of mind and soul. The Lord's soul was more sorrowful than any outward manifestation could display, contrasting with other experiences in His lifetime, such as when He "rejoiced in spirit" (Luke 10:21). This sorrow was "even unto death". This does not refer primarily to physical death, when He dismissed His spirit into the Father's hand, when He went into paradise which was no place of suffering, though entirely different from anything through which He had passed before. Rather He more particularly referred to the process of death, the shame of the cross, the associated pain caused by man's cruelty, and the spiritual sufferings through which He would pass at the hand of the Judge on high. His soul would be made an offering for sin; He would see the travail of His soul; He would pour out His soul unto death (Isa 53:10-12). Here was the darkness and the forsaking of His God (Ps 22:1-2; 69:1-3, 14-17). Here were the agonies as He tasted the judgment of the second death due to all men apart from redemption through His blood. No wonder His perfect soul shrank from this death that was so near at hand, but He knew that the Father's will was the only way forward.

The request "watch with me" is amplified in Luke 22:40, "Pray that ye enter not into temptation". After the first hour in Matt 26:41, the Lord said, "Watch and pray, that ye enter not into temptation", as if Satan was abroad in the darkness, waiting for any whom he could devour. Being divine, the Lord could not fail, but He knew the weakness of the disciples, and their lack of prayer may have contributed to their failure shortly afterwards.

39 "Little" in "a little further" is the word *mikron*, an adverb meaning small in both space and time. Thus in Matt 26:73, time is implied: "after a while", namely "after a little". The word is used seven times in John 16:16-19 meaning "a little while" in time. In Gethsemane, the "little further" implies typically that the Lord was within the vail, showing the complete difference between Himself and those on the outside. It is the little further that costs, and the little further that counts: the cost for Christ was His agony in the garden when He prayed more earnestly, and it counted, for had it not been for His work then there could be no believers today. We too must go a little further to be effective, since if it costs, then it counts. This feature distinguishes the service of the most devoted of the Lord's people.

The Lord addressed the Father as always in His prayers – the exception being in Matt 27:46 when in the darkness He said "My God, my God". His statement, "If it be possible", did not denote His will, but the sensitivity of a true human heart shrinking from the worst. Our constitution is made that way; it is not a question of weakness or failure, but an inevitable reaction produced by the way we are made. Christ, being human, shared the same reaction. The vital question is, what happened next? An ordinary man may well flee from the cause, or he may seek to alter the situation, or have someone else alter it. But in the Lord's case, He went straight forward, knowing that the cup was the Father's will, and He would not exercise a will independent of His Father's. Throughout life and death, the will of Christ was always that of His Father; the whole of John's Gospel is a living testimony to that fact. Concerning His *word*, He said, "the word which ye hear is not mine, but the Father's which sent me" (John 14:24); concerning His *will*, He said, "I came down from heaven, not to do mine own will, but the will of him that sent me" (John 6:38; 5:30; Heb 10:7); concerning His *works*, "I have finished the work which thou gavest me to do" (John 17:4; 14:10); concerning His *witness*, "I have greater witness than that of John: for the works which the Father hath given me to finish, the same works that I do, bear witness of me" (John 5:31, 36).

In Luke 22:41, we read that the Lord "kneeled down" to pray, but according to Matthew, He "fell on his face", namely the lowest position for the deepest prayer. Others had done this in Matt 17:6; Luke 5:12; 17:16, while the elders in heaven will also fall upon their faces in worship (Rev 11:16), but the Lord was unique in the extremity of His soul. In the OT, the idea behind a "cup" is sometimes one of blessing (Ps 23:5), but often of judgment at the hand of God (Isa 51:17; Jer 25:15); it was a picture of what had to be partaken. In the NT, believers partake of "the cup of blessing" (1 Cor 10:16), and in a measure partake of the cup of Christ (Matt 20:22,23) referring to His sufferings at the hands of men. Mystery Babylon will partake of a cup of wrath in the future (Rev 16:19), but believers will never partake of a cup of judgment. This aspect of the Lord's cup – the partaking of judgment on the cross at the hands of God – will never be the portion of believers, since He exhausted it once and for all.

40-41 When the Lord returned to His disciples from the "stone's cast" (Luke 22:41), He found them asleep instead of watching and praying, in keeping with Ps 69:20, "I looked for some to take pity, but there was none; and for comforters, but I found none". Both the Lord and His disciples had had sleepless nights no doubt before, but here only One overcame the physical difficulties. We recall that these three men had fallen asleep before (Luke 9:32) under completely opposite circumstances – when the Lord was transfigured before them on the mount. Luke 22:45 adds that they were "sleeping for sorrow", but they had not gone a little further so as to keep awake. Previously, the Lord had prayed for the disciples and for Peter (John 17:9, 15; Luke 22:32), but here the Lord had to watch and pray alone for Himself – there was no reciprocation. For "Watch and pray", see Eph 6:18; 1 Pet 4:7; temptation would arise and sin would follow if the mind were not occupied with Christ alone, for an empty mind is soil prepared for one to act upon temptation. But the Lord conceded that the spirit was willing even though the flesh was weak. In other words, there were natural limitations in their physical make-up, yet the Lord overcame under similar circumstances. No doubt here the Lord implied "flesh" physically, yet in other places it has a spiritual or metaphorical meaning: "It is the spirit that quickeneth; the flesh profiteth nothing" (John 6:63), the natural man cannot understand the things of the Spirit of God; "the flesh lusteth against the Spirit, and the Spirit against the flesh" (Gal 5:17), and Paul provided two lists, the works of the flesh and the fruit of the Spirit.

42-44 According to Luke 22:44, this second prayer was "in an agony", and the Lord "prayed more earnestly" (or, more intently). Men have an uncontrolled dread of certain things; how much more the Lord as He knew beforehand the details of that which He was about to pass through – yet He went straight forward. In Matt 26:39, the divine Man was contemplating the Father's will consistent with the eternal counsels; here He contemplates the fact that the cup cannot pass, and that He was prepared to drink it. Heb 5:7, 8 has explained it thus: "in the days of his flesh, when he had offered up prayers and supplications with strong crying and tears unto him that was able to save him from (out of, JND) death", for He "learned ... obedience by the things which he suffered". His prayer was answered at the resurrection. The Lord did not learn obedience as we do from the opposite position of disobedience; rather He learnt it by experiencing obedience to the uttermost after a life that had always manifested obedience. Obedience was nothing new to the Lord, but the depth of it was new in Gethsemane.

Three times the Lord said similar words, and three times He found the three disciples asleep. In 2 Cor 12:8 Paul prayed three times that his thorn in the flesh might depart. These three times were sufficient for the apostle to know what the mind of the Lord was, for the answer came, "My grace is sufficient for thee: for my strength is made perfect in weakness". (Consider Daniel, who prayed "three times a day" in Dan 6:10.) There is nothing mechanical in praying a similar prayer three times when this prayer comes from the heart. This has no connection with the vain repetitions of the Pharisees or the heathen (Matt 6:7), or with the multitude of formal prayers that have been read in identical form for hundreds of years, obviously with no discernment as to whether God would answer these prayers or not, else such prayers would either cease or would turn into thanksgiving. In 2 Cor 11:28 we have Paul's constant and daily prayers for the churches, but for himself he would pray only three times. He was in touch with God to know that that was enough.

45-46 "Sleep on now", said the Lord to His disciples when His prayer was complete. There was no more time available for watching and praying on their part; man's hour was at hand for doing the worst, and the Lord assessed the true nature of the religious leaders; they were "sinners". We believe that the Lord spoke to His disciples in sympathy, and allowed them to sleep for as long as possible: "for thou, Lord, only makest me dwell in safety" (Ps 4:8), since Satan and evil men were nigh at hand. This permitted time of sleep comes between v.45 and v.46; the Lord watched over them although they had not watched with Him. Of course He knew what was happening outside the garden, and He could trace the approach of the great multitude with Judas at its head. Only at the last moment did the Lord awaken the disciples, saying "Rise, let us be going". In other words, He was going to meet the enemy, so that Judas might know once again that his deed had been foreknown by the Lord.

47-50 John 18:4 informs us that the Lord went forth to meet the "band of men" since He knew "all things that should come upon him". In John's account, the Lord took the initiative, while in Matthew's account Judas took the initiative. Since the Lord was in ultimate control, we believe that He spoke first, "Whom seek ye?", and when He replied "I am he" (*egō eimi*, I am), the power of His word caused the men to fall to the ground, repelled as sinners by the power of One divine. We harmonise the recorded events as follows: Judas had agreed with the leaders that he would identify the Lord with a kiss (Matt 26:48); he would not be outdone although the Lord had independently identified Himself. So he approached the Lord to carry out his dastardly sign, but again the Lord prevented him by saying, "betrayest thou the Son of man with a kiss?" (Luke 22:48). Judas persisted, the Lord allowing his deed: "he came to Jesus, and said, Hail, master; and kissed him" (Matt 26:49), the word for "master" being Rabbi. The closest contact was made, John "leaning on Jesus' bosom" (John 13:23) in perfect love, and Judas kissing Him in the depths of treachery. In speaking to His Father, the Son referred to Judas as "the son of perdition" (John 17:12), but in speaking directly to Judas, He said "Friend". This particular word for "friend" (*hetairos*) occurs four times and only in Matthew's Gospel, - viz. 11:16; 20:13; 22:12; 26:50. It does not involve affection, rather companionship, reflecting on the fact that Judas, as one of the twelve, had accompanied the Lord for several years in His ministry. This scene being over, the Lord was taken prisoner for the first and the last time. Men thought that they had triumphed, but the triumph of the Lord would soon be demonstrated in resurrection, when they would never again be able to touch Him personally. The Jewish religious leaders and the Roman authorities in Judaea were those who thought that they had triumphed, corresponding to the two beasts in Rev 13 who will be "taken" ultimately when the Lamb "shall overcome them" (Rev 19:20; 17:14).

51-52 The multitude came "with swords and staves" (vv.47, 55), as if expecting trouble from the "King of peace" and His small band of disciples. The word for sword is *machaira*, a short sword, dagger or knife; the word for stave is *xulon*, meaning wood as a material, or a cudgel made of wood. When a weapon is not implied, the word is translated tree or wood, as in 1 Cor 3:12; Gal 3:13; 1 Pet 2:24 (the cross being described five times by this word). The band of apostles also had "two swords" (Luke 22:38), which they showed to the Lord in the upper room; He said, "It is enough", namely that their conversation should come to an end. One of them was prepared to be bold in an unspiritual manner (identified as Peter in John 18:10), cutting off the ear of a servant of the high priest, his name being Malchus (John 18:10). Luke has provided more details of the incident: they had actually asked the Lord, "shall we smite with the sword?" (Luke 22:49), though the Lord did not answer this question. And it was then that the Lord performed His last miracle before His death: "he touched his ear, and healed him" (v.51). Normally men would marvel, but their hardened hearts could no longer marvel at the Lord's miracles, even though they had never seen that particular miracle performed before. If this were a sign, they would not believe because of a sign. The Lord rebuked Peter; he had to put away the weapon, "for all they that take the sword shall perish with the sword". A similar statement is found in Rev 13:10, referring to the offensive warfare made by the future beast against the saints (v.7). In other words, the beast would suffer in a worse way than that which he inflicts upon God's people. The King of kings comes with "a sharp sword" proceeding out of His mouth, and at His command this beast and the anti-Christ are cast alive into the lake of fire (namely, not killed with any physical sword, Rev 19:15, 20). In Peter's case, he was wrong in his action, since it might almost have prevented the OT Scriptures from being fulfilled! See also John 18:36, "… then would my servants fight".

53-54 Angels were prominent during the lifetime of the Lord Jesus on earth (Matt 1:20; 2:13; 4:11; Ps 91:11; Luke 22:43; Matt 28:2). They acted in a protective and ministerial capacity, not only for the Lord but also for His people (Acts 5:19); 12:7; Heb 1:14). However, in order that the Scriptures might be fulfilled at the cross, no angels were forthcoming to protect the Son of God from the hands of evil men. Had His hour not yet come, then more than twelve legions of angels would have been available to protect Him if men had taken Him under similar circumstances. In Elisha's day there was the mountain "full of horses and chariots of fire" around about him (2 Kings 6:17), usually unseen, but then made visible to Elisha's servant. Taking a legion as 6,000 (for the word refers to the Roman army), and recalling that one angel "smote in the camp of the Assyrians an hundred fourscore and five thousand" (2 Kings 19:35), then the Lord was protected by angels who had the capacity to slay 12 x 6,000 x 185,000, namely, 13,320,000,000 enemies of the Lord. Indeed, "greater is he that is in you, than he that is in the world" (1 John 4:4).

55-56 The Lord asked a question, and made a statement. They considered Him as a thief and came to arrest Him, whereas He had been a teacher and they made no attempt to arrest Him. During the past few previous days, He "was teaching in the temple", coming in early from the mount of Olives to do this, since some of the people in Jerusalem were attentive to hear Him (Luke 21:37-38). The word for "temple" is, as usual, *hieron*, referring in this case to the temple courts where the people could congregate. The reason why the leaders had made no attempt to arrest Him in public was that this had to be done "in the absence of the multitude" (Luke 22:6), otherwise there would have been an uproar. In Matt 26:54, the Lord referred to the Scriptures being fulfilled, but in v.56 Matthew the author added a similar statement as the answer to the Lord's question. The multitudes could not or would not answer the question, but Matthew provided a deeper answer.

So the disciples "forsook him, and fled", as the Lord had predicted in Matt 26:31, "the sheep of the flock shall be scattered abroad". However, John and Peter followed to the palace of the high priest (John 18:16 Matt 26:58).

No eye was found to pity,
No heart to bear Thy woe;
But shame, and scorn, and spitting —
None cared Thy name to know.

Man's boasting love disowns Thee;
Thine own Thy danger flee;
A Judas only owns Thee
That Thou may'st captive be.

JND, *The Man of Sorrows* (1867)

The Lord had allowed them to flee from Him, for we read in John 18:8-9, "let these go their way: That the saying might be fulfilled, which he spake, Of them which thou gavest me have I lost none". He desired to protect them, though their motives were wrong.

4. *The Trial before the Sanhedrin and Peter's Denial* 26:57-75

v.57 "And they that had laid hold on Jesus led *him* away to Caiaphas the high priest, where the scribes and the elders were assembled.
v.58 But Peter followed him afar off unto the high priest's palace, and went in, and sat with the servants, to see the end.
v.59 Now the chief priests, and elders, and all the council, sought false witness against Jesus, to put him to death;
v.60 But found none: yea, though many false witnesses came, *yet* found they none. At the last came two false witnesses,

v.61 And said, This *fellow* said, I am able to destroy the temple of God, and to build it in three days.
v.62 And the high priest arose, and said unto him, Answerest thou nothing? what *is it which* these witness against thee?
v.63 But Jesus held his peace. And the high priest answered and said unto him, I adjure thee by the living God, that thou tell us whether thou be the Christ, the Son of God.
v.64 Jesus saith unto him, Thou hast said: nevertheless I say unto you, Hereafter shall ye see the Son of man sitting on the right hand of power, and coming in the clouds of heaven.
v.65 Then the high priest rent his clothes, saying, He hath spoken blasphemy; what further need have we of witnesses? behold, now ye have heard his blasphemy.
v.66 What think ye? They answered and said, He is guilty of death.
v.67 Then did they spit in his face, and buffeted him; and others smote *him* with the palms of their hands,
v.68 Saying, Prophesy unto us, thou Christ, Who is he that smote thee?
v.69 Now Peter sat without in the palace: and a damsel came unto him, saying, Thou also wast with Jesus of Galilee.
v.70 But he denied before *them* all, saying, I know not what thou sayest.
v.71 And when he was gone out into the porch, another *maid* saw him, and said unto them that were there, This *fellow* was also with Jesus of Nazareth.
v.72 And again he denied with an oath, I do not know the man.
v.73 And after a while came unto *him* they that stood by, and said to Peter, Surely thou also art *one* of them; for thy speech bewrayeth thee.
v.74 Then began he to curse and to swear, *saying*, I know not the man. And immediately the cock crew.
v.75 And Peter remembered the word of Jesus, which said unto him, Before the cock crow, thou shalt deny me thrice. And he went out, and wept bitterly."

57-58 All the four Gospels must be consulted to gain a complete picture of what happened at the trial of the Lord Jesus before the Jewish Sanhedrin. According to John 18:13, He had appeared before Annas first, who had been the high priest previously, before he was deposed by the Romans. Annas had then sent Him bound to Caiaphas (v.24), whose counsel was that "one man should die for the people" (v.14). In Matt 26:57, the Lord was brought before the high priest, the scribes and the elders; the Sanhedrin was waiting for Him to be brought, since they had sent the multitude with Judas to arrest Him (v.47). The procedure for a trial before the Sanhedrin was elaborate and well-defined (see the article "Sanhedrin" in any Bible dictionary, such as *The New IVF Bible Dictionary*). By the deliberate introduction of false witnesses, these procedures were violated; the high priest had pronounced the verdict before the trial commenced, so he manipulated the proceedings to achieve his end.

It was "into the high priest's house" (*oikos*) that they brought the Lord (Luke 22:54), though Peter followed "unto the high priest's palace" (*aulē*), meaning the courtyard around which the house was built. In Matt 26:57, they led the Lord to the religious authorities, while later in Luke 22:66 they led Him to the legal authorities (a meeting of the Sanhedrin when it was day; the word for "council" in this verse is Sanhedrin). In Matt 27:2, they led Him to the Roman political authorities; In Luke 23:7, He was sent to Herod the regal authority, and then in Matt 27:31 they led Him to the military authorities for crucifixion. All this was physically exhausting, but the scourging was the worst part of all.

Peter followed "afar off" This position "afar off" is that which characterises Jews and Gentiles prior to conversion (Acts 2:39; Eph 2:17). The positions of the unconverted and of Peter are in sharp contrast to that of the faithful women who in the tragedy of their hearts, stood "afar off" (Matt 27:55). Peter's object was to see "the end" (*telos*), namely, the absolute end when the Lord would be condemned to death. But fellowship with men of the world Is not helpful to spirituality. Peter "sat with the servants" (*hupēretēs*); originally *hupēretēs* meant an under-rower, and hence a subordinate or officer; it appears 20 times in the NT with various designations and applications. Thus it is used of the Sanhedrin court officers; of "ministers of the word" (Luke 1:2); of the synagogue attendant (Luke 4:20); of the Lord's servants (John 18:36); of Mark (Acts 13:5); and of Paul (Acts 26:16; 1 Cor 4:1).

Peter remained in "the hall" (*aulē*, Luke 22:55), the courtyard, and sat down with the ungodly to warm himself. It is a danger to be in the company of those who are antagonistic to the Lord, while waiting to accomplish the evil decisions of their superiors. Peter's position was unlike the Lord's words in John 17:14-16, where His own were seen as in the world but not of it. Peter did not go as far as having the friendship of the world, which is "enmity with God" (James 4:4), but he sat down with these officers, in contrast to the time a few hours earlier when he had sat with the Lord (Matt 26:20). They had kindled a fire (Luke 22:55), but the fires of the world are dangerous, for a fire had burnt up the Word of God (Jer 36:23), and a fire had burnt up "our holy and our beautiful house" (Isa 64:11).

59-60 The whole of the Sanhedrin was of one mind in their objective and how to attain it. They knew that they had to use false witness in order to condemn the Lord to death, for everything was true about the Lord and this was of no use as evidence. Religious false witness was sufficient for the Sanhedrin, but political false witness would be necessary before Pilate. Many false witnesses testified before the Sanhedrin, but the evidence that they brought forward was not sufficient for the pronouncement of the death sentence. In the OT the law recognised the importance of true witness, but when it pleased the Sanhedrin, they were quite content to break the ninth commandment, "Thou shalt not bear false witness" (Exod 20:16). They overlooked the provision of Deut 19:16-19: if false witness caused a man's death, then the false witnesses should also put to death. "A false witness shall not be unpunished" (Prov 19:5, 9) is repeated twice because of its importance. It is interesting to note that the first Christian martyr suffered the same injustice at the hands of the Sanhedrin; they "set up false witnesses" (also concerning "this holy place") against the teaching of Stephen, because they could not resist his wisdom (Acts 6:10-14). But at last they found "two false witnesses", two being necessary because "the testimony of two men is true" (John 8:17; Deut 19:15), though Mark 14:59 informs us that their false witness did not agree together. See also 1 Kings 21:9-14.

61-62 In John 2:18 the Jews who had witnessed the Lord's cleansing of the temple in Jerusalem asked for a sign to prove that He had the authority to do such things. His reply, "Destroy this temple, and in three days I will raise it up", seemed incomprehensible to the natural mind. Forty-six years had already been spent on the building of this remarkable edifice, and it was finally completed just before its destruction in AD 70. However, the Lord spoke of "the temple of his body". Note that the Lord implied that the Jews would destroy this temple, but divine power would raise it in resurrection. The tabernacle had taken five months to build, and Solomon's temple and the second temple after the return of the captivity had both taken many years to complete. The Jews would recall that Solomon's temple had been destroyed by Nebuchadnezzar, and they did not want a repetition of that in their day. When the Lord used the word "temple", the special word *naos* appears in Greek, being the inner shrine, which more properly typified the holy shrine of His body. Only after the resurrection did the disciples remember the Lord's words (John 2:22), but the Jews remembered them, and recalled them against the Lord during His trial, and when He was on the cross (Matt 27:40).

In both cases, the false witnesses and the Jews ascribed to the Lord the destruction of the temple: "I am able to destroy", "Thou that destroyest the temple". They had to twist the Lord's words that they, the Jews, would perform the destroying process; they could not have used that in their false witness. Its rebuilding in three days implied, to the believing mind, His resurrection after the appointed time. The disciples did not understand any reference to "the third day" (Luke 18:33-34), but the Pharisees remembered and knew what this period of time implied, and were quick to use it when necessary (Matt 27:63). The Lord had predicted the destruction of Herod's temple by the Romans only to His disciples (Matt 24:2), and Stephen must have used this prophecy in his teaching. False witnesses changed his teaching, asserting that "this Jesus of Nazareth shall destroy this place", namely, "this holy place" (Acts 6:13, 14).

In Mark 14:58, to add spice to their false witness, the words "made with hands" and "made without hands" were added. Because of these additions and changes, the false witness of these two men did not "agree together" (v. 59). Yet the high priest accepted the evidence, and expected the Lord to answer the charge of damage to, and destruction of the temple, what would be called terrorism today.

63 The Lord remained silent; He would not defend Himself against such lying charges. He knew that, without repentance, all liars would ultimately find themselves in the lake of fire (Rev 21:8). As Isa 53:7 puts it, "he opened not his mouth … as a sheep before her shearers is dumb, so he openeth not his mouth". In Ps 38:12-14 "I was as a dumb man" because of what men did; in Ps 39:9 "I was dumb" because of what God did. Yet in resurrection "he hath put a new song in my mouth" (Ps 40:3). However, when the high priest said, "I adjure thee by the living God, that thou tell us whether thou be the Christ, the Son of God", it was necessary for the Lord to answer. Effectively, Caiaphas said, "I put Thee on Thy oath"; under these circumstances the law demanded an answer (Lev 5:1).

64 Caiaphas had asked about "the Christ" and "Son of God", and by saying "Thou hast said" (*su eipas*), the Lord answered in the affirmative. However, He then referred to Himself as "the Son of man".

The names associated with the Lord during this period should be noted.

1. **In the form of questions:** "Art thou the Christ?" (the chief priests and Caiaphas, Luke 22:67; Matt 26:63); "Art thou then the Son of God?" (Caiaphas and all the accusers, Matt 26:63; Luke 22:70); "Art thou the King of the Jews?" (Pilate, Matt 27:11; Luke 23:3; John 18:33). No question was asked about the title "Son of man".

2. **In the form of supposition with an "if":** "If he be Christ" (rulers and one malefactor, Luke 23:35, 39); "If thou be the Son of God" (passers by, Matt 27:40), "If thou be the king of the Jews" (soldiers, Luke 23:37).

3. **In the form of a true confession:** "Thou art the Christ" (Peter, Matt 16:16; Luke 9:20; John 6:69); "The Son of God" (apostles and Peter, Matt 14:33; 16:16); "The King of Israel" (Nathaniel, John 1:49).

4. **In the form of a divine testimony.** "Mine anointed (lit. my Christ) (Ps 132:17); "Thou art my Son" (Ps 2:7; Matt 3:17; 17:5); "My king" (Ps 2:6).

To His answer, the Lord added His stupendous declaration, "Hereafter shall ye see the Son of man sitting on the right hand of power, and coming in the clouds of heaven" – His ascension position as seated on the right hand of the power of God, and the time of His future vindication. Whatever Caiaphas and Pilate might do, His resurrection was assured as based on this prediction. Previously, such truth was spoken only to His disciples (Matt 24:30), but now it was made known to religious unbelief. The word "power" (*dunamis*) implies absolute power in judgment, to be distinguished from "All power is given unto me" (Matt 28:18), where the word is *exousia*, meaning absolute authority.

In our verse, note that the Lord said "Thou" in the singular, but "you, ye" in the plural. Modern translations of the Scriptures that use "you" for both singular and plural must be treated with great caution and suspicion, since the meaning of many verses is deliberately confused and distorted by this device, and these modern translations cannot be used for detailed Bible study with any assurance of safety. In other places (such as Ps 2:7; Heb 1:5) they also introduce heresy as well as distortion.

65-68 The rending of clothes was an outward display of inner emotion, whether justified or not. In Lev 10:6; 21:10 it suggests the ending of the priesthood. In some contexts it denoted an expression of the horror of blasphemy. Thus Hezekiah rent his clothes when he heard of Rab-shakeh's blasphemy against the living God (2 Kings 19:1; 18:37); Paul and Barnabas rent their clothes when the people of Lystra sought to offer sacrifice believing that they were gods come down in the likeness of men (Acts 14:14). The word "blasphemy" (*blasphēmia*) refers to an utterance that is defamatory against God and sacred things. To accuse the Lord of this is itself blasphemy; and is equivalent to calling light dark. It shows the darkness of Jewish religion to make such a statement against the Lord of life and glory. No doubt Caiaphas believed what he said, but the belief of unbelievers is unbelief. He suddenly ended the trial, no more witnesses were needed, the Lord's own words were sufficient. Of unbelievers, the Lord had said, "by thy words thou shalt be condemned" (Matt 12:37), but the high priest effectively twisted this statement so as to apply it to the Lord!

The whole council thus condemned the Lord to death; Mark 14:64 states that they "all" condemned Him. It was a unanimous vote, with none standing for the Lord. We can presume that Nicodemus "being one of them" (John 7:50), and Joseph of Arimathaea who "had not consented to the counsel and deed of them" (Luke 23:51), were absent.

Physical indignities were then heaped upon the blessed Lord, who deliberately took the position of not seeking to defend Himself. They spat, buffeted and smote with their hands, they blasphemously spoke against Him (Luke 22:65). They blindfolded Him, seeking to test His ability to prophesy: "Who is he that smote thee?" Of course the Lord would not demonstrate this ability, though He did know before each blow descended who it was who was delivering the blow. This fulfilled Isa 50:6, "I gave my back to the smiters, and my cheeks to them that plucked off the hair: I hid not my face from shame and spitting". He added, "therefore have I set my face like a flint" (v.7). But worse was to come at the hands of Pilate.

69-70 The fear of man rather than the strength of the Lord was the ultimate cause of Peter's downfall, though his compromising position with the servants laid him right open for the attack. Taking all the Gospel accounts together, it appears that Peter was surrounded by several people all speaking to him at once, and at each denial he answered two or three, the different authors of the Gospels taking up differing accusations and answers. We trace these through the four Gospels in order:

Peter's first denial. The speakers: "a damsel" (Matt 26:69); "one of the maids of the high priest" (Mark 14:66); "a certain maid" (Luke 22:56); "the damsel that kept the door" (John 18:17).

The accusation against Peter: "Thou also wast with Jesus of Galilee" (Matt 26:69); "thou also wast with Jesus of Nazareth" (Mark 14:67); "This man was also with him" (Luke 22:56); "Art not thou also one of his disciples?" (John 18:17).

Peter's response: "I know not what thou sayest" (Matt 26:70); "I know not, neither understand I what thou sayest" (Mark 14:68); "Woman, I know him not" (Luke 22:57); "I am not" (John 18:17).

Consequences: "When he was gone out into the porch" (Matt 26:71); "he went out into the porch; and the cock crew" (Mark 14:68); "a little while" (Luke 22:58); "the servants and officers stood there ... they warmed themselves: and Peter stood with them, and warmed himself" (John 18:18).

71-72 Peter's second denial. The speakers: "another (*allos*, of the same kind) maid" (Matt 26:71): "a maid" who spoke to those that stood by, (Mark 14:69); "another" (*heteros*, a man of a different kind, Luke 22:58); "They" (the Sanhedrin court officers, John 18:25).

The accusation against Peter: "This fellow was also with Jesus of Nazareth" (Matt 26:71); "This is one of them" (Mark 14:69); "Thou art also of them" (Luke 22:58); "Art not thou also one of his disciples?" (John 18:25).

Peter's response: "he denied with an oath, I do not know the man" (Matt 26:72); "he denied it again" (Mark 14:70); "Man, I am not" (Luke 22:58); "I am not" (John 18:25).

Consequences: "after a while" (Matt 26:73); "a little after" (Mark 14:70); "about the space of one hour after" (Luke 22:59); no comment in John's Gospel.

73-74 Peter's third denial. The speakers: "they that stood by" (Matt 26:73); "they that stood by" (Mark 14:70), "another" (*allos*, a man of the same kind, Luke 22:59); "One of the servants of the high priest, being his kinsman whose ear Peter cut off" (John 18:26).

The accusation against Peter: "Surely, thou also art one of them; for thy speech bewrayeth (makes manifest) thee" (Matt 26:73); "Surely, thou art one of them: for thou art a Galilaean, and thy speech agreeth thereto" (Mark 14:70); "Of a truth this fellow was with him: for he is a Galilaean" (Luke 22:59); "Did not I see thee in the garden with him?" (John 18:26).

Peter's response: "Then began he to curse and to swear, saying, I know not the man" (Matt 26:74); "I know not this man of whom ye speak" (Mark 14:71) "Man, I know not what thou sayest" (Luke 22:60); "Peter then denied again" (John 18:27).

Consequences: "immediately the cock crew" (Matt 26:74); "the second time the cock crew" (Mark 14:72) – the only Gospel containing the two-fold crow; "immediately, while he yet spake, the cock crew" (Luke 22:60); "immediately the cock crew" (John 18:27).

75 The cock indicated the dawn of the last day of the Lord's life on earth. It was during the night that the Lord had warned that the denial would take place in a few hours' time. In Mark 14:68, the cock crew after the first denial, as if to have been a warning to Peter, to call him to his senses to seek spiritual courage. But he remembered the Lord's words only at the end of the three denials. No doubt on a balcony, the Lord turned and looked upon Peter below in the court. Elsewhere, His eyes could be as a flaming fire (Rev 1:14), yet here there would be love and sympathy in His eyes as they looked on poor Peter.

Peter wept tears of repentance (recorded in the three Synoptic Gospels), and he had to depart even from the Lord's presence. Yet this repentance was confirmed by the Lord in His three-fold question after His resurrection: "Lovest thou me?" (John 21:15-17). After that Peter was bold and courageous with strength granted by the Lord (Acts 4:29, 31), though he lapsed again in Gal 2:12; he was finally crucified for His Master's sake (John 21:18). It was with this experience of failure and strength that he could later write, "that the trial of your faith ... might be found unto praise and honour and glory" (1 Pet 1:7).

II. The Trial before Pilate, and the Crucifixion (27:1-66)

1. *The Suicide of Judas* 27:1-10

v.1 "When the morning was come, all the chief priests and elders of the people took counsel against Jesus to put him to death:
v.2 And when they had bound him, they led *him* away, and delivered him to Pontius Pilate the governor.
v.3 Then Judas, which had betrayed him, when he saw that he was condemned, repented himself, and brought again the thirty pieces of silver to the chief priests and elders,
v.4 Saying, I have sinned in that I have betrayed the innocent blood. And they said, What *is that* to us? see thou *to that.*
v.5 And he cast down the pieces of silver in the temple, and departed, and went and hanged himself.
v.6 And the chief priests took the silver pieces, and said, It is not lawful for to put them into the treasury, because it is the price of blood.
v.7 And they took counsel, and bought with them the potter's field, to bury strangers in.
v.8 Wherefore that field was called, The field of blood, unto this day.
v.9 Then was fulfilled that which was spoken by Jeremy the prophet, saying, And they took the thirty pieces of silver, the price of him that was valued, whom they of the children of Israel did value;
v.10 And gave them for the potter's field, as the Lord appointed me."

1-2 In v.66 of the previous chapter, the Sanhedrin had agreed that "He is guilty of death". There may have been a break in the court hearing until the time "when the morning was come". A decision now had to be taken as to how "to put him to death". In 26:4, they consulted how they might take Him and kill Him, but when the actual time came, they had no authority to put any man to death. They said to Pilate, "It is not lawful for us to put any man to death: That the saying of Jesus might be fulfilled, which he spake, signifying what death he should die" (John 18:31-32). The Romans had taken away the Jewish right to stone those condemned to death; Jewish criminals had to be crucified according to the Roman method by Roman soldiers. (In John 12:32-33, the Lord had spoken of being "lifted up", signifying that He would die by crucifixion.) Hence the Sanhedrin needed Roman co-operation to get their false condemnation based on religions grounds accepted by Pilate. Thus they "took counsel" together to decide what arguments to place before Pilate; they had to use political persuasion and not religious arguments. Pilate, like Gallio the deputy of Achaia, was not concerned with religious matters, "if it be a question … of your law, look ye to it; for I will be no judge of such matters" (Acts 18:12-16). They would raise the following points: He perverted the nation,

1. forbidding to give tribute to Caesar,

2. claiming to be a King instead of Caesar (Luke 23:2).

The following mockery of a trial before Pilate revolved around this accusation that the Lord claimed to be King.

They "bound him" to ensure that He could not escape, in just the same way as later they sealed the tomb to ensure that His body could not be removed (Matt 27:64). The Lord was thus "delivered … to Pontius Pilate the governor (*hēgemōn*), a name given to the Roman procurators. Pilate, as procurator in Judaea, was the Roman administrator and judge, with full powers over life and death; as an unjust man, he was guilty of countless murders without trial (see Luke 13:1 for the coarse kind of activity to which he could sink). Thus there was a dual aspect to the trial of Christ: political power and religious intrusion joined hands together, in keeping with Ps 2:1-2; Acts 4:27. A fusion of state and church is loved today, having the effect that the true gospel is effectively barred from public utterances made by the leaders of either side of the dividing line.

3-4 There is now recorded the end of Judas, the son of perdition, this name being used by the Lord in the context where He prayed for the preservation of His own left in the world (John 17:12). It appears that Judas killed himself at about the same time as the Lord gave Himself in death on the cross – two contrasting deaths in every respect.

Judas seemed to have been a witness of the decisions of the Sanhedrin – he saw that the Lord "was condemned", something that his treachery had not foreseen, since it appears that Judas wanted both the money and the Lord's release. So Judas "repented himself" – the word used is *metamelomai* and not *metanoeō*; the former means to regret, while the latter means to repent. Certainly Judas did not repent in the Christian sense of the word – neither did Esau though he tried to reverse the effect of his deed (Heb 12:17). Natural remorse has no status before God. In Judas' case, the situation had gone beyond what he had intended or anticipated, but there was no way back – no way of undoing what he had done. His act was judged by divine standards, and there was no place for repentance of any sort, for he was beyond divine mercy.

To satisfy his mind, Judas sought to return the thirty pieces of silver to the priests, since he could not rectify the consequences of his deed. The lesson for us is that we should think carefully before we act, since usually we cannot alter the course of events if things go wrong. Judas confessed "I have sinned" to sinful priests, something not unknown in Christendom today; by confessing to men he confessed in the wrong direction. By contrast, it was to Nathan that David said, "I have sinned" (2 Sam 12:13); this confession was really directed to God (Ps 51:3-4), so in this case the iniquity of his sin was forgiven (Ps 32:5).

Judas rightly referred to "the innocent blood". In v.19 Pilate's wife called Him "that just man", while in v.24 Pilate called Him "this just person". The one thief on the cross said, "this man hath done nothing amiss" (Luke 23:41), and the Roman centurion claimed that "this was a righteous man" (v.47). In other words, there was a great testimony from unrighteous men to the righteousness of Christ. The priests, of course, now cast off Judas; their ends had been achieved, and they were no longer interested in the means: "What is that to us? see thou to that".

5 The word for "temple" in this verse is *naos*, the inner shrine reserved for the priests alone. The Lord and the apostles never went into this temple, only into the courts where the Lord taught: thus, in John 2:14, He was found in the temple (*hieron*), the courts and the totality of the buildings. How Judas cast down the pieces of silver in the inner shrine we are not told. He may have followed the priests into the temple in a state of desperation, but in any case, he was out of bounds and profaned the sanctuary, as men were doing to the holy temple of the Lord's body. Acts 1:18 then informs us that he "purchased a field with the reward of iniquity", though Matt 27:7 states that the priests bought the field. Strictly, the Greek word for "purchased" in Acts 1:18 is *ktaomai*, meaning to obtain or acquire rather than to purchase. We suspect that Judas acquired the field before the betrayal, and before handing over the money. But then he disposed of the money before the transaction was complete, and after his death the priests completed the transaction perhaps at the insistence of the original owner. Certainly, Matthew stated that Judas "hanged himself", but Peter in Acts 1:18 stated that he fell headlong, and that "he burst asunder in the midst, and all his bowels gushed out". The contraption (perhaps a branch of a tree) on which he intended to hang himself collapsed, and he fell to a worse death. Such was the manner in which he went "to his own place" (Acts 1:25), a place in hades, and then to "the blackness of darkness for ever" (Jude 13).

6-8 In the OT, God would have only holy things in His house: "holiness becometh thine house, O Lord" (Ps 93:5); "be ye clean, that bear the vessels of the Lord" (Isa 52:11). Evil money was not to be brought into the house of the Lord, as Moses said, "Thou shalt not bring the hire of a whore, or the price of a dog, into the house of the Lord ... these are abomination unto the Lord thy God" (Deut 23:18). The attitude of the priests in not allowing money that was the price of blood to be brought into the treasury was hypocritical, since they had just broken the moral law many times in allowing false witness to be the sole evidence by which they had condemned the Lord to death. So the price of blood was used in the service of death, for they completed the purchase of the potter's field and there strangers would be buried. No doubt it seemed a good opportunity to ensure that unclean foreigners were buried separately from the Jews. This field was therefore given an unpleasant name "Aceldama" (Acts 1:19), "the field of blood", and this name persisted for a considerable time, "unto this day". Judas' deed was known far and wide, and they kept alive his memory through the name attached to this field, rather than the memory of the Lord Jesus. In other words, memory was perpetuated, either by a field with the name of blood, or through a cup speaking of the blood of the new covenant.

9-10 The deed of Judas was so bad that it can be traced prophetically through the OT Scriptures. The NT writers have drawn attention to some of these references. Thus Peter in Acts 1:20 quoted from Ps 69:25 and 109:8, while Ps 41:9 is quoted in John 13:18. In fact, the Lord assessed the sin of Judas as being greater than that of Pilate: "he that delivered me unto thee (Pilate) hath the greater sin" (John 19:11). But the quotation from Zech 11:12-13 modified in Matt 27:9-10 has caused commentators the most difficulty, since v.9 states that it was spoken by "Jeremy" (Jeremiah) the prophet rather than by Zechariah. Explanations are varied, and we will quote a few that we have come across.

1. When the Gospel was written, Matthew did not have a copy of the OT prophets with him, and accidentally used the name Jeremiah rather than Zechariah. No doubt all preachers fail in this respect sometimes, but this suggestion does not honour the principle of inspiration.

2. Matthew had Jeremiah in mind because of references to the potter in Jer 18:1-4; 19:1. But this seems unlikely, since the wording in Zech 11:12-13 is so like Matthew's quotation, while those in Jeremiah have hardly anything in common.

3. The prophets were arranged in groups, and Matthew referred to the first one in the group rather than to the particular one from which the quotation was made.

4. There existed in Matthew's time a portion of Jeremiah's prophecy now lost from which Zechariah took his material.

5. When Matthew wrote his Gospel, he only wrote "by the prophet" without his name, as in Matt 21:5 where Zech 9:9 is quoted. Some manuscripts actually exist without the name appearing. A later ignorant copyist then inserted "Jeremy" perhaps in the margin, which was subsequently incorporated in the text. However, this suggestion contains many speculations that are mere hypotheses!

It will be seen that none of these explanations is "spiritual", and we prefer not to be dogmatic, but to keep an open mind on the issue until further light is available.

2. *The Judgment before Pilate* 27.11-31

v.11 "And Jesus stood before the governor: and the governor asked him, saying, Art thou the King of the Jews? And Jesus said unto him, Thou sayest.
v.12 And when he was accused of the chief priests and elders, he answered nothing.
v.13 Then said Pilate unto him, Hearest thou not how many things they witness against thee?
v.14 And he answered him to never a word; insomuch that the governor marvelled greatly.
v.15 Now at *that* feast the governor was wont to release unto the people a prisoner, whom they would.
v.16 And they had then a notable prisoner, called Barabbas.
v.17 Therefore when they were gathered together, Pilate said unto them, Whom will ye that I release unto you? Barabbas, or Jesus which is called Christ?
v.18 For he knew that for envy they had delivered him.
v.19 When he was set down on the judgment seat, his wife sent unto him, saying, Have thou nothing to do with that just man: for I have suffered many things this day in a dream because of him.
v.20 But the chief priests and elders persuaded the multitude that they should ask Barabbas, and destroy Jesus.
v.21 The governor answered and said unto them, Whether of the twain will ye that I release unto you? They said, Barabbas.
v.22 Pilate saith unto them, What shall I do then with Jesus which is called Christ? *They* all say unto him, Let him be crucified.
v.23 And the governor said, Why, what evil hath he done? But they cried out the more, saying, Let him be crucified.
v.24 When Pilate saw that he could prevail nothing, but *that* rather a tumult was made, he took water and washed *his* hands before the multitude, saying, I am innocent of the blood of this just person: see ye *to it*.
v.25 Then answered all the people, and said, His blood *be* on us, and on our children.
v.26 Then released he Barabbas unto them: and when he had scourged Jesus, he delivered *him* to be crucified.
v.27 Then the soldiers of the governor took Jesus into the common hall, and gathered unto him the whole band *of soldiers*.
v.28 And they stripped him, and put on him a scarlet robe.
v.29 And when they had platted a crown of thorns, they put it upon his head, and a reed in his right hand: and they bowed the knee before him, and mocked him, saying, Hail, King of the Jews!

v.30 And they spit upon him, and took the reed, and smote him on the head.
v.31 And after that they had mocked him, they took the robe off from him, and put his own raiment on him, and led him away to crucify *him*."

11 "Jesus stood before the governor", and was questioned by him, these questions deriving from accusations made by the Jews. John, in his Gospel, has provided more details. The Lord was led to Pilate's "hall of judgment" (John 18:28), strictly the Praetorium, the official residence of Pilate in Jerusalem: this word is variously translated in the AV. John has informed us that the Jews "went not into the judgment hall, lest they should be defiled; but that they might eat the passover". This was hypocrisy indeed: they would not go into a Gentile house, yet they were hounding to death One who was innocent. The extended conversation between Pilate and the Jews on the one hand, and Pilate and the Lord on the other, demanded that Pilate should constantly move "in" to speak to the Lord and "out" to speak to the Jews. Thus in v.29 he went "out" to the Jews, and in v.33 he went "into" the Praetorium. In v.38, he went "out" again, while 19:1 implies that he went "in". Following this, he went "out" in 19:4, and the Lord also came out dressed up as a King by the soldiers in mockery, at which Pilate said, "Behold the man!". In v.9 he went "in" again, seeking to release the Lord. Finally, he came "out" again in v.13 for the last time, when the Lord was delivered to the Jews to be crucified.

The Lord did not answer false accusations, but testified simply of the truth. To Pilate's question, "Art thou the King of the Jews?", He simply answered in the affirmative, "Thou sayest" (*su legeis*). Note, in 26:64 the Lord answered in the past tense, "Thou hast said", but here He answered in the present (continuous) as if Pilate was repeating himself (as indeed he was: see John 18:33,37). Of course this was a vital question as far as Pilate was concerned, for it suggested a new rival to Caesar. This He was, but not in the sense that Pilate thought, for regarding the fourth Roman beast in Dan 7:26, the Roman dominion will be taken away, to be replaced by the kingdom of the most High (v.27).

12-14 Pilate brought in from the outside further questions and accusations against the Lord on the inside, but the Lord "answered nothing" and "he answered him to never a word". We have already commented on this silence in our remarks on Matt 26:63; truly, "when he was reviled, (he) reviled not again; when he suffered, he threatened not" (1 Pet 2:23). However, the tables will be turned in the future day of judgment, for "kings shall shut their mouths at him" (Isa 52:15), "that every mouth may be stopped, and all the world may become guilty before God" (Rom 3:19).

The priests attempted to affect Pilate in every possible way. Thus they "accused" Him of "many things", putting false thoughts into Pilate's mind. One false accusation is found in Luke 23:5, "He stirreth up the people, teaching throughout all Jewry, beginning from Galilee to this place". They arranged for a clamour of voices to ask for the release of Barabbas (Matt 27:20), and demanded His crucifixion (v.22). Their loud voices prevailed over Pilate (Luke 23:23), and they suggested that Pilate would not be Caesar's friend if the Lord were released (John 19:12). So Pilate collapsed under the onslaught, and the trial was no righteous trial at all. Judas had had no idea that his treachery would cause the unrighteousness in others to reach such heights: "Behold, how great a matter a little fire kindleth! And the tongue is a fire, a world of iniquity ... it defileth the whole body, and setteth on fire the course of nature; and it is set on fire of hell" (James 3:5-6).

Pilate realised that the Lord was innocent (Matt 27:23), because the Jews had delivered Him "for envy" (*phthonos*), indicating their displeasure at the Lord's ability to live morally, to teach and to do miracles; so the Jews sought to remove from Him once and for all the opportunity to be so different from themselves. Further, Pilate claimed that both he and Herod found no fault in Him (Luke 23:14, 15); nevertheless he was "willing to content the people" (Mark 15:15). He saw that "he could prevail nothing", since if righteous decisions were made, a tumult would arise amongst the Jews (Matt 27:24). This shows Pilate's complete indifference to righteous judgment, and an unjust death. After all, he was the ultimate authority in Judaea, and had plenty of Roman soldiers to assist him in his work. But he preferred the easy way out.

At the same time, he tried to extricate himself from his self-imposed difficulty. He did this by sending the Lord to Herod (Luke 23:7), by trying to release Him instead of Barabbas, by seeing if scourging would satisfy the Jews (Luke 23:16), and by washing his hands to claim innocency (Matt 27:24). However, his efforts were fruitless; he did not know that the Lord had to be "lifted up" according to the OT Scriptures, and that he, Pilate, was the tool to effect this.

In v.4 we have already commented upon the testimony to this "just man". The most unrighteous of men recognised this fact. The rest of the NT also provides adequate witness to this truth: He was known as "the Just One" (Acts 3:14; 7:52; 22:14); He is "the righteous judge" (2 Tim 4:8), and "faithful and just" (1 John 1:9), He "suffered for sins, the just for the unjust" (1 Pet 3:18). This, then, was the common testimony of believers and unbelievers, yet Pilate allowed Him to be crucified. His action stands in contrast to that of Agrippa, who would have released Paul in spite of the activity of the Jews, though the apostle's appeal to Caesar prevented this release (Acts 26:32).

15-18 Pilate had a custom with the Jews whereby, at the Passover feast, he released to them a prisoner of their choice. It appears that Barabbas had already been selected for this favour, though Pilate evidently thought that the King of the Jews would be a useful alternative to solve his dilemma. The name Bar-abbas obviously means "son of his father", so he stood in contrast to the Lord who was the Son of His Father. Barabbas had been cast into prison "for sedition and murder" (Luke 23:25), yet the religious Jews preferred this to the infinite purity of the Son of His Father in whom they found no fault except that derived from false witness and false insinuations. Barabbas took character from his first father, Adam, through whom sin passed upon all men: the Lord took character from His Father (being the last Adam, and the second man from heaven, 1 Cor 15:45, 47). Pilate asked the Jews for their choice; he asked the question again in Matt 27:21, knowing the reason why they had delivered the Lord, and no doubt sensing the answer that the Jews would give.

19 This verse contains a brief interlude that is peculiar to Matthew's Gospel. Pilate was sitting "on the judgment seat" (*bēma*); this was the tribunal, a platform on which a Roman magistrate sat to administer justice. The word appears more than ten times in the NT, mostly in the Acts (12:21; 18:12,16,17; 25:6,10,17). This is a case where a natural word is imported into a spiritual truth, for it is used twice of "the judgment seat of Christ" (Rom 14:10; 2 Cor 5:10), a tribunal in heaven before which believers will appear after the rapture, when their lives and service will be reviewed so that appropriate rewards may be given.

Pilate's wife had had an unpleasant dream – the description of it does not state that it was a divinely arranged angelic visitation. No doubt she had known beforehand what the Jews were plotting, and that the Lord was a "just man", so her worried conscience brought about the unpleasant dream or nightmare. At least she was bold enough to interrupt the proceedings, though without recorded effect.

20-23 The narrative returns to Barabbas; the multitudes were under the sway of their leaders, the chief priests and elders. They "persuaded the multitude", an example of mass-manipulation based on the psychological emotionalism of the hour. Other examples of such manipulation are found in Dan 3:4-7; Acts 12:21-22; 19:25-29; 21:27-31. Certainly a Christian should not allow his mind to be bent by mass movements, protests and demonstrations. It appears that this persuasion took place between Pilate's first question about Barabbas (v.17) and the second.

In vv. 21-23, Pilate asked three questions.

1. "Whether of the twain (*apo tōn duo*, of the two) will ye that I release unto you?" The answer "Barabbas" meant that he could not abide by his wife's request, although the Lord was a "just man", and Barabbas had made insurrection with murder (Mark 15:7).

2. "What shall I do then with Jesus which is called Christ?" Note that Pilate used the title "Christ", derived from the Jew's accusation in Luke 23:2, "saying that he himself is Christ a King". Pilate intended that his decision should be made by the Jews who had already decided that the Lord's death should of necessity be by the Roman method of crucifixion, so they answered, "Let him be crucified".

3. "Why, what evil hath he done?" Pilate knew the answer to that; he had said, "I ... have found no fault in this man" and "I have found no cause of death in him" (Luke 23:14,22). The Jews did not take the trouble to repeat their accusations, but shouted with venom again, "Let him be crucified".

24 In Deut 21:6, we read of the washing of hands of the elders of the city nearest to a place where a man was found slain; they had to declare, "Our hands have not shed this blood". Pilate adopted this practice to satisfy his conscience. In Ps 73:12-13, because of the prosperity of the ungodly, Asaph said, "I have ... washed my hands in innocency"; likewise in Ps 26:5-6, because of the congregation of evil doers, "I will wash mine hands in innocency: so will I compass thine altar, O Lord". All this was true, but Pilate's action was but a vain gesture, for he did not "judge righteous judgment" (John 7:24). He could have called Roman soldiers to his rescue, but he would not. Scripture holds Pilate guilty: "of a truth against thy holy child Jesus ... both Herod, and Pontius Pilate ... were gathered together, For to do whatsoever thy hand and thy counsel determined before to be done" (Acts 4:27-28). His guilt matched the rest of his life; later he killed some Samaritans on mount Gerizim, and he was recalled to Rome to explain his action before the emperor; shortly afterwards he committed suicide. Some years ago, the author recalls reading that Pilate had been canonised by one African church!

25 The Jews were not interested in the niceties of Pilate's innocence or otherwise. They placed both themselves and their descendants under a curse, "His blood be on us, and on our children", though they had no understanding whatsoever as to the results of this curse. Effectively the children of Israel had placed themselves under a curse before, when they boasted "All that the Lord hath spoken we will do" (Exod 19:8), for "Cursed is every one that continueth not in all things which are written in the book of the law to do them" (Deut 27:26; Gal 3:10); the results of that are traced throughout the rest of OT history. Similarly with the Jews in NT times. The apostles spoke openly of Jewish guilt – that they had by wicked hands crucified and slain the Lord Jesus (Acts 2:23; 3:14-15); the Sanhedrin interpreted this kind of preaching as an intent "to bring this man's blood upon us" (Acts 5:28). This was not true, since they themselves had bound themselves under the curse. And this curse remained, until grace changed the blood of the curse into the blood of expiation in the experience of any who repented and trusted by faith in the Lord. The curse's first dreadful manifestation was in AD 70 when Jerusalem was destroyed by the Romans. Yet the Lord could weep for this people (Luke 19:41), because of what their enemies would do to the city (Luke 21:20). And when the faithful women wept for Him, he said that they should weep for themselves because of what was going to happen (Luke 23:28). This curse will remain, until the "spirit of grace" is poured out upon the inhabitants of Jerusalem, enabling faith to gaze upon Him whom they had once pierced (Zech 12:10). Only in the coming kingdom of Messiah's glory "there shall be no more curse" (Rev 22:3).

26 Thus Barabbas was released, whether to commit further acts of sedition and murder, or whether to repent and believe like one of the crucified malefactors (Luke 23:40-42), we do not know. And Pilate "delivered (*paradidōmi*) him to be crucified". It is interesting to note that this verb "deliver" (or "betray") is used more times in Matthew's Gospel than in the others. Pilate delivered Him to the centurion and soldiers responsible for the crucifixion: John 19:16 suggests that it was to the Jews that He was delivered.

At the same time, Pilate "scourged Jesus", something that the Lord had predicted to His apostles (Luke 18:33). According to John 19:1-16 a further conversation took place between Pilate and the Lord, after the release of Barabbas and before the Lord was finally condemned by Pilate. Scourging is one of the most wicked and cruel devices invented by man, and we are not surprised that Rome used it, since the fourth beast was "dreadful and terrible ... it had great iron teeth: it devoured and brake in pieces" (Dan 7:7). The Roman method of scourging (*phragelloō*) was to tie the victim in a bent position to a post, or to stretch him on a frame. The whip consisted of leather thongs, with sharp pieces of metal or bone attached; these lacerated the back and front of the victim's body, tearing the flesh with great wounds. "I gave my back to the smiters", said the Lord prophetically (Isa 50:6). Such treatment reduced a man to a state of indescribable suffering, weakness and helplessness, while some victims died under this torture. Such sufferings in others seemed to make no impression on Roman and Jewish spectators; it was common practice, and men appeared to gain sadistic pleasure in watching. The Lord warned that believers would likewise suffer (Matt 10:17; 23:34), and Paul wrote that he had suffered five times at the hands of the Jews (2 Cor 11:24-25). The fact that the Lord of life and glory, as God manifest in flesh, suffered such inhuman treatment, should reduce the Christian to lowly worship, wonder and adoration, for the result of this treatment was that "his visage was so marred more than any man, and his form more than the sons of men" (Isa 52:14).

27-30 Verse 26 must have taken place outside the Praetorium, for the soldiers took the Lord back into "the common hall", namely the Praetorium, in order to dress Him up as a King, so that Pilate could bring Him forth to the people (John 19:4-5). The Lord had predicted that He would be "mocked, and spitefully entreated" (Luke 18:32) by the Gentiles; this statement must have sounded strange to the disciples' ears, since they understood none of the Lord's predictions. But now this was being enacted (perhaps watched by the apostle John). Here was coarse Gentile play by the basest of Pilate's men, coldly disregarding the Lord's sufferings, and watched over by Pilate so as to mock both the Lord and the Jews. The "whole band of soldiers" (*speira*) consisted of several hundred men, for the Roman military presence in Jerusalem was strengthened on the occasions of the Jewish feasts.

These soldiers rejoiced in the sufferings of Christ, knowing that these and the trial were unlike anything that they had witnessed before, and also knowing that the Lord would shortly be crucified at their hands. So they presented the kingship of Christ in mockery as they saw it; heaven still refrained from interfering, but in a future day, every aspect of this mockery will be reversed: as we sometimes sing, "Told in answering glory now". Psalm 2 describes how God will reverse what men have done; it is the great Psalm of divine reversals. In vv.1-3, men sought to remove divine restrictions from them, saying in effect that they would not have the Lord to rule over them. They would break the divine bands and cords, so that they could live without the divine presence, equivalent today to men denying the Lordship of Christ so that they can do as they please. Such men are effectively fighting against God, seeking to overthrow His work being done by His servants (Acts 5:39). We may note the following reversals:

"A crown of thorns". The fact that these were available recalls to mind that thorns are the product of a cursed ground (Gen 3:17-18); in the same context, the statement is made that the first Adam would return unto dust (v.19). On the contrary, the last Adam did not see corruption (Acts 2:31). This crown of thorns was a mark of cruelty, as well as of mockery. One prick on a finger with a piece of barbed wire yields pain enough, how much more many thorns pressed around the head? In our v.31 the articles of regal mockery were taken off the Lord; this suggests that the Lord did not wear this crown when He was on the cross, although this is usually depicted by artists. The word used here for crown is *stephanos*, a token of public honour woven as a garland of various twigs; the word for a crown displaying regal dignity is *diadēma*, which could not be used here, since the crown was a woven garland. However, when God reverses this, "on his head were many crowns (*diadēma*)" (Rev 19:12).

"A scarlet robe". This was indicative of regal majesty. But the vesture of the King of kings will be "dipped in blood" (Rev 19:13), referring not to the sacrificial blood shed on the cross, but to the blood of His enemies which will have already been shed during the prior period of the great tribulation.

"A reed in his right hand". This represented a sceptre; a rod in the hand is a symbol of regal authority. This mockery will be reversed in the coming kingdom when a king shall reign in righteousness; "Thy throne, O God, is for ever and ever: a sceptre of righteousness is the sceptre of thy kingdom" (Heb 1:8; Ps 45:6-7). This regal authority shall not depart from Judah, until Shiloh come (Gen 49:10).

"They bowed the knee before him". This act of mockery will be reversed when "at the name of Jesus every knee should bow, of things in heaven, and things in earth, and things under the earth" (Phil 2:10).

"Hail, King of the Jews". In the reversal, God will say, "Yet have I set my king upon my holy hill of Zion" (Ps 2:6); the Lord had taught that the unbelieving

Jews would not see Him again until they greeted Him with the words, "Blessed is he that cometh in the name of the Lord" (Matt 23:39).

"They spit upon him", as a sign of contempt. In the reversal, God will vex or trouble them "in his sore displeasure" (Ps 2:5). Instead of spitting, leaders should "Kiss the Son" (v.12), namely, turn to love and not to hatred.

"They ... smote him on the head", supposedly on the crown of thorns, so as to embed the thorns more deeply. In the reversal, He will break the nations with a rod of iron, dashing them into pieces like a potter's vessel (Ps 2:9; Rev 2:27).

"They ... mocked him". In the reversal, "He that sitteth in the heavens shall laugh: the Lord shall have them in derision" (Ps 2:4). Mockery of those who love the Lord has sometimes been a favourite occupation of those who hate His truth. As soon as Paul mentioned the resurrection in Athens, "some mocked" (Acts 17:32). In Hezekiah's time, messengers from Jerusalem were mocked when they came to the northern kingdom suggesting that they should come to the south to keep the restored Passover in Jerusalem (2 Chron 30:10), while in the last days there will be scoffers and mockers (the same word, 2 Pet 3:3; Jude 18).

"They took the robe off from him". In the vain minds of these soldiers, there was nothing lasting about this mock kingship – it was merely an event hastening to His crucifixion. But it had already been declared that "he shall reign over the house of Jacob for ever; and of his kingdom there shall be no end" (Luke 1:33); "he shall reign for ever and ever" (Rev 11:15).

31 The session of mockery came to an end; they would not crucify Him in these garments representing mock-kingship, though a notice would be placed on the cross to denote His title. His own garments were returned to Him, no doubt being those that had previously been supplied by the faithful women who ministered to Him in His lifetime, and still bearing the odour of the ointment (at least to those whose senses could discern it). The outer garments would later be distributed by lot amongst some of the soldiers (v.35). After these scenes of suffering and humiliation, they led Him away for crucifixion.

3. *The Crucifixion of the Lord* 27:32-50

v.32 "And as they came out, they found a man of Cyrene, Simon by name: him they compelled to bear his cross.

v.33 And when they were come unto a place called Golgotha, that is to say, a place of a skull,

v.34 They gave him vinegar to drink mingled with gall: and when he had tasted *thereof*, he would not drink.

v.35 And they crucified him, and parted his garments, casting lots: that it might be fulfilled which was spoken by the prophet, They parted my garments among them, and upon my vesture did they cast lots.

v.36 And sitting down they watched him there;

v.37 And set up over his head his accusation written, THIS IS JESUS THE KING OF THE JEWS.
v.38 Then were there two thieves crucified with him, one on the right hand, and another on the left.
v.39 And they that passed by reviled him, wagging their heads,
v.40 And saying, Thou that destroyest the temple, and buildest *it* in three days, save thyself. If thou be the Son of God, come down from the cross.
v.41 Likewise also the chief priests mocking *him*, with the scribes and elders, said,
v.42 He saved others; himself he cannot save. If he be the King of Israel, let him now come down from the cross, and we will believe him.
v.43 He trusted in God; let him deliver him now, if he will have him: for he said, I am the Son of God.
v.44 The thieves also, which were crucified with him, cast the same in his teeth.
v.45 Now from the sixth hour there was darkness over all the land unto the ninth hour.
v.46 And about the ninth hour Jesus cried with a loud voice, saying, Eli, Eli, lama sabachthani? that is to say, My God, my God, why hast thou forsaken me?
v.47 Some of them that stood there, when they heard *that*, said, This *man* calleth for Elias.
v.48 And straightway one of them ran, and took a spunge, and filled *it* with vinegar, and put *it* on a reed, and gave him to drink.
v.49 The rest said, Let be, let us see whether Elias will come to save him.
v.50 Jesus, when he had cried again with a loud voice, yielded up the ghost."

32 The word for "cross" is *stauros*, and that for "crucify" is *stauroo*. Crucifixion originated before Roman times, but the Romans used this method of execution as consistent with the inherent cruelty of the nation and its emperors. There were four forms of cross, shaped as **I, T, X, †,** the first being an upright stake on which the victim was crucified with arms vertical. Vine, in his *Expository Dictionary of New Testament Words,* is dogmatic that the Lord was crucified on a vertical stake, claiming that the traditional shape (the last of the four depicted) was imported into Christianity from pagan sources: "By the middle of the third century AD the churches had either departed from, or had travestied, certain doctrines of the Christian faith. In order to increase the prestige of the apostate ecclesiastical system pagans were received into the churches apart from regeneration by faith, and were permitted largely to retain their pagan signs and symbols. Hence the Tau or **T**, in its most frequent form, with the cross-piece lowered, was adopted to stand for the cross of Christ."

However, it must be pointed out that compilers of Bible Dictionaries and expositors of Holy Scripture do not agree with this even on historical grounds. This painful form of death is described by the following details. The victim was made to carry, not the whole cross, but the cross-beam (in Latin, the *patibulum*). The man was laid across this on the ground, and his hands were tied or nailed to it. In the Lord's case, the accuracy of the prophetic Scriptures prove that He was nailed to the cross (Ps 22:16; see John 20:25, 27). The cross-beam was then fixed to the upright post already in position, the victim's feet being attached to this post. A lingering death of pain, hunger and exhaustion was the portion of the one crucified, though in the Lord's case He brought His life to a voluntary end at the appropriate time.

As the Lord left the scene of the trial, He was carrying His cross (John 19:17), though His physical weakness unsupported by special angelic strength caused other arrangements quickly to be made. Simon of Cyrene was forced to carry the Lord's cross (though metaphorically, a disciple must carry his own cross, according to the Lord's teaching in Matt 16:24). This man Simon is described as "coming out of the country" (Luke 23:26). Perhaps he had arrived late for the Passover, it being the duty of Jewish males in far-off countries to come to Jerusalem for the principal feasts. Mark 15:21 has informed us that he was "the father of Alexander and Rufus", the latter usually being understood to be the same Rufus as mentioned in Rom 16:13, in which case Paul sent greetings to Simon's wife, the mother of Rufus.

33 It is at this stage that the Lord made His last public utterance (Luke 23:27-31). He spoke to the women of Jerusalem who were weeping for Him, and He concluded with the words, "If they do these things in a green tree, what shall be done in the dry?". He was the green tree, while the nation was the dry tree. He thereby anticipated the terrible judgment that would fall upon the nation in AD 70; He Himself had wept for the city in Luke 19:41-42. Under Titus and the Roman army, Jerusalem lay in ruins and the temple in ashes. The priestly hierarchy, from the days of Aaron and Eli in the OT, to Annas and Caiaphas in the NT, was no longer in existence. The Sanhedrin as a Jewish governing institution and the kingdom of Judaea had all disappeared. Forty years later, under the Roman emperor Hadrian, a further siege and military intervention destroyed anything that was left, and the ground was ploughed up to prevent any rebuilding of the city. All Jews were forbidden to enter the city and its vicinity again. And so the nation remained scattered for 1850 years, though retaining a hope to return to their capital city occupied for so long by Gentile powers. As the Lord went to the cross, He knew all this by divine foreknowledge, so we can understand what He meant by the question, "what shall be done in the dry?". Truly God so loved the world when He gave His Son, but this can never be divorced from the necessity of judgment against the ungodly.

Golgotha and the corresponding Roman name Calvary (Luke 23:33) both mean "skull" – hence Matthew's interpretation "a place of a skull". Various reasons have been suggested why the place had this name; for example, because the shape of the place resembled a skull. Typically, however, the name speaks of the apex of human wisdom, for those who crucified the Lord of glory possessed this wisdom, the opposite to the wisdom of God (1 Cor 2:6-8). It speaks of the unsanctified intelligence of men who still reject Christ in unbelief.

It must be pointed out that the Roman name "Calvary" occurring in Luke 23:33 does not appear in the Greek text; both the RV and JND use "Skull" corresponding to the Greek word *kranion*. The use of the title Calvary has been imported from the old Latin Vulgate translation.

34 Before the crucifixion, the Lord was offered "vinegar to drink mingled with gall", to which there is added "myrrh" in Mark 15:23. This corresponds to the prophetic word in Ps 69:21, "They gave me also gall". This "vinegar" (*oxos*) was a sour wine, though some Greek texts substitute *oinos*, meaning "wine"; the RV has "wine" but JND retains "vinegar" which conveys a wrong impression to the English reader. Mark 15:23 definitely has the word *oinos*, "wine". This was a stupifying drink to minimise pain. The Lord refused to partake of it, since His mind was going to be clear to the end; with human and divine clarity of consciousness, He issued the seven words from the cross in spite of the pain He was suffering, in order to partake of the cup from the divine hand. There may be a reference to this in the words of the mother of king Lemuel, "Give strong drink unto him that is ready to perish" (Prov 31:6), though crucifixion could not have been in the mind of the speaker.

35 "And they crucified him" is rendered "And when they had crucified him" (RV) and "And having crucified him" (JND). Grammatically, this is the aorist participle of the verb "crucify" (*stauroō*), and strictly is the subject of the following verb "parted"; no corresponding English words exactly match this very common Greek construction. A literal rendering might be, "the having crucified-Him ones parted His garments", though only by reading the Greek text and letting the mind become used to the grammar can a reader gain the flavour of the Greek construction.

This proper translation shows that the actual act of crucifixion is not dwelt on, so focusing attention (in the Acts and the Epistles) on God's side relating to the sufferings of Christ. Behind the historical deed, we think of sin that needed it, love that ordained it, malice that wrought it, and patience that endured it. Truly, "he humbled himself, and became obedient unto death, even the death of the cross" (Phil 2:8). On the cross, He was "made a curse for us: for it is written, Cursed is every one that hangeth on a tree" (Gal 3:13; Deut 21:22-23). Not that the OT actually implied crucifixion! A man would be stoned to death (Lev 20:2; 24:14; Num 15:35); as an example to others his dead body might then be hung upon a tree for a few hours. Though the circumstances in the Lord's case were different, the quotation was very apt. The cross is therefore often referred to as a "tree" (*xulon*, Acts 5:30; 10:39; 13:29; 1 Pet 2:24).

A team of men consisting of a centurion and four soldiers was responsible for the crucifixion (John 19:23); they regarded the Lord's clothes as a reward for their work. The "garments" (*himation*) were the outer garments, for which they cast lots. In John 19:23 there was also the "coat" (*chiton*), an inner garment. (Dorcas made both kinds of garments in Acts 9:39.) This one inner garment was not rent, but lots were cast as to which soldier should have it. In Matt 27:35, the

AV (following the TR) gives the quotation from Ps 22:18, "that it might be fulfilled which was spoken by the prophet, They parted my garments among them, and upon my vesture did they cast lots". Other Greek texts omit all these words in Matt 27:35, and they do not appear in the RV and JND. However, the quotation rightly appears in John 19:24, in which case the quotation in Matt 27:35 may have been a reader's marginal note taken from John 19:24, and a later copyist may then have unwittingly incorporated it into the text. There is, of course, the other point of view, that the TR is correct, and the other manuscripts that omit the quotation are wrong.

36 They were content to sit down and watch Him there. This was to protect the Lord from any savage attack by the Jews, and they also joined in the mockery of the crowds around (Luke 23:36); Prophetically in Ps 22:16-17, the Lord had said, "For dogs have compassed me ... they look and stare upon me", dogs being a reference to the unclean Gentiles. In Ps 69:12, He had said, "They that sit in the gate speak against me; and I was the song of the drunkards" (or, drinkers of strong drink). In Ps 118:10-12, we read a metaphorical description of the inner thoughts of the Lord, "All nations compassed me about ... They compassed me about; yea, they compassed me about ... They compassed me about like bees" .

37 The wording "This is Jesus the King of the Jews" was Pilate's own choice, in spite of objections from the chief priests (John 19:21-22). They thought that this accusation read too much like fact, and wanted to substitute "I am the King of the Jews" in keeping with their accusation (Luke 23:2). At last Pilate found himself in control again; resisting the Jews, he declared, "What I have written I have written". The four Gospels give the wording of this title: "This is Jesus the King of the Jews" (Matt 27:37); "The King of the Jews" (Mark 15:26); "This is the King of the Jews" (Luke 23:38); "Jesus of Nazareth the King of the Jews" (John 19:19). Totally, the wording must have been "This is Jesus of Nazareth the King of the Jews", written in Hebrew (for the Jews), Greek (for strangers from Greek- speaking lands), and in Latin (for the Roman soldiers). Pilate thereby declared to all mankind the Roman rejection of divine authority. Conversely, the gospel had to be preached in "all the world" (Mark 16:15) and to "the uttermost part of the earth" (Acts 1:8), for if the Lord were lifted up, He declared "I will draw all men unto me" (John 12:32), whether for salvation or for judgment. Note that the Lord is declared to be both King of the Jews and "King of nations" (Rev 15:3, JND), but not King of the church.

38 These "two thieves" are described as "two other, malefactors" in Luke 23:32. The word for "other" (*heteros*) means others of a different kind, so distinguishing them completely from the Lord. (The second Greek word for "other" is *allos*, of the same kind, a word that could not possibly have been used in this context. The reader may care to note that both words occur in Gal 1:6-7 and 1 Cor 12:8-10 where the passages can only be properly understood by observing the difference in meaning.) The author has read one strongly-argued assertion that there were four malefactors crucified around the Lord, but expositors generally do not adhere to this argument. The full story is given in Luke 23:39-43 (note that *heteros* is used appropriately for "the other" in v.40, thus distinguishing between the two malefactors). In Mark 15:28, this is seen as fulfilling Isa 53:12, "he was numbered with the transgressors", and appears to have been the Roman method to implicate the Lord, by placing Him on the lowest level with them. However, their scheming misfired, for one of the two malefactors repented and expressed faith in the Lord. These two men may have been one of the same band as that to which Barabbas belonged, but their deaths represented a parting of the ways: one leading to paradise, the other to judgment. The Romans wanted shame to accrue to the Lord as associated with these two men, but the Father had already arranged for infinite glory to radiate from the Son when He appeared with two men, Moses and Elijah, on the mount (Matt 17:2-3).

39-40 The Lord was surrounded by evil men; in vv.39-44 there are described the insults rendered by the passers-by, the chief priests with the scribes and elders, and the two thieves. The Lord referred prophetically to these men in Ps 22:7,12,13, saying, "All they that see me laugh me to scorn", "Many bulls have compassed me ... They gaped upon me with their mouths", the bulls typically denoting the Jews, while the dogs denoted the Gentiles. In Ps 69:19, His words were "mine adversaries are all before thee". The description "wagging their heads" uses the verb *kineō*, meaning to move; men were moving their heads to what they regarded as a centre of attraction; see also Ps 22:7; 109:25. In just the same way as the false witnesses before the Sanhedrin misquoted the Lord's words in John 2:19, so these people also misquoted the Lord's words. They insinuated that the Lord would destroy the temple, whereas His words had indicated that *they* would destroy the temple (*naos*), "the temple of his body" The disciples remembered the Lord's words after His resurrection, evidently by the Holy Spirit, but these men remembered them before His death, no doubt by the agency of Satan. They did not realise that the temple referred to the temple of His body. Thinking that He claimed miraculous powers to rebuild their huge temple in three days, they taunted Him with "save thyself"; this temptation should be taken in conjunction with "cast thyself", "pity thyself", "shew thyself" (Matt 4:6; 16:22, marg; John 7:4). Instead, He humbled Himself and gave Himself. These men continued to taunt the Lord with His Sonship and miraculous powers. But no signs, no miracles would be forthcoming. He would neither keep Himself alive by a miracle at His temptation in the wilderness, nor here on the cross, for He was about to give up His life. In His own country, He "did not many mighty works there because of their unbelief" (Matt 13:58), but here on the cross He would do no miracles at all because of the depths of their unbelief.

41-43 Here we find the religious element mocking the Lord on the cross. These priests correspond to Christendom today, rejecting the cross and the blood as God's means of salvation. They have trodden under foot the Son of God, having "counted the blood of the covenant … an unholy thing" (Heb 10:29).

These men of the Sanhedrin recalled the saving power that the Lord had shown to men in need, whether mentally, physically or even in death. But they were bold to assert, "himself he cannot save". Here, in the moment of their apparent triumph, they ridiculed His past power. Using the title "King of Israel" rather than "Son of God" (based on their political and not religious accusations), they placed a condition upon the exercise of their own personal faith: "let him now come down from the cross, and we will believe him". But conditions of any sort are invalid before God; miracles might bring wonder and fear, but they do not grant faith. Previously, the Lord had quoted the words of Abraham, "neither will they be persuaded, though one rose from the dead" (Luke 16:31). In other words, the Lord never worked miracles to satisfy the curiosity of unbelief.

In Ps 22:8, it had been foreseen that men would say, "He trusted on the Lord that he would deliver him: let him deliver him, seeing he delighted in him". Note that they were not quoting the words of this psalm; rather the psalm was quoting their words (over 1,000 years in the future when the Psalm was written). So this religious mockery overall in these verses took in divine words, the divine temple, divine relationships ("Son of God"), divine kingship, divine power, divine trust. It all amounted to the apex of blasphemy, and no doubt these men were quite satisfied with their efforts at the end of the day.

44 To start with, the two thieves engaged in the general mockery. This was prior to the repentance of the one thief documented In Luke 23:39-43, where the title "Christ" was also used in addition to "Son of God" and "King of Israel". So Matthew has viewed the complete rejection of the King, making no reference to the faithful remnant also at the cross. Only in the other Gospels do we find the repentant thief (Luke 23:42), the faithful women (John 19:25), and John the apostle (v.26). In any mixed company, "The Lord knoweth them that are his" (2 Tim 2:19).

45-50 These verses cover the final period. A considerable part of the afternoon is covered in v.45, but Matthew is silent as to what was happening during these hours of darkness. The unseen work of redemption is passed over in silence in Matthew's record, and the Epistle writers have explained their understanding of the death of Christ, without mentioning the hours of darkness. Both v.45 and Mark 15:33 give the figures "from the sixth hour … unto the ninth hour"; additionally Mark 15:25 states that the Lord was crucified at the third hour. However, John 19:14 informs us that it was "about the sixth hour" when He was led away to be crucified. There is no inconsistency here. The day was divided into these periods; people had no watches or clocks, and many times were therefore only approximate in assessment. The Spirit of inspiration did not seek to improve on human observation. Consequently the word "about" would allow a deviation either way of one-and-a-half hours (in our exact reckoning).

There had been light from heaven when the birth of the Saviour was announced (Luke 2:9-11), but there was darkness at His death when salvation was accomplished. Men were allowed no sight of the Lord suffering as the sin offering. This darkness was "over all the land" (*gē*), a word which means both land locally and all the earth; JND allows either word. It is therefore not possible to assess whether this darkness was confined to the area around Jerusalem, to the land of Judaea, or to the whole earth. God had interfered with the sun before (Josh 10:12-14; 2 Kings 20:9-11); in which the whole of the earth would have been affected. So we would feel that the whole of the earth was affected at the crucifixion of the Lord, God's greatest work, during which He interfered with the shining of the sun.

The "ninth hour" would be half way between noon and sunset. Of the seven sayings from the cross, only one has been related by Matthew and Mark, three by Luke and three by John. In historical order, these are:

> "Father, forgive them; for they know not what they do" (Luke 23:34); in the immediate context, this referred to the Roman soldiers who nailed Him to the cross.
> "Verily I say unto thee, Today shalt thou be with me in paradise" (Luke 23:43).
> "Woman, behold thy son! … Behold thy mother!" (John 19:26-27).
> "My God, my God, why hast thou forsaken me?" (Matt 27:46; Mark 15:34).
> "I thirst" (John 19:28).
> "It is finished" (John 19:30).
> "Father, into thy hands I commend my spirit" (Luke 23:46).

This great cry of dereliction given in Aramaic and translated as "My God, my God, why hast thou forsaken me?" appears in Ps 22:1. The Spirit of prophecy and inspiration enabled David over 1,000 years previously to hear the voice of the Saviour and to record it for posterity. As a human being, Asaph once gave expression to a similar thought, "Will the Lord cast off for ever? and will he be favourable no more? Is his mercy clean gone for ever? doth his promise fail for evermore? Hath God forgotten to be gracious? hath he in anger shut up his tender mercies?" (Ps 77:7-9). The Lord can therefore be "touched with the feeling of our infirmities" (Heb 4:15), since He passed through quite a deeper and different experience.

The Jewish bystanders reinterpreted the Aramaic "*Eli*" as "Elias". The Aramaic words are inserted in the Greek text to explain why the people suddenly referred to Elias, since the Greek word *Theos* would provide no clue. Some expositors think that the people, awed by the darkness, really thought that the Lord was calling for Elijah (since they were expecting his return), but others think that this was wilful mockery (and v.49 suggests this).

One man, rebuked by the others in v.49, showed a little mercy; John 19:28-30 gives further details. The "vinegar" (*oxos*) was a sour wine drunk by labourers and soldiers, obtained from a vessel "full" for that purpose (John 19:29). Thirst was a suffering that accompanied crucifixion, and the Lord had said, "I thirst" in keeping with Ps 69:21.

In v.50, some have doubted whether the Lord's final loud cry consisted of actual words. But the word – "again" suggests that it repeated what had just happened before; namely, He spoke. So we believe that this final cry was the sixth and seventh saying from the cross, after which He "yielded up the ghost" (*pneuma*, spirit). This was in keeping with His declaration, "I lay down my life … No man taketh it from me, but I lay it down of myself" (John 10:17-18). This was the final act in His voluntary sacrifice; the fact that He could yield up His spirit shows that He was different from all other men. Death by crucifixion usually overcame the victim after a much longer time, so that Pilate marvelled that the Lord had died so quickly (Mark 15:44). Thus the Lord "gave himself", a truth recorded six times in the NT: Gal 1:4; 2:20; Eph 5:2, 25; 1 Tim 2:6; Tit 2:14. Note that Matthew, who recorded the Lord's words "my blood of the new testament, which is shed for many for the remission of sins" (Matt 26:28), made no reference to the historical event when the Lord's blood was shed at His death. John, who made no reference to "the blood of the new testament" in the upper room, gave details of the soldier, the spear, and that "blood and water" emerged from the Lord's side (John 19:32-37). The two records are therefore complementary the one to the other.

After the Lord's death, the four evangelists recorded only what happened to the Lord's body. In quoting Ps 16:10, Peter (in Acts 2:27) and Paul (partially in Acts 13:35) have shown what happened to the Lord's soul. For a brief time, He was found in hades, otherwise "paradise", though He was not left there, and neither did His body see corruption, for all was reunited in resurrection on the third day, after which "Christ … dieth no more; death hath no more dominion over him" (Rom 6:9). Certainly He did not descend into the hades of Luke 16:23.

4. *Events between the Lord's Death and His Resurrection 27:51-66*

v.51 "And, behold, the veil of the temple was rent in twain from the top to the bottom; and the earth did quake, and the rocks rent;
v.52 And the graves were opened; and many bodies of the saints which slept arose,
v.53 And came out of the graves after his resurrection, and went into the holy city, and appeared unto many.
v.54 Now when the centurion, and they that were with him, watching Jesus, saw the earthquake, and those things that were done, they feared greatly, saying, Truly this was the Son of God.

v.55 And many women were there beholding afar off, which followed Jesus from Galilee, ministering unto him:
v.56 Among which was Mary Magdalene, and Mary the mother of James and Joses, and the mother of Zebedee's children.
v.57 When the even was come, there came a rich man of Arimathaea, named Joseph, who also himself was Jesus' disciple:
v.58 He went to Pilate, and begged the body of Jesus. Then Pilate commanded the body to be delivered.
v.59 And when Joseph had taken the body, he wrapped it in a clean linen cloth,
v.60 And laid it in his own new tomb, which he had hewn out in the rock: and he rolled a great stone to the door of the sepulchre, and departed.
v.61 And there was Mary Magdalene, and the other Mary, sitting over against the sepulchre.
v.62 Now the next day, that followed the day of the preparation, the chief priests and Pharisees came together unto Pilate,
v.63 Saying, Sir, we remember that that deceiver said, while he was yet alive, After three days I will rise again.
v.64 Command therefore that the sepulchre be made sure until the third day, lest his disciples come by night, and steal him away, and say unto the people, He is risen from the dead: so the last error shall be worse than the first.
v.65 Pilate said unto them, Ye have a watch: go your way, make it as sure as ye can.
v.66 So they went, and made the sepulchre sure, sealing the stone, and setting a watch."

51 The temple referred to here is the *naos*, the inner shrine, where the veil separated between the holy place and the holiest of all (Heb 9:3). Moses' first tabernacle (Exod 33:7-11; 34:34) had no veil as far as can be ascertained. But the second tabernacle had a veil (Exod 26:31; 40:3, 21), indicating that the way into the holiest was not yet made manifest (Heb 9:8). David's tabernacle is not described as possessing a veil (1 Chron 16:1), though Solomon's temple had a veil to separate the two parts of the sanctuary (2 Chron 3:14). We presume that the temple built after the captivity had a veil; certainly Herod's temple had one. In the OT, those structures that had been built according to the commandments of God had a veil, but Herod's temple was just a copy, with no divine command for its building. The veil, therefore, did not possess the same significance as in the OT. When the Lord died, this veil was rent from top to bottom as a divine act, thereby destroying an object devised by man. In the NT, the true veil is interpreted as "his flesh", a new and living way through which we pass with boldness into "the holiest by the blood of Jesus" (Heb 10:19-20). The rending of the veil in Herod's temple is hardly typical of this great spiritual reality in Christ. Rather it marked the fact that God was declaring that the old ceremony was at an end, particularly as it showed to the priests ministering in the temple that the holiest of all was empty: there was no ark there as in Moses' tabernacle and Solomon's temple. The ritual in Herod's temple was shown to be a sham; ceremonial worship therein was hollow and empty without the presence of its centrepiece. The priests may arrange for the veil to be restored, but not for long; all was destroyed in AD 70 when fire gutted the building and its contents. Today,

Christians must avoid all ceremony that seeks to maintain a veil in one form or other, for it is equivalent to building again the things that have been destroyed (Gal 2:18). Temples that God values today are found in 1 Cor 3:16; 6:19; Eph 2:21; Rev 21:22 (the word *naos* always being used).

Just as an earthquake had introduced the first covenant (Exod 19:18), so it introduced the second covenant; another occurred at the resurrection (Matt 28:2). A further earthquake will remove unwanted things, so that what is immoveable will remain (Heb 12:26-27).

52-53 The rending of the rocks enabled certain graves to be opened. There are times when men want to reverse this process, in fear and desperation seeking to hide themselves from calamities (Hos 10:8 in the OT times of judgment; Luke 23:30 referring to AD 70: Rev 6:16 after the rapture of the church). Here was a "miniature" resurrection of "the saints which slept", taking place "after his resurrection" and not immediately after His death.

There are two words for the verb "sleep" in the NT. The verb *katheudō* is used largely in the Synoptic Gospels of physical sleep, though in the case of Jairus' daughter it is used of the body in death (Matt 9:24). The other verb *koimaomai* is used mainly of the body in death (such as in our v.52; John 11:11; Acts 7:60), though occasionally for physical sleep (Matt 28:13; Acts 12:6). Both words are used of the disciples in the garden of Gethsemane (Matt 26:40; Luke 22:45). The word applies to the body in death, not to the soul; the fathers fell asleep (2 Pet 3:4), yet Abraham is seen as talking to the rich man in hades (Luke 16:23, 25), and Lazarus is described as "comforted" in Abraham's bosom.

The Lord Jesus was the firstfruits in resurrection, with men in their own order afterwards. These were raised, and entered into Jerusalem, appearing to many. This was no miracle akin to the bringing back to life of Jairus' daughter, of the widow of Nain's son, and of Lazarus, all of whom died again as a natural process. Rather, we feel that the divine work in vv.52-53 was the genuine resurrection of these saints as to their bodies, though how they entered heaven is not described. It was a pre-enactment of the resurrection of Christians at the rapture. Since Scripture provides no further light on this event, any suggestive interpretation by expositors must be somewhat speculative.

54 The unusual events caused fear in the Roman centurion and others who were watching (namely, the darkness, the Lord's sudden decease, and the earthquake). Their confession was, "Truly this was the Son of God". The centurion had heard the priests use this name (John 19:7; Matt 27:43), and also the Jewish passers-by (Matt 27:40), so he came to believe that it was a true name. Whether this was a confession that led to salvation is not clear. In Luke 23:47, "he glorified God, saying, Certainly this was a righteous man", copying the testimony given at the trial by Pilate and his wife (Matt 27:19, 24). We heard an address once that stressed the word "was" in this confession, as if they were glad that He was no longer alive. He still allowed a soldier under his charge to pierce the Lord's side with a spear!

55-56 Faithful women had followed the Lord from Galilee. Although they are not often mentioned in the Gospels, they were with Him and ministering (*diakoneō*) to Him. Normally, the disciples were with the Lord, and sometimes they are seen ministering to His needs – for example in John 4:8,31, where they had gone to purchase food, after which they said, "Master, eat". We find these "certain women" in Luke 8:2-3, "which ministered (*diakoneō*) unto him of their substance". These include Mary Magdalene from whom had gone seven demons, Joanna the wife of Chuza, Herod's steward, Susanna, with many others. In the Lord's absence, many things can be done unto Him (giving drink, food and clothing) by doing them unto His brethren, chiefly the household of faith (Matt 25:35-40; Gal 6:10).

Originally, these women had stood by the cross, so that the Lord could talk to them (John 19:25-27), but at the end they were "beholding afar off" no doubt in much distress. Matthew has named them as Mary Magdalene, Mary the mother of James and Joses, and the mother of Zebedee's children, James and John. The record has been silent about Mary Magdalene since Luke 8:2, but now she reappears in the narrative at the Lord's death and resurrection (Matt 28:1; John 20:1, 11-18). Not all faithful souls are always in the limelight or noted by name, but her constant service is recognised in our verse 55 – she was "unknown, and yet well known" (2 Cor 6:9). Likewise Zebedee's wife had accompanied the Lord: James and John had left their father in Matt 4:22, but their mother had quietly been there, and that accounts for the sudden appearance of the mother in Matt 20:20, worshipping and desiring something from the Lord. "Mary the mother of James and Joses" was the sister of Mary, the Lord's mother (John 19:25), no doubt the "other Mary" in Matt 27:61 watching at the sepulchre. This James was the apostle named in Matt 10:3 as "James the son of Alphaeus". If the reader will examine carefully the two names "Cleophas" and "Alphaeus", he will note the identical letters l-ph-s, for there were two different pronunciations of the same word. There is therefore no inconsistency in the sacred text in the name of Mary's husband and father of James and Joses.

57-61 "When the even was come" shows that there was a considerable lapse of time after the Lord's decease. In fact, nothing could be done until the death of the two malefactors had been hastened by the breaking of their legs (John 19:32). Joseph of Arimathaea suddenly appears in the Gospel record. He is described as

1. "a rich man", being linked with Isa 53:9, "with the rich in his death".

2. "Of Arimathaea", "a city of the Jews" (Luke 23:51), believed by ancient writers to be Ramah where Samuel was born.

3. "Himself was Jesus' disciple", although we do not read of him before this event; this discipleship was in secret because of his fear of the Jews (John 19:38).

4. "An honourable counsellor" (Mark 15:43), a member of the Jewish Sanhedrin.

5. He "waited for the kingdom of God" (Mark 15:43), that is, for the kingdom in glory to replace the Roman kingdom under which the Jews were suffering.

6. He "boldly" went to Pilate. In other words, the Lord's death now gave him courage, whereas previously he had lived in fear of the Jews.

7. He had not consented to the "counsel and deed" of the Sanhedrin in condemning the Lord to death (Luke 23:51).

8. He was "a good man, and a just" (v.50), a suitable commendation for his discipleship.

Legend is a strange partner to truth, but there are stories that he founded the first Christian settlement in Britain at Glastonbury, and that he brought the holy grail with him.

Someone had to deal with the Lord's body, else He would have been disposed of with criminals. The disciples had fled, Peter had disappeared, and John, though present, could apparently do nothing. The women, too, were present, but could do nothing, though they knew immediately when Joseph and Nicodemus boldly came forward lovingly to attend to the matter; see John 19:39. Before Pilate allowed the body to be taken down, he had to obtain confirmation from the centurion that the Lord had died (Mark 15:44-45), since it was unusual for death to take place so quickly. At the same time, the Jews (so unjust in their condemnation of the Lord) once again took refuge in their law; bodies should not be left on the cross on the following Sabbath day, so they definitely wanted death to be hastened when necessary, in order that the bodies should be removed immediately (John 19:31). But the Lord's voluntary act in yielding up His own life, and Joseph's loving deed in asking for permission to take the Lord's body down from the cross, solved the Jews' problem for them.

The day in which these events took place was called "the day of the preparation" (*paraskeuē* v.62; Mark 15:42; Luke 23:54; John 19:31,42); Mark 15:42 had defined this day to be "the day before the sabbath". The title of this day (the sixth day of the week) arose from the necessity to prepare food on that day for the following Sabbath day. The origin of this is found in Exod 16:22-26, where an extra portion of manna had to be gathered and baked on the sixth day, for no manna was provided on the seventh day. In the Gospel narrative, both the ritualistic ungodly Jews (John 19:31) and the few spiritual godly men and women (Luke 23:54) were concerned about this day of preparation and the following Sabbath day. Today, when Christendom and true Christians apparently do the same thing on occasions, God knows the motives and accepts only what is spiritually the work of faith from the heart.

It is remarkable that Joseph had to beg (or crave, as in Mark 15:43) for the Lord's body, as if Pilate was a resistive force to be overcome. All four Gospels record that he took the body down, a tragic experience for a secret disciple. Others had handled Him in His lifetime, a fact that John recalled many years later (1 John 1:1), while others were invited to handle Him in resurrection (Luke 24:39); the ungodly and sinners had handled Him when He had been taken captive, at His trial, and when they placed Him on the cross. But in death, the Lord's body was handled by reverent hands; God had arranged for His selected servants to be available and exercised at the right time. Who helped Joseph in his painful task of taking the body down we are not told; no doubt it was Nicodemus, who was helping him afterwards according to the record (John 19:39).

Joseph provided the linen cloth, fine and clean (Mark 15:46), while Nicodemus provided the myrrh, aloes and spices (John 19:39-40), "as the manner of the Jews is to bury". The cloth reminds us of the "fine twined linen" from which the inner curtains of the tabernacle were made (Exod 26:1), suitable to form the surrounds of the ark of the covenant where the presence of God amongst His people was recognised. No women were involved at this stage; their duty had been done by faith before He had died (Matt 26:12; John 12:7). Other women came later but not those who had already anointed Him before His death.

Joseph had provided for himself; when he had hewn out in the rock "his own new tomb", "wherein was never man yet laid" (John 19:41), he had had no idea that the tomb would be used for Another. This is a lesson indeed for Christians: even the most unlikely of possessions should be held for the Lord's use. The way in which this was done in the early church is found in Acts 4:32, "neither said any of them that ought of the things which he possessed was his own". The Lord had the first place in birth and in death; He had been the firstborn of Mary His mother, and now His body was the first to occupy this new tomb, that "in all things he might have the preeminence" (Col 1:18). A "great stone" was rolled in front of the entrance, as the custom was, to separate the living from the dead – as Abraham said "that I may bury my dead out of my sight" (Gen 23:4). There was no thought in Joseph's mind that the Lord's resurrection was just round the corner!

Mary Magdalene and Mary the mother of James and Joses could not leave the scene (v.61); they sat and watched, hopeless and not expecting the resurrection. The other women who had followed from Galilee saw the tomb, but returned home afterwards (Luke 23:55, 56). Those who remained were sitting and watching over Him in death, a contrast to Peter, James and John, who slept in the garden instead of watching over the Lord in His life (Matt 26:40). How long they remained, we are not told; in Matt 28:1 they are seen as coming to the sepulchre in order to see it.

62-66 "The next day" was the Jewish Sabbath. An argument has been put forward that there were two Sabbath days immediately following one another, in which case the Lord would have been crucified on a Thursday. The reason for this is found in Lev 23:5-7. The Passover was the fourteenth day of the first month, while the feast of unleavened bread commenced on the fifteenth day, this day being an additional Sabbath regardless of the day of the week on which it fell (v.7). If this were the sixth day of the week, then two Sabbaths would follow one another. John 19:31 is quoted, when John stated that "that sabbath day was an high day", as if it were something special and distinct from an ordinary Sabbath. Moreover, the argument runs, this would be more in keeping with verses such as Matt 12:40, where the Lord would lie in death for "three days and three nights". The extra day provided by this argument would enable this statement to be interpreted literally instead of idiomatically in which parts of three days and two nights would be involved. However, expositors generally do not even mention the existence of this argument, though readers may care to consider it. However, the difference is vital in one scheme of scriptural chronology.

People's activity on the Sabbath should be noted. The women who had previously prepared spices rested on the Sabbath day (Luke 23:56). The Lord's body lay in the tomb, though it would not see corruption (Acts 13:35, 37), and His soul would remain in hades (paradise) only until His resurrection; this would release those who in faith were already there, and prevent others from going there. The priests and Pharisees (who readily criticised the Lord for His activity on Sabbath days during His life) showed their hypocritical inconsistency, by using the day to consult with Pilate. This shows their plight in having to rely upon the Romans for a guard (as the Israelites once had to rely on the Philistines to sharpen their tools, 1 Sam 13:19-22).

In their statement to Pilate, the priests interpreted the "three days" literally; one day had passed already. "We remember" contrasts with the memory of the apostles, "this saying was hid from them" (Luke 18:34). They did not believe the Lord's prediction, but thought that the disciples would engage in trickery and steal the body. Then "the last error shall be worse than the first": the first error – the people believing on Him in His life; the second error – the people believing after His death, supposing Him to be alive again. This was the beginning of intrigue to prevent faith in the truth. The act of securing the sepulchre and setting a watch was not an attempt to prevent the resurrection, for they did not believe this would occur.

The seal on the stone was to ensure that it could not be moved without a clear indication of this fact becoming apparent; we recall that a seal had been placed on the stone guarding Daniel in the den of lions (Dan 6:17). Pilate said, "Ye have a watch", referring to Roman soldiers (Matt 28:12) granted to the Jews for this purpose. We cannot imagine how the women on the following day would have gained an entry into the sepulchre. They were going to come to anoint the Lord's body with the sweet spices that they had prepared (Mark 16:1), yet both the seal and the Roman guard constituted a barrier to be overcome; in effect they were shutting up the kingdom of heaven against men (Matt 23:13). In the event, divine intervention had solved the problem for them before they arrived.

III. The Resurrection of Christ (28:1-20)

1. *The Resurrection Day* 28:1-10

v.1 "In the end of the sabbath, as it began to dawn toward the first day of the week, came Mary Magdalene and the other Mary to see the sepulchre.
v.2 And, behold, there was a great earthquake: for the angel of the Lord descended from heaven, and came and rolled back the stone from the door, and sat upon it.
v.3 His countenance was like lightning, and his raiment white as snow:
v.4 And for fear of him the keepers did shake, and became as dead *men*.
v.5 And the angel answered and said unto the women, Fear not ye: for I know that ye seek Jesus, which was crucified.
v.6 He is not here: for he is risen, as he said. Come, see the place where the Lord lay.
v.7 And go quickly, and tell his disciples that he is risen from the dead; and, behold, he goeth before you into Galilee; there ye shall see him: lo, I have told you.
v.8 And they departed quickly from the sepulchre with fear and great joy; and did run to bring his disciples word.
v.9 And as they went to tell his disciples, behold, Jesus met them, saying, All hail. And they came and held him by the feet, and worshipped him.
v.10 Then said Jesus unto them, Be not afraid: go tell my brethren that they go into Galilee, and there shall they see me."

The resurrection of Christ is that glorious fact against which unbelief raises its ugly voice. "Slow of heart to believe" said the Lord (Luke 24:25); "they ... believed not", "neither believed they them", "their unbelief and hardness of heart" (Mark 16:11-14);– "some doubted" (Matt 28:17). The empty tomb was quickly explained by lies on the part of the priests and elders (Matt 28:13). There were those who mocked at the concept of resurrection (Acts 17:32). The Corinthians could not understand how Christians will be raised, so they denied it; Paul then showed that this was equivalent to denying the resurrection of Christ (1 Cor 15:12-13). Later, the denial of future resurrection became a body of false doctrine (2 Tim 2:18). Today, unbelievers consider the resurrection of Christ to be an anachronistic irrelevant doctrine emanating from the past. Some have propounded the theory that Christ did not actually die, that he revived in the cool of the tomb, and eventually made His way to India; this denies the power of God in resurrection. Men have invented infant baptism to discard the resurrection of Christ and its moral effect upon believers, for Rom 6:4-11 clearly links believer's baptism to His resurrection. Mark 16:9-20 is a particularly open paragraph dealing with unbelief in the resurrection of Christ; it is common these days for modern translations to eliminate this passage from Scripture, so that this condemnation of unbelief is expunged, in an attempt to satisfy the consciences of many. The omission of this vital passage is justified by the policy of producing translations from the "best" Greek texts, such texts being the oldest, omitting this passage in Mark 16. But the whole policy is dishonest in the extreme, for the oldest manuscripts, although omitting the passage, nevertheless provide incontrovertible proof that the passage actually existed when the manuscripts were first produced. (Gaps exist in the places where the passage would normally go.) Hence the passage is older than the "best" old manuscripts. So if age is the criterion for judging what is "best", then the passage should be included, as in the TR, from which the AV is derived. Thus unbelief seeks to introduce uncertainty in the minds of true believers regarding this passage; this in turn is calculated to lead to other uncertainties, for a little leaven leavens the whole lump unless action is taken.

1. The word "sabbath" literally appears twice in this verse, both times in the genitive plural (*sabbatōn*). The AV rendering "In the end of the sabbath, as it began to dawn toward the first day of the week" is replaced in the RV by "late on the sabbath day, as it began to dawn toward the first day of the week", and in JND by "now late on sabbath, as it was the dusk of the next day after sabbath", though his last French revision has "Or, sur le tard, le jour du sabbat, au crepuscule du premier jour de la semaine". The reader may well wonder why there are such variations, and where the second word "sabbath" has disappeared to. Expositors differ in their explanations, while some make no reference to the somewhat strange verbal situation. "In the end of the sabbath" really means "late on the sabbath", that is, late after the sabbath, the point in time being not dusk of the departing day, but early on the next morning. Vine, in his *Expository Dictionary of New Testament Words,* explains the matter linguistically and idiomatically, in which case the plural form *sabbata* is rightly translated in the singular. Thus "the first day of the week" is, in Greek, "one of sabbaths" meaning "the first day after the sabbath". Others try to explain the plural form "sabbaths" as if the Jews regarded every day as a Sabbath; "late on sabbaths" would then mean after the last Sabbath, and "first of sabbaths" would mean the first day of the seven. Another explanation based on a scheme of Bible chronology requires these "sabbaths" to be taken literally, with the word "began to dawn" being translated as "getting dusk"; this would ensure that the Lord was actually raised at the end of the Jewish Sabbath exactly three days and three nights after His death. What we do know is that the manifestation of the Lord's resurrection took place on the first day of the week, and that this became the special day of the week for Christian worship and service. Thus in Acts 20:7 it was on "the first day of the week" (namely, one, or first, of the sabbaths) that the disciples in Troas came together to break bread. This was also known as "the Lord's day" (*hē kuriakē hēmera*, Rev 1:10) – "the dominical day", to be distinguished from "the day of the Lord" (*hē hēmera tou kuriou*).

A whole series of detailed events then took place, many of which are recorded in the four Gospels; it may not be completely clear how all these events fit together to form a continuous narrative. Matt 28:1 informs us that Mary Magdalene and the other Mary came "to see the sepulchre". Salome is included in Mark 16:1, and they had spices to anoint the body of the Lord. "The other Mary" (Matt 27:56, 61) is Mary the mother of James and Joses, stated to be the sister of the Lord's mother in John 19:25. In other words, the women who had ministered to the Lord in His life were now going to minister to Him in His death; their actions of love show that they, had no expectation of His resurrection.

2-4 It was not the earthquake that caused the removal of the stone from the entrance to the tomb, but the angel who descended from heaven. The power behind the removal of the stone extended beyond the stone, and strong seismic waves radiated out from that epicentre, causing the "great earthquake". This was a foretaste of how the power of the resurrection of Christ was to spread around the world in the Gospel message, bringing salvation through the same power that raised Christ from the dead (Eph 1:19, 20). Earthquakes were to cause fear in the hearts of unbelievers. This happened at the Lord's death (Matt 27:51); here the Roman soldiers "did shake, and became as dead men" upon seeing the angel sitting on the stone, with a face like lightning. The Lord's people too can be fearful when confronted with terrifying circumstances, as Moses when he trembled on mount Sinai (Heb 12:21), and the women who feared at the tomb, for the angel said to them "Fear ye not" (Matt 28:5). The keeper of the prison in Philippi was also trembling with fear because of an earthquake and the associated opening of all the doors (Acts 16:26-29).

In Matt 28:2-4, the earthquake manifesting divine power over nature did not cause faith in the unbelievers who witnessed it. No comfort was offered them, and they sought fellowship with the chief priests (Matt 28:11). Similarly, divine intervention in Rev 9 brought no repentance to those who suffered under it (v.21). The same may be said of Pharaoh during the plagues in Egypt. On the other hand, the rolling away of the stone was a sign from heaven, inviting the women to see that a greater work had been accomplished in the raising of the body of the Lord. God allowed the seal to be broken, thwarting all the efforts of men in a moment, yet He knew that strange explanations would be invented and circulated both by the Jews and for the Jews. The faith of believers today must overcome when faced by supposedly-rational explanations of men.

Usually, angels appeared on earth to be seen by men of faith. Thus Gideon saw an angel (Jud 6:12), as did Manoah and his wife (Jud 13:3, 8-21). Additionally, there was angelic visitation to the Lord Himself (Matt 4:11; Luke 22:43). But for an angel radiating glory to be seen by unbelievers such as the Roman soldiers was very unusual. They explained to the priests what they had seen, but the priests disregarded the evidence of the miraculous, evidently thinking that a heavenly intervention was something that they could lie about.

In the Lord's transfiguration His face had shone as the sun, and His raiment had become white as the light (Matt 17:2). This was a character of Christ that was visible to the chosen three, and certainly is visible in heaven above. So the angel took character from the Lord; his face and raiment are described in a similar way. Moses' face shone when he came out from the presence of the Lord (Exod 34:29-30). Just before his death, Stephen's face was as the face of an angel, and as he looked upwards he saw the glory of God which evidently was transferred to him at the moment of crisis (Acts 6:15; 7:55). Our bodies too shall be fashioned like unto His body of glory (Phil 3:21) as were the bodies of Moses and Elijah on the mountain top with the Lord.

Thus we have the physical manifestation (v.2), the angelic manifestation (vv.2-7), and the divine manifestation (vv.9-10). God has provided plenty of evidence for faith to accept the resurrection of Christ without any doubt.

5-7 In just the same way as the Lord had calmed the fears of the apostles (Matt 17:6, 7; Rev 1:17), so too the angel said to the women, "Fear not ye". The angel knew (and so does the Lord) the motives and objectives of these women, "I know that ye seek Jesus, which was crucified", stressing that the Lord really had died, and that He had really risen from the dead. Inside the sepulchre, there were two angels, asking "Why seek ye the living among the dead?" (Luke 24:4-5). The angel on the outside invited the women to look inside, and to "see the place where the Lord lay". The stone was like the veil of the temple; when the stone was rolled away by divine power, an empty tomb was revealed; when the veil was rent by divine power from on high, an empty inner sanctuary was revealed since the ark and glory were absent.

In his testimony the angel stated, "as he said", implying that the Lord's resurrection was wholly in keeping with His previous teaching. We are not informed whether Mary Magdalene had been with the Lord during His lifetime ministry, but the other Mary certainly was, and must have heard His teaching. The women were to spend no more time at the sepulchre; the message of resurrection had to be told quickly to the disciples – "not to all the people, but unto witnesses chosen beforehand of God" (Acts 10:41). These other witnesses were not all resident in the vicinity of Jerusalem, but there were many disciples living to the north in Galilee where most of the Lord's ministry had been accomplished; hence He would revisit in resurrection the familiar scenes of the greatest fruitfulness of His lifetime ministry. This visit to Galilee enabled the event "at the sea of Tiberias (Galilee)" to take place (John 21:1); it was here that the Lord gave a commission to His eleven apostles (Matt 28:16). (He may have taken them away from Jerusalem to Galilee for a rest after the physically and mentally strenuous days of the past week.) It may have been in Galilee that "above five hundred brethren at once" saw the Lord (1 Cor 15:6).

8-10 Here, the emotions of "fear and great joy" were mingled. Greater joy would shortly be theirs, since they did not have to wait until the visit to Galilee before they saw the Lord; they would see Him almost immediately. The same can be said about the Lord's words in v.10; they saw Him long before they all met again in Galilee (Luke 24:33-48; John 20:19-29).

Before proceeding further, we supply a table of all the recorded manifestations of the Lord to individuals and groups; numbers in bold type denote the number of disciples involved.

Witnesses Chosen Beforehand of God												
	Mary Magda.	Two Marys	Peter	Emmaus Road	Apos-tles	Apos-tles	Tiber-ias	Gali-lee?	James	Apos-tles	Apos-tles	Paul
Matt	–	**2** 28:9	–	–	–	–	–	–	–	**11** 28:16	–	–
Mark	**1** 16:9	–	–	**2** 16:12	**11** 16:14	–	–	–	–	–	**11** 16:19	–
Luke	–	–	**1** 24:34	**2** 24:15	**13** 24:36	–	–	–	–	–	**11** 24:50	–
John	**1** 20:16	–	–	–	**10** 20:19	**11** 20:26	**7** 21:2	–	–	–	–	–
Acts	–	–	–	–	–	–	–	–	–	–	**11** 1:4	–
1 Cor	–	–	**1** 15:5	–	**12** 15:5	–	–	**500** 15:6	**1** 15:7	**11** 15:7	–	**1** 15:8

As the women departed their obedience brought a reward beyond anticipation; as we have noted, they would see the risen Lord long before He and they would meet in Galilee. We know that we will see Him on high for evermore, but there will be the sudden moment of grace when we see Him at His coming again. As the Lord met them, He said "All hail" (*chairete*), from a verb meaning to rejoice, used as a greeting; Judas (Matt 26:49) and the soldiers (Matt 27:29) used this mockingly when they addressed the Lord, while Gabriel used the word when he first addressed Mary (Luke 1:28). As the women "held him by the feet", here was humility, wonder, love and faith mingled as an act of worship. This word "worshipped" (*proskuneō*), meaning to make obeisance, occurs many times in the NT, most frequently in Matthew, John and Revelation. Thus Satan wanted worship (Matt 4:9), and as the dragon he obtains it (Rev 13:4). The emperor-beast of the future will receive worship (Rev 13:4, 8, 12), as will his image (16:2). John even attempted to worship an angel (Rev 19:10), but was stopped immediately. In John 4:21, 23, 24 the Father is worshipped, while in Revelation it is God as seated on the throne who is worshipped (Rev 4:10). The angels worship the Son (Heb 1:6). In the Gospels, individuals worshipped the Lord Jesus (Matt 8:2; 9:18; 15:25; 20:20; John 9:38), and also small groups of men and women (Matt 2:11; 14:33; 28:9, 17; Luke 24:52). J. N. Darby, in his translation, has used the rendering "to do homage", explaining his choice in his preface "for simple souls"; the word "worship" gives the wrong meaning in some cases where individuals worshipped the Lord without realising that He was God. He has quoted 1 Chron 29:20, where they "worshipped the Lord, and the king", observing that this "is simple blasphemy, if it (the word worshipped) be used in the modern sense".

Thus the women engaged in the touch of worship; in Luke 24:39 the touch was an invitation that faith should perceive Him as a body and not as a spirit; in John 20:27, the invitation to touch Him was that Thomas should "be not faithless, but believing". In John 20:17, the Lord said to Mary, "Touch me not", which was the true position of faith, for she recognised Him at His word "Mary".

The Lord repeated to the women what the angel had said, "tell my brethren that they go into Galilee, and there shall they see me", though they would see Him in the upper room later that evening. The description "my brethren" is one of grace, introducing them into the heavenly family. Elsewhere, He called His own by the names "my servant" in relation to Him as Lord (John 12:26; 18:36); "my disciples" in relation to Him as Master (John 15:8); "my sheep" in relation to Him as Shepherd (John 10:26, 27); "my friends" in relation to Him as Man (John 15:14); "my brethren" in relation to Him as Son (Matt 12:48; 28:10; John 20:17). Conversely, His people are privileged to call Him "my Lord": Elizabeth before His birth (Luke 1:43); Mary Magdalene at the sepulchre (John 20:13); Thomas in the upper room (John 20:28); David (Ps 110:1; Matt 22:44; Mark 12:36; Luke 20:42; Acts 2:34); and Paul (Phil 3:8).

2. *Events after the Resurrection* 28:11-20

v.11 "Now when they were going, behold, some of the watch came into the city, and shewed unto the chief priests all the things that were done.
v.12 And when they were assembled with the elders, and had taken counsel, they gave large money unto the soldiers,
v.13 Saying, Say ye, His disciples came by night, and stole him *away* while we slept.
v.14 And if this come to the governor's ears, we will persuade him, and secure you.
v.15 So they took the money, and did as they were taught: and this saying is commonly reported among the Jews until this day.
v.16 Then the eleven disciples went away into Galilee, into a mountain where Jesus had appointed them.

v.17 And when they saw him, they worshipped him: but some doubted.
v.18 And Jesus came and spake unto them, saying, All power is given unto me in heaven and in earth.
v.19 Go ye therefore, and teach all nations, baptizing them in the name of the Father, and of the Son, and of the Holy Ghost:
v.20 Teaching them to observe all things whatsoever I have commanded you: and, lo, I am with you alway, *even* unto the end of the world. Amen."

11-15 Human scheming immediately comes to the fore. The soldiers must have known that a miracle had taken place, because of the appearance of the angel shining in glory, and because of the empty tomb that they had been guarding so carefully. They knew but they did not believe – knowledge is not faith, yet true faith has knowledge. So the watch went to the priests, not to Pilate; they thought that this was a highly-religious matter that the priests could cope with, rather than a political matter that Pilate could have dealt with. The Sanhedrin had to decide what to do, "for that indeed a notable miracle hath been done ... and we cannot deny it" (Acts 4:16). But they could take steps to ensure that the news travelled no further. So money was used both to gain the betrayal of the Lord, and then to ensure the denial of His resurrection. Whereas Judas attempted to return the money, the soldiers kept it and spread the lie around. So the Jews believe the lie that "His disciples came by night, and stole him away while we slept", in just the same way as men will believe a lie in the future (2 Thess 2:11). This was Satan's first attack on the resurrection; he had failed all through the Lord's lifetime to deflect Him, so now he sought immediately to deflect men from faith in the resurrection of Christ. The Spirit of inspiration has left the event clearly on the pages of Holy Scripture, so we know the source of all denial of the resurrection. Heretics said that the resurrection was past, obliterating the hope of believers in the future resurrection day (2 Tim 2:18). Today, many relegate the Lord's resurrection to a theory; explanations that are offered are equivalent to a denial, since no explanation is necessary save that this resurrection was the work of God (Acts 2:32; Eph 1:19-20). Like the Jews of old, the masses today are easily convinced by error, but seldom by the truth.

There would have been danger for these soldiers if Pilate had heard that they had been sleeping while on guard, just as the Philippian jailor would have been in danger if the prisoners under his charge had escaped (Acts 16:27). So the Sanhedrin promised to manipulate Pilate, so as to "secure" the soldiers (*amerimnos*). This adjective means "without anxiety", and is translated "we will ... rid you of care" in the RV. So the lie was "commonly reported among the Jews" in the same way as the good news was taught among all nations (Matt 28:19). One led to faithlessness while the other to faith and salvation.

16-17 The rest of the chapter is occupied with divine plans, revealed to the eleven apostles in Galilee. Matthew passes over the resurrection manifestations to the apostles in Jerusalem (John 20:19-29), and in keeping with the main themes of his Gospel he concludes with a brief mention of the Lord's manifestation to the eleven in Galilee. It is stated that the meeting took place in "a mountain where Jesus had appointed them". We are not told when the appointment was made; it may have been an unrecorded appendix to Matt 26:32 when the Lord mentioned Galilee the night before He was crucified, or it may have been an appendix to Matt 28:10 when the Lord mentioned Galilee to the women. The "mountain" was, no doubt, familiar to the apostles, and it has been suggested that it was the mount of transfiguration (Matt 17:1). This would have been a very suitable venue, combining kingdom glory, and resurrection glory. The remarkable thing is that His presence brought both worship and doubt. All four Gospels present various aspects of doubt, but we do not feel that the doubt in our v.17 was in the hearts of the eleven apostles, for they had already seen the Lord twice in Jerusalem. The doubt in v.17 is very serious, since the Lord was actually present; this is unlike Thomas, who doubted only when he was not in the Lord's presence. Many had not believed when present with Him in His lifetime, but this was doubt when actually in the presence of His miraculous state. Perhaps there were some in Galilee who doubted that He had actually died, since He obviously looked so real in resurrection!

18 The Lord expressed His "power" (*exousia*, authority, absolute freedom of action) to commission His apostles. In Luke 24:47-48, a commission was given in the upper room in Jerusalem; in John 21:15, a commission was given to Peter by the Sea of Tiberias: in Acts 1:8, a commission was given on Olivet where the Lord ascended. To fulfil this commission, the apostles would be filled with the Spirit (who is suddenly introduced in v.19); the Lord would receive the Spirit from the Father in heaven, and would then shed Him forth on earth (Acts 2:33). The Lord had authority to send His disciples forth, to achieve results in men, and to change the direction of the testimony to embrace not only the Jews but also the nations. Today likewise, all service is subject to divine authority and power – the Spirit gives gifts for service, the Lord provides opportunities for service, God works out the results of service (1 Cor 12:4, 5, 6).

19-20 The commission to "teach all nations" reverses the Lord's principal object during His lifetime ministry, when the message went forth mainly to the Jews (Matt 10:5-6; 15:24); now it would go forth to the nations, as in Matt 21:43; 22:9. This was in keeping with God's promise to Abraham, that in him "shall all families of the earth be blessed" (Gen 12:3; Gal 3:8). The clause "teach all nations" is *mathēteuō ta ethnē*, namely, make disciples of all nations, an expression also occurring in Acts 14:21. Through the apostles' preaching, Christ worked "to make the Gentiles obedient, by word and deed" (Rom 15:18).

The new disciples were to be baptised. Thus there are three new concepts introduced in v.19: the nations, baptism, the Holy Spirit. For this was an advance on John's baptism in Matt 3:6; his baptism was unto repentance that led to faith in Christ (Acts 19:4); Christian baptism, on the other hand, is an intelligent sign by a believer of new moral and spiritual conditions by faith that is already possessed. It is the abandonment of the old life practically, so as to take up a new life in Christ (Rom

6:6-11). Moreover, this baptism is "in the name of the Father, and of the Son, and of the Holy Spirit". The three Persons of the Godhead are described under one "name", implying one true God. Mostly, when we read "in my name", the word "name" is in the dative case (Matt 12:21; 24:5, *tō onomati*), but a few times in the accusative case implying direction (*eis to onoma*, Matt 10:41, 42; 18:20; 28:19); see 1 Cor 10:2; Gal 3:27. Believers are baptised into the authority of the Name, for this is the basis of discipleship and of observing all things. The Persons of the Trinity were evident at the Lord's baptism (Matt 3:16-17). There are many other contexts where the three Persons are found or implied; a list is provided in the author's article "The Unity of the Godhead" in *Treasury of Bible Doctrine*. Three particularly interesting examples are:

1. the giving of gifts (Rom 12:3; Eph 4:7; 1 Cor 12:11);
2. divine work in hard hearts (Isa 6:10; John 12:39-41; Acts 28:25);
3. the Speakers at the anointing of the Lord (Isa 61:1-3; 42:1-4; 11:1-9).

"Teaching" (v.20) is the basis of spiritual instruction; the Lord's words and commandments are not to be neglected. This is the same word as in v.15; in other words, the soldiers did as they were "taught" by the priests, and the new disciples had to do what they were taught by the apostles. Teaching is the method by which truth is passed on; see John 17:20. Several stages are indicated in 2 Tim 2:2, these stages being Paul, Timothy, faithful men, others also.

When the Lord sent forth His disciples in Matt 10:5, His personal presence was not with them. Now this would be changed because of His ascension; He would be with them always, as the Lord said to Paul in Corinth, "I am with thee" (Acts 18:10). In Mark 16:20, the promise is taken further: "the Lord working with them". In other words, His presence and His working are the secret of success in Christian service. This presence was promised "unto the end of the world", namely, "unto the completion of the age". The word for "end" is *sunteleia*, whose meaning we have explained in our introduction to Matt 24. In other words, the Lord's presence is promised not only for the apostolic and church period, but also for the last seven years before it is known in manifested glory during His coming reign of triumph and authority.

The Gospel opened with the King, the "son of David", and His genealogy. The rejection of the King and the introduction of the kingdom in mystery (not seen, but known only by revelation to the initiated) have caused the Gospel to end on a different note, namely "the Father, the Son, and the Holy Spirit" relating to the Christian age. The Jews as a nation have been put on one side until the fulness of the Gentiles be come in (Rom 11:25). In particular, the Acts traces the transfer of the Gospel message from the Jews to the Gentiles. Matthew has ended his Gospel with a precious promise, but Mark and Luke with a brief statement of the Lord's ascension. Subsequently, the King and His kingdom in glory have been largely forgotten by men, yet the Gospel has promised that the King will come, and His kingdom will come; God's purpose will be worked out in His own good time.

MARK

H. S. Paisley

MARK

Introduction

1. Authorship
2. Recipients
3. Date
4. Purpose
5. Theme
6. Features
7. Bibliography
8. Outline

1. Authorship

Mark's name is not found in the Gospel attributed to his penmanship, but there is general agreement among Bible scholars that he was the inspired writer. Mark, also called John Mark, is mentioned ten times in the Acts and the Epistles (Acts 12:12, 25; 13:5, 13; 15:37, 39; Col 4:10; 2 Tim 4:11; Philem 24; 1 Pet 5:13).

These references suggest a threefold relationship:

i. Natural: Mark was the son of a God-fearing mother, whose name was Mary. She was a woman of means as her house was large enough for many believers to gather for prayer. The entrance to the house was by a gate and a girl was the portress. When Peter was delivered from prison "he came to the house of Mary the mother of John, whose surname was Mark, where many were gathered together praying" (Acts 12:12). This is the first historical reference to John Mark in the Scriptures. He was a Jew: John ("the grace of God") being his Hebrew name, and Mark ("the hammer") his Roman surname. From his home in Jerusalem Mark went forth as a servant to the two apostles Barnabas and Saul. He first journeyed to Antioch, then from Antioch to Perga (Acts 12:25; 13:5, 13). Mark was also the cousin of Barnabas (Col 4:10, RV).

ii. Spiritual: it seems evident that Mark owed his conversion to the instrumentality of Peter, who writes of him as "Marcus my son". He was Peter's son in the faith. His close friendship with Peter accounts for the eye-witness accounts of the Lord's miracles in his Gospel. It has been said that Mark received his facts of the gospel from Peter, and the explanation of the gospel from Paul

(1 Pet 5:13). Peter's sermon to Cornelius describing the earthly ministry of the Lord Jesus is an epitome of Mark's Gospel. Peter outlined: the path of the Saviour from the beginning of His Galilean ministry following the ministry of John the Baptist; the anointing of the Lord with the Holy Spirit and power at His baptism; His mission of healing all that were oppressed of the Devil; His sufferings, death, resurrection and ascension (Acts 10:37-43).

The Gospel according to Mark is a catechetical expansion of Peter's words, although Mark must have drawn information from other sources as well.

iii. Subservient: Mark's association with Barnabas and Saul during their first missionary journey from Antioch ended abruptly at Perga. Luke uses a laconic sentence to describe the termination of this first phase of Mark's public service: "John departing from them returned to Jerusalem" (Acts 13:13).

This breakdown in service became the cause of a breakdown in fellowship between the two apostles. On the second missionary journey Barnabas was determined that Mark should accompany them again. Paul strongly refused this proposal. He "thought it not good to take him with them, who departed from them from Pamphylia, and went not with them to the work" (Acts 15:37, 38). Barnabas took Mark and sailed to Cyprus. Concerning the journey and the result Luke has left no record. The loyalty of Barnabas has been ascribed to the blood relationship between the two men. Paul's choice of Silas for the visitation of the churches in Syria and Cilicia had the approval of the brethren in Antioch (Acts 15:36-41). For the next ten years a veil is drawn over the events in Mark's life.

The restoration of Mark to the confidence of Paul and to fruitful service is referred to by the apostle in his epistles. In writing to the Colossians he includes the greetings of Mark, and an injunction for his hearty reception. He had been with Paul as a comforter in the prison. In the letter to Philemon Mark is associated with Luke and others as a fellow-labourer of the apostle (Col 4:10; Philem 24). During his final imprisonment Paul instructed Timothy to bring Mark with him as he would be profitable for service (2 Tim 4:11).

Paul who once refused the company of Mark, now desires him as an attendant. We are not given any account of the cause of the failure of Mark in going back from Perga. In Paul's estimation it was serious enough to hinder him from further service with the apostles at that time.

How refreshing to find that God called one who had failed to write of the one perfect Servant who never failed. Mark's tongue became the pen of a ready writer. His Gospel reveals the love in his heart for the Person of the Lord Jesus. His meditation of Him as the Servant is sweet.

2. Recipients

According to the early Church Fathers Mark wrote his Gospel from Rome for the Christians there. The character of his writings give credence to this belief.

The Gospel, which outlines the violent acts of men to Christ, and His passivity, was to be a source of strength to the Roman Christians, who were suffering for their faith. To those who first read the Gospel the Lord Jesus was presented in such a manner that in the hour of their severe persecutions they received power to endure and remain faithful even to death. The ceaseless activities of the Lord recorded by Mark would be of great interest to the Romans. To a people of proud military achievement the virtues of true service, absolute obedience, unflinching faithfulness and indomitable courage, seen in the perfect Servant of Jehovah, would have special appeal. In addition Jewish words and customs, unknown to Romans, are explained: 5:41; 7:1-4; 15:34, 42. The few OT references: 1:2-3; 15:28 and the many uses of Latinism i.e. Latin terms transliterated into Greek, (12:42; 15:16) also point to the Roman origin of the Gospel.

Mark's Gospel has been described as the neglected book of the NT, for it is the least studied. God gave it primarily for the first century Christians, but also that Christians throughout the age might profit by the pattern of the perfect Servant.

3. Date

It must be confessed that we do not possess the information for a definite dating of Mark. It is generally accepted that the time of writing must have been between AD 50 and AD 68. The book may have been the first of the four Gospels. It is one of the earliest books of the NT.

The time period covered in the Gospel by Mark extends from the opening ministry of John the Baptist to the early preaching of the apostles after the ascension of the Lord to heaven (1:2-8; 16:19, 20).

4. Purpose

Three areas of emphasis may be observed:

i. Informative: To outline in an orderly way the works of the Son of God, Mark discloses the ministry of the Lord by His own words. These words form a key to the Gospel: "The Son of Man came not to be ministered unto, but to minister, and to give his life a ransom for many" (10:45).

Here the perfect Servant states the objective of His daily life of ministry, and the vicarious nature of His death.

Jesus, the Son of God, is presented as God's suffering Servant who performs 18 miracles.

ii. Apologetic: The Gospel by Mark stresses the rising tide of enmity towards the Servant, and the plotting of the Jewish leaders to put Him to death. A rapid review of the Gospel will show Christ encountering great opposition (2:6, 7; 3:2, 6, 22; 5:17, 40; 6:3, 5; 11:18, 27, 28; 12:13, 18, 28).

All the way through the Servant experienced increasing enmity, at every step fresh persecution. These things are written for the instruction of all the servants of Christ. The animosity of this world system will be encountered, and will become greater as the church comes to the end of the age.

iii. Practical: He serves best who is most like the perfect Servant. He has left us a pattern that we should follow His steps (1 Pet 2:21). Mark presents much more than the correct theology concerning the mercy and might of the Person of the Lord; there are actions to be observed and followed by every one who has been called to serve. We serve the Lord Christ, and He is the example of all acceptable service to God. For our emulation this Gospel reveals His tenderness, His love, His faithfulness, His devotion, His courage, His dependence, His determination, His wisdom, and His unostentatiousness.

5. Theme

The Lord Jesus is presented in this Gospel as the Servant of Jehovah and the Prophet of God. Isaiah prophesied of the coming Messiah as the Servant: "Behold my Servant, whom I uphold; mine elect, in whom my soul delighteth; I have put my Spirit upon him: he shall bring forth judgment to the Gentiles. He shall not cry, nor lift up, nor cause his voice to be heard in the street. A bruised reed shall he not break, and the smoking flax shall he not quench: he shall bring forth judgment unto truth. He shall not fail nor be discouraged, till he have set judgment in the earth: and the isles shall wait for his law" (Isa 42:1-4).

Moses predicted the raising up of a Prophet whose word would be final on all subjects: "The Lord thy God will raise up unto thee a Prophet from the midst of thee, of thy brethren, like unto me; unto him ye shall hearken... I will raise them up a Prophet from among their brethren, like unto thee, and will put my words in his mouth; and he shall speak unto them all that I shall command him" (Deut 18:15-18).

Mark was the instrument chosen by God to portray the Son of His love in these two wondrous offices, the Servant of Jehovah and the Prophet of God.

The hand of the Lord Jesus is frequently mentioned in Mark which is fitting to the Gospel of service. The book could be called: "The Ministry of the Hand of Christ". The prophetic ministry of Christ is also emphasised. There are three Passion prophecies: 8:27-33; 9:30-32; 10:32-34. There are two great prophecies of Preview concerning the Servant's advent the second time as the Sovereign: 13:3-37; 14:62. We see the hand of the Servant in the Gospel by Mark, and we hear the voice of the Prophet.

6. Features

Mark is the shortest of the four Gospels; yet it contains the most picturesque details of the life and service of the Lord Jesus. Matthew has painted a full length portrait of the Sovereign, while Mark has portrayed the Servant in a series of vignettes. Matthew presents His Supremacy and Mark His Submissiveness. He who is highest in majesty was also humblest in ministry. The pen-portraits of Christ by Mark are drawn in such a way that they enable us to appreciate Him as if He were here at the present time. There are at least seven unique features concerning the Servanthood of the Lord in this Gospel:

i. The Hand of the Servant: One of the outstanding features of Mark is the manner in which the Lord used His hands in the healing of the people, as the following passages show:

"He came and took her by the hand, and lifted her up" (1:31).

"And Jesus, moved with compassion, put forth his hand, and touched him" (1:41).

"And he took the damsel by the hand, and said unto her, Talitha cumi" (5:41),

"And they bring unto him one that was deaf, and had an impediment in his speech; and they beseech him to put his hand upon him" (7:32).

"He put his hands again upon his eyes, and made him look up" (8:23-25).

In these and other mentions of His hand we learn the tenderness and interest of the Servant toward the suffering ones. The ultimate in Christian service is to reach the hearts of men with the Gospel. To accomplish this the servant of Christ must have tenderness and compassion for the needy.

ii. The Eyes of the Servant: The Spirit through Mark also draws attention in a unique way to the eyes of the Servant: "And when he had looked about on them with anger, being grieved for the hardness of their hearts..." (3:5). His eyes flashed upon them for they had condemned him for healing the man with the withered hand on the Sabbath day.

Concerning the rich young ruler who came to him, and asked him, "What shall I do that I may inherit eternal life?" we read a statement only once used in all the Gospels: "Then Jesus beholding him loved him" (10:21). What boundless pity and compassion shone in His eyes on that occasion.

"And Jesus entered into Jerusalem, and into the temple: and when he looked round about upon all things, and now the eventide was come, he went out unto Bethany with the twelve" (11:11). Here His eyes revealed the indignation of His heart as He beheld the desecration of the Father's House. There are also other records of His eyes but these will be sufficient to show the attention of the Lord to the details of every situation. It was true of him "Mine eye affecteth mine heart" (Lam 3:51).

iii. The Voice of the Servant: Mark also helps us to hear the voice of the Servant. He alone records the actual words of the Saviour, before he translates them into Greek, the language familiar to literate Romans of the first century. There was something familiar in their tones that could not be translated. The preservation of the actual Aramaic words used by the Lord on several occasions is one of the highlights of Mark's Gospel. The circumstances of the following seven occurrences are a subject for holy meditation:

> "Boanerges" (3:17); "Talitha cumi" (5:41); "Corban" (7:11); "Ephphatha" (7:34); "Abba" (14:36); "Golgotha" (15:22); "Eloi, Eloi, lama sabachthani?" (15:34).

By recording these actual words of Jesus, Mark enables the reader to imagine the quality and timbre of the voice of the Saviour.

iv. The Promptitude of the Servant: The adverb *eutheōs*, variously translated in the Gospel by the words "immediately", "straightway", "forthwith" and "anon", is found forty-two times and has been described as Mark's signature word. In the first chapter it is used on eleven occasions, e.g.:

> "And straightway coming up out of the water, he saw the heavens opened" (1:10);
>
> "And immediately the Spirit driveth him into the wilderness" (1:12);
>
> "But Simon's wife's mother lay sick of a fever, and anon they tell him of her" (1:30);
>
> "And forthwith he sent him away" (1:43).

The constant repetition of this word is indicative of the promptness of the Servant. He was always ready, willing and on time. There was no reluctance but an immediate response in the path of service. We do well to follow His example.

v. The Continuity of His Service: The connecting of one narrative to another and one chapter to another with the conjunction "and" is another unusual feature of Mark's Gospel. Thirteen of the sixteen chapters open in this way. The word occurs more than any other in this Gospel and is recorded at least twelve hundred times. In this manner the record moves on in unbroken continuity. Even a slow reader can read through Mark in two hours. It should be read at one sitting. In this way the wonderful unceasing labours of the Servant will be more fully appreciated.

From a literary point of view the opening of a chapter with the conjunction "and" is extraordinary. In the realm of human authorship not a single book is known with even one chapter commencing with the word.

The conjunction "and" is a bonding word. It links two things together. The service of the Lord was characterised as one complete and perfect whole. He was instant in season and out of season, and never weary in well-doing. Every other servant has experienced times of slackness, inactivity, and breakdown. The service of the perfect Servant was fitly joined in one unbroken continuity. God would teach us great lessons from the little conjunction "and".

vi. The Objective of the Servant: This Gospel describes in greater detail than the others the sufferings and death of the Servant. This was the objective of His mission. Three times He predicts His Passion:

> "And he began to teach them, that the Son of Man must suffer many things, and be rejected of the elders, and of the chief priests, and scribes, and be killed, and after three days rise again" (8:31);
>
> "He ... said unto them, the Son of Man is delivered into the hands of men, and they shall kill him; and after that he is killed, he shall rise the third day" (9:31);
>
> "And he took again the twelve, and began to tell them what things should happen unto him, Saying, Behold we go up to Jerusalem; and the Son of Man shall be delivered unto the chief priests, and unto the scribes; and they shall condemn him to death, and shall deliver him to the Gentiles; And they shall mock him, and shall scourge him, and shall spit upon him, and shall kill him: and the third day he shall rise again" (10:32-34).

These predictive words of the Lord Jesus speak of His outward sufferings from human hands. They point to the violence of His death. Again He said "For even the Son of Man came not to be ministered unto, but to minister, and to give His life a ransom for many" (10:45). This is one of the greatest declarations concerning the final goal of His mission to earth. He came to give His life a ransom for many. His death was voluntary, vicarious, and victorious.

vii. The Exaltation of the Servant: The ending of Mark's Gospel is also unique. There has been much controversy among Bible scholars whether the last twelve verses are part of this Gospel. The internal evidence indicates that they are rightly included in our Bibles. The theme of the Gospel is the Son of God as the lowly Servant of Jehovah and these closing verses perfectly fit the portrait. Mark presents Him as the One, who being in the form of God, took the form of a bondservant; and being found in fashion as a man He humbled Himself, and became obedient unto death, even the death of the cross. Now in the closing verses of this Gospel we behold Him highly exalted by God, and seated at the right hand of God. This Gospel seems to be epitomised in Paul's great Christological statement (Phil 2:5-11).

Matthew and John give no account of the ascension of the Lord, while Luke gives the fullest account (Luke 24:50,51; Acts 1:9-11). Mark is the only Gospel writer who uses the word "received up" which indicates "welcome". Mark alone adds the last particular, "And sat on the right hand of God" (16:19). This glorious fact was attested by Peter (Acts 2:34) and Stephen (Acts 7:56). It is Mark alone who describes this event beyond the cloud, when the Servant passed into the glory from whence He came to minister.

7. Bibliography

Alford, Henry. *The Greek Testament.* London: Revingtons, 1863.
Baxter, J. Sidlow. *Explore the Book; Vol 5.* Grand Rapids: Zondervan Publishing House, 1966.
Bellett, John G. *The Evangelists.* Oak Park: Bible Truth Publishers, 1920.
Cole, Alan. *The Gospel according to St. Mark.* Grand Rapids: Wm. B. Eerdmans Publishing Co., 1961.
Darby, John Nelson. *Mark's Gospel.* London: Moorish, 1900.
Dunnett, Walter. *New Testament Survey.* Chicago: Moody Press, 1975.
Earle, Ralph. *The Gospel according to Mark.* Grand Rapids: Zondervan Publishing House, 1957.
Edersheim, Alfred. *The Life and Times of Jesus the Messiah.* Grand Rapids: Wm. B. Eerdmans Publishing Co., 1921.
English, Schuyler. *Studies in Mark's Gospel.* New York: Our Hope Publications, 1943.
Erdman, Charles. *The Gospel of Mark.* Philadelphia; Westminster Press, 1975.
Falwell, Jerry. *Liberty Bible Commentary of the New Testament.* Nashville: Thos Nelson Inc, 1978.
Gaebelein, Arno. C. *The Annotated Bible.* Vol. 6. South Carolina: The Southern Bible Book House, 1920.
Harrison, Everett F. *Introduction to the New Testament.* Grand Rapids: Wm. B. Eerdmans Publishing Co., 1971.
Ironside, H. A. *Expository Notes on Mark.* Neptune: Loizeaux Brothers, 1930.
Kelly, Wm. *Lectures on Mark.* London: Moorish, 1920.
Luck, Coleman. *An Introduction to Bible Synthesis.* Chicago: Moody Press, 1955
McGee, J. V. *Through the Bible.* Vol. 4. Nashville: Thos. Nelson, 1983.
McNichol, John. *Thinking through the Bible.* Grand Rapids: Kregel Press, 1976,
Morgan, Campbell. *The Gospel according to Mark.* Old Tappen: Fleming Revell Co., 1927.

Ryrie, Charles. *The Ryrie Study Bible.* Chicago: Moody Press, 1976.
Schofield, A. T. *The Journeys of Jesus Christ.* London: Oxford University Press, 1913.
St. John, Harold. *An Analysis of the Gospel of Mark.* London: Pickering & Inglis, 1956.
Swete, H. B. *The Gospel according to St. Mark.* London: Macmillan, 1927.
Scroggie, Wm. Graham. *A Guide to the Gospels.* London: Pickering & Inglis, 1948.
Stuart, C. E. *Sketches from the Gospel of Mark.* Neptune: Loizeaux Bros., 1920.
Thompson, E. T. *The Gospel according to Mark.* Richmond: John Knox Press, 1954.
Vincent, Marvin. *Word Studies in the New Testament.* New York: Charles Scribners, 1887.
Vine, W. E. *Expository Dictionary of New Testament Words.* London: Oliphants, 1940.
Vos, Howard F. *A Study Guide Commentary of Mark.* Grand Rapids: Zondervan Publishing House, 1978.
Walvoord, F. W. & Zuck, Roy B. *The Bible Knowledge Commentary.* Wheaton: Victor Books, 1983.

8. Outline

Key: "For even the Son of Man came not to be ministered unto, but to minister, and to give his life a ransom for many" (10:45).

On the premise of the two parts of this statement of the Lord Mark's Gospel is divided into two main sections as follows:

1. The Service of the Servant
   His Galilean Ministry, around the Sea of Galilee. — Chapters 1-10

2. The Sufferings of the Servant
   His Judean Ministry, around the city of Jerusalem. — Chapters 11-16

Sub-Divisions:

I.	The Person of the Servant	1:1
Key:	"Jesus Christ, the Son of God".	1:1
II.	The Preparation of the Servant	1:2-13
Key	"Thou art my beloved Son, in whom I am well pleased".	1:11
III.	The Preaching of the Servant.	1:14-3:6
Key:	"They came to him from every quarter".	1:45

IV.	The Parables of the Servant.	3:7-4:34
Key:	"And he began to teach by the sea side".	4:1
V.	The Power of the Servant.	4:35-7:23
Key:	"What manner of man is this, that even the wind and the sea obey him?"	4:41
VI.	The Prerogatives of the Servant.	7:24-8:26
Key:	"He hath done all things well".	7:37
VII.	The Purpose of the Servant.	8:27-10:52
Key:	"Behold, we go up to Jerusalem; and the Son of Man shall be delivered unto the chief priests, and unto the scribes; and they shall condemn him to death".	10:33,34
VIII.	The Presentation of the Servant.	11:1-12:44
Key:	"Blessed is he that cometh in the name of the Lord".	11:9
IX.	The Presage of the Servant.	13:1-37
Key:	"Then shall they see the Son of Man coming in the clouds with great power and glory".	13:26
X.	The Passion of the Servant.	14:1-15:47
Key:	"They bring him unto the place Golgotha, which is, being interpreted, The place of a skull".	15:22
XI.	The Resurrection and Appearances of the Servant.	16:1-18
Key:	"When Jesus was risen early the first day of the week".	16:9
XII.	The Pre-eminence of the Servant.	16:19, 20
Key:	"He was received up into heaven, and sat on the right hand of God".	16:19

Text and Exposition

I. The Person of the Servant (1:1)

v.1 "The beginning of the gospel of Jesus Christ, the Son of God."

Mark's thought-provoking beginning to his Gospel makes no reference to the genealogy of the Lord, no mention of the miracle of His conception, and no allusion to His virgin birth. The visit of the wise men from the east to worship the King, and the years of His submission at Nazareth are passed over without comment. These omissions reveal the handiwork of the divine Spirit in the grand purpose and design of the Gospel. Mark is presenting Christ as the perfect Servant of Jehovah. In this connection a genealogy, details of birth and early life are of little importance to the portrait. It is essential for Matthew to trace the royal line of the Sovereign. The virgin birth and true manhood must be attested by Luke as he presents the Son of Man. John, setting forth the deity of the Word incarnate, begins with His pre-existence and eternal union with God. All these are important facts concerning Christ, but they were not requisites in writing of His Servanthood.

So Mark commences with the words, "The beginning of the Gospel of Jesus Christ, the Son of God".

The term "gospel" occurs more frequently in Mark than any other of the Gospels. The word Gospel is "good news" (*euangelion*) and refers here to the glad tidings concerning Jesus Christ Himself. The perfect Servant of Jehovah was also the Herald of the Gospel.

The "beginning" of this good news suggests its continuance, which is evident in the closing verse, where the disciples went forth into the world to preach the Word of the good news. This still goes on, and will to the end of the age (16:20).

The theme and centre of the "good news" is the Person of the Lord Jesus Christ. How significant is Mark's description of Him. The good news is concerning Jesus Christ, the Son of God.

He is Jesus, which is His name as Man here upon the earth. This wondrous name is the Greek form of the Hebrew "Joshua", meaning Jehovah the Saviour. The name declares the moral glory of His manhood (Matt 1:21).

He is Christ which is the Greek form of the Hebrew Messiah, or "The Anointed". Through the glorified Christ God will fulfil the deliverance and destiny of Israel as predicted in many OT prophecies as Gen 49:10; Ps 110; Isa 9:1-7. This precious title unfolds the official glory of God's Vicegerent.

He is also the Son of God. In this Gospel of His lowliness as the Servant, the Holy Spirit guards the unique relationship of Jesus Christ as the Son of God. His Sonship is confirmed by His Father on two occasions (1:11; 9:7), confessed by demons on two occasions (3:11; 5:7), affirmed by Christ Himself (13:32; 14:36,61-62) and acknowledged by the Roman centurion after His death upon the cross (15:39). This peerless relationship of Sonship asserts His essential glory.

Notes

1 Sonship and service are joined together by God. Only the Son of God could render perfect service. The redeeming grace experienced by believers on the Lord Jesus has made them sons of God. The enjoyment of this sonship should produce acceptable service to the Lord. Only those in this blessed position truly serve God. Faithful servants of God will be heralds of the Gospel of Christ.

II. The Preparation of the Servant (1:2-13)

1. *By His Herald* 1:2-8

v.2 As it is written in the prophets, Behold, I send my messenger before thy face, which shall prepare thy way before thee.
v.3 The voice of one crying in the wilderness, Prepare ye the way of the Lord, make his paths straight.
v.4 John did baptise in the wilderness, and preach the baptism of repentance for the remission of sins.
v.5 And there went out unto him all the land of Judaea, and they of Jerusalem, and were all baptised of him in the river of Jordan, confessing their sins.
v.6 And John was clothed with camel's hair, and with a girdle of a skin about his loins; and he did eat locusts and wild honey;
v.7 And preached, saying, There cometh one mightier than I after me, the latchet of whose shoes I am not worthy to stoop down and unloose.
v.8 I indeed have baptised you with water: but he shall baptise you with the Holy Ghost."

2-3 There are only three occasions when Mark cites directly from the Old Testament; twice in these verses, and once in 15:28. Other quotations are the recorded words of the Lord Himself. The coming of the Messiah and His forerunner was the subject of divine prophecy, given hundreds of years before their fulfilment. The first of these quoted by Mark was written in the last (Mal 3:1) and the second in the first of the prophetic books (Isa 40:3).

Malachi predicted John as the messenger to announce the advent of the Messenger. Jehovah speaks: "I will send my messenger, and he shall prepare the way before me". The Holy Spirit changes the "me" to "thy face". Thus Jehovah of the OT is Jesus of the NT. Again Mark quotes from Isaiah: "The voice of him that crieth in the wilderness. Prepare ye the way of the Lord, make straight in the desert a highway for our God". The glorious truth of the deity of Jehovah's perfect Servant is again attested. This is the foundation of His perfect service, His sin-atoning sacrifice and final exaltation. Mark unites the two prophecies, but names only Isaiah. There is no inaccuracy in his design. Isaiah being the chief exponent of the Servanthood of Christ filled the thoughts of Mark as he wrote his Gospel. The Servant of Jehovah is mentioned twenty-seven times in the latter part of Isaiah, which has been called, "The Book of Consolation".

Mark quotes from the introduction to this section of Isaiah which includes four great songs, known as "The Songs of Jehovah's Servant". Isaiah 40:3 presents the herald, John the Baptist, calling upon Israel to prepare for the advent of the Shepherd Sovereign. The Servant is the subject of the songs that follow. It is interesting to see that the divine features of the Servant in these songs are fully developed in the Gospel by Mark. The limits of the songs are as follows:

First Song	: Isaiah 42:1-9
Content	: The Servant's relationship to God, His teaching of the Truth, the meekness of His manner, and the scope of His mission.
Second Song	: Isaiah 49:1-13
Content:	The Servant as the Prophet of God and the severe opposition to His ministry by the nation.
Third Song	: Isaiah 50:4-11
Content	: The Servant's communion, His steadfastness, His sufferings at men's hands, and His final vindication by God.
Fourth Song	: Isaiah 52:13-53:12
Content	: The vicarious death of the Servant and His ultimate exaltation.

It is remarkable to see the correlation between these songs and the theme of Mark's writings. It indicates that the author of the Scriptures was the Holy Spirit Himself (2 Pet 1:20–21).

4-8 These verses cover the brief record by Mark of the ministry, dress, diet and proclamation of John the Baptist.

The baptism administered by John in the river Jordan was a sign of repentance; the subjects confessed their sins. It was a necessary preparation for the coming of the Messiah. Water-baptism in the Scripture is never said to have any saving value. John's baptism was unto repentance with a view to the forgiveness of sins, while Christian baptism is a public confession of the Lordship of Christ by those who are already forgiven.

The success of John's ministry is recorded in the vivid language of Mark that "all" went out to John to be baptised. All kinds of people formed the great multitude at Jordan.

The garment of camel's hair and the girdle of skin are reminiscent of the dress of the prophet Elijah, for John came in the spirit and power of that great prophet (Luke 1:17). The diet of John was locusts (Lev 11:22) and wild honey (Ps 19:10). John was marked by simplicity of dress and plainness of food. He was truly a remarkable character. The Lord said of him, "Of them that are born of women there hath not risen a greater" (Matt 11:11).

The proclamation of the herald announcing the coming of Christ was the highlight of John's ministry. He recognised the superiority of the Lord in His personal glory and greater service. John exalted the Person of Christ in his preaching. He also expressed his own unworthiness even to stoop down and untie the thong of His sandal, the task of a menial slave. John contrasted his ministry with the ministry of Christ. He had baptised with water but the Lord would baptise with the Spirit. This was fulfilled at Pentecost (Acts 1:8; 2:1-4) and whenever a believing soul trusts the Saviour (Acts 10:44; 11:15-17; 1 Cor 12:13).

2. *By His Baptism* 1:9-11

v.9 "And it came to pass in those days, that Jesus came from Nazareth of Galilee, and was baptised of John in Jordan.
v.10 And straightway coming up out of the water, he saw the heavens opened, and the Spirit like a dove descending upon him:
v.11 And there came a voice from heaven, *saying*, Thou art my beloved Son, in whom I am well pleased."

9-11 The Lord Jesus came from Nazareth, where for thirty years He had served in obscurity, to be baptised of John in Jordan. This baptism of the Lord was His public consecration to the great work He had come to accomplish. The blessed Lord had no sins to confess as others, but at the Jordan he signified His willingness to take the sinner's place in death. In anticipation of Golgotha He identified Himself with sinful men (10:38). The word "straightway" occurs for the first time in connection with the Lord coming up out of the water of Jordan. It is the great characteristic word of Mark, and its usage describes the Lord's promptness in His service.

The language of Mark is graphic as he details the activities of the Trinity at the Jordan. The Father expressed His greeting to His beloved Son (Isa 42:1). He had been well-pleasing in the obscurity of the despised city of Nazareth, and now also in the hour of His entrance into public ministry. The Holy Spirit confirmed the Father's thoughts, descending like a dove upon Him. The Son received the opened Heaven's approval and anointing for the work of the ministry.

The voice specially marked out the Lord as unique. Others in the Scriptures have been called beloved of God, as Solomon (Neh 13:26) or pleasing to God, as Enoch (Heb 11:5) but He alone can be called by God "My Son".

3. *By His Temptation* 1:12-13

v.12 "And immediately the Spirit driveth him into the wilderness.
v.13 And he was there in the wilderness forty days, tempted of Satan; and was with the wild beasts; and the angels ministered unto him."

12 The third event which was preparatory to the public ministry of the Servant is mentioned briefly by Mark. The forms of temptation recorded by Matthew and Luke are entirely omitted. There are, however, certain details which add uniqueness to the Temptation narrative. The other accounts state that He was led by the Spirit into the desert to be tempted of the devil, but Mark uses a more forceful word translated "driveth", suggesting compulsion of the Spirit. This reveals the extent of His submission to the Spirit of God.

13 The name of the enemy is also distinctive of Mark. Mark does not use the title "the devil", who is the slanderer, as the other Synoptists (Matt 4:1; Luke 4:2) but the term "Satan", the adversary. The purpose of this is seen throughout the Gospel, for Satan caused intense opposition to the Servant. The fact that the victory over Satan in this temptation is passed over by Mark suggests that the conflict with Satan is an on-going one leading to the final confrontation at the cross.

The reference to the wild beasts being present with Him is recorded only by Mark. The closing phrase recalls David's words, "Bless ye the Lord ... ye ministers of his, that do his pleasure" (Ps 103:21).

These closing verses unveil four interesting vignettes of the Servant.

1. In the river	: The Son	— The delight of the Father.
2. In the wilderness	: The Seed of the woman	— The object of Satan's enmity.
3. With the wild beasts	: The Creator	— The Controller of a marred creation.
4. The Angels with Him	: The Lord of Hosts	— The subject of angelic ministration.

Notes

2-3 The Deity of the Lord is asserted three times in the first three verses.

It is a curious feature in Mark to note the enclosing of one statement with another, as in verses 2 and 3, and one miracle with another (5:21-43).
6 John's diet of locusts and wild honey suggests that the spiritual diet of every servant of Christ should be pure (locusts are among the clean to be eaten, Lev 11:22) and sweet (honey suggests the Word of God, Ps 19:10).
13 The reference to "wild beasts" would have a special appeal to Romans accustomed as they were to seeing men engaged in conflict with wild beasts in the unnatural surroundings of the arena. Here was a Man who suffered no danger from wild beasts in their own natural habitat. Servants of Christ should be conscious of the call of God, be obedient to divine ordinances, realise Heaven's approval, expect times of testing, and enjoy angelic ministry (Heb 1:1,4).

III. The preaching of the Servant (1:14-3:6)

1. *The Initial Preaching* 1:14-15

v.14 "Now after that John was put in prison, Jesus came into Galilee, preaching the gospel of the kingdom of God,
v.15 And saying, The time is fulfilled, and the kingdom of God is at hand: repent ye, and believe the gospel."

14 The time, place and theme of the preaching of Jesus is indicated. The ministry of the Servant in Galilee commenced following the arrest of John the Baptist by Herod. The reason and result of John's imprisonment are fully stated in Mark 6:14-29. Prior to the coming of Jesus into Galilee He had performed miracles and ministered in Judea and Samaria for several months (John 1:19-4:45). These are omitted by Mark, which underlines that his purpose was not to give a complete chronological summary of the life of Jesus.

The ending of the public testimony of John the Baptist signalled the beginning of the Servant ministry of Jesus in Galilee. The words "Jesus came... preaching the gospel" indicate the predominant feature of His ministry. He emphasised the source of His message: it was the gospel from God.

15 There were two declarations made by Jesus which summarised His preaching. These were followed by two instructive terms to be obeyed in view of receiving the blessings of the message of the gospel. The first declaration "The time is fulfilled" showed that God's appointed time for His kingdom had arrived. The Messiah was now present on earth (Gal 4:4; Heb 1:2). The second "the kingdom of God is at hand" announced the availability of the royal rule of the King.

The promise of a glorious Messianic kingdom, established on earth and centred in Jerusalem, was the hope of Israel. It is the subject of OT prophecy (Isa 9:6-7; 11:1-9; Micah 4:6-7; Zech 14:9). But Jesus presented the terms upon which His hearers might immediately enter into the benefits of this long-expected Messianic reign, by repentance and belief in the gospel. The word "repent" is derived from the Greek *metanoia* which means a change of mind, and turning away from an existing source of trust.

He also added the command to "believe" the gospel. Mark is the only writer in the NT who uses the term "believe in" from the Greek combination *pisteuete en*, meaning a complete trust in the subject of the gospel. The entrance into the kingdom on these terms was finally rejected officially by the leaders of the nation of Israel, as Mark shows later (12:1-12; 14:1-2, 61-64; 15:31-32). The earthly kingdom therefore could not be initiated immediately (Luke 19:11).

God's present purpose is the saving of men from all nations, and the building of His church, composed of all who repent and believe the message of the gospel of the grace of God. This is the aspect of the gospel preached by the disciples following the finished work of Christ upon the cross and His glorious resurrection and visible ascension to the right hand of God (16:15-20). When this purpose of God is completed the Messiah will return and set up His kingdom on the earth (Zech 14:4; Acts 15:14-18; Rev 19:15). The nation of Israel will be fully restored and redeemed, acclaiming Jesus as their King and Saviour, and will enjoy the fulfilment of the prophetic promises (Isa 53; Zech 12:9-14; 13:1; Rom 11:25-29).

2. *The Call of the First Disciples* 1:16-20

v.16 "Now as he walked by the sea of Galilee, he saw Simon and Andrew his brother casting a net into the sea: for they were fishers.
v.17 And Jesus said unto them, Come ye after me, and I will make you to become fishers of men.
v.18 And straightway they forsook their nets, and followed him.
v.19 And when he had gone a little further thence, he saw James the *son* of Zebedee, and John his brother, who also were in the ship mending their nets.
v.20 And straightway he called them: and they left their father Zebedee in the ship with the hired servants, and went after him."

16-18 This scene, as he walked by the sea of Galilee, is very instructive. The extraordinary One called four ordinary ones from their trade as fishers to become fishers of men. These four fishermen, Simon and Andrew, James and John, had an earlier contact with Jesus. Andrew and John had beheld Him as the Lamb of God at the river Jordan, and had left John the Baptist to follow Him (John 1:35-37). Andrew, as a result, found Simon his brother and brought him to Jesus. When James first saw Jesus is not recorded, but it must have been prior to this memorable occasion on the sea shore.

At the first meeting with Christ the affections of these men were won to the Saviour, and they received a definite call to His service. The Lord is selective in the choice of servants. He calls those who have proved themselves efficient in their daily task. There is no room for idlers in His work. In OT days God called men from following sheep to become shepherds of His people (Gen 37:2; Exod 3:1; Ps 78:70-72). Paul, who was a tent-maker by trade, became a planter of assemblies (Acts 18:3). Here four fishermen were called to become fishers of men.

The word used for net here is *amphiblestron* in contrast to *sagene* (Matt 13:47). The first required great skill, acquired after long usage in the art of casting aright. The net was thrown over the right shoulder where it must spread into a circle before entering the water. This type of net used for inshore fishing was unlike the second, which was a drag net for the deeper parts of the sea. The Lord chose these two brothers, who were casting their net skilfully, because they would prove suitable in the greater work of casting the gospel net to catch sinful men. Upon hearing the call the first two brothers forsook their nets and followed Him. The salvation of God is free, but the service of God is costly.

19-20 Farther along the beach two other brothers, James and John, were preparing to fish in the deeper waters of the lake, and were mending their nets for the expedition. This work required great patience. In His service men of patience are as needful as men of skill. The call and obedience of these two sons of Zebedee is another illustration of the sacrifices demanded by true discipleship. Christ and His claims were foremost, so they forsook home and business for His sake and the gospel.

Mark adds a picturesque detail. He says they left their father Zebedee in the ship with the hired servants, and went after Him. In this Mark paints another vignette of exceptional interest: a little boat pulled up on the shore of the tranquil lake; two brothers, who have been fishers since childhood, leaving their aged father, the hired servants, and the family business, follow Jesus along the shore to the new occupations of "catching men" and "mending broken lives".

The important words of Jesus spoken to these fishermen are vital to all soul winners: "Come ye after me, and I will make you to become fishers of men". Following the example of the Lord's dealings with people, as recorded in the gospels, is the only way to be fully equipped for success in evangelism.

3. *First Sabbath Day in Capernaum* 1:21-34

a. *The Power of the Servant over a Demon (vv.21-28)*

v.21 "And they went into Capernaum; and straightway on the sabbath day he entered into the synagogue, and taught.
v.22 And they were astonished at his doctrine: for he taught them as one that had authority, and not as the scribes.
v.23 And there was in their synagogue a man with an unclean spirit; and he cried out.
v.24 Saying, Let *us* alone; what have we to do with thee, thou Jesus of Nazareth? art thou come to destroy us? I know thee who thou art, the Holy One of God.

v.25 And Jesus rebuked him, saying, Hold thy peace, and come out of him.
v.26. And when the unclean spirit had torn him, and cried with a loud voice, he came out of him.
v.27 And they were all amazed, insomuch that they questioned among themselves, saying, What thing is this? what new doctrine *is* this? for with authority commandeth he even the unclean spirits, and they do obey him.
v.28 And immediately his fame spread abroad throughout all the region round about Galilee."

21 Following the call of the four disciples they accompanied Jesus into the city of Capernaum. This city became the centre of the Galilean ministry of the Servant after His rejection by His own city of Nazareth (Luke 4:16-31). Capernaum was on the north-west shore of the sea of Galilee, the site of a Roman garrison, a custom's post, and the home of the four fisherman Peter, Andrew, James and John (Matt 8:5-13; Mark 2:14; 1:29).

The record of the Lord's first Sabbath day in the city is the most complete account of a day in the service of Christ. In the morning He addressed the synagogue congregation, and cured the demoniac who interrupted His preaching. In the afternoon He entered the home of Peter and raised up his wife's mother, who lay prostrate with a fever. In the evening He went into the street where He healed many that were sick with various diseases. After a short night, He rose up a great while before daybreak, and departed into a desert place to pray.

Mark in the closing of his gospel tells of another full day. Comparing the two is a subject of great interest. The second day began with His betrayal and arrest in the evening, followed by a night of mockery which preceded the false trial and crucifixion in the morning, and ending with His death and burial in the evening (14:32-15:47).

The key to the gospel is illustrated in these two days: the early day "The Son of man came not to be ministered unto, but to minister", and the second "to give his life a ransom for many" (10:45).

22-26 Demonology is a reality as this incident and others in Mark plainly reveal. There are about twelve instances of the Lord dealing with evil spirits in this gospel. He had come to destroy the works of the devil (1 John 3:8), hence the special activity of Satan's kingdom in opposing the Person of the Servant, by hindering His ministry. Satan is aided by demons, who do his will and serve him. He is not omnipresent, omnipotent, nor omniscient, but with the aid of wicked spirits he is in touch with all the world. That these demons are capable of indwelling and controlling men and animals is evident through the pages of this gospel (5:2-5, 11-13). It is solemn to realise that demons have an apparent desire to be possessed of physical bodies (Mark 5:10-12). Satan is the head of this vast host of unclean spirits which are called demons. Paul mentions in his epistles the fact of the powerful influence of the powers of darkness in this Christian age (Eph 6:12; 1 Tim 4:1-3).

While demons may possess the unsaved, no born-again person could ever be in that condition due to the blessed fact that all believers are indwelt by the Holy Spirit. Nevertheless demons hinder the work of God, oppose the preaching of sound doctrine and wage an unseen warfare against the Lord's people and holy angels.

The teaching of the Servant in the synagogue in the morning of the Sabbath day at Capernaum astonished His hearers, but stirred up the antagonism of Satan. In the midst of the preaching a man with an unclean spirit cried out, saying, "Let us alone...I know thee who thou art, the Holy One of God". The words of the demoniac were very unusual, being spoken in the singular and plural numbers. The man was the mouthpiece of the unclean spirit. Demonism is often dismissed as a form of insanity, but this is not the case; it is rather a sinister form of evil, being the indwelling of a human by a demon. This terrible condition has always existed among pagan people in the heathen world. In Christendom it is found lurking in subtle guise in spiritism.

The miracle shows the usual manner in which Jesus dealt with demon possession. He addressed the unclean spirit as distinct from the man himself, and commanded the demon to come out immediately. The evil spirit was unwilling but had to submit to the authority of Christ; it submitted, convulsing the man, and with a loud shriek leaving him. It is notable that the Lord refused testimony concerning His Person from the demon. Witness to Him can be given only by a clean vessel like Peter (8:27-29).

27-28 The question of the amazed witnesses: "What thing is this? what new doctrine is this?" shows that they could discern something altogether new in teaching. They were in the presence of One whose authority in preaching and speaking reached even to the unseen realm of evil spirits, who were forced to obey His Word.

In summing up the incident Mark says that His fame spread throughout all the region. It should be noted that this is the first miracle recorded by Mark and Luke.

b. *The Power of the Servant over a Disease (vv.29-31)*

v.29 "And forthwith, when they were come out of the synagogue, they entered into the house of Simon and Andrew, with James and John.
v.30 But Simon's wife's mother lay sick of a fever, and anon they tell him of her.
v.31 And he came and took her by the hand, and lifted her up; and immediately the fever left her, and she ministered unto them."

29 Upon leaving the synagogue Jesus came around mid-day to the home of Peter and Andrew, accompanied by James and John.

30 The fact that Peter's wife's mother lay prostrate with fever, refutes the tradition of the celibacy of Peter. Some suggest that his wife was dead, and later he had taken the vow of celibacy. That his wife was still alive is clearly stated by Paul: "Have we not power to lead about a sister, a wife, as well as other apostles, and as the brethren of the Lord, and Cephas (Peter)?" (1 Cor 9:5).

31 The ear of the Servant was open to the appeal of the household on behalf of the one who was taken with a great fever (Luke 4:38). Mark graphically details the actions of the Servant. He came near, he took her by the hand, lifted her up, and the fever left her immediately. A miracle revealing the compassion of His heart and the tenderness of His hand, had taken place. The cure was perfect, leaving no aftermath of weakness, for the woman was well enough to minister to them.

c. *The Servant healing at Sunset (vv.32-34)*

v.32 "And at even, when the sun did set, they brought unto him all that were diseased, and them that were possessed with devils.
v.33 And all the city was gathered together at the door.
v.34 And he healed many that were sick of divers diseases, and cast out many devils; and suffered not the devils to speak, because they knew him."

32 In his gospel Mark particularises times in a way peculiar to himself: "And in the morning, rising up a great while before day..." (1:35); "And the same day, when the even was come..." (4:35); "And it was the third hour, and they crucified him." (15:25); "And very early in the morning the first day of the week..." (16:2). Here Mark says, that it was "at even, when the sun did set...".

The mention of the time makes it clear that the people of Capernaum waited until the Sabbath Day was ended before bringing the diseased and demoniacs to Jesus, lest they would break the law, for burdens could not be carried on that day (Exod 20:10; Jer 17:24). The cool of the day was also a suitable time to bring or to "keep on carrying", as the term reads in the literal text, those who were fevered and feeble.

They brought those that were possessed of devils. The word is demons. The Greek distinguishes between the devil (*diabolos*) and demons (*diamonion*). The former is always singular, for there is only one devil, but many demons. The unusual interest was evidently stirred by the events earlier in the day, but most of them sought only physical healing and not salvation from the more serious disease of sin.

33 The expression "all the city was gathered at the door" is a hyperbole. It seemed to Simon and the disciples that the whole community had come to the door of the fisherman's cottage.

34 In great compassion and tenderness the untiring Servant manifested His love for the needy, and healed many that were brought into His presence (Matt 8:16). Various diseases were cured and many demons were driven out. The demons knew Him. Some ancient authorities add "they knew him to be the Christ", which expression is found in Luke's record of the same event (Luke 4:41). He would not accept the testimony of demons, but silenced their tongues, showing His supreme authority over the power of the devil.

4. *The Communion of the Servant* 1:35-38

v.35 "And in the morning, rising up a great while before day, he went out, and departed into a solitary place, and there prayed.
v.36 And Simon and they that were with him followed after him.
v.37 And when they had found him, they said unto him, All *men* seek for thee.
v.38 And he said unto them, Let us go into the next towns, that I may preach there also: for therefore came I forth."

35 The Lord had spent a full day of ministry in Capernaum, but He rose up early to commune in the secret place with God in prayer, and to refresh His spirit. There are two adverbs in the Greek text which indicate how early it was when He left the home of Simon and resorted to a solitary place: very early, and by night. This valuable information left in sacred writing by Mark only, is reminiscent of the prophetic words concerning the Servant: "He wakeneth morning by morning, he wakeneth mine ear to hear as the learned" (Isa 50:4). It emphasises the complete dependence of the Servant, though He was the Son of God, as He moved here serving Jehovah. Prayer is the expression of dependence. Jesus felt the need for times of retirement and communion in which to cast Himself anew upon the Father whose honour He sought and for whose glory He had come to serve and suffer. Before entering upon another tour of service He spent time alone with God. He is our example. Often we fail in our service because we have failed in holy intimacy with the Father. Every servant must feel the importance of being alone in prayer with God, for only there can the true secret of power to serve be known.

36-37 When the others awoke they found Him missing from the home. Peter and the disciples followed after Him, as crowds of people seeking His healing power had again assembled at the door. The word "following after him" (*katadioko*) is used only once in the NT, and means to hunt for Him. He was evidently in such a secluded place that it was with some difficulty that they finally found Him. They interrupted His holy time of prayer, saying "All men seek for thee". He gave them no rebuke for disturbing His time of communion with His God.

38 The Servant outlines His future purpose, which was contrary to the thinking of the disciples. He must go into the next towns rather than back to Capernaum, for His primary objective was not to heal the diseased, but to proclaim the gospel. The words of Jesus reaffirm His glorious objective: "therefore came I forth". Students differ as to the meaning of His saying. Where did He come forth from? Some answer Capernaum, others Nazareth. When the parallel section in Luke is read there is no doubt that He is speaking of His coming forth from the Father to make known the gospel, and give His life a ransom. "And he said unto them, I must preach the kingdom of God to other cities also: for therefore am I sent" (Luke 4:43; John 16:27-28).

5. *His Preaching Tour of Galilee* 1:39-45

v.39 "And he preached in their synagogues throughout all Galilee, and cast out devils.
v.40 And there came a leper to him, beseeching him, and kneeling down to him, and saying unto him, If thou wilt, thou canst make me clean.
v.41 And Jesus, moved with compassion, put forth *his* hand, and touched him, and saith unto him, I will; be thou clean.
v.42 And as soon as he had spoken, immediately the leprosy departed from him, and he was cleansed.
v.43 And he straitly charged him, and forthwith sent him away;
v.44 And saith unto him, See thou say nothing to any man: but go thy way, shew thyself to the priest, and offer for thy cleansing those things which Moses commanded, for a testimony unto them.
v.45 But he went out, and began to publish *it* much, and to blaze abroad the matter, insomuch that Jesus could no more openly enter into the city, but was without in desert places: and they came to him from every quarter."

39 In a single verse Mark summarises the extensive tour of the Servant in Galilee, preaching the gospel and exorcising demons.

40 In the course of the journey a leper came to Him beseeching Him for cleansing. Mark noted the reverent attitude of this poor leper, kneeling down before the Saviour, and repeating "if thou wilt, thou canst make me clean". He had recognised in the lowly Servant the mighty Messiah, whose kingdom would be established with physical healings, when the subjects shall not say, "I am sick" (Isa 33:24; 35:3-6).

41 His imploring cry drew forth the compassion of Jesus, a fact specially noted by Mark alone in reporting this miracle. Again the Holy Spirit of God testifies to the tender love of the perfect Servant for the distressed and helpless. The gentle touch of the Master's hand, and the gracious word of authority saying, "I will; be thou clean", must have filled with unspeakable joy the heart of this man, who had been full of leprosy (Luke 5:12). The Lord cleansed him by an act of His own will and by the fiat of His word. The touching of the leper exposed the Servant to the charge of defilement, but no taint could ever be transmitted to the impeccable Christ of God. The holy Law of God drove lepers from society, but the sovereign grace of God drives leprosy away, but not the leper. In the Servant power and love are combined.

43-44 The Lord charged the man solemnly to say nothing to any man. The question is asked: Why? Some scholars say that in this command the Servant manifested His humility, serving without ostentation. It seems more in keeping with the context that Jesus did not want at this stage of His ministry to be thronged with multitudes coming to Him merely for physical healing, as the great objective of this tour of Galilee was to preach the Word of God, and proclaim the gospel. The Lord also gave the man something to do which would be a wonderful testimony, the signs of the presence of Messiah in the land. He commanded him to appear before the priest to be pronounced clean, and to offer for his cleansing those things commanded by Moses, for a testimony unto them. For centuries no leper had been certified clean by a priest. As there is no record given by Mark of his compliance with the command of the Servant, in all likelihood he failed to respond to that which he should have done for the Lord.

45 In the closing remark on the cleansed leper Mark states that he disobeyed the injunction not to say anything to any man, but began to publish it much, and to blaze the matter everywhere. By his actions he brought to an end the ministry of the Servant in the cities, forcing Him to continue His ministry in remote and uninhabited places. Even there multitudes kept coming to Him from every direction. The result of the leper's failure to obey forms the background to the withdrawal of the Lord to the desert.

Notes

Two important features of the ministry of the Servant are foremost.

1. The ceaseless activity is marked by the eleven usages of the word *eutheos* (1:10,12,18,20,21,28,29,30,31,42,43) translated straightway, forthwith, immediately, and anon.
2. The popular enthusiasm which His miracles and teaching evoked (1:27,28,33-37,45).

26,34,42 The spiritual application of the three types of miracles.

1. Exorcism of demons	Power over sin's domination.
2. Healing of various diseases	Power over varied forms of sin.
3. Cleansing of leprosy	Power over sin's defilement.

39-40 A comparison of the parallel accounts given by Matthew (4:23; 8:1) and Mark (1:39, 40) shows the Sermon on the Mount comes between verses 39 and 40 of Mark 1. This sermon therefore is a sample of the preaching of the Servant during His Galilean visits to their synagogues.

44-45 The disobedience of the leper and the result of his failure is a reminder of the words of Samuel: "Hath the Lord as great delight in burnt offerings and sacrifices, as in obeying the voice of the Lord? Behold, to obey is better than sacrifice, and to hearken than the fat of rams" (1 Sam 15:22).

6. *The Beginnings of Opposition to the Preaching of the Servant 2:1-3:6*

From 2:1 to 3:6 Mark, the beginning of a movement of enmity and antagonism to Christ from the religious leaders of Israel is introduced. This opposition is seen to intensify as the writer proceeds, consummating in the plot to destroy Him. The rising tide of conflict between the Servant and the scribes and Pharisees is one of the background themes of Mark's Gospel.

The popularity and wonder among the people is overshadowed by this underground dissension. The causes are indicated in the incidents recorded in this section.

a. *The Claim of the Servant to forgive sins (vv.1–12)*

v.1 "And again he entered into Capernaum, after some days; and it was noised that he was in the house.
v.2 And straightway many were gathered together, insomuch that there was no room to receive *them*, no, not so much as about the door: and he preached the word unto them.
v.3 And they come unto him, bringing one sick of the palsy, which was borne of four.
v.4 And when they could not come nigh unto him for the press, they uncovered the roof where he was: and when they had broken *it* up, they let down the bed wherein the sick of the palsy lay.
v.5 When Jesus saw their faith, he said unto the sick of the palsy, Son, thy sins be forgiven thee.
v.6 But there were certain of the scribes sitting there, and reasoning in their hearts,
v.7 Why doth this *man* thus speak blasphemies? who can forgive sins but God only?
v.8 And immediately when Jesus perceived in his spirit that they so reasoned within themselves, he said unto them, Why reason ye these things in your hearts?
v.9 Whether is it easier to say to the sick of the palsy, *Thy* sins be forgiven thee; or to say, Arise, and take up thy bed, and walk?
v.10 But that ye may know that the Son of man hath power on earth to forgive sins, (he saith to the sick of the palsy,)
v.11 I say unto thee, Arise, and take up thy bed, and go thy way into thine house.
v.12 And immediately he arose, took up the bed, and went forth before them all; insomuch that they were all amazed, and glorified God, saying, We never saw it on this fashion."

1-2 The journey through Galilee being ended, Jesus returned to Capernaum. The news soon spread that He was at home, in all likelihood in the house of Peter. The house was soon filled, until there was no access by the door. The Servant had His desire and delight by preaching the Word to them.

3-4 As He was preaching a group came to the house seeking His presence. They brought one who suffered from paralysis. He was carried on a mat by four others. Mark is the only one who gives this added information. The crowded conditions made an approach to the Lord impossible by the door, but in their compassion for their helpless neighbour, they climbed up the outside stair to the roof, and removed the clay tiling (Luke 5:19) and lowered the paralytic on his pallet into the presence of Jesus.

5 Jesus saw this visible evidence of their faith, and gave them no rebuke for interrupting His preaching, but said to the sick man "Son, thy sins be forgiven thee". Their desire was physical healing, but Jesus revealed the solemn truth that the sin of the soul is a more serious problem than the sickness of the body. The Lord placed the most important matter first. The greatest need of all is the forgiveness of sins.

6-8 The Servant's deity was revealed, for only God can forgive sins. This raised the antagonism among the scribes, who reasoning in their hearts ascribed blasphemy to Him, although their opposition was not verbalised. The Servant confronted them with their own thoughts, establishing proof that while they looked upon Him as a mere man, He possessed the divine power of omniscience.

9 The counter questions of the Lord were a direct challenge. Which was easier, to speak forgiveness, or to tell the paralytic to take up his bed and walk? The answer was evident: it was easier to say to the man, "Thy sins be forgiven thee". None could tell if this had been effective, but to cause the man to arise and walk was a visible display of omnipotent power.

10-11 The forgiving of sins and the raising of this man were both acts of God. To display that this authority was His, and to make it known to all present, and to later readers of the gospel, He said "but that ye may know that the Son of Man hath power on earth to forgive sins", and He commanded the sick of the palsy to arise, and take up his bed, and return to his own house. For the first time Jesus used the title "Son of Man" which appears fourteen times in Mark. He was the Son of God from all eternity but in wondrous grace became the Son of Man in time. The title was Messianic (Dan 7:13).

12 An instantaneous cure was performed. The formerly paralysed man arose, rolled up his pallet, and walked before all the observers. The crowd, amazed at this display of Jesus' power, gave glory to God. They were forced to accept the fact that the man had received forgiveness of sins, but on this they made no comment. The enmity of the critics became more vehement.

b. *The Companionship of the Servant with publicans and sinners (vv.13-17)*

v.13 "And he went forth again by the sea side; and all the multitude resorted unto him, and he taught them.

v.14 And as he passed by, he saw Levi the son of Alphaeus sitting at the receipt of custom, and said unto him, Follow me. And he arose and followed him.
v.15 And it came to pass, that, as Jesus sat at meat in his house, many publicans and sinners sat also together with Jesus and his disciples: for there were many. and they followed him.
v.16 And when the scribes and Pharisees saw him eat with publicans and sinners, they said unto his disciples, How is it that he eateth and drinketh with publicans and sinners?
v.17 When Jesus heard *it*, he saith unto them, They that are whole have no need of the physician, but they that are sick: I came not to call the righteous, but sinners to repentance."

13 Following the miracle of the healing of the paralytic, Jesus walked along the shore of the Sea of Galilee, and the multitudes kept resorting to Him and He kept on teaching them. The tenses being imperfect imply continuous activity. Various groups kept coming to Him and His untiring service in teaching them continued without intermission.

14 Capernaum was situated on the main highway from Damascus to the Mediterranean Sea. Near to the city was a Roman customs station. One of the officials was Levi, later surnamed Matthew (meaning "the gift of God", 3:18). He was employed by Herod Antipas, son of Herod the Great, the ruler of Galilee. Tax-gatherers were often guilty of exacting by fraudulent means. The Jews despised them and looked upon them as hirelings of the Romans. What grace on the part of the Saviour to call one like this to follow Him, to fill the new office of an apostle, and to use the pen of a ready writer to speak of the King in his Gospel (Ps 45:1). On hearing the voice of the Servant, Levi made a complete break with the civil service and immediately followed his new Master.

15-16 Some time later he made a great feast in his own house in honour of Jesus, but also to bring his old associates into close contact with Him. Matthew showed his love for the Person of Christ and his love for the perishing of the world. These are still the marks of reality in a follower of Christ.

The Pharisees are first introduced in this gospel as observers of the scene. They are named over one hundred times in the NT. The name "Pharisee" means "a separated one". They were a Jewish sect which came into being in the days of the Maccabees. Their prime objective was to enforce strict observance of the Law of Moses in times of worldliness and departure. When Christ was on earth the Pharisees were marked by legality without compassion, hypocrisy and an inveterate enmity towards Jehovah's Servant, whom they believed to be an impostor. Their opposition to the Lord became vital in this incident, discrediting Him to His disciples, and expressing their disapproval of His conduct in eating with publicans and sinners. They failed to recognise the condescension of the Servant-Son, and His love for sinners whom He came to save.

17 The Lord answered their criticism by using a well known proverb: "They that are whole have no need of the physician, but they that are sick". He then added a statement which summarised His mission to the world, and justified His conduct and attitude to sinners: "I came not to call the righteous, but sinners". Those, who assume themselves righteous, as these Pharisees, place themselves beyond the skill of the great Physician.

c. *The Change of Dispensation announced by the Servant (vv.18-22)*

v.18 "And the disciples of John and of the Pharisees used to fast: and they come and say unto him, Why do the disciples of John and of the Pharisees fast, but thy disciples fast not?
v.19 And Jesus said unto them, Can the children of the bridechamber fast, while the bridegroom is with them? as long as they have the bridegroom with them, they cannot fast.
v.20 But the days will come, when the bridegroom shall be taken away from them, and then shall they fast in those days.
v.21 No man also seweth a piece of new cloth on an old garment: else the new piece that filled it up taketh away from the old, and the rent is made worse.
v.22 And no man putteth new wine into old bottles: else the new wine doth burst the bottles, and the wine is spilled, and the bottles will be marred: but new wine must be put into new bottles."

18 A coalition of the disciples of John and of the Pharisees approached the Lord with a question concerning fasting. It took place on a day when these disciples were fasting (JND). In all likelihood it was while Jesus and His disciples were feasting in the house of Levi. The Law commanded fasting as an act of repentance on one day every year: the Day of Atonement (Lev 16:29). Legalism had introduced many fast days in memory of calamitous events in the history of the Jewish people. The Pharisees also prescribed voluntary fastings two days every week as acts of devotion (Luke 18:12).

19-20 Jesus showed how incongruous it would be for His disciples to fast while He was with them. It would be as inappropriate as guests at a wedding mourning in the presence of the bridegroom (Ecc 3:1-4). This figure was suitable to the disciples of John, as he had spoken of Jesus as the Bridegroom, and of himself as one of His friends (John 3:29). Conditions, however, would change, for the time would come when the Bridegroom would be taken away. This is the first indication in Mark's Gospel of the violent death of the Servant. The word for "shall be taken away" (*aparthe*) means to be violently removed; this was fulfilled in His crucifixion (Isa 53:8; Dan 9:26). When this event would take place sorrow, like fasting, would be the experience of His disciples.

21-22 The Servant now announces in two simple parables a change of dispensation. The first supposes patching a garment, worn out by usage, with a new unshrunk piece of cloth. When the garment is washed the new piece will shrink and cause the rent to be worse. Likewise a wineskin which has been used for the fermentation of wine is already stretched to its limit; if new wine is poured into this container, worn out by usage, the skin will burst and the wine be spilled. The old garment and the old wineskins are symbols of Judaism. The new cloth and the new wine are symbols of the Gospel of God's grace. Law and grace cannot and must not be mixed. Christ had not come to add any new rites or obligations to the old system of the Jews' religion, but to introduce something entirely new. "The law was given by Moses, but grace and truth came by Jesus Christ" (John 1:17).

d. *The Conduct of the Servant on the Sabbath (vv.23-28)*

v.23 "And it came to pass, that he went through the corn fields on the sabbath day; and his disciples began, as they went, to pluck the ears of corn.
v.24 And the Pharisees said unto him, Behold, why do they on the sabbath day that which is not lawful?
v.25 And he said unto them, Have ye never read what David did, when he had need, and was an hungered, he, and they that were with him?
v.26 How he went into the house of God in the days of Abiathar the high priest, and did eat the shewbread, which is not lawful to eat but for the priests, and gave also to them which were with him?
v.27 And he said unto them, The sabbath was made for man, and not man for the sabbath:
v.28 Therefore the Son of man is Lord also of the sabbath."

23 On the sabbath day Jesus and His disciples walked through the corn fields (grain fields of barley or wheat). The disciples, being hungry, began to pluck the heads of the ripened grain, rubbing off the husk with their hands, and eating the kernels.

24 The Pharisees saw in this a breach of the Law of the sabbath and they brought their accusation of the disciples to the Lord. The Law, however, allowed a hungry man to pluck and eat standing corn: "When thou comest into the standing corn of thy neighbour, then thou mayest pluck the ears with thine hand; but thou shalt not move a sickle into thy neighbour's standing corn" (Deut 23). Why then the complaint of the Pharisees? Their objection was that the disciples were breaking the sabbath by working (Exod 20:10). Plucking heads of wheat was said to be reaping, rubbing away the husk, threshing, and blowing the chaff, winnowing; therefore the Pharisees concluded this to be unlawful on the sabbath.

25–26 In answering the fastidious Pharisees the Lord Jesus cited a familiar incident in the life of David (1 Sam 21:1-6). Although David was the anointed king, he had been rejected and a plot to destroy his life was afoot. He and his followers fleeing from Saul came hungry to the house of God at Nob, where he asked five loaves of common bread from the priest. The priest informed him that only the shewbread, which was sacred and exclusively eaten by the priest, was available (Lev 24:5-9). Yet David ate this bread and distributed it to the men that were with him. Was David justified in this action? The answer must be, yes. Why then should these Pharisees condemn Jesus and His disciples, who in their need had eaten grain by the way. The application silenced the critics.

The parallel between David, the rejected king and Jesus, the rejected Messiah, was obvious. The Holy Spirit would also link the plot to murder David, with the similarly murderous resolve already in the hearts of these men, who charged Jesus and His disciples with a minor infraction of the Law. The important teaching of the Servant is that the supplying of human need is of more interest to God than strict adherence to a religious rite.

Mark records the Lord as saying that David "went into the house of God in the days of Abiathar the high priest". There seems to be a discrepancy, for in the OT account we are told David came "to Nob to Ahimelech the priest" (1 Sam 21:1). Those who accept and trust the Word of God believe that there are no inaccuracies in the Bible. A number of solutions have been suggested by scholars as follows:

1. There may be a copyist's error.

2. In Scripture it was common for a father and a son to take the same name: for Abiathar and Ahimelech, sometimes Abimelech (1 Sam 22:20; 2 Sam 8:17; 1 Chron 18:16).

3. The expression "in the days of Abiathar" has been taken to mean that the happening transpired during the lifetime of Abiathar.

4. The most satisfactory explanation is to render the phrase "In the section of Abiathar the high priest" (2:26, JND). This was the Jewish manner of indicating the section of a book in the OT where an incident could be found. The Lord Himself used this method when speaking of an experience of Moses: "Have ye not read in the book of Moses, in the section of the bush?" (12:26, JND).

27-28 Mark gives an appendage in which two great principles are stated. The first is a quotation of the Lord's words showing that the sabbath was made by God for man's blessing, rest and refreshment, not to bring hardship and bondage by the burdens of legalism.

The second principle is Mark's own commentary on the teaching of Jesus: "Therefore the Son of man is Lord also (even) of the Sabbath". The Lordship of Christ, which extended even to the sabbath, gave Him the sovereign right of its administration, regulation and the interpretation of its meaning. The lowly Servant was the Lord of the sabbath.

The sabbath no longer exists. Grace has given a new day: the Lord's day (Rev 1:10), the first day of the week (Acts 20:7). On that day it is the privilege of the saints to enjoy communion with the risen and exalted Lord and fellowship with His people (John 20:19-20).

e. *The Compassion of the Servant on the Sabbath (3:1-6)*

v.1 "And he entered again into the synagogue; and there was a man there which had a withered hand.
v.2 And they watched him, whether he would heal him on the sabbath day; that they might accuse him.
v.3 And he saith unto the man which had the withered hand, Stand forth.
v.4 And he saith unto them, Is it lawful to do good on the sabbath days, or to do evil? to save life, or to kill? But they held their peace.
v.5 And when he had looked round about on them with anger, being grieved for the hardness of their hearts, he saith unto the man, Stretch forth thine hand. And he stretched *it* out: and his hand was restored whole as the other.
v.6 And the Pharisees went forth, and straightway took counsel with the Herodians against him, how they might destroy him."

The first six verses of this chapter are linked with the events of the previous chapter. They mark the termination of the preaching of the Servant during His early Galilean ministry. The healing of the man with the withered hand stands in close relationship to the incident in the corn fields, as both took place upon a sabbath day.

The Lord performed seven miracles on the sabbath. Three of these are recorded by Mark:

1.	The demoniac in the synagogue at Capernaum	1:21-27
2.	Peter's wife's mother	1:29-31
3.	The man with the withered hand	3:1-6

Two are recorded by Luke:

1.	The paralytic woman	13:11-17
2.	The man with dropsy	14:1-6

Two are recorded by John:

1. The cripple at the pool of Bethesda	5:1-16
2. The blind man at the pool of Siloam	9:1-41

1 The Lord entered into the synagogue and a man was there with a withered hand. The Greek participle indicates that his hand had become withered by accident or disease, and was not a congenital defect. The hand was atrophied and palsied. It was his right hand (Luke 6:6).

2 Some who were present kept watching Him, spying on Him, secretly hoping He would shew mercy to this man and heal him, in order that they might accuse

Him of violating the holiness of the sabbath. To provide medical attention on the sabbath day was considered by the Rabbinical schools as working, thereby desecrating that holy day. Healing was only permitted in grave conditions where the person would not be likely to live another day. The case of this man was not in the emergency class.

3 Jesus knew the condition of heart amongst the Pharisees, but He chose to perform this miracle in full view of all who were present. He called upon the man to rise up and come into the midst, where everyone could witness the miracle.

4 Every eye must have been directed towards the Servant, waiting for the next event in the drama. Jesus asked them two questions. Firstly: "Is it lawful to do good on the sabbath days, or to do evil?" They were in a dilemma. All would admit that it is lawful to do good, and unlawful to do evil. The Lord was about to do good. How evil of them to leave this man with his withered hand hanging paralysed by his side, when there was a remedy available. The second question was even more direct: "Is it lawful on the sabbath days to save life, or to kill?" This man was an exposure of their hypocrisy. He was about to save life for a man is dependent upon his right hand, while they were contemplating killing Him. It is no wonder that Mark records their unanimous silence.

5 The Lord looked round about on them with anger, being grieved or distressed with the hardness of their hearts. The expression "looked round about" is from the Greek verb *periblepomai* which means to look with a penetrating gaze. The word is unusual to the NT being found only seven times, and six of these are in the gospel by Mark (3:5,34; 5:32; 9:8; 10:23; 11:11).

This is the only reference to the anger of Jesus in the Gospels. In the vivid language so often repeated by Mark we see the deep stirring of the emotions of the Servant. He looked upon them with anger and was grieved for the hardness and unmerciful state of their hearts. The Greek aorist participle shows that the look of anger was but for a moment, but His grieving was continuous, as the present participle of the verb shows.

The voice of the Saviour broke the stillness with His compassionate command to the man to stretch forth his hand. The man had faith in the power of the Lord Jesus and immediately obeyed His word. A mighty miracle took place before them all: the hand was restored to normality, as whole as the other. No one could accuse Him of working on the sabbath, as no visible means had been used in the healing. His spoken word was sufficient.

6 It is sad to note that no thanksgiving came from the hearts of those who witnessed the power of God manifested in their midst, but an opposite effect now appeared, revealing more fully the hardness of the human heart. The Pharisees left in fury and called a counsel of the Herodians to join with them in hatching a plot to kill Jesus.

The Herodians were the political supporters of the Herod line of rulers. The religious and political establishments, at variance before, formed a league to destroy Him. This is Mark's first reference to the death of the Saviour: the shadow of Golgotha is now cast upon the ministry of the Servant.

IV. The Parables of the Servant (3:7-4:34)

1. *The Popularity of the Servant* 3:7-12

v.7 "But Jesus withdrew himself with his disciples to the sea: and a great multitude from Galilee followed him, and from Judaea,
v.8 And from Jerusalem, and from Idumaea, and *from* beyond Jordan; and they about Tyre and Sidon, a great multitude, when they had heard what great things he did, came unto him.
v.9 And he spake to his disciples, that a small ship should wait on him because of the multitude, lest they should throng him.
v.10 For he had healed many; insomuch that they pressed upon him for to touch him, as many as had plagues.
v.11 And unclean spirits, when they saw him, fell down before him, and cried, saying, Thou art the Son of God,
v.12 And he straitly charged them that they should not make him known."

These verses form an introduction to the later ministry of Jesus in Galilee.

7-8 He withdrew from the opposition of the leaders of the people in the city of Capernaum to the shores of the sea of Galilee. His disciples withdrew with Him. They shared in both His rejection and His acceptance.

The antagonism of the Pharisees did not hinder the popularity of Jesus. The more they opposed Him, the more the common people flocked to Him. In these verses they are seen coming to Him from all parts of the land, some even from remote areas. Walking many miles, hundreds of them were drawn by His fame as a healer, and many doubtless brought their sick into His presence.

9 The crowds were so great that He arranged with His disciples to have a little boat set in the sea lest the throng would crush Him. Mark is the only writer who refers to this remarkable scene.

Multitudes pressing around Him, He moves into a little ship and it is pushed out from the beach, where all may see Him. The crowds line the shore; the Servant preaches to the vast throng; the eyes of all are fastened upon Him; they listen spell-bound to His gracious words. Here we have another of those delightful vignettes so often scattered throughout this Gospel.

10-12 He had healed many, which caused others with plagues to press upon Him to touch Him, making the little ship a necessity to escape being thronged by the crowd. Demons confessed Him to be the Son of God, but as before He silenced them. The Servant would receive no testimony from unclean sources to the glory of His Person as the Son of God (1:25, 34).

2. *The Personnel of the Servant* 3:13-19a

v.13 "And he goeth up into a mountain, and calleth *unto him* whom he would: and they came unto him.
v.14 And he ordained twelve, that they should be with him, and that he might send them forth to preach,
v.15 And to have power to heal sicknesses, and to cast out devils:
v.16 And Simon he surnamed Peter;
v.17 And James the *son* of Zebedee, and John the brother of James; and he surnamed them Boanerges, which is, The sons of thunder:
v.18 And Andrew, and Philip, and Bartholomew, and Matthew, and Thomas, and James the *son* of Alphaeus, and Thaddaeus, and Simon the Canaanite,
v.19a And Judas Iscariot, which also betrayed him:"

13 There were many disciples who followed Jesus in His Galilean ministry (2:15) but from among them He chose twelve, who were to be His most intimate associates and, excepting one of them, would be His witnesses after His death and resurrection and ascension. They were to carry on His ministry when He had gone back to heaven; for this, preparation and training were specially needed.

14 He made "the twelve" a separate group from all others. They are designated "the twelve" throughout the remainder of the gospel (4:10; 6:7; 9:35; 10:32; 11:11; 14:10, 17, 20, 43) and once as "the Eleven", after the sad end of Judas Iscariot (16:14). As there were twelve tribes in OT times, here we have twelve apostles in NT times, expressing the claims of the Messiah over the whole nation of Israel. It is not for men to choose or appoint themselves special servants of God. The choice of these twelve was by the sovereign appointment of Christ. Today the risen Head of the Church still chooses those who will serve Him, as evangelists or pastor-teachers (Eph 4:11). The principle remains: "Ye have not chosen me, but I have chosen you, and ordained you, that ye should go and bring forth fruit" (John 15:16). The Twelve were to be with Him, and then to go from Him to preach. The order was: with Him for communion, instruction, training, teaching and preparation, then to be sent forth by Him, to evangelise the world. The school of Christ must precede the service of Christ.

15 They also had delegated authority to heal sickness and to cast out demons, so that they might have credibility and power in the message they would carry to Israel (16:17,18).

16-19 The selection of these men was of great importance to the Servant, and was made after He had spent the whole of the previous night in prayer (Luke 6:12). There are four listings of their names in the NT: Matt 10:2-4; Luke 6:14-16; Mark 3:16-19: Acts 1:13. The arrangements of the list may have been the order in which they were called out from the others present and ordained by Jesus. Peter was first and Judas Iscariot is always mentioned last, until missing altogether from the last list.

There are three sets of four names:

1. Peter, James, John and Andrew;
2. Philip, Bartholomew, Matthew and Thomas;
3. James, the son of Alphaeus, Thaddaeus, Simon the Canaanite, and Judas Iscariot.

Eleven of these men were Galileans, all except Judas Iscariot, who is described as a man from Kerioth a village in Judaea.

The first five came from Bethsaida. Four of these were fishermen and represent two sets of brothers: Peter and Andrew (John 1:40, 41); James and John (1:19). Bartholomew is the Nathaniel of John's Gospel (1:45). Simon is called the Zealot, probably on account of his zeal for the Lord. The Twelve would never have been chosen by men of this world, as they had no special qualifications by earthly standards. They were unlearned and without social standing or influence; they came from poor families, and held no religious recognition. In this we have the great principle illustrated, as it was in the choice of David, "Look not on his countenance, or on the height of his stature ... for the Lord seeth not as man seeth; for man looketh on the outward appearance, but the Lord looketh on the heart" (1 Sam 16:7). Paul writing to the Corinthians expressed the same principle: "For ye see your calling, brethren, how that not many wise men after the flesh, not many mighty, not many noble, are called: But God hath chosen the foolish things of the world to confound the wise; and God hath chosen the weak things of the world to confound the things which are mighty; And base things of the world, and things which are despised, hath God chosen, yea, and things which are not, to bring to naught things which are: That no flesh should glory in his presence" (1 Cor 1:26-29). These men had many flaws and faults, but they had two outstanding features that gave them a high standing in heaven's reckoning: they loved the Lord Jesus with all their hearts (excepting Judas, who betrayed Him) and had great courage to follow Him in a world where He was despised and rejected.

3. *The People of the Servant* 3:19b–35

There are three distinct parts to this section. It is an example of one of the peculiar features of Mark's manner of narration: the enclosing of one episode within another (5:21-43). The beginning and ending of the passage speak of the anxiety of His kinsmen and interwoven into the central part is the accusation of His foes.

a. *The Anxiety of His Kinsfolk (vv.3:19b-21)*

v.19b "...and they went into an house.
v.20 And the multitude cometh together again, so that they could not so much as eat bread.
v.21 And when his friends heard *of it*, they went out to lay hold on him: for they said, He is beside himself."

19b-20 These verses are only found in Mark's Gospel. The events took place in a house in the city of Capernaum. Again large crowds flocked to Him seeking His ministry. The demands upon Jesus and His disciples were so pressing that they had no time to eat (6:31).

21 When His kinsmen heard of the continuous activity of Jesus, they became anxious concerning Him. His brethren did not believe in His claims; indeed He was an alien to His mother's children (Ps 69:8) and His zeal was misunderstood by them. The people kept repeating that His mind was unbalanced (compare Acts 26:24). Fearing that this was the case His family decided to journey from Nazareth to control Him and remove Him from the arduous labours which prevented Him having rest and sustenance. The word for "laying hold upon him" is from the Greek *kratesai* which means to "make an arrest", and is used again of Herod laying hold upon John the Baptist (6:17).

b. *The Accusation of His Foes (vv.3:22-30)*

v.22 "And the scribes which came down from Jerusalem said, He hath Beelzebub, and by the prince of the devils casteth he out devils.
v.23 And he called them *unto him,* and said unto them in parables, How can Satan cast out Satan?
v.24 And if a kingdom be divided against itself, that kingdom cannot stand.
v.25 And if a house be divided against itself, that house cannot stand.
v.26 And if Satan rise up against himself, and be divided, he cannot stand, but hath an end.
v.27 No man can enter into a strong man's house, and spoil his goods, except he will first bind the strong man; and then he will spoil his house.
v.28 Verily I say unto you, All sins shall be forgiven unto the sons of men, and blasphemies wherewith soever they shall blaspheme:
v.29 But he that shall blaspheme against the Holy Ghost hath never forgiveness, but is in danger of eternal damnation:
v.30 Because they said, He hath an unclean spirit."

22 Before His kinsmen arrived to hinder Him from further ministry, a company of scribes, who were teachers of the Law, came from Jerusalem to investigate the healings of Jesus. They laid two serious charges against him:

1. He was possessed of Beelzebub, having an unclean spirit (3:30).
2. He was in league with Satan.

It is significant that they did not deny that demons were being cast out, but they ascribed the work to Satanic power. Baalzebub was the name of the god of the heathen Philistines at Ekron, named in the OT (2 Kings 1:2), the Hebrew interpretation being "Lord of the Flies". It was a clear indicating to them that He was indwelt by the prince of demons. These men were repeatedly stating this to the multitudes, evidently out of the immediate presence of the Lord.

23-27 These charges were known to the omniscient Servant, so He called His accusers into His presence, and confronted them with an unanswerable question, which showed the absurdity of their claims: "How can Satan cast out Satan?". He then uses two short parables to refute their evil insinuations. If a kingdom or a house is divided internally in objectives, it cannot survive. The same must be true of Satan's empire. He, the prince of that kingdom, will be at the end of his control, although not at the end of his existence. The second charge, which He dealt with first, was therefore proved false. The exorcisms were not accomplished by any league with Satan. He then refuted the false charge that He was possessed by Beelzebub, using His second parable. It is impossible for one to break into a strong man's house and plunder his possessions unless he has power to overcome and bind the strong man first, then he can spoil his house. The analogy was clear: Satan is the strong man, his house the unfortunate beings controlled by demoniac power, but the Lord was the Stronger One, who by the enabling of the divine Spirit, had defeated Satan, and had the mastery over demons.

28-30 He now issued a most solemn warning, prefaced by the phrase "Verily I say unto you". This is an affirmative clause used only by Jesus, appearing exclusively in the Gospel narrative, and occurring thirteen times in Mark. By the gracious words that all sins shall be forgiven unto the sons of men, and blasphemies wherewith they shall blaspheme, Jesus declared that through the grace of God provision to meet the vilest was available. All kinds and classes may obtain the forgiveness of sins. However He draws an exception in one case, which He described as "eternal sin"; for this there can be no forgiveness. What is the nature of this terrible sin? It is the sin of maliciously attributing the exorcism of demons to Satanic power, thus misrepresenting the reality of the power of the Holy Spirit by which this work had been accomplished. The sin had become aggravated in the case of these scribes for they "kept on saying, He hath an unclean spirit". They were denominating the Holy Spirit "Satan". Continuing in this state of mind excludes from pardon, entangling in guilt from which there is no deliverance.

c. *The Adoption of His New Family (vv.31-35)*

v.31 "There came then his brethren and his mother, and, standing without, sent unto him, calling him.
v.32 And the multitude sat about him, and they said unto him, Behold, thy mother and thy brethren without seek for thee.
v.33 And he answered them. saying, Who is my mother, or my brethren?
v.34 And he looked round about on them which sat about him, and said, Behold my mother and my brethren!
v.35 For whosoever shall do the will of God, the same is my brother, and my sister, and mother."

33-35 When the Lord was told of the presence of His mother and brethren outside, He asked a question worthy of consideration: "Who is my mother or my brethren?" Then He looked around at His disciples, who sat in the circle with Him, and indicated that they were His true kinsfolk.

The Lord was not breaking the ties of ordinary family relationships, but showing that there is a closer bond, for "whosoever shall do the will of God, the same is my brother, and my sister, and mother". Here He announces the adoption of His spiritual family. These spiritual ties are more to the child of God than earthly ties, even in our day. The figure of the threefold relationship suggests: devotion in a sister, fellowship in a brother, and succour in a mother. The words brother, sister, and mother have no article in the Greek, thus pointing to the qualities of such ties in a family.

Notes

28-30 The nature of the unpardonable sin is such that it is unlikely to be committed in this age. The circumstances in which it occurred were unique to the presence of Christ on earth, when He went about healing all that were oppressed of the devil, for the Holy Spirit wrought through Him in unusual power. The substituting of Satan for the Holy Spirit was the essence of this eternal sin. It is debatable whether this could now take place.

34-35 It should be specially noted that there is no reference that any in the spiritual family stands in relationship to the Lord as father. There is only One who could ever hold that place. There is "One God and Father of all, who is above all, and through all, and in you all" (Eph 4:6). The thought of "fathers" in John's Epistle is of spiritual attainment and experience in the things of God, rather than a place in the spiritual family.

4. *The Three Parables of the Servant (4:1-34)*

The Lord spent many busy days as already seen in the opening chapter of this Gospel. These parables, recorded in the fourth chapter, were spoken in the midst of one of those days. The events at the end of the previous chapter (3:15–30) took place in the house; the preaching in parables recorded here by the side of the sea, to be followed in the evening by the storm on the sea.

Mark's Gospel, the Gospel of action, is more concerned with the works of Jesus than His words, for while there are eighteen miracles there are only four parables: the sower and the soils, the growing of the seed, and the mustard seed, recorded in this chapter, and the murderous tenants of the vineyard in 12:1-12.

There are a number of proverbial sayings earlier in this gospel: fishers of men (1:17), the physician and the bridegroom (2:17, 19), old garments and new wine (2:21-22), the house and kingdom divided (3:24-25) and the strong man and his goods (3:27). In this chapter, however, there are parables, discourses making comparisons, usually spoken to convey a special single truth.

It is evident that since the Lord would send out the twelve to preach they must be instructed ere they went forth, both as to the character of the times and the manner in which God works among men. The lessons of these parables were therefore of great value to them.

The kingdom of God was to be advanced, not by the sword, but by the sowing of the Word. Hearts were to be won, and not simply knees bent in homage to military might. Israel had fought under Joshua and David, and the kingdom had been extended to the pre-determined limits by the power of the sword (Gen 15:18; 2 Chron 9:26). The Lord's presence on earth, however, was the beginning of a new order. The kingdom was to be advanced by the Word being sown in the heart. When any would receive the Word fruit would be produced. This is the teaching of this parable.

a. *The Parable of the Sower and the Soils Stated (vv.1-9)*

v.1 "And he began again to teach by the sea side: and there was gathered unto him a great multitude, so that he entered into a ship, and sat in the sea; and the whole multitude was by the sea on the land.
v.2 And he taught them many things by parables, and said unto them in his doctrine,
v.3 Hearken; Behold, there went out a sower to sow:
v.4 And it came to pass, as he sowed, some fell by the way side, and the fowls of the air came and devoured it up.
v.5 And some fell on stony ground, where it had not much earth; and immediately it sprang up, because it had no depth of earth:
v.6 But when the sun was up, it was scorched; and because it had no root, it withered away.
v.7 And some fell among thorns, and the thorns grew up, and choked it, and it yielded no fruit.
v.8 And other fell on good ground, and did yield fruit that sprang up and increased; and brought forth, some thirty, and some sixty, and some an hundred.
v.9 And he said unto them, He that hath ears to hear, let him hear."

1-2 Again Jesus taught a great multitude by the side of the sea of Galilee, following the events recorded at the end of the preceding chapter. As on a previous occasion He was in a ship pushed out a little way from the shore, because of the pressing crowd that thronged Him. The sloping banks formed a natural amphitheatre where the seated thousands could easily see and hear Him. It was with this background that He taught them many things by parables. There is in the use of this form of address a divine insight into the construction of the human mind, which is receptive to instruction by illustration. The Greek word *parabole* expresses the thought of something placed beside as a compassion. These parables vividly unfolded great truths.

3 Jesus called upon the multitude on the shore to hearken, implying the need for careful attention. He also used the same warning for "a hearing ear" at the end of this first parable (4:23).

4-9 It may have been within the view of the crowd, that the familiar sight of a sower scattering seed with wide sweeps of his hand could be seen. Jesus therefore commenced His parable with the words "Behold, there went out a sower to sow". It is thought-provoking to realise that although He was a carpenter, He never used His trade to illustrate the principles of the kingdom. These were taught from the work of the farmer, the fisherman, the physician and the shepherd.

As the sower scattered his seed it fell into four types of ground. Some fell along the pathway, some fell on rocky places where there was no depth of earth, others fell among thorns, and still other seeds fell into good ground. Only one of the four soils produced fruit. Birds ate the seed from the wayside, the sun scorched the tender plants that quickly sprung up in the shallow soil covering the limestone rock, and thorns choked other plants. The seed, however, that fell into the good ground took root, grew, and became productive bringing yields of thirty, sixty, and an hundredfold.

b. *The Parable Explained (vv.10-20)*

v.10 "And when he was alone, they that were about him with the twelve asked of him the parable.

v.11 And he said unto them, Unto you it is given to know the mystery of the kingdom of God: but unto them that are without, all *these* things are done in parables:

v.12 That seeing they may see, and not perceive: and hearing they may hear, and not understand: lest at any time they should be converted, and *their* sins should be forgiven them.

v.13 And he said unto them, Know ye not this parable? and how then will ye know all parables.

v.14 The sower soweth the word.

v.15 And these are they by the way side, where the word is sown; but when they have heard, Satan cometh immediately, and taketh away the word that was sown in their hearts.

v.16 And these are they likewise which are sown on stony ground; who, when they have heard the word, immediately receive it with gladness;

v.17 And have no root in themselves, and so endure but for a time: afterward, when affliction or persecution ariseth for the word's sake, immediately they are offended.
v.18 And these are they which are sown among thorns; such as hear the word,
v.19 And the cares of this world, and the deceitfulness of riches, and the lusts of other things entering in, choke the word, and it becometh unfruitful.
v.20 And these are they which are sown on good ground; such as hear the word, and receive *it*, and bring forth fruit, some thirtyfold, some sixty, and some an hundred."

10-12 The change of circumstances is important. He had stated the parable in the presence of a great multitude. He was now alone and was asked privately by the Twelve and some others with them the meaning of the parable. They had the great privilege of understanding the mystery of the kingdom. The word *musterion* used once in the Gospels in connection with this parable, appears over twenty times in other parts of the NT. A mystery is not something mysterious or strange but simply truth that was previously hidden from the prophets, but is now revealed to people of God's choice (Rom 16:25-27). The secret made known on this occasion was the fact that the kingdom of God in its present form would be an age of sowing seed. To those who were content to go on in ignorance, He would still teach in parables, but unless they sought the truth, the parable would result in their condemnation (Isa 6:9-10). This method of divine teaching impressed the interested seeker, but veiled the mind of the antagonistic. As Matthew Henry has aptly summarised "A parable is a shell that keeps good fruit for the diligent, but withholds it from the slothful".

13 The Lord's two questions emphasised the vital importance of the parable of the sower, the seed and the soils. If this is not comprehended, then other kingdom parables cannot be understood.

14-20 He now proceeds to interpret the parable. The sower is not identified, but the context shows that he is a representation of the Servant Himself, and all others who will follow Him preaching the gospel. The seed is the Word of God (Luke 8:11). Religious training, education, social improvement and civilisation are all useful, but cannot substitute the Word. The sower must sow the seed if any lasting fruit is to be produced. The response to the gospel is envisaged in the kinds of soils, which represent various types of hearers in whom the seed is sown. It is solemnly shown that when Christ is preached most of those who hear are unfaithful. Some, like the wayside ground, are hard-hearted in their indifference to the gospel. Satan's action, like the birds, steals away the word, and therefore the heart is unresponsive. Others, like stony ground, have shallowness of heart, responding quickly with emotional gladness to the Word, but having no depth to their spiritual character, soon wither away. When hardship or persecution comes on account of the gospel they quickly turn from their profession, bringing disappointment to the sower. The actings of the flesh become evident in the starvation of the seed. Those among thorns are like those who hear the Word, but the message is choked out of their hearts, by the actions of the world, in its threefold form: firstly "the cares of this world", which are the distracting anxieties of the present age, also "the deceitfulness of riches" which has temptation and snares, and lastly "the lusts of other things" which drown men in destruction (1 Tim 6:9-10). There is the fourth soil, where the receptive heart is seen, and the sower's reward for His labour enjoyed. The action of faith has welcomed the Word and a spiritual harvest is the result. These alone are genuine disciples. But even in them there is a graduation of fruit bearing. In the Christian life various degrees of productiveness exist: thirtyfold, sixtyfold, an hundredfold. This varying degree may be due to circumstance, or faithfulness. Some can only bear a certain amount and will have a full reward, but others bear less than they should and will suffer loss in the harvest of recompense. The longer the parable is studied the more practical are its implications.

c. *The Lamp (vv.21-25)*

v.21 "And he said unto them, Is a candle brought to be put under a bushel, or under a bed? and not to be set on a candlestick?
v.22 For there is nothing hid, which shall not be manifested; neither was any thing kept secret, but that it should come abroad.
v.23 If any man have ears to hear, let him hear.
v.24 And he said unto them, Take heed what ye hear: with what measure ye mete, it shall be measured to you: and unto you that hear shall more be given.
v.25 For he that hath, to him shall be given: and he that hath not, from him shall be taken even that which he hath."

21-23 The Lord used parabolic sayings on various occasions, as noted in the introductory paragraph to this section. The plain teaching of these words of Jesus was given lest the disciples should fail in the task of diffusing the illumination of the Word. The mystery was not to be kept to themselves alone, but to be held forth as a bright shining lamp (Phil 2:15-16). The word "candle" should be translated "lamp", which was a lighted wick in a shallow vessel full of oil. He asked the question: "Is the lamp to be set under a measuring bowl or under a couch or on a lampstand?" There are three places where a lamp may be placed, but only one is the correct place. Placing it under the measuring bowl was the usual means at bedtime of extinguishing the light, a lamp under the dining couch would cause conflagration, but placed on its stand it would illuminate, and thus fulfil its purpose. The application given by the Lord shows that the divine intention is that the precious things of the kingdom are to be displayed. Valuable items are kept hidden for use at the appropriate time. The many aspects of truth made known to His disciples, may be reserved for a time, but following the Servant's exaltation to the right hand of God, they must go into all the world and display the excellencies of the Saviour, by preaching the gospel (16:15-20). The seed speaks of life and the lamp speaks of light. The Word of God is both (1 Pet 1:23; 2 Pet 1:19).

24-25 The acquisition and distribution of material goods is not the subject of these verses, but rather the accumulation of spiritual perception. The receiving and assimilating of the Word produces enlargement of capacity. The effective exercise of ability to comprehend truth will sharpen spiritual understanding.

Incapacity to receive truth leads to the loss of truth already possessed. This is the meaning of the Lord's word, "from him shall be taken even that which he hath". Failure to use spiritual comprehension will blunt the conception of divine truth. The writer to the Hebrews reminded some of this danger, for while the time had come when they should have been teachers, they required to be taught again the basics of Christianity, which they had once possessed (Heb 5:11-12).

d. *The Seed Growing Secretly (vv.26-29)*

v.26 "And he said, So is the kingdom of God, as if a man should cast seed into the ground;
v.27 And should sleep, and rise night and day, and the seed should spring and grow up, he knoweth not how.
v.28 For the earth bringeth forth fruit of herself; first the blade, then the ear, after that the full corn in the ear.
v.29 But when the fruit is brought forth, immediately he putteth in the sickle, because the harvest is come."

26-27 This parable is unique to Mark's Gospel. It is suitable in the Gospel of the mighty Servant, the Son of God, for it is a parable for the servants of Christ. In the parable of the sower the emphasis is upon the responsibility of the hearers of the message of the gospel; this parable contains a lesson for those who preach the Word. The work of the sower ends with the sowing, the reaper begins His task at the harvest, in between lies the mysterious period when the production is in the hand of God. The parable, therefore, depicts three distinct periods in the experience of the farmer: first a time of faithful sowing, then of patient waiting and lastly of joyful reaping. The Christian worker must sow the seed faithfully, then he can rest from his labour, and can sleep and rise night and day, for by means of which he is ignorant, the seed will spring up and grow. There is an adaptation between the Word of God and the heart of man, which like the earth itself has properties adapted to the seed, and the seed possesses the germ of life which only the earth can mature.

28-29 The word for the development of grain in the soil "of herself" is the

Greek word *automate* from which the English word "automatic" is derived. It suggests "without visible cause" and thus refers to a divine work. God alone produces the harvest without human agency. The parable may have three applications. Some see a picture of evangelism, others of spiritual growth in a believer. The last view, that of the mysterious growth of the kingdom of God between the initial sowing of Christ and His apostles, and the final manifestation of the Kingdom with Christ as the Harvester, seems to suit the context. Whatever view is taken, (all have elements of truth) this parable is a very encouraging one. The psalmist's words are suited to the ideas it expresses: "They that sow in tears shall reap in joy. He that goeth forth and weepeth bearing precious seed, shall doubtless come again with rejoicing bringing his sheaves with him" (Ps 126:5, 6).

e. *The Mustard Seed (vv.30-34)*

v.30 "And he said, Whereunto shall we liken the kingdom of God? or with what comparison shall we compare it?

v.31 *It is* like a grain of mustard seed, which, when it is sown in the earth, is less than all the seeds that be in the earth:

v.32 But when it is sown, it groweth up, and becometh greater than all herbs, and shooteth out great branches; so that the fowls of the air may lodge under the shadow of it.

v.33 And with many such parables spake he the word unto them, as they were able to hear *it.*

v.34 But without a parable spake he not unto them: and when they were alone, he expounded all things to his disciples."

30-32 The parable of the mustard seed is closely related to the two previous parables. It is found in all three Synoptic gospels (Matt 13:31-32; Luke 13:18-19).

In the first parable the seed is sown, in the second it is growing, and in the last it has grown. The preceding parable describes the manner of growth internally; this one the extent of the growth externally. The double question of the Servant introduces the comparison of the kingdom of God to a tiny mustard seed sown in the ground. This seed when it is planted is described by Jesus as less than all seeds to be planted in the earth. The statement has been challenged as a mustard seed is not the smallest seed known to botany. The answer simply is that it was the smallest seed in common use in Palestine. To the Jews its small size was proverbial, since it was the smallest of all seeds sown in their land. On another occasion the Lord stated that faith as small as a mustard seed was all that was required to move a mountain, providing of course that it be the will of the Father (Matt 17:20). Yet this smallest of all seeds can produce a growth greater than all herbs, and shoots out great branches.

Two opposite interpretations have been given to the parable. One is that it pictures the extension of Christianity, which although starting from small beginnings, finally spreads over the whole world. The other, which is more suited to the context, shows that the growth of the mustard seed represents the abnormal development of professing Christendom. The "birds" are the key to this interpretation, for if they represent the evil activities of Satan in the first parable they must do so here, to be consistent with the Lord's clue to the understanding of parables. He had said "Know ye not this parable? and how then will ye know all parables?" (v.13). The birds which removed the seed from the wayside, are seen in this parable sheltering under the branches of the mustard tree. In the final phase of Christendom revealed as Babylon the great, birds are seen in a cage in the system which they had sought to develop (Rev 18:2). These birds depict the ways of the false teachers often mentioned by Paul, Peter, and John in their epistles.

33-34 Mark knew of many such parables which Jesus had spoken, but these are not recorded. Those selected were suitable in the Gospel of Jehovah's perfect Servant, the wonder-working Son of God. The purposeful selection was made under the divine direction of the Holy Spirit. John speaks of many other things which Jesus did which he did not record (John 20:30). There are many things which the Servant said and many things which the Son accomplished of which we have no account, but all has been written that is necessary for faith to say of the Servant, "He hath done all things well" and of the Son, "My Lord and my God (7:37; John 20:28). The Lord continued to teach in this parabolic form, for "without a parable spake he not" unto the people. He used simple illustrations. If any hearer desired further enlightenment He was always ready to minister the truth, for His purpose in coming was "not to be ministered unto, but to minister". When He was alone with His disciples, however, He kept on explaining everything concerning His objectives as they related to the kingdom of God. This twofold approach, so clearly seen in this chapter, is further developed throughout the final chapters of the Gospel.

Notes

14-20 The parable has been often designated the Parable of the Soils. The reason is obvious. The main point of the parable is the difference between the four soils, rather than the person of the sower.

23 The expression "If any man hath ears to hear, let him hear" is a call by the Lord to underline the vital importance of the subject. There are five other occasions in the Gospels when He used this form of speech, and also eight times in the Revelation. Every person is responsible to listen with understanding to His words, and then obey the truth unto salvation.

28 As shown in the exposition, the Greek word concerning the earth bringing forth fruit by itself is *automatē* which means of its own accord. The only other occurrence is Acts 12:10 concerning the "iron gate...which opened to them of his own accord".

29 The development of the plant life is in three stages: first the blade, then the ear and the full corn in the ear. The sower plants in the spring, the seed germinates and the plant grows in the summer, and the reaper goes forth to harvest in the autumn. Christ is the sower, God causes the seed to sprout and produce, and the Son of Man is the reaper (Rev 14:14-16). The proclamation by the servants of God of the glorious gospel is also a time of sowing, then a time of patient waiting follows when the sower rests from his labours; finally the sickle of grace gathering the ripened grain is used by the reapers of the harvest. The principle for service is "one soweth, and another reapeth" (John 4:37-38). There should be no envy on the part of either, but he that soweth and he that reapeth should rejoice together. A beautiful example of this is seen in the sowing of the men of Cyprus and Cyrene at Antioch and the reaping of Barnabas, who rejoiced with them when he came and saw the grace of God. The full result was that much people were added to the Lord (Acts 11:19-24).

34 The added word in the RV is interesting, thus reading "his own disciples" instead of "his disciples". The intimacy and uniqueness of the Servant's relationship to them is underscored. To them He explained all things. What a wonderful Teacher, having divine affection for His scholars. He is the perfect example to all who would teach His truth.

V. The Power of the Servant (4:35–7:23)

The first section (4:35–5:43) contains four of the greatest miracles performed by the Lord. Mark's selection by the Holy Spirit of the parables is followed by his selection of miracles of the Servant. The words of Christ are authenticated by His works. Mark vividly describes these more than the other writers. They are parables in action, wrought one after the other, within the course of a few days.

1. The Storm at Sea (4:35-41)	The Power of the Servant over the forces of nature.
2. The Demoniac (5:1-20)	The Power of the Servant over the world of spirits.
3. The Incurable Disease (5:25-34)	The Power of the Servant over physical illness.
4. Death (5:35-43)	The Power of the Servant over the realm of death.

In each case the power of Christ is presented overcoming hostile forces. The emphasis is placed on the fact that man's extremity is God's opportunity.

There is:

1. A storm no seaman could overcome.
2. A demoniac no man could tame.
3. A disease no physician could cure.
4. A tragedy no parent could avert.

The storm affected a company of men on the sea. The demon affected one man among the tombs. The disease affected one woman, who sought to hide in the crowd. The death affected a child in her father's house. The Servant proved His sufficiency for every circumstance.

1. *The Power of the Servant Over the Storm (4:35-41)*

v.35 "And the same day, when the even was come, he saith unto them, Let us pass over unto the other side.
v.36 And when they had sent away the multitude, they took him even as he was in the ship. And there were also with him other little ships.
v.37 And there arose a great storm of wind, and the waves beat into the ship, so that it was now full.
v.38 And he was in the hinder part of the ship, asleep on a pillow: and they awake him, and say unto him, Master, carest thou not that we perish?
v.39 And he arose, and rebuked the wind, and said unto the sea, Peace, be still. And the wind ceased, and there was a great calm.
v.40 And he said unto them, Why are ye so fearful? how is it that ye have no faith?
v.41 And they feared exceedingly, and said one to another, What manner of man is this, that even the wind and the sea obey him.

35 The vivid account of Mark indicates that he received his information from an eye-witness, probably Peter. The miracle is closely connected with the preceding ministry, for it was the same day at even that Jesus said to His disciples, "Let us pass over unto the other side". It was at the end of a busy day, in which earlier He had encountered the opposition of His foes, and the misunderstanding of His kinsfolk. He had preached several times to great multitudes along the sea shore, and had interpreted the parables privately to His disciples, and some others who desired the truth. At the end of the day He was wearied and as soon as opportunity came He slept. The "other side" of the lake was the eastern shore, which lay some six miles away. He was concerned about the need of this new locality and was anxious to make the journey.

36 "They took him even as he was in the ship" seems to show that without any provisions or preparations they pushed off to sea immediately, taking Him in the same ship from which He had preached during the hours of the afternoon. Other little ships accompanied them. They would share the perils of the sea, but also the peace of the calm.

37 The storm that arose was, and is, a common occurrence on the Lake of Galilee, but on this occasion it was more severe than usual. The waves were filling the ship, so that the seasoned fishermen were afraid they would perish.

38 The Lord, asleep on the steersman's pillow, was truly a perfect Man, but He was also truly God, who being awakened by the distressful cries of His disciples, arose, and hushed the stormy gale and calmed the raging sea.

39 He rebuked the wind and said to the sea "Be silent" or "Be muzzled". This was the form of address He had used when exorcising demons (1:25) and may suggest that He recognised the malignant power of Satan at work in the storm.

40 The disciples had inferred that He was indifferent to their danger when they asked the question, "Master, carest thou not that we perish?". He then rebuked them with His questions: "Why are ye so fearful? how is it that ye have no faith?". Despite His gracious ministry concerning Himself, they had not learned that He was the Son of God in possession of all power. The calming of the sea was a divine act, ascribed to Jehovah alone in the OT: "Jehovah, God of hosts, who is like unto thee, the strong Jah ... Thou rulest the pride of the sea: when its waves arise, thou stillest them" (Ps 89:8-9; Ps 107:23-32, JND).

41 The disciples feared exceedingly when they realised the power of God evidenced in Jesus. According to W. E. Vine's Expository Dictionary, there are three words translated "fear" in the NT: firstly *deilos* which means cowardly, used in the question: "Why are ye so fearful?" (v.40); the second word is *phobos* used in this verse, meaning reverential fear in the presence of divine power; the other word *eulabeia* appears twice only in the NT, on both occasions in the Epistle to the Hebrews (Heb 5:7; 12:28).

They said to one another: "What manner of man is this that even the wind and the sea obey him?". He had revealed Himself in this miracle as the powerful Creator. Creation had heard the Creator's voice, yet how slow the minds of men to realise the significance of His actions. They should have acknowledged that Jehovah of the OT is Jesus of Galilee. The Lord appears in this verse as the representative Man to whom God has given dominion over all creation (Heb 2:5-9).

Notes

35-41 The raging sea is a picture of the storms of life through which believers are called to pass. Oftentimes the circumstances may be so perplexing that the heart may wonder if the Saviour cares. The compassion of Christ and His control of the situation is encouraging and reassuring.

Peter recalling the case, wrote in his epistle: "Casting all your care upon him, for he careth for you" (1 Pet 5:7).

38 Measure the degree of His weariness by the fact that the violence of the squall did not awaken Him, but the cries of His disciples aroused Him immediately. A mother may sleep through a thunderstorm, but the faintest whimper of her baby instantly awakens her from rest. This is the only record in the gospel of the Servant sleeping, yet He interrupted it in the service of others (Matt 8:24; Luke 8:24).

2. *The Power of the Servant Over Demons (5:1-20)*

This miracle manifested the power of the Servant over the spirit world, in casting out a host of demons. It is the most circumstantial of all the miracles in Mark's Gospel.

v.1 "And they came over unto the other side of the sea, into the country of the Gadarenes.
v.2 And when he was come out of the ship, immediately there met him out of the tombs a man with an unclean spirit,
v.3 Who had *his* dwelling among the tombs; and no man could bind him, no, not with chains:
v.4 Because that he had been often bound with fetters and chains, and the chains had been plucked asunder by him, and the fetters broken in pieces: neither could any *man* tame him.
v.5 And always, night and day, he was in the mountains, and in the tombs, crying, and cutting himself with stones.
v.6 But when he saw Jesus afar off, he ran and worshipped him,
v.7 And cried with a loud voice, and said, What have I to do with thee, Jesus, *thou* Son of the most high God? I adjure thee by God, that thou torment me not.
v.8 For he said unto him, Come out of the man, *thou* unclean spirit.
v.9 And he asked him, What *is* thy name? And he answered, saying, My name *is* Legion: for we are many.
v.10 And he besought him much that he would not send them away out of the country.
v.11 Now there was there nigh unto the mountains a great herd of swine feeding.
v.12 And all the devils besought him, saying, Send us into the swine, that we may enter into them.
v.13 And forthwith Jesus gave them leave. And the unclean spirits went out, and entered into the swine: and the herd ran violently down a steep place into the sea, (they were about two thousand;) and were choked in the sea.
v.14 And they that fed the swine fled, and told it in the city, and in the country. And they went out to see what it was that was done.
v.15 And they came to Jesus, and see him that was possessed with the devil, and had the legion, sitting, and clothed, and in his right mind: and they were afraid.
v.16 And they that saw *it* told them how it befell to him that was possessed with the devil, and *also* concerning the swine.
v.17 And they began to pray him to depart out of their coasts.
v.18 And when he was come into the ship, he that had been possessed with the devil prayed him that he might be with him.
v.19 Howbeit Jesus suffered him not, but saith unto him, Go home to thy friends, and tell them how great things the Lord hath done for thee, and hath had compassion on thee.
v.20 And he departed, and began to publish in Decapolis how great things Jesus had done for him: and all *men* did marvel."

1 His disciples and the Lord arrived together on the other side of the sea, but in the events to take place there, the disciples were silent observers of His power over a host of unclean spirits. The country of the Gadarenes should be Gerasenes, a locality midway along the eastern shore of the sea of Galilee. Most of its inhabitants were Gentiles (v.11).

2-5 When the Lord disembarked from the ship, immediately there met Him a man out of the tombs. Matthew mentions two men (Matt 8:28) while Luke and Mark speak of only one, likely the most degraded of the two. It was customary for tombs to be the haunts of the demented. This man was uncontrollable, for none could subdue him, not even with chains or fetters. His piercing cries day and night rang through the mountains, as he cut himself with sharp stones. He was under the complete domination of Satanic forces.

6-7 The man ran towards Jesus and did homage to him. The demon recognised Him, acknowledging Him to be the Son of the Most High God. The appeal of the demon was that he would not be tormented by being sent to his final punishment immediately (Matt 8:29; Luke 8:31). Demons not only know the Person of Jesus, who He is, but are aware of their ultimate destiny, which is in the hand of the Lord. They must have some understanding also of the divine programme of the Judgments.

8 The demon sought to parley with Jesus about his future, and did not come out of the man at the first command of Christ.

9 Jesus asked the demon's name. The demon answered through the man saying: "My name is Legion: for we are many". He was indwelt by a host of unclean spirits. Two other cases of multiple demon possession are recorded in the gospels. Mary Magdalene was indwelt by seven demons (Luke 8:2) and an unknown man with seven also (Luke 11:24-26). A legion was a division of the Roman army, having six thousand men at full strength. As the Romans had oppressed the land at this time, the name Legion was a symbol of power and oppression.

10 The spokesman for the other demons besought the Lord not to send them out of the country, to the abyss, before the time (Luke 8:31).

11-13 Swine were unclean to the Jewish people (Lev 11:7), but the farmers of this area, to make gain of the many Gentiles living in the ten cities of the region, raised swine for the meat markets of Decapolis. The demons desired to enter into the swine in a desperate attempt to evade being confined to a disembodied state until their final judgment. They acknowledged the absolute authority of Jesus. When Jesus granted permission, they left the man, and entered into the swine, causing the whole herd to stampede down the steep bank, and be drowned in the lake.

14-17 The herdsmen fled in fear and reported the event in the city and country, which caused many to investigate the incident. When they came to Jesus they saw the great contrast in the appearance and conduct of the former demoniac. He was sitting peacefully at the feet of the Lord instead of running madly among the tombs, clothed instead of naked, in his right mind instead of in frenzied insanity. He was no longer under the control of a legion of unclean spirits, but under the control of the Saviour. The sight filled the onlookers with awe. They also heard the strange happening which incurred the loss of the herd of swine. The result of the investigation was that they besought the Lord to depart out of their coasts. Their major concern was the loss to the economy in the death of the herd of swine rather than the deliverance of the man from the power of Satan. They unanimously begged Jesus to leave them, apparently fearing further losses.

18-20 In these verses we have another of those vignettes so familiar to the reader of Mark. The Lord turning His back upon a community walks slowly down to the ship; one of the community follows Him and desires to journey with Him. The Lord points to the cities without a witness and sends the former demoniac to proclaim the good news concerning Jesus the Christ. It is likely that the man had been estranged from his family for years, but immediately be returns to tell of the mercy of the Lord to him. He was a personal testimony in an area without a disciple. In his faithfulness he published in the ten cities the great things Jesus had done, causing all men to marvel.

Jesus did not place the injunction of silence upon this man as He had done with the cleansed leper (1:44), because, this man was a Gentile and his testimony was limited to the Gentile locality where Christ was not welcomed.

3. *The Power of the Servant Over Physical Disease* (5:21-34)

The account of the raising from the dead of Jairus' daughter is divided by the incident of the healing of the woman with the haemorrhage. Earlier in the Gospel a similar form of recording has been noted (3:22-30). This enclosing of one episode within another is one of the curious features of the narrative. This is the only case of two distinct healings being linked together, the one within the other. The same time scale measures the miracles. The girl had lived twelve years of continual happiness, while during the same period the woman had experienced continual suffering. The girl died after living for twelve years. The woman was a living *dead* person for the same twelve years. The restoration to fulness of life for the woman anticipated the resuscitation to fulness of life for the child.

v.21 "And when Jesus was passed over again by ship unto the other side, much people gathered unto him: and he was nigh unto the sea.
v.22 And, behold, there cometh one of the rulers of the synagogue, Jairus by name; and when he saw him, he fell at his feet,
v.23 And besought him greatly, saying, My little daughter lieth at the point of death: *I pray thee*, come and lay thy hands on her, that she may be healed; and she shall live.
v.24 And *Jesus* went with him; and much people followed him, and thronged him.
v.25 And a certain woman, which had an issue of blood twelve years,
v.26 And had suffered many things of many physicians, and had spent all that she had, and was nothing bettered, but rather grew worse,
v.27 When she had heard of Jesus, came in the press behind, and touched his garment.
v.28 For she said, If I may touch but his clothes, I shall be whole.
v.29 And straightway the fountain of her blood was dried up; and she felt in *her* body that she was healed of that plague.
v.30 And Jesus, immediately knowing in himself that virtue had gone out of him, turned him about in the press, and said, Who touched my clothes?
v.31 And his disciples said unto him, Thou seest the multitude thronging thee, and sayest thou, Who touched me?
v.32 And he looked round about to see her that had done this thing.
v.33 But the woman fearing and trembling, knowing what was done in her, came and fell down before him, and told him all the truth.
v.34 And he said unto her, Daughter, thy faith hath made thee whole; go in peace, and be whole of thy plague."

21-24 When the Lord arrived again on the west side of the sea, probably near Capernaum, great crowds again gathered to Him on the shore. Out of this vast company one man came and fell down at the feet of Jesus. He was Jairus by name, a ruler of the synagogue. He thus held a high office, as these rulers arranged the service of those who would read the appointed portions of Scripture every Sabbath day. He was held in high esteem among all the people. Jairus had one little daughter who was dying, as he came humbly seeking the Lord to lay His healing touch upon her that she might not die. Jairus had witnessed His power previously in the synagogue, and believed He had power to save the life of his daughter (1:21-28; 3:1-6). The tender-hearted Servant needed no further urging. He was always ready to answer the plea of the needy and the sorrowful (1:33-34). So he went along the highway to the ruler's house, with great crowds following them and pressing around him.

25-27 As they slowly made their way to Jairus' house, an interruption took place. An unnamed woman, who had an incurable disease, in all likelihood uterine haemorrhage, joined the multitude. Her serious condition had baffled many physicians. She had spent all her living upon various treatments, which had caused her to suffer more, and her case was now hopeless. The disease had also rendered her unclean by the law of Moses (Lev 15:25-27)

With faith in her heart she came behind Him, and touched His garment, saying to herself, "If I may touch but his clothes, I shall be whole".

29-34 Immediately she was healed of her plague, and she knew it in her body. The Lord also knew power had gone out of Him. A better rendering is: "power from Him, on account of who He was, had gone out to someone". Jesus desired to honour her faith and had extended His saving virtue to her in her great need. The Lord's question, "Who touched Me?" was asked to establish a relationship and personal contact with the woman. He was aware, of course, who it was that had exercised faith. The disciples seemed to consider His question unreasonable, as many were pressing around Him, touching His garment. Jesus, however, knew the vital difference between the touch of faith, and the touch of indifference. He looked around to see her that had touched the hem of His garment. The woman came forward in humble reverence, falling down in His presence, telling Him all the truth. Jesus addressed her in a unique manner calling her "daughter". This is the only time He ever used this form of address to any, thus revealing her new relationship in the family of God (3:33-35). He also said, "Thy faith had made thee whole; go in peace, and be whole of thy plague". The cure had been affected by her act of faith, and not the touch of His clothes. The words, "Thy faith hath made thee whole" mean also "Thy faith hath saved thee". "Go in peace" seems to indicate spiritual salvation, while "be healthy" her physical recovery.

4. *The Power of the Servant Over Death (5:35-43)*

v.35 "While he yet spake, there came from the ruler of the synagogue's *house certain* which said, Thy daughter is dead: why troublest thou the Master any further?
v.36 As soon as Jesus heard the word that was spoken, he saith unto the ruler of the synagogue, Be not afraid, only believe.
v.37 And he suffered no man to follow him, save Peter, and James, and John the brother of James.
v.38 And he cometh to the house of the ruler of the synagogue, and seeth the tumult, and them that wept and wailed greatly.
v.39 And when he was come in, he saith unto them, Why make ye this ado, and weep? the damsel is not dead, but sleepeth.
v.40 And they laughed him to scorn. But when he had put them all out, he taketh the father and the mother of the damsel, and them that were with him, and entereth in where the damsel was lying.
v.41 And he took the damsel by the hand, and said unto her, Talitha cumi; which is, being interpreted, Damsel, I say unto thee, arise.
v.42 And straightway the damsel arose, and walked; for she was *of the age* of twelve years. And they were astonished with a great astonishment.
v.43 And he charged them straitly that no man should know it; and commanded that something should be given her to eat."

35-36 The faith of Jairus was severely tried by the delay caused by the interruption of the woman. His daughter was at the point of death, and he feared they might not reach home in time. A message sent to him from the house confirmed those fears concerning his only child, for she had just died. The message advised him not to trouble the Lord further, as all hope was now gone, but to return with all haste alone. The gracious Servant encouraged Jairus by saying, "Be not afraid, only believe". Jairus took fresh courage and they continued together on their way to his house.

37 The Lord took three of His disciples, who composed the inner circle of the twelve: Peter, James and John. There were three special occasions on which the Lord took the same three apart from the rest, giving them the opportunity of learning wonderful lessons as they witnessed His grace as the Saviour, His glory as the Sovereign (9:2-3) and His grief as the Sufferer (14:33).

38 The tumult at the house of Jairus was occasioned by the hired professional mourners who wept and wailed, joined by the noise of the sorrowing neighbours.

39 The Lord rebuked the mourners, telling them that the child was not dead but asleep. The mourners laughed scornfully at His words. We have assurances from Luke's account that she was indeed dead for he adds that "her spirit came again" when the Lord raised her to life (Luke 8:55). The words "the damsel is not dead, but sleepeth" refer to the NT understanding of death to a believer as falling asleep, as far as the body is concerned. The awakening will follow when the Lord shall descend at the Rapture of the church to raise the dead in Christ and reunite them with those who may be alive and remain. Then the complete company will be forever with the Lord in glorified bodies (1 Cor 15:51-54; 1 Thess 4:13-18). The Lord only raised three persons from the dead during His earthly ministry. This child who had just died, the young man on his way to the place of burial (Luke 7:11-17) and the older man already in the grave four days (John 11:38-44). Each one was raised again by the mighty power of God. When the Lord comes again, some will have just died, others being carried to the place of burial, and many others already in the graves for centuries, but He will resurrect all who have died in faith.

40-41 The Lord excluded all the mourners from the house, and, taking only the father and mother of the child and His three disciples, He entered into the room where the girl lay. Then in the hushed and silent atmosphere of reverence, He took the maid's hand, and spake in the Aramaic, "Talitha cumi". The words literally mean "Little lamb, I say unto thee arise". The Great Shepherd called her back into a world of sorrow, but it had temporary joy for her parents. The words "Talitha cumi" were so impressive that Mark retains His actual words in calling the girl back to life. He implies by this that there was a quality in their tones that could not be fully translated. Aramaic, a Semitic language related to Hebrew, was the mother-tongue of the Galileans and the usual language of Jesus.

42 At the command of the Lord, the child arose and walked, for she was twelve years old. The five onlookers were astonished.

43 The Lord gave two important commands to them as they watched her walking about the room: firstly that no one should know it, and also that she should be given some food. Both these manifest the thoughtfulness and consideration of the Servant. He desired the parents and the child to enjoy a brief time of privacy, ere the facts would be widespread, and crowds of curious neighbours would surround the door of their home. In their excitement they could easily overlook the needs of the child for sustenance. She likely had not eaten for days before her death, and although raised up in perfect health, she was still in a body subject to weakness and therefore required food. The resurrected bodies of believers will require no material sustenance, in contrast to this case of a resuscitation (1 Cor 15:51-57).

Notes

23-41 Jairus desired the Lord to lay His hand upon his child. This is what he did when He entered into the room where the maid lay: "He took the damsel by the hand". This is one of the outstanding features of the Servant's ministry. He used His hand in touching people when He healed them. He took Peter's wife's mother by the hand and raised her up. He stretched forth His hand and touched the leper (1:31,41). He tenderly received little children that were brought to Him taking them up in His arms, blessing them, laying His hands upon them (9:36; 10:16). The hand which was nailed to the tree was a hand of infinite tenderness, and is still the hand of sympathy. Servants of Christ must have a hand of tender compassion.

On another occasion we read "Jesus took him by the hand, and lifted him up" (9:27). How blessed for every believer to know that he is safely held in that same blessed hand (John 10:28).

The Scriptures present the Lord in incarnation as possessing two perfect natures coexisting in His one glorious Person. These two natures must never be separated or divided. The usage of statements saying that "as Man" He did certain things and "as God" other things, should be avoided. It was One who was both God and man who did these things. Human logic cannot be applied in the "things concerning Himself". Neither should the Lord be spoken of as "the God-Man" for this makes the word God an adjective. In speaking of the blessed Lord Jesus it is safe ground to adhere to what is written in the Word of God. This great truth is known as the Hypostatic Union, that is, the union of two perfect natures in one Person. Deity and humanity in equal relationship are found alone in the eternal Son of God, the perfect Servant of Jehovah. This wondrous foundation of Christian Faith often appears in the same context. In this chapter there are clear examples of this truth recorded by Mark.

The Servant who fed five thousand men with five loaves and two fishes, who walked upon the angry waves of the stormy sea, and who healed all who touched the hem of His garment, also marvelled at unbelief, required retirement, and in dependence prayed upon the mountainside. He who was the Carpenter of Nazareth was at the same time the Creator of all things.

This sixth chapter contains six further manifestations of the perfect Servant's wonderful power.

1.	The Servant rejected at Nazareth.	Power restrained	6:1-6
2.	The Twelve sent forth to preach.	Power reproduced	6:7-13
3.	The Beheading of John the Baptist.	Power reported	6:14-29
4.	The Feeding of the Five Thousand.	Power revealed	6:30-44
5.	Jesus walking on the water.	Power realised	6:45-52
6.	Healing the sick at Gennesaret.	Power recognised	6:53-56

5. *The Power of the Servant Restrained* (6:1-6)

v.1 "And he went out from thence, and came into his own country; and his disciples follow him.
v.2 And when the sabbath day was come, he began to teach in the synagogue: and many hearing *him* were astonished, saying, From whence hath this *man* these things? and what wisdom *is* this which is given unto him, that even such mighty works are wrought by his hands?
v.3 Is not this the carpenter, the son of Mary, the brother of James, and Joses, and Juda, and Simon? and are not his sisters here with us? And they were offended at him.
v.4 But Jesus said unto them, A prophet is not without honour, but in his own country, and among his own kin, and in his own house.
v.5 And he could there do no mighty work, save that he laid his hands upon a few sick folk, and healed *them.*
v.6 And he marvelled because of their unbelief. And he went round about the villages, teaching."

1 The Lord went out from Capernaum and walked the twenty miles to His own country which was Nazareth. This is the second recorded visit of the Lord to His home town, and it was evidently His last. On the previous occasion He preached, and afterwards they sought to cast Him over the brow of the hill upon which the city was built (Luke 4:16-30).

2 There seems to have been no such outward display of enmity on this visit, but there was severe criticism and disapproval from the crowds who heard Him teaching in their synagogue. They questioned in a scornful manner the source of His wisdom. They could not reconcile the fact that the village carpenter could be a prophet of God.

3 The question, "Is not this the carpenter, the son of Mary?" is peculiar to this Gospel. It verifies the earthly secular calling of the Lord. What grace that the great Creator should wear the garb of a village carpenter! The remark that He was the son of Mary was a slur against His mother. It was their suggestion that He was illegitimate (John 8:41).

As no mention of Joseph appears it is implied that he was dead. All the five sons of Mary reveal by their names the godliness of Joseph and Mary in the giving of Bible names. Four of the Lord's brothers (they had the same mother, but unlike Jesus, who had no earthly father, Joseph was their father) are named: James, Joses, Judah, and Simon. The record is silent as to the last two, also the two sisters who still resided in Nazareth. James was an unbeliever until after the Lord's resurrection when the Lord appeared to him. He became prominent in the Jerusalem church and it is generally accepted that he authored the epistle that bears the name of James (John 7:5; 1 Cor 15:7; Acts 15:13-31; James 1:1). Judah was the Jude who became the author of the Epistle of Jude (Jude 1).

The people of Nazareth, being unable to understand that One with such a humble background could be the Messiah were offended at Him. They were repelled and scandalised at the idea of Jesus the carpenter claiming to be God's anointed.

4 The answer of Jesus to them was the quotation of a proverb which He used on three separate occasions: "A prophet is not without honour, but in his own country, and among his own kin, and in his own house" (Luke 4:24; John 4:44). Today we use the similar saying "Familiarity breeds contempt". In the statement He asserts His claim to be a prophet. Like many of the prophets of the OT, whose ministry was refused by those who knew them best, He was rejected in the village where he had lived for thirty years.

5-6 The solemn words, "He could there do no mighty work", shows the restraining of His power on account of their unbelief. There was no limitation on His part, but repentance and faith were missing on theirs. Only a few sick folk had faith to come to Him for healing. He marvelled at their unbelief. The Lord only marvelled on one other occasion, in every way a contrast to the result of His visit to His home town. He marvelled when He saw the faith of a Roman centurion, and called it great, for it was the faith He desired in Israel (Matt 8:10). Unbelief is still found in those most likely to have faith, while faith is evidenced in those whose opportunities have been limited.

The Lord left Nazareth. Their attitude had robbed them of the further ministry of the divine Servant. He moved to other villages, teaching, where His presence was welcomed. Nazareth in its blindness represents the blindness of the nation of Israel today (Rom 11:7-10).

6. *The Power of the Servant Reproduced* (6:7-13)

v.7 "And he called *unto him* the twelve, and began to send them forth by two and two; and gave them power over unclean spirits;

v.8 And commanded them that they should take nothing for *their* journey, save a staff only; no scrip, no bread, no money in *their* purse:
v.9 But *be* shod with sandals; and not put on two coats.
v.10 And he said unto them, In what place soever ye enter into an house, there abide till ye depart from that place.
v.11 And whosoever shall not receive you, nor hear you, when ye depart thence, shake off the dust under your feet for a testimony against them. Verily I say unto you, It shall be more tolerable for Sodom and Gomorrha in the day of judgment, than for that city.
v.12 And they went out, and preached that men should repent.
v.13 And they cast out many devils, and anointed with oil many that were sick, and healed *them*."

7 The Lord had appointed the twelve to be with Him, for instruction and training, that He might eventually send them forth to preach, and have power to heal the sick, and to cast out demons (3:13-15). This period had now ended and the time of their going forth on their mission had arrived. They were sent out by two and two, which fact is alone noted by Mark. There are great advantages to co-operation and companionship.

Solomon had emphasised the value of this fellowship in a remarkable proverb: "Two are better than one" (Ecc 4:9). If they fall, one will lift up his fellow, if two lie together there will be warmth, and if one prevail against one, the two can overcome. Therefore the great benefits of two together. There is assistance, comfort, and defence. Solomon also stated that three would even provide greater reward and victory: "A threefold cord is not quickly broken" (Ecc 4:9-12). The greater than Solomon, the Son of God, sent forth the Twelve in pairs, but He Himself, working with them, would provide the threefold cord of fellowship (16:20).

As they went forth He gave them power over unclean spirits. The word *exousia* is authority. They were given authority to exorcise demons. His power would be reproduced in them (1:26). These men were His representatives, being sent forth by Him on a special mission, and to return to Him with an account of their labours.

8-11 The unusual instructions given by the Lord were unique for this mission alone, and not for any future occasion.

Because of the urgency and shortness of their journey, they were to travel with minimum burden. Each disciple was allowed one staff, but no scrip for carrying provisions, no bread, no money in their purse, nor extra tunic.

The confidence and trust of the Twelve was to be in God, who would provide food and shelter through the warm hospitality which marked the Jewish households. They must be careful that their first abode would be the base of their service in any community, and not to seek more attractive lodgings. By this procedure there was an avoidance of offence to a household by leaving for better surroundings.

They could expect some places to refuse their message and presence. If such circumstances arose He gave them their plan of procedure. They were to leave that place, and shake the dust off from under their feet. This was for a public testimony against them. The shaking off the dust was a symbol of dissociation. The rejectors would then be responsible to God for their treatment of the message of the gospel, and the faithful servants who had visited them. Paul and Barnabas shook the dust from their feet later, when the citizens of Antioch in Pisidia had rejected the gospel of the grace of God (Acts 13:51).

12-13 The Twelve preached repentance, cast out demons and anointed the sick with oil, healing many. The same message and power seen in the perfect Servant's ministry, was reproduced in the servants (1:14-15, 32-34; 3:10). The "anointing with oil" is noted only by Mark in the gospels, but James mentions it in his epistle (James 5:14). Olive oil was used in the east because of its medicinal value (Luke 10:34; Ps 23:5). On this occasion it may also have been a symbol of the authority of the One they represented. The healing of the sick was by His power and none of their own.

7. *The Power of the Servant Reported* (6:14-29)

The sordid story is recorded in three parts:

a.	Herod's Explanation of the Identity of Jesus	vv.14-16
b.	The details of John's Execution	vv.17-28
c.	The burial of John's Decapitated Corpse	v.29

a. *Herod's Explanation of the Identity of Jesus (vv.14-16)*

v.14 And king Herod heard of *him*; (for his name was spread abroad:) and he said, That John the Baptist was risen from the dead, and therefore mighty works do shew forth themselves in him.
v.15 Others said, That it is Elias. And others said, That it is a prophet, or as one of the prophets.
v.16 But when Herod heard *thereof*, he said, It is John, whom I beheaded: he is risen from the dead."

14 The report of the Servant's ministry and miracles caused the guilty conscience of Herod to be awakened. He is called Herod the king by Mark, but actually he was only the tetrarch of Galilee and Perea, which was a fourth part of the Roman province (Matt 14:1; Luke 9:7).

15-16 Various views were current in the land as to the identity of Christ. Some said that He was Elijah, or one of the prophets. Herod, however, insisted that it was John the Baptist, whom he had beheaded, risen from the dead. This was a remarkable confession of one who was a Sadducee for they said that there was no resurrection and denied the existence of angel or spirit (Acts 23:8).

The statement revealed the fact that while he had silenced the preacher, he was unable to silence the voice of conscience.

b. *The Details of John's Execution (vv.17-28)*

v.17 "For Herod himself had sent forth and laid hold upon John, and bound him in prison for Herodias' sake, his brother Philip's wife: for he had married her.
v.18 For John had said unto Herod, It is not lawful for thee to have thy brother's wife.
v.19 Therefore Herodias had a quarrel against him, and would have killed him; but she could not:
v.20 For Herod feared John, knowing that he was a just man and an holy, and observed him; and when he heard him, he did many things, and heard him gladly.
v.21 And when a convenient day was come, that Herod on his birthday made a supper to his lords, high captains, and chief *estates* of Galilee;
v.22 And when the daughter of the said Herodias came in, and danced, and pleased Herod and them that sat with him, the king said unto the damsel, Ask of me whatsoever thou wilt, and I will give *it* thee.
v.23 And he sware unto her, Whatsoever thou shalt ask of me, I will give it thee, unto the half of my kingdom.
v.24 And she went forth, and said unto her mother, What shall I ask? And she said, The head of John the Baptist.
v.25 And she came in straightway with haste unto the king, and asked, saying, I will that thou give me by and by in a charger the head of John the Baptist.
v.26 And the king was exceeding sorry; yet for his oath's sake, and for their sakes which sat with him, he would not reject her.
v.27 And immediately the king sent an executioner, and commanded his head to be brought: and he went and beheaded him in the prison,
v.28 And brought his head in a charger, and gave it to the damsel: and the damsel gave it to her mother."

This section is a flashback to the brief detail in the first chapter: "Now after that John was put in prison, Jesus came into Galilee preaching the gospel of the kingdom of God" (1:14). It is also an explanation of the previous verses (6:14-16).

17-18 Herod was living with the wife of his half brother. Herodias had deserted her former husband Philip to live with Herod, contrary to the law of God. John the Baptist, being a faithful servant of God, rebuked Herod saying: "It is not lawful for thee to have thy brother's wife". The force of this expression is "that John kept on repeating the charge". It was no isolated rebuke.

19-20 Herodias was enraged by John's interference, and bore him a continual grudge, seeking to have him killed but was continually thwarted in her purpose, because Herod, fearing John and knowing that he was a just man and holy, protected him from the murderous intentions of Herodias. He therefore kept him bound in prison, where he was out of the reach of this evil woman. Meanwhile Herod visited John in the prison and in spite of his own sinful behaviour gladly listened to John's ministry, although it left him greatly puzzled. The words "greatly puzzled" from *polla ēporei* seem to have better manuscript support than the words "he did many things". Herod was unable to comprehend the attraction he had for John's preaching which was a rebuke to his immoral manner of life.

Herod and Herodias bear a remarkable likeness to Ahab and Jezebel in the OT (1 Kings 21). Both Herod and Ahab had evil wives, and were themselves vacillating in character. Concerning Jezebel it is said that she "stirred up" her husband to do wickedly". As a result Ahab sold himself to work wickedness in the sight of the Lord. The parallel is evident between these two guilty pairs. Jezebel schemed the death of Naboth, as Herodias did the assassination of John. Both women finally gained their evil objectives.

21-28 The detail of the martyrdom of John also parallels the teaching of Christ in the following chapter: "For from within, out of the heart of men, proceed evil thoughts, adulteries, fornications, murders, Thefts, covetousness, wickedness, deceit, lasciviousness, an evil eye, blasphemy, pride, foolishness" (7:21, 22). These thirteen evils (the number thirteen is the number which indicates the fulness of rebellion, Gen 14:4) were fully developed in Herod, Herodias, and Salome.

Herod, on his birthday, held a great supper to which the notables of his realm were invited. Salome, who was the daughter of Herodias by a former marriage, danced in a sensual manner to entertain the company. Herod was so pleased with the exhibition that he made a foolish promise to the damsel, confirming it by an oath, to give her whatever reward she desired, even to the half of his kingdom. Salome evidently wanted something for herself, but upon asking her mother's advice, Herodias grasped the opportunity to remove John, and instructed the damsel to ask for his head. Salome hurried back into the presence of the king with her demand for the head of John the Baptist immediately in a great dish. The dilemma of the king, caught in the trap, makes sordid reading. He respected and feared John, yet for his oath's sake, and to save face in the company of the grandees of his realm, he would not reject the damsel. The executioner was immediately sent to carry out the beheading of John in the prison. The gruesome platter with the head of the faithful servant was carried to the damsel, who immediately brought it to her mother. The voice of John had been silenced, but his message could never be overthrown.

c. *The Burial of the Decapitated Body (v.29)*

v.29 "And when his disciples heard *of it*, they came and took up his corpse, and laid it in a tomb."

29 The disciples of John took the corpse of their faithful leader and laid it in a tomb, to wait the resurrection of the just, when the body will be raised in honour and completely glorified (1 Cor 15:42,43). The words added by Matthew tell that they came into the presence of Jesus following the burial, expressing their grief over what had taken place (Matt 14:12). Herod, having rejected John, later sought to kill the perfect Servant (Luke 13:31). His apostasy was complete, and his doom sealed. In the final meeting with Jesus, Herod interrogated Him with many words, but the Lord remained silent. There was no further message.

The sad episode of John's martyrdom was inserted by Mark in this section of his Gospel to explain why Jesus left Galilee to minister elsewhere.

8. *The Power of the Servant Revealed (6:30-44)*

a. *The Return of the Twelve (vv.30-32)*

v.30 "And the apostles gathered themselves together unto Jesus, and told him all things, both what they had done, and what they had taught.
v.31 And he said unto them, Come ye yourselves apart into a desert place, and rest a while: for there were many coming and going, and they had no leisure so much as to eat.
v.32 And they departed into a desert place by ship privately."

30 The unique feature of Mark's arrangement enclosing one happening within another is seen again in the placing of John's martyrdom between the sending forth of the Twelve and their return from their mission. This is the first and only occasion the Twelve are named apostles in this Gospel, although they are called "the Twelve" ten times. The Greek word *apostolos* means one who has been sent on a mission. Having completed their mission they now gather to report their activities and teaching to the Lord.

31 The greater than Solomon, who initiated their going forth by two and two for comfort and companionship (Eccl 4:9-12), took care of His wearied servants as Solomon did, as he "sent them ... ten thousand a month by courses, a month they were in Lebanon, and two months at home" (1 Kings 5:14). Following their strenuous labours the Lord said to them: "Come ye yourselves apart into a desert place, and rest a while". They were so busy with the many who gathered around the Lord, that as on a former occasion there was not leisure time to partake of a meal (3:20).

32 Hence they left privately by ship to seek quiet and rest in some lonely place such as was found on the eastern side of the lake.

b. *The Feeding of the Five Thousand (vv.33-44)*

v.33 "And the people saw them departing, and many knew him, and ran afoot thither out of all cities, and outwent them, and came together unto him.

v.34 And Jesus, when he came out, saw much people, and was moved with compassion toward them, because they were as sheep not having a shepherd: and he began to teach them many things.
v.35 And when the day was now far spent, his disciples came unto him, and said, This is a desert place, and now the time *is* far passed:
v.36 Send them away, that they may go into the country round about, and into the villages, and buy themselves bread: for they have nothing to eat.
v.37 He answered and said unto them, Give ye them to eat. And they say unto him, Shall we go and buy two hundred pennyworth of bread, and give them to eat?
v.38 He saith unto them, How many loaves have ye? go and see. And when they knew, they say, Five, and two fishes.
v.39 And he commanded them to make all sit down by companies upon the green grass.
v.40 And they sat down in ranks, by hundreds, and by fifties.
v.41 And when he had taken the five loaves and the two fishes, he looked up to heaven, and blessed, and brake the loaves, and gave *them* to his disciples to set before them; and the two fishes divided he among them all.
v.42 And they did all eat, and were filled.
v.43 And they took up twelve baskets full of the fragments, and of the fishes.
v.44 And they that did eat of the loaves were about five thousand men."

This remarkable miracle is the only one recorded in all the four Gospels. Therefore it is of great importance, showing that the Servant of Jehovah has unlimited supplies for the need of mankind.

33 The Servant and His men crossed the sea of Galilee in the ship to avoid the pressing throngs. The Lord made several withdrawals from Galilee to minister elsewhere (6:31; 7:24, 31; 8:22). On those occasions He taught the Twelve how interested He is in the needs of His people and of men in general. The people saw the Lord and His disciples as they cast off from the shore, and followed them around the sea on foot. As they went they were joined by many others from all the cities, and were in the desert place before the arrival of the ship.

34 When the Lord saw the great multitude waiting for Him on the shore, He was moved with deep compassion towards them, for He saw them as sheep not having a shepherd, lost and wandering, helpless and without protection. He availed Himself of the opportunity to teach them concerning the kingdom of God, until the day was drawing to a close. Such service of the Lord was prompted by love. Mark is the only one of the four evangelists that brings this lovely feature into this scene. Without compassionate love service is barren.

35-36 As the day was ending, the disciples became anxious, and came to the Lord to remind Him that the people had nothing to eat, and being a desert place no nearby markets were available. They advised sending them away to the villages to buy bread.

37 The reply of Christ presented them with a dilemma when He said, "Give ye them to eat". The project seemed impossible to them, as two hundred pennyworth of bread would not even be sufficient to feed such a throng. The Roman penny (denarius) was a day's wages of a man in Palestine.

38 The Lord sent them to find out what provision was available. They returned to Him with only five loaves and two fishes. What would they be among so many?

39-40 On that spring evening in Palestine (the grass is green only in springtime) the Lord gave instructions for the crowd to be seated upon the green grass of the hillside, in companies of hundreds and fifties. David's words seem in keeping with the scene: "The Lord is my shepherd…He maketh me to lie down in green pastures" (Ps 23:1-2). Mark is the only writer who adds these picturesque details. The service of the Servant was conducted in an orderly manner. This fact is mentioned in several statements found only in Mark. Two of these are in this chapter: "He called unto him the twelve, and began to send them forth by two and two" (v.7). In these verses "he commanded them all to sit down by companies upon the green grass. And they sat down in ranks, by hundreds and by fifties". The attention to detail is instructive. God is never the author of confusion, as the example of Christ here plainly shows. Service for God calls for careful and prayerful attention. The arranging of the crowd in this manner provided for their comfort, reclining upon the soft green grass, and also allowed the food to be distributed with ease.

The vivid description of Mark indicates an eye-witness account, which in all probability he received from Peter. The original word for "ranks" is *prasiai* which literally means flower beds. The people, in their colourful dress, reclining upon the green grass, in the light of the declining sun, on the hillside overlooking the still waters of the lake, appeared as beautiful as flower beds.

41 The anxious disciples, and the waiting company now seated with expectancy, presented a challenge to faith. The Host of the great multitude took the loaves and the two fishes into His hands, looked up to His Father in Heaven and blessed God who had given the food which was about to be multiplied to feed the great crowd. The loaves were then broken into pieces and the fishes divided into portions. He then gave them to the disciples to set before the people. The imperfect tense of the verb "gave" denotes that He "kept on giving" more and more pieces of bread and fish, which were ever present in His hands.

42-44 All were finally supplied and fully satisfied. Twelve small baskets were used to gather the fragments of that which was left, probably one for each of the twelve. About five thousand men had been fed, as well as many women and children. It is noteworthy that the men who partook of His bounty were counted.

Notes

a. The Lord provided the supply, but it was the responsibility of the disciples to distribute the food.
b. Those who minister to the needs of others must fill their hands from the hands of Christ. He alone is the Source of supply.

9. *The Power of the Servant Realised* (6:45-52)

v.45 "And straightway he constrained his disciples to get into the ship, and to go to the other side before unto Bethsaida, while he sent away the people.
v.46 And when he had sent them away, he departed into a mountain to pray.
v.47 And when even was come, the ship was in the midst of the sea, and he alone on the land.
v.48 And he saw them toiling in rowing; for the wind was contrary unto them: and about the fourth watch of the night he cometh unto them, walking upon the sea, and would have passed by them.
v.49 But when they saw him walking upon the sea, they supposed it had been a spirit, and cried out:
v.50 For they all saw him, and were troubled. And immediately he talked with them, and saith unto them, Be of good cheer: it is I; be not afraid.
v.52 And he went up unto them into the ship; and the wind ceased: and they were sore amazed in themselves beyond measure, and wondered.
v.52 For they considered not *the miracle* of the loaves: for their heart was hardened."

This miracle reveals the absolute omnipotence of the Servant: He is the Son of God, for only God can tread upon the waves of the sea (Job 9:8). The aftermath of the miracle shows that as yet the Twelve were not fully convinced of the absolute glory of His Person.

45-46 When the five thousand had been fed the Lord immediately constrained the disciples to embark in the ship, and go before Him to the other side of the lake to Bethsaida, which seems to have been the fishing harbour of Capernaum (John 6:17). This urgent action of Christ seems, at first, difficult to explain. The parallel reading of John's account throws light on the reason. It lay in the fact that the people were so attracted to Him on account of the miracle of feeding so many with so little, that they were desirous to take Him immediately and crown Him as their King. Such an action would have interfered with the divine prophetic programme for Christ, and would have been premature. The ultimate purpose of the Servant was "to give his life a ransom for many" (10:45). The Lord, therefore, intervened to prevent the intention of the crowd, and hastened His disciples away lest they should support the possibility of His present coronation (John 6:15).

Having dismissed the disciples and the multitude, He departed to the loneliness of the mountain side to pray. The ministry of the Servant was preceded and concluded by prayer. Mark is the only one who records His prayer at the commencement of a day of untiring service: "And in the morning, rising up a great while before day, he went out and departed into a solitary place, and there prayed" (1:35). This statement, placed in the first chapter, discloses the secret of the uniqueness and perfectness of His service. Here after a tiring day of ministry, He again seeks the solitary place upon the hillside to continue with His Father. In this He is the example to all His servants.

47-48 By evening the ship was well out into the midst of the sea, while the Saviour was alone on the land. On the previous occasion of the storm He was with them in the ship, but here He had gone up to pray in the mountain (4:35-41). In the days of His flesh He was with them, but the time was coming when He would leave them to return to the Father (John 16:16). He was teaching them great principles of faith. One of the great themes of Mark is the preparatory ministry given by the Servant, so that they might be ready to carry on His interests following His ascension.

It may have appeared to them that He had forgotten them, but His eye saw them in their distress and perplexity upon the sea, where they had encountered a contrary wind, hindering their progress. In the fourth watch, between three and six o'clock Roman time, He went out to them, walking on the surface of the troubled waters.

The words; "He ... would have passed by them" have been interpreted in various ways. Some suggest He was teaching them that He could cross the sea without their aid; others that He desired them to invite Him into the ship. The expression "He ... would have passed by them" may be read "He would have passed alongside them". The idea then is that He would draw so near the ship that they would be reassured that it was Himself. This is preferable. He would not bypass His disciples in their need.

49-50 Before He could reach the ship to identify Himself, they saw Him walking on the water, and they cried out in terror supposing Him to be a spirit. The word used for "spirit" (*phantasma*) literally means a water phantom. The words of Jesus were encouraging: "Be of good cheer". The Lord Jesus used this form of greeting on six recorded occasions in the NT: Matt 9:2,22; 14:27; Mark 6:50; John 16:33; Acts 23:11. He also added "It is I". The Greek words *ego eimi* mean "I am". They identify Jesus Himself, but also are a cast back to God identifying Himself to Moses as "I AM THAT I AM" (Exod 3:14). Jehovah of the OT is Jesus of the NT. He also added: "Be not afraid" which recalls the promise of God to His people of old in their distress: "Fear not: for I have redeemed thee...When thou passest through the waters, I will be with thee" (Isa 43:1-2). Matthew records the walk of Peter on the water to meet the Lord at this point (Matt 14:28-32).

51 As the Lord went up into the ship, the wind ceased; evidently another miracle took place showing the infinite power of the Servant. The storm being ended they were soon moored on the shore near Capernaum.

52 The disciples were sore amazed beyond measure, which expression is used by Mark on two previous occasions. Following the healing of the sick of the palsy, and the raising of Jairus' daughter, the onlookers were amazed, which literally means out of their minds (2:12; 5:42). Mark is the only writer who states the reason for the disciples' attitude: "they considered not the miracle of the loaves: for their heart was hardened". The miracle of the loaves was a powerful display of the real identity of Jesus; He was the omnipotent Son of God, the Creator of all things. The lack of consideration of the miracle is ascribed to their spiritual dullness. They failed to recognise His true identity in the desert place, as He multiplied the loaves and fishes, hence they did not recognise Him when He walked across the surface of the sea.

Notes

The actions of the Lord in the afternoon (v.41), in the evening (v.45) and in the morning (v.51) suggests three great foundations of Christian faith:
a. His sacrificial death typified in the breaking of the bread (John 6:51),
b. His sympathetic priesthood pictured as He ascended into the mountain to pray (Heb 9:24).
c. His sovereign advent pre-figured in His descent to the troubled sea to deliver His own. Dispensationally the incident figures the coming of Christ as Israel's King to deliver them in their darkest hour (13:26–27).
Three great truths to live by:
Live as though the Saviour died yesterday; ascended as the shepherd today; and is returning as the Sovereign tomorrow (From the oral ministry of Hawthorn Baillie).

10. *The Power of the Servant Recognised* (6:53-56)

v.53 "And when they had passed over, they came into the land of Gennesaret, and drew to the shore.
v.54 And when they were come out of the ship, straightway they knew him,
v.55 And ran through that whole region round about, and began to carry about in beds those that were sick, where they heard he was.
v.56 And whithersoever he entered, into villages, or cities, or country, they laid the sick in the streets, and besought him that they might touch if it were but the border of his garment: and as many as touched him were made whole".

The ship arrived at Capernaum where Jesus gave His discourse on the subject of the Bread of life, therefore between v.53a and v.53b, the whole of the section recorded in John 6:22-71 must be inserted.

53-54 Later the Lord and His disciples went southward along the shoreline from Capernaum to the land of Gennesaret, which was a short journey by ship.

It was a beautiful fertile plain stretching four miles along the coastline and two miles inland. The Jews called it "Paradise". When they arrived on the beach the people immediately recognised Him.

55 The whole community was aroused by the visit of the Servant. In every place that He ministered, whether in the city, village or countryside, crowds of sick were carried on pallets and laid at His feet in the streets and marketplaces. The great multitudes of diseased folk in this area were ascribed to the many medicinal mineral springs, which attracted the invalids.

56 The needy kept on asking again and again if they could touch the fringe of blue of His garment (Num 15:37-41). The words "as many as touched him were made whole" do not imply that there was any virtue in the hem of blue. The touch was the expression of their faith, but the healing was brought about by the power of Jehovah's perfect Servant, not by His garment.

11. *The Power of the Servant In His Teaching* (7:1-23)

This section has two main parts.

a. The Tradition of the Pharisees concerning Ceremonial Defilement (1-13).
b. The Teaching of the Servant concerning Moral Defilement (14-23).

a. The Tradition of the Pharisees concerning Ceremonial Defilement (vv.1-13)

The Galilean ministry of the Lord had been attended by great popularity with the multitudes. There was also a striking contrast of great opposition from the Pharisees and the scribes. They had shown their enmity at the commencement of His ministry and now at the conclusion of His service in Galilee their animosity was more virulent (2:6, 7, 23-28; 3:1-6, 22).

v.1 "Then came together unto him the Pharisees, and certain of the scribes, which came from Jerusalem.
v.2 And when they saw some of his disciples eat bread with defiled, that is to say, with unwashen, hands, they found fault.
v.3 For the Pharisees, and all the Jews, except they wash *their* hands oft, eat not, holding the tradition of the elders.
v.4 And *when they come* from the market, except they wash, they eat not. And many other things there be, which they have received to hold, as the washing of cups, and pots, brasen vessels, and of tables.
v.5 Then the Pharisees and scribes asked him, Why walk not thy disciples according to the tradition of the elders, but eat bread with unwashen hands?
v.6 He answered and said unto them, Well hath Esaias prophesied of you hypocrites, as it is written, This people honoureth me with *their* lips, but their heart is far from me.

v.7 Howbeit in vain do they worship me, teaching *for* doctrines the commandments of men.
v.8 For laying aside the commandment of God, ye hold the tradition of men, *as* the washing of pots and cups: and many other such like things ye do.
v.9 And he said unto them, Full well ye reject the commandment of God, that ye may keep your own tradition.
v.10 For Moses said, Honour thy father and thy mother; and, Whoso curseth father or mother, let him die the death:
v.11 But ye say, If a man shall say to his father or mother, *It is* Corban, that is to say, a gift, by whatsoever thou mightest be profited by me; *he shall be free.*
v.12 And ye suffer him no more to do ought for his father or his mother;
v.13 Making the word of God of none effect through your tradition, which ye have delivered: and many such like things do ye."

1-2 These Pharisees and scribes which had journeyed from Jerusalem to investigate Jesus, came to Him with a complaint against His disciples. They had observed some of them eating food with unclean hands. This does not mean that the disciples ate their food with hands physically unwashed but rather that they had neglected the ceremonial washings required by the tradition of the law teachers. The interpretation of the law by the Rabbinical schools was more important to the Pharisees than the Word of God itself.

3-4 These verses form a parenthesis. Mark explains the various customs of the Jews, in their ceremonial washings of hands, cups, pots, vessels and tables, for the benefit of his Gentile readers who were unfamiliar with Jewish ritual cleansings. For any Jew to disregard these traditions was a serious sin: to observe them was, in their view, honouring to God.

5 The charge against the disciples was brought to the Lord, as their guide and teacher. They asked Him: "Why walk not thy disciples according to the tradition of the elders, but eat bread with unwashed hands?".

6-9 The reply, of the Lord carried a stern rebuke. He quoted and applied one of the solemn prophecies of Isaiah: "This people honoureth me with their lips, but their heart is far from me" (Isa 29:13). The hypocrisy that marked the men of Isaiah's times was repeated in these Pharisees and scribes, and the Lord called them hypocrites. This is the only time that Mark uses the word hypocrites. The very essence is shown to be an outward profession with the lip of great devotion to God, and yet the heart to be without worship or true holiness of thought. Like the people in Isaiah's day, they also had replaced the truth of God's Word with the tradition of men.

10-13 They had laid aside God's commandments to keep their own tradition. To support this charge He gave them an illustration of their hypocrisy. The commandment of God stated that a man was to honour his father and mother by providing for their need in old age or sickness. One of the traditions of the elders to bypass this responsibility was the introduction of the vow of "Corban". A man could pronounce over the amount to support his father or his mother "Corban", which means a gift specially devoted to God by unchanging vow. This caused the amount to be exempt from usage in the care of a man's parents, as commanded by the law. The man was not under pressure to give the Corban to the temple; he could use it for himself. In this way it was possible to allow parents to suffer need and the son yet possess wealth. The plain commandment could be broken, but the tradition of the elders provided an outward observance to excuse the guilt. The Lord pressed the exposure of the hypocrisy of the religious leaders, stating that they were making the Word of God of none effect. They nullified its truth by their tradition. This Corban vow was only one of their many distortions of Scripture.

b. *The Teaching of the Servant concerning Moral Defilement (vv.14-23)*

v.14 "And when he had called all the people *unto him*, he said unto them, Hearken unto me every one *of you*, and understand:
v.15 There is nothing from without a man, that entering into him can defile him: but the things which come out of him, those are they that defile the man.
v.16 If any man have ears to hear, let him hear.
v.17 And when he was entered into the house from the people, his disciples asked him concerning the parable.
v.18 And he saith unto them, Are ye so without understanding also? Do ye not perceive, that whatsoever thing from without entereth into the man, *it* cannot defile him;
v.19 Because it entereth not into his heart, but into the belly, and goeth out into the draught, purging all meats?
v.20 And he said, That which cometh out of the man, that defileth the man.
v.21 For from within, out of the heart of men, proceed evil thoughts, adulteries, fornications, murders,
v.22 Thefts, covetousness, wickedness, deceit, lasciviousness, an evil eye, blasphemy, pride, foolishness:
v.23 All these evil things come from within, and defile the man."

14-15 The teaching of the Lord is in two parts: in His address to the crowd He states the general principle of moral defilement, while in the private address in the house to His disciples He develops the principle more fully (vv.17-23). In these verses He traces the source of real defilement. It is not from without. A man is not defiled morally by what he eats, even if his hands have not been washed. Defilement is from within. One could observe ceremonial cleansing, but have a defiled heart. Jesus taught plainly that evil comes from within and not from without.

17-18 In the privacy of the house, His disciples desired an explanation of His address to the crowd outside. He chided them for not having a better understanding of His ministry. They were slow learners in the school of discipleship.

19 The Lord therefore enlarged upon His earlier teaching and emphasised the fact that nothing eaten can defile a man morally. Food cannot enter into the heart, but into the stomach to be eliminated by the natural function of the body.

20-23 The thing that comes out of a man is the defilement. Wickedness arises from within, and proceeds from the heart of man. The first thing mentioned is the key to the other twelve items in the dreadful catalogue of evil things. "Evil thoughts" are the indication of a man's heart. The thought life is therefore vital to moral character. "For as he (a man) thinketh in his heart, so is he" (Prov 23:7). It is of great importance to have right thoughts. Paul also stressed this when writing to the Philippians: "...whatsoever things are true, whatsoever things are honest, whatsoever things are just, whatsoever things are pure, whatsoever things are lovely...think on these things" (Phil 4:8). The defilement of the human heart is an evidence of the reality of the fallen state of the whole Adamic family. The stream of human nature is polluted by sin. The Lord discloses in a terrible catalogue twelve wicked things which originate in man's heart. They are not the result of taking something into our mouth with unwashed hands, but are already in the heart in seed form, and are in danger of developing into various acts of impurity. This plain and searching ministry of Christ was a severe rebuke to the religious leaders who heard Him, but it is needed in every age, and never more so than today. This final ministry of the Servant in Galilee was a fitting prelude to His further ministry in Tyre and Sidon among Gentiles.

Notes

In light of the foregoing, David's prayer should be prayed by every disciple: "Search me, O God, and know my heart; prove me, and know my thoughts; And see if there be any grievous way in me; and lead me in the way everlasting" (Ps 139:23-24 JND).

In contrast to all others Christ was the embodiment of absolute purity of heart. Of no other person could it even be stated that he was without spot. In the person of the Lord Jesus Christ is a concentration of all the wondrous features of dignity, majesty, perfection, and glory. He was unblemished in character, untainted in conduct, unimpeachable in consistency, because He was impeccable in His nature. In the human heart is sin, but in Him there was and is no sin.

VI. The Prerogatives of The Servant (7:24-8:26)

In this section Mark presents the royal rights which belong exclusively to Jehovah's perfect Servant.

The Lord left the coasts of the sea of Galilee and journeyed northward some fifty miles to the borders of Tyre and Sidon. His objective was a season of retirement from the crowded areas, where He was continually pressed by the multitudes seeking healing, that He might have private fellowship with

His disciples. He was anxious to prepare them for their future ministry when finally He would have ascended to the Father. The journey to the northern regions took Him into a mainly Gentile part of the land. Following His visit to the borders of Tyre He returned by a roundabout route to the coasts of Decapolis, on the east of the sea of Galilee (v.31). Then He crossed the sea to Dalmanutha (8:10) and finally to Northern Galilee again, to Bethsaida (8:22).

The incidents recorded by Mark reveal the prerogatives and power of the Lord, in His service:

1. The curing of the daughter of the Syrophenician woman	7:24-30
2. The healing of the deaf man, who had an impediment in his speech	7:31-37
3. The feeding of the four thousand	8:1-9
4. The Pharisees demand for a sign	8:10-13
5. The teaching concerning leaven	8:14-21
6. The giving of sight to a blind man	8:22-26.

The miracles of opening the ears of the deaf man and the eyes of the blind man are recorded only in Mark's Gospel. They have many similar features, and both signs took place with a Gentile background.

1. *The curing of the daughter of the Syrophenician woman 7:24-30*

v.24 "And from thence he arose, and went into the borders of Tyre and Sidon, and entered into an house, and would have no man know *it*: but he could not be hid.
v.25 For a *certain* woman, whose young daughter had an unclean spirit, heard of him, and came and fell at his feet:
v.26 The woman was a Greek, a Syrophenician by nation; and she besought him that he would cast forth the devil out of her daughter.
v.27 But Jesus said unto her, Let the children first be filled: for it is not meet to take the children's bread, and to cast *it* unto the dogs.
v.28 And she answered and said unto him, Yes, Lord: yet the dogs under the table eat of the children's crumbs.
v.29 And he said unto her, For this saying go thy way; the devil is gone out of thy daughter.
v.30 And when she was come to her house, she found the devil gone out, and her daughter laid upon the bed."

24 The Lord arose from Capernaum and journeyed to the far north of Palestine to the borders of Tyre and Sidon. This was known in those days as Phoenicia; today it is Lebanon. On His arrival He withdrew into a house to teach His disciples. His desire was to remain in obscurity, but He could not be hid. The news soon spread abroad that the mighty miracle-worker was amongst them, and doubtless many soon gathered, but only one incident of healing is on record.

25-26 A Gentile woman, a Syrophenician by nation, who had a little daughter with an unclean spirit, came to Him. She fell down at the feet of Jesus and entreated Him many times to cast forth the demon from her child. The continuous pathetic cries of the mother moved the tender heart of the Lord with compassion, yet His attitude towards her at first, seems difficult to understand.

27 The Lord stated that it was not a right thing to take the children's bread and cast it to the dogs. This remarkable figurative language was not a rebuke to the woman, but a test of her faith. The Lord had indicated that His objective in being there in retreat was to minister spiritual food to His disciples and it would not be in keeping with that purpose to interrupt the family table by feeding dogs. The word that He used here for dogs is not that which is commonly used in the NT, meaning the unclean dogs that roamed the streets, but rather little house-trained pet dogs that sat under their master's tables at mealtime.

28 The answer of the woman shows her intelligence and faith in God. She is the only person in this Gospel written by Mark who addressed Jesus as Lord. She also accepted His royal rights to refuse her request, but added that even the dogs under their master's tables may eat of falling crumbs without interfering with the continuance of the meal.

29 The answer drew out the prerogative of the Servant. He admired her saying, and told her to go home, giving her the glad assurance that the demon had left her daughter. The words denoted that the cure had already taken place.

30 On arriving at her house, the woman found that the demon had gone, and her dear child was lying peacefully in bed.

The miracle is the only one recorded by Mark where an exorcism took place without the spoken command of the Lord, and when He was at a distance from the subject.

Notes

Some teach that the children represent Israel who had the first claim upon the ministry of Christ, and their bread or privileges must not be given to Gentiles, who are pictured in the dogs, because their time for having the gospel preached to them had not yet arrived. This application is correct, but the primary point in the account must not be overlooked: that is, that the Lord saw the great importance of preparing the disciples for their mission, and it was not an appropriate time for Him to be occupied with service to a Gentile woman. The triumphant faith of this woman is an example of true motherhood, who sought nothing for herself but everything for her daughter. There is a marked contrast between the mother of ch.6, Herodias, who sought evil for her daughter, and this mother, who sought the welfare of her daughter.

2. *The Healing of the deaf man, who had an impediment in his Speech* 7:31-37

v.31 "And again, departing from the coasts of Tyre and Sidon, he came unto the sea of Galilee, through the midst of the coasts of Decapolis.
v.32 And they bring unto him one that was deaf, and had an impediment in his speech, and they beseech him to put his hand upon him.
v.33 And he took him aside from the multitude, and put his fingers into his ears, and he spit, and touched his tongue;
v.34 And looking up to heaven, he sighed, and saith unto him, Ephphatha, that is, Be opened.
v.35 And straightway his ears were opened, and the string of his tongue was loosed, and he spake plain.
v.36 And he charged them that they should tell no man: but the more he charged them, so much the more a great deal they published *it*;
v.37 And were beyond measure astonished, saying, He hath done all things well: he maketh both the deaf to hear, and the dumb to speak."

31-32 Leaving Tyre and Sidon the Lord journeyed to the south-eastern region of the coasts of Galilee, to the region of Decapolis. There they brought to Him a deaf man, who also had defective speech. They begged Him to place His hand upon the unfortunate man. This is one of two miracles recorded only in Mark's Gospel. The other is the opening of the eyes of a blind man (8:22-26).

The healing processes of these two cases have many features in common. Firstly, both were healed in Gentile surroundings. In each case the afflicted one was brought to Jesus by others, who besought Him to put His hand upon them. Each healing was performed in stages. They are the only two miracles recorded in the Synoptic gospels where the Lord used His own saliva. John records one incident of a similar nature (John 9:6). Finally in both these healings a charge was given afterwards to the multitude to keep the matter unknown.

This man had a twofold problem. He was deaf, but he also had great difficulty in speaking. He was not a deaf mute. The Spirit through Mark uses an unusual word in the Greek to represent the six words describing his defective speech; "had an impediment in his speech" is one word, *mogilalos*. It is derived from *mogis*, with difficulty, and *laleō*, to speak. This unusual word is not found in any other part of the NT, but appears once in the OT (LXX). Used in the Septuagint Version of Isa 35:6 it previews the kingdom of God on earth during the reign of Christ, "when the ears of the deaf shall be unstopped, and the tongue of those who speak with difficulty shall sing". In the present account, the same miracle to be performed in the future was a sign of the Messiah's credentials, but Israel rejected Him. The condition of the man is a spiritual picture of the ruin of the human family. They have no ear for the voice of God, and are unable to speak clearly of divine things.

33-34 The Lord's actions in healing this man are remarkable and instructive to all who serve Him. There are seven important steps detailed:

1. Jesus took him aside from the crowd.
2. He put his fingers into his ears.
3. He spat.
4. He touched his tongue.
5. He looked up into heaven.
6. He sighed.
7. He said "Ephphatha" which means "Be opened".

All these were features of sympathy in the process of the man's recovery. In taking him away from the curious crowd, He desired to communicate alone with the man in a quiet atmosphere. Deaf people are confused in a crowd. The presence of so many onlookers could have hindered the great work. The Lord then used sign language for the benefit and encouragement of the man's faith. The putting of His fingers into his ears and the touching of his tongue with His own saliva were symbolic actions, showing the man His divine intentions to heal him. He looked up to heaven in prayer to God. His deep emotion at the ravages of sin, and His tender compassion for the subject to be healed caused Him to groan deeply.

Having looked up to heaven, an attitude which revealed His prayerful spirit (6:41) the Lord used the beautiful Aramaic word "Ephphatha" which means "Be opened". There was something in the quality of His voice which the Spirit of God would have the reader of the Gospel hear, hence Mark records the actual word of the Saviour before he conveys the meaning. There was a tenderness in the tone of His voice. The man could easily lip-read this one word of the Lord. The whole detail of the process of healing is a lesson to servants in their personal dealings with needy souls. Each must be met on the level of his understanding. Personal contact is of vital importance; absolute dependence upon God for success, and the right word to be spoken to affect the remedy are of equal importance.

35 Immediately at the command of Jesus, the ears of the man were opened to hear, the string of his tongue was loosed, so that he could speak clearly, confessing Christ before them all.

36-37 Again the Lord charged that the matter would not be published, but the more He commanded them, the more they told abroad the news of the miracle. The Lord had used this charge of silence previously (1:44-45; 5:43). He desired to minister in Decapolis and not be known as a popular Healer.

The miracle caused the people to be astonished beyond measure and their ascription of praise was, "He hath done all things well". When the Creator had finished His mighty work at the beginning, His verdict upon the whole was, "It was very good" (Gen 1:31). Here men join in a similar sentence of approval of the work of His Son, for all He has done is also very good. Everyone who has known His saving touch in his life can bear this testimony; "He hath done all things well". It should also be true of all those who follow the example of the perfect Servant in service; that "Well done" should be the assessment (Matt 25:21,23).

Notes

34 Jesus looked up to Heaven. Mark emphasises the looks of the Servant. It is one of the distinctive features of this Gospel. It was the Lord's way to look round about at the crowds around Him, at subjects for healing, at His disciples, at places on earth and into the face of God in Heaven. His face revealed His indignation when He "looked round about" on those who did not desire the man with the withered hand to be healed on the Sabbath (3:5). Deep affection for His disciples was displayed in His "look on them" as they sat in the house at Capernaum, when His mother and His brethren came seeking Him (3:34). A tender interest was in the "look around the crowd" to see who had touched the border of His garment (5:32).

On two occasions He "looked up to Heaven". His spirit of thanksgiving was seen in His blessing of God for the loaves (6:41), while in the second He intimated to the deaf man that power to heal him must be given from on high. There was a look of love in His face during the interview with the rich young ruler: "Jesus beholding him loved him" (10:21), but also a look of disappointment when the young man went away sad from His presence without eternal life. The most significant look took place in the Temple, following His triumphal entrance into the city of Jerusalem: "When he had looked round about upon all things, and now the eventide was come, he went out unto Bethany with the twelve" (11:11). Jehovah's perfect Servant, the Messiah of Israel, had come to His own, but His own received Him not, hence He turned away with sadness on His countenance.

3. *Four Thousand Fed*
(8:1-9)

v.1 "In those days the multitude being very great, and having nothing to eat, Jesus called his disciples *unto him*, and saith unto them,
v.2 I have compassion on the multitude, because they have now been with me three days, and have nothing to eat:
v.3 And if I send them away fasting to their own houses, they will faint by the way: for divers of them came from far.
v.4 And his disciples answered him, from whence can a man satisfy these *men* with bread here in the wilderness?
v.5 And he asked them, How many loaves have ye? And they said, Seven.
v.6 And he commanded the people to sit down on the ground: and he took the seven loaves, and gave thanks, and brake, and gave to his disciples to set before *them*; and they did set *them* before the people.
v.7 And they had a few small fishes: and he blessed, and commanded to set them also before *them*.
v.8 So they did eat, and were filled: and they took up of the broken *meat* that was left seven baskets.
v.9 And they that had eaten were about four thousand: and he sent them away."

1-3 Presumably as a result of the healing of the deaf man who had the impediment in his speech, a great crowd gathered "in those days" around the Servant. The Lord was on His way to the Sea of Galilee when the multitude gathered. Following the feeding of the four thousand He entered into the ship with His disciples to cross the lake to the western shore.

The great crowd, having nothing to eat, became the object of the compassion of the Lord. He called the disciples and said "I have compassion on the multitude". They had been listening to Him for three days without food. He therefore feared if they went away fasting many would become exhausted on the long way home.

4 The answer of the disciples to His challenge was their question, "From whence can a man satisfy these men with bread here in the wilderness?". Many see in this statement of the apostles their lack of faith, and forgetfulness of the Servant's power in the previous miracle of feeding the five thousand (6:30-44). Their question does not necessarily suggest such an interpretation. It appears to be a confession of the powerlessness of mere men to satisfy such a crowd, and their absolute dependence upon the Lord Himself. He, being God, was the only One who could furnish a table in the wilderness. The fact that Jesus did not rebuke them gives credence to the fact that the question was not an evidence of their lack of understanding of the situation. They realised that no man could supply the need. The solution lay with Him.

5-7 The Lord asked them how many loaves were available. Their answer was "Seven". As on the previous occasion the great company was commanded to recline on the ground. His procedure followed the same pattern as before (6:41). He took the loaves, gave thanks, and brake them, and began to pass them to His disciples to impart to the multitude. The same was done with the few small fishes. He provided; the disciples dispensed. The spiritual lesson is evident: Christ is the Bread of Life for the world, but this Bread must be passed to hungry souls by disciples.

8-9 The outcome was that everyone had plenty to eat and was satisfied. All were filled, for "he hath filled the hungry with good things" (Luke 1:53).

The Lord would not allow any waste. Seven baskets were filled with broken bread that was left. In God's economy it is sinful to waste either time or food. This is a needful lesson for our times.

This miracle has been titled "The Forgotten Miracle" as some have viewed it as a mere duplication of the earlier feeding of the five thousand. A careful, reverent reading of the accounts cannot permit such a supposition. There are similarities but the differences are such that two separate events are indicated.

The places of the feeding were different, the first near Bethsaida, the latter nigh unto the Sea of Galilee (Matt 15:29). Previously, the crowd were with Jesus one day, but here three days. Then there were five thousand beside women and children, fed with five loaves and two fishes, twelve baskets of fragments taken up, but in this record there were four thousand men, and no mention of women and children, fed with seven loaves and a few fishes, and seven baskets of fragments collected.

The word for basket is also different in each case. In the feeding of the five thousand they were small baskets, *kophinos*, but in the second they are hampers, *spuris*. The first feast is recorded in all four Gospels, but this one by the first two writers only (see Matt 15:30-39).

It is also noteworthy that the compassion of Jesus in the first was primarily for spiritual needs, whereas in the second it was the physical need of the multitude that touched His heart. This tender compassion of the Servant for men in need is one of the outstanding features of His ministry and should be an example for all who serve the Lord Christ.

Here He had consideration for a hungry crowd as He realised the distance they had to walk home. It is human to avoid giving help to those in distress, but divine compassion should motivate a service of pity in stretching out hands to the needy.

The five thousand who were fed by Christ were all Jewish people, coming from the west and northern shores of the Lake of Galilee, whereas the four thousand were Gentiles from the north-east of the sea. The response of the five thousand Jews would have been to crown Him as their King (John 6:15) but no response is recorded of the Gentile crowd, for they had no Messianic hope.

In the two accounts there is a picture of the progress of the Gospel of the grace of God, going out first to the Jew, and then to the Gentile (Rom 1:16).

Notes

1-9 The mathematics of the miracle is suggestive. He fed fewer with greater provision, and the larger number less. A weighty lesson for every servant to consider.

4. *Pharisees Condemned* (8:10-13)

v.10 "And straightway he entered into a ship with his disciples, and came into the parts of Dalmanutha.
v.11 And the Pharisees came forth, and began to question with him, seeking of him a sign from heaven, tempting him.
v.12 And he sighed deeply in his spirit, and saith, Why doth this generation seek after a sign? verily I say unto you, There shall no sign be given this generation.
v.13 And he left them, and entering into the ship again departed to the other side."

10 Having sent the people away the Lord entered into the ship with His disciples to cross the lake to Dalmanutha, a location unknown today, but situated on the western side of the sea. All that history records of this place is found in this section.

11 Again the Pharisees came to confront the Lord. On this occasion they sought a sign from heaven, tempting Him. One of the teachings of the Pharisees at that time was the appearance of the Messiah upon the pinnacle of the temple, proclaiming deliverance to Israel, and displaying light from heaven as the sign of Messiahship. This was known as the *Pesikta Rabbati*. The same was evidently in the mind of Satan in the Temptation (Matt 4:5-7). The many signs with which He had filled the land were the true credentials of His Messiahship. The Pharisees, however, discounted all His miracles and sought this particular sign from heaven.

12 Instead of a sign from heaven, He sighed toward heaven. The unusual word used to signify His groaning deeply in His spirit is *anastenazo*, which means a sighing upward from the depths of His being. This compound verb is never used again in the Scriptures. It is one of the graphic descriptive words used by Mark, which was in all likelihood passed on by word of mouth by Peter, who could never forget that sigh. The wilful unbelief of these men grieved the Lord deeply and He declared "There shall no sign be given unto this generation".

In the parallel passage it is added that one sign will be given, even the sign of the prophet Jonah (Matt 16:4). How can the two statements harmonise? What Jesus declared in Mark was that a sign, such as the Pharisees demanded would not be given. The sign of Jonah was already given in the Scriptures of truth.

13 The words of this verse are exceedingly solemn: "He left them" and entering into the ship departed to the other side. His forbearance was exhausted. There is mercy for those who repent, but wilful rejection will close the door of salvation forever.

5. *The Disciples instructed* (8:14-21)

v.14 "Now *the disciples* had forgotten to take bread, neither had they in the ship with them more than one loaf.
v.15 And he charged them, saying, Take heed, beware of the leaven of the Pharisees, and *of* the leaven of Herod.
v.16 And they reasoned among themselves, saying, *It is* because we have no bread.
v.17 And when Jesus knew *it*, he saith unto them, Why reason ye, because ye have no bread? perceive ye not yet, neither understand? have ye your heart yet hardened?
v.18 Having eyes, see ye not? and having ears, hear ye not? and do ye not remember?
v.19 When I brake the five loaves among five thousand, how many baskets full of fragments took ye up? They say unto him, Twelve.
v.20 And when the seven among four thousand, how many baskets full of fragments took ye up? And they said, Seven.
v.21 And he said unto them, How is it that ye do not understand?"

14 The exodus from Dalmanutha had apparently been taken in haste for the disciples had forgotten to take bread. Mark records that they had only one loaf in the ship, a provision inadequate for their needs.

15 The Servant used the occasion of being alone with them to warn of the "leaven of the Pharisees" and of "the leaven of Herod". "Take heed" and "beware" are imperatives in the present tense, literally meaning to continually take heed and be watchful.

Leaven is a substance which ferments. In the Scriptures it is always a symbol of secretly spreading evil (Exod 12:15; Lev 2:11; 1 Cor 5:6-9; Gal 5:9). The leaven of the Pharisees referred to hypocrisy and legality, while the leaven of Herod to worldliness and political power. These influences would prove disastrous to disciples of Christ. Against these forms of evil, believers today should be on constant alert also.

16 The disciples thought that Jesus was speaking of literal leaven in the one loaf that they had brought. Their reasonings grieved Him. He was teaching important spiritual lessons but they were thinking only of material bread. They were disputing one with another and could not agree on the meaning of the Lord's words.

17-21 In order to reveal the true facts of His ministry Jesus asked them nine pointed questions.

1. Why reason ye, because ye have no bread?
2. Perceive ye not yet, neither understand?
3. Have ye your heart yet hardened?
4. Having eyes, see ye not?
5. Having ears, hear ye not?
6. Do ye not remember?
7. When I brake the five loaves among five thousand, how many baskets full of fragments?
8. When the seven among the four thousand, how many baskets full of fragments?
9. How is it that ye do not understand?

He reminded them of the two miracles which He had wrought in feeding multitudes. In this there is definite proof that the feeding of the four thousand was not a mere duplication of the feeding of the five thousand. The feeding of the five thousand is reported in all the four Gospels (Matt 14:20; Mark 6:43; Luke 9:17; John 6:13), while the four thousand only by Matthew and Mark and it is mentioned twice by each writer (Matt 15:37; 16:10; Mark 8:8,20).

He was showing them that He was able to supply their physical needs, but His chief concern was their supply of spiritual bread. Hence His solemn warning concerning the evil quality of false teaching. The peril of a leavened ministry is as great today as it was when He gave the warning in the ship on the sea of Galilee. Food for the body seems to be a greater concern among many Christians than food for the soul.

The vital lesson of this section is to realise the ability of the Lord to supply both wholesome physical bread for the body, and pure spiritual food for the soul. He Himself is the Bread of life.

6. *A Blind Man Healed* (8:22-26)

v.22 "And he cometh to Bethsaida; and they bring a blind man unto him, and besought him to touch him.
v.23 And he took the blind man by the hand, and led him out of the town; and when he had spit on his eyes, and put his hands upon him, he asked him if he saw ought.
v.24 And he looked up, and said, I see men as trees, walking.
v.25 After that he put *his* hands again upon his eyes, and made him look up: and he was restored, and saw every man clearly.
v.26 And he sent him away to his house, saying, Neither go into the town, nor tell *it* to any in the town."

22-26 The ship finally arrived at Bethsaida Julias, near to the place where He had fed the five thousand. These miracles of the healing of the blind man and the opening of the ears of the deaf man in Decapolis are recorded only by Mark. They are unique to the Servant Gospel and are of great value to all who are His servants.

The remarkable similarities in the two cases are important:

1. In each the afflicted one was brought to Jesus by others, and an urgent plea was made for the touch of His hand in healing power.
2. The deaf man was taken aside from the crowd as was also the blind man. In this was seen the tenderness and thoughtfulness of Jehovah's Perfect Servant.
3. Jesus had put His fingers into the ears of the deaf man, and touched his tongue with His spittle, and had looked to heaven with a sigh and had said, *"Ephphatha"*. In this case He again used His spittle, touching his eyes and laying His hands upon him asked him if he saw anything.

The important difference in the miracles is the fact that the deaf man, who had the impediment in his speech was cured at the first touch, but the blind man had a second touch which fully restored his vision. This marks the healing as unique; it is the only recorded miracle where the cure was gradual.

After the first touch, in answer to His query if he saw anything the man replied: "I see men as trees, walking". This fact, and the later addition that his sight was restored, indicates that he had not been born blind, but that he had suffered the loss of eyesight at some stage of his life. When the Lord placed His hands upon him the second time and made him look up the mist was gone and he saw every man clearly. The cure was finally perfected, and he was sent home with the same admonition given previously to the deaf man. He was to tell the miracle to no one.

The great question arising from this miracle is: "Why did the cure take place in two stages?". The first was partial and incomplete, but the second full and perfect. No explanation is given by Mark. The genuineness of the miracle is, however, assured as none would ever have invented such an unusual detail. The Lord could have healed the blind man instantly as there was no limitation with Him. Any limitation is found only on the human side, usually in lack of faith. It is safe to conclude from the incident that the Lord's methods in affecting spiritual cures, as in the physical cures, are not always exactly the same, neither are the spiritual experiences of all who are blessed always alike.

There are a number of important Scriptural principles illustrated in this remarkable incident.

1. The miracle may be an illustration of the Lord's purpose for His people as stated by Paul, who assured the saints at Philippi that "He which hath begun a good work in you will perform it until the day of Jesus Christ" (Phil 1:6).

2. Similar experiences may by known by soul-winners, who meet some at the time of their conversion, who may be unclear in their spiritual perception, but later as a result of instruction have clear spiritual enlightenment.

3. For all believers an application can also be made to profit and comfort. Perfect vision will never be ours while in the body, but when the Lord shall come, the shadows will flee away, and we shall see Him face to face (1 Cor 13:12).

4. Mark, who recorded this unique miracle, may be an example in his own experience. At first his spiritual vision was poor and his service incomplete, but later he became a faithful companion of the apostles, and the biographer of the pathway of the beloved Servant.

5. The partial vision of this man could also picture the spiritual outlook of the disciples while Jesus was yet with them. They seemed to but dimly grasp the true purpose of His mission. The sufferings and death of the long-expected Messiah were an enigma to their minds. Later, in His post-resurrection ministry their eyes were opened through His exposition of the Scriptures concerning Himself (Luke 24:45-47). From that time they could see clearly the absolute necessity of His sufferings, prior to the glory of His future kingdom, and to this they bore faithful testimony in their ministry.

VII. The Purpose of the Servant (8:27–10:52)

1. *Predictions of the Servant* (8:27-9:1)

This first section has two sub-sections:

a. The Person of Christ and the First Prediction of His Passion (vv.27-33).
b. Prediction concerning the Cost of Discipleship (vv.34-9:1).

a. Predictions of the Servant: The Person of Christ and His Passion (vv.27-33)

v.27 "And Jesus went out, and his disciples, into the towns of Caesarea Philippi: and by the way he asked his disciples, saying unto them, Whom do men say that I am?
v.28 And they answered, John the Baptist: but some *say,* Elias; and others, One of the prophets.
v.29 And he saith unto them, But whom say ye that I am? And Peter answereth and saith unto him, Thou art the Christ.
v.30 And he charged them that they should tell no man of him.
v.31 And he began to teach them, that the Son of man must suffer many things, and be rejected of the elders, and *of* the chief priests, and scribes, and be killed, and after three days rise again.
v.32 And he spake that saying openly. And Peter took him, and began to rebuke him.
v.33 But when he had turned about and looked on his disciples, he rebuked Peter, saying, Get thee behind me, Satan: for thou savourest not the things that be of God, but the things that be of men."

27 In preparation for His final journey to Jerusalem the Lord walked northward from Bethsaida some thirty miles to Caesarea Philippi. This place is to be distinguished from the capital city of Herod on the Phoenician coast. This city was famous for the temple to the great god Pan. He desired to spend some time in retirement with His disciples in view of His approaching death. It was to be a period of special training and instruction. The Lord had important teaching to impart to them concerning the great doctrines which embody the sum of the Christian faith. These teachings concerned His Person, His death, His resurrection and His glory. He makes known the truth of His deity, atonement and second advent. These are the cardinal foundations of the faith, once for all delivered to the saints, for which all believers must earnestly contend (Jude 3).

28 Jesus commenced His ministry by asking the question. "Whom do men say that I am?" Various answers were given: some said John the Baptist, others Elias, and others one of the prophets. The natural man can only offer speculation concerning the Person of Christ.

29 Jesus then asked them: "But whom say ye that I am?" Peter's answer, as the spokesman, reflects his faith in Him: "Thou art the Christ". He owned Him as the true Messiah. The Greek word *Christos*, means "the Anointed".

30 The Lord's charge that they should tell no man reveals that the time for the public manifestation and proclamation of the Messiah had not yet arrived.

31 This verse is the first of three great predictions made by the Servant concerning His coming sufferings, death and resurrection (9:31; 10:23-34). In each of these predictions certain matters are emphasised. In the first His rejection by the three groups who comprised the Sanhedrin in Jerusalem: the elders, the scribes, and the chief priests. In the second the treachery of the betrayer is predominant (9:31). In the third the terrible indignities which He must endure are delineated (10:34) followed by the atoning character of His death (10:45).

The introductory words "He began to teach" mark the mid-point of this Gospel. The confession of His Messiahship by Peter is now followed by a new theme, that of the Passion of the Son of Man.

The concept of a suffering Messiah was foreign to Jewish theology. The OT foretold a sufferer and a Sovereign, but the Jews did not combine the two in one person. They looked for the glorious throne but not for a shameful cross. Hence Jesus began to teach the truth as to His Person and mission in precise yet plain language.

The title Son of Man does not mean son of *a* man, but expresses His deity as the ideal Man (Dan 7:13-14).

The necessity of His sufferings is stressed: he "must suffer many things". The final teaching discloses the violent character of His death, and the victorious triumph of His resurrection after three days. We rejoice that He who made the prediction fully performed the act.

32 The uttering of the saying "openly" does not mean publicly in this context, but rather "plainly", without any parabolic language. But Peter, who had just made such a wonderful confession, now took the Lord aside and began to rebuke Him. Jesus, when He turned and looked on His disciples, rebuked Peter in return.

33 The style of His rebuke is surprisingly strong: "Get thee behind me, Satan". They are a repetition of His words to Satan in the Temptation (Matt 4:10). The statement does not imply that Peter was indwelt by Satan, but rather the same mind of Satan in the Temptation is now voiced by Peter, that the Lord should avoid suffering and ascend the throne by an easier way. Peter's mind was not in harmony with the Lord's on this occasion. Jesus said to him that he was speaking after the thoughts of men. He was showing him that he had no understanding of God's plan of redemption, and establishing His kingdom through suffering and death. Peter's conception was that One with such power as Christ should sit upon His throne as King without the shame of a cross.

b. Prediction of the Servant concerning the Cost of Discipleship (vv.34-9:1)

v.34 "And when he had called the people *unto him* with his disciples also, he said unto them, Whosoever will come after me, let him deny himself, and take up his cross, and follow me.
v.35 For whosoever will save his life shall lose it; but whosoever shall lose his life for my sake and the gospel's the same shall save it.
v.36 For what shall it profit a man, if he shall gain the whole world, and lose his own soul?
v.37 Or what shall a man give in exchange for his soul?
v.38 Whosoever therefore shall be ashamed of me and of my words in this adulterous and sinful generation; of him also shall the Son of man be ashamed, when he cometh in the glory of his Father with the holy angels.
9v.1 And he said unto them, Verily I say unto you, That there be some of them that stand here, which shall not taste of death, till they have seen the kingdom of God come with power."

34 Peter had expressed his abhorrence of suffering. He was for the saving of his life, but this would end in loss. The Lord's way was to give up His life and this would end in gain.

Discipleship is a path to be chosen. It is the path of following Christ. Every Christian is a disciple by choice. The terms are plainly presented in a threefold cord: deny self, take up the cross, follow Christ. The words "deny" and "take up" being Greek aorist tenses, suggest actions of definite decision, while "follow" is in the tense of continuous action. A disciple must follow all the days of his life. Following the Lord is a lifelong path.

35 Here the Servant shows that one who would save his life from suffering for Christ, and the hardship of service, will eventually lose it. But another who loses his life, as far as worldly greatness is concerned in self-denying service for others, for Christ's sake and the gospel's, will ultimately save his life.

36 The well known question of this verse is solemn and searching. The answer is, "Nothing". What good is a fortune if the soul is lost? The soul is of incomparable value.

37 The word "exchange" expresses the idea of a price for something purchased. The whole world cannot bring back a soul that is lost, or a life that has been wasted. It should be noted that the same Greek word *psuchē* is used for "life" and "soul" in these verses.

38 Following the death of Christ lies His glory. Here is stated the truth of the glory of the Sovereign, when He comes again with His holy angels. In that day He will be ashamed of those who have been disloyal to Him and His words.

9:1 In this verse which rightly belongs to chapter 8, the Lord promises that some standing there will not taste death till they have seen the kingdom. As the verse stands it would appear to be an introduction to the Transfiguration scenes to follow (9:2–8). Some present on this occasion were to have a preview of His glorious Kingdom, on the mount of Transfiguration. The promise of the Lord and the fulfilment in the verses following were before Peter later when he wrote of the "power and coming of our Lord Jesus Christ" (2 Pet 1:16-18).

2. *The Display of the Servant's Future Glory and Present Power 9:2-29*

This section has two sub-sections:

a. The Display of the Glory of the Servant Foreshadowed (vv.2-13)
b. The Display of the Power of the Servant (vv.14-29).

a. *The Display of the Glory of the Servant Foreshadowed (vv.2-13)*

v.2 "And after six days Jesus taketh *with him* Peter, and James, and John, and leadeth them up into an high mountain apart by themselves: and he was transfigured before them.
v.3 And his raiment became shining, exceeding white as snow; so as no fuller on earth can white them.
v.4 And there appeared unto them Elias with Moses: and they were talking with Jesus.
v.5 And Peter answered and said to Jesus, Master, it is good for us to be here: and let us make three tabernacles; one for thee, and one for Moses, and one for Elias.
v.6 For he wist not what to say; for they were sore afraid.
v.7 And there was a cloud that overshadowed them: and a voice came out of the cloud, saying, This is my beloved Son: hear him.
v.8 And suddenly, when they had looked round about, they saw no man any more, save Jesus only with themselves.
v.9 And as they came down from the mountain, he charged them that they should tell no man what things they had seen, till the Son of man were risen from the dead.
v.10 And they kept that saying with themselves, questioning one with another what the rising from the dead should mean.
v.11 And they asked him, saying, Why say the scribes that Elias must first come?
v.12 And he answered and told them, Elias verily cometh first, and restoreth all things; and how it is written of the Son of man, that he must suffer many things, and be set at nought.
v.13 But I say unto you, That Elias is indeed come, and they have done unto him whatsoever they listed, as it is written of him."

The display of His glory on the mount was a foreshadowing of His return in majesty to reign. The occasion was a prelude to His sufferings and death, and therefore was to be a source of assurance to His disciples of future victory. His present rejection and sufferings would be followed by His future reign and glory. Peter later recorded the glorious event, how that he and James and John had been eye-witnesses of His Majesty, when He received from God the Father honour and glory (2 Pet 1:16-18). The vision was not one of His glorious resurrection or enthronement in heaven, but the power and coming of His earthly Kingdom. The subject is therefore enthralling.

2 The expression "after six days" refers to the time lapse since the first announcement of His death and resurrection (8:31).

Three chosen disciples, Peter, James and John, were taken by Him into the high mountain, apart from the others. There are three special occasions in this Gospel on which the perfect Servant took these same three apart to teach them important lessons and also to show them His Person as the Saviour (5:37), the Sufferer (14:33) and the Sovereign (9:2).

He was transfigured before them for their special benefit. They beheld His glory. It was to be a source of inspiration to them.

James was the *martyr.* He was the first of the three to die (Acts 12:2). Was the Lord worth dying for? The glory of the mount, and His divine instruction was such that James was ready to die for His Lord.

John was the *minister.* He was to write as no other of the glory of the Son, and the glorious Kingdom of Christ. The preview on the mount lent inspiration to his pen.

Peter was the *messenger.* He also beheld the glory of the Servant on the mount, and listened to Moses and Elias speak of His death. He was therefore specially equipped to preach the gospel with "Jesus only" as his theme. Peter, the great soul-winner was inspired to point men to the glorified Christ: "God hath made this same Jesus, whom ye crucified, both Lord and Christ" (Acts 2:36).

The location of this transfiguration is unnamed. The word "transfigured" is *metemorphothe* from which is derived the word metamorphosis, which means to be changed into another form. On the mount the Lord was transformed and seen by His disciples as He will appear when He returns in power and great glory to establish His earthly Kingdom (1 Cor 15:20-28; Rev 1:14-15; Rev 19:15).

3 Mark was impressed with His shining raiment, exceeding white as snow, as no fuller on earth could whiten. This mention of supernatural whiteness is unique to Mark, where the spotless purity of the Servant is his theme. Matthew in his account writes that His face did shine as the sun (Matt 17:2). In keeping with the character of that gospel the sovereign Ruler is as the sun, for He made the sun to rule the day.

4 Two great men of the OT appeared and talked with Jesus. The name of Elijah, the servant prophet, is placed by Mark before the name of Moses, the Law-giver. Three great deliverers were present. Moses was the great deliverer from Egypt, Elijah from the false worship of Baal, and Christ who would deliver from sin. Elijah and Moses left this life under unusual circumstances. Elijah was raptured and Moses buried secretly. In the appearance of the representatives of the Law and the Prophets, the disciples saw the unlimited power of the Sovereign to summon the illustrious dead to His coronation. The theme of their conversation was His exodus to be accomplished at Jerusalem.

5-6 Peter was overwhelmed by the scene and proposed the prolongation of the experience for he said "It is good for us to be here". The idea of making three booths arose from the feeling in his heart that the Kingdom had arrived and therefore the Feast of Tabernacles should be celebrated (Lev 23:33-43; Zech 14:16). Mark adds that the suggestion was made because Peter did not know what to say and they were all terrified by the display of the dazzling glory.

7-8 Peter's implication in placing Moses and Elijah on the same level as Jesus was to be quickly rebuked by God Himself. The cloud that overshadowed them was, in all likelihood, the Shekinah of God's presence (Exod 40:35). The voice from the cloud said: "This is my beloved Son: hear him". The Father's voice, heard at the commencement of His ministry giving witness to His Sonship, is again heard on the eve of the conclusion of His ministry attesting the glory of His well beloved Son. His Sonship places Him above all others. "Hear him" means "Listen only to Him". This is a reminder that Jesus is the Prophet greater than Moses (Deut 18:15).

The disciples looked again and saw that Moses and Elijah had gone leaving none save "Jesus only". They were superseded by the Son of God, who is greater in His rule than Moses and greater in His speaking than Elijah.

9-10 As they were descending from the mountain Jesus charged them to tell no man what they had seen until He had risen from the dead. The full meaning of the happening would only be evident to them after His resurrection, for then His Sonship would be fully attested.

The disciples were unable to understand "rising from (among) the dead". They believed in the resurrection of the dead, but One rising from among the dead was beyond their conception. Concerning this they held a discussion, questioning one another as they came down the mountain side.

11 Following the scene which they had witnessed came the idea that the kingdom was about to be established, so they asked the question: "Why did the scribes say Elijah must first come?". Elijah was expected to precede the coming Messiah.

12 Jesus confirmed that Elijah must come first and restore all things (Mal 4:5-6). They were right about Elijah but wrong concerning the Son of Man, since they did not include the necessity of His rejection and suffering (Isa 53:3). He must suffer many things and be set at nought.

13 "But I say unto you" is a strong introductory phrase. The "but" in Greek here is a strong adversative. Elijah had already come. The Lord identified John the Baptist as the one who fulfilled the ministry of Elijah. John had denied in his day that he was Elijah, but his career bears a close affinity to the prophet. They dressed alike, ate the same desert food, rebuked great kings for their sin, and placed their lives in danger of resentful queens. The Lord gave John the Baptist and His ministry a significance that John did not realise in himself (John 1:21). As John fulfilled the prophecy of Elijah's coming in type at the first advent of Christ, so another witness, also Elijah-like, will appear to finally fulfil the prophecy of Malachi, before the second advent of the Lord (Mal 4:5-6; Rev 11:6).

To the first witness they did to him what they desired. His message was rejected and he died at the hands of Herod. This rejection will be repeated and the death of the other Elijah-like witness will take place in the days of the Beast (Rev 11:7-8).

Notes

Many commentators teach the resuscitation of Elijah, but the view expressed here seems preferable in the context of the words of the Lord.
The phrase "Elijah ... restoreth all things" must be understood as the divine purpose, which was thwarted by the intervention of Herod in the martyrdom of John. The witness of the second Elijah-like prophet will likewise be interrupted by the Man of Sin.

b. *The Display of the Power of the Servant (vv.14-29)*

v.14 "And when he came to *his* disciples, he saw a great multitude about them, and the scribes questioning with them.
v.15 And straightway all the people, when they beheld him, were greatly amazed, and running to *him* saluted him.
v.16 And he asked the scribes, What question ye with them?
v.17 And one of the multitude answered and said, Master, I have brought unto thee my son, which hath a dumb spirit;
v.18 And wheresoever he taketh him, he teareth him: and he foameth, and gnasheth with his teeth, and pineth away: and I spake to thy disciples that they should cast him out; and they could not.
v.19 He answereth him, and saith, O faithless generation, how long shall I be with you? how long shall I suffer you? bring him unto me.
v.20 And they brought him unto him: and when he saw him, straightway the spirit tare him; and he fell on the ground, and wallowed foaming.
v.21 And he asked his father, How long is it ago since this came unto him? And he said, Of a child.
v.22 And ofttimes it hath cast him into the fire, and into the waters, to destroy him: but if thou canst do any thing, have compassion on us, and help us.
v.23 Jesus said unto him, If thou canst believe, all things are possible to him that believeth.
v.24 And straightway the father of the child cried out, and said with tears, Lord, I believe; help thou mine unbelief.

v.25 When Jesus saw that the people came running together, he rebuked the foul spirit, saying unto him, *Thou* dumb and deaf spirit, I charge thee, come out of him, and enter no more into him.
v.26 And *the spirit* cried, and rent him sore, and came out of him: and he was as one dead; insomuch that many said, He is dead.
v.27 But Jesus took him by the hand, and lifted him up; and he arose.
v.28 And when he was come into the house, his disciples asked him privately, Why could not we cast him out?
v.29 And he said unto them, This kind can come forth by nothing, but by prayer and fasting."

In this incident there is a wonderful display of the tender compassion and unique power of the Servant; following the Sovereign's glory is the Servant's grace. The miracle shows the inability of the servants in the absence of Christ. Power could only be obtained by prayer and faith in God alone. The lesson is timely for all who serve during the "little while" of His absence.

14-15 When Jesus and His three disciples reached the nine at the foot of the mount they found a great multitude gathered around them. A dispute was in progress with the scribes. As soon as Jesus came near the people ran to greet Him.

16-18 The Lord asked the meaning of the argument. A father in the audience explained the situation. He had a son possessed of a dumb spirit. The demon often caused him to have violent seizures, and had made numerous attempts to destroy his life. In his great need he had brought him to Jesus, but in Jesus' absence he had spoken to the disciples to exorcise the demon, but they could not.

19 Jesus used sad questions which revealed His distress at their lack of faith. He then asked them to bring the boy to Him. He would act in power where they had failed.

20 The presence of Jesus aroused the demon to take control of the boy more fully, throwing him to the ground in violent spasms. The boy lay down on the ground wallowing and foaming – a sad sight of one in a helpless and hopeless state.

21-22 The tender enquiry of Jesus as to the duration of the condition brought the father's sad account of the long-standing plight of his son. The demon had often cast him into fire, and into water to destroy him. The father's pathetic plea for help touched the compassionate heart of the Servant.

23 The reply of Jesus is a classic statement of the dependence of faith for blessing. The power of God is always available, but faith in God is essential. "All things are possible to him that believeth".

24 The response was immediate and sincere. With tears flowing down his cheeks the father expressed his faith, "Lord, I believe", but he also added "Help thou mine unbelief". He felt his need, as all Christians, for the strengthening of faith by the One who is its object.

25 The curious crowd began to converge on the father and his son and the Saviour. Jesus rebuked the unclean spirit and gave two commands: firstly "Come out of him", and then "Enter no more into him".

26 The evil spirit cried out in a rage and convulsed him much and came out of him, leaving the boy as one dead. Many of the people concluded that he was dead.

27 But Jesus took him by his hand. Here we see the tender touch of the Servant's hand. He also lifted him up, a special help given to those cases of extreme weakness (5:41). The boy now arose completely cured.

28-29 This expression "coming into a house" is very common in Mark's writing. There are six separate occasions when the Lord entered into the house of an unnamed person. A careful connecting of these will show that in each case He gave private instruction concerning His works or words for the education of His servants (3:19; 7:17, 24; 9:28, 33; 10:10). The matters spoken "in the house" were for His disciples alone. He would teach them the secrets of the kingdom,

The question of the disciples on this occasion was "Why could not we cast him out?" The reply was definite: "This kind can come forth by nothing, but by prayer". The explanation of their inability was neglect of prayer and lack of faith. They, like us, may have depended on past successes, instead of depending alone on God (6:7, 13). The early church, when feeling human weakness and Satanic power, found grace in their prayers of faith (Acts 4:24-33). And the greatest need of the churches of God today is for a revival of prayer and dependence upon God for real power in testimony.

Notes

29 In the original text there is no reference to fasting. The added words "and fasting" are omitted in the oldest manuscripts.

3. *The Final Phase of the Servant's Galilean Ministry* 9:30-50

a. *The Disclosure of His Passion (vv.30-32)*

v.30 "And they departed thence, and passed through Galilee; and he would not that any man should know *it*.

v. 31 For he taught his disciples, and said unto them, The Son of man is delivered into the hands of men, and they shall kill him; and after that he is killed, he shall rise the third day.
v.32 But they understood not that saying, and were afraid to ask him."

30 Retiring from the north, Jesus and His disciples passed through Galilee. His ministry in Galilee was now ended and His last journey to Jerusalem had commenced. He desired His presence to be unknown to the multitudes. His ministry was now to be mainly for His disciples in preparation for their service in the future, when He would be no longer on earth.

31 As they walked along the way Jesus made known to them the second time His coming death (8:31). On this occasion He emphasised His betrayal into the hands of men. The violence of His death is implied by the words "they shall kill him and after that he is killed, he shall rise the third day". These vital and important truths were the constant theme of His teaching as they journeyed.

32 The disciples were dull of hearing. They could not understand the meaning of His death and the miracle of His resurrection. Mark writes with Peter in the shadows, and likely was informed by him of their fear to ask Jesus for further enlightenment, and of their remaining in ignorance.

b. *The Discourse on Humility (vv.33-41)*

v.33 "And he came to Capernaum: and being in the house he asked them, What was it that ye disputed among yourselves by the way?
v.34 But they held their peace: for by the way they had disputed among themselves, who *should be* the greatest.
v.35 And he sat down, and called the twelve, and saith unto them, If any man desire to be first, *the same* shall be last of all, and servant of all.
v.36 And he took a child, and set him in the midst of them: and when he had taken him in his arms, he said unto them,
v.37 Whosoever shall receive one of such children in my name, receiveth me: and whosoever shall receive me, receiveth not me, but him that sent me.
v.38 And John answered him, saying, Master, we saw one casting out devils in they name, and he followeth not us: and we forbad him, because he followeth not us.
v.39 But Jesus said, Forbid him not: for there is no man which shall do a miracle in my name, that can lightly speak evil of me.
v.40 For he that is not against us is on our part.
v. 41 For whosoever shall give you a cup of water to drink in my name, because ye belong to Christ, verily I say unto you, he shall not lose his reward."

33-34 Jesus and His disciples came to Capernaum. It was His last visit to this city, and probably the last time He would enter the house of Peter.

In the house He asked the disciples an embarrassing question: "What were ye disputing about in the way?". They were silent, for their argument was concerning which one of them would be the greatest. The thoughts of Jesus, on the journey, were of His sacrifice, yet His followers were filled with selfish thoughts of elevation to chief positions in the Messianic Kingdom, which they expected to be set up upon their arrival at Jerusalem.

35 The Lord sat down, as was the custom of all Jewish teachers, and called them around Him. He taught them the true principles of elevation: "If any desire to be first, the same shall be last of all, and servant of all". The basis of true greatness is humility and self-effacing service. A servant is one who attends freely to the needs of others with a lowly spirit and without any desire for elevation as a result.

36-37 Jesus took a little child and placed him in the central place. To be a "servant of all" one must give attention even to the very least among them, even to a little child. It is in keeping with the character of this Gospel of the perfect Servant that the beautiful note is added that, "Jesus took the child in His arms". To be a true servant we must welcome and embrace in His Name one of these little children as such represented the lowliest and poorest of the disciples. Receiving the least on behalf of His Name is equivalent to receiving the Son Himself, and also the Father who sent Him. The humblest service is crowned with the highest dignity.

38 At this point John speaks of seeing a man exorcising demons in Christ's name, and they had sought to stop him, because he followed not with them.

39 The answer of the Lord was plain: "Do not forbid him, as no man performs a miracle in My Name, and will speak evil of Me".

40 He then introduced the well-known statement, "He that is not against us is on our part". Every servant must acknowledge that while some do not follow the Lord in exactly the same manner, nevertheless they may be following and opposing Satan's kingdom. It should have given the disciples great searching of heart that this man was more successful than nine of them who had been duly commissioned by Christ (6:7-13; 9:14-18).

41 The Lord concludes this teaching about humility by showing that anyone who does the least act of kindness, even giving a cup of cold water to drink, will not lose his reward.

Notes

37–41 The fourfold mention of the Name in this section is thought-provoking.

1. The least of the saints are welcomed because of the Preciousness of His Name (v.37);
2. The power of Satan is overcome because of the Authority of His Name (v.38);
3. The service of Christ is acceptable because of the Value of His Name (v.39);
4. The servant of the Lord is refreshed because of the Sweetness of His Name (v.41).

c. *The Danger of Hell Fire (vv.42-48)*

v.42 "And whosoever shall offend one of *these* little ones that believe in me, it is better for him that a millstone were hanged about his neck, and he were cast into the sea.
v.43 And if thy hand offend thee, cut it off: it is better for thee to enter into life maimed, than having two hands to go into hell, into the fire that never shall be quenched:
v.44 Where their worm dieth not, and the fire is not quenched.
v.45 And if thy foot offend thee, cut it off: it is better for thee to enter halt into life, than having two feet to be cast into hell, into the fire that never shall be quenched:
v.46 Where their worm dieth not, and the fire is not quenched.
v.47 And if thine eye offend thee, pluck it out: it is better for thee to enter into the kingdom of God with one eye, than having two eyes to be cast into hell fire:
v. 48 Where their worm dieth not, and the fire is not quenched."

These verses contain some of the most solemn words ever spoken by the faithful Servant. Every servant must be faithful in warning of the eternal reality of hell.

42 The Lord gave serious warning to any who turn away from believing in Him. The severity of the punishment is indicated in His words: "it is better ... that a millstone were hanged about his neck, and he were cast into the sea". This was the manner adopted for punishment by drowning.

43 He then speaks of the possibility of one being led into sin by the hand or foot or eye. Whatever tempts one to turn away from Christ must be removed, as a surgeon amputates a gangrenous limb. The argument of the Lord is plain. It is better to enter into life and into God's kingdom without earthly things that would hinder, than to remain in unbelief, and finally be cast into hell, into the fire that never shall be quenched. The word used for hell here is not *hades*, the place of disembodied spirits (Luke 16:23), or *tartaros*, the place where sinful angels are reserved for judgment (2 Pet 2:4), but *gehenna*. Our Lord Jesus used this solemn word eleven times out of its twelve occurrences in the NT (James 3:6 being the one exception). Gehenna, or the valley of Hinnom, was a place south of Jerusalem. It was a place of pagan worship where children were offered in fire to appease the heathen god Molech (2 Chron 28:3; 33:6). The good king Josiah turned the place into the city dump-heap, where fires burned day and night to consume the worm-infested garbage.

Jesus used this place as an illustration of the place of future eternal punishment. Three times He stated that the fire never shall be quenched, referring to hell's external torment; "where their worm dieth not" could refer to the unending remorse of the damned in their internal anguish. The lake of fire is to be greatly feared, to be faithfully preached, and solemnly believed. It is a fundamental doctrine. Those who deny it are outside of the kingdom now, and should be outside of any local church, and will finally be outside of heaven for all eternity.

Gehenna is the final eternal place of torment where both soul and body of every unbeliever shall be punished in conscious existence with everlasting fire. Let all be warned for "Whosoever was not found written in the book of life was cast into the lake of fire" (Rev 20:11-15).

d. *The Distinctiveness of Salt (vv.49-50)*

v.49 "For every one shall be salted with fire, and every sacrifice shall be salted with salt.
v.50 Salt *is* good: but if the salt have lost his saltness, wherewith will ye season it? Have salt in yourselves, and have peace one with another."

These two verses have been spoken of as the most difficult in the NT.

49 Everyone shall be salted with fire. This problem statement has been given at least twelve suggested explanations. The first word "for" and the last word "fire" in the clause link the verse with the previous context of vv.43–48. This would refer the meaning to the unbeliever who is finally cast into hell-fire, being salted with fire. The preservation of the bodies and souls of those who perish in the lake of fire seems to be the teaching of the verse.

The second clause (omitted in the RV) could refer to believers, who offer their bodies a living sacrifice. They are thus preserved from the corruption in the world, even as the meal-offering was seasoned with salt (Lev 2:13). The conversation of the believer should be full of grace, yet seasoned with salt (Col 4:6).

50 Salt is good. The meaning being that it is a useful substance for preservation. If the quality of saltness is lost it becomes utterly worthless. The application was specially for the disciples who were disputing at that time who should be the greatest. They were losing their saltness. Their savour for one another's fellowship and with the Lord was in jeopardy. So Jesus said to them, "Have salt in yourselves and be at peace with one another". The influence for good of the Christian in the world is only possible as he retains a Christ-like savour. There are three mentions of a "covenant of salt" in the OT: Lev 2:13; Num 18:19; 2 Chron 13:5. In each one a contract is ratified between God and man. A "covenant of salt" is one ratified by sacrifice of which salt was the accompaniment. It was therefore made sure.

In the East, once a stranger has shared salt at the table, his host becomes his friend. Hence the Lord said to His disciples, who were contrary one to another: "have salt between you and be at peace". This injunction is as needful today as then.

4. *The Last Journey to Jerusalem* 10:1-52

The key to this chapter is found in the words "We go up to Jerusalem" (vv.33-34).

The journey is described in two chapters in Matthew, and ten in Luke (Matt 19-20; Luke 9:51-19:28). The account by Mark is briefer than the others, but he gives graphic touches enhancing the beauties and perfections of Jehovah's Servant. The first nine chapters of Mark focus mainly on His Galilean ministry, the remainder on His Perean and Judean ministry. Between Mark 9:50 and 10:1, the events of Luke 9-19 and John 7-11 should be placed.

v.1 "And he arose from thence, and cometh into the coasts of Judea by the farther side of Jordan; and the people resort unto him again: and, as he was wont, he taught them again."

1 Jesus left Galilee for the last time and came into the region beyond Jordan, where He commenced to teach in public again, after the months of retirement spent in the private instruction of His disciples. The gathering of the crowds "again" and His teaching them "again" is an indication of His fame in Judea as in Galilee.

The ministry of Jesus in His last journey covers a number of important subjects:

a. Concerning Marriage	vv.2-12
b. Concerning Children	vv.13-16
c. Concerning Eternal Life	vv.17-31
d. Concerning His Death and Resurrection	vv.32-34
e. Concerning Ambition	vv.35-45
f. Opening the Eyes of Blind Bartimaeus	vv.46-52.

4. *The Teaching of the Servant concerning Marriage* 10:2-12

a. *The Teaching of the Servant concerning Marriage (vv.2-12)*

v.2 "And the Pharisees came to him, and asked him, Is it lawful for a man to put away *his* wife? tempting him.
v.3 And he answered and said unto them, What did Moses command you?
v.4 And they said, Moses suffered to write a bill of divorcement, and to put *her* away.

v.5 And Jesus answered and said unto them, For the hardness of your heart he wrote you this precept.
v.6 But from the beginning of the creation God made them male and female.
v.7 For this cause shall a man leave his father and mother, and cleave to his wife;
v.8 And they twain shall be one flesh: so then they are no more twain, but one flesh.
v.9 What therefore God hath joined together, let no man put asunder.
v.10 And in the house his disciples asked him again of the same *matter.*
v.11 And he saith unto them, Whosoever shall put away his wife, and marry another, committeth adultery against her.
v.12 And if a woman shall put away her husband, and be married to another, she committeth adultery."

2 The hostile Pharisees followed the Lord relentlessly seeking to trap Him in His words. Here they questioned Him on the subject of a man putting away His wife. The question of divorce was a cause of division among the Pharisees. One school of thought followed Rabbi Shammah, who taught adultery was the only just cause for divorce. The more liberal followers of Rabbi Hillel, held that a man could sever his marriage for every cause (Matt 19:3). The question of these men was not intended for correct information, but as a subtle trap to condemn His teaching.

3 Jesus did not relate their present teaching, but directed their attention back to Moses and to the origin of marriage in the garden of Eden. "What did Moses command you?", He asked.

4 In reply, they quoted Deut 24:1-4, where Moses allowed a writing of divorcement to put her away.

5 The perfect Servant expounded the meaning of this law. It was given by Moses because of the hardness of men's hearts. It was far from the ideal purpose of God, but was added on account of low moral conditions of Israel.

6-8 Jesus then refers the Pharisees to the original institution of marriage in the garden of Eden. In the first arrangement it was to be an indissoluble union: "From the beginning of the creation God made them male and female". The union was both spiritual and physical.

There is no human relationship so sacred and binding. The whole structure of society is built upon the enjoyment of this divine union. Marriage is divine in its origin under the bands of divine laws, and therefore to tamper with the holy bond is to incur divine displeasure.

Divorce is a mere legal enactment of men, and cannot set aside a union of divine constitution.

9 Jesus said, "What therefore God hath joined together, let not man put asunder". One who sunders, may be one of the parties by infidelity, or a third person who may intrude and cause the marriage to be shipwrecked, or a legal officer who may issue a bill of divorcement. The world today, and all Christians, have special need to consider these solemn words of the perfect Servant and Teacher.

10-12 The second part of the teaching was given in private to His disciples in the house, in answer to their question on the same matter of marriage and divorce. The action of Herod illustrated the sin of v.11. Mark added v.12 for his Gentile readers, since unlike Jewish women, under Roman law a wife could obtain divorce.

The ideal for a broken marriage is not divorce, but reconciliation in the spirit of forgiveness.

b. *The Servant and the Little Children (vv.13-16)*

v.13 "And they brought young children to him, that he should touch them: and *his* disciples rebuked those that brought *them*.
v.14 But when Jesus saw *it*, he was much displeased, and said unto them, Suffer the little children to come unto me, and forbid them not: for of such is the kingdom of God.
v.15 Verily I say unto you, Whosoever shall not receive the kingdom of God as a little child, he shall not enter therein.
v.16 And he took them up in his arms, put *his* hands upon them, and blessed them".

13-16 This episode of the parents who kept bringing their children to Him, that He might touch them in blessing, is made important by the context. It follows the subject of divorce, for it is usually the children who are the innocent and pathetic victims of suffering and loss in such cases. Many have been damaged emotionally for life as a result. This is one of the saddest outcomes of divorce.

The connection between this incident and the unscriptural ordinance of "infant-sprinkling" is without warrant although used by many theologians to bolster their practice.

The disciples could see no value or importance in these children. To them it was a waste of time. Therefore they sought to hinder their coming into His presence.

14-15 Jesus showed His strong displeasure to their attitude. He rebuked them saying: "Allow these little children to come to Me, do not hinder them coming to Me". The added expression "for of such is the kingdom of God" indicates that children enter His kingdom, and all those who have childlike faith.

16 Mark now presents one of the most intriguing portraits of the compassion and tenderness of the Servant. He took the little children up in His arms, which is a throwback to the beautiful words of the prophet Isaiah: "He shall gather the lambs with his arm, and carry them in his bosom" (Isa 40:11). He then put His hands upon them and blessed them. It is worthy of special attention that the Greek verb for "blessed" used here (*kateulogei*) in some manuscripts is unique to this verse in all the NT. Thus the gracious attitude of the Servant is emphasised to each child whom He received.

Servants of Christ should never be too busy to overlook the vital importance of ministry among children.

c. *The Servant and Eternal Life (vv.17-31)*

v.17 "And when he was gone forth into the way, there came one running, and kneeled to him, and asked him, Good Master, what shall I do that I may inherit eternal life?
v.18 And Jesus said unto him, Why callest thou me good? *there is* none good but one, *that is*, God.
v.19 Thou knowest the commandments, Do not commit adultery, Do not kill, Do not steal, Do not bear false witness, Defraud not, Honour thy father and mother.
v.20 And he answered and said unto him, Master, all these have I observed from my youth.
v.21 Then Jesus beholding him loved him, and said unto him, One thing thou lackest: go thy way, sell whatsoever thou hast, and give to the poor, and thou shalt have treasure in heaven: and come, take up the cross, and follow me.
v.22 And he was sad at that saying, and went away grieved: for he had great possessions.
v.23 And Jesus looked round about, and saith unto his disciples, How hardly shall they that have riches enter into the kingdom of God!
v.24 And the disciples were astonished at his words. But Jesus answereth again, and saith unto them, Children, how hard is it for them that trust in riches to enter into the kingdom of God!
v.25 It is easier for a camel to go through the eye of a needle, than for a rich man to enter into the kingdom of God.
v.26 And they were astonished out of measure, saying among themselves, Who then can be saved?
v.27 And Jesus looking upon them saith, With men *it is* impossible, but not with God: for with God all things are possible.
v.28 Then Peter began to say unto him, Lo, we have left all, and have followed thee.
v.29 And Jesus answered and said, Verily I say unto you, There is no man that hath left house, or brethren, or sisters, or father, or mother, or wife, or children, or lands, for my sake, and the gospel's,
v.30 But he shall receive an hundredfold now in this time, houses, and brethren, and sisters, and mothers, and children, and lands, with persecutions: and in the world to come eternal life.
v.31 But many *that are* first shall be last; and the last first."

17 Mark's is the Gospel of action. This is apparent in the account of this man who came running and kneeling before the Servant in deep respect. It took place at the very time when Jesus was setting out on His way to Jerusalem. This eager enquirer desired to know the terms on which he could inherit eternal life. This man was young, wealthy and influential, being a ruler (Matt 19:20-22; Luke

18:18). With all his earthly security he felt insecure for the life to come. His question, "Good Master, what shall I do to inherit eternal life?" indicated his thought that he must do something to obtain an entrance into the kingdom.

18 The answer of Jesus has been misunderstood. He sought to show this man that no one is good, absolutely perfect, but God alone. The Lord Jesus was God. This was a challenge to the ruler to perceive that Jesus was the Messiah of Israel and the Son of God.

19 The Lord quoted five commandments from the second table of the Law (Exod 20:12-16; Deut 5:16-20). These all have to do with conduct in human relations. The final command "Defraud not", occurring only in Mark, was substituted by the Servant in the place of the tenth commandment. This precept is found in relationship to the matter of paying the wages of a hired servant (Deut 24:14).

20 The young man stated that he had kept all these from his youth. He had taken the responsibility of obedience to the commandments, as a son of the law, at his Bar Mitzvah, at the age of twelve (Luke 2:42-47).

21 Jesus beholding him loved him. He saw into his heart and knew that one thing was lacking. In faithfulness to his soul Jesus declared that God demanded unrivalled Lordship in his life. He therefore commanded him to sell all that he had and distribute it to the poor. This would remove the god of his life which was worldly possessions. Then he was to follow the perfect Servant in a path of poverty and reproach. This way to eternal life is by turning from all trust in earthly things to childlike faith and confidence in Christ alone. The Lord does not make this demand from all His disciples. He was dealing here with a special and unusual case. The great principle taught is that all who would be in His kingdom must part with anything which would hinder entrance.

22 This earnest enquirer failed the great test. He became sad and went away in sorrow for he had great possessions. The sad spiritual history of many is seen in this incident. Those who go away from the Saviour can never find true happiness in this life. It is possible to be loved by Christ and yet lost forever.

23-27 Jesus now told His disciples that it was a hard matter for the rich to enter God's kingdom. This statement surprised them as in Israel riches were counted a mark of divine favour, which seemed an added help in entering the kingdom. Jesus repeated the same truth again, and addressed them as children. This was significant. It is the sole occasion in this Gospel that He called them children. The use of such a form of address in this context revealed their immaturity in spiritual perception.

The Lord then used graphic hyperbole to illustrate the insuperable difficulty of entering the kingdom when burdened with earthly riches. It is easier for the camel, the largest animal known in Palestine, to go through the eye of a common needle, the smallest opening known, than for one who trusts in riches to enter the kingdom of God. The word used by Mark for the needle is *raphis*, the ordinary domestic needle. The idea that the "needle's eye" was the name of a small gate in the city wall should not be entertained, as such a name was unknown until centuries later. The disciples carried His words to their logical conclusion and said, "Who then can be saved?" To this the Lord replied that salvation is impossible with men, but God is able. All things have been made possible by divine grace. No man can obtain his own salvation by any work or merit, but God is able and willing to save to the uttermost.

28-30 Peter now acted as spokesman for the others saying "We" (in contrast to the rich young ruler) "have left" (aorist, meaning a complete break with the past) and "have followed thee".

In the same context he also asked what the reward would be for their service (see Matt 19:27). This feature is often emphasised by Mark, how that they were constantly occupied with gaining an honourable place in the earthly Messianic Kingdom of Christ.

Jesus promised that rewards will be given and will extend to all who have sacrificed for Him. That which is left for Him will bring a hundredfold by new relationships with fellow-believers in this age (Mark 3:31-35; Acts 2:41-47) and in the future age following His advent the ultimate enjoyment of eternal life. This is not inferring that they must wait for that blessing. The Lord also said "I *give* unto them eternal life" as a present gift (John 10:28).

31 This verse has been described as "a floating statement" because of its use in various contexts (Matt 20:16; Luke 13:30). Rewards will not be based on priority of position, or length of time served, but on devotion to Christ.

d. *The Teaching of the Servant concerning His Own Death and Resurrection (vv.32-34)*

v.32 "And they were in the way going up to Jerusalem; and Jesus went before them: and they were amazed; and as they followed, they were afraid. And he took again the twelve, and began to tell them what things should happen unto him,
v.33 *Saying,* Behold we go up to Jerusalem; and the Son of man shall be delivered unto the chief priests, and unto the scribes; and they shall condemn him to death, and shall deliver him to the Gentiles:
v.34 And they shall mock him, and shall scourge him, and shall spit upon him, and shall kill him: and the third day he shall rise again."

32 Jesus went before them, leading them to Jerusalem; this is the first mention of their ultimate destination. The mention of His going before is unique to Mark. He is the Leader of His people in suffering, but also in glory (16:7).

In the way, He now speaks to them for the third time of His impending sufferings (8:31; 9:31). On the first occasion He mentioned suffering, rejection, death and resurrection; in the second He added His betrayal.

33-34 This third Passion Prophecy contains new information. Seven phases are enumerated: His sufferings will take place at Jerusalem; Israel will not only reject Him as the Messiah, but will deliver Him into the hands of the Gentiles; the Romans shall mock Him, spit upon Him, scourge and kill Him; He shall be vindicated on the third day by resurrection. This final prediction disclosed the violence of His death, and the victory of His resurrection. We rejoice that He who made the prediction fully performed the act.

e. *The Teaching of the Servant concerning Ambition (vv.35-45)*

v.35 "And James and John, the sons of Zebedee, come unto him, saying, Master, we would that thou shouldest do for us whatsoever we shall desire.
v.36 And he said unto them, What would ye that I should do for you?
v.37 They said unto him, Grant unto us that we may sit, one on thy right hand, and the other on thy left hand, in thy glory.
v.38 But Jesus said unto them, Ye know not what ye ask: can ye drink of the cup that I drink of? and be baptised with the baptism that I am baptised with?
v.39 And they said unto him, We can. And Jesus said unto them, Ye shall indeed drink of the cup that I drink of; and with the baptism that I am baptised withal shall ye be baptised:
v.40 But to sit on my right hand and on my left hand is not mine to give: but *it shall be given to them* for whom it is prepared.
v.41 And when the ten heard *it*, they began to be much displeased with James and John.
v.42 But Jesus called them *to him*, and saith unto them, Ye know that they which are accounted to rule over the Gentiles exercise lordship over them; and their great ones exercise authority upon them.
v.43 But so shall it not be among you: but whosoever will be great among you, shall be your minister:
v.44 And whosoever of you will be the chiefest, shall be servant of all.
v.45 For even the Son of man came not to be ministered unto, but to minister, and to give his life a ransom for many."

35-37 Following the second Passion Prophecy (9:30-32) a question of greatness had arisen among His disciples. After the third announcement the same question arose again. In a context of prediction concerning His sufferings and shameful death it is difficult to understand His followers arguing about leadership roles in an earthly kingdom. The flesh yearns for a position of pre-eminence.

James and John are concerned about reigning. Salome, their mother, also joined in requesting a place for her sons, one or the right hand and the other on the left when Jesus would reign in majesty over all the earth.

38 The perfect Servant rebuked their ignorance. He presented them with a cup rather than a crown. Two symbols of His sufferings were chosen by the Lord: a cup and a baptism. In the first, the drinking of the cup, activity is suggested. The contents of a cup are taken by the one who drinks. In the second, the baptism is passive. Jesus asked the two brothers, were they able to drink the cup that He drinks, or to be baptised with the baptism that He was baptised with. The use by Him of the present tense show the sufferings were already a reality to Him.

39-40 The reply of James and John showed their utter lack of understanding of the words of Jesus. He therefore applied the two symbols of suffering to them. In following Him they would indeed suffer even unto death. The cup was drunk by James, who was the first apostle to be martyred (Acts 12:2). John endured many years of exile even in his old age, and was the last apostle to die (Rev 1:9). They would share His sufferings, but not in an atoning sense. The positions of honour they sought were not promised them, as they were not in His power to give, but will be assigned by God to those for whom it is prepared.

41-44 The ten were moved with indignation against the two. The blessed Peacemaker called them all around Him and gave them some needful ministry as to the essence of true greatness. He called attention to the character of Gentile rulers: those who rule exercise lordship over their subjects, and the great ones exercise authority upon them. This type of rule would not be known in His kingdom. Whoever desired greatness among them must be their servant, and whoever desired to be chiefest must be slave of all. The mark of true greatness in God's kingdom is humility and service.

45 This verse is the greatest and most significant in this gospel. In its two clauses it forms the key to the whole ministry of the perfect Servant. The first clause covers the first ten chapters of this Gospel: "For ... the Son of man came not to be ministered unto, but to minister"; and the last clause "to give His life a ransom for many" covers the last chapters, eleven to sixteen. The Lord of glory had veiled His glory and come into the world as God's perfect Servant (Phil 2:6-8). His service was climaxed in His death as a ransom for many. His death was voluntary, violent, vicarious and victorious.

The word ransom is *lutron*, used only here and Matt 20:28, and means the price of release. The preposition is important. Here Mark uses *anti* which means in the stead of. It is the great preposition of substitution. He made provision for all, but He died in the place of many.

Notes

38 The cup is a Jewish metaphor for divine judgment against sin; see Ps 75:7-8; Hab 2:16; Zech 12:2.

Baptism was an OT picture of overwhelming sufferings; see Ps 69:2; Isa 43:2.

45 A number of words are used in the NT for redemption, and should be distinguished.
1. *Lutron*. A ransom, meaning a release by a price; see Mark 10:45.
2. *Exagorazo*. To redeem, meaning to purchase out of the slave market (Gal 3:13; Eph 5:16; Col 4:5).
3. *Apolutrosis*. Redemption, meaning "a buying back" (Rom 3:24; 1 Cor 1:30; Eph 1:7).

f. *The Servant opening the eyes of Blind Bartimaeus (vv.46-52)*

v.46 "And they came to Jericho: and as he went out of Jericho with his disciples and a great number of people, blind Bartimaeus, the son of Timaeus, sat by the highway side begging.
v.47 And when he heard that it was Jesus of Nazareth, he began to cry out, and say, Jesus, *thou* Son of David, have mercy on me.
v.48 And many charged him that he should hold his peace: but he cried the more a great deal, *Thou* Son of David, have mercy on me.
v.49 And Jesus stood still, and commanded him to be called. And they call the blind man, saying unto him, Be of good comfort, rise; he calleth thee.
v.50 And he, casting away his garment, rose, and came to Jesus.
v. 51 And Jesus answered and said unto him, What wilt thou that I should do unto thee? The blind man said unto him, Lord, that I might receive my sight.
v.52 And Jesus said unto him, Go thy way; thy faith hath made thee whole. And immediately he received his sight, and followed Jesus in the way."

46 This unique miracle is the last recorded by Mark. It reveals the tenderness of the perfect Servant, as well as His majesty and power as the Son of David and the Son of God. The last journey to Jerusalem traced by Mark emphasises the preaching and teaching of the Servant, but now as the journey was ending a mighty miracle took place. The entrance of the Lord into Jerusalem will not only be in lowliness as King, in might as Prophet, but in power as Saviour.

The Lord passed through the city of Jericho on His way to Jerusalem situated fifteen miles further south-west. As Jesus and His disciples, with a great multitude, likely pilgrims going up to the Passover, were on the outskirts of Jericho, a blind beggar-man named Bartimaeus sat on the wayside. Mark uses the beautiful Aramaic name Bartimaeus, which means son of Timaeus. Mark is the only writer who records his name (Matt 20:29-34; Luke 18:35-43).

It was a common sight to see blind beggar-men along the Jericho road.

47 When Bartimaeus heard that it was Jesus of Nazareth who was passing by, he cried out for attention saying, "Jesus, thou Son of David, have mercy on me".

48 The crowd began to rebuke him as a nuisance, and may also have objected to his acknowledgment of Jesus as Son of David. The attitude of the crowd only increased the calls of the beggar-man. The wonderful faith of this blind beggar-man is in marked contrast to the blind unbelief of the vast majority of the Jews. The beautiful title Son of David occurs in Mark for the first time. It marks out the King Messiah as David's Son (2 Sam 7:8-16; Matt 1:1; Rom 1:3).

49 The Saviour of the world stood still at the cry of a blind beggar man. He accepted the testimony and answered his appeal for mercy. As He commanded him to be called, the crowd encouraged Bartimaeus to come saying, "Be of good cheer, arise, He calleth thee".

50 What joy filled his heart as he learned of the willingness of the Servant to receive and heal him. He cast away his garment, allowing nothing to impede him in reaching the Lord immediately.

51 The question of the Saviour was to encourage the blind man's faith. His response was definite and delightful: "Rabboni, that I might receive my sight". Lord (*Rabbounei*) means my Lord and Master. Only two persons ever addressed the Lord in this manner: a blind beggar-man, and a woman who was once possessed with seven demons (John 20:16).

52 The answer of the Lord was brief and powerful "Go thy way, thy faith hath saved thee". The result was immediate; his eyes were opened, and he followed Jesus in the way.

The miracle is a picture of the saving work of Christ, who opens the eyes of those who are spiritually blind. Concluding this section which has had true discipleship as one of its themes, the miracle is a living parable of its meaning (8:31; 10:45). Trust in the Lord lies at the commencement of the path of following Him. The imperfect tense of the verb means that Bartimaeus kept on following Jesus all the way to Jerusalem. Luke adds the note of praise that came from Bartimaeus, and all the people, when they witnessed the power of the Servant (Luke 18:43).

Notes

46 The accounts of Bartimaeus by Mark differs from the records of Matthew and Luke, which has given rise to the critics casting doubts upon the perfection of the Word of God.
An explanation is therefore useful.

1. Mark and Luke mention one blind man, while Matthew states there were two.
2. Matthew and Mark report the miracle as taking place when Jesus was departing from Jericho, whereas Luke states it was as he approached the city.

It is clear that there were two blind men. Bartimaeus, being more earnest in his plea for mercy, is given the prominent place. Matthew, being the dispensational Gospel required a twofold witness of Messiah's power (Matt 18:16).

To answer the geographical difference, the fact of the two Jericho's explain the incident. One was a small village built on the site of the OT Jericho, the other, the NT Jericho about a mile south. The miracle took place between the two. Matthew and Mark record it as Jesus came out of one of the cities, while Luke reports it as taking place on His way to the other.

VIII. The Presentation of the Servant (11:1-12:44)

There are three complete divisions in Mark:

1.	The Servant and His Service	1:1-10:52
2.	The Servant and His Sacrifice	11:1-15:47
3.	The Servant and His Supremacy	16:1-16:20

The second division has three sections:

a.	The Presentation of the Servant	11:1-12:44
b.	The Presage of the Servant	13:1-13:37
c.	The Passion of the Servant	14:1-15:47

The chronological framework covers eight days extending from His entrance into Jerusalem to His emergence from the tomb. It is the greatest week ever known.

1. Sunday	The Day of Acclamation	11:1-11
2. Monday	The Day of Authority	11:12-19
3. Tuesday	The Day of Antagonism	11:20-13:37

These were days of action. They present the public ministry of the Servant in Jerusalem, and are marked by many teachings of the Lord.

4. Wednesday	The Day of Anointing	14:1-11
5. Thursday	The Day of Anticipation	14:12-31

These two days were days of solitude. They present the private ministry of the Servant at Bethany, and are marked by the compassionate teachings of the Lord.

6. Friday	The Day of Atonement	14:32-15:41

This day presents the sin-offering character of the Lord's death. The silence of the Servant is prominent.

7. Saturday	The Day of Absence	15:42-47
8. Sunday	The Day of Appearance	16:1-18
Forty days later	The Day of Ascension	16:19-20

During this last week the Lord is presented in contrast to great men of the OT.

He is greater than all, fairer than the children of men, and altogether lovely.

1. Sunday	In contrast to Joash	2 Kings 11:12; 12:2-16
2. Monday	In contrast to Moses	Deut 14:24-26; 18:18-19
3. Tuesday	In contrast to Solomon	1 Kings 10:1-3; Matt 12:42
4. Wednesday	In contrast to David	1 Sam 16:12-13; Ps 78:70-72
5. Thursday	In contrast to Adam	Gen 3; Rom 5:14
6. Friday	In contrast to Isaac	Gen 22:8-9; Rom 8:32
7. Saturday and Sunday	In contrast to Jonah	Jonah 2; Matt 12:40-41

The links with these men will be developed in the text of the exposition.

1. *Sunday The Day of Acclamation* 11:1-11

v.1 "And when they came nigh to Jerusalem, unto Bethphage and Bethany, at the mount of Olives, he sendeth forth two of his disciples,
v.2 And saith unto them, Go your way into the village over against you: and as soon as ye be entered into it, ye shall find a colt tied, whereon never man sat; loose him, and bring *him*.
v.3 And if any man say unto you, Why do ye this? say ye that the Lord hath need of him; and straightway he will send him hither.
v.4 And they went their way, and found the colt tied by the door without in a place where two ways met; and they loose him.
v.5 And certain of them that stood there said unto them, What do ye, loosing the colt?
v.6 And they said unto them even as Jesus had commanded: and they let them go.
v.7 And they brought the colt to Jesus, and cast their garments on him; and he sat upon him.
v.8 And many spread their garments in the way: and others cut down branches off the trees, and strawed them in the way.
v.9 And they that went before, and they that followed, cried, saying, Hosanna; Blessed *is* he that cometh in the name of the Lord:
v.10 Blessed *be* the kingdom of our father David, that cometh in the name of the Lord: Hosanna in the highest.
v.11 And Jesus entered into Jerusalem, and the temple: and when he had looked round about upon all things, and now the eventide was come, he went out unto Bethany with the twelve."

There are two events on this day. The first is His royal entry into the city (vv.1–10) and the second His entry into the temple (v.11).

1-2 These verses present the Lord's triumphal entrance into Jerusalem, riding upon a colt. Each of the four Gospels record the event; see Matt 21:1-11; Luke 19:28-44; John 12:12-19. Bethany was on the eastern slope of the Mount of Olives about two miles from Jerusalem. The exact location of Bethphage is unknown. Bethany means the "house of figs" and Bethphage the "house of unripe figs".

3 Jesus sent two of His disciples to Bethphage to find the unbroken colt. They were to untie it and bring it to the Lord. If challenged, they were to say "The Lord hath need of him". The colt will be sent back again shortly. Jesus required the colt for a little while to carry out a prophetic programme. Matthew includes the mother also (Matt 21:2). The colt was a Messianic sign. Jacob had prophesied of Shiloh that He would come binding His colt to the vine (Gen 49:10-12). The Lord was the true Vine and the colt represented the repentant nation in subjection to Messiah. Both the animals represent phases in Israel's history.

Daniel also foresaw the time of His royal entrance. Gabriel had announced that after sixty-nine weeks of prophetic years (483 years), Messiah the Prince would present Himself to His people and be cut off and have nothing (Dan 9:23-28). Sir Robert Anderson in his excellent book *The Coming Prince* shows the exact fulfilment of this prophecy to the very day when Jesus rode down the slopes of Olivet and entered the city.

Jacob had seen the Messianic character of the event, and Daniel its time in the prophetic calendar, but Zechariah had written of the Person of the King, saying "Behold thy King cometh unto thee: he is just and having salvation; lowly, and riding upon an ass, even upon a colt the foal of an ass" (Zech 9:9).

The disciples carried out the Lord's instructions and found that all the events reflected the divine omniscience of the Servant. The detailing implies an eyewitness account. It is thus probable that Peter was one of the two sent to bring the colt to Jesus.

7 The casting of the disciples' garments on the colt was a makeshift saddle. The Lord sat upon the colt. He who was to lie in the tomb wherein never man was laid, sat upon a colt whereon never man sat. Mark is the only writer who notes that the colt was unbroken, and had never carried a burden.

He who had called the animal for His service would supply the strength for the burden, would calm the unbroken spirit, and speak words of guidance for the way. The lowly Servant is also the great Creator in perfect control.

8 The spreading of the garments in the way is a throwback to the royal acclaim given to Jehu (II Kings 9:13). The cutting down of the branches of the palm trees in the pathway of the King symbolised the final victory of the Messiah.

9-10 The unusual arrangement of these verses is suggestive of antiphonal singing by two companies. Those who led the procession and those who followed in the rear. The words are taken from Psalm 118:25-26.

"Hosanna" literally means "Save us now" followed by "Hosanna in the highest", which means:" Save us, Thou who livest in Heaven".

The singers, however, did not perceive in Him the Messiah who must suffer before the glories of the kingdom could be established. To them it was a Passover celebration, though it appeared to the Pharisees that the world had gone after Him (John 12:19).

11 Following His triumphal entry into the city came His inspectoral entry into the temple. The crowd who sang His praise is not necessarily the same who cried for His death. The crowd disappeared soon after the city was reached. Mark alone gives the brief record of the visit of the Lord to the temple courts (*hieron*). The visit was a survey, in which He saw that the precincts were not being used as God intended, which gave rise to His actions on the next day. The first day of the last week was now ending as Jesus and the twelve passed through the city gates ere they closed, and they walked over the mount of Olives to Bethany for the night.

On this day He is seen as greater than Joash. Joash was the king's son who, after years in hiding, came forth to be presented to Israel in pomp. When they saw Him they cried, "God save". There is a marked contrast to the lowly grace of Christ. Joash served the Lord as long as Jehoida instructed him, but no lapse was ever seen in the perfect Servant; see 2 Chron 24:17. Joash failed to cleanse the land of the "high places" but the Lord cleanses the temple; see 2 Kings 12:2.

2. *Monday The Day of Authority* 11:12-19

v.12 "And on the morrow, when they were come from Bethany, he was hungry:
v.13 And seeing a fig tree afar off having leaves, he came, if haply he might find any thing thereon: and when he came to it, he found nothing but leaves; for the time of figs was not *yet.*
v.14 And Jesus answered and said unto it, No man eat fruit of thee hereafter for ever. And his disciples heard *it.*
v.15 And they come to Jerusalem: and Jesus went into the temple, and began to cast out them that sold and bought in the temple, and overthrew the tables of the money changers, and the seats of them that sold doves;
v.16 And would not suffer that any man should carry *any* vessel through the temple.
v.17 And he taught, saying unto them, Is it not written, My house shall be called of all nations the house of prayer? but ye have made it a den of thieves.
v.18 And the scribes and chief priests heard *it,* and sought how they might destroy him: for they feared him, because all the people was astonished at his doctrine.
v.19 And when even was come, he went out of the city."

There are two events on this day. The first was the cursing of the fig tree (vv.12-14) and the second the cleansing of the temple (vv.15-19).

12-13 These are very important verses. As Jesus walked from Bethany to Jerusalem early in the morning He became hungry. It is possible He had spent the night on the mount of Olives, and unlike His disciples had eaten nothing. His hunger manifests His true humanity, as jurisdiction over the fig tree reveals

His absolute deity. The great truth of His two natures in one Person is basic to the Christian faith.

The Lord saw the solitary fig tree afar off by the wayside, and coming to it searched its foliage for fruit, but He found nothing but leaves. Leaves upon a fig tree was the usual harbinger of the season of figs (13:28). In the power of His jurisdiction He pronounced a sentence of permanent fruitlessness upon the tree.

14 This remarkable sentence was a prophetic indication of God's impending judgment upon Israel. It must not be understood as an angry reaction of Jesus against a tree which had no fruit. The tree was a figure of the spiritual state of Israel, in spite of the outward glories of their temple (Judg 9:11; Micah 7:1). As He was the Creator He had sovereign rights over the tree.

15-16 John writes of a similar cleansing at the beginning of the ministry of the Lord, and the Synoptics, as Mark, at the end of His ministry. Some consider both events to be identical, but there is no evidence of such a conclusion. The first cleansing required to be repeated as impurity had continued (John 2:13-17).

The high priest had permitted a market in the court of the Gentiles, for sale of items used in the temple ritual, as wine, salt, oil, and birds and animals. There also moneychangers produced large revenues, often by fraud. There were those also who carried baggage of merchandise from the markets through the sacred temple area, as a short cut home. Mark is the only writer who records this added act of irreverence.

The Lord was outraged at this commercial disregard for the special area set apart for the Gentiles, so He cast out them that sold and bought, and overthrew the tables of the moneychangers, and the seats of them that sold doves, neither would He permit any to use the precincts as a thoroughfare.

The Lord is seen in His actions here as One greater than Moses. Moses had considered the fact that some who would worship had a long journey to travel. "And if the way be too long for thee, so that thou art not able to carry it; or if the place be too far from thee…Then thou shalt turn it into money, and bind up the money in thy hand…And thou shalt bestow that money for whatsoever thy soul lusteth after, for oxen, or for sheep, or for wine" (Deut 14:24-26). The present priesthood had gone far beyond Moses and the sacred courtyard had become a place of commerce. The Lord, as greater than Moses, exposed these abuses and sought to cleanse the temple.

17 The Lord began to teach the true purpose of God's temple. He asked them a solemn question; "It is not written, My house shall be called of all nations the house of prayer?" (Isa 56:7). It was to be a place of joy for visiting Gentiles, but now those who came to worship from afar found only a commercial bazaar. He then quoted; "Ye have made it a den of thieves" (Jer 7:10-11). The divine jurisdiction of Jesus as the Messiah, whose rights were asserted over the temple and its courts, was made evident (Mal 3:1-3).

18 The outcome of the event was a plot by the religious leaders to destroy Jesus. They sought some method to remove Him without a disturbance among the multitudes. Mark adds the explanation of their secrecy. They were afraid of Him because of His popularity with the people who were astonished at His teaching.

19 The Lord again left the city with the twelve in the evening and returned to the village of Bethany.

Notes

15-16 There is a grave danger of desecrating His sanctuary and commercialising His service in our day. Holiness and reverence become His spiritual house now, as they did His earthly house then.

3. *Tuesday The Day of Antagonism* 11:20-13:37

In this section the Lord is seen as greater than Solomon in His wisdom. Solomon answered all the hard questions of the queen of Sheba, but could not outline the future, for "Who, as I shall ... declare it, and set it in order for me, since I appointed the ancient people? and the things that are coming, and shall come, let them show unto them" (1 Kings 10:1; Isa 44:7). The ministry of the Lord on this day is the most comprehensive in the Gospel, revealing the grace and wisdom of the perfect Servant, indicating practical lessons for His servants. He also concludes the day's ministry with an outline of prophetic unfoldings. The questions manifest the hostility of the religious leaders to Christ.

The ministry on this last Tuesday may be divided as follows:

a.	The lesson of the withered fig tree	11:20-26
b.	The question of His authority	11:27-33
c.	The parable of the wicked husbandmen	12:1-12
d.	The question of taxes	12:13-17
e.	The question of resurrection	12:18-27
f.	The question of the greatest commandment	12:28-34
g.	The question of the Lord Himself concerning His deity	12:35-37

a. *The lesson of the withered fig tree (vv.20-26)*

v.20 "And in the morning, as they passed by, they saw the fig tree dried up from the roots.
v. 21 And Peter calling to remembrance saith unto him, Master, behold, the fig tree which thou cursedst is withered away.
v.22 And Jesus answering saith unto them, Have faith in God.
v.23 For verily I say unto you, That whosoever shall say unto this mountain, Be thou removed, and be thou cast into the sea; and shall not doubt in his heart, but shall believe that those things which he saith shall come to pass; he shall have whatsoever he saith.
v.24 Therefore I say unto you, What things soever ye desire, when ye pray, believe that ye receive *them,* and ye shall have *them.*
v.25 And when ye stand praying, forgive, if ye have ought against any: that your Father also which is in heaven may forgive you your trespasses.
v.26 But if ye do not forgive, neither will your Father which is in heaven forgive your trespasses."

20 The account given in this paragraph is the sequel to the previous verses (vv.12-14). As the disciples passed by in the morning of the Tuesday of the last week of the Servant's ministry on earth, they saw the same fig tree which Jesus had cursed completely withered already in fulfilment of His word.

21 Peter said "Rabbi, behold, the fig tree which thou cursedst is withered away". There was an element of surprise among the disciples that judgment against the tree had taken place so quickly.

22 It is thought-provoking that Jesus did not detail the spiritual meaning of the fig tree, but evidently it was a figure of the nation of Israel, and God's judgment upon that people. Rather the Lord exhorts the disciples to have faith in God.

23 The statement of Jesus that whosoever shall say unto this mountain, be thou removed and cast into the sea, is not to be taken as literal but rather as hyperbole. We are not called to remove a geographical mountain, but to do the works of the Father who is in heaven. We can do things which appear impossible, if we have unwavering faith in God. The mountain like the fig tree represents Israel which later was removed from the land, and cast into the sea of the Gentile world. The sentence on the tree, and the removal of the mountain need not be final. He can speak again to the fig tree, or command the mountain and it shall be done (Job 14:7-9; Mark 13:28; Dan 2:35).

24-25 The plain direction for a successful prayer life is of great value to all who serve: "What things soever ye desire, when ye pray, believe that ye receive, and ye shall have them". Unbelief is the greatest hindrance to answered prayer.

The Lord gave a final condition: "When ye stand praying, forgive." This is essential if we expect the Father to forgive us our trespasses. An unforgiving spirit will hinder the blessing of God on our service (Eph 4:32).

26 This verse is omitted in the most reliable manuscripts. It is usually considered to be an insert from Matt 6:15, where it is in the rightful context.

b. *The First Question: Concerning the Authority of Christ (vv.27-33)*

v.27 "And they come again to Jerusalem: and as he was walking in the temple, there come to him the chief priests, and the scribes, and the elders.
v.28 And say unto him, By what authority doest thou these things? and who gave thee this authority to do these things?
v.29 And Jesus answered and said unto them, I will also ask of you one question, and answer me, and I will tell you by what authority I do these things.
v.30 The baptism of John, was *it* from heaven, or of men? answer me.
v.31 And they reasoned with themselves, saying, If we shall say, From heaven; he will say, Why then did ye not believe him?
v.32 But if we shall say, Of men; they feared the people: for all *men* counted John, that he was a prophet indeed.
v.33 And they answered and said unto Jesus, We cannot tell. And Jesus answering saith unto them, Neither do I tell you by what authority I do these things."

27-28 In the temple courts the Lord's credentials were challenged by the chief priests, and the scribes and elders, who together composed the Sanhedrin. Their questions were asked in guile to place the Lord in a dilemma: "By what authority doest thou these things? and who gave thee this authority?" Their reference was to His driving out the traders from the courts, the overthrowing of the tables of the moneychangers, and the seats of them that sold doves. They demanded the source of His authority. Was it divine or human?

29-30 The Lord met their questions with a counter question concerning John's baptism. This was a common form of Rabbinic debating practice. He demanded of them an answer to His question: "Was John's baptism of divine or human origin?". Their answer would be His answer to their question.

31-32 They had set a trap for the Lord in the framework of their questions, but were now placed in a great difficulty by Him. As they reasoned together they could see that if they answered "from heaven", they would be condemned for not accepting John's testimony. They would also have to acknowledge that the authority of Christ was from His God. The evident answer was the truth but they rejected it in their hostility to Him.

They feared to say that John's ministry was by human authority, for this would discredit them in the eyes of all the people, who regarded John as a prophet of God. They preferred this answer although erroneous, but could not express it openly, because of the people.

33 In order to hide their thoughts they claimed ignorance, and would not answer His question: therefore He was not required to answer their questions. He had shown, however, that the authority to cleanse the temple and teach the truth was like John's from heaven.

The attitude of these leaders in rejecting God's prophets and finally God's Son, was a repetition of their former leaders', and would bring God's judgment upon the nation. This great truth is underlined in the parable of Christ which followed.

c. *The Parable of the Wicked Husbandmen (vv.12:1-12)*

v.1 "And he began to speak unto them by parables. A *certain* man planted a vineyard, and set an hedge about *it,* and digged *a place for* the wine-fat, and built a tower, and let it out to husbandmen, and went into a far country.
v.2 And at the season he sent to the husbandmen a servant, that he might receive from the husbandmen of the fruit of the vineyard.
v.3 And they caught *him,* and beat him, and sent *him* away empty.
v.4 And again he sent unto them another servant; and at him they cast stones, and wounded *him* in the head, and sent *him* away shamefully handled.
v.5 And again he sent another; and him they killed, and many others; beating some, and killing some.
v.6 Having yet therefore one son, his well-beloved, he sent him also last unto them, saying, They will reverence my son.
v.7 But those husbandmen said among themselves, This is the heir; come, let us kill him, and the inheritance shall be ours.
v.8 And they took him, and killed *him,* and cast *him* out of the vineyard.
v.9 What shall therefore the lord of the vineyard do? he will come and destroy the husbandmen, and will give the vineyard unto others.
v.10 And have ye not read this scripture; The stone which the builders rejected is become the head of the corner:
v.11 This was the Lord's doing, and it is marvellous in our eyes?
v.12 And they sought to lay hold on him, but feared the people: for they knew that he had spoken the parable against them: and they left him, and went their way."

This chapter is a continuation of Tuesday, known as the Day of Antagonism. It commences with the parable of the wicked husbandmen, and ends with the praise of the widow.

1 This is the fourth and final parable preserved for us in Mark. The others are the sower, the automatic seed, the mustard seed (4:1-9, 26-29, 30-34).

The Lord began to speak to them by parables. The word being in the plural refers to the many similitudes in the parable. When He had ended they knew that He had spoken the parable against them. The word parable being in the singular (v.12) presents the unity of its many figures as an allegory.

The details of this parable are derived from the law of Moses (*Torah*), the Prophets (*Neviim*) and the Psalms (*Ketuvim*), the three divisions of the Jewish OT. The description of the vineyard is a cast back to the song of the Well Beloved (Isa 5:1-7). The attitude of the tenants to the well-beloved Son and Heir is reflected in their exact usage of the words of Joseph's brethren: "Come let us kill him" (Gen 37:20). The builders were refusing the Stone, which in God's purpose becomes the capstone, as the quotation from the same Psalm from which the triumphal "Hosanna" had been taken, shows (Ps 118:22-23).

The blessed Lord is presented in this beautiful parable in His Sonship, mission, death, resurrection, exaltation and coming glory.

The man who planted the vineyard represents God's relationship with Israel. The furnishing of the vineyard with a wall for shelter, a place for the wine-fat for storage, a tower for security shows the extent of God's interest to make the vineyard fruitful. It was leased to the tenants, the leaders of Israel, while He was absent in the far country.

2-5 At the vintage the owner sent a servant to receive the fruit of the vineyard. The first slave was taken and beaten and sent away empty. The second was stoned, wounded in the head and insulted. A third was killed and many others who came were beaten and slain. These servants represent the OT prophets and John the Baptist.

6-8 The owner had one final messenger to send, His only Son, His well-beloved. This title was given to the Lord Jesus at His baptism and on the Holy Mount (1:11; 9:7). The expression "last of all" is part of Mark's graphic descriptive language.

He expected the tenants to respect and reverence His well-beloved Son, but the husbandmen expressed the very words of Joseph's brethren, when they saw him in his coat of many colours, the sign of heirship: "The is the heir come let us kill him, and the inheritance shall be ours". What was planned was carried out and they killed the Son of His love.

9 The solemn question of Jesus called upon His hearers to decide the action of the owners: "What shall therefore the lord of the vineyard do? he will come and destroy the husbandmen, and will give the vineyard unto others". The final rejection of Christ by the nation's leaders would bring judgment upon Israel and their privileged position would be transferred to others for a season (Rom 11:25-31).

This judgment fell upon them in the destruction of the city in AD 70.

10-11 Jesus finally quoted: "The stone which the builders rejected is become the head of the corner: This was the Lord's doing and it is marvellous in our eyes" (Ps 118:22-23).

These precious words are Messianic in context (Acts 4:11). The figure changes from the Son slain, to a Stone exalted. The tenants, who had rejected the Son, were also builders, who had refused the Stone. God has raised His Son from among the dead and has highly exalted Him as the living Stone (Rom 1:4; 1 Pet 2:4-8). This reversal of man's opposition is seen as a marvellous thing. It is a display of God's sovereign ways which are past finding out (Rom 11:33-36).

12 The Pharisees were hostile towards Him and sought to arrest Him. They realised this parable was aimed at their conscience. They feared that their interfering with Him might occasion an uprising amongst the people. An open display of hatred would also have shown that they understood the implications of the parable, something they wished to hide. They knew that He had spoken this parable against them, and "they left him, and went their way".

d. *The Second Question: Concerning Taxes (vv.13-17)*

v.13 "And they send unto him certain of the Pharisees and of the Herodians, to catch him in *his* words.
v.14 And when they were come, they say unto him, Master, we know that thou art true, and carest for no man: for thou regardest not the person of men, but teachest the way of God in truth: Is it lawful to give tribute to Caesar, or not?
v.15 Shall we give, or shall we not give? But he, knowing their hypocrisy, said unto them, Why tempt ye me? bring me a penny, that I may see *it*.
v.16 And they brought *it*. And he saith unto them, Whose *is* this image and superscription? And they said unto him, Caesar's.
v.17 And Jesus answering said unto them, Render to Caesar the things that are Caesar's, and to God the things that are God's. And they marvelled at him."

13 The Sanhedrin in their animosity wasted no time in conceiving another plot to discredit Jesus. This time they planned a political charge against Him which would incur the death penalty. Like Pilate and Herod later, who, although bitter enemies, became friends in their common hatred of Jesus (Luke 23:12) the Pharisees and Herodians formed a coalition. The Pharisees were in opposition to their Roman rulers, and therefore hated the imposition of paying taxes, but the Herodians were supporters of the Empire and were favourable to such payments. These two groups had earlier joined together against Jesus, whom they hated (3:6).

This principle operates today when various factions of differing views join forces against Christ (Ps 2:1). On this occasion they came to catch Him in His words. The word "catch" here is to snare, as a hunter would when stalking his prey.

14-15 Their insincerity is shown in their approach to Jesus, with flattering words. Their question was: "Is it lawful to give tribute to Caesar, or not? Shall we give, or shall we not give?" They desired a yes or no to their question.

This question is important, for it raises the principle of responsibility and obligations to an earthly state and to the heavenly Kingdom. These men thought that they had finally trapped the Lord. If His answer was in the affirmative, the Pharisees could denounce Him as a traitor before the people, and if He answered in the negative the Herodians would charge Him to the Roman authority for treason against the Emperor. To all who were present it appeared as a snare without an escape, but Jesus said "bring me a penny, that I may see it". This "penny" was the *denarion*. It was a silver coin minted in Rome and used in every part of the Roman Empire. The tax must always be paid in this coinage. On one side of this penny was the head of Caesar, and on the other a pagan god. The coin was offensive to a Jew. It became the cause of a rebellion at a later date (Acts 5:37).

16 They brought Him the denarius and He showed them the answer to their question was on the coin. He used it as a visual aid. Having turned to the side with Caesar's likeness and title, He asked them "Whose are these?" They acknowledged it was Caesar's.

17 The Roman coin was therefore not for God, but for Caesar. They had asked, "Shall we give, or shall we not give?" His answer was not give (*didomi*) but give back (*apodidomi*) to Caesar. All citizens owe something to the State. There are civil responsibilities which must be rendered, unless they conflict with our conscience to the higher rule of God. We have obligations to the government of the land where we reside and also to the government of the land to which we journey. Our earthly and heavenly responsibilities should be understood by all His disciples (Rom 13:7; 1 Pet 2:13-14).

The Lord silenced His enemies; they marvelled at Him. This incident was important to the first readers of the Gospel, who were Romans. Servants of Christ must be loyal to the state in paying taxes, which is their debt for the benefits of government. Yet Caesar must also be denied Emperor worship; this belongs to God only.

3e *The Third Question: Concerning Resurrection 12:18-27*

e. *The Third Question: Concerning Resurrection (vv.18-27)*

v.18 "Then come unto him the Sadducees, which say there is no resurrection; and they asked him, saying,
v.19 Master, Moses wrote unto us, If a man's brother die, and leave *his* wife *behind him,* and leave no children, that his brother should take his wife, and raise up seed unto his brother.
v.20 Now there were seven brethren: and the first took a wife, and dying left no seed.

v.21 And the second took her, and died, neither left he any seed: and the third likewise.
v.22 And the seven had her, and left no seed: last of all the woman died also.
v.23 In the resurrection therefore, when they shall rise, whose wife shall she be of them? for the seven had her to wife.
v.24 And Jesus answering said unto them, Do ye not therefore err, because ye know not the scriptures, neither the power of God?
v.25 For when they shall rise from the dead, they neither marry, nor are given in marriage; but are as the angels which are in heaven.
v.26 And as touching the dead, that they rise: have ye not read in the book of Moses, how in the bush God spake unto him, saying, I *am* the God of Abraham, and the God of Isaac, and the God of Jacob?
v.27 He is not the God of the dead, but the God of the living: ye therefore do greatly err."

18 Sadducees now came to Him to ensnare Him by their question. This group was largely made up of the priesthood. They held the controlling position of the temple. Following the destruction of the city and the temple in AD 70 they disappeared from history. They differed in doctrine from the Pharisees. They denied bodily resurrection, future punishment, and the existence of angel or spirit (Acts 23:8). On this occasion they thought they would bring into public ridicule the great doctrine of the resurrection.

19-23 Their case was built upon the law of levirate marriage given by Moses (Deut 25:5). When a man died childless, then his brother was to take the widow. The first male child would become the legal heir of the deceased first husband. The provision was to preserve the family line. The case they cited was likely hypothetical. Seven brethren, each in turn, married the same woman, but there was no child. "In the resurrection therefore, when they shall rise, whose wife shall she be?"

24 Jesus' answer was in the form of a rebuke. "Do ye not err therefore, because ye know not the scriptures, neither the power of God?" They were ignorant of the true interpretation of the Scriptures.

25 In the resurrection there will be no conjugal union. There will be no marriage, and no further need of the propagation of the human race. Like the angels, believers will be deathless. Their eternity will be taken up solely with fellowship with God and His Son,

26-27 The Sadducees wrongly asserted that there was no scriptural proof of resurrection in the writings of Moses, upon which they based their doctrines. Therefore Jesus asked them: "Have ye not read in the book of Moses, in the passage called The Bush (there were no chapter and verse divisions at the time in the Hebrew Bible) how God spake unto him saying: I am the God of Abraham, and the God of Isaac, and the God of Jacob?" (Exod 3:6). The Lord then applied the passage saying, "He is not the God of the dead but of the living".

God is still the God of the patriarchs. If death had ended the existence of Abraham, Isaac and Jacob, He never could have said "I am (at that moment) their God".

The final word of Mark concerning this interview is unique to his gospel. Jesus said to them, "Ye do greatly err". The word He used was *planasthe* (from which is derived the English "planet"), meaning "wanderer". The planets seemed to wander to the early astronomers. Jude described the apostates in his day, as wandering planets for whom is reserved the blackness of darkness forever (Jude 13).

It is a serious matter to deny life after death and a future resurrection. Many with Sadducean ideas will not discover this until eternity is reached.

f. *The Fourth Question: Concerning the Greatest Commandment (vv.28-34)*

v.28 "And one of scribes came, and having heard them reasoning together, and perceiving that he had answered them well, asked him, Which is the first commandment of all?
v.29 And Jesus answered him, The first of all the commandments *is,* Hear, O Israel; The Lord our God is one Lord:
v.30 And thou shalt love the Lord thy God with all thy heart, and with all thy soul, and with all thy mind, and with all thy strength: this *is* the first commandment.
v. 31 And the second *is* like, *namely* this, Thou shalt love thy neighbour as thyself. There is none other commandment greater than these.
v.32 And the scribe said unto him, Well, Master, thou has said the truth: for there is one God; and there is none other but he:
v.33 And to love him with all the heart, and with all the understanding, and with all the soul, and with all the strength, and to love *his* neighbour as himself, is more than all whole burnt offerings and sacrifices.
v.34 And when Jesus saw that he answered discreetly, he said unto him, Thou art not far from the kingdom of God. And no man after that durst ask him *any question.*"

28 An impression was made upon this scribe as He listened to Jesus answering the Sadducees so clearly. He was not hostile to Jesus. He desired an answer to a question which was the cause of many legal debates among the law-teachers: "Which is the first commandment of all?" Rabbinical schools taught that there were 613 precepts in the law, divided into 365 prohibitions and 248 commandments. They taught all were binding but some were weighty and some were light. In their debates they had even sought to sum up the whole of the 613 precepts in one single sentence. This is the background to the question of the scribe.

29-31 The Lord immediately quoted the Shema (Deut 6:4-5). It was so called because of the first word "hear" from the Hebrew *Sema.* Every pious Pharisee repeated the Shema twice a day, in the morning when he rose and in the evening before lying down.

The Shema was the foundation of Jewish faith: "Hear O Israel: the Lord is our God, the Lord alone". Here the Jew declared the uniqueness of His God. This God demanded total devotion of love with all the heart, soul and mind.

Jesus then added "This is the first commandment". He also added the words "Thou shalt love thy neighbour as thyself" (Lev 19:18) and "There is none other commandment greater than these" (Rom 13:8; 1 John 4:19-21). To fulfil this commandment with its two separate parts is to fulfil all the others, hence it is the summation of all the 613 precepts known to the Pharisees.

32-34 This answer impressed the scribe and he addressed the Lord as the excellent Teacher. The scribe added to Jesus' statement a true assessment of devotion to God and one's neighbour as being of greater value than all burnt offerings and peace sacrifices.

When Jesus saw his wise response He gave him a commendation followed by a challenge. "Thou art not far from the kingdom of God". He was on the right path and now near to entering the kingdom by faith. There is no further record given of him ever entering. How sad if like Agrippa he was almost persuaded, yet finally lost (Acts 26:28).

From that point no further questions were asked of the Lord by His enemies. He had silenced every opponent. He had also exposed their hostility and error. The greater than Solomon was amongst them, yet they knew Him not.

g. *The Fifth Question: Concerning the Deity of Christ (vv.35-37)*

v.35 "And Jesus answered and said, while he taught in the temple, How say the scribes that Christ is the Son of David?

v.36 For David himself said by the Holy Ghost, The LORD said to my Lord, Sit thou on my right hand, till I make thine enemies thy footstool.

v.37 David therefore himself calleth him Lord; and whence is he *then* his son? And the common people heard him gladly."

35 This question was asked by the Servant Himself of the leaders of Israel. He turned to His former inquisitors with His own question: "How say the scribes that Christ (Messiah) is the Son of David?" The Davidic Sonship of the Christ was believed by the Jews (John 7:41-42). But Jesus added that the Messiah is also David's Lord, and asked, "How can this be?"

36 He then ascribed the Davidic authorship and divine inspiration of Psalm 110 to the King of Israel. This Psalm is the most quoted in the NT (Acts 2:29-35; Heb 1:5-13; 5:6; 7:17-21). The Lord (*Jehovah*) said unto my Lord (*Adonai*), Sit thou at my right hand, until I make thine enemies thy footstool".

37 The wondrous fact was that David called the Messiah his Lord. How can this One be David's son and yet David's Lord? The answer is that He is both God and Man at the same time. Jesus was the Son of David according to the flesh, but He was also the Son of God. Our blessed Lord was earlier than David and yet later than David (Rom 1:3-4; 2 Tim 2:8; Rev 22:16). The law-teachers had no answer, but the common people heard Him with delight.

h. *The Servant's Condemnation of Religious Pride (vv.38-40)*

v.38 "And he said unto them in his doctrine, Beware of the scribes, which love to go in long clothing, and *love* salutations in the marketplaces,
v.39 And the chief seats in the synagogues, and the uppermost rooms at feasts:
v.40 Which devour widows' houses, and for a pretence make long prayers: these shall receive greater damnation."

38-40 The Lord did not condemn all the scribes for religious pride. He had just commended one who was a seeker, and others did receive Him as the Messiah. Here He warns His hearers to be on guard against the evil influence of some of the scribes.

This group will be characterised by four features:

1. They go in long clothing. Their personal appearance in long robes with a broad blue fringe demanded reverence among men.
2. They sought the chief places in the synagogues, and the uppermost rooms at feasts.
3. They took advantage of people of limited means. They were marked by greed.
4. They made long public prayers for a pretence.

What a marked contrast to the perfect Servant of Jehovah: "He shall not cry, nor lift up, nor cause His voice to be heard in the street. A bruised reed shall He not break and the smoking flax shall He not quench" (Isa 42:2-3).

Jesus finally announced that they would receive greater damnation at the judgment day. This denunciation of these scribes concluded His public ministry. The remainder of His ministry on this day took place in the womens' court of the temple, and on the Mount of Olives, and was specially for His disciples alone.

i. *The Servant's Commendation of a Widow's Devotion (vv.41-44)*

v.41 "And Jesus sat over against the treasury, and beheld how the people cast money into the treasury: and many that were rich cast in much.
v.42 And there came a certain poor widow, and she threw in two mites, which make a farthing.
v.43 And he called *unto him* his disciples, and saith unto them, Verily I say unto you, That this poor widow hath cast more in, than all they which have cast into the treasury:
v.44 For all *they* did cast in of their abundance; but she of her want did cast in all that she had, *even* all her living."

41 The account of this widow's devotion is in marked contrast to the outward display of religious fervour manifested in the scribes. The touching scene took place in the court of the women. The Lord sat down and beheld how the gifts were given into the treasury. Along the wall were thirteen copper chests each with a trumpet-like receptacle into which the offerings were dropped. Nine were designated "Jehovah's Offering" and four "The Offering for the Poor". The phrase "sounding the trumpet" was derived from throwing the coins into the receptacle so as to attract attention (Matt 6:2). Jesus saw many that were rich casting in much.

42 His eye finally rested on a destitute widow, who was making her way to the chests. She cast in two mites (*lepta*) which were the smallest of all coins in the land. Mark, for the sake of his Roman readers, states that they were equal to a farthing, which was a quadron in Roman coinage. The value of one mite was a one hundred and twenty-eighth part of a denarius (v.15). The great importance of the incident is not in the value of her gift, but in its value to her; it was all she had.

43-44 The blessed Lord deeply appreciated her devotion and commended her to His disciples. The Lord is concerned with the amount of the sacrifice entailed in a gift, rather than its value.

The simple action of the widow brought joy to the heart of the perfect Servant, and was a fitting summation to His teachings of that day. She had shown a true understanding of what faith meant in the removing of a mountain of difficulty. She would go to bed hungry unless God supplied her need (11:22). She had likely suffered wrong from the scribes, but she could give her gift with a forgiving spirit (11:25; 12:40). She also gave back to God the things that were His (12:17). She obeyed from her heart the first and greatest commandment. She loved the Lord with all her heart and showed this by giving one mite to Jehovah, but she also loved her neighbour as herself and cast one mite to the offering for the poor. This widow was the living embodiment of the ministry of Christ on that day. She shall receive recompense at the resurrection of the just. No person addressed her on that day, and she conversed with none. Having dropped her coins in silence she slipped unnoticed through the crowd. But the all-seeing eye of the Lord had seen her secret sacrifice and had assessed its heavenly value. It is likely that she lived and died without ever knowing that One in the shadowy precincts of the women's court had said to His followers, "More than they all". The smallest gift which is prompted by divine love is of more value to God than the largest offering given for display. Most givers retain the most for self.

The perfect Servant gave also all that He had (Matt 13:45-46). God gave the only Son He had (12:6, John 3:16). What have we given?

IX. The Presage of the Servant (13:1-37)

The Olivet Discourse concerns the future. Now the final ministry of the long Tuesday of controversies moved into the subject of eschatology. The presaging of the Servant is also reported by Matthew and Luke (Matt 24:1-25:46; Luke 21:5-36).

This important chapter may be divided into three main sections:

1.	The Destruction of the Temple Predicted	vv.1-2
2.	The Disciples' Perplexity	vv.3-4
3.	The Discourse on Prophetic Events	vv.5-37.

The third section has four main parts:

a.	The Beginning of the Sorrows	vv.5-13
b.	The Great Tribulation	vv.14-23
c.	After the Tribulation	vv.24-27
d.	The Exhortations to Vigilance	vv.28-37.

It must be clearly understood that the Church is not included in the events outlined by the Lord in His Olivet Discourse. Preceding the prophetic happenings of this chapter is the Rapture of the Church. The great truth of a pre-tribulation Rapture is not mentioned in the Synoptics. It was first made known to the same disciples by the Lord Jesus two days after His ministry on this occasion (John 14:1-3).

The glorious hope of the Church is the coming of the Son of God as the Bridegroom to remove all the saints of this age (1 Thess 4:13-18; 5:9-11; 1 Cor 15:51-53). The church will be spared the final judgments of God upon the earth, and will not go through either the Beginning of the Travail or the Great Tribulation itself (Rev 3:9-10). The return of the Lord for His own will take place prior to the 70th week of Daniel's great prophecy (Dan 9:27). The Rapture is outside of the sphere of prophetic events foretold by the Servant on this occasion. It will not be conditioned by preliminary signs, but is an imminent event for present-day believers, who should be watching, working and waiting in the spirit of expectancy for His arrival.

Having established that the initial phase of His return is not the subject of the Olivet Discourse, the programme of God's dealings especially with Israel will appear evident.

1. *The Destruction of the Temple Predicted* 13:1-2

v.1 "And as he went out of the temple, one of his disciples saith unto him, Master, see what manner of stones and what buildings *are here!*

v.2 And Jesus answering said unto him. Seest thou these great buildings? there shall not be left one stone upon another, that shall not be thrown down."

1 As Jesus left the temple area for the last time, one of His disciples called His attention to the great stones and the outward splendour of the temple building with its complexity of porches, colonnades and courts. The area covered one sixth of the city of Jerusalem. To every Jew it was the sum of all magnificence.

2 The reply of Jesus foretold a day when the great buildings would be totally destroyed. The whole would be levelled to the ground and not one stone left upon another. This would be God's ultimate judgment upon the nation of Israel for their departure from Him and their rejection of His Son as their Messiah, as foretold by the prophets (Jer 26:3-7; Micah 3:11-12). The prophecy given by Jesus was literally fulfilled in the destruction of Jerusalem in AD 70. It is significant to learn from Josephus in his book *The Jewish Wars* that Titus ordered the Roman legions to demolish the temple stone by stone to the ground.

2. *The Disciples Perplexity* 13:3-4

v.3 "And as he sat upon the mount of Olives over against the temple, Peter and James and John and Andrew asked him privately,
v.4 Tell us, when shall these things be? and what *shall be* the sign when all these things shall be fulfilled?"

3-4 Jesus and His disciples now silently walked across the brook Kedron to a point on the side of the Mount of Olives opposite the temple. When He sat down, the four leading disciples came to Him enquiring of the time of the temple's destruction and the sign of the event. The Lord did not answer their question, nor is there any reference made in this chapter to the city of Jerusalem or the temple. Mark's account differs from Luke in this significant fact. Luke presents a double perspective of the destruction of Jerusalem in AD 70, and the Tribulation days just prior to His second coming (Luke 21:8-19, 20-24).

It is of great importance to notice that the four disciples Peter, James, John and Andrew are on this occasion representative of the faithful remnant of Israel who will witness for the Lord during the Tribulation period. Later in the upper room the same men are representative of the Church of this age, and are given the new prospect of the Rapture, in response also to their question (John 13:36-14:30).

3. *The Discourse of Prophetic Events* 13:5-37

a. *The Beginning of the Sorrow (vv.5-13)*

v.5 "And Jesus answering them began to say, Take heed lest any *man* deceive you:
v.6 For many shall come in my name, saying, I am *Christ;* and shall deceive many.

v.7 And when ye shall hear of wars and rumours of wars, be ye not troubled: for *such things* must needs be: but the end *shall* not *be* yet.
v.8 For nation shall rise against nation, and kingdom against kingdom: and there shall be earthquakes in divers places, and there shall be famines and troubles: these *are* the beginnings of sorrows.
v.9 But take heed to yourselves: for they shall deliver you up to councils; and in the synagogues ye shall be beaten: and ye shall be brought before rulers and kings for my sake, for a testimony against them.
v.10 And the gospel must first be published among all nations.
v.11 But when they shall lead *you,* and deliver you up, take no thought beforehand what ye shall speak, neither do ye premeditate: but whatsoever shall be given you in that hour, that speak ye: for it is not ye that speak, but the Holy Ghost.
v.12 Now the brother shall betray the brother to death, and the father the son; and children shall rise up against *their* parents, and shall cause them to be put to death.
v.13 And ye shall be hated of all *men* for my name's sake: but he that shall endure unto the end, the same shall be saved."

5 It is vitally important to see that the apostles to whom Jesus addressed Himself represented the godly remnant of Israel, who will live and testify for the Lord during the time of Jacob's trouble (Jer 30:7) or the Tribulation days. He speaks to them of events over 2,000 years ahead, yet places them as present in the centre of all the happenings. These instructions will be of very special interest to those who read them when the time has come. The forecast given by the Lord introduces a series of conditions which will prevail on earth immediately following the Rapture of the Church. The recurring phrase "take heed", mentioned four times, is important (vv.5, 9, 23, 33).

6 The events predicted in vv.6–13 should be placed alongside the Seal judgments (Rev 6:1-17). It is obvious that events in the last apocalyptic book have a background in the earlier prophecies. Evidential proof of this lies in the fact that the 70th week of Daniel's prophecy is both the subject of the Olivet Discourse and the section of Revelation taken up with "things which shall be after these things", i.e. after the things of the Church age (Dan 9:27; Mark 13:14; Rev 4:1-19:21).

The Lord warns of the appearance on earth of pretenders who will claim His authority and deity, saying "I am". Many will be led astray by this deception. Following the opening of the first seal, a white horse with a rider holding a bow and wearing a victor's crown comes forth conquering and to conquer (Rev 6:1-2). This ruler is a false Messiah, a sinister victor.

7-8 A period of wars and rumours of wars, aggression among nations and kingdom rising against kingdom is forecast by the Lord. This condition correlates with the opening of the second seal when in contrast to the rider upon the white horse, a second rider upon a red horse and carrying a great sword takes peace from the earth (Rev 6:3-4). It is a time of serious anarchy, but is only the beginnings of sorrow.

There shall be many earthquakes and famines and troubles. These are also more fully described in Revelation. When the third seal is opened famine is seen as the terrible aftermath of war, and the time of inflated prices causes the poor to perish. The black colour of the horse is death. The pale horse represents the troubles mentioned by Jesus, while the earthquake is an introduction to the fearful judgments of the sixth seal (Rev 6:5-12).

The term "the beginnings of sorrows" is literally "the beginning of birth pains". It is clear that this term is an overall description of the first half of the prophetic week of years, a period of 42 months or 1,260 days, to be followed by the Great Tribulation in the last three and a half years, (Dan 9:27; Rev 11:3; 12:6; 13:5). Beyond this period of intense suffering is the final birth of the Messianic Kingdom of our Lord Jesus Christ.

9-13 A period of persecution, betrayal and hatred is predicted. These will be arranged by religious leaders, political dictators and domestic relations. Trials have been the portion in other times but nothing to equal the future Great Tribulation, which will be introduced by these early sufferings during the first three and a half years, or the beginnings of the travail. Those arrested in those days have a special promise of the assistance of the Holy Spirit to advocate their cause, in the absence of earthly defence. Martyrs will be many during this period. When the fifth seal was opened, John had a revelation of the souls of these martyrs in heaven, who asked the question: "How long, O Lord, holy and true, dost thou not judge and avenge our blood on them that dwell on the earth?". The answer shows that they are indeed the martyrs of this period, and that the time of the Great Tribulation, in which many others will be martyred, is about to commence (Rev 6:9-11).

The fact that the gospel must first be published among all nations is more fully given by Matthew: "And this gospel of the kingdom shall be preached in the whole world, for a witness to all nations, and then shall the end come" (Matt 24:14). The gospel always means "good news" and has its foundations upon the death and resurrection of Christ, but its content differs in various ages. The message to be preached here is unique and should not be confused with the gospel of the grace of God of this present age. It is a message concerning the coming Messianic Kingdom on earth and the imminent advent of the King Himself.

The expression "he that shall endure unto the end, the same shall be saved" must not be construed as a condition of eternal salvation. The basis of that salvation is the finished work of Christ upon the cross. The endurance here is the enduring of the severe persecutions in faithfulness to the Lord, and the salvation is physical. Those who survive will join the great company who shall come out of the Great Tribulation, and enter into the earthly department of the Kingdom (Rev 7:13-17). It is thus established that this "Little Apocalypse" (Mark 13) forms part of the key to the understanding of that which is amplified in the "Greater Apocalypse", Revelation.

b. *The Great Tribulation (vv.14-23)*

v.14 "But when ye shall see the abomination of desolation, spoken of by Daniel the prophet, standing where it ought not, (let him that readeth understand,) then let them that be in Judaea flee to the mountains:
v.15 And let him that is on the housetop not go down into the house, neither enter *therein,* to take any thing out of his house:
v.16 And let him that is in the field not turn back again for to take up his garment.
v.17 But woe to them that are with child, and to them that give suck in those days!
v.18 And pray ye that your flight be not in the winter.
v.19 For *in* those days shall be affliction, such as was not from the beginning of the creation which God created unto this time, neither shall be.
v.20 And except that the Lord had shortened those days, no flesh should be saved: but for the elect's sake, whom he hath chosen, he hath shortened the days.
v.21 And then if any man shall say unto you, Lo, here *is* Christ; or, lo, *he is* there; believe *him* not:
v.22 For false Christs and false prophets shall rise, and shall shew signs and wonders, to seduce, if *it were* possible, even the elect.
v.23 But take ye heed: behold, I have foretold you all things."

14 This solemn section deals with details of the Great Tribulation. It is described by Jeremiah as "the time of Jacob's trouble" (Jer 30:7) and by Daniel as "a time of trouble, such as never was, since there was a nation" (Dan 12:1). The signal of the beginning of this period is the abomination of desolation or sacrilege that shocks. This awful abomination is first mentioned by Daniel and on three separate occasions: Dan 9:27; 11:31; 12:11.

The original has reference to the desecration of the temple by the Syrian invader, Antiochus Epiphanes in 167 BC. To this Daniel refers in Dan 11:31. This evil man erected an altar to the pagan god Zeus on the site of the altar of burnt offerings, and sacrificed swine upon it. This event in the past foreshadows the more serious abomination that will be the cause of desolation in the future. Mark altered the neuter "it" to "he" (RV) and applies it to the evil person who will stand where he has no right to be found. This person is the "Man of Sin" (2 Thess 2:3-4). He is described as sitting in the temple, proclaiming himself to be God. This requires the rebuilding of the temple in which the detestable abomination will be enacted (Rev 11:1). This abomination of desolation is specially linked with Daniel's prophecy of the 70th week of years. Antichrist will make a covenant with the Jewish people for a seven-year period, but in the middle of the period he will break his covenant, cause all temple sacrifices to cease, desecrate the holy place, and finally proclaim himself to be God Almighty (Matt 24:15; 2 Thess 2:3-4; Rev 11:2). When this takes place it will be the world-wide signal that the Great Tribulation has commenced. All who fail to bow to the beast will suffer the severity of his wrath, and therefore should make haste to flee to the mountains.

15-18 Jesus describes the haste and urgency that the crisis will demand of those who would escape. One working upon a roof should in no case even enter his house for his possessions, and one in the field should never return to take his coat. A special compassion was expressed by the perfect Servant as He spoke of pregnant women and nursing mothers forced to run from their homes. A special prayer should be offered that the Great Tribulation will not commence in winter, when the rains and storms would impede progress to the place of safety.

19-20 Those days have never been equalled for distress since the beginning of creation, nor shall the like ever be known again.

The prophecies of the OT fixed the duration of the Great Tribulation as three and a half years, 42 months or 1,260 days. The blessed Lord, however, has other plans, and in His sovereign mercy the days will terminate earlier, otherwise no person would survive. This limitation is for the sake of the elect, His chosen and redeemed people of those difficult days.

21-23 In those terrible days it is amazing to read of the many false Christs and false prophets that will arise. They will display signs and wonders, under the influence of seducing spirits. Their supernatural demonstrations will deceive multitudes, but no true believer will follow them or be seduced. Jesus again uses the warning "Take heed" or "Be Alert". He had given them ample warning of the serious nature of those days, and His words were well ahead of the time.

c. *After the Tribulation (vv.24-27)*

v.24 "But in those days, after that tribulation, the sun shall be darkened, and the moon shall not give her light,
v.25 And the stars of heaven shall fall, and the powers that are in heaven shall be shaken.
v.26 And then shall they see the Son of man coming in the clouds with great power and glory.
v.27 And then shall he send his angels, and shall gather together his elect from the four winds, from the uttermost part of the earth to the uttermost part of heaven."

This wonderful section points to the triumphant Advent of Christ.

24-25 The time of the glorious advent of the Messiah is indicated as being after the Tribulation. Preceding His arrival a number of cosmic signs shall appear: the sun shall be darkened; the moon shall not give her light, and stars shall fall one after the other. These disturbances in the heavens need not be symbolised, but rather accepted as literal happenings.

26 When these final signs in the heavens have taken place, everyone on earth shall see the Son of Man coming in clouds with great power and glory.

Every eye shall see Him; He will be visible to the whole world (Rev 1:7). This is the visible personal advent of the glorified Son of Man, as described by Himself here and at His trial (14:62); He said to the high priest "Ye shall see the Son of man, sitting on the right hand of power, and coming in the clouds of heaven".

27 He shall also send His angels into new service. They shall gather His elect from the four winds, which means every part of the earth. This wonderful re-gathering of Israel is the subject of many OT prophecies (Isa 11:12; Jer 31:7-9). Many of His elect, His chosen and redeemed, will be in the land already, but this final gathering will bring all the redeemed of Israel around their Messiah to gladly own Him as their Lord and King (John 1:49; 20:28; Rom 11:25-27).

d. *The Exhortations to Vigilance (vv.28-37)*

v.28 "Now learn a parable of the fig tree; When her branch is yet tender, and putteth forth leaves, ye know that summer is near:
v.29 So ye in like manner, when ye shall see these things come to pass, know that it is nigh, *even* at the doors.
v.30 Verily I say unto you, that this generation shall not pass, till all these things be done.
v.31 Heaven and earth shall pass away: but my words shall not pass away.
v.32 But of that day and *that* hour knoweth no man, no, not the angels which are in heaven, neither the Son, but the Father.
v.33 Take ye heed, watch and pray: for ye know not when the time is.
v.34 *For the Son of man is* as a man taking a far journey, who left his house, and gave authority to his servants, and to every man his work, and commanded the porter to watch.
v.35 Watch ye therefore: for ye know not when the master of the house cometh, at even, or at midnight, or at the cockcrowing, or in the morning:
v.36 Lest coming suddenly he find you sleeping.
v.37 And what I say unto you I say unto all, Watch."

28-29 The fig tree in these verses is in marked contrast to the fig tree at the commencement of the day's ministry (11:20), although in both Israel is typified. In the first the tree was withered and cursed, but here the tree is sprouting again. The fig tree is not an evergreen, but loses its leaves in winter and blooms in the late spring. When the dried twigs become tender, as the sap rises and the leaves appear, the tree becomes a sure harbinger of the approach of summer. Israel, as a nation, will be seen in wondrous glory in the Messianic Kingdom of the Lord Jesus Christ. For them the winter will be past, and the rain over and gone, "the flowers appear on the earth; the time of the singing of birds is come, and the voice of the turtle is heard in our land; The fig tree putteth forth her green figs" (Song of Songs 2:11-13). The Lord therefore states that when that glorious time is near, Israel's springing to life will be the true indication. When these things come to pass it will be known also that "he (RV) is near", i.e. the Son of Man is near.

30 This verse is best understood as meaning that the generation of Jesus living in the end of the Great Tribulation who will witness the events of those final days, will not come to an end or pass off the earth, until the things pertaining to the advent of the Messiah have been consummated.

31 Jesus states clearly that these words pertaining to these events will remain, even when the present heavens and earth have come to a cataclysmic end. This statement of Jesus shows His words to be eternal, and every detail of prediction will surely come to pass.

32 The nearness of the coming of the Son of Man is sure, but the exact time as to the day and the hour no one knoweth, not even the angels, neither the Son but the Father. Date-setting is impossible.

To understand the expression "neither the Son, but the Father", the spheres of the administrations and purposes of the Persons of the Godhead must be considered. The Son is co-equal with the Father, but He voluntarily accepted the place of subjection in coming into the world in Manhood. Yet at no time was He inferior to the Father, or limited in His knowledge (1 Cor 11:3). The Son took the place of subjection as Jehovah's perfect Servant in order to achieve the eternal counsels of the Godhead. These counsels were worked out by the Son, as He fulfilled the will of the Father in the power of the Holy Spirit. It is very important to realise that each Person in the Godhead has His own sphere of divine action. The Son states that positions in the kingdom, and times and seasons, are in the authority and domain of the Father (10:40). He acknowledges willingly that dates, hours and times are not in His hand, and as the perfect Servant He acknowledges the Father's administration.

Later He said to His disciples "It is not for you to know the times or the seasons, which the Father hath put in his own power" (Acts 1:7). What He, as the Servant of Jehovah, acknowledged concerning times and seasons and dates should be true of every servant. This would save from the folly of date-fixing, a trap into which even some Christians have fallen.

There is no question of limitation or self-limitation in this verse. The blessed Lord Jesus is at one and the same time both God and Man. He embodied in Himself two whole and perfect natures, each in fulness co-existing in one glorious Person. He remains in the realm of inscrutability, and it is beyond any to understand the mystery of His Person.

33-37 Vigilance is incumbent upon all the servants of Christ in all the age, hence the use of the verb "watch" four times in this short section: "Watch and pray"; He "commanded the porter to watch"; "Watch ... for ye know not when the master ... cometh": "I say unto all, Watch" (vv.33, 34, 35, 37).

The reference to the four watches of the night is according to the Roman division of the night. It suggests the whole period of His absence (Rom 13:11-

12): in the even He was taken up as the glorified Shepherd at His ascension (Luke 24:50, 51); at midnight His hands are lifted up as the tender Sympathiser (Matt 14:22ff.); at cockcrowing He will catch up His blood-bought Church as the coming Saviour (Rev 22:16); in the morning He will set up His Messianic Kingdom as the supreme Sovereign (Zech 14:4).

His people in every part of the night should be watching and waiting. The imminence of His return is impressive truth for all saints. Jesus said, "What I say unto you (Great Tribulation saints) I say unto all (Church age saints), Watch."

Notes

3 The Four Representative Disciples

1. *Peter.* Delivered from the sword of Herod and brought out of the prison safely, he pictures the godly remnant in their preservation from the sword of the beast and brought through the Great Tribulation alive.
2. *James.* Beheaded by Herod, he is a picture of the martyrs of the Tribulation period.
3. *John.* Jesus said "If I will that he tarry till I come" concerning him, Later he was caught up in vision to heaven, prior to the awful visions of the Tribulation days (Rev 4:1 John 21:22). He is, therefore, a picture of the Church raptured into Heaven before the Great Tribulation.
4. *Andrew.* Having brought his brother to the Lord for salvation, and later the Greeks (John 1:41; 12:22), he is a picture of the remnant in testimony to Jew and Gentile during the Tribulation.

35 The Lord as Master of the House

Four aspects of the coming of Christ in the four Gospels.

1. In Matthew the King is coming to reign	Matt 25:34
2. In Mark the Master of the house is coming to regulate	Mark 13:35
3. In Luke the Nobleman is coming to reward	Luke 19:12
4. In John the Bridegroom is coming to receive	John 14:3.

X. The Passion of the Servant (14:1-15:47)

This section presents the Servant giving His life a ransom for many (10:45). There are four great days in this section:

1	Wednesday	The Day of Anointing	14:1-11
2.	Thursday	The Day of Anticipation	14:12-31
3.	Friday	The Day of Atonement	14:32-15:41
4.	Saturday	The Day of Absence	15:42-47

1. *Wednesday The Day of Anointing* 14:1-11

There are three paragraphs which cover the events recorded by Mark on this day. The last Wednesday seems to have been spent in the quietness of the village of Bethany in the enjoyment of the love of devoted hearts. Like other sections in this Gospel this one has an alternating construction. The conspiracy of men to destroy the Servant and to betray Him is in contrast to the consecration of a woman to honour Him.

a.	The Decision of the Rulers to kill Christ	vv.1-2
b.	The Devotion of Mary to anoint Christ	vv.3-9
c.	The Determination of Judas to betray Christ	vv.10-11.

a. *The Decision of the Rulers to destroy Jesus (vv.1-2)*

v.1 "After two days was *the feast of* the passover, and of unleavened bread: and the chief priests and the scribes sought how they might take him by craft, and put *him* to death.
v.2 But they said, Not on the feast *day*, lest there be an uproar of the people."

1 This is the first mention by Mark of the Passover. It was one of the three annual Jewish feasts. It was celebrated in Jerusalem in the month Nisan (March-April) on the fourteenth and fifteenth day of that month, which coincided with the Thursday and Friday of Passion week.

The celebration commenced with the death of the Passover lamb near the end of the fourteenth Nisan, or Thursday afternoon. The Passover meal, eaten at the beginning of the fifteenth Nisan between sunset and midnight on Thursday, marked the commencement of the feast of Unleavened Bread which continued until the twenty-first Nisan. Then the Jewish people commemorated their Exodus from Egypt (Exod 12:1-20). These two feasts were often spoken of as one, and called the Jewish Passover (2 Chron 35:17).

2 Two days before the Passover would be Nisan thirteenth, or Wednesday. The counsel of the Sanhedrin sought a secret plan by which they could arrest Jesus, and put Him to death. They had a great difficulty, as the thousands of pilgrims at the feast were favourable to Jesus. They therefore feared an uprising. It was decided to postpone their actions for a week, when the city would have returned to normality. The programme of God, however, demanded the death of the Lamb at the Passover. He overruled the intentions of the chiefs and the scribes who had said "not on the feast day".

b. *The Devotion of Mary to anoint Christ (vv.3-9)*

v.3 "And being in Bethany in the house of Simon the leper, as he sat at meat, there

came a woman having an alabaster box of ointment of spikenard very precious; and she brake the box, and poured *it* on his head.
v.4 And there were some that had indignation within themselves, and said, Why was this waste of the ointment made?
v.5 For it might have been sold for more than three hundred pence, and have been given to the poor. And they murmured against her.
v.6 And Jesus said, Let her alone: why trouble ye her? she hath wrought a good work on me.
v.7 For ye have the poor with you always, and whensoever ye will ye may do them good: but me ye have not always.
v.8 She hath done what she could: she is come aforehand to anoint my body to the burying.
v.9 Verily I say unto you, Wheresoever this gospel shall be preached throughout the whole world, *this* also that she hath done shall be spoken of for a memorial of her."

3 This anointing of Jesus at Bethany is also recorded by Matthew and John (Matt 26:6-13; John 12:1-8), but should not be equated with the anointing of the Lord recorded by Luke (Luke 7:36-50). This anointing was by Mary of Bethany in Judaea, whereas the latter was by an unnamed sinful woman in Galilee.

A chronological problem arises from the misunderstanding of John's account: "Then Jesus six days before the Passover came to Bethany" (John 12:1). It is not necessary to conclude that the supper in His honour was held on that day, which would place it on the Saturday before His triumphal entry into Jerusalem. Mark, who wrote his Gospel first usually details his material chronologically. He states that the anointing took place on the Wednesday of Passion week. Matthew also states this. The placing of the anointing two days before the Passover on Wednesday, is more suitable to the context, as it is in sharp contrast to the treacherous actions of the Sanhedrin and Judas, the betrayer.

The anointing is said to have taken place in the house of Simon the leper, as Jesus sat at meat. Nothing is known of this Simon and speculation is unreliable. The woman who came with the alabaster flask of ointment of genuine nard – a very costly oil, obtained from an aromatic Indian plant – was of Bethany (John 12:3). She is not named by Mark.

The graphic language of Mark concerning the woman's actions reveals the devotion of her heart and the value of her service: "she brake the box" showing that she would not withhold a drop, but pour all upon her Lord. Her worship was after the same order as the widow of the previous day, who gave all that she had (12:41-44). This unreserved devotion brought delight to the perfect Servant, and is still acceptable to God (Heb 13:16).

Matthew and Mark state that she poured the ointment upon His head. The King of glory and the Servant of grace was anointed upon His head. John, however, records the fact that she anointed His feet also and wiped them with her hair. Here the worshipper takes the lowly place at the feet of the Son of God.

The scene recalls the anointing of David in the midst of his brethren before he faced the enemy, and was rejected by the world and his brethren. He was anointed upon his head to be the servant of God and as the sovereign of Israel (Ps 78:70-71; 1 Sam 16:12-13). Only the greater than David could have anointed feet; the pathway of David was defiled. Concerning David, "he was ruddy" but only of the Lord, "He is white and ruddy". Samuel was confused as to the person who should have the anointing, but Mary knew that Christ was the only One worthy of the oil.

The pouring forth of the ointment revealed the fragrance of His Name and the greatness of His Person (Song 1:3).

4-5 Judas became the leader of an opposition movement against her action, in which the disciples joined. They looked upon the ointment as wasted. Since the ointment was valued at 300 denaria it equalled the wages of a labouring man for a year. The contention of the disciples was that it could have been sold and distributed to the poor. To be concerned for the poor was right, but here it was a mere cloak to hide their lack of appreciation of the woman's devotion and also the greed of Judas. They began to murmur, which means to scold her for her deed. This record is unique to Mark.

6-8 The Lord defended Mary and praised her. His estimation of her act was "she hath wrought a good work on me". It is interesting to note that the word "good" is ***kalon*** which literally means "an excellent work". Jesus placed great value upon her expression of love.

He then shows them that they will always have opportunity to help the poor, but as He would soon be leaving them the opportunity to express their devotion to His Person was limited. The opportunity to serve others is always available, but occasions to worship the Lord are restricted.

The beautiful words "She hath done what she could" are also preserved alone by Mark, being a true standard for all service. The Lord only expects what there is ability to perform.

The secret of the Lord belonged to Mary for she not only anointed Him in view of His kingly glory at His Messianic coronation, but also with His death and burial before her heart. She had evidently learned as she sat at His feet and heard His word that His holy body would never see corruption, and therefore would require no spices for burial (Ps 16:8-11). Peter learned the same truth later and quoted this Psalm in his great Pentecost sermon (Acts 2:24-29). The flask that she had kept for the day of His burying would be useless then, so she would pour it upon the living Christ. In this connection it is interesting to notice that Mary did not join the other women who brought sweet spices to the tomb to anoint Him; she knew better (Mark 16:1).

9 Jesus promised that her act would be remembered long after His death, burial and resurrection, right down through the centuries of time. Wherever the gospel, the record of the perfect Servant's activities would be told throughout the whole world, the influence of Mary's sacrificial act of devotion would be known. Jesus gave her a unique place in the spiritual hall of fame. It is interesting also that Matthew and Mark, who alone report the Saviour's praise, withheld her name. It can be said of her: "Many daughters have done virtuously, but thou excellest then all. Favour is deceitful and beauty is vain, but a woman that feareth the Lord she shall be praised" (Prov 31:29-30).

c. *The Determination of Judas to betray Christ (vv.10-11)*

v.10 "And Judas Iscariot, one of the twelve, went unto the chief priests, to betray him unto them.
v.11 And when they heard *it,* they were glad, and promised to give him money. And he sought how he might conveniently betray him."

10-11 In the background of this beautiful vignette is the sinister form of the betrayer. He left the scene of worship and the house that was filled with fragrance for the presence of the chief priests, to offer assistance by betraying Jesus into their wicked hands at a time and place which would be unknown to the multitudes. His visit and promise to betray Jesus made them glad, and they promised to give him money. Matthew states that they gave him thirty pieces of silver (Matt 26:15). It was not simply the price of a slave, but a slave gored by an ox (Exod 21:32). It was also the price of the services of the rejected shepherd (Zech 11:12). From that moment Judas kept looking for the opportune time to betray Him into their hands.

2. *Thursday The Day of Anticipation* 14:12-31

There are four main parts in Mark's account of the Servant's private ministry on the Thursday of Passion week.

a.	The Passover Prepared	In the Morning	vv.12-16
b.	The Passover Celebrated	At Sunset	vv.17-21
c.	The Lord's Supper Instituted	In the Evening	vv.22-25
d.	The Lord's Denial Predicted	At Nightfall	vv.26-31.

a. *The Passover Prepared (vv.12-16)*

v.12 "And the first day of unleavened bread, when they killed the passover, his disciples said unto him, Where wilt thou that we go and prepare that thou mayest eat the passover?
v.13 And he sendeth forth two of his disciples, and saith unto them, Go ye into the city, and there shall meet you a man bearing a pitcher of water: follow him.

v.14 And wheresoever he shall go in, say ye to the goodman of the house, The Master saith, Where is the guestchamber, where I shall eat the passover with my disciples?
v.15 And he will shew you a large upper room furnished *and* prepared: there make ready for us.
v.16 And his disciples went forth, and came into the city, and found as he had said unto them: and they made ready the passover."

12 The Passover lamb was killed on the first day of unleavened bread, which was the afternoon of the 14th day of the month Nisan. The meal was eaten in the evening which marked the commencement of the 15th day of Nisan.

The disciples spoke to Jesus, apparently at Bethany in the morning of that day, concerning His instructions for the preparation of the Passover. They were anxious to know where the preparation would take place.

13 Jesus sent two of them, whom we learn from Luke's account were Peter and John (Luke 22:8), into the city of Jerusalem with definite instructions. A man would meet them bearing a pitcher of water. This one would become their guide to the place. Usually a woman did this kind of work. They would therefore have no difficulty in knowing the one to follow. He would be a servant marked by humility, doing a woman's task.

14 They were to ask the goodman of the house for the location of the guest chamber. Mark's inclusion of the personal pronoun is significant: "The Teacher saith: Where is my guest-chamber?" (RV). That the owner knew Jesus and the Lord also had supplied the disciples with his name is implied by Matthew, but he remains nameless in the records (Matt 26:18).

15 The Lord also informed them of the result to be expected. They would be shown a large upper room furnished for the passover. The two were then to make ready the passover supper for Jesus and the rest of the twelve.

16 Mark describes in graphic language the exact fulfilment of the words of Jesus. Peter, who is always in the shadows of Mark's reporting, doubtless supplied this added information. It is a demonstration of the omniscience of the perfect Servant, who knew all things, and had power to induce the goodman of the house to show favour to Him and His disciples by having a suitable room prepared for their Sedar.

b. *The Passover Celebrated (vv.17-21)*

v.17 "And in the evening he cometh with the twelve.
v.18 And as they sat and did eat, Jesus said, Verily I say unto you, One of you which eateth with me shall betray me.
v.19 And they began to be sorrowful, and to say unto him one by one, *Is* it I? and another *said, Is it* I?

v.20 And he answered and said unto them, *It is* one of the twelve, that dippeth with me in the dish.
v.21 The Son of man indeed goeth, as it is written of him: but woe to that man by whom the Son of man is betrayed! good were it for that man if he had never been born."

The brief account of the events in the upper room cover eight verses in Mark, in John five chapters. The emphasis on Mark's record is upon the announcement of the betrayal, and the institution of the Lord's Supper.

17 In the evening, at sunset, Jesus came with the twelve to the large upper room.

18 Between these two verses two events not recorded by Mark took place; the contention between the disciples as to which of them should be the greatest, and the washing of the disciples feet by Jesus (Luke 22:24-30; John 13:1-20). The sad words of Jesus concerning the fact that one of the number would betray Him caused them to be sorrowful.

19 One by one they asked Him "Is it I?". They showed no suspicion of Judas, else they would have not suspected themselves.

20 Jesus identified the betrayer as the one that dipped with him in the dish. This revealed the treachery of Judas, but also gave him an opportunity to retract and repent.

21 The Lord now made a plain statement concerning His death. "The Son of man indeed goeth, as it is written of Him." His death will fulfil all the prophecies of the Scriptures (Ps 22; Isa 53). His death was by the determinate counsel of God, but the betrayer was also responsible, being the agent of Satan (John 13:2, 27). The solemn words of Jesus show the awful destiny of Judas. His non-existence would have been preferable to his future in hell. Divine arrangements do not minimise human responsibility.

At this point Judas went out from the company into the night (John 13:30).

c. *The Lord's Supper Instituted (vv.22-25)*

v.22 "And as they did eat, Jesus took bread, and blessed, and brake *it*, and gave to them, and said, Take, eat: this is my body.
v.23 And he took the cup, and when he had given thanks, he gave *it* to them: and they all drank of it.
v.24 And he said unto them, This is my blood of the new testament, which is shed for many.
v.25 Verily I say unto you, I will drink no more of the fruit of the vine, until that day that I drink it new in the kingdom of God."

22 It is clearly stated by Paul that Judas was not present when the Lord instituted the Lord's Supper: "the Lord Jesus the same night in which he was betrayed" – or rather while He was being betrayed, as the imperfect tense signifies, that is, as the negotiations between Judas and the Sanhedrin were in progress – Jesus instituted the supper. Judas had therefore left the upper room before the institution of the Supper (1 Cor 11:23).

As they were eating He took bread, and blessed God (not the bread) and brake it, giving it to His disciples. He then said "Take, eat: this is my body". The verb "is" means "represents". It is obvious that this is the true meaning, for He was there present in His body as He spake these words. The disciples did not eat His body literally or drink His blood. The dogma of transubstantiation has no scriptural foundation, but is a fabric of human invention.

23 He also took the cup, containing wine, and when He had given thanks He gave it to them, and they all partook of it.

24 He then explained the meaning of the cup. It represented His blood of the New Testament, which is shed for many. The word "covenant" is the accurate translation of "testament".

A testament is a will, but the covenant was God's new arrangement in dealing with men in grace on the grounds of the sacrifice of His Son. The covenant was established by God. Its infinite blessings may be accepted by men or finally rejected.

The word *huper* in the phrase "the blood ... shed for many" means shed "on behalf of many" being a clear reference to the vicarious character of the Lord's death.

25 The Lord now spake to them of a future banquet. It would result in the reunion of His people in the glorious Messianic kingdom with its joy and fellowship.

The Lord's Supper replaced the Passover. It was to be continued in the simplicity of its institution by companies of believers who gather upon the Lord's Day, to break bread in remembrance of Him, and to proclaim His death, till He come (Acts 2:42; 20:7; 1 Cor 11:23-26).

d. *The Lord's Denial Predicted (vv.26-31)*

v.26 "And when they had sung an hymn, they went out into the mount of Olives.
v.27 And Jesus saith unto them, All ye shall be offended because of me this night: for it is written, I will smite the shepherd, and the sheep shall be scattered.
v.28 But after that I am risen, I will go before you into Galilee.
v.29 But Peter said unto him, Although all shall be offended, yet *will* not I.
v.30 And Jesus saith unto him, Verily I say unto thee, That this day, *even* in this night, before the cock crow twice, thou shalt deny me thrice.

v.31 But he spake the more vehemently, If I should die with thee, I will not deny thee in any wise. Likewise also said they all."

26 It was the usual custom at the Passover to sing the Hallel Psalms, which were the great praise Psalms of Israel (Ps 113-118). The first two were sung before the Sedar and the last four at its conclusion. A consideration of some of the beautiful words of the last Psalm (118) will show how appropriate was the language upon the lips of the blessed Lord, as He led the singing of His disciples:

"The Lord is on my side; I will not fear: what can man do unto me?" (Ps 118:6)

"I shall not die, but live..." (v.17)

"The stone which the builders refused is become the head stone of the corner." (v.22)

"Bind the sacrifice with cords, even unto the horns of the altar." (v.27)

The singing of the Lord on the way to His sufferings should touch the heart of all those who have been redeemed.

It was near midnight when the little group left the seclusion of the upper room, walked along the valley of the Kedron and finally crossed the brook to the western slope of Olivet, where the garden of Gethsemane was located.

27 Jesus warned His disciples that they would all stumble because of Him that night. The events about to take place would shake all their faith. He then quoted the beautiful words in keeping with His prediction "I will smite the shepherd, and the sheep shall be scattered" (Zech 13:7). The change by the Lord of the written prophesy shows that He viewed Himself as the Shepherd, who would be smitten by God, and His disciples would be scattered. Although smitten He would later turn His hand upon the little ones (Zech 13:7).

28 The Shepherd will rise again, and will go before His sheep into Galilee. He will gather again His scattered flock. The wondrous promise of His resurrection passed unnoticed by the eleven.

29 Peter in self-confidence affirmed that though all others would stumble he would remain faithful and steadfast.

30 Jesus informed him other-wise: "This day, even in this night, before the cock crow twice, thou shalt deny me thrice".

The time factor is specially recorded by Mark alone, as "before the cock crow twice".

31 Mark also adds a detail passed over by the other writers concerning Peter's assertion of his faithfulness. He describes the manner of Peter's address as being vehement. He uses the compound adverb *ekperissos* which means "exceeding vehemently".

Peter, who is in the shadow of Mark's account, recalled these two important details of the event. Jesus had given him a special warning as to the timing of his denial, and he also remembered the strength of his objection to the prediction of his fall. These intimate details from Peter's memorabilia add an intimate graphic touch to the writing of Mark.

The "cock crowing" was an expression describing the early morning, or the third watch of the night (13:35). On this occasion this particular cock would crow twice in quick succession. The Creator Himself would arrange the unusual occurrence, so that all of them might be reminded of the forewarning of Jesus when the incident took place (v.72).

All the disciples expressed their loyalty to the Lord, but all of them were unaware of their human weakness.

Notes

29-31 It is not the uniform that tests the soldier, but the conflict.
It is not the classroom that tests the student, but the examination.
It is not the time of hymn singing that tests the believer, but the persecution.
Our only strength is in God (W. G. Scroggie).

3. *Friday The Day of Atonement* 14:32-15:41

This day begins and ends in a garden.

a.	Gethsemane	14:32-42:	The sufferings of the Servant in anticipation.
b.	Betrayal	14:43-52:	The sufferings at the hand of a former disciple.
c.	The Trial	14:53-65:	The sufferings from false accusations. (The first hearing: His religious trial before the Sanhedrin in the palace of the high priest).
d.	The Denial	14:66-72:	The sufferings from one of His own.
e.	The Trial	15:1-15:	The sufferings from unrighteous judgment. (The second hearing: His civil trial before Pilate in the palace of the governor).
f.	Praetorium	15:16-20:	The sufferings from the soldiers.
g.	Golgotha	15:21-41:	The sufferings from the hand of God, as the Sin-Offering.

This wonderful day, the greatest in time, and the centre of the ages, begins in the garden of Gethsemane and ends in the garden of the tomb or the memorial garden.

It is with washed feet and bowed hearts that we commence the study of this record of the sufferings of the perfect Servant of Jehovah, on the day when His soul was made an offering for sin. Mark specially relates to the sin-offering aspect of the Lord's death. Matthew, who presents the trespass-offering aspect, emphasises the supernatural happenings surrounding His death. The peace-offering is presented by Luke, and in that Gospel the sympathy of the suffering One is pre-eminent, while in John's record the Lord is seen fulfilling the Scriptures in the events around His sacrifice, for there the theme is the burnt-offering. In Mark the Saviour is viewed as the bearer of sin and in His sufferings the perfect Servant is marked by His silence under all the pressures and circumstances associated with the atonement. This day is the epitome of all His service. He offered no resistance to the abuse, mockery, spitting, beatings and agonising death by crucifixion.

The climax of all His sufferings was the hours of sin-bearing, when Jehovah laid upon Him the iniquity of us all. It was then, on the cross, that He died for our sins according to the Scriptures (Isa 53:5-6; Ps 22:1-21; 2 Cor 5:21; 1 Pet 2:24). This is the outstanding feature of His Servanthood. He came not to be ministered unto, but to minister; this is the substance of Mark 11-15 (see 10:45b). And to rise again the third day is the substance of Mark 16 (see 9:31).

a. *Gethsemane: Sufferings of Anticipation (vv.32-42)*

v.32 "And they came to a place which was named Gethsemane: and he saith to his disciples, Sit ye here, while I shall pray.
v.33 And he taketh with him Peter and James and John, and began to be sore amazed, and to be very heavy;
v.34 And saith unto them, My soul is exceeding sorrowful unto death: tarry ye here, and watch.
v.35 And he went forward a little, and fell on the ground, and prayed that, if it were possible, the hour might pass from him.
v.36 And he said, Abba, Father, all things *are* possible unto thee; take away this cup from me: nevertheless not what I will, but what thou wilt.
v.37 And he cometh, and findeth them sleeping, and saith unto Peter, Simon, sleepest thou? couldest not thou watch one hour?
v.38 Watch ye and pray, lest ye enter into temptation. The spirit truly is ready, but the flesh *is* weak.
v.39 And again he went away, and prayed, and spake the same words.
v.40 And when he returned, he found them asleep again, (for their eyes were heavy,) neither wist they what to answer him.
v. 41 And he cometh the third time, and saith unto them, Sleep on now, and take *your* rest: it is enough, the hour is come; behold, the Son of man is betrayed into the hands of sinners.
v.42 Rise up, let us go; lo, he that betrayeth me is at hand,"

In this paragraph the Servant Son is presented suffering in anticipation of the bearing of sins upon the cross. No saintly mind can ever comprehend the profound mystery and depths of His suffering in Gethsemane as He began to be sore distressed, and His sweat became, as it were, great drops of blood (Luke 22:44).

32 Gethsemane means the "oil press". The olives when pressed yield their oil which is used for healing and light. It is believed that the garden was located in an olive orchard on the western side of the mount of Olives. Here the Lord and His disciples often met for rest in seclusion (John 18:1-2). On this occasion He requested eight of His disciples to sit near the entrance until He had prayed.

Mark records three separate occasions when Jesus prayed; see 1:35; 6:46; 14:32ff. In the first the Servant commenced the day in prayer: "rising up a great while before day, he...departed into a solitary place, and there prayed". In the second He went up into the mountain side to pray in the evening. Here He prayed in the night, and repeated His prayer three times. Dependence, devotion, and determination marked the perfect Servant in each case.

33-34 He selected the favoured three to accompany Him. On two previous occasions reported by Mark, Jesus had taken Peter, James and John apart from the others to teach them important lessons, and also to reveal Himself as the Saviour (5:37), the Sovereign (9:2) and the Sufferer (14:33). It is interesting to notice that death was associated with each of the scenes.

On entering the garden He began to be sore amazed and full of heaviness. He requested the three to remain behind and watch. He did not shrink from death, nor was His anguish on account of the approaching physical sufferings from the hands of men, nor was it as though Satan would kill Him in the garden, as some have wrongly suggested. Jesus was in no danger of dying in the garden. All such statements are God-dishonouring to the blessed Person of the Son. This Gospel presents the sacrifice of Christ as the sin-offering, hence the grief of the Servant is detailed in graphic terms. The sinless Son of God was soon to become the bearer of human guilt upon the cross. This was the cause of His sorrow in the garden. He was viewing the hour when He would be made the sin-offering (2 Cor 5:21).

35-36 The Lord's three prayers contained words common to each: "Abba, Father, all things are possible unto thee; take away this cup from me: nevertheless not what I will, but what thou wilt". He bowed Himself to the will of His Father, as the obedient Servant. As was underlined earlier Mark alone preserves the actual utterances of Jesus in His native Aramaic language. Here *Abba* is linked with the Greek equivalent, Father. *Abba* is said to be the simplest sound an infant's lips can frame. The title conveys the intimacy and affection of the Son for the Father. It was a unique form of address. We believe God never heard such an expression of approach from any other man before. The title occurs twice elsewhere in the NT, where by sovereign grace, the sons of God may claim this precious word (Rom 8:15; Gal 4:6).

The use of these titles of His God is appropriate to the circumstance and substance of His prayer. The hour of His deepest woe on the cross, when He would drink the cup of wrath on account of sin, would be the occasion of the turning of the face of God from Him. He would cry soon "Eloi, Eloi, lama sabachthani?" (15:34). A comparison of these two Aramaic expressions is an exposition of the sufferings of Christ: in Gethsemane in anticipation of sin-bearing and at Golgotha in the endurance of sin-bearing.

37-42 The three disciples' failure to stay awake is the focus of attention in these verses. Jesus found them sleeping on the three occasions that He returned to them from His place of prayer. He had requested them to stay alert to spiritual danger, and pray lest they should come into temptation. He had indicated by this the approach of severe testings. The moment of His betrayal and arrest was nearing, and they would require strength found alone in dependence upon God. In the case of Peter, his denial of the Lord three times followed closely on his failure to watch and pray three times.

When the Lord found them sleeping on the third occasion, He said, "Sleep on now and take your rest". This statement, understood as a question, "Are you still sleeping?", gives the sense more clearly. It is likely that a short interval occurred between the words "Sleep on, and take your rest" and the words "It is enough". They had now slept long enough, for the hour had now come when the Son of Man would be betrayed into the hands of sinners. They must rise up, not to leave Gethsemane, but to join the other eight disciples and go forth with Him to meet the betrayer and his companions.

b. *Gethsemane: The Betrayal and Arrest (vv.43-52)*

v.43 "And immediately, while he yet spake, cometh Judas, one of the twelve, and with him a great multitude with swords and staves, from the chief priests and the scribes and the elders.
v.44 And he that betrayed him had given them a token, saying, Whomsoever I shall kiss, that same is he; take him, and lead *him* away safely.
v.45 And as soon as he was come, he goeth straightway to him, and saith, Master, master; and kissed him.
v.46 And they laid their hands on him, and took him.
v.47 And one of them that stood by drew a sword, and smote a servant of the high priest, and cut off his ear.
v.48 And Jesus answered and said unto them, Are ye come out, as against a thief, with swords and *with* staves to take me?
v.49 I was daily with you in the temple teaching, and ye took me not: but the scriptures must be fulfilled.

v.50 And they all forsook him, and fled.
v. 51 And there followed him a certain young man, having a linen cloth cast about *his* naked *body;* and the young men laid hold on him:
v.52 And he left the linen cloth, and fled from them naked."

43 As Jesus was speaking these words to His disciples, Judas came with a great multitude armed with swords and staves, sent to arrest Him with the authority of the Sanhedrin.

44-46 The vileness of the crime of Judas to betray Jesus was signalled by his deceitful kiss, given lest, in the uncertain light, one of the other disciples might be mistaken for Him. The One kissed should be arrested. Judas gave instructions to seize Him and lead Him away safely. He feared that there might be an attempt to rescue Jesus. When they laid their hands on Jesus, He offered no resistance. The dignity of the perfect Servant, surrounded by the armed band, and His fearful followers, is a vignette of supreme majesty.

47 The attempted armed intervention of an unnamed disciple (Peter, as John 18:10 shows) is recorded by Mark. He drew his sword and aimed what was intended to be a fatal stroke upon a servant of the high priest. The attempt failed but he cut off the ear of the man. Luke adds the information that Jesus restored the ear, and with the accuracy of a physician records that it was his right ear (Luke 22:50-51). Peter's intervention, like the untimely action of Moses to the Egyptian, was an exhibition of fleshly energy which failed to further the purpose of God.

48-49 Jesus rebuked those who had arranged His arrest for their clandestine approach and their display of force against Him as if He were a thief. Why did they not arrest Him in the daytime as He moved openly in the temple? They were afraid of an uproar among the common people who heard Him gladly.

Throughout the ordeal the dignity of the Lord, as the Servant of Jehovah, in His moral loveliness was displayed. His arrest was according to the prophetic plan of the Scriptures. The reference may be to the words of Isaiah: "he was oppressed, and he was afflicted, yet he opened not his mouth: he is brought as a lamb to the slaughter, and as a sheep before her shearers is dumb, so he openeth not his mouth" (Isa 53:7).

50 The eleven fled the scene. Fear filled their hearts. Their hopes of the Messianic kingdom collapsed. His prediction, given earlier in the night, had come to pass (v.27): He was deserted. The fearless composure of the Servant is contrasted with the failing courage of the eleven disciples. God had said of Him: "He shall not fail nor be discouraged" (Isa 42:4).

51-52 A unique episode is recorded of one unnamed young man who was the last to leave Jesus. It would appear that he had hurried to the garden from his bedroom, putting only a Roman cape of linen around him, possibly to warn Jesus of the treachery of Judas. On his arrival at the scene the crowd were already leading the Lord away to the high priest, so he followed in the way. Finally some of the young men in the mob laid hold of him but he managed to escape, leaving behind his linen cloth. It seems to be a case of the veiling of Mark's own identity. The graphic description of his flight, leaving Jesus alone to face his accusers, is the writer's manner of autographing his eye-witness account.

Notes

47 Mark knew from Peter's account that it was Peter who used the sword, but having respect to him, withheld his name, as Peter was still alive when the Gospel was written. John, writing many years later, mentions Peter by name, and also the name of the high priest's servant, apparently when both men were dead. In this, the consideration of the disciples one for another is evidenced.

A contrast between Eden and Gethsemane

The Lord Jesus is greater than Adam, who was a figure of Christ (Rom 5:14). Eden was a garden of delight, but Gethsemane was a garden of distress. Adam sinned and fell in Eden, but Jesus suffered and triumphed in Gethsemane. Adam received fruit from Eve's hand in disobedience to God's will, but Jesus accepted the cup from the Father's hand in obedience to God's will. God sought Adam in the garden of Eden but the Son sought His God in Gethsemane.

A sword was drawn at Eden, but a sword was sheathed in Gethsemane. Adam was driven out of the garden, but the Lord was led away from Gethsemane. Adam faced his own guilt and its consequences in Eden, but the Lord Jesus faced the sin and guilt of others, and the consequences in Gethsemane. In the garden as in all else He is pre-eminent and excels all others.

c. *The Palace of the High Priest: The Ecclesiastical Trial (vv.53-65)*

v.53 "And they led Jesus away to the high priest: and with him were assembled all the chief priests and the elders and the scribes.
v.54 And Peter followed him afar off, even into the palace of the high priest: and he sat with the servants, and warmed himself at the fire.
v.55 And the chief priests and all the council sought for witness against Jesus to put him to death; and found none.
v.56 For many bare false witness against him, but their witness agreed not together.
v.57 And there arose certain, and bare false witness against him, saying,
v.58 We heard him say, I will destroy this temple that is made with hands, and within three days I will build another made without hands.
v.59 But neither so did their witness agree together.
v.60 And the high priest stood up in the midst, and asked Jesus, saying, Answerest thou nothing? what *is it which* these witness against thee?
v.61 But he held his peace, and answered nothing. Again the high priest asked him, and said unto him, Art thou the Christ, the Son of the Blessed?
v.62 And Jesus said, I am: and ye shall see the Son of man sitting on the right hand of power, and coming in the clouds of heaven.

v.63 Then the high priest rent his clothes, and saith, What need we any further witnesses?
v.64 Ye have heard the blasphemy: what think ye? And they all condemned him to be guilty of death.
v.65 And some began to spit on him, and to cover his face, and to buffet him, and to say unto him, Prophesy: and the servants did strike him with the palms of their hands."

He was first tried by the religious power and then by the political authorities. The indictment before the Sanhedrin was the charge of blasphemy. The religious leaders could find Him guilty but had no power to exercise the punishment of death (John 18:31). They therefore delivered Him to civil judgment. The indictment before the political court was treason against the Roman Emperor.

Each of the two trials of Jesus had three distinct hearings:

The Ecclesiastical Trial:

1 First hearing before Annas	John 18:12-14.
2. Second hearing before Caiaphas	Mark 14:53-65.
3. Third hearing before the Sanhedrin	Matt 27:11; Mark 15:1; Luke 22:66-71.

The first two hearings were in the night, and at the final hearing at dawn the verdict of guilty was passed. The sentence was death by stoning for blasphemy. Between the two trials Judas committed suicide (Matt 27:3-10).

The Civil Trial:

1. The first hearing before Pilate	John 18:28-38; Mark 15:1-5.
2. The second hearing before Herod	Luke 23:7-12.
3. The third hearing before Pilate	Matt 27:15-26; Mark 15:6-20; John 18:39; 19:16; Luke 23:13-25.

The final verdict of death by crucifixion for treason was passed around six o'clock in the morning (John 19:14-16).

53 Jesus was led away to the high priest Caiaphas, where the Sanhedrin had assembled. The seventy members of the Sanhedrin and the high priest were met together in a private room upstairs in the palace of Caiaphas (v.66). It was only on some serious circumstances that a trial could be conducted on a feast day, and in normal proceedings no hasty verdict was determined. On this occasion the Sanhedrin had already been unanimous in their common decision to kill Him. They had passed the verdict of capital punishment upon

Him long before His arrest (14:1-2). They now sought the needed evidence to justify His death.

54 Peter had regained some courage and had followed Jesus afar off, and had finally entered into the courtyard in the centre of the high priest's palace. Being a cold night he sat down with the servants and warmed himself at the charcoal fire.

55-59 The trial was led by two chief priests, and they, with all the council sought evidence by witness to justify the death of Jesus, but their search was unfruitful. The numerous false witnesses that arose disagreed in their testimony. To convict a person under the law of Moses, an agreement must be procured from at least two witnesses (Num 35:30; Deut 17:6). Some of the witnesses gave a distorted account of the words of Jesus (John 2:19-20). They claimed He had said "I will destroy this temple that is made with hands, and within three days I will build another made without hands". The disagreement in this further witness made it useless also in evidence.

60-61a Caiaphas became frustrated and standing up in the midst of the council, asked Jesus two questions, hoping to find Him guilty. The first demanded a positive answer: "Answerest thou nothing?" and the second; "What are these charges witnessed against thee?" Jesus remained silent. He stood as a sheep dumb before her shearers and opened not His mouth (Isa 53:7). This silence of the Servant brought the proceedings to a climax.

61b The high priest now asked Him an emphatic question, which he kept repeating: "Art thou the Christ, the Son of the Blessed?" The title "The Blessed" is the Jewish substitute for God. They considered it irreverent to speak directly of God, or to God, and so used euphemisms.

62 The answer of Jesus was "I am". Here for the first time in this Servant Gospel, Jesus declared His Messiahship. He also added a remarkable prophecy, quoting from Daniel, and applying it to Himself, as definite proof of His true Messiahship. He was indeed the Christ, the Son of the Blessed: "...and ye shall see the Son of man sitting on the right hand of power, and coming in the clouds of heaven" (Dan 7:13). Here He states that He will be exalted to the highest place of authority. The day was coming when His judges would be raised from their graves to stand before Him as their Judge. In that day, they would realise that He who was rejected by them was indeed the Christ of God.

63-64 On hearing this solemn statement the high priest rent his clothes. The Mosaic Law forbade a high priest to rend his garments (Lev 10:6; 21:10). Later the Rabbinical writings allowed this act in the case of outrageous blasphemy. Those present realised this expression of horror by Caiaphas meant the death penalty for Jesus. There was now no need of any further witness. They regarded His words as blasphemy, for He had claimed the authority and prerogatives of God.

The penalty for blasphemy was death by stoning (Lev 24:15-16). On the basis of this Sanhedrin trial He was condemned to death, but they had no authority under Roman law to carry out the penalty.

65 They began, however, to display their contempt and hatred for Him. The account is sad reading. They began to spit in His face. This was an act of personal insult and dishonour (Deut 25:9; Isa 50:6). They also blindfolded Him and struck Him severe blows on the face with their fists, demanding that He would reveal the smiter's name. They applied the traditional test of Messiah status which had its conception from a wrong understanding of the prophecy: "He shall not judge after the sight of his eyes, neither reprove after the hearing of his ears" (Isa 11:3). The lesser servants followed the example of their officers and received Him with blows, beating Him with their open hands. In all these insulting and shameful happenings the Servant opened not His mouth (Isa 53:7; 1 Pet 2:23).

In the incredible brutality of these men, who claimed to represent God on earth, we see that envy and hatred which cause men to act as demons. Man's inhumanity to man has produced bloodshed, violence, torture, and war among nations. In this scene we see the inhumane treatment sinful men heaped upon the holy Son of God.

d. *The Palace of the High Priest: Peter's Denial (vv.66-72)*

v.66 "And as Peter was beneath in the palace, there cometh one of the maids of the high priest:
v.67 And when she saw Peter warming himself, she looked upon him, and said, And thou also wast with Jesus of Nazareth.
v.68 But he denied, saying, I know not, neither understand I what thou sayest. And he went out into the porch; and the cock crew.
v.69 And a maid saw him again, and began to say to them that stood by, This is *one* of them.
v.70 And he denied it again. And a little after, they that stood by said again to Peter, Surely thou art *one* of them: for thou art a Galilaean, and thy speech agreeth *thereto.*
v.71 But he began to curse and to swear, *saying,* I know not this man of whom ye speak.
v.72 And the second time the cock crew. And Peter called to mind the word that Jesus said unto him, Before the cock crow twice thou shalt deny me thrice. And when he thought thereon, he wept."

The denial of Peter is recorded in all the four Gospels; see Matt 26:69-75; Luke 22:55-62; John 18:15-18. The account given by Mark is the most graphic and vivid of all, showing that he received his information from Peter himself.

66-69 The denial of Peter in the courtyard coincided with the confession of Christ before His accusers. The perfect Servant witnessed a good confession in contrast to the denial of an imperfect one.

One of the maids of Caiaphas saw Peter's face in the light of the fire and recognised him as one of the disciples of Jesus, and said to him "Thou also wast with Jesus of Nazareth". Peter denied all knowledge of what she had said. To escape further investigation he went out into the porch. The same maid approached him again and said to the guards standing by: "This is one of them". Again Peter denied his discipleship of Christ.

70-71 Later, others accused him of being one of Jesus' disciples. They identified him by his accent. The Galilaeans spoke in the Aramaic dialect, which had notable differences of pronunciation. This time Peter began to curse and to swear, saying "I know not this man of whom ye speak".

What is spoken of today as "cursing and swearing" is not what is meant here. It was not profane cursing, but rather Peter placed himself under a curse from God if he were lying, and under an oath, as in court, to establish the truth of his denial.

71 The cock crowed the second time. The other writers only mention one crowing of the cock in the parallel passages; see Matt 26:74; Luke 22:60; John 18:27. Mark is more specific. He punctuates Peter's denial by the cock crowing twice in quick succession (vv.68, 72). The first cock crowing did not awaken Peter's conscience as it was a common occurrence every morning, but when the cock crowed the second time, which was unusual, he immediately remembered the words of Jesus: "Before the cock crow twice, thou shalt deny me thrice". Peter was overwhelmed with sorrow at what he had done and wept bitterly. This contribution was the forerunner of true repentance which led to Peter's restoration to the joy of His Lord.

He would know Him in a new way as the risen One, who would be his Shepherd (John 21:15-17).

e. *Before Pilate: The Civil Trial (15:1-15)*

v.1 "And straightway in the morning the chief priests held a consultation with the elders and scribes and the whole council, and bound Jesus, and carried *him* away, and delivered *him* to Pilate.

v.2 And Pilate asked him, Art thou the King of the Jews? And he answering said unto him, Thou sayest *it*.

v.3 And the chief priests accused him of many things: but he answered nothing.

v.4 And Pilate asked him again, saying, Answerest thou nothing? behold how many things they witness against thee.

v.5 But Jesus yet answered nothing; so that Pilate marvelled.

v.6 Now at *that* feast he released unto them one prisoner, whomsoever they desired.

v.7 And there was *one* named Barabbas, *which lay* bound with them that had made insurrection with him, who had committed murder in the insurrection.

v.8 And the multitude crying aloud began to desire *him to do* as he had ever done unto them.
v.9 But Pilate answered them, saying, Will ye that I release unto you the King of the Jews?
v.10 For he knew that the chief priests had delivered him for envy.
v.11 But the chief priests moved the people, that he should rather release Barabbas unto them.
v.12 And Pilate answered and said again unto them, What will ye then that I shall do *unto him* whom ye call the King of the Jews?
v.13 And they cried out again, Crucify him.
v.14 Then Pilate said unto them, Why, what evil hath he done? And they cried out the more exceedingly, Crucify him.
v.15 And *so* Pilate, willing to content the people, released Barabbas unto them, and delivered Jesus, when he had scourged *him,* to be crucified."

1 The Sanhedrin were united in their condemnation of Jesus. They bound Him and led Him through the streets of the city, from the residence of the high priest to the place where Pilate had taken up residence for the Passover season. Pilate's usual headquarters were at Caesarea, on the sea coast, but as religious uprisings were frequent in Jerusalem at the feast days, he moved into the city to obviate any riots. Extra soldiers of the Roman legion were also on duty. The Jews, being unable to inflict the supreme penalty of death, brought Jesus to Pilate in the early morning for the endorsement of their verdict and its execution.

2-5 The charge before Pilate was treason against the Roman Emperor. Pilate therefore interrogated Jesus asking Him if He was the King of the Jews. Jesus' answer was in the affirmative. This claim to kingship was spiritual in meaning, as later recorded alone by John (John 18:34-38). He had declared Himself to be Messiah, but not a political king. Pilate realised there was no valid charge of treason against Him, and was determined to set Him free. However he had no control over the passions of the religious leaders whose influence was stirring up the mob to clamour for the death of the Saviour.

The profound silence of Jesus during the preliminary hearing to the many allegations witnessed against Him confounded Pilate. The example of the perfect Servant was later underscored by Peter: "Who, when he was reviled, reviled not again; when he suffered, he threatened not; but committed Himself to him that judgeth righteously" (1 Pet 2:23). Are we silent in the face of false accusation, leaving matters in the hand of God? The Servant only answered questions concerning His wondrous Person and glorious offices.

In His ecclesiastical trial Jesus remained silent during the preliminary investigation and then spoke, whereas in His civil trial He answered the early charge and then remained silent. Solomon wrote of a time to keep silent, and a time to speak (Eccl 3:7). This was exemplified in the perfect Servant during His trials.

The silence of Jesus, as recorded by Mark, is impressive. From the time of

His arrest in the garden until He died near the other garden, His words were few. John records over one hundred and fifty words, but Mark has preserved only thirty. This silence of the Servant is one of the unique features of this Gospel (Isa 53:7-9). Pilate was impressed with the quiet, majestic dignity of the Lord.

6-14 One of the prevailing Passover customs was the release of a prisoner of the people's choice. Pilate considered this as an opportunity to liberate Jesus. He had in custody a very disreputable character called Barabbas, who had shared in insurrection and had committed murder. Pilate believed that the common people would never choose Barabbas before Christ. When he placed the alternatives before the crowd he expected a different reaction, but the presence of the chief priests incited the mob to cry out for the release of Barabbas, and the death of Jesus by crucifixion. History has often repeated itself. Those who have witnessed the mass hysteria of a mob, urged on by a few radicals, can appreciate the graphic scene outlined by Mark. Pilate found himself in a helpless dilemma.

The means of execution demanded by the people was not the normal Jewish method of execution, which was by stoning, nor Roman, which was by beheading. Death by crucifixion was reserved for the vilest criminals. Usually only slaves or foreigners suffered such a terrible end. Pilate made a final effort to save Jesus, but the fierce enmity of the crowd became more intense. They cried out more exceedingly: "Crucify him". Crucifixion, the means of His death foretold in the Scriptures, must be the manner of His execution (Ps 22:16).

15 Pilate therefore released Barabbas. His punishment would be borne by the Saviour. The vilest wretch in Jerusalem, though guilty and condemned, was set free, because the Lord Jesus took his place. Barabbas may never have grasped the spiritual truth of substitution, but this event in his life is a blessed illustration of the doctrine. The moral glory of Christ in the perfection of His grace to deliver from dying and bless another by His own death, reveals the absolute perfection of the Servant.

Pilate finally delivered Jesus to be crucified, after he had ordered His scourging. The brutality of scourging was often inflicted as separate punishment, but in the case of the Lord it was added to His sufferings. The victim was stripped, bound to a pillar, and beaten on the back by the Roman guards, who used a short whip of leather studded with the sharp bones of animals. The number of stripes was unlimited, unlike the limited beating of Paul by the Jews (2 Cor 11:24). This great indignity in its severity was the portion of the Holy Son of God, Jehovah's perfect Servant. Scourging often proved fatal. The Scriptures were fulfilled: "I gave my back to the smiters" and "The plowers plowed upon my back: they made long their furrows" (Isa 50:6; Ps 129:3).

f. *The Praetorium: Mocked by the Soldiers (vv.16-20)*

v.16 "And the soldiers led him away into the hall, called Praetorium, and they call together the whole band.
v.17 And they clothed him with purple, and platted a crown of thorns, and put it about his *head,*
v.18 And began to salute him, Hail, King of the Jews!
v.19 And they smote him on the head with a reed, and did spit upon him, and bowing *their* knees worshipped him.
v.20 And when they had mocked him, they took off the purple from him, and put his own clothes on him, and led him out to crucify him."

16 The Roman soldiers led Jesus from the outer square, where He had been flogged, inside the palace to Praetorium. He was bruised and bleeding when they called together the cohort, which may have numbered six hundred men. A cohort was the tenth part of a Roman legion of six thousand soldiers.

17 This section records some of the terrible indignities heaped upon the Saviour, which never cease to touch the hearts of those who love Him. The enactment of the mock coronation of Jesus was a ridicule of His claims to sovereignty. They arrayed the King in a robe of imperial purple. A crown of thorns was hastily prepared and placed upon His brow. Grievous pain was inflicted upon His holy head. Caesar wore a laurel wreath upon his brow, so cruel soldiers wreathed the brow of the Redeemer with thorns in mockery. Their action was significant since thorns are an emblem of the curse (Gen 3:17-18). The Saviour voluntarily wore the thorns which were a symbol of the reality of the curse which He was to bear on the cross (Gal 3:13). The word for crown is *stephanos,* a victor's crown, usually worn when the conflict has been won. The Saviour was a victor before He entered into death.

18 The plaudit "Hail, King of the Jews" was borrowed from their usual acclamation "Ave Caesar" when in the presence of the Emperor,

19 They then smote Him upon the head with the reed, which was His mock sceptre, causing severe bruising and pain. As for homage they kept on spitting on Him, bending their knees in mock submission to His majesty. The verbs in this verse are all in the imperfect tense in the Greek text, suggesting the fact of continued action.

20 Finally the chosen execution squad of four hand-picked soldiers, under the special supervision of a centurion, came to take Him from the Praetorium to the place of crucifixion. The mock regalia was removed from His bleeding back and they dressed Him in His own clothes. From the fortress of Antonia He was led into the open street. The Servant went forth to die for the redemption of the race. The Scripture had foretold that He would be led as a lamb to the slaughter; here it was fulfilled (Isa 53:7).

4c. *The Crucifixion and Death of the Servant* 15:21-41

g. *Golgotha: The Crucifixion and Death of the Servant (vv.21–41)*

v.21 "And they compel one Simon a Cyrenian, who passed by, coming out of the country, the father of Alexander and Rufus, to bear his cross.
v.22 And they bring him unto the place Golgotha, which is, being interpreted, The place of a skull.
v.23 And they gave him to drink wine mingled with myrrh: but he received *it* not.
v.24 And when they had crucified him, they parted his garments, casting lots upon them, what every man should take.
v.25 And it was the third hour, and they crucified him.
v.26 And the superscription of his accusation was written over, THE KING OF THE JEWS.
v. 27 And with him they crucify two thieves; the one on his right hand, and the other on his left.
v.28 And the scripture was fulfilled, which saith, And he was numbered with the transgressors.
v.29 And they that passed by railed on him, wagging their heads, and saying, Ah, thou that destroyest the temple, and buildest *it* in three days,
v.30 Save thyself, and come down from the cross.
v.31 Likewise also the chief priests mocking said among themselves with the scribes, He saved others; himself he cannot save.
v.32 Let Christ the King of Israel descend now from the cross, that we may see and believe. And they that were crucified with him reviled him.
v.33 And when the sixth hour was come, there was darkness over the whole land until the ninth hour.
v.34 And at the ninth hour Jesus cried with a loud voice, saying, Eloi, Eloi, lama sabachthani? which is, being interpreted, My God, my God, why hast thou forsaken me?
v.35 And some of them that stood by, when they heard *it,* said, Behold he calleth Elias.
v.36 And one ran and filled a spunge full of vinegar, and put it on a reed, and gave him to drink, saying, Let alone; let us see whether Elias will come to take him down.
v.37 And Jesus cried with a loud voice, and gave up the ghost.
v.38 And the veil of the temple was rent in twain from the top to the bottom.
v.39 And when the centurion, which stood over against him, saw that he so cried out, and gave up the ghost, he said, Truly this man was the Son of God.
v.40 There were also women looking on afar off: among whom was Mary Magdalene, and Mary the mother of James the less and of Joses, and Salome;
v.41 (Who also, when he was in Galilee, followed him, and ministered unto him;) and many other women which came up with him unto Jerusalem."

The death of crucifixion which was meted out to the blessed Lord was the most terrible of all forms of capital punishment. Mark, with great reverence, records the outward physical sufferings in graphic language, but he emphasises more the overwhelming spiritual sufferings of Christ as He became the sin-bearer.

Each Gospel presents the mighty sacrifice from a different viewpoint in keeping with the ancient offerings (Lev 1-6). Matthew presents the trespass-offering; Mark presents the sin-offering; Luke the peace-offering and John the burnt-offering.

21 It was part of the shame associated with death by crucifixion that the condemned carry the cross-beam, *patibulum,* which was a heavy piece of wood. This was borne by the victim publicly through the city streets to the place of execution. The Lord Jesus though bruised and marred thus commenced His journey to Golgotha. The teaching that He faltered, and became so weak that He stumbled under the cross is dishonouring to His Person, and foreign to the God-given records. To the eyes of His guards it seemed He might not reach Golgotha, so they seized a passer-by at random, Simon by name, and he was compelled to carry the cross-beam the remainder of the way. Mark alone supplies the detail that he was the father of Alexander and Rufus (see Rom 16:13).

22 The account of the sufferings of the Servant in Mark's Gospel stresses the things which were done to Him. The other three witnesses wrote of what the Lord did and said. It is an interesting study to parallel the literary form of language used by Mark, with the record of Moses of the offering up of Isaac (Gen 22). Each uses a succession of short sentences beginning with the conjunction "and". The Holy Spirit moved both these writers to use the word "and" some forty times in each section (Gen 22:1-15; Mark 15:16-41). This is an infallible proof of the divine interest in, and authorship of, the Scriptures. At Moriah, the submission of Isaac the son to his father was displayed. At Golgotha, in the same place, the submission of the Son of God was displayed. Christ is greater than Isaac. Isaac almost died on the altar, but Christ did die on the cross.

Golgotha was reached, which was a place nigh to the city, but outside its gates (John 19:20). Golgotha means the place of a skull. It is believed that its contour resembled a human skull. The actual spot cannot be known with certainty, but "Gordon's Calvary" seems by popular consent to identify the location.

23 Prior to the actual crucifixion of the Saviour He was offered wine mingled with myrrh. This drink was an anaesthetic usually presented by the compassionate women of the city, to ease the severity of the pain of this form of death. The Servant refused the drink, choosing rather to have an unclouded mind as He assumed the task of giving His life a ransom and bearing the sin of the world.

The Lord was offered drink on three occasions at Golgotha: Mark 15:23; Luke 23:36; John 19:29-30. The first was before He was crucified, the second after He was uplifted, and the last before He died. He refused the first two, but received the last. The first was a cup of mercy, the second of mockery, and the last of majesty. The offices of the Lord are seen on these three occasions. The greatness of the Priest is established by His refusal of the wine mixed with myrrh, as no offering priest was to approach God having drunk wine (Lev 10:9). The grandeur of the Potentate is seen as they mocked His kingship with a drink of celebration which He refused (Luke 23:36). The glory of the Prophet in fulfilling every obligation of Scripture caused Him to request vinegar, to complete prophetic revelation (Ps 69:21; John 19:28-30).

24-25 Finally the Servant was crucified, but Mark is silent as to the details of the terrible act. He was nailed to the tree by His hands and feet (Ps 22:16; John 20:25). The parting of His garments, and the casting of lots upon them for the treasured inner seamless garment of linen, which was woven from the top throughout, was a direct fulfilment of prophecy. The soldiers unwittingly carried out the divine programme of events: "They pierced my hands and my feet ... they look and stare upon me. They part my garments among them, and cast lots upon my vesture" (Ps 22:16-18).

Mark states that it was the third hour when He was crucified. John indicates that the sentence of death was passed upon Him at the sixth hour (John 19:14). There is no discrepancy. Mark used the Hebrew method of reckoning time, so the third hour was three hours after sunrise, or nine o'clock in the morning. John used the Roman method which counted the hours from midnight and noon, thus the sentence of death was passed upon Jesus by Pilate at six o'clock in the morning. The interim hours were the hours of mockery by the soldiers in preparation for His execution.

26 It was customary for the criminal's name and crime to be carried on a placard before Him, and then nailed above his head upon the cross. One went before Jesus carrying His Name and accusation, which was nailed over His thorn-crowned brow. The superscription is briefest in Mark. He gives the substance of the official charge: "The King of the Jews". Pilate, who dictated the writing, intended it to be an insult to any Jewish aspiration for independence. This was the cause for the chief priests' objection to the wording, but Pilate refused any alteration (John 19:21-22).

27-28 The perfect Servant of Jehovah, who had so delighted God's heart in all His ministry, was crucified in the midst of thieves who had robbed both God and men. The action of Pilate, having Jesus thus placed between two robbers, unwittingly fulfilled another ancient prophecy: "He was numbered with the transgressors" (Isa 53:12).

29-32 The insults of the representatives of the Jews' religion had three degrees of mockery, which must have been painful to the tender heart of the Saviour. The first was the vile insinuation that since He claimed ability to rebuild the temple in three days, had He not power to save Himself? The wagging of their heads in derision was a fulfilment of David's prophetic words (Ps 22:7). They further taunted Him saying that He who saved so many from disease was now unable to save Himself. Their implication was that the power by which He had worked miracles was not the power of God at all. Finally they jeered at His claims to be the Messiah, and challenged Him to come down from the cross and prove that He was the true King. Their mocking title "King of the Jews" appears five times in Mark's record. The two thieves also reviled Him. Luke relates the final repentance of one of them who obtained forgiveness (Luke 23:39-43).

33 Mark is the only writer who gives an accurate timetable of that day: he mentions the cockcrowing (14:72), the morning (15:1), the third hour (15:25), which was nine in the morning, the sixth hour or twelve noon (15:33), the ninth hour or three in the afternoon (15:34) and the even (15:42). Mark's usage of the Jewish computation of time is in contrast to John, who made use of the Roman manner of reckoning time. This accounts, as noted above (vv.24-25), for what appears to be a discrepancy between the two narratives. John states that it was about the sixth hour when Pilate passed the final verdict of death, while Mark writes that when the sixth hour was come, there was darkness, as Jesus suffered on the cross.

At the birth of the Saviour the midnight darkness was illuminated by the glory of the Lord; at the death of the Servant the midday light was draped in supernatural darkness. It was a cosmic display of God's intervention and cannot be explained by any natural cause. It was co-incidental with the judgment of sin borne by the Lord Jesus. The whole land means the whole earth, and should not be limited to the land of Israel. During the three hours of darkness silence marked the suffering Christ.

34 The only word from the cross recorded by Mark is the cry of abandonment from the lips of the Lord at the ninth hour. Matthew quotes the Hebrew "Eli'' but Mark retains the actual words of Jesus in Aramaic "Eloi, Eloi''. The cry contains the mystery of atonement. The loneliness and deep anguish of the sin-bearer cannot be translated. Mark thus preserves the actual words before rendering them in the language of his text. This cry expresses more than physical pain or mental grief. The sinless Lamb of God endured the wrath of God upon the tree. It was then that He put away sin by the sacrifice of Himself (Heb 9:26) and became the propitiation for the whole world (1 John 2:2). This cry of desolation is a quotation from the greatest of all the Messianic Psalms (Ps 22:1). It is the Psalm of the sin-offering and is the key to the understanding of the meaning of Golgotha.

The cross of our Lord Jesus Christ is the foundation of Christian faith and the central doctrine of the gospel of God's redeeming grace (Gal 6:14).

35 It is difficult to account for the misconception of those who heard Him cry with the loud voice. The Roman soldiers would have no knowledge of Elias

(Elijah), but the Jews should have known their own tongue. They turned the cry to mockery, and said: "He calleth Elias".

36 At this point Jesus had said "I thirst" (John 19:28). One of the soldiers dipped a sponge in vinegar, and held it to the lips of the Saviour to drink. The vinegar was not the same as the pain-deadening wine offered earlier, but was a sour wine to quench thirst, thus fulfilling the prophetic Scriptures (Ps 69:21). The crowd sought to hinder the soldier, but he said "Let me alone". Others spoke in derision, "Let us see whether Elias will come to take him down".

37 Jesus uttered a loud cry, evidently the triumphant "It is finished" (John 19:30). He gave up His spirit. Having completed His perfect service of atonement, the Servant by an act of His own will dismissed His spirit (John 10:17-18).

38 The beautiful vail which separated the Holy place from the Holiest of all in the temple was a curtain of blue, purple and crimson upon fine linen, adorned with figures of cherubim (2 Chron 3:14). The hanging vail announced that the way into the Holiest was not yet made manifest. When Christ died the vail was rent in twain from the top to the bottom by the hand of God. This was a glorious sign that all religious ceremony was ended. The way into the presence of God is opened to every believer on the ground of the blood of Christ (Heb 10:19-25). The priesthood of the Judaic order was finished, and a new order of priesthood which includes all believers in Christ had commenced.

Many of the priests who saw the actual rent vail became believers later (Acts 6:7). They were influenced towards obedience to the gospel of Christ by the rending of the vail.

39 The centurion, as Mark describes the officer in charge of the soldiers who carried out the crucifixion of Jesus, made a wonderful confession saying: "Truly this man was the Son of God". There is no definite article in the original, so many conclude he was simply classifying the Servant as a hero, a son of God. However, he had observed the patience of the Saviour during the long ordeal, and had listened to all His words, and therefore concluded that He was indeed the Son of God.

40 Mark also comments on the devotion of certain women, who were witnesses of a different kind. There was Mary Magdalene, Mary the mother of James the less and of Joses, and Salome, the wife of Zebedee and the mother of James and John (Matt 27:56; John 19:25).

41 These women, who had ministered to Him in Galilee, became witnesses of

His death, burial, and resurrection (Luke 8:1-3; Mark 15:47; 16:1). One of them was chosen by the risen Lord to be the first to see Him in resurrection (16:9).

Notes

40 Mary of Magdala (on the western shore of Galilee) was a woman out of whom the Lord had cast seven demons. It is not to be supposed that she was an immoral woman. She should not be confused with Mary of Bethany nor with the woman who was a sinner, who anointed the feet of Jesus with tears and wiped them with the hairs of her head (John 11:1; Luke 7:37).

34 The Seven Words of Jesus on the cross.

1. Before the darkness – from nine in the morning to noon.

a. "Father, forgive them; for they know not what they do".
A prayer for His enemies. Luke 23:34.
b. "Verily I say unto thee, To day thou shalt be with me in paradise".
The promise to the repentant thief. Luke 23:43.
c. "Woman, behold thy son…Behold thy mother". John 19:26-27.
The provision for His mother.

2. After the darkness.

d. "My God, my God, why hast thou forsaken me?"
The cry of desertion. Mark 27:46; Mark 15:34.
c. "I thirst".
The cry of accomplishment. John 19:28.
f. " It is finished".
The cry of triumph. John 19:30.
g. "Father, into thy hands I commend my spirit".
The cry of completion. Luke 23:46.

4. *Saturday The Day of Atonement* 15:42-47

v.42 "And now when the even was come, because it was the preparation, that is, the day before the sabbath,
v.43 Joseph of Arimathaea, an honourable counsellor, which also waited for the kingdom of God, came, and went boldly unto Pilate, and craved the body of Jesus.
v.44 And Pilate marvelled if he were already dead: and calling *unto him* the centurion, he asked him whether he had been any while dead.
v.45 And when he knew *it* of the centurion, he gave the body to Joseph.
v.46 And he bought fine linen, and took him down, and wrapped him in the linen, and laid him in a sepulchre which was hewn out of a rock, and rolled a stone unto the door of the sepulchre.
v.47 And Mary Magdalene and Mary *the mother* of Joses beheld where he was laid.

42 When the evening of Friday came, which was called the preparation, that is the beginning of the sabbath, which commenced after sunset, the burial of Jesus took place.

43 Joseph of Arimathaea, himself a member of the Sanhedrin, came boldly to Pilate and asked the body of Jesus. Joseph was rich (Matt 27:57), a good and a righteous man (Luke 23:50) and a disciple of Jesus (John 19:38). Mark adds that he was an honourable counsellor, who waited for the kingdom of God. Luke supplies the information that he had not consented to His death.

44 Pilate was amazed that Jesus should die so quickly, as crucifixion was usually a slow and torturous death. Jewish law did not permit a body to be left overnight to exposure (Deut 21:23). More importantly, God would not allow the body of His Son to remain longer on the cross to be maltreated when His glorious work was ended. The Scripture was also fulfilled in detail: "They made His grave with the wicked (plural number) but He was with the rich (singular number) in His death" (Isa 53:9). The human intention was to cast His body into a common grave with the thieves, but God intervened and He was with the rich man in His death.

45 Pilate having ascertained from the centurion the reality of the death of the Saviour, gave the body to Joseph. Mark uses two different words to describe the body of Jesus. "Joseph craved the body of Jesus": the word he used was *soma,* meaning the holy temple in which the Holy Spirit could dwell. His body could never see corruption (Ps 16:10). Pilate "gave the body to Joseph", here the word is *ptoma,* meaning a corpse. To Joseph the body was precious, but to Pilate it was a worthless thing.

46 It is not to be supposed that the linen was bought hastily, or the tomb given at the last moment. Joseph had already procured the linen and had prepared the tomb, specially for this occasion. He knew he was the rich man, chosen by God, to do this important service. He was no cowardly secret follower, but rather one who had served in secret, lest his labour of love in arranging the sepulchre would be interfered with by the hostile members of the Sanhedrin. Joseph, assisted by Nicodemus, lovingly enwrapped the body in the linen with spices, and laid Him in the tomb which was hewn out of a rock, and rolled a stone upon the entrance.

47 Two Marys were witnesses to His burial. They saw where He was laid. They could bear reliable testimony on the morning of the first day of the week that the tomb was empty.

Notes

The burial of Christ is an integral part of the gospel message (1 Cor 15:4). Only four persons attended it. No psalm or hymn was sung, no prayer was offered, no Scripture read, no eulogy given, and we read of no tears being shed. His burial was unique, He was buried in the manner of the Jews. The Romans removed vital organs from their dead, and the Egyptians embalmed, but His holy body was not tampered with in death, God preserved that body from all heathen indignities. His body being untainted by sin was therefore not subject to corruption.

The fact of His burial verified His death, as His appearances later verified His resurrection. The death, burial and resurrection of Christ form the very heart of the Christian faith, and are described by Paul as of first importance (1 Cor 15:3-5).

XI. The Resurrection and Appearances of the Servant (16:1-18)

The predominant importance of the resurrection of Christ is revealed in the fact that it is interwoven into the entire fabric of the Scriptures. In the OT, His resurrection was foreshadowed, foretold and foreknown (Gen 22:5; Ps 16:10; 22:22; Isa 52:13). The Lord also predicted His rising from among the dead (Matt 17:9; Mark 8:31; Luke 9:22; John 2:19-21). The four Gospels contain the historical evidences (Matt 28:6-7; Mark 16:6; Luke 24:6; John 20:17). The fact is declared in the Acts (1:3; 2:24; 10:41-42). The Epistles declare the doctrine (Rom 4:24; 1 Cor 15:4; 1 Pet 1:3). The Revelation testifies to His resurrection (Rev 1:18). The resurrection is the keystone of the Christian arch. It shows the Servant's approval by God; see Romans 1:4

The basic difference between Christianity and the great religions of the world is the fact that it was founded by the only Person who once lived and died but is now alive. Confucius and Muhammad, the originators of great religions, are dead today. Hinduism and Buddhism are based on the teachings of gods and heathen deities who never lived. But Christ is alive for evermore. God marked out Aaron by the dead rod which came alive and bore bud, blossom and fruit. He was the man of God's choice. All the other eleven rods were dead and remained lifeless. So the Lord Jesus is the only One whom God owns, for He alone is alive.

It may be difficult to harmonize the various appearings of the risen Lord, but the records are not contradictory. The fourfold account of the evangelists forms an irresistible proof of the glorious reality of His resurrection. Matthew shows it was an invincible act (Matt 27:62-65). Luke claims it was indispensable (Luke 24:13-53). John sets forth indisputable evidences (John 20). Mark emphasises that it was inevitable (Mark 16:7).

He was seen in the early morning (John 21:4), in the afternoon (Luke 24:13ff.) and in the evening (John 20:19). He appeared in a garden to one woman, on a highway to two men, in an upper room to more than eleven, by the seashore to seven disciples, and to over 500 in another place. He appealed to their senses: He ate with them (Acts 10:41); He spoke to them and breathed upon them (John 20:19, 22); He showed them His wounded hands, feet, and side (Luke 24:40; John 20:20). There is no doubt that this same Jesus, who died and was buried, is alive.

1. *His Resurrection: God's Approval of the Servant* 16:1-8

The resurrection is the crown of the Servant's ministry, the God-given vindication of His Person and Work. The Son who served on earth is now the Son seated at God's right hand in heaven. His redemptive work finished at Calvary was followed by His present unfinished work in heaven as the great High Priest and Advocate of His people. He is coming again for His blood-bought church to take her to Himself, and later He will come to Israel to reign as King of kings. His resurrection is the proof that the penalty for sin has been paid once for all; it provides a new power for Christian service, and is the guarantee of the final resurrection of all believers who have fallen asleep (1 Cor 15:20).

a. *Women at the Sepulchre (vv.1-4)*

v.1 "And when the sabbath was past, Mary Magdalene, and Mary the *mother* of James, and Salome, had bought sweet spices, that they might come and anoint him.
v.2 And very early in the morning the first *day* of the week, they came unto the sepulchre at the rising of the sun.
v.3 And they said among themselves, Who shall roll us away the stone from the door of the sepulchre?
v.4 And when they looked, they saw that the stone was rolled away: for it was very great."

1 When the sabbath was over certain women had bought sweet spices that they might anoint Jesus. They would place these inside the sepulchre in loving adoration of His Person. The passing of the sabbath marked the end of an old dispensation, and the beginning of a new day and age.

2 These women – Mary Magdalene, Mary the mother of James, and Salome – had stayed to behold His death at Calvary, and had been present at His burial in the rock-hewn tomb. They now arrived at the garden tomb very early in the morning, upon the first day of the week, as the sun was rising.

3 As they walked along the way they remembered that a stone had been rolled to the door of the sepulchre, and they began to question: "Who shall roll us away the stone from the door?".

4 To their amazement they found the stone rolled away. The stone was very great indicating that the entrance to the tomb was a large opening.

b. *The Angels at the Sepulchre (vv.5-8)*

v.5 "And entering into the sepulchre, they saw a young man sitting on the right side, clothed in a long white garment; and they were affrighted.

v.6 And he saith unto them, Be not affrighted: Ye seek Jesus of Nazareth, which was crucified: he is risen; he is not here: behold the place where they laid him.
v.7 But go your way, tell his disciples and Peter that he goeth before you into Galilee: there shall ye see him, as he said unto you.
v.8 And they went out quickly, and fled from the sepulchre; for they trembled and were amazed: neither said they any thing to any *man*; for they were afraid."

5 When the women entered seeking the body of Jesus they had no thought of His resurrection. They saw an angelic being sitting on the right side, clothed in a long white garment. He appeared as a young man. The awesome sight filled them with fear.

6 The angel quickly calmed their fear and supplied them with wonderful information: the One they seek, Jesus of Nazareth, who has been crucified, is not in the tomb; He is risen; His glorious work is completed; the mighty victory is won; He has conquered death and the grave.

The angel then invited them to enter further and behold the place where they laid Him. The tomb was empty. The linen clothes lay in their original windings, but they found not the body of the Lord Jesus (Luke 24:3). No human eye saw Him rise from the dead. It was first announced by angelic messengers, witnessed by the empty tomb, and confirmed by the personal appearances of the Lord Himself. These are the infallible proofs (Acts 1:3).

The angel gave the women directions to go and tell His disciples and Peter. The special inclusion of Peter is unique to Mark, and is a revelation of the unchanging friendship and forgiving love of the Servant. The words "and Peter" also impress the influence of Peter present in the background with Mark as He wrote his Gospel.

The disciples would see Him in Galilee. He would go before them there. He had already made that promise before His death: "After that I am risen, I will go before you into Galilee" (Mark 14:28). His resurrection was inevitable. He must fulfil His word.

8 The women were overwhelmed with the experience of meeting the angel and hearing his message. Trembling and astonished, they fled from the sepulchre. At first they said nothing to any man, for they were afraid.

2. *The Appearances of the Servant on Earth* 16:9-18

v.9 "Now when *Jesus* was risen early the first *day* of the week, he appeared first to Mary Magdalene, out of whom he had cast seven devils.
v.10 *And* she went and told them that had been with him, as they mourned and wept.
v.11 And they, when they had heard that he was alive, and had been seen of her, believed not.
v.12 After that he appeared in another form unto two of them, as they walked, and went into the country.

v.13 And they went and told *it* unto the residue: neither believed they them.
v.14 Afterward he appeared unto the eleven as they sat at meat, and upbraided them with their unbelief and hardness of heart, because they believed not them which had seen him after he was risen.
v.15 And he said unto them, Go ye into all the world, and preach the gospel to every creature.
v.16 He that believeth and is baptised shall be saved; but he that believeth not shall be damned.
v.17 And these signs shall follow them that believe; In my name shall they cast out devils; they shall speak with new tongues;
v.18 They shall take up serpents; and if they drink any deadly thing, it shall not hurt them; they shall lay hands on the sick, and they shall recover."

The closing verses of Mark have been a great difficulty to many students. Are these last twelve verses genuine? Were they written by Mark? Were they added centuries later by an unknown penman? These are some of the questions concerning these verses, for the last twelve verses are not found in the two oldest Greek manuscripts of the NT: the Vaticanus and Sinaiticus. Therefore many textual critics omit them.

The following should be considered:

It is not tenable that this Gospel (Matthew is a book, Luke a letter, and John a treatise) would end at v.8 with the word "afraid" in the English text. It is even more evident that such is unthinkable when it is understood that the last word in the Greek text is the conjunction "for" (*gar*).

The usual "long ending" in our English Bible was quoted by Irenaeus in the second century. The Vaticanus manuscript leaves a space after verse eight. This is an indication of the known absence of the completion of the Gospel.

Internal evidence suggests that Mark himself later added the verses as a postscript, as John did in his Gospel (cf. John 21). The character of Mark's manner of reporting events in rapid succession, moving quickly from one scene to another, is in keeping with the tenor of these closing verses. Without the "long ending" the Gospel would be unfinished. It is therefore without doubt part of the verbally-inspired Word.

There are at least ten appearances of the risen Lord during the forty days before He ascended to the right hand of God in heaven. Five of these were on the day of His resurrection, one a week later, three at times not stated, and one on the day of His ascension. He appeared to individuals and to companies, privately and publicly. The locations and times differed. They are all infallible proofs of His physical literal resurrection.
Mark records four appearances.

1. To Mary	vv.9-11 (see John 20:14)
2. To two disciples	v.12 (see Luke 24:13-35)
3. To the eleven	v.14
4. At the commission	vv.15-18 (see 1 Cor 15:16).

He appeared in resurrection only to His disciples.

9 An important fact is stated: "Jesus was risen early the first day of the week". This is the only place in the NT where it is clearly stated that He arose upon the first day of the week.

His first appearance was to Mary of Magdala, out of whom He had cast seven demons. This appearance to Mary is given in greater detail by John (John 20:11-18).

10-11 Mark emphasises the unbelief of the disciples concerning the visual appearances of the Lord. When Mary came with the news of His resurrection to the weeping disciples, they did not believe her testimony that she had seen the risen Lord.

12-13 The appearance to the two as they walked and went into the country is related fully by Luke (Luke 24:13-35). He appeared to them in another form (*en hetera morphe*). He was as a stranger. This matter is left indefinite by Mark. Luke says "their eyes were holden". It was an appearance of His Person. He was visible and human. He walked with them, conversed, entered their house, sat at their table and handled a loaf. The teaching is that He is a real Person in resurrection. These were not visions but appearances. More is concealed than revealed. Again the unbelief of the disciples is mentioned, when the two disciples came and told of the things that happened to them in the way, and how He was made known to them in the breaking of bread.

14 He appeared to the eleven as they sat at meat. He reproached them for their unbelief in refusing the testimony of the eye-witnesses of His resurrection.

15-18 This appearance should be equated with the records of Matthew and Paul (Matt 28:16-20; 1 Cor 15:6). On this occasion he appeared to 500, including the eleven, at a mountain in Galilee. It ranks as His eighth appearance. He gave the great commission. Every person in the whole world comes within the scope of the message of the gospel of God's grace. It was His desire that every man, woman and child, of every tongue and colour, should have the opportunity to hear the gospel. Every Christian is responsible to further the gospel, and every church should be evangelistic.

16 The person who believes the gospel and confesses outwardly by being baptised shall be saved. The baptism is believers' baptism by total immersion in water. The person who does not believe shall be finally damned. The omission of baptism in this clause shows that faith alone saves the soul. Baptism followed faith in Christ and was practised by all believers at the beginning (Acts 2:41-42; 18:8).

17-18 The signs mentioned – casting out demons, speaking with new tongues, taking up serpents, drinking any deadly thing, and laying hands on the sick for their recovery – were given to accredit the message, and were confined to that period of time. These can be traced in the Acts (2:4; 8:7; 9:32ff; 28:1-6).

Today, with the complete revelation of God in the writings of the NT, the signs which were unique to the infant church are no longer manifest (1 Cor 13:8-13).

XII. The Pre-eminence of the Servant (16:19-20)

v.19 "So then after the Lord had spoken unto them, he was received up into heaven, and sat on the right hand of God.
v.20 And they went forth, and preached every where, the Lord working with *them*, and confirming the word with signs following. Amen."

The ascension is also recorded by Luke (24:50-51; Acts 1:9-12). It proclaims the supremacy of the Servant, marking the culmination of His earthly ministry. It is the final and greatest proof of His resurrection and is the commencement of His heavenly ministry.

19 When the Lord Jesus had spoken His final word to His disciples, He was received up into heaven. His Servant work being finished, God highly exalted Him and seated Him at His own right hand. He has been given the place of honour and power. The Epistles affirm this glorious position (Rom 8:34; Eph 1:20; Col 3:1; Heb 1:3; 10:12; 12:2). Three men have seen Him there (Acts 7:54-56; 9:3; Rev 1:12, 13).

Mark ends with the emphasis on faith in contrast to the unbelief of the earlier verses. The ascension in Mark is linked with faith, in Luke with love and hope (Luke 24:50; Acts 1:11).

In Mark the ascended Lord assists His servants as they evangelise. In Luke He sympathises with His people in their sorrows. In the Acts He is ascended but will finally return to reign over Israel as their sovereign. He is the Prophet to bring God's message to the world, He is the Priest to bear the burdens of His saints, and He is the King who is coming back to reign over all the earth.

20 They went forth, and preached everywhere. Their efforts were followed with success for the risen Lord worked with them. This Gospel which commences with a servant going before the Lord, ends with servants going forth after the Lord had gone into glory. The service of the Lord has not terminated, He is everywhere working with His faithful servants. He is in heaven physically but yet spiritually near. His servants are not alone as they spread the news of His salvation. He is still working and confirming the Word with power in conversions.

In the days of the apostles, the co-operation of the ascended Christ was manifested by the accompanying signs which had been promised. In later days servants have other indications of His continual presence working with them in the confirmation of the Word.